Psychology of Learning and Memory

Psychology of Learning and Memory

Henry C. Ellis, *University of New Mexico*
Thomas L. Bennett, *Colorado State University*
Terry C. Daniel, *University of Arizona*
Edward J. Rickert, *University of Alabama*

Brooks/Cole Publishing Company
Monterey, California
A Division of Wadsworth Publishing Company, Inc.

Consulting Editor: *Edward L. Walker*

Printed in the United States of America

10 9 8 7 6 5 4 3 2 1

Library of Congress Cataloging in Publication Data

Main entry under title:

Psychology of learning and memory.

Bibliography: p. 429
Includes index
1. Learning, Psychology of. 2. Memory. I. Ellis, Henry Carlton, 1927–
BF318.P78 153.1 78-16292
ISBN 0-8185-0267-3

Acquisition Editor: *William H. Hicks*
Manuscript Editor: *Grace Holloway*
Production Editor: *John Bergez*
Interior and Cover Design: *Jamie S. Brooks*
Illustrations: *Ayxa Art*
Typesetting: *Graphic Typesetting Service*

This book is dedicated with affection to our wives,
Florence, Jackie, Caroline, and Donna

Preface

We have written this book for the typical first course in the psychology of learning or learning and memory. Our aim has been to provide a comprehensive survey that is intelligible to students who are studying these topics in detail for the first time.

The capacities to learn and to remember are critically important features of living organisms. Consequently, the psychology of learning and memory is a fascinating and rewarding field of study. Although it involves some fairly technical material, we have tried to make the field accessible for students by providing the background necessary for an understanding of complex concepts and by defining unfamiliar terms as they are introduced. We have also used many examples from everyday life to clarify important principles and concepts. For example, we frequently discuss practical applications of our knowledge of reinforcement and punishment, forgetting, decision making, discrimination learning, and other topics. In short, we have aimed for a readable, straightforward presentation that will be both clear and interesting to undergraduates.

We wrote this book partly to satisfy our own needs as instructors. We wanted a text that included several topics frequently omitted in learning and memory texts. For instance, because of the growing recognition of the biological bases of learning and memory, we have devoted an entire chapter to this topic. Similarly, we wanted a text that dealt in some detail with developmental factors and with perceptual processes as they relate to learning and memory. Thus, the traditional topics in this field are supplemented by some that are less commonly included in basic texts.

Another of our objectives has been to show the commonalities between animal and human learning. At the same time, we recognize that these two areas of study have increasingly gone their separate ways in recent years, and we have tried to accurately represent this development while striving for an integrated presentation of the principles of learning and memory.

In writing this book, we have tried to apply what we know about learning and memory. Since what is usually retained from a college course is the gist, we have highlighted major concepts, and we have cited experiments only with the clear objective of illustrating them. Similarly, since we know that spaced repetition aids in learning and retention, we have emphasized review. Later chapters do not assume that students remember everything they have read in earlier chapters. We remind our readers of the meanings of important terms and concepts, and we occasionally reexamine experiments in new contexts. In addition, the chapter summaries review the major points, concepts, and principles covered in each chapter. These devices have the additional benefit of making the chapters somewhat more self-contained than they would be otherwise, so that instructors can assign them in the order that best suits their purposes.

The book is organized in a way that we hope makes it both comprehensive and flexible. Instructors who wish to emphasize either animal or human memory and learning will find that the book falls naturally into two parts. Following an introductory chapter, the first part (Chapters 2 through 8) deals with animal learning, conditioning, and biological and developmental aspects of behavior. The second part (Chapters 9 through 15) focuses on human memory and learning, including language, thought, and other complex processes. Each part begins with an overview chapter; Chapter 2 introduces the major concepts in animal learning and conditioning, and Chapter 9 introduces the topic of memory from an information-processing viewpoint. The remaining chapters provide detailed coverage of more specialized topics. Thus, instructors who wish to emphasize animal learning and give only light coverage to human processes may want to assign Chapters 1 through 8 plus one or two chapters from the second half of the book. Instructors who want to stress human processes might want to assign Chapters 1, 2, 3, and 9–15. In short, we believe that the book is sufficiently flexible that it could serve as a text in courses covering either animal learning or human memory and learning alone, as well as in the typical comprehensive course, which covers both areas.

It is always a pleasure to acknowledge individuals who have played a role in the development of a book. Several colleagues were especially helpful to us. We are particularly grateful to Judith Goggin, University of Texas, El Paso, for her careful and thoughtful reviews, notable for their detail and wit. In addition, we wish to thank our other reviewers: Delos D. Wickens, Ohio State University; Roger L. Mellgren, University of Oklahoma; and Edward L. Walker, University of Michigan, Consulting Editor for Brooks/Cole. We also thank the following colleagues who reviewed one or more chapters: Henry A. Cross, Colorado State University; Harold D. Delaney, University of New Mexico; John P. Gluck, University of New Mexico; Charles R. Grah, Austin Peay State University; R. Reed Hunt, University of North Carolina, Greensboro; David Kieras, University of Arizona; Frank A. Logan, University of New Mexico; Frederick J. Parente, Towson State University; James R. Ranck, Jr., State University of New York, Downstate Medical Center; and Chris Tanz, University of Arizona. In addition, we wish to thank the following students who provided useful feedback: Paula Hertel, Sherman Tyler, Marvin McCallum, Merith Cosden, June Hargrove, and Donald Taylor.

A competent production staff is essential for this kind of effort. We were fortunate in having the support of a truly superb group of people at Brooks/Cole. In particular we express our gratitude to William Hicks, our editor and friend; to administrative assistant Vena Dyer; to John Bergez, our production editor; to Grace Holloway, our manuscript editor; to Jamie Brooks, art director; to J. Richard Verduin, our permissions editor; and to the ever-helpful Terry Hendrix, publisher.

Finally, we are grateful to a number of people who provided clerical and other assistance. In particular, we wish to acknowledge the work of Eleanor Orth, LaNelle Ruebush, Jill Ngola, Virginia Moore, Joan Block, Mary Ann Ward, and Kenney McLain.

Henry C. Ellis
Thomas L. Bennett
Terry C. Daniel
Edward J. Rickert

Contents

Psychology of Learning and Memory

Chapter 1

Introduction to Learning and Memory

The topics of learning and memory occupy a central position in contemporary psychology. One of the most important features of human beings is that we can *learn* to modify our behavior to adapt to new situations. A second important feature is that we can *remember* the results of past experiences. The range of things that we can learn and remember is vast. Even the simplest behaviors exhibited by the infant at birth come to be modified by the learning process. In turn, our most complex behaviors, such as language, reasoning, and thinking, are partly dependent on the processes of learning and memory. For example, we could engage in very little effective thinking if we were unable to retain the products of our thoughts.

The significance of learning can also be seen by noting its role in specific areas of psychology. In social psychology the study of attitude formation can be viewed as the study of how complex attitudes and belief systems are learned. Similarly, the study of personality traits represents the study of characteristics that are partly the result of the learning process. Finally, our conceptions of therapy and behavior modification depend upon assumptions about the nature of the learning process. For instance, behavior-modification approaches to therapy make the general assumption that many maladaptive or inappropriate behaviors are the result of the learning process and that therapy requires the application of basic principles of learning. Thus, the pervasiveness of learning is a major reason for its central role in psychology.

Our daily activities regularly involve learning and memory. We encourage those behaviors we regard as desirable, and we may ignore or punish behaviors we disapprove of, usually on the assumption that rewards or punishments will lead to changes in behavior. We exhort others (sometimes ourselves) to study harder, to organize their thinking, to search their memories more carefully, and so forth in an effort to stimulate more effective performance. We assume that good study habits lead to better retention of information. Probably most of us take our learning and memory for granted and often only become aware of them when they fail us. We are sometimes concerned if we fail to remember the name of someone we met the previous week, or fail to remember an appointment, or forget information we thought we had learned. A particularly frustrating experience is to be unable to recall information on an exam and yet recall it moments after leaving the examination room. You are also experiencing this "perversity" of memory, in which information present in memory is not always easily accessible, when you feel that something is on the tip of your tongue but you cannot quite recall it.

If you have any doubt about the pervasiveness of learning and memory in your daily life, examine a short period of activity such as a lunchtime conversation with friends. You may have spent some of the time describing events, such as what you did, where you went, and whom you saw over the weekend. As you conversed, you were recalling information and bringing it forward to your immediate consciousness. You may also have been aware of organizing your thoughts as you prepared to regale your friends with an especially amusing happening. While your friends talked, you may have found yourself gaining new information that was useful and/or interesting. Thus, learning and memory play a major part in the ordinary flow of consciousness.

The Concept of Learning

In the course of reading this book, your definition of learning will become refined and sharpened. At this point it would be useful to look at one view of learning so that you have a working definition of the concept. Psychologists do not completely agree on a precise definition of learning, in part because we never see learning directly. Learning is something we infer from observed changes in behavior. However, we cannot infer learning simply because behavioral changes have occurred; we must first rule out the possibility that the changes are due to temporary drug influences, maturation or growth, fatigue, or motivation. Only changes in behavior due to practice are attributed to learning. Finally, learning is viewed as relatively permanent.

This definition has four salient features. First, the focus is on learning as an *inference;* it is not directly observed. Concepts in physics such as energy, mass, and force are also inferences because we never see them directly. Second, learning is dependent upon *practice* as distinct from maturation, drugs, or other effects. If some behavior develops through regular maturational stages rather than training, we conclude that the behavior is not due to learning. An example of this kind of behavior is the flying of birds. However, many behaviors are not simply the result of either learning or maturation but are due to a complex interaction of the two processes. In such cases we must be able to attribute at least some of the observed change in behavior to practice or training in order to conclude that learning has occurred. A third feature of our definition is that learning is tied to *performance* but is not the same as performance. The distinction between learning and performance is that learning may have occurred in a situation, yet the performance from which we infer the learning may not happen until some later time. For example, a child may have learned new words as a result of silent reading but may not exhibit knowledge of the words until called upon by the teacher. Finally, our definition calls attention to the relative *permanence* of learning. This is a useful assumption because it allows us to distinguish learning from more temporary changes in behavior resulting from fatigue or other factors.

The Concepts of Stimulus and Response

The concepts of stimulus and response are fundamental to the psychology of learning. Because these words are part of our everyday vocabulary, this section provides a general description of how they are used in the psychology of learning. The term *stimulus* is used in several ways. One way is simply to denote a physical stimulus, such as an object in our environment. A related notion is that a stimulus is any effective change in energy at our receptors. A loud noise, a flash of light, the spoken language, and so on all function in this fashion.

Psychologists also distinguish between a *nominal* and a *functional* stimulus. A nominal stimulus is whatever an experimenter decides to vary in an experiment. For example, an animal could be required to discriminate between two shapes, a circle and a triangle. The two shapes constitute the nominal stimuli because they are what the experimenter actually manipulates. But suppose there are differences in the brightness of the stimuli, with the circle being the brighter stimulus. The animal may choose to respond to the circle because of its brightness rather than its shape. If so, the functional, or effective, stimulus is a brightness difference. The significance of this distinction between the stimulus as defined by the experimenter and the stimulus as used by the subject will be seen throughout this book.

Another aspect of a stimulus is that it can be viewed as a *stimulus-as-coded.* It has long been recognized that the effective stimulus may be the stimulus as it is perceived and represented by the subject. For instance, a smile can serve as a stimulus event. But our interpretation of the smile (for example, approval versus amusement) affects our reaction. Thus, it is not the smile itself but our manner of representing, or coding, the event that is the important stimulus. The stimulus-as-coded is related to the functional stimulus in that the coded stimulus is the representation of the functional stimulus in memory.

Just as the term *stimulus* has several meanings, so does the term *response.* Responses can vary from very simple events, such as muscle twitches, to very complex sequences of behavior. Typically, the function and the *molar,* or general, features of a response are emphasized rather than its minute aspects. Responses such as recalling a list of words, driving a car, and brushing one's teeth are molar responses viewed in terms of their functions.

It has been noted, however, that consideration of just the molar features of a response may be insufficient. For example, the speed or force of a response also appears to be the result of learning; not only do we learn to talk but we learn to talk at a certain characteristic rate and loudness. This approach to a response, which emphasizes that certain quantitative properties of the response are learned, is called a *micromolar* approach. As you read this book, you will have ample opportunity to see the many different ways of looking at responses as well as stimuli.

What Is Learned: Associations or Knowledge and Skills?

A longstanding issue that has led to much debate in the psychology of learning is the question of what is learned. In the classical view, learning is the formation of an *association* between a stimulus and a response. In its simplest form this association means learning when and/or where to make a response. For instance, when you can connect a particular name with a particular person, you can be said to have learned a stimulus-response (S-R) association.

Another approach, still within the associationistic framework, proposes that we actually form associations between stimuli. In other words, when stimulus-stimulus (S-S) connections are established, we have learned to expect a particular stimulus whenever some other stimulus event occurs. According to this view, we learn the meaning of stimuli rather than learning to make particular responses to stimuli. The distinction between the S-R and S-S conceptions of learning can be illustrated by the following example. Consider the matter of learning to drive from your home to that of a new friend. We will assume that the sequence consists of a number of turns in the order left, left, right, left, right. From the viewpoint of the S-R psychologist, what you learn is a series of left-and-right turns—that is, responses. The S-S psychologist conceives of the process in more cognitive terms, in which you learn the location of your friend's house. To oversimplify, the first approach contends that you are learning responses, whereas the second proposes that you are learning ideas.

In recent years an increasing number of theorists have questioned the associationistic approach to learning. They contend that many learning situations do not lend themselves readily to associationistic interpretation, especially of the S-R variety. Central to this approach is the notion that complex cognitive processes are important in the understanding of learning and memory and that the human is an active processor of information rather than a passive organism in which associations become strengthened through practice. Symbolic mental processes, such as reasoning, thinking, abstraction, organizing, and memory searching, are emphasized. From this perspective, the study of learning is the study of how we acquire *knowledge and skills,* as distinct from associations. Knowledge is regarded as having an understanding of events, or possessing conceptual information. Recalling the topic of conversation at dinner last night, being able to solve quadratic equations, and understanding complex legal issues are all aspects of behavior that allow us to infer knowledge. The learning of skills involves the development of proficiency in perceptual-motor skills, such as swimming, golf, tennis, and dancing.

Closely related to cognitive conceptions of behavior are information-processing conceptions of learning and memory. An increasing number of psychologists have begun to view much behavior from the perspective of an information-processing system. According to these theorists, information in the form of input from the external environment impinges on the organism and flows through successive stages or sequences in the organism. Information-processing approaches generally view humans as though they behaved like the processing mechanisms in computers. Humans, of course, are not computers as such, but certain aspects of our behavior, such as perception, learning, memory, and abstraction, can be analyzed from the viewpoint of information processing.

Although psychologists can agree on a working definition of learning to some degree, there is greater diversity over conceptual/theoretical approaches to studying it. The same researchers working on a problem in human learning may treat it differently from, say, a problem in animal learning. This diversity in approaches should not be of concern to you at this stage. Indeed, such diversity can be seen as evidence of richness, ferment, and activity. In this book we have adopted no single conceptual/theoretical approach to the study of learning and memory. Instead, we have attempted to explain the major conceptual approaches in the particular experimental context in which they seem most appropriate.

The Concept of Memory

Regardless of how we decide to describe what is learned, if it is to be useful it must somehow be stored, and it must be accessible at a later time. In general, memory is regarded as involving three processes: *encoding, storage,* and *retrieval.* We will discuss these processes at length in subsequent chapters but will briefly note them here. The first process, encoding, involves transforming or arranging information so that it can be stored in memory. For example, as you hear someone describe an idea, you do not normally store every sentence in the description verbatim. Rather, you select certain features, reduce the idea to its essentials, and try to remember the key propositions of the idea. Much of your effort is directed toward analyzing the most meaningful aspects of the information you hear. This process of analyzing the information and extracting the essential features is called encoding. The second process in memory is the storage of information. Because we can remember events for days, weeks, and years, we need to assume some kind of storage of the representation of these events. The third process is retrieval. We must assume the existence of this process, because we sometimes have to search our memory store for information before we can recall it. As noted earlier, the search may not be successful; information can be stored in memory and still not be accessible at a particular time.

Biological Constraints on Learning

Psychologists in the late 19th and early 20th centuries viewed behavior as having instinctive, genetic, and biological determinants. However, the development of behavioristic psychology under the leadership of John Watson led to the view that learning is the major determinant of behavior. Watson (1924) argued persuasively for the dominant role of learning in behavior and for the importance of environmental rather than genetic and biological factors. This position was adopted by other behavioristic psychologists, such as B.F. Skinner (1938), who has defended the view of strong environmental determinism. Skinner has stressed the importance of environmental conditions in controlling and maintaining behavior and has noted that behavior can be controlled via reward contingencies without resorting to internal processes or biological events as explanations of behavior. This viewpoint remained influential into the 1960s but has met with increasing opposition since then.

Despite the pervasiveness of learning, there is now substantial evidence of biological constraints on the learning process. An early warning of this development was noted by Breland and Breland (1961) in their efforts to teach a wide range of behaviors to different species. They found that certain kinds of behavior would not remain easily conditioned in particular species. For example, they trained a pig to pick up a wooden coin and place it in a "piggy bank." At first the pig performed this task well, but with further training, behavior characteristic of pigs in general began to appear and disrupt the learned behavior. Instead of carrying the coin in its mouth and depositing it in the bank, the pig would drop it, root it, pick it up again, then drop it and root it again. In brief, the instinctive pattern of rooting behavior intruded and disrupted the learned pattern of behavior. As a result of this and related findings, behaviors that were previously thought to be learned across a wide range of species began to be seen as more restricted in scope, and the idea of species-specific behavior began to emerge. The importance of biological constraints on learning will be discussed in more detail in Chapter 3.

Philosophical Influences on Theories of Learning and Memory

Differences in current approaches to the study of learning and memory can be partly understood by reference to philosophical approaches to the theory of knowledge. The fundamental questions within the theory of knowledge include how we know something, how ideas are related and organized, and what the relation is between experience and knowledge. Philosophers have distinguished between two views of these issues, which are known as *empiricism* and *rationalism*.

The position of empiricism is that our knowledge about our world arises directly from experience, not from innate ideas. In addition, our ideas about the world are thought to be established via sense impressions. The ideas may be simple, in which case they are direct copies of sense impressions, or they may be complex, in which case they are combinations of several simple ideas. Simple ideas are linked to form more complex ideas by the process of association. Ideas become associated when the sensory experiences occur close together in time or space, and the strength of the association is a function of the frequency with which the experiences occur contiguously. Finally, once knowledge is gained from sensory experiences, additional knowledge can be achieved by reflections on the experiences.

In contrast to empiricism, the rationalist school holds that reason is the principal source of knowledge. Information coming from the senses must be interpreted and organized by the mind in accordance with certain innate predispositions. The mind is not a tabula rasa (blank slate) but is so constructed as to place constraints on what it accepts. In the extreme form, classical rationalism postulates that all knowledge is innately present in the human mind and that the function of experience is merely to bring the knowledge forward. Most rationalist philosophers, however, have been more modest and have argued that only certain forms or classes of knowledge are innate. This emphasis on innate factors in learning is akin to the idea that the learning process is constrained by biological predispositions.

This brief sketch of empiricism and rationalism will suffice for our purposes. The interested reader may pursue these topics in the history of psychology in Boring (1950) or Mandler and Mandler (1964). Let us now turn our attention to how empiricist and rationalist conceptions influenced developments in the psychology of learning and memory.

It was the associationistic bent of empiricism that led to the experimental investigation of human learning and memory under the direction of Hermann Ebbinghaus (1885). He attempted to understand association formation by using materials that were thought to be largely outside the past experiences of the learner. Thus, a major objective was to study how associations are learned from scratch. In the domain of animal learning, the first major studies, by Edward L. Thorndike (1898), were also directed toward understanding associative processes. Developments within behavioristic psychology continued the associative emphasis, since learning was viewed as the acquisition of S-R (or S-S) associations, and forgetting was regarded as the weakening of these associations. Indeed, theories of learning and memory were largely associationistic until the early 1960s. Research on human learning and memory, influenced by the functionalist school of psychology, also maintained an associative cast during the same period (for example, McGeoch, 1942; Underwood & Schulz, 1960). The functionalist school was concerned with describing empirical relationships between independent and dependent variables.

Despite the long-dominant role of associationism in North American psychology, rationalist arguments have been advanced by some theorists. Perhaps the most forceful proponents of rationalism have been the Gestalt psychologists and contemporary researchers in psycholinguistics. Gestalt psychology was developed in Germany under the leadership of Max Wertheimer, who was joined in his efforts by Kurt Koffka (1924) and Wolfgang Köhler (1925). Gestalt psychology began in part as a reaction against associationistic conceptions of psychology, especially as they were applied to perception. The Gestalt argument is that certain phenomena, such as motion perception and perceptual grouping, cannot be explained in terms of discrete associations. Perceptions are influenced by certain organizational characteristics of the brain, which predispose us to perceive our world in certain predictable ways. Thus, we group stimuli in accordance with similarity, proximity, and the like as a result of built-in properties of the nervous system. The grouping methods are known as the laws of perceptual organization. Learning is viewed as of secondary interest, since what is learned is determined by these laws. The Gestaltists also applied their ideas about perception in efforts to account for memory. Although unsuccessful in some ways, Gestalt theory has been important in its emphasis on organizational and constructive processes in memory. These issues will be discussed more fully in chapters on memory, especially chapter 12.

In the field of psycholinguistics, controversy has arisen during the past decade over the nature of language acquisition. Basically, the dispute is between empiricist and rationalist conceptions of language. A prominent spokesman for the former view is Skinner (1957), who has argued for a descriptive approach to language acquisition, emphasizing that language behavior is learned just as are other behaviors observed in the laboratory. In contrast, Noam Chomsky (1972) has argued that descriptive, associative conceptions are too simple to account for the richness of human language. Chomsky's view is that the very complexity of language demands the assumption of a set of linguistic universals, which are presumed to be innate. These issues can be only briefly noted here, but they serve to illustrate how empiricist and rationalist conceptions affect our current thought about language.

In summary, the study of learning and memory has been influenced by philosophical conceptions of how knowledge is acquired. These influences still operate in modern psychology, and in later chapters you will have an opportunity to see them at work.

The Plan of This Book

This book outlines the major principles of learning and memory, ranging from the basic processes of conditioning and animal learning to the complex processes of language, memory, thought, and conceptual behavior. The organization is quite straightforward. Chapters 2 through 8 deal with conditioning, animal learning, and developmental and physiological processes in learning and memory. The remaining chapters cover human learning and memory, language, conceptual behavior, and other complex processes.

The emphasis of the book is on the major findings and generalizations in learning and memory. We have adopted no single theoretical approach but describe associative, cognitive, and information-processing conceptions where seemingly most appropriate. Although our preference is to be systematic rather than eclectic, the wide range of topics covered in this survey precludes, at least for the present, our adopting a single conceptual approach. Our belief is that the richness and diversity of the field of learning and memory make it exciting and challenging despite the lack of any unifying single theory.

Chapter 2

Classical and Instrumental Conditioning

Psychologists generally agree that classical and instrumental conditioning represent the simplest forms of learning. There are two reasons for this view. One is that conditioning is observed in lower organisms as well as humans. The other is that conditioning procedures are fairly simple, although the resulting behavioral changes may turn out to be quite complex (G. A. Kimble, 1971).

A third reason for this view of conditioning is historically interesting but now generally discredited. At one time some theorists thought that conditioning processes might serve as the building blocks for more complex forms of learning and that, once we had a thorough understanding of conditioning, we might be able to account for more complex behaviors. However, in the past 25 years psychologists have increasingly come to believe that such complex learning processes as concept learning, language, and memory can be explained only by principles derived from studying these behaviors directly.

This chapter describes and illustrates the basic procedures of classical and instrumental conditioning and then discusses some research findings. A very brief introduction to some applications of conditioning principles is also presented.

Classical Conditioning

In the course of conducting experiments on the digestive processes of dogs, the Russian physiologist and Nobel Prize winner Ivan Pavlov developed a training procedure that has come to be known as classical or Pavlovian conditioning. A brief description of one of his experiments will make this procedure clear. Pavlov used dogs as subjects and typically studied salivation as the response. Prior to the experiment the dog received a minor operation in which the opening of the salivary duct was moved from the mouth to the outside skin, so that the amount of salivation could be easily observed. In the experiment the dog was placed in a soundproof compartment and restrained in a harness-like device. The dog was taught to salivate at the sound of a beating metronome by presenting meat powder to the dog after each of a number of presentations of the sound. After a number of trials, the dog began to salivate at the sound itself.

The terminology of classical conditioning can also be illustrated by this experiment. The meat powder, which automatically produces salivation, is called the *unconditioned stimulus* (US). The US produces the *unconditioned response* (UR) of salivation. After a number of pairing trials, the sound of the metronome itself comes to produce the salivation. Hence, the metronome is called a *conditioned stimulus* (CS), which produces a *conditioned response* (CR). Classical conditioning is thus seen as the formation of an association between a conditioned stimulus and a response by repeated presentation of the conditioned stimulus in conjunction with the unconditioned stimulus. The conditioned stimulus is originally "neutral" for the organism; the CS itself normally has no capacity or a relatively limited capacity to evoke the response. It is through training that the CS acquires the capacity to evoke the response. This procedure is summarized in Figure 2–1.

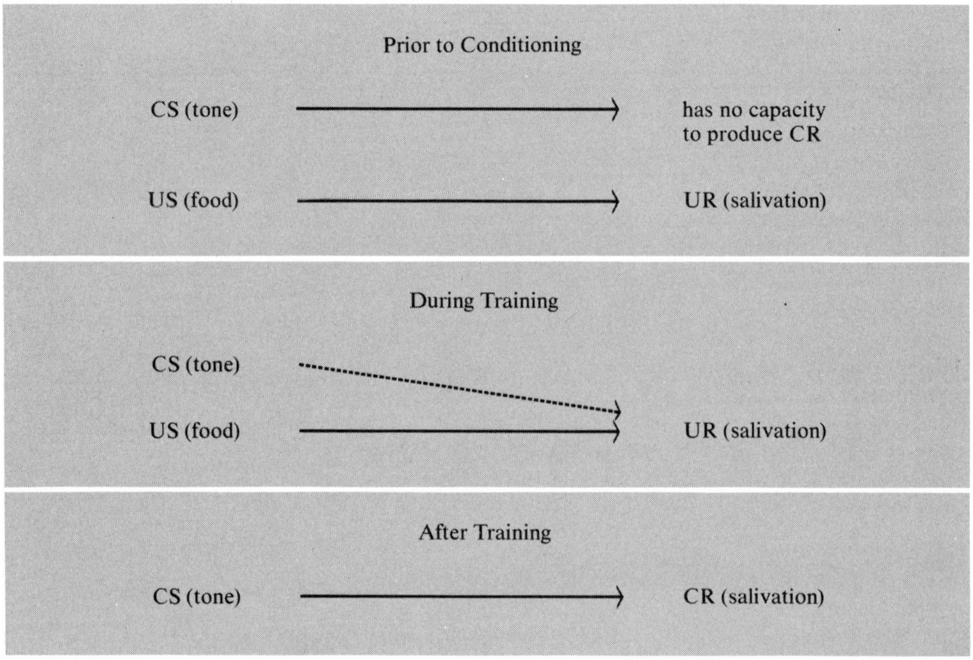

Figure 2–1. Diagram of the classical-conditioning procedure. At the start of training, the US will evoke the UR, but the CS does not have the capacity to evoke the appropriate response. During training the CS and the US are presented such that the CS comes to evoke the response. The development of a CS-CR association is the result of conditioning.

Another aspect of this procedure is the dog's attentional activity. When first exposed to the sound, the dog pricks up its ears and moves its head in the direction of the sound. This reaction is called an *orienting response* and is generally observed when an animal is exposed to an unfamiliar stimulus. The response is viewed as an index of the attention-demanding properties of the CS (Sokolov, 1963) and also indicates that more than one response system is involved in conditioning.

Noting three other features of this procedure is important for a proper understanding of classical conditioning. First, the presentation and temporal sequencing of the CS and the US are made without reference to what the organism does; in other words, the US follows the CS regardless of what the subject may do. Since the occurrence of the US depends only upon the presentation of the CS, the procedure is said to be *noncontingent;* that is, the US follows the CS without being dependent on the response. A second feature of this procedure is that the CS is a clearly identifiable, easily specified event. Normally, there is no doubt about what event constitutes the CS. Finally, the CR may be almost identical to the UR in appearance but usually differs in amount. In our example the CR and the UR are both salivary responses, but the amount of the CR is usually less. Sometimes the CR appears to be only a fractional portion of the UR. For example, food powder may elicit both salivation and chewing responses, whereas the sound may produce only salivation.

Procedural Variations

There are several ways in which the CS and the US may be presented in classical-conditioning experiments. The most commonly used procedure is called *delayed* conditioning. In this procedure the CS is presented sometime prior to the US and normally continues until the onset of the US. The CS may also be presented at various times during or after US presentation.

A second procedure, called *trace* conditioning, requires that the CS be presented and terminated before the onset of the US. Although the CS is no longer physically present when the US occurs, the assumption is that the residual effects of the CS in the nervous system, in the form of a neural trace, are still present and that conditioning develops on the basis of the trace of the CS.

Other variations include *simultaneous, backward,* and *temporal* conditioning. Simultaneous conditioning is the simultaneous presentation and termination of the CS and the US, a procedure that produces very little conditioning. Backward conditioning is the presentation and termination of the US prior to presentation of the CS. Finally, temporal conditioning involves presenting the US at regularly spaced intervals without presentation of a specifiable CS. If this is done often enough, a CR will occur shortly before the onset of the US. This procedure is called temporal conditioning because time itself is presumably functioning as the CS. It is in temporal conditioning that the CS is not clearly specified. Otherwise, the CS is normally clearly identified. Figure 2–2 outlines the various arrangements of the CS and the US in classical conditioning.

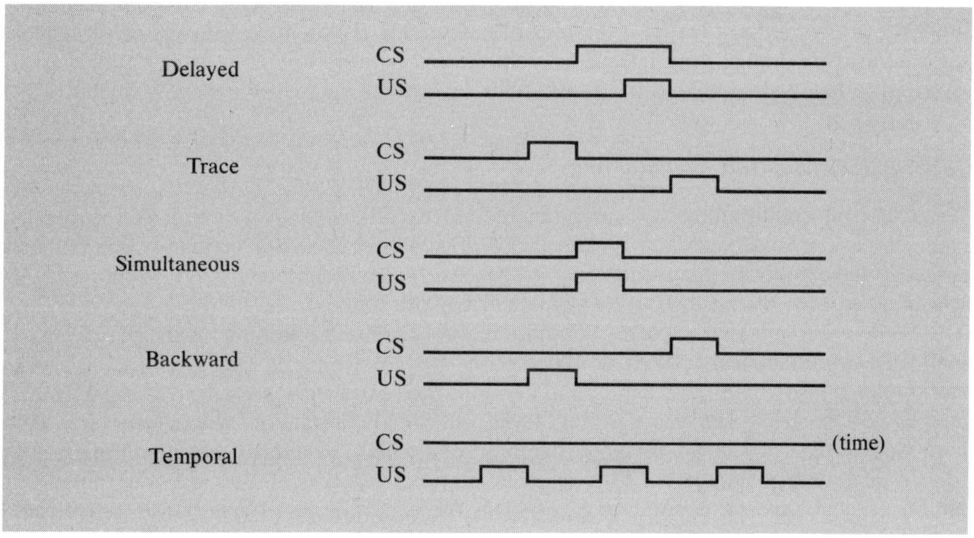

Figure 2–2. Some experimental variations of CS-US intervals in classical conditioning.

Appetitive and Defense Conditioning

Another distinction that can be made between types of conditioning concerns the effects of the US. In *appetitive* conditioning the US is some pleasant, satisfying event. Pavlov's basic procedure is an example of appetitive conditioning in that the US (food) that followed the CS was satisfying. In contrast, in *defense* conditioning the US is noxious or unpleasant. For example, a US such as a mild acid solution applied to the mucous membranes of the mouth or an electric shock to a dog's foot pad would set up defensive reactions.

This distinction between the two kinds of US has consequences for the conditioning process. First, in order for a CR to be elicited by a CS when a pleasant or benevolent US is used, the subject must be motivated. Obviously, when food is used as a US, it would be difficult to condition a salivary response in a dog if the animal was not hungry. In contrast, most noxious USs provide their own motivation—that is, motivation to escape the unpleasant event. A second consequence is that, as mentioned earlier, the CR established by the pleasant US is usually not identical to the UR. When a noxious US is used, the situation is more complex. In some cases the CR to the CS may initially be extremely variable and then become more precise with increasing numbers of trials, yet it may still differ from the UR (Liddell, 1954). In other cases the CR may appear to be identical to the UR in virtually every respect. For example, after a dog has received several injections of morphine (which produces a variety of symptoms such as nausea, salivation, vomiting, and sleep), it has been observed that the mere sight of the syringe is sufficient to produce all the symptoms previously produced by the morphine itself (Pavlov, 1927; Krylor's experiments, p. 35).

Some of you may have experienced similar situations when you have taken the family dog to the veterinarian. If the dog has learned to fear going to the vet as a result of painful injections or other unpleasant experiences, it may begin to show emotional reactions such as increased agitation, whimpering, and so on when you simply drive into the parking lot by the vet's office. Indeed, the dog may show these classically conditioned responses while you are merely driving in the vicinity of the office. And the annual trip to the vet for rabies and distemper shots is frequently sufficient to maintain these CRs throughout the life of your pet. As another example, you may recall an instance in which a person became quite upset or even ill when faced with receiving an injection or even going for a physical checkup. Similarly, a few adults still report feelings of nausea and incipient movements of regurgitation when served orange juice because, as children, they were forced to drink castor oil (an unpleasant medicine) mixed with orange juice as a home remedy for some ailment.

The Range of Classical Conditioning

Classical conditioning is clearly not limited to situations in which dogs salivate to tones. It can be observed in a wide variety of situations, occurs in many different organisms, and results in many different responses. We will note only a few of these to provide some idea of the diversity of classical conditioning.

Some observers have reported conditioning in organisms as simple as the planarian, a small flatworm (Jacobson, 1963; R. Thompson & J. McConnell, 1955). Chick embryos and human fetuses have also undergone conditioning. And responses such as heart rate, pupillary dilation, eye blink, finger withdrawal, intestinal contractions, blood pressure, and brain waves (recorded in an EEG), to mention just a few, have all been conditioned.

A particularly interesting kind of conditioning, because of its enormous potential significance, is *semantic* conditioning, which is the conditioning of a response to a verbal stimulus, such as a word or a sentence (Razran, 1961). In semantic conditioning the "meaning," or emotional significance, of a word is established by classical-conditioning procedures. For example, Lacey, Smith, and Green (1955) presented subjects with a list of words and asked the subjects to give verbal associates. For selected words the experimenters gave a shock when an association was produced. One of these words, for example, was *cow*. They recorded the subjects' heart rate for each trial and found that it became conditioned to those words that had been followed by a shock. Not only was there an increase in heart rate to the shocked words, but there was an increase in heart rate to words that might be related in some way, such as the farm-related words *chicken* and *tractor*. This type of finding indicates that our emotional reactions to words can be conditioned and may help explain why humans react in certain ways to verbal stimuli. Indeed, our prejudices and strong feelings about various verbal labels may be developed via classical conditioning in the sense that words, symbols, and the like may take on meaning as the result of the particular stimuli with which they are associated.

Control Procedures

In classical conditioning a critical question is whether the previously neutral stimulus, the CS, has actually acquired control in producing the CR. In other words, has an association truly been established between the CS and the CR, or is the occurrence of the CR a consequence of other factors? Obviously, if the CR appears but a CS-CR association has not been established, something other than the conditioning procedure itself is producing the CR. To ensure that conditioning has actually taken place, researchers use a number of important control procedures.

First, it is essential to demonstrate that a CR will occur in the presence of the CS alone. However, the appearance of the CR is not sufficient in itself as a demonstration of conditioning, because presentation of the CS alone might elicit some responses even though no CS-US pairings had been made. Therefore, one type of control procedure, called the *CS alone control,* is commonly used to measure the effects of any familiarity with the CS itself. Control subjects are given CS presentations without any CS-US pairing. Their performance in the presence of the CS alone is then compared with that of experimental subjects who receive explicit training with the CS-US pairing. For conditioning to have truly occurred, responding following CS-US pairing must be greater than responding to the CS alone.

But there is a problem with this control procedure. Subjects will *habituate* to a CS that is presented repeatedly. (Habituation refers to a decrease in responding following repeated presentations of the CS alone.) Since the rate of habituation to the CS alone may be different from habituation to the CS previously paired with the US, this procedure may not permit an accurate assessment of habituation.

A second type of control is needed because the US may also produce responding independently of the CS-US pairing. With this type of control, called a *US alone control,* subjects receive the same number of US presentations as the experimental (CS-US training) subjects. The CS is not presented. This control provides a way of assessing the degree of responding to the US in the absence of CS-US pairing.

Finally, another control is now recognized as important. As we have noted, conditioning assumes that the subject learns that the CS and the US occur together. Rescorla (1967) points out that there must be some positive contingency between a CS and a US for conditioning to occur; in effect, the CS must convey some reliable information about the US (predict the US) if the subject is to learn what goes with what. Therefore, Rescorla has proposed that the proper control procedure is one in which the CS and the US are presented but bear no relation to each other. The idea is to make the occurrence of the CS and the US *truly random* and thus prevent the CS from conveying reliable information about the US. Since the CS conveys no reliable information to the subject about the occurrence of the US, no association between the two should develop. Thus, the truly random control measures the effects of CS and US without association formation. Of course, the truly random procedure does allow for an occasional pairing of the CS and the US; that is, even though the CS occurs independently of the US, there will be some trials in which they occur together, and some association formation might occur. Nevertheless, even if some association formation does occur in the truly random control, this provides a rather conservative baseline against which to evaluate the effects of conditioning (Rescorla & Wagner, 1972).

In summary, we have briefly described the logic of the CS-alone control, the US-alone control, and the truly random control in classical conditioning. The interested reader should consult Rescorla (1967) for more detail.

Factors Influencing Classical Conditioning

A number of factors are known to affect classical conditioning. In this section we will examine a few of the major ones: the amount of training, the CS-US interval, the stimulus intensity, the role of instructions and awareness, and the frequency of the US.

Amount of Training. A basic factor in classical conditioning is the amount of training, which is the number of times the CS and the US are paired. Conditioning has occurred when the CR appears in the presence of the CS alone. The tendency for this event to develop is usually a gradual process in most conditioning experiments. In an early study Anrep (1920), working in Pavlov's laboratory, demonstrated the learning of salivation in which the CS was a tone and the US was food powder. Dogs were given a total of 50 CS-US pairings over 16 days, and the amount of salivation to the CS regularly increased up to 30 pairings, beyond which no increase was observed.

Similarly, Hovland (1937c) showed that the strength of a galvanic skin response (GSR) increased in a systematic fashion with the number of CS-US pairings. In this study, which used human subjects, a tone was the CS, and a mild electric shock applied to the wrist was the US. The UR to the shock was a decrease in skin resistance—that is, a GSR change. Hovland's subjects received either 8, 16, 24, or 48 pairings of the CS and the US and were then tested for the strength of the conditioning by the presentation of the CS alone. A control group received no training in order to obtain a measure of responding at baseline conditions. The measure of conditioning was simply the amplitude of the GSR to the CS in the absence of the US. Figure 2–3, which indicates the basic results, shows that the magnitude of the GSR increased with the amount of training. The curve shows the rather typical negatively accelerated function of many conditioning studies and indicates that some responding occurs even without training. In this case we can conclude that some learning had taken place prior to conditioning and that training served to increase the strength of the CR. In situations in which no previous learning is effective, the curve is essentially *S*-shaped. In this latter case early training produces relatively little strengthening of the response; only after extended training does substantial conditioning occur.

The CS-US Interval. The interval between the CS and the US is an important variable, and it has received a good deal of attention. Many studies have attempted to identify the optimal CS-US interval for conditioning to occur, and the variable has been of theoretical interest because the role of contiguity of stimulus events is an issue in many theories of learning.

It was believed for some time that the optimal CS-US interval for conditioning is usually .5 seconds. Either longer or shorter intervals were generally found to decrease the amount of conditioning. A classic study on this issue was conducted by Spooner and Kellogg (1947). In this study the UR was finger withdrawal, the CS was a short buzz, and the

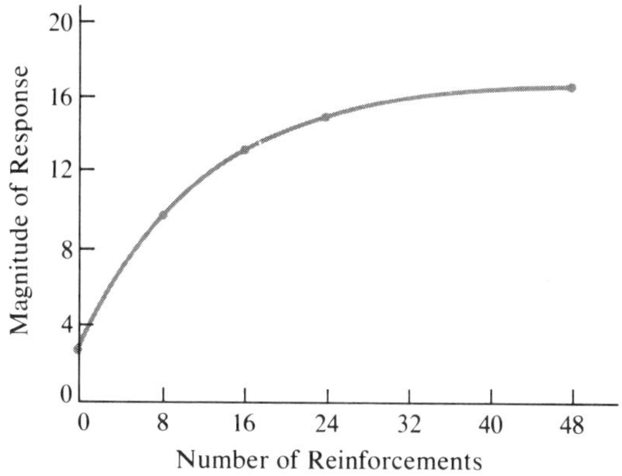

Figure 2–3. Amplitude of the galvanic skin response (GSR) as a function of number of reinforcements. (From "The Generalization of Conditioned Responses: IV. The Effects of Varying Amounts of Reinforcement upon the Degree of Generalization of Conditioned Responses," by C.I. Hovland, *Journal of Experimental Psychology,* 1937, *21,* 261–276. Copyright 1937 by the American Psychological Association. Reprinted by permission.)

US was an electric shock delivered by electrodes strapped to the finger. The CS was occasionally presented alone throughout the course of conditioning, and the presence of a finger-withdrawal CR was measured. Six separate groups of subjects were used, each having a different CS-US interval. One group received simultaneous conditioning, in which the CS and the US were presented together. Three groups received trace conditioning in which the CS preceded the US by an interval of either .5, 1.0, or 1.5 seconds. The other two groups received backward conditioning in which the US preceded the CS by either .25 or .50 seconds. The results, shown in Figure 2–4, indicate that the optimal interval was .5 seconds.

Subsequent investigations have found that the .5 second interval is optimal in some situations but not in others. The optimal interval depends upon the kind of subject, the particular response system, and the type of experimental procedure used. Experimental subjects have included rabbits, fish, pigs, and cats; response systems have included eye blinks, finger withdrawal, leg flexion, and the nictitating membrane of the rabbit. For example, Noble and Adams (1963) used fish as experimental subjects and found that 2.0 seconds was the optimal interval for conditioning. As a result, contemporary investigators have generally accepted the view that there is no single optimal interval for all situations (see, for example, Gormezano & Moore, 1969; Hall, 1976). Indeed, Bitterman (1965) has argued that the search for an optimal interval is a fruitless enterprise.

Stimulus Intensity. The role of stimulus intensity has also received a good deal of attention. The general finding has been that the strength of conditioning increases as a function of the intensity of the US up to some limit. For example, Beck (1963) reported that eyelid conditioning in humans was greater with stronger air puffs to the eye. Similarly, a series of experiments by Spence and his associates demonstrated stronger conditioning with a more intense US (for example, Trapold & Spence, 1960).

But what about the role of CS intensity? For a number of years, investigators were unable to find a systematic relationship between the strength of conditioning and CS intensity. For example, Grant and Schneider (1949) conditioned the GSR response in humans by

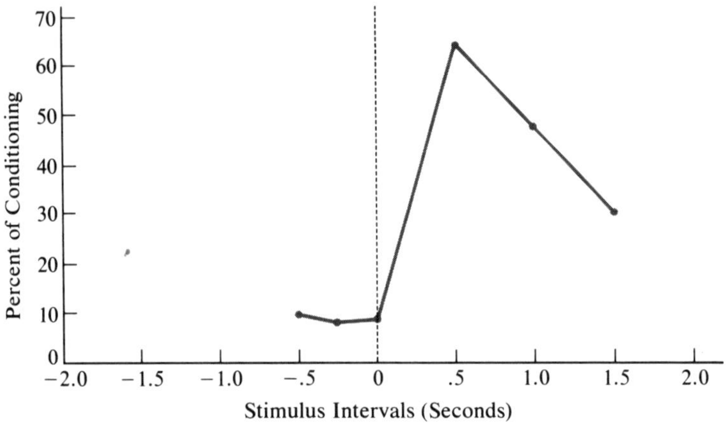

Figure 2–4. Effect of the time interval between the CS and the US, and the order of the CS and the US, on conditioning. Minus values on the horizontal axis indicate that the CS follows the US; positive values indicate that the CS precedes the US. (From "The Backward Conditioning Curve," by A. Spooner and W.N. Kellogg, *American Journal of Psychology,* 1947, *60,* 321–334. Reprinted by permission of the University of Illinois Press.)

pairing a tone CS with shock as a US. Using four different CS intensities, they were unable to find an orderly relationship between CS intensity and strength of conditioning. However, subsequent studies by Beck (1963) and Grice and Hunter (1964) were able to show clear-cut evidence for the effects of CS intensity. The critical feature of the last two studies was the use of between-subject and within-subject designs. Between-subject designs present the subject with only one level of a variable, in this case only one level of stimulus intensity, whereas in within-subject designs the subject receives all levels of the variable. The major finding of both Beck and Grice and Hunter was that CS-intensity effects were clearly present with a within-subject procedure but were minimal with a between-subject procedure. Let us examine the Grice and Hunter study in more detail.

In this study Grice and Hunter examined the effects of CS intensity on human eyelid conditioning in which the CS consisted of a tone. Two groups of subjects were conditioned for 100 trials with either a loud tone of 100 decibels (db) Sound Pressure Level (SPL) or a soft tone of 50 db SPL. A third group, the within-subject condition, received 50 conditioning trials with each tone, with the order of presentation of the tones being random. The results, shown in Figure 2–5, were quite dramatic. As you can see, there was a pronounced effect of CS intensity when the subjects received both stimuli during conditioning and a quite marginal effect when the subjects received only one stimulus. Clearly, the effects of CS intensity depend on the procedure used.

The interpretation of this finding is rather complex and has gone through something of an evolution in recent years. Obviously, any interpretation has to do with the fact that the subjects who received both tones had some opportunity to *compare* them, whereas the subjects who received only one tone did not. In other words, the CS-intensity phenomenon is due to some kind of contrast effect. Initially, the explanation offered was in terms of an adaptation-level principle, in which the subject's adaptation level for stimulus intensity was thought to be located between the two stimuli. In short, a perceptual contrast between the

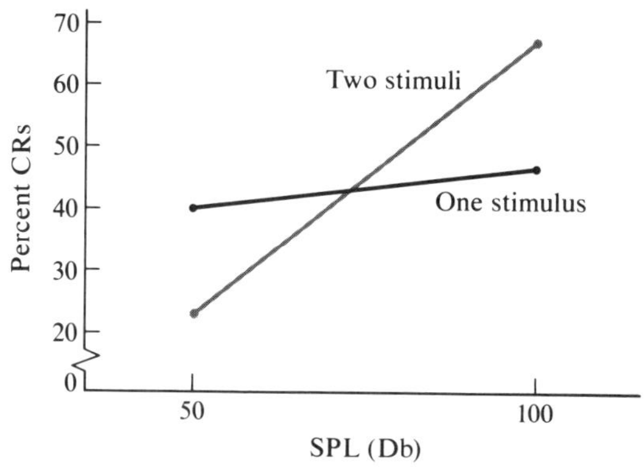

Figure 2–5. Percentage of CRs during the last 60 trials to the loud and soft tones under the one-stimulus and two-stimulus conditions. (From "Stimulus Intensity Effects Depend upon the Type of Experimental Design," by G.R. Grice and J.J. Hunter, *Psychological Review,* 1964, *71,* 247–256. Copyright 1964 by the American Psychological Association. Reprinted by permission.)

two CSs would amplify their effects. Subsequently, Grice (1968, 1972, 1977) proposed a new interpretation of this finding and a number of related phenomena as well. The interpretation is based upon the idea of a variable criterion that makes the assumption that subjects adopt a criterion for whether or not to respond in a situation and that the criterion a subject adopts may vary over a range of experimental conditions. Variable-criterion theory is a form of decision theory concerned with the evocation of simple responses. It simply states that response evocation will occur when the information produced by a stimulus exceeds a subject's criterion. The criterion is thought to be distributed normally as a random variable. The stimulus is thought to produce two kinds of information, sensory and associative, which combine in an additive fashion.

The Role of Instructions and Awareness. With human subjects it is possible to change performance in classical conditioning by instructions. This simply emphasizes that cognitive factors are important in the sense that human subjects are usually trying to figure out what is going on, perhaps so they can attempt to master the situation.

An early study by Norris and Grant (1948) illustrated that instructions can inhibit the course of conditioning. Human subjects received eyelid conditioning in which half the subjects were given no verbal instructions, while the remaining half were warned not to blink before they felt the air puff. The results indicated that the instructions clearly depressed performance. Similar results have been reported by Nicholls and Kimble (1964). They gave one group of subjects instructions designed to facilitate conditioning—such as "Relax and let your eye reactions take care of themselves"—whereas another group of subjects were told not to blink until they felt the puff of air. Subjects who received facilitative instructions showed substantially greater conditioning.

Related to the role of instructions is the role of awareness. In this context the term *awareness* refers to the subject's knowledge of the CS-US contingency. Some researchers have argued that human subjects must be aware of this contingency if conditioning is to occur, and a large number experiments have examined this factor. The results have been mixed. One of the critical problems has been to define a subject's awareness in a valid way. After conditioning, subjects are usually given a questionnaire designed to assess their state of awareness, but, unfortunately, we cannot be sure that their responses constitute a valid measure of awareness. Consequently, some investigators, such as Grant (1973), conclude that evidence for a positive relationship between awareness and conditioning is as yet rather weak, whereas others, such as Spielberger & DeNike (1966), believe that the relationship is strong.

The Frequency of the US. In general, the acquisition of a CR is directly related to the frequency of the US during training. In classical conditioning the US constitutes a reinforcing stimulus, so varying the frequency of the US is equivalent to varying the frequency of reinforcement. For the present the reader can regard a reinforcer as any event that increases the strength or probability of a response. Several studies of human eyelid conditioning have shown that the percentage of CRs produced increases with the percentage of reinforcement (US). For example, Hartman and Grant (1960) presented the US for 25%, 50%, 75%, or 100% of the acquisition trials and found a direct relation between percentage of reinforcement and acquisition of the CR. Similar findings have been reported by Moore and Gormezano (1963).

Instrumental Conditioning

The essential feature of instrumental conditioning is that a response is instrumental in obtaining some goal. In this situation the subject's behavior determines the outcome. For example, Thorndike (1898), in his early investigations, studied the behavior of hungry cats in a locked puzzle box. The cats were able to escape from the box by hitting a latch that opened a door allowing them access to food. When placed in the box, the cats would at first move around vigorously, making many responses. But during repeated trials the cats began to learn the appropriate response of hitting the latch. Today, a commonly used device in instrumental conditioning is an enclosed chamber sometimes called a Skinner box (Skinner, 1938). A hungry or thirsty animal placed in the box must press a bar to obtain food or water. Initially, an animal such as a rat will move about, making a variety of responses, but will gradually learn to press the bar, the response that achieves a reward, and to eliminate responses that do not produce a reward.

Instrumental conditioning differs from classical conditioning in several ways. In instrumental conditioning a contingency is established between some stimulus situation, a response, and a reinforcer; in classical conditioning a contingency is established between two stimuli. In instrumental conditioning a response must occur before a reward, or a reinforcing stimulus, is obtained; in classical conditioning the US occurs prior to and produces the response. Another distinguishing feature is that the stimulus eliciting the response in classical conditioning is well specified, but the "stimulus situation" in instrumental conditioning is not. Indeed, it may not be possible to identify the stimuli in many instrumental-conditioning experiments. Finally, instrumental conditioning involves greater variability of behavior than does classical conditioning. In instrumental conditioning the subject may be faced with a variety of response alternatives and must come to *select* the appropriate response.

Although the procedures of classical and instrumental conditioning differ, the behavior acquired under these procedures is similar across a wide range of variables. The validity of this generalization will become apparent as we review the factors affecting instrumental conditioning in subsequent chapters.

Outcomes in Instrumental Conditioning

We can classify various kinds of outcomes in instrumental conditioning by distinguishing between *reinforcers* and *punishers*. In instrumental conditioning a response is made that is followed by some stimulus event or consequence. If the stimulus event, whatever it may be, has the effect of increasing the frequency of the response, the stimulus is called a reinforcer. For example, food is a reinforcer for a hungry animal if the food leads to an increase in a particular response, such as bar pressing. Conversely, if the response is weakened or suppressed as a result of its outcome, the stimulus event is called a punisher. Accordingly, the stimulus events in instrumental conditioning are defined in terms of their effects on behavior; the reinforcing or punishing properties of the stimulus are inferred from response changes. These definitions are circular, but the circularity is avoided as long as it can be shown that a stimulus has similar effects on different response classes. For example, since food has the effect of increasing the rate of bar pressing, it should have a similar effect on a locomotive response; that is, running speed in a straight alley should also increase when the locomotive response is followed by food. In brief, the circularity argument can be "escaped" by demonstrating that reinforcers and punishers are transsituational (Meehl, 1950).

Another distinction is that reinforcers and punishers can be classified as *positive* or *negative*. A reinforcer is identified as positive when its occurrence results in an increase in response probability. For instance, candy can be said to be a positive reinforcer for a young child if it increases the probability of the child's saying "please." In contrast, a reinforcer is negative if there is an increase in response probability following termination of a noxious stimulus event. For example, if cleaning up your room prevents or terminates parental nagging, nagging is said to be a negative reinforcer. Thus, response probability increases with either a positive or a negative reinforcer; the difference between them resides in whether the response is followed by an occurrence or a termination of the stimulus event.

A similar distinction is made for punishers. Positive punishers are indexed by responses producing the onset of an aversive stimulus, which decreases response probability. Negative punishers also produce decrements in the probability of the response, but response suppression ensues because a benevolent stimulus is removed. Usually, reinforcers and punishers produce reciprocal effects. Both positive and negative reinforcers increase response probability when the onset of a benevolent or the termination of an aversive event occurs. Conversely, with punishers the onset of an aversive or the termination of a benevolent stimulus results in a decrease in response probability. Classifying reinforcers and punishers in this way is important because the nature of the contingent event permits a classification of various kinds of instrumental conditioning.

Basic Processes in Conditioning

In this section we will provide a very brief description of basic processes in both classical and instrumental conditioning. These processes will be discussed in much greater detail in subsequent chapters, but a short description is useful at this point for understanding certain features of conditioning.

Acquisition. The process of acquisition is simply the occurrence of conditioning. In classical conditioning, acquisition takes place when the CS can reliably produce the CR. In instrumental conditioning, acquisition is the strengthening of the reinforced response.

Extinction and Spontaneous Recovery. Extinction is the weakening or elimination of a response. In instrumental conditioning a response is said to undergo extinction when reinforcement no longer follows the response. In classical conditioning, extinction will occur when the CS is repeatedly presented without the US. Extinction is usually thought to be some sort of active inhibitory process, not simply a passive process of nonresponding. One piece of evidence for this conclusion is that responses will undergo spontaneous recovery after some period of time following non-reinforcement. For instance, if, after extinction of a bar-pressing response, an experimental animal is removed from the chamber in which it was trained and later returned to the chamber, the animal may press the bar again, sometimes with a burst of responses.

Stimulus Generalization. The term *stimulus generalization* refers to the finding that stimuli similar to the CS, or training stimulus, also acquire the capacity to evoke a response. A study by Hovland (1937a) will illustrate the process of stimulus generalization in classical conditioning. Hovland conditioned the GSR in human subjects with an auditory stimulus of 153 hertz (hz). Shock was the US. He then tested for generalization by presenting the subjects with tones of 486, 1000, and 1967 hz, which were judged to be equidistant from one another in judged frequency. He observed that the subjects would respond to the tones and that the amplitude of the GSR decreased as the test stimuli became progressively less similar to the CS. Similar findings occur in instrumental conditioning (Grice & Saltz, 1950).

One point to note about the process of stimulus generalization is that it indicates that our learning is not necessarily tied to specific stimuli. Rather, the process emphasizes that behavior can be controlled by a range of stimuli similar to those used in conditioning training.

Discrimination. Related to generalization is the process of discrimination. Discrimination is the ability of a subject to respond differentially in the presence of two stimuli. This simply means that a subject learns to respond in the presence of one stimulus and not in the presence of another.

Types of Instrumental Conditioning

Instrumental conditioning can be classified into several types. We will describe several types whose features depend on whether reward or punishment is given and on whether the subject must produce or withhold a response.

Reward Training. Any training procedure in which the subject receives positive reinforcement for making an appropriate response is called reward training. We have already discussed several examples: rats pressing levers to obtain food or water, children saying "please" to obtain candy. With lower animals the reinforcer is usually food or water; with humans the rewards may be, for example, candy, money, praise, movies, or tokens of some kind that can be exchanged for some desired object. The term *reward* is used because the objects are typically valuable or pleasant for the subject. Generally, a distinction is made between reinforcers and rewards. Reinforcers are defined by their effects on behavior; nothing is implied about whether they produce pleasure. In contrast, calling a stimulus event a reward connotes that it produces pleasure.

An important aspect of reward training involves the use of *shaping* procedures. Ordinarily, in teaching a subject to make a particular response, it is desirable to reinforce a response that only approximates the desired response. For example, in teaching a rat to press a bar for food, responses are reinforced that are only grossly related to bar pressing, such as placing a paw on a lever, touching the lever with the nose, or even getting near the bar. Gradually, only those responses that successively approximate the correct response are reinforced. Good teachers may use the same procedure. At first they may reinforce behaviors that only roughly approximate the desired outcome; later they can demand more precise and appropriate behaviors.

Omission Training. In omission training the subject must learn to *withhold* a response to obtain a reward. In other words, if a response is made no reward occurs, and nonresponding leads to a reward. Since nonresponding is rewarded, this procedure leads to an increase in nonresponding.

Escape and Avoidance Training. Negative reinforcers were defined as stimuli whose removal results in an increase in the probability of some response. If we focus on the response in question rather than the reinforcing event, it should be noted that the response allows the subject to escape the noxious stimulation. *Escape* responses, then, are responses that result in the termination of aversive stimuli. And escape learning is a training procedure in which the probability of a response increases when aversive stimuli are removed. A rat's pressing a lever to terminate shock and your taking off your coat on a hot day qualify as escape responses. Common to each example is that the negative reinforcer is applied independently of the subject's behavior and that the occurrence of a particular response terminates the event.

Escape learning is such a commonplace occurrence that it may remain undetected by the individual engaging in it. The reason is that the stimuli are usually only mildly aversive. But for noxious events that produce considerable pain or fear, the subject usually takes preparatory action to prevent them. This type of response is classified as an *avoidance* response. Avoidance learning is an interesting phenomenon because so much of our behavior appears to involve it. Paying one's bills on time, filing income-tax forms before the deadline, and perhaps even studying for an examination can be viewed as avoidance responses because the effect of such responses is to prevent the occurrence of aversive stimulation. Escape responses, in contrast, terminate aversive stimuli.

Punishment. Punishment training is defined as a situation in which a noxious stimulus is applied as the result of some response. Punishment is similar to reward training except that the stimulus is aversive or unpleasant. In general, responses are suppressed or weakened by punishment, whereas they are strengthened by reinforcement. If the inappropriate or punished response fails to occur, the punisher is not presented. This is a typical consequence of the punishing procedure; the subject can avoid the onset of noxious stimulation by *not* making the response. For this reason the term *passive avoidance* is used by some psychologists to refer to the punishment procedure. This is to say, the subject can passively avoid the punisher by not engaging in the inappropriate behavior. Characterizing punishment in this way suggests that avoidance and punishment have reciprocal effects. In avoidance, if the subject makes the appropriate response, the aversive stimulus is not presented. In punishment, if an inappropriate response is made, aversive stimulation occurs. Furthermore, in punishment, if the inappropriate behavior does *not* occur, the punisher is *not* applied, whereas in avoidance the punisher is presented when the avoidance response fails to occur.

Comparison of Classical and Instrumental Conditioning

When classical and instrumental conditioning are compared, one issue is whether they differ only in their procedures or whether the procedures actually reflect different processes as well. Many psychological concepts refer to both procedure and process (J.S. Brown, 1965). For example, *extinction* may indicate a decrease in response probability when a reinforcer is removed, but the term may also be used to refer to a hypothetical weakening of an S-R connection that results from that procedure. Similarly, the terms *classical* and *instrumental conditioning* may describe different procedures, or they may refer to the processes responsible for the learned associations established by the paradigms.

It is easy to distinguish between classical and instrumental conditioning procedurally, but more difficult to differentiate between them as processes. For example, classical conditioning may take place in the course of instrumental conditioning. Furthermore, the responses investigated with the two conditioning paradigms usually differ, so it is difficult to make comparisons between them. Indeed, some theorists (for example, Skinner, 1938) argue that since the responses produced by each training procedure are mediated by two functionally distinct divisions of the nervous system, the laws of these forms of learning are different.

One way to determine whether an organism learns different things within the two paradigms is to ask whether the behavioral effects observed with one paradigm also occur with the other. The strategy has been to examine an effect produced by experimental manipulation of a variable in classical conditioning and determine whether the same or a similar effect will occur when the same manipulation is performed in instrumental conditioning. Presumably, if the same behavioral phenomenon is observed with two procedures when the same variable is manipulated, a sufficient condition exists for supposing that the laws governing the establishment of the associations are the same. G.A. Kimble (1961) provides an excellent review of the earlier literature and concludes, in the main, that the findings suggest that the same behavioral phenomena observed in classical conditioning are also found in instrumental learning.

One exception to these findings is the effects of intermittent or partial reinforcement. Here reinforcement is given for only some portion of the responses. Pavlov (1927) noted that CRs could not be established if the US was presented on only every fourth trial. Learning of classically conditioned responses is also seriously impaired when the US appears on only half the trials after terminal or asymptotic performance (where the performance levels off) is reached (Ross, 1959; Runquist, 1963). In contrast, the effects of partial reinforcement may lead to asymptotic performance levels equal or superior to those found with continuous reinforcement in instrumental conditioning (see, for example, Goodrich, 1959). Moreover, responding is not impaired when animals are shifted gradually from continuous to intermittent reinforcement (see, for example, Ferster & Skinner, 1957). The differential effects of partial reinforcement on classical and instrumental conditioning have led some theorists (for example, Razran, 1971) to view the paradigms as reflecting the operation of two different processes.

At one time, further support for two-process theories rested on observations that organisms' responses in experiments were of two basic sorts. The majority of responses conditioned with Pavlovian procedures involved the glands or viscera and were apparently mediated by the autonomic nervous system. In contrast, responses investigated using instrumental procedures involved the movement of the organisms or their parts in space, which obviously required the use of skeletal muscles that are controlled by the cerebral/spinal system. Although some muscular responses could be conditioned classically—for example, leg flexion—it appeared that visceral and glandular reactions could not be modified instrumentally.

Illustrative of the supposed inability to modify glandular responses instrumentally was an experiment by F.D. Sheffield (1965). Using omission training procedures, he was unable to inhibit a dog's salivary response to the US even after 800 trials. (The dog received the US only when the salivation failed to occur; if the CR appeared during the CS presentation, the US was withheld.) Sheffield concluded on the basis of this finding that glandular responses are not modifiable by reinforcement. He suggested that an organism's inability to modify responses mediated by the the autonomic nervous system is a result of those responses being deficient in sensory aftereffects; that is, given the paucity of stimulation resulting from those responses, they remain undetected by the nervous system.

However, shortly after Sheffield's work appeared, N.E. Miller and his co-workers published reports contradicting Sheffield's conclusions. Miller and Carmona (1967) trained dogs to increase or decrease salivation for a water reward, demonstrating that an autonomically innervated response could be modified by instrumental training procedures. But since the dogs' skeletal muscles were intact, it was possible that salivary responding was indirectly controlled through skeletal mechanisms. To control for this problem, d-tubocurarine, a pure form of curare isolated in 1935, was used in subsequent experiments to induce muscle paralysis. Preventing the transmission of impulses at the neuromuscular junction produced a further problem: food and water could not be used as reinforcers because the organism lacked the means to consume them. Therefore, stimulation of a reward center in the brain, the medial-forebrain bundle in the hypothalamic region, was used to reinforce changes in visceral activity. This technique used with curarized rats has produced either increases or decreases in visceral responses such as heart rate (Miller & DiCara, 1967), blood pressure (DiCara & Miller, 1968b), vasomotor responses (DiCara & Miller, 1968c), intestinal motility (Miller & Banuazizi, 1968), and renal blood flow (Miller & DiCara, 1968). Criticism that visceral learning might be due to the nature of the reward was obviated when DiCara and Miller (1968a) showed that heart rate could be modified by escape from or avoidance of electric shock.

The visceral learning was also revealed to be highly specific. Miller and Banuazizi (1968) showed that curarized rats rewarded for either increases or decreases in heart rate did not show any change in intestinal relaxation or contraction, while animals trained to alter intestinal motility showed no change in heart rate. The specificity of the responses learned indicated that visceral learning was not mediated by heightened arousal or by an imbalance between the sympathetic and parasympathetic systems. Since instrumental training procedures could be used to modify responses innervated by both the central and the autonomic system, Miller (1969) concluded that the functional division of the nervous system could not be sustained and that the laws permitting the modification of responses by Pavlovian or instrumental procedures reflected a single process. At this juncture the uniprocess theory looked strong.

Shortly afterward, however, DiCara, Braun, and Pappas (1970) demonstrated that removal of the neo-cortex in rats prevented the modification of heart rate by instrumental procedures but not by classical conditioning. Normal rats learned to change heart rate with both procedures. The results suggest that the neuroanatomical loci for visceral learning may be different for instrumental and classical conditioning. Presumably, if the neural mechanisms responsible for classical and instrumental modification of visceral reactions are different, the processes mediating their formation may also differ.

A more serious objection to a uniprocess theory of learning based upon the instrumental modification of visceral reactions stems from recent failures to replicate the early experiments (for example, Miller & Dworkin, 1974). Although other workers report reliable changes in heart rate (Hothersall & Brener, 1969; Slaughter, Hahn, & Rinaldi, 1970), there has been a progressive decline in learned heart-rate changes since the inception of the work (see Figure 2–6).

The reasons for the failure to induce changes in heart rate are unclear, but a strong contender for the anomalous results may be the drug itself. Early work (Smith, Brown, Toman, & Goodman, 1947; Unna & Pelikan, 1951) suggested that d-tubocurarine did not affect the autonomic and cerebral systems; its action was apparently confined to the neuromuscular junction. The evidence of curare's effect on the central nervous system is still equivocal (for an excellent review, see Howard, Galosy, Gaebelien, & Obrist, 1974),

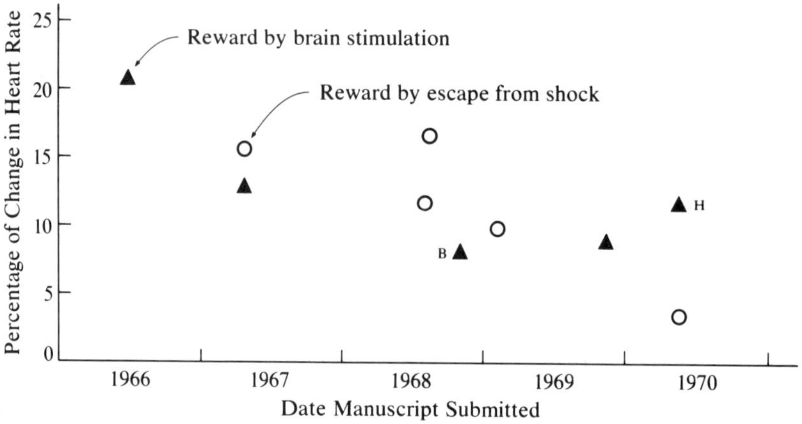

Figure 2–6. Progressive decline in learned heart-rate changes during five years. The experiments were performed under approximately similar conditions in Miller's laboratory, except for point B, from data by Hothersall and Brener (1969), and point H, from data by Slaughter, Hahn, and Rinaldi (1970). For each experiment, increases and decreases were converted into percentage changes and then averaged. (From "Interactions between Learned and Physical Factors in Mental Illness," by N.E. Miller, *Seminars in Psychiatry,* 1972, *4,* 239–254. Reprinted by permission of Grune & Stratton, Inc.)

but recent work suggests that it may affect the autonomic system either directly or indirectly. As an illustration of an indirect action, it is known that d-tubocurarine releases histamine (W.W. Douglas, 1970). Histamine produces many changes in the body: capillary dilation, bronchiolar constriction, stimulation of the smooth muscles of arteries and veins. These effects could conceivably alter heart rate indirectly via blood-pressure changes. But another problem still exists. If Miller and others used the same drug throughout this five-year period, it is unclear why the amount of conditioning decreased.

Even acknowledging that autonomic functioning may be changed by curare, it is difficult to account for the specificity of visceral learning, especially in the Miller and Banuazizi experiments, which show changes in intestinal motility but no change in heart rate. In short, it would be premature to dismiss the results as artifacts of the drug.

In any event, firm conclusions about the learning of visceral responses by instrumental training procedures cannot be made at this time. But the resolution of this issue is important for theories of learning, of the functional division of the nervous system, and of psychosomatic ailments (Miller, 1975). More specifically, future research will increase our understanding of what is meant by voluntary control, whether one's behavior alters physiological functioning to the degree that homeostatic mechanisms may be affected, and whether behavioral techniques can be developed to cure or prevent peptic ulcers, colitis, and other ailments presumably caused by environmental stress.

Higher-Order Conditioning

In 1927 Pavlov described a phenomenon in conditioning that has come to be known as *higher-order* or second-order conditioning. Higher-order conditioning can be understood as follows. Assume that a hungry dog has been conditioned to salivate in the presence of a tone. We can now build upon this CS (tone)–CR (salivation) connection by introducing a *new* CS, pairing it with the old CS. In this fashion we treat the old CS as if it were the US. The new CS is some other stimulus such as a light or some visual pattern such as a black square. With this procedure we can train the dog to salivate in the presence of the new CS. The new CS is itself originally a neutral stimulus, but after a few pairings with the old CS, it begins to elicit the salivary response.

Higher-order conditioning has been assigned a heavy explanatory burden by a number of learning theorists. It has been used to account for the establishment of learned rewards (Hull, 1943) and for the maintenance of locomotive and manipulatory responses by those who wish to account for learning with Pavlovian-conditioning principles (Sheffield, 1966). Despite the theoretical uses to which higher-order conditioning has been put, many experimenters have regarded the evidence as insufficient for higher-order conditioning to carry this burden of explaining more complex behavior. In Pavlov's experiments, for example, attempts to extend the conditioning to a third neutral stimulus—that is, pairing a black square with another stimulus—failed to produce salivation to the new stimulus. Furthermore, the effects of higher-order conditioning are typically unstable, with the CRs weakening rapidly when the US is no longer presented.

Recently, however, Rescorla and his associates (Rescorla, 1973; Rizley & Rescorla, 1972) have provided evidence showing that substantial second-order conditioning can be obtained. In addition, their work clarifies the processes that underlie this form of learning. Rizley and Rescorla, in Experiment 1, employed a procedure in which classical conditioning is indexed by disruption of bar pressing. They trained four groups of eight rats each to press a bar under circumstances in which food was delivered on the average of once every minute. The behavior generated under these conditions produces a stable rate of bar pressing and enables the experimenter to assess the effect of other manipulations on this baseline. Three of the four groups then received eight paired presentations of a 10-second flashing light and a .5-second foot shock superimposed on their bar pressing. The four groups received eight lights and eight shocks with an "explicitly unpaired" procedure.

After first-order conditioning a 1800-Hz tone 30 seconds long was paired with the light for three of the groups; the fourth group received the same number of tones and lights, but the stimuli were unpaired. During the second-order phase of conditioning, no shocks were delivered. To index the effects of the second-order stimulus on the bar-pressing rate, the experimenters calculated a suppression ratio, $A/(A+B)$. The symbol A denotes the response rate during the tone, and B is the rate for a comparable period before its onset. A suppression ratio of .5 indicates that the CS has not had an effect; the rate of responding before and during the CS would be identical. A 50% reduction in bar-pressing rate yields a ratio of .33, while a ratio of 0 means that the CS has completely suppressed the bar-pressing behavior.

Figure 2–7 shows the disruption of response rate to the second-order stimulus for the four groups. As can be seen, the groups receiving paired presentation of CS_1 and the US followed by the second-order pairing of CS_2 and CS_1 (Groups PPN and PPE) showed significant disruption of response rate, suggesting a substantial amount of second-order conditioning. Groups UPE and PUE served as controls: light and shock were never paired for the UPE group, and, consequently, no first-order conditioning occurred. Second-order conditioning was prevented for Group PUE because the tone was never paired with the light. The suppression of response rate by the PPE and PPN groups shows that second-order stimuli can have profound effects on behavior.

More generally, Rescorla's findings support the idea that the association formed during second-order conditioning is between the second-order stimulus and the conditioned response. As a result of Rescorla's work, interest in the phenomenon of second-order conditioning can be expected to increase.

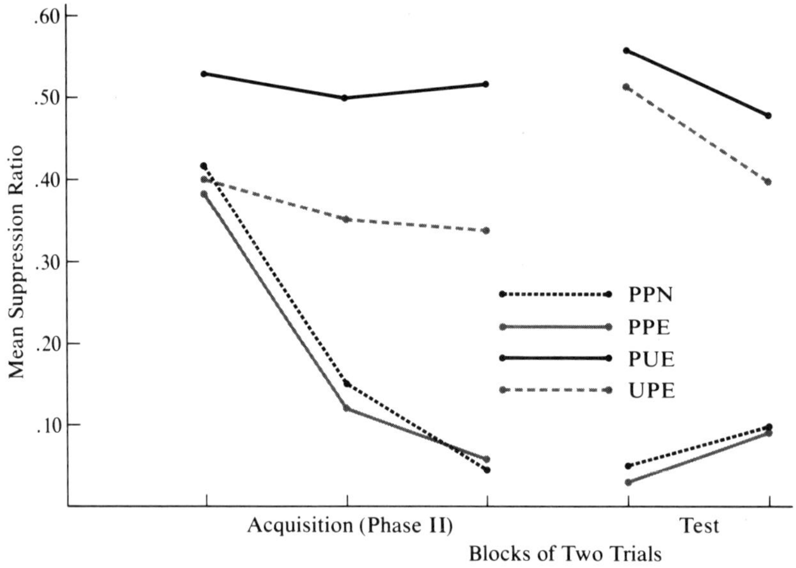

Figure 2–7. Mean suppression ratio during the second-order stimulus. Extinction of the first-order stimulus intervened between acquisition and test of the second-order stimulus. (From "Associations in Second-Order Conditioning and Sensory Preconditioning," by R.C. Rizley and R.A. Rescorla, *Journal of Comparative and Physiological Psychology*," 1972, *81*, 1–11. Copyright 1972 by the American Psychological Association. Reprinted by permission.)

Applications of Conditioning

Psychologists have been successful in applying the principles of conditioning to several areas, notably education, behavior therapy, and child development. This is not surprising, since the principles of classical and instrumental conditioning also describe ways of changing behavior. Effective use of the principles of conditioning has led to a new technology of managing behavior, particularly in the classroom and in the clinic. In this section we will briefly examine two kinds of applications that have received a good deal of attention.

Instructional Technology

One major application of principles of conditioning is in the teaching/learning process. In a series of papers, Skinner (1958, 1961) outlined the way these principles could be applied in educational settings. His contribution was the "teaching machine" and, more important, the idea of programmed learning. Programmed learning involves breaking down a body of instructional material into relatively small, discrete steps. Students advance through each step until they eventually master the material. At each step they are presented a question or problem to which they must respond. For example, the students may be presented a sentence with a blank and asked to fill it in. They receive immediate feedback on the correctness of their answer by consulting an answer sheet. If they are correct, they continue on to the next item; if they are incorrect, they are alerted that they are having difficulty, and they may be directed to a remedial question. The teaching machine is simply a mechanical device for presenting the material; there is nothing special about such devices other than that they conveniently control the material presented. Most programmed-learning materials are now prepared in book form, so that use of the machine itself has become unimportant.

Programmed learning applies the principles we have described in this chapter. First, the procedure emphasizes that students must actively respond for learning to occur. The sequence of the problems keeps the learners actively responding at each step. Second, the learners are given feedback at each step. This is somewhat akin to receiving reinforcement but is not exactly the same process. Third, the learners are led through a series of steps in which progress is gradual and continuous. Finally, the students are free to progress at their own rate.

An interesting extension of programmed learning is the Keller plan, developed by Fred Keller. He described a plan by which an entire course, such as introductory psychology, can be programmed. In this plan, lectures are optional. The course is broken up into a number of mastery units, and the students must individually complete and master each unit before proceeding to the next one. The students study a given unit, and as soon as they feel prepared, they take a quiz on it. If they pass, they progress to the next unit; if not, the instructor evaluates weaknesses and assists the students. The Keller plan appears to be successful, and experimental tests of the plan indicate that students respond quite favorably. Its effectiveness is apparently due to the same features noted in programmed learning: active responding, feedback, self-pacing, and requiring high levels of mastery before going on to the next unit.

Behavior Therapy

Another application of the principles of conditioning is in the area of behavior therapy. Behavior therapy makes the basic assumption that most abnormal behaviors are the result of the learning process. Therefore, this approach views therapy as a process of teaching patients both to extinguish old, ineffective ways of coping with problems and to strengthen new, effective coping strategies. The basic task of the therapist is to identify the maladaptive, ineffective behaviors that are part of the patient's problem and to extinguish these behaviors. In addition, the therapist must attempt to reinforce new, adaptive behaviors that will enable the patient to cope more effectively with life problems.

A variety of behavior-therapy techniques have been developed (see, for example, Kanfer & Phillips, 1970; Krasner & Ullman, 1965). It is beyond the scope of this chapter to review these in detail, but we will mention two of them. One technique is called aversion therapy, in which subjects are taught to "dislike" some stimulus through classical-conditioning procedures. For example, the therapist may treat alcoholic patients by conditioning some aversive consequence (nausea, shock) with the taste and smell of alcoholic beverages. The other technique is called implosion therapy, in which patients are taught to imagine or visualize whatever fear-provoking stimuli concern them. For example, if a patient has an extreme fear of heights, the patient imagines being on top of a mountain. Since presumably no actual punishing consequences follow, the fear will gradually extinguish.

Behavior therapy has become a useful set of procedures for the therapist. This approach has been found effective where others have failed. It is not, however, the only approach to therapy, and it is recognized that there are some areas in which it may not be as effective as other approaches.

Summary

This chapter described the basic procedures and processes of classical and instrumental conditioning. Classical conditioning was seen as a training procedure in which a previously neutral stimulus, the CS, acquires the capacity to elicit a CR. We saw that the US follows the CS regardless of what the subject may do, making the procedure noncontingent. The CS is a clearly identifiable event, and the CR may be similar to the UR but may differ in certain ways. The wide range of classical conditioning was noted, and the importance of control procedures was emphasized. Factors affecting classical conditioning include amount of training, the CS-US interval, stimulus intensity, the frequency of the US, and instructions and awareness.

Instrumental conditioning was described as a procedure in which a response is instrumental in obtaining some goal. Several features differentiating between classical and instrumental conditioning were noted. Reinforcers and punishers were distinguished by noting that reinforcers have the effect of increasing the frequency of a response, whereas punishers have the effect of weakening or suppressing a response. Basic processes in both classical and instrumental conditioning include acquisition, extinction, spontaneous recovery, generalization, and discrimination. Types of instrumental conditioning described are reward training, omission training, escape and avoidance training, and punishment.

One major objective of comparisons of instrumental and classical conditioning has been to determine whether they differ only procedurally or reflect different processes as well. Much of this research has focused on instrumental conditioning of autonomic responses. Although there is some evidence for such conditioning, the evidence is still equivocal.

Higher-order conditioning has long been of interest to psychologists. One reason for this interest is that higher-order conditioning can account for several features of learning. Although earlier studies indicated only limited effects, recent studies have indicated substantial evidence for second-order conditioning.

Finally, some applications of conditioning principles were described. Two major kinds of applications were seen in instructional technology and in behavior therapy.

Chapter 3

Reinforcement and Learning

Reinforcements and punishments are widely used to influence behavior. In fact, we spend a good deal of our daily lives responding in such a way that we will achieve as much reinforcement and avoid as many punishing experiences as possible. We also reinforce in others those behaviors that we find desirable and punish those behaviors that we find objectionable.

At a conceptual level our current views of reinforcement and punishment can be traced back to biological ideas about evolution and natural selection (Darwin, 1859; Spencer, 1855). For Charles Darwin, the diversity occurring in nature reflected the operation of natural selection: organisms struggle to survive; those that are successful possess characteristics that aid in the struggle. These traits are eventually transmitted to the organisms' offspring. Through this process a species gradually acquires new characteristics that allow it to adapt to its changing environment. Those species that do not change will perish, as the large number of extinct forms of plant and animal life attests.

Herbert Spencer, one of the early proponents of evolutionary theory, was among the first to suggest that if natural selection can explain the evolution of species, then possibly a similar principle can be used to explain why adaptive changes occur in the behavior of *individual* animals (Postman, 1947). Essentially, Spencer extended the principle of natural selection from describing the survival of species to describing the survival of individuals. He suggested that through the course of evolution, associations had been established between subjective states of pleasure and responses beneficial for survival and between subjective feelings of pain and responses that lessen the chances for survival. He thought that animals that learned to repeat responses that produced pleasure while refraining from responses that produced pain were likely to produce offspring with similar behavior characteristics.

If natural selection as a process resulted in the survival of some individuals and the elimination of others, depending on how well they adapted to their environment, learning was probably a similar process that ensured "survival" of adaptive responses and "extinction" of nonadaptive responses. Although Spencer's primitive psychology of learning was highly speculative, it was important because it treated behavior as a biological process. In his view, rewards and punishers were biologically significant events that affected later behavior. This means that rewards and punishers ultimately influenced the survival of both an individual organism and its species. For this reason, he felt, psychologists should determine possible relationships between behavior and the various properties of rewards and punishments.

One effect of Spencer's ideas was to encourage the application of scientific methods to the study of behavior. One of the first psychologists to do so was Thorndike (1898). He conducted many experiments, and on the basis of his work, he formulated his famous law of effect. The law, which shares many similarities with Spencer's basic view, states:

> Of several responses made to the same situation, those which are accompanied or closely followed by satisfaction to the animal will, other things being equal, be more firmly connected with the situation, so that, when it recurs, they will be more likely to recur; those which are accompanied or closely followed by discomfort to the animal will, other things being equal, have their connections with that situation weakened, so that when it recurs, they will be less likely to occur. The greater the satisfaction or discomfort, the greater the strengthening or weakening of the bond. [Thorndike, 1911, p. 244].

The early version of the law of effect, stated above, assigns equal weights to reward and punishment; rewards strengthen S–R associations, while punishers weaken them. Thorndike later modified his law so that punishment is given far less importance than reinforcement. In his revised law, punishment does not directly affect learning; that is, punishment has no inherent weakening effects on those behaviors it follows. Instead, the effect of punishment is thought to be limited to increasing the opportunity for responses other than the one punished to occur. However, as we shall see in the next chapter, which examines punishment phenomena in detail, punishment can actually produce a dramatic and long-lasting suppression of behaviors that it follows. The present chapter will be confined to the topic of reinforcement. We will first explore the law of effect more thoroughly and see that the effectiveness of reinforcement can vary from one animal species to another. Next, the nature of and the mechanisms that underlie reinforcement will be described. Finally, the ways in which different properties of reinforcers differentially affect behavior will be discussed.

The Learning of Contingencies: Is the Law of Effect Automatic?

Thorndike's law of effect specifies the conditions that are necessary for the formation of response–reinforcer contingencies. In other words, the law describes the dependency that exists between behavior and its consequences (either reinforcement or punishment). We learn about contingencies in our own environments in that we acquire information about what leads to what. More specifically, we learn correlations between behaviors that we emit and the outcomes they produce. For example, if children learn that they must emit a certain behavior, such as cleaning their bedroom, to obtain reinforcement, such as a dessert, they will probably act accordingly. If they learn that they must wash the dishes before they can obtain money for the movies, the dishes will probably get washed. Animals will learn to do similar things. If an animal must press a lever at a certain rate in an experimental chamber or run at a certain speed down a straight-alley runway to obtain a food reinforcement, it will adjust its response rate accordingly; infrahuman species, like humans, will learn to run or press a bar at a rapid or a slow rate in order to optimize the amount, frequency, or immediacy of reward.

Superstitious Behavior

Learning about response–reinforcer contingencies requires, in part, that they occur in temporal contiguity. One issue, then, is whether the occurrence of contiguous events (events occurring close together in time) is a sufficient condition for animals to learn an association between those events. In a classic experiment Skinner (1948) attempted to answer this question by presenting food at a fixed interval to eight hungry pigeons independently of their behavior. In other words, the pigeons were reinforced regardless of how they were behaving at a particular moment. Even though no specific response was required to produce reinforcement, Skinner reported that the birds developed stereotyped, idiosyncratic behavior patterns. The pigeons were observed to walk around in circles or scratch the floor or wave their heads from side to side. Furthermore, they would engage in these long sequences of behavior during the intervals between reinforcement. Such behavior was called *superstitious* because the relationship between the emission of a response and the occurrence of a reinforcer was only accidental.

One significance of superstitious behavior is the implication that the effects of reward are automatic and mechanical. Any arbitrary response immediately preceding reward was thought to be strengthened by the blind action of the law of effect. The superstitious-conditioning hypothesis was later treated as an important corollary of operant-conditioning principles (operant conditioning refers to any situation in which the subject is free to respond). It was even used to account for the development of idiosyncratic behavior patterns in humans, such as the athlete who wears the same pair of socks, without washing them, during the team's entire winning streak (for example, Herrnstein, 1966).

More recently, an interesting study by Staddon and Simmelhag (1971) has questioned the hypothesized automatic, mechanical action of the law of effect. Their procedure was an extension of Skinner's demonstration, and it involved a systematic examination of *all* behaviors occurring in the experimental setting. They found that the response observed to follow reinforcement most often early in training was not the same response that occurred following reinforcement after extended exposure to the training situation. Specifically, during early training the most frequent response was "head-in-food-magazine." In contrast, the most frequent response observed late in training was pecking. This is an important finding. If responses are strengthened solely by accidental, or noncontingent, reinforcement, then the response that occurred most often early in training should also have been the response observed most often after extensive training. Thus, Staddon and Simmelhag's results are inconsistent with the superstitious-behavior hypothesis and the view that the law of effect is automatic. In fact, the high degree of similarity between the response observed after extensive training and normal patterns of feeding behavior suggests that, in general, *only those responses compatible with consummatory responding are learned*. This possibility would fit in nicely with Spencer's view of the biological significance of reinforcers.

Shettleworth (1975) has reported observations consistent with this compatibility view of what gets learned. She found that hamsters will increase their rate of emitting responses appropriate to food gathering (for example, digging) when food is used as a reward, but they will show little change in their rate of emitting responses that seldom lead to food in their natural environment (for example, grooming) when food is made contingent on them.

Autoshaping

Support for the compatibility view is also provided by a phenomenon called *autoshaping,* which has recently received a good deal of attention. Suppose we put a pigeon into a chamber like the one used by Skinner and by Staddon and Simmelhag, but with a lighted disk. The light behind the disk goes off at the same time that food is delivered. Again in this case the bird is reinforced at a fixed interval (for example, every 8 seconds) regardless of what it is doing. The behavioral outcome is quite striking. The pigeon quickly acquires a behavior of pecking the key even though pecking in no way affects whether food will be delivered. P.L. Brown and Jenkins (1968) called this phenomenon autoshaping, since the pigeon shapes itself to a key-pecking response rather than being shaped by an experimenter who reinforced behavior that more and more closely approximated key pecking. Autoshaping is a very easy phenomenon to demonstrate in a number of animals.

A fascinating difference between autoshaping and the usual operantly conditioned key-pecking response is that the birds cannot learn to inhibit it when they are subjected to omission training; that is, they will not stop pecking even though their pecking ensures that food will *not* be delivered (D.R. Williams & Williams, 1969). Moreover, even if they enter the training situation under these conditions, in which pecking postpones food delivery, they will still acquire the pecking response.

Autoshaping probably occurs because of the animals' natural tendency to emit responses normally associated with feeding when food is presented. This view would fit in nicely with the compatibility hypothesis, that only those responses compatible with the relevant consummatory behavior will be learned. Technically, the occurrence of autoshaping is best explained as the result of some sort of reflexive, Pavlovian-conditioning process. Pecking may be a highly reflexive UR to food in pigeons, just as salivation is for dogs. Since pecking is so closely tied to food, it may be readily associated with any neutral stimulus that reliably predicts the arrival of food. In other words, the US is the food, and it regularly elicits the reflexive behavior of pecking (UR) at the food. When conditioning occurs, because of the association between the light and food, the pigeon gradually comes to peck at the light, which then becomes the CS (Hearst & Jenkins, 1974). This analysis of the pecking response as an unconditioned response elicited by the unconditioned stimulus of food is fascinating because operant conditioners have always used key pecking as an example of how a response can be shaped and brought under experimental control by applying the proper reinforcement contingencies. *This reinterpretation argues that this response is probably innate, or already wired into the brain of pigeons.* It argues that what we teach animals to do is to associate an already innate response pattern with whatever stimulus we choose for the CS. It makes one wonder about how "voluntary" instrumental responses really are.

Biological Constraints

Breland and Breland (1961, 1966) have described many situations in which species-specific behavior has circumvented the effects of reinforcement. As noted in Chapter 1, they trained a pig to pick up a wooden coin and place it in a piggy bank. The pig learned well initially, but as training progressed, behavior characteristic of this species began to disrupt the instrumental sequence. Instead of carrying the coin in its mouth and depositing it in the bank, the pig would drop the coin, root it, pick it up again, then drop and root it. Continued reinforcement only worsened the situation. In another case they trained a raccoon to pick up a wooden egg and drop it down a chute for a food reward. After only one or two sessions, the raccoon became reluctant to drop the egg. The animal kept it in its paw, fondled it, mouthed it, put it in the chute, pulled it back, chewed it, and so on. Obviously, the delay of reinforcement caused by these intrusions is inconsistent with classical principles of reinforcement theory. Breland and Breland (1966) suggest that for both pig and raccoon the object became a food surrogate; both animals treated it like a piece of food with behavior appropriate to the animal's ecological niche. Presumably, stimuli predicting reinforcement serve as surrogates of the reinforcer and facilitate certain sensorimotor patterns that are characteristic of the food-gathering behavior of the particular species. Thus, instrumental responses that are incompatible with species-specific behavior patterns are weakened rather than strengthened.

Perhaps the most striking illustration of the selectivity of associations among stimuli and responses is the work of Garcia and his associates. This work grew out of attempts to assess the effects of toxins, drugs, and x-rays on behavior. Nonlethal dosages of radiation make animals sick, but the symptoms (such as nausea, vomiting, loss of appetite, and inactivity) typically appear several hours after exposure to radiation.

An early experiment (Garcia, Kimeldorf, Hunt, & Davies, 1956) exposed rats to a low radiant flux from a radioactive-cobalt source for 8 hours once a week. Food and water consumption was depressed during the exposure period without affecting consumption in the home cages. When the rats were tested in the radiation chambers a week later but without exposure to gamma radiation, their food and water consumption remained suppressed. They had apparently learned an aversion to these substances. These investigators had discovered what is now called the *Garcia effect: learning occurred even when responses were separated from their consequences by a number of hours.* Learning over long delays stands in contrast to the contiguity principle, which specifies that punishing or rewarding outcomes must follow stimuli or responses immediately to ensure effective learning.

Initially, Garcia and his colleagues (for example, Garcia, Kimeldorf, & Hunt, 1961) treated these conditioned aversions as though they were based on classical conditioning. For example, tasty water may serve as a CS and the digestive disturbance produced by irradiation or toxins as the US. Other investigators quickly challenged this interpretation of the Garcia effect by showing that backward and pseudoconditioning paradigms can also produce conditioned aversions (McLaurin, 1964; McLaurin, Farley, Scarborough, & Rawlings, 1964). This development led to a new interpretation, which is best illustrated in an experiment by Garcia and Koelling (1966).

Garcia and Koelling trained two groups of rats by pairing a compound stimulus with administration of a toxin or a shock to the paws. When a rat's tongue touched a bottle containing saccharin, an electronic circuit produced an audiovisual signal, light/click. Thus, the rats had two cues, sweet taste and light/click, that preceded nausea induced by the toxin or pain produced by electric shock. Figure 3–1 summarizes the results of the experiment. As can be seen, if punished by nausea, the rat will acquire an aversion to the

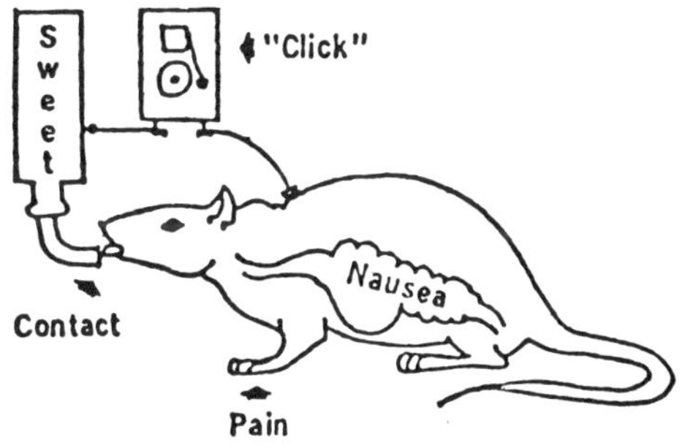

		Consequences	
		Nausea	Pain
Cues	Sweet	Aquires aversion	Does not
	"Click"	Does not	Learns defense

Figure 3–1. The effects of pairing a gustatory or an auditory cue with internal illness or external pain in an experiment by Garcia and Koelling (1966). (From *Perspectives in Ethology,* by J. Garcia, J.C. Clarke, and W.G. Hankins. Copyright 1966 by Plenum Publishing Corporation. Reprinted by permission.)

sweet taste, but it will not learn to avoid the light/click cue. Conversely, if punished by shock, the rat will learn to defend against shock by backing away from the water spout, but if the audiovisual cue is eliminated, the rat will continue to drink the sweet water. In summary, if the rat is made ill, it will avoid the sweet water, but if the rat gets shocked, it will develop an aversion to the "bright, noisy" water.

Several features of the experiment are of particular interest. First, the conditioned aversion to sweet water is no longer regarded as a case of classical conditioning; emphasis has shifted to the response and its consequences. Second, although the procedure shares certain properties with the punishment paradigm, a long delay between response and punishment, the limited number of punishments, and the specificity of learning suggest that the laws of learning may not be uniform. Third, that stimulus and consequence jointly determine whether a response is learned challenges the assumption that any stimulus capable of detection can be converted into a conditioned stimulus signaling that reward or punishment is imminent (Pavlov, 1928). If the assumption that all perceptible stimuli are equivalent is rejected, then no theory of learning is tenable without knowledge of the biological substrate upon which learning is based. In short, explaining behavioral events must ultimately entail a knowledge of the animal's anatomical structure and of the neurophysiological determinants of behavior.

Garcia, Hankins, and Rasiniak (1974) have further suggested that the laws governing the adaptive behavior of the organism in regulating its external and internal environment may be different. They point out that to survive the animal must use information received by exteroceptive and proprioceptive stimuli to avoid painful attacks upon it or to locate food or mates; that is, the organism must process spatiotemporal information from its exteroceptors and proprioceptors in order to avoid punishing features of the environment or to bring it into contact with naturally rewarding events. Presumably, survival is enhanced if the animal acquires contingencies of this sort: if this stimulus, then that consequence; or, given this response, then that outcome will occur. In other words, the organism learns what leads to what.

In coping with the internal environment, however, survival depends upon responses to demands from internal receptors. Thus, gustatory stimulation is used to select nutrients or to avoid toxins. But since reward or punishment may occur hours after eating, precise time discriminations would be of little value. Further, since motor behavior following ingestion cannot help achieve well-being or avoid illness, spatial discriminations would not enter into such associations either. This analysis rationalizes observations of the sort that wild rats, after an illness resulting from consuming poisoned bait, will avoid that type of food but not the location where the food was found (Barnett, 1963). Apparently, animals do not acquire "if/then" strategies in the regulation of their internal environment. Rather, the rewarding or punishing effect of various substances alters the hedonic quality of external stimuli sensed by peripheral receptors, and these changes in the incentive value of stimuli enhance or inhibit feeding activity (Garcia, Hankins, & Rasiniak, 1974).

Summary

In this section we have seen that the earlier view of the automatic action of the law of effect has come under serious attack. A new way of viewing superstitious behavior, the significance of autoshaping, and learning over long delays indicate that the law of effect cannot, at least in a number of circumstances, be viewed as a simple, automatic process.

The Nature of Reinforcers

In this section we examine the concept of reinforcement. We shall review the definition of positive and negative reinforcers, note the technical distinction between rewards and reinforcers, and explore the theoretical properties of the concept of reinforcement. What is of special importance is to note that there are several kinds of theoretical interpretations of reinforcement and that there is evidence in support of each type of interpretation.

Reinforcers and Rewards

Reinforcers are stimuli that increase the relative frequency of responses. We have noted that when response probability is increased by the *introduction* of a stimulus, the stimulus is called a *positive reinforcer*. On the other hand, when response probability increases as a consequence of the removal or *termination* of a stimulus, the stimulus is referred to as a *negative reinforcer*. Since reinforcers are identified by their behavioral effects, it is unnecessary to attribute affective or emotional properties to them. However, rewards are thought to produce changes in the organism's affective or hedonic state; positive affect is presumed to result from the occurrence of a pleasurable stimulus, while the termination of an aversive stimulus reduces a negative emotional state.

All rewards are reinforcers, but not all reinforcers are rewards. For example, a rat will learn to press a bar either to turn on or to turn off a light (Berlyne, 1969). Since the rate of bar-pressing increases as a consequence of the stimulus change, both the onset and the termination of the light qualify as reinforcers. But we would hardly regard the light as a rewarding event. A similar comparison can be made in classical conditioning. For example, a mild acid solution is sometimes used to elicit salivation. When a CS, such as a tone, precedes the application of acid to the mouth, a salivary response eventually occurs to the CS. The acid reinforces the connection between the CS and the CR, but again it can hardly be considered rewarding. We call your attention to this technical distinction between a reinforcer and a reward, although the terms are frequently used synonymously.

Definitions of Reinforcement

Thorndike's law of effect defines reinforcers empirically. An empirical definition of reinforcement identifies reinforcers by their behavioral effects and specifies the operations or procedures that produce an increase in responding. One consequence of defining reinforcement empirically is that a large number of stimuli that function as reinforcers must be identified. Another problem with this approach is that recent work on the biological boundaries of learning indicates that reinforcers may differ from species to species; indeed, even different response systems within the same organism may be affected differently by the same reinforcer. Therefore, some psychologists have attempted to develop theoretical definitions of reinforcement. A theoretical definition treats reinforcement as a hypothetical process that affects associative or motivational mechanisms in such a way that the probability of responding increases. Identifying the processes that produce the behavioral change would explain the mechanisms by which reinforcers produce their reinforcing effect and strengthen behaviors that they follow. If the properties of reinforcers that produce the reinforcing effect could be identified, it would help to clarify why reinforcers function differently in different species.

Psychologists who are committed to a theoretical approach to reinforcement seek to identify those characteristics of reinforcers that serve as a mechanism for reinforcement. In this section we will examine three kinds of interpretations of the effects of reinforcement. The first deals with the *sensory consequences* of reinforcers, the second focuses on the *nature of the responses* made in the presence of the reinforcers, and the third focuses on *motivational changes* following reinforcement.

Stimulus Properties of Reinforcers. The first theoretical approach to reinforcement identifies stimulation of the organism's receptors as the reinforcement mechanism. Rats, for example, learn to press a bar when the outcome of their responding is nothing more than turning on a light (for example, Hurwitz, 1956). Responses are also acquired when electrical stimulation of certain parts of the brain is made contingent on those responses (for example, Olds & Milner, 1954). These findings suggest that stimulation alone may be sufficient to produce reinforcement (Pfaffman, 1960). Experimenters using conventional reinforcers have found similar effects; when taste stimulation was varied by changing the concentration of a sweet sucrose solution, performance increased as the intensity of the taste stimulation increased (Guttman, 1953; Stebbins, 1962).

Although stimulation appears to be a necessary condition for identifying reinforcers, it seems unlikely that stimulation itself is also sufficient for reinforcement. Some stimuli produce decrements rather than increments in responding, while other stimuli apparently produce no change in behavior. Moreover, when food or water is used as a reinforcer, the stimulation arising from their ingestion is typically confounded with other possible sources of reinforcement, such as a reduction in hunger.

Response Properties and Reinforcers. There are two contrasting positions on the role of response factors in reinforcement: *empirical* and *theoretical.* The starting point of the empirical approach is to group responses into different classes (for example, eating, walking) and then to record the number of responses that fall into each class. The rule for determining whether one response class increases relative to another depends on the temporal sequencing of responses occurring with different frequencies (Premack, 1959). As an example of an empirical approach, consider two response classes, A and B. If B occurs with a higher probability than A, then the relative frequency of A will increase when B is made contingent upon A. Conversely, and again assuming B more probable than A, B will decrease in frequency if followed by A, the less probable response. For example, suppose the probability of a child's reading a book is low (Response A) but the probability of the same child's watching a movie is high (Response B). To increase the likelihood of reading, watching a movie should be made contingent upon reading a book. This phenomenon is called *Premack's principle.* More generally, Premack's principle contends that high-probability behavior can serve to reinforce low-probability behavior.

One interesting implication of the Premack principle is that the reinforcement relation is reversible. For example, Premack and Premack (1963) have shown that rats will eat in order to run as well as run in order to eat. Keep in mind that the reinforcement relation is reversible because a low-probability behavior can become a high probability behavior and hence serve as a reinforcer. This finding also appears applicable to human situations. Very young children will perform a variety of academic tasks if other activities, such as running, are made contingent on learning arithmetic or reading (Homme, deBaca, Devine, Steinhorst, & Rickert, 1963).

Although Premack's principle has a certain utility, especially in circumstances requiring self-control, there is a problem in comparing responses. Response probability is usually indexed by response rate, and it is assumed that the higher the response rate, the better the response is learned. However, since some responses are more difficult to make than others, it may be inappropriate to equate response rate with how well a response is learned. Responses may simply have a low rate either because making them requires more effort or because they have not been well learned.

In contrast, the theoretical approach to reinforcement, which emphasizes the response as crucial for determining whether a stimulus is reinforcing, argues that the *source of reward resides in the quantitative dimensions of consummatory activity.* Consummatory responses satisfy biological drives. Eating, drinking, copulating, and fleeing are consummatory responses because they reduce the drives of hunger, thirst, sexual arousal, or fear. Since these responses bring striving to an end, the *consummatory-response hypothesis* predicts that the more vigorous the consummatory activity, the greater its reward value. The reinforcing value of the consummatory response is usually determined by its effect on instrumental activity. This implies a positive correlation between the strength of instrumental responding and the amount of consummatory activity. In general, this prediction has been confirmed. For example, linear relationships have been found between the drinking rates of rats and the speed with which they traverse an alley runway (F.D. Sheffield, Roby, & Campbell, 1954). Higher rates of drinking are correlated with faster running speeds.

Usually, however, the greater the vigor of consummatory activity, the more intense the stimulation received by the organism. In many instances, then, the vigor of consummatory responding and the stimulation resulting from that activity are confounded. In an attempt to disentangle the effects of the consummatory response and its accompanying stimulation, Kraeling (1961) independently assessed the effects of these factors on response strength. The intensity of stimulation was varied by different sucrose concentrations, and the vigor of responding (number of licks) to each concentration was used as the measure of the duration of the consummatory response. Kraeling's results appear in Figure 3–2. The top graph shows the relation between the strength of the instrumental response and the three concentrations of sucrose solution. This graph indicates that the final performance level varied directly with the amount of sucrose concentration; the rats ran faster to secure higher concentrations of the sucrose solution. The bottom graph shows the consummatory-response curves for the three different sucrose concentrations. The animals licked each solution equally except during early trials. Taken together, the results indicate that stimulation arising from consummatory behavior has more reward value than the duration of the consummatory response.

One complication for the hypothesis that the effects of reward are due to the elicitation of predominant consummatory responses was noted by N.E. Miller and Kessen (1952). They trained three groups of rats to select the correct side of a *T* maze for a milk reward. One group received milk for a correct response and saline for an incorrect response. Both substances were injected directly into the rats' stomachs via an implanted tube. This procedure eliminated the occurrence of peripheral consummatory activity. Miller and Kessen reasoned that if consummatory responses are necessary for reinforcement, this group would not learn the task. The other groups, similarly implanted, received reward by mouth either immediately or after a delay of 7 minutes and 35 seconds, a time period corresponding to how long it took the group receiving reward via the tube to receive the 14 cubic centimeters of milk. Contrary to the consummatory-response hypothesis, all the groups learned the task, though the group receiving the milk by injection directly into the stomach learned at a slower rate than the other two groups. The findings (see Figure 3–3) indicate that the elicitation of prepotent consummatory activity enhances the reward value of the consummatory stimuli but that consummatory responding itself is not necessary for learning. Since the animals that had the milk injected directly into their stomachs still learned, Miller and Kessen's data also suggest that the source of reward results from a change in the motivational state of the organism. It is to this hypothesis on the nature of reinforcers that we now turn.

Motivation and Reinforcement. Reward and motivation are closely related. For example, food serves as an effective reinforcer only when the animal is hungry. Conversely, if an animal is not motivated by hunger, responses immediately preceding food will not be strengthened. Observations of this sort and the functional emphasis on the organism's adaptability to its environment have suggested that the process whereby new associations are made results from a change in the organism's motivational state. According to this view, learning is thought to be a process of organic evolution that helps ensure the survival of organisms by reducing biological needs. The process of strengthening specific stimulus–response connections results from the reduction of a drive arising from a need or

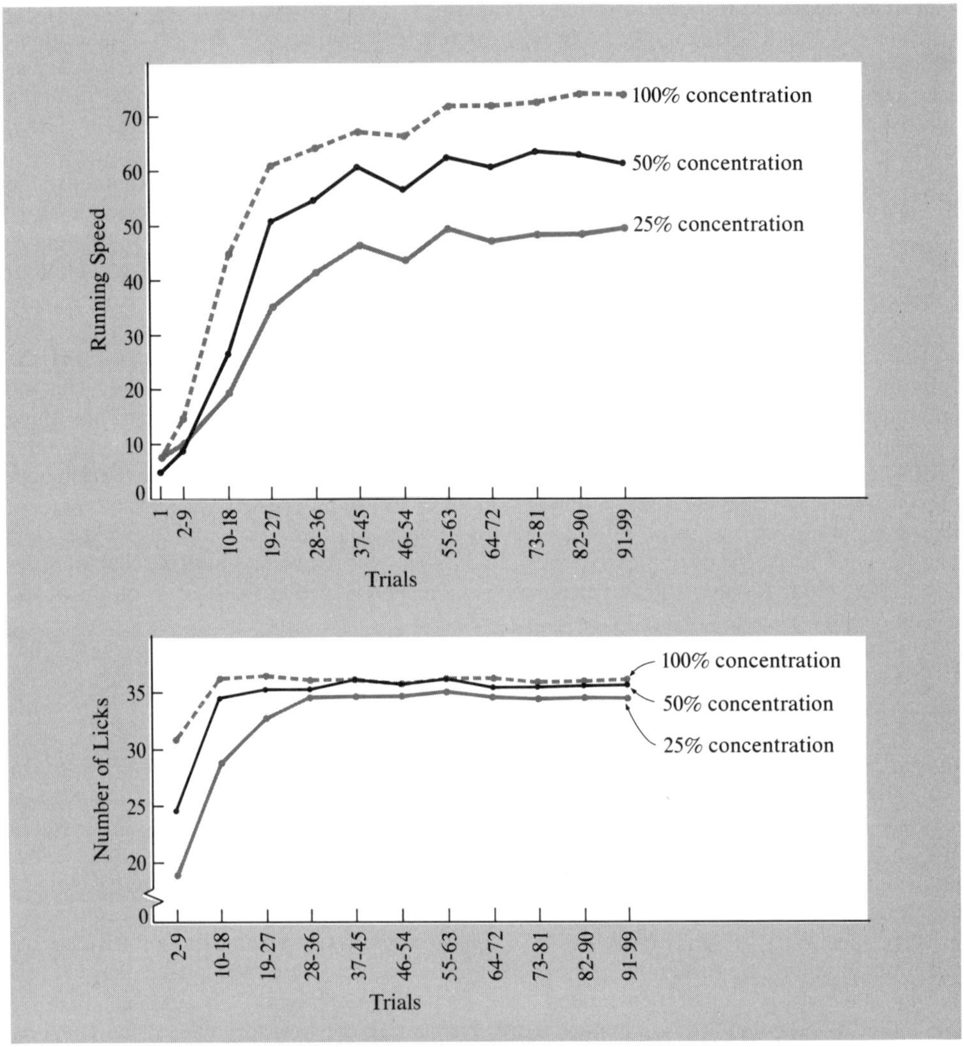

Figure 3–2. The top graph illustrates speed of running as a function of concentration of sucrose solution. The bottom graph shows the relation between vigor of consummatory responding and concentration of sucrose solution. (From "Analysis of Amount of Reward as a Variable in Learning," by D. Kraeling, *Journal of Comparative and Physiological Psychology,* 1961, *54,* 560–565. Copyright 1961 by the American Psychological Association. Reprinted by permission.)

the reduction in stimuli characteristic of the need. Thus, reinforcers strengthen behaviors immediately preceding them when those behaviors are instrumental in reducing a drive. The idea that drive reduction is a necessary condition for learning is known as the *law of primary reinforcement* (Hull, 1943). It assumes that no learning will occur when a response fails to produce a reduction in drive.

Hull assigned at least two properties to the drive concept. One property is to *energize behavior;* responses are more vigorous when the animal is motivated. The second property of drive is its *stimulus function.* The stimulus function of drive makes it possible for the

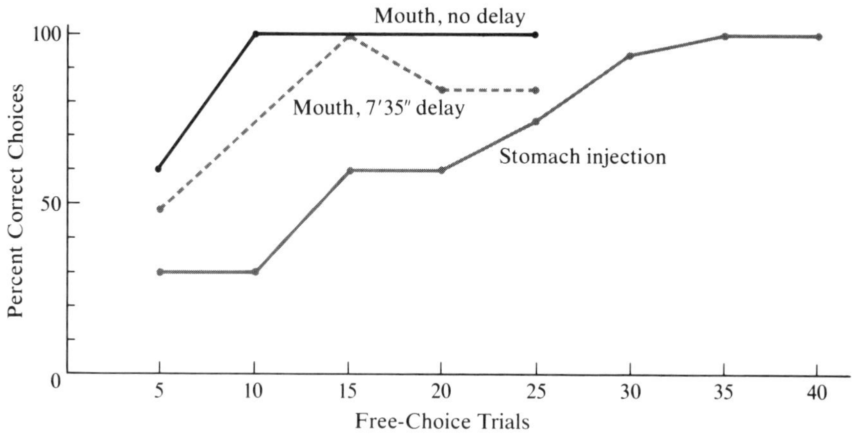

Figure 3–3. Learning of a *T* maze by rats receiving reward in different ways. (From "Reward Effects of Food via Stomach Fistula Compared with Those of Food via Mouth," by N.E. Miller and M.L. Kessen, *Journal of Comparative and Physiological Psychology,* 1952, *45,* 555–564. Copyright 1952 by the American Psychological Association. Reprinted by permission.)

animal to determine the nature of its motivational state by discriminating among stimuli characteristic of each state. For example, fear "feels" different from hunger because the stimuli resulting from these different drives are different. In addition to these relatively primitive features of drives, stimuli produced by each drive become part of the total stimulus complex to which responses are made.

Although intuitively reasonable, Hull's theory of the dual nature of drive presented problems for the interpretation of experimental results and for the determination of the mechanism responsible for reinforcement. For instance, performance changes resulting from changes in motivation might be due to either a change in arousal or a change in drive stimuli. For example, suppose a hungry rat is allowed to eat. Both the energizing and the directive aspects of drive would be altered. A decline in responding might be due to either a lower level of arousal or the fact that the change in the stimulus complex controlling the response weakened the tendency for the response to be made. This latter explanation is known as *generalization decrement.* Hull's early theory was equivocal about whether reinforcement results from a decrease in arousal or a reduction in drive stimuli. Hull (1952) later proposed that the removal of drive stimuli is indeed the reinforcement mechanism. In any case, the crucial feature of the primary law of reinforcement is that a reduction in motivation is a necessary condition for learning. If responses do not reduce the prevailing level of motivation, no associations will be formed between them and the accompanying stimuli.

But how do tests of the drive-reduction hypothesis fare? F.D. Sheffield and Roby (1950) were among the first investigators to provide evidence against the strong form of the hypothesis. They demonstrated that rats will learn in the *absence* of need reduction. In one of their experiments, hungry rats acquired a simple response as a result of drinking a saccharin solution, even though this sweet-tasting substance has no nutritive value and hence could not affect the animals' hunger. In a subsequent experiment Sheffield, Wulff, and Backer (1951) showed that male rats will learn an instrumental response of copulating with estrous females without consummating the act of coitus. Because the male rats were allowed to mount females in heat but were removed from the experimental setting prior to ejaculation, no reduction in sex drive occurred. Nevertheless, learning occurred when the consequence of responding involved an *increase* rather than a decrease in sexual excitement. Other work showed that animals acquire responses that produce increases in novel stimulation (compare Harlow, Harlow, & Meyer, 1950; Montgomery, 1954). These data suggest that learning may occur when the consequence of responding is to increase motivation rather than decrease it. Finally, the drive-reduction hypothesis does not indicate how natural selection managed to make need-reducing events reinforcing; there is no provision to indicate how a reduction in drive facilitates the formation of stimulus–response associations. Despite this difficulty, however, there is considerable evidence that responses are strengthened when they produce a reduction in drive (for example, N.E. Miller & Kessen, 1952). Therefore, drive reduction is a sufficient, but not a necessary, condition for reinforcement.

Summary. This section indicates that it is extremely difficult to separate the effects of stimulation, consummatory responses, and motivation from one another, but each of these factors under certain conditions is involved in strengthening responses. Although stimulation is apparently a sufficient condition for reinforcement, it is not a necessary condition because many stimuli either produce no behavioral change or actually result in impaired performance. Hypotheses that assign a crucial role to consummatory responses are supported to the extent that the occurrence of these responses facilitates learning, but since learning may occur in their absence, they are not a necessary condition for reinforcement. Finally, a similar situation exists for motivational interpretations: learning occurs when drives are reduced, but learning is also found when drives increase in intensity. Thus, the factors of stimulation, consummatory responses, and motivation are all involved in learning, but no one factor is seen as a necessary condition for learning.

Mechanisms of Reinforcement

In this section we turn our attention to interpretations of reinforcement. The fundamental question is just how reinforcement exerts its effects on behavior. Conceivably, reinforcement may directly strengthen stimulus–response associations; alternatively, reinforcement may affect the "willingness" or motivation of the organism to engage in certain behaviors. Probably reinforcement affects both of these processes.

Associative Interpretations of Reinforcement

Many early versions of learning theory proposed that reinforcers directly affect what organisms learn. For example, the law of effect attributes the strengthening of S–R connections to the rewarding properties of stimuli. Reinforcement "stamps in" S–R associations and is thus the "glue" binding responses to stimuli. Theorists after Thorndike treated the learning process in a similar way. For example, rewards were thought to contribute directly to the formation of associations by building reflex reserve (Skinner, 1938) or by producing increments in habit strength (Hull, 1943). How reinforcement affects learning obviously differed for these theorists, but a common feature of their theorizing was that rewarded responses are learned.

Hullian learning theory provided the most detailed, systematic explanation of how reinforcement affects learning. For Hull, the strengthening of specific S–R connections was a gradual, incremental process that varied directly with the number of experiences with reward. In addition to the number of reinforcements, the strength of the S–R connections, or *habit strength,* as Hull called it, was also affected by the amount and the delay of reinforcement. These two properties of reinforcers theoretically determined the associative strength between specific stimuli and responses by setting a limit on the final level of habit strength. Amount and delay produced inverse effects: habit strength was stronger (had a higher asymptote) the greater the magnitude of reward, while increases in delay weakened habit strength and resulted in lower asymptotes. Figure 3–4 represents Hull's theoretical curves showing the growth of habit strength with different amounts and different delays of reward when the number of rewarded trials are equal.

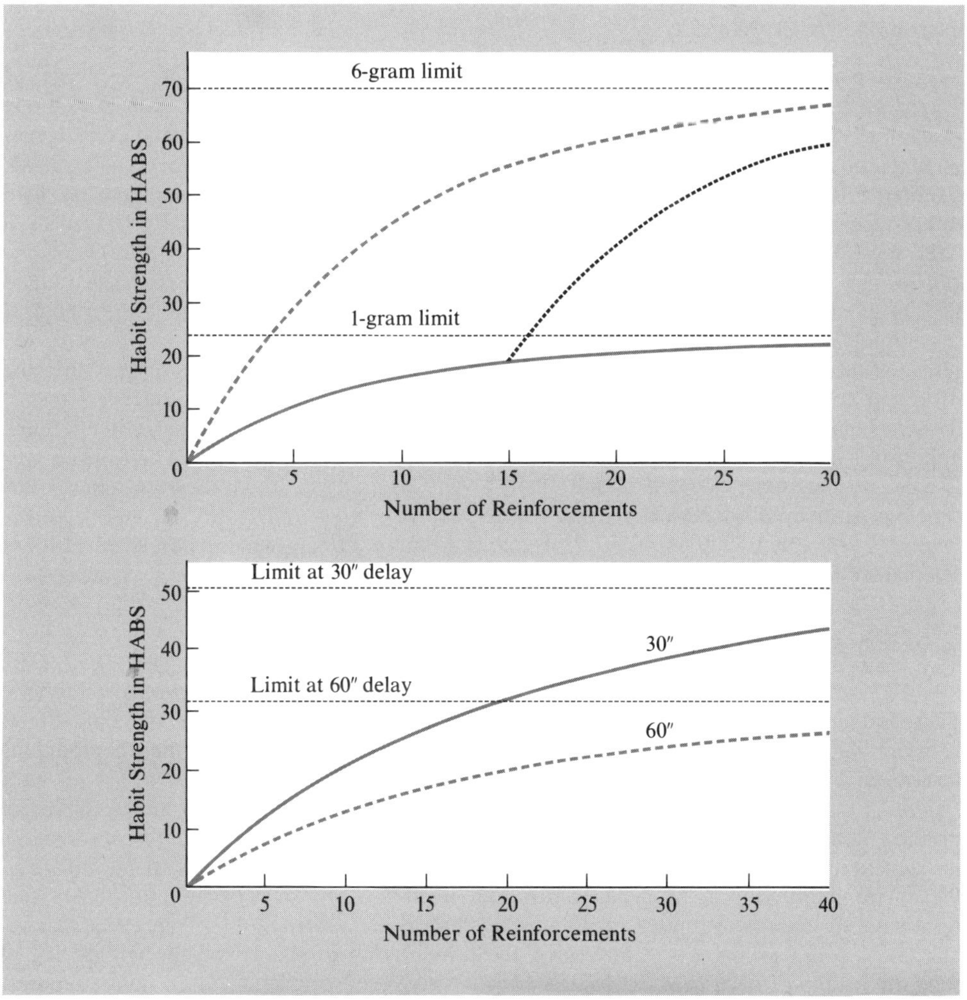

Figure 3–4. Two theoretical illustrations of the hard-reinforcement principle. The top graph illustrates the effect of reward magnitude on associative strength (HABS). The dotted curve shows the course of associative strength following an abrupt shift in reward magnitude. The bottom graph shows the effect of delay of reward on associative strength. (From Hull, 1943.)

The top graph shows the growth of habit strength with two amounts of food reinforcement. The graph shows that the upper limit of the curves varies directly with reward magnitude; the larger reward has a higher asymptote. A shift from a small to a large reward gradually increases the habit strength until an asymptotic level is attained that is appropriate to the large amount of reinforcement. The two delay conditions appear in the bottom graph. With amount and number of rewards equated, an increase in the delay of reward results in a lower maximal level of habit strength. The notion that the properties of reward affect learning in such a direct manner is known as the *hard principle of reinforcement* (E.J. Capaldi, 1967).

Motivational Interpretations

Motivational interpretations of reinforcement have been made on the basis of *reward-shift* experiments. A reward-shift study is one in which a subject is trained with one level of reward and then suddenly shifted to another level—that is, to smaller or larger amounts of reward. Early studies of reward shift (for example, Crespi, 1942, 1944; Zeaman, 1949) found that changes in the prevailing condition of reinforcement produce abrupt changes in performance. Specifically, Zeaman found that rats initially trained on a small reward, and then shifted to a large reward, "overshot" the performance levels of rats trained on a large reward from the beginning of training. Conversely, rats initially trained on a large reward, and then shifted to a small reward, performed below the level of control rats initially trained on a small reward. The effect of shifting the amount of reward was quite abrupt, and was also apparently transitory, which led theorists to suspect that the effects of reinforcement might be motivational rather than associative. Indeed, Crespi's (1944) choice of terms for the phenomena carries motivational/emotional connotations: *elation* was assigned to the overshooting of the large-reward asymptote, and *depression* was assigned to the undershooting of the small-reward asymptote. Today a more neutral terminology is favored: *elation* has given way to *positive-contrast effect* (PCE), and *negative-contrast effect* (NCE) has replaced *depression*. Contrast effects will be described in more detail later in this chapter.

Secondary Reinforcement and Acquired Motivation

The previous chapter developed a fourfold classification of reinforcers and punishers. These outcomes were identified as positive or negative, but in all cases the outcome affects behavior independently of the organism's prior experience with them. Stimuli producing behavioral effects without the benefit of previous learning are defined as either *primary reinforcers* or *primary punishers*. Food, water, and escape from shock are examples of primary reinforcers. Food and water are classified as *primary positive reinforcers* because instrumental responses are strengthened as a consequence of these events' being *added* to the environment. Shock escape is a *primary negative reinforcer* because responses that terminate an aversive stimulus result in the removal, or *subtraction,* of an event that increases response probability. Conversely, the presentation of shock and the withdrawal of food are examples of primary punishers because both outcomes result in response suppression. Shock onset is an instance of *primary positive punishment* because the effect of the response is to bring about the occurrence of an event that suppresses behavior. In contrast, the withdrawal of food is a *primary negative punisher* because the response results in the removal of a stimulus, the effect of which is to reduce further responding.

This classificatory scheme has been extended to stimuli that acquire reinforcing or punishing properties because of their association with primary reinforcers or primary punishers. Such stimuli are designated as *secondary reinforcers* or *secondary punishers*. For example, if a previously neutral stimulus, such as a tone, signals the occurrence of food, and if when food is later absent the tone has the effect of maintaining the previously acquired response or of increasing the probability of a new response that it follows, the tone would qualify as a *secondary positive reinforcer*. On the other hand, if the tone predicts the occurrence of shock, and if in the later absence of shock the tone suppresses instrumental appetitive behavior or causes the animal to flee or escape from it, the tone would qualify as a *secondary positive punisher*.

Complementary operations are required for the establishment of *secondary negative reinforcers* and *secondary negative punishers*. Stimuli correlated with the termination of aversive stimuli qualify as secondary negative reinforcers if they maintain previously acquired behavior or facilitate the learning of new responses. The behavioral effects of secondary negative punishers, on the other hand, should be identical to those produced by secondary positive punishers. Cues associated with the removal or absence of pleasurable stimuli qualify as secondary negative punishers if the animal is motivated to avoid or escape them.

This classification of learned rewards and punishers is empirical. It was developed by defining the concepts in terms of operations that are necessary for their establishment. But, as we have seen, reinforcers and drives are intimately related theoretically. Many contemporary theories of motivation also link the concepts of secondary reinforcers and punishers to motivation by distinguishing between stimuli that motivate or elicit behavior and those that reinforce or strengthen behavior. Moreover, some theorists conclude on the basis of the available evidence that an asymmetry exists between the capacity of a stimulus to acquire learnable motivating versus reinforcing properties (Logan, 1968). The basis for this asymmetry depends upon the nature of the drive with which the stimulus is paired. This analysis divides drives into two theoretically distinct categories: *deprivation drives* and *stimulation drives*.

Deprivation drives are those that are evoked by the withdrawal of substances necessary for the maintenance of the organism or for the preservation of the species. Conversely, *stimulation drives* are those that are evoked by the occurrence of stimuli that are painful or injurious to the organism. In simpler terminology the absence of appetitive stimuli (for example, food, water, sex) evokes deprivation-drive states; the presence of noxious or aversive stimuli (for example, electric shock, loud noise, extreme heat or cold), evokes stimulation-drive states. According to this analysis, any stimulus that reduces a deprivation drive constitutes a primary positive reinforcer, while any event that diminishes a stimulation drive is characterized as a primary negative reinforcer. Given this distinction, a previously neutral stimulus associated with the onset of a stimulation drive can acquire secondary motivating properties, but a stimulus paired with the reduction of a stimulation drive will not possess reinforcing properties. Conversely, a neutral stimulus predicting the reduction of a deprivation drive acquires conditioned reinforcing properties, but stimuli paired with the onset of these drives do not become acquired motivators. The results of most experiments attempting to condition stimuli to these two classes of drives are consistent with this analysis.

Although the theoretical structure relating reinforcement to motivation still requires further clarification, the concepts of secondary reinforcement and secondary motivation have proved useful for describing the effects of stimuli that, though originally ineffective in governing behavior, may become effective in guiding behavior through conditioning. Keeping in mind this description of the nature of reinforcers as well as the suggestions about how reinforcers produce their effects, let us turn to the ways by which different properties of reinforcers differentially influence behavior.

Conditions of Reinforcement

Several conditions of reinforcement can affect rate of learning and final performance level attained. Among these are the magnitude of reward, the delay of reward, and the frequency of reward. Their general effects on behavior can be summarized as follows.

The Magnitude of Reward

The amount of a reward is considered to be an important variable in both the associative and the motivational interpretation of reinforcement. In both of these theories, the strength of an association is thought to increase with increases in reward magnitude. Many experiments have supported this prediction (see Bitterman & Schoel, 1970, for a review), but these findings are complicated by the fact that the amount of a reward is a complex variable that can be further divided into such factors as weight, number of units comprising the reward, duration of consummatory activity, caloric value, and even perceived size (Logan, 1960). For example, consider an experiment by Logan (1960) designed to isolate the motivational value of the number of units comprising a reinforcer from its total weight. Two groups of rats were run in a straight-alley runway to a .5-gram food reward. One group initially received this amount in one pellet, while the second group was given the same weight in six pellets. The animals were administered one trial per day for 70 days, and then the conditions of reinforcement were reversed. The group shifted from one to six units of reward (Group 1–6) thereafter ran faster than the group shifted from six pellets to one (Group 6–1). This finding suggests that the multiple pellets had more value to the animals than did the single pellet even when the total magnitude of the reward, as measured by weight, was the same. This result also suggests that the number of units comprising a reward can affect behavior in a manner similar to simple differences in reward magnitude.

McCain (1969) reported results consistent with Logan's findings. He also used a straight-alley runway in which two groups of rats ran to either one 1000-milligram food pellet or 22 45-milligram food pellets (total weight = 990 milligrams). During the initial training period the group given 22 pellets ran faster than the group receiving approximately the same weight of food in one pellet. However, a shift in the conditions of reward reversed the running times of the two groups; the group transferred to the single unit of reward ran slower than the group shifted to the multiple pellets.

Why do the animals run faster to multiple pellets? There are at least two possible explanations. One is that the physical magnitude of a reward—that is, its weight—is not equivalent to its perceived magnitude. In everyday life it is generally thought that many units of an item may appear to be more of that item than a single unit of equivalent magnitude. A number of pieces of chocolate that have a total weight of 8 ounces will appear to be more candy than a single 8-ounce chocolate bar. If a steak is very thinly sliced, it will look like more than a single intact piece. Another explanation for the differences in running speed under single versus multiple units of reward centers on the idea that consummatory activity may be quite different under the two reward conditions. This possibility has been formally addressed by Amsel and his associates with their *miniature-trial hypothesis*.

Amsel, Hug, and Surridge (1968) have suggested that the number of rewards given on a single trial affects the rate of approach to the asymptotic level, but that the final performance level for multiple and single units of reward varies only with the physical magnitude of reward. In brief, they propose that when multiple pellets are involved, the eating of each pellet comprises a miniature trial for the animal. Under conditions of limited practice, rats getting multiple pellets make more goal responses than rats receiving a single unit and consequently achieve an asymptotic level of responding more rapidly. With extended training, however, rats exposed to the single unit of reward eventually attain the same asymptotic level (Amsel, Surridge, & Hug, 1969).

Traupmann (1971) has reported data consistent with the miniature-trial hypothesis. Rats were given five, 15, or 60 acquisition trials under either a multiple-pellet or a single-pellet condition, with equal physical magnitudes of reward. As expected from the miniature-trial hypothesis, rats receiving 15 training trials under the multiple-pellet condition were running faster than those given a single pellet, but after 60 trials no reliable differences were found between single-pellet and multiple-pellet conditions. The results of an experiment by Daly (1972) are also compatible with the miniature-trial hypothesis. Rats given 25 20-milligram pellets approached asymptote faster than animals getting one 500-milligram pellet, but with extended practice the two groups ran at the same speed. Apparently, more frequent elicitation of consummatory responding results in a more rapid rate of learning, but with equal magnitudes of reward the ultimate level of habit strength is regulated by the overall amount consumed.

These experiments used equal weights of reward but varied the number of units of reward. In an analogous manner the number of units may be equated and the physical magnitude of reward allowed to vary. Recently a number of studies (for example, R.W. Black, 1969; McCain, 1970; McCain, Dyleski, & McElvain, 1971) have challenged the generalization that reward magnitude determines asymptotic level. Rats receiving different reward magnitudes (as indexed by the length of time they had access to food) either show no difference in terminal performance (for example, McCain, 1970), or those that receive the smaller of the two magnitudes have a higher asymptote (for example, R.W. Black & Ekstand, 1964). For example, Figure 3–5 shows the curves of two groups of rats that differed in the time spent with food reward in the Black and Ekstand experiment. As the figure indicates, the group given the small reward (10-second food access) had a higher asymptotic level than the large-reward group (30-second food access).

R.W. Black (1969) points out that as the quantity of reward increases, the length of time required to consume the reward will also increase. In brief, whenever reward mag-

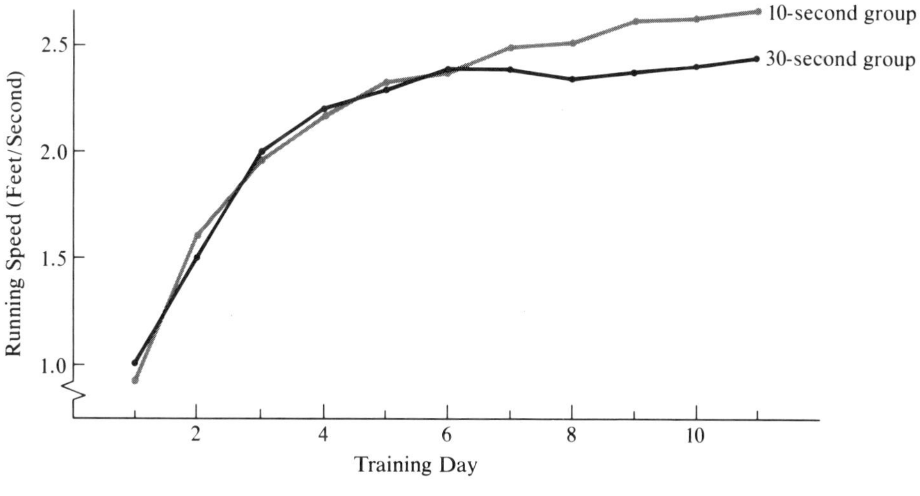

Figure 3–5. Speed of running in rats as a function of length of access to food reward. (From "Instrumental and Consummatory Behavior as a Function of Length of Reward Period," by R.W. Black and P. Ekstand, *Psychonomic Science,* 1964, *1,* 301–302. Reprinted by permission of the Psychonomic Society, Inc.)

nitude is varied, at least three variables are confounded: amount of reward, duration of consummatory activity, and duration of nonconsummatory responding. Nonconsummatory behavior is important because eating typically occurs in bursts, and animals given the large reward spend more time in nonconsummatory activity such as retracing and scratching the goal-box door than do rats receiving the small reward. Accordingly, there may be a greater opportunity for them to "unlearn" the response. Rats are usually removed from the goal box immediately after eating a food reward, and since the ratio of consummatory to nonconsummatory responding is greater with smaller quantities of food (they do not engage in large amounts of nonconsummatory activity), the association between the alley cues and running will be protected.

In summary, it is apparent that amount of reward is a complex variable. Intensity of stimulation, duration of consummatory behavior, and changes in drive may all have different effects on associative and motivational mechanisms. Supporting evidence for this view is provided by experiments (for example, Traupmann, 1971) showing that the number of reward units on a single trial affects the rate of approach to asymptote, a typical index of learning. On the other hand, the weight of reward determines terminal asymptotic level (the final level of performance), a measure usually regarded as reflecting motivational processes. Furthermore, the many procedural differences among the experiments may affect one source of reward more than another. For example, when rats are run to large rewards for more than one trial per day, they may become less motivated (Wike, 1969). In addition, the "rule" for removing the animal from the goal box, after a fixed period of time or after consummation of reward, may influence the extent to which it engages in nonconsummatory activity in the goal box (for example, Cilluffo & Black, 1970). Finally, the number of acquisition trials given may affect not only the rate of approach to asymptote but whether rats even attain a terminal level of performance (Traupmann, 1971).

Delay of Reward

Delay is regarded as a crucial property of reinforcers, since many studies indicate that performance is inferior if reward is delayed (for example, Grice, 1948b; Logan, 1960; Perin, 1943). We noted earlier that in Hull's 1943 version of learning theory, delay of reward affected habit strength directly. Specifically, the limit of associative strength was regarded as an inverse function of increasing delay. In Hull's early theorizing, the time interval between an S–R association and the reward was presumed to produce a gradient of reinforcement expressing how an increase in habit strength would vary with delay of reward. To determine the shape of the reinforcement gradient and its temporal extent, it is necessary to make the stimulus context as constant as possible. Stimuli occurring coincidentally with reward tend to acquire rewarding properties. Accordingly, if the stimuli associated with reward are similar to those conditioned to the response, then stimuli present with reward would acquire the capacity to evoke the response. To circumvent the effects of the acquired reward value of stimuli, the context should be as constant as possible during both the delay and the reinforcement.

Perin (1943) attempted to maximize the constancy of the stimulus conditions between a response and the subsequent reward by training rats to press a bar under different conditions of delay of reward (either 0, 2, 5, 10, 20, or 30 seconds). After the response was made, the bar was withdrawn and the delay interval before reinforcement began. Using latency to press the bar as a measure of learning, Perin found that rats showed learning up to the 10-second delay, but no appreciable learning was evident with the 30-second delay condition. Although the external-stimulus conditions were relatively constant throughout training, proprioceptive stimuli arising from responses made during the delay interval could themselves have acquired rewarding properties. Conceivably, this type of stimulation could have been a learned source of reward mediating the response over the interval of delay.

Grice (1948a) eliminated the problem of proprioceptive cues by using a visual-discrimination procedure. He trained all of his rats to choose between black or white entrance corridors that led into delay chambers painted a neutral gray. After the appropriate delay had elapsed, different groups of rats were exposed to the goal boxes. For one group the goal boxes were black or white, which corresponded to the positive or negative entrance cues used in training. Another group was required to make differential responses at the time of discrimination by twisting around blocks placed in the alley or by running up an inclined plane. Both of these groups experienced a 5-second delay.

Grice reasoned that the different external or internal cues associated with delayed reward or nonreward would maximize the likelihood that stimuli associated with delayed reward would acquire reinforcing properties. In contrast, control animals, which experienced delays of .5, 1.2, 2.0, 5.0, or 10.0 seconds, had goal boxes identical to the delay boxes; that is, the goal boxes were a neutral gray. As expected, the 5-second-delay groups provided with the differential external or proprioceptive stimulation learned the task. However, the group exposed to the neutral-gray goal boxes during the reinforcement delay showed no appreciable learning, even after 700 trials. Figure 3–6 shows the performance

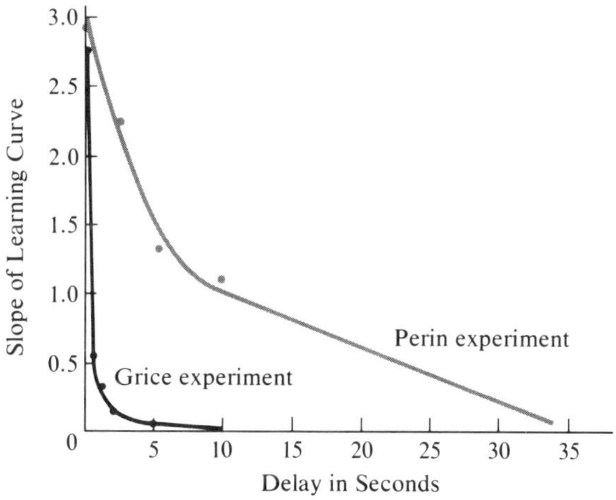

Figure 3–6. Delay-of-reinforcement gradients obtained by Perin (1943) and Grice (1948b). Note that almost no learning occurred with the elimination of secondary reinforcement. (From "The Relation of Secondary Reinforcement to Delayed Reward in Visual Discrimination Learning," by G.R. Grice, *Journal of Experimental Psychology,* 1948, *38,* 1–16.)

of this latter group compared to the results reported by Perin. The Grice experiment, which minimized the role of exteroceptive and proprioceptive cues, showed almost no learning for the 2-second-delay and 5-second-delay groups. Indeed, it appears from the Grice data that there is no gradient of primary reinforcement. Accordingly, Grice's results suggest that *learning involving delay of reward arises from the action of secondary reinforcement.*

If no gradient of primary reinforcement exists, how does the association between specific stimuli and responses get learned? K.W. Spence (1947) suggested that the S–R association is strengthened by *immediate secondary* reinforcement; that is, he assumed that stimuli occurring with reward acquire reinforcing properties and that these learned properties of reward generalize to other stimuli that precede them according to some temporal gradient. Early experimental tests of Spence's theory of delayed reward supported his theory. In addition, they suggested that the processes that resulted in previously neutral stimuli's acquiring reward value were Pavlovian in nature. A study by W.O. Jenkins (1950) supports this possibility.

Jenkins presented a discrete 3-second buzzer to five groups of rats that was followed by food after a period of either 1, 3, 9, 27, or 81 seconds. After 80 to 100 such buzzer/food pairings, the rats were placed in an operant-conditioning apparatus. Bar pressing in this second apparatus produced the buzzer but not the food. If the buzzer had acquired reinforcing properties during the first phase of training because it reliably predicted food, then it was thought that the rats should learn to emit a response that immediately preceded the buzzer (that is, bar pressing). The results supported this hypothesis. The principal finding was that the number of bar-pressing responses emitted was a decreasing function of the time interval, between the buzzer and the food, experienced during the first phase of training. Rats that had been exposed to the 1-second, 3-second, and 9-second buzzer/food intervals pressed the bar significantly more often than did a group of control animals that had not received the original training in the Pavlovian procedure. The groups that had been exposed to either a 27-second or an 81-second buzzer/food interval did not press the bar any more than the control group. Research published by Bersh (1951) also suggests that learning under conditions of delayed reinforcement is mediated by secondary reinforcement arising from Pavlovian-conditioning processes.

The Frequency of Reward

Behavior in learning situations is influenced not only by the magnitude and delay of reward but also by the frequency with which reward is given. As you know, a common feature of our everyday world is that rewards occur infrequently or even rarely. It is unusual for a reward to be given for every correct response except perhaps in highly controlled learning environments. In the laboratory the effects of frequency of reward have been extensively studied using both *discrete-trial* and *free-responding* procedures.

Discrete-Trial Procedures. With a discrete-trial procedure the subject makes a response and then, typically, is removed from the training apparatus for some period and then returned and allowed to make another response. One of the simplest laboratory procedures used to study the effects of frequency of reward is to vary the reward so that rewarded and nonrewarded trials are alternated. If goal events have stimulus properties, then behavior should be responsive to this alternating pattern of reward and nonreward. If reward and nonreward have stimulus properties, they should become part of the stimulus complex that guides behavior on later trials. For example, consider a rat exposed to alternating reward and nonreward on successive trials. When the rat is given a reward, its occurrence may provide information that there will be no reward on the next trial. Conversely, the occurrence of nonreward may tell the rat that reward will be available on the next trial.

Evidence bearing on this issue appears in Figure 3–7. In the figure, which presents latency measures in an alley runway, the reward (R) and nonreward (N) trials are plotted separately for two groups of rats. One group was trained 12 trials per day on a single-alternating (Group SA) schedule of reward (RNRN and so on). The other group was given a double-alternating (Group DA) schedule of reward (RRNNRRNN and so on) under an equivalent practice regimen. The figure shows that the single-alternating group learned to run slowly on nonrewarded trials, which suggests that the previously rewarded trial was a

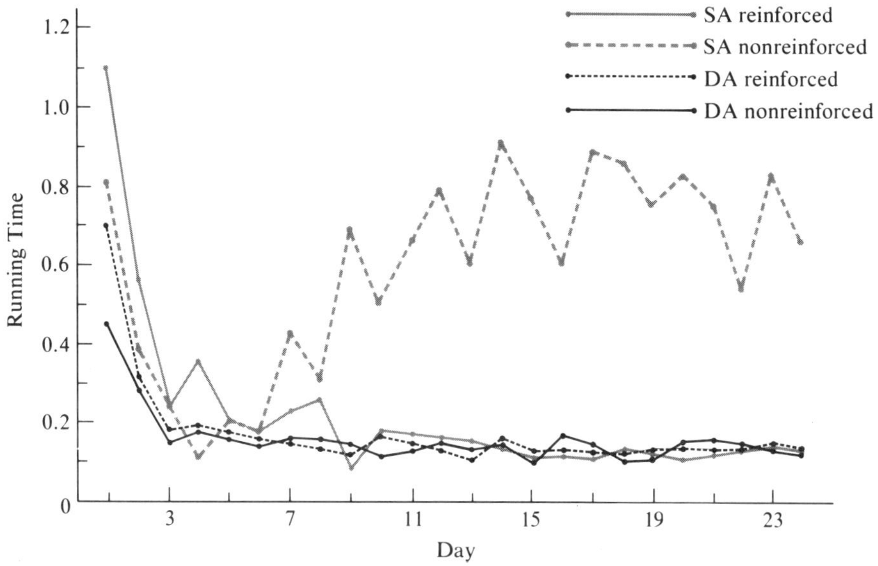

Figure 3–7. Running times on reinforced and nonreinforced trials for single-alternating (SA) and double-alternating (DA) groups of rats. (From "The Behavior of Rats in Relation to Complex Patterns of Partial Reinforcement," by J.M. Bloom and E.J. Capaldi, *Journal of Comparative and Physiological Psychology,* 1961, *54,* 261–265. Copyright 1961 by the American Psychological Association. Reprinted by permission.)

signal not to run. In contrast, the group receiving the double-alternating schedule ran at the same speed on both rewarded and nonrewarded trials. These results suggest that when reinforcement is administered in a single-alternating sequence, rewarding trials may function as negative stimuli because they predict nonreward on the next trial, and nonrewarded trials function as positive stimuli because they predict reinforcement. No patterning effect develops with a double-alternating sequence because neither a rewarded nor a nonrewarded trial reliably predicts the occurrence of reinforcement on the next trial.

Although pattern running is not found with a double-alternating schedule, it does develop with more complex schedules of reinforcement if the outcomes are made more distinctive and consistent. For example, Pschirrer (1972) obtained pattern effects when he trained rats on a complex R_1R_2N sequence, in which the first reward of the sequence (R_1, which was milk) was made discriminably different from the second reward (R_2, which was food pellets). In the milk/pellet/nonreward sequence used by Pschirrer, the stimulus trace of pellets functioned as a negative stimulus predicting nonreward. On the other hand, when the rats received milk or no reward, these specific stimuli served as discrimination cues predicting either pellets or milk. Pschirrer's data are presented in Figure 3–8, which shows speed of running plotted against training trials. Note that speeds on nonrewarded trials became slower than speeds on rewarded trials as training progressed. The results indicate that rats may use not only the presence or absence of reinforcement but also particular properties of reward as discriminative stimuli to guide their behavior. The pattern effect on single-alternating schedules is enhanced when reward magnitude is larger on rewarded trials (P.E. Campbell, Crumbaugh, Rhodus, & Knouse, 1971; Gonzalez, Bainbridge, & Bitterman, 1966) or when drive level is increased (E.D. Capaldi, 1972). Patterning has also been found when rats are given alternating schedules of immediate and long-delayed reward (Burt & Wike, 1963).

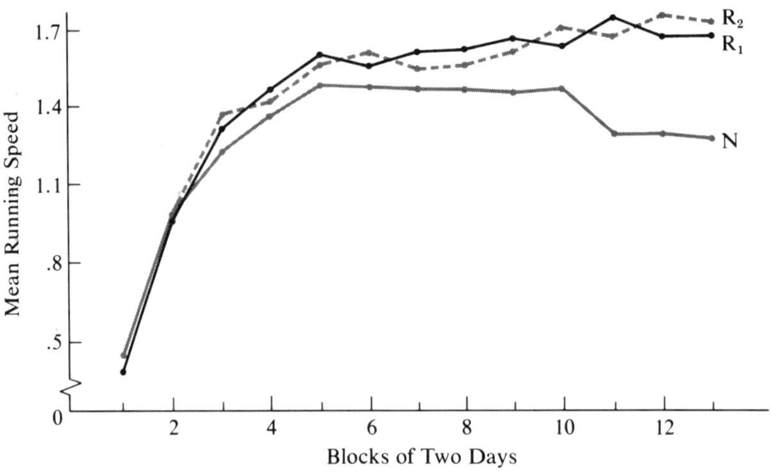

Figure 3–8. Speed of running in rats on a reward/reward/nonreward sequence with different rewards. (From "Goal Events as Discriminative Stimuli over Extended Intertrial Intervals," by M.E. Pschirrer, *Journal of Experimental Psychology,* 1972, *96,* 425–432. Copyright 1972 by the American Psychological Association. Reprinted by permission.)

Although many theorists acknowledge that the consequences of a response may provide cues that direct later responses (for example, Amsel, 1967; E.J. Capaldi, 1967; Logan & Wagner, 1965), the question of whether patterning occurs when long time periods intervene between trials is still unanswered. This question is important because its answer determines what mechanism may be involved in the patterning effect. Clearly, reward and nonreward produce stimuli, but the properties theorists assign to these stimuli differ. Some psychologists treat the stimuli as memory traces of limited duration (for example, Surridge & Amsel, 1966), while others treat the stimulus consequences as longer-lasting memories that can be recalled when the alley cues are reinstated (for example, E.J. Capaldi & Lynch, 1967).

In support of a memory mechanism, E.J. Capaldi and his co-workers have reported the same pattern running under single-alternating schedules when trials were separated by 15 seconds, 2 minutes, 10 minutes, or 20 minutes (Capaldi & Stanley, 1963). In a later experiment Capaldi and Spivey (1964) found a patterned effect even when trials were separated by 24 hours. In contrast, Amsel and his associates (Surridge & Amsel, 1965, 1966, 1968) have not found a pattern effect with trials spaced a day apart.

Another procedure used in reward-pattern studies is to present rewarded and nonrewarded trials randomly or quasi-randomly. With this procedure the stimulus properties from preceding outcomes cannot be used by the organism to guide its behavior because reward and nonreward have no consistent role in predicting the occurrence of the next outcome. Schedules of partial reward are of interest because they more closely approximate the conditions of the natural environment. Moreover, since prior outcomes do not reliably predict the nature of the next behavioral consequence, the behavioral effects of partial reward on acquisition and extinction differ from those found when the conditions of reward remain constant. One consequence of partial reinforcement is that responding is more persistent than it is following continuous reward, once reinforcement for making a given response is discontinued. This phenomenon is known as the *partial-reinforcement effect* (PRE). The PRE refers to the finding that resistance to extinction, as measured by a persistence of a previously reinforced response pattern, is greater following partial reinforcement. We will examine the probable mechanisms of the PRE in Chapter 5.

Partial reinforcement also produces different behavioral effects during acquisition. Consider two groups of rats, one given reward on every trial and the other receiving reward and nonreward in an unpredictable sequence with reward occurring on the average of half of the trials. During the early phase of training, the partially rewarded animals run slower, but as training progresses, their running speed increases so that eventually they are running faster than the group rewarded continuously. This crossover from slower to faster running for the partially rewarded group is called the *Goodrich effect* (see, for example, Goodrich, 1959; Haggard, 1959; Wagner, 1961). If, after extended training, overall running speed is broken down into start, runway, and goal-box measures, partially rewarded rats are observed to run faster in the start and runway sections but slower than continuously rewarded subjects in the goal segment. Figure 3–9 shows the performance of partially and continuously rewarded rats over the course of training in the three alley segments. Note the crossover from slower to faster speeds in the partially rewarded group in the start and run segments of the alley and the absence of this effect in the goal segment. The basis for the crossover effects in running speed is far from clear. Different theorists have suggested that it is mediated by motivational (for example, Amsel, 1967) and memory (for example, Gamboni, 1973) mechanisms.

A recurrent theme in this chapter has been the adequacy of associative and motivational hypotheses in providing an explanation of reinforcement. Conceivably, both interpretations may eventually be incorporated into a comprehensive theory of reinforcement. Goal events are devoid of neither emotional nor stimulus consequences. Since the behavioral laws assigned to each of these consequences appear identical, the different behavioral effects probably reflect the extent to which motivational and associative processes are present in a given situation. For example, the greater the incompatibility between instrumental and consummatory behavior, the more likely that associative processes would be predominant, *but* the more palatable the reward, the stronger the motivational process.

Free-Responding Procedures. The pattern of reinforcement and nonreinforcement has been discussed so far in the context of situations in which a subject makes a response in a specific, externally controlled stimulus situation. In contrast, behavior in free-responding situations is freely available to the organism. The measures used to index behavior also differ between discrete-trial and free-responding situations. Whereas response latency is employed in discrete-trial settings, *response rate* is the measure used in free-responding (operant) tasks. Response rate reflects the length of time elapsing between successive responses. Since behavioral change is measured as time intervening between responses in free-responding, or operant, experiments, the number of responses is plotted against time rather than trials. The dependent variable is expressed as a rate measure—that is, number of responses per unit of time.

In free-responding situations the pattern of reinforcement and nonreinforcement is called a *schedule of reinforcement*. Schedules are defined by the number of responses and the elapsed time since either the last response or the last reinforcer. Schedules can be classified on the basis of the number of responses required to produce reinforcement—that is, *ratio schedules*—and on the basis of elapsed time between successive reinforcers—that is, *interval schedules* (Ferster & Skinner, 1957).

Ratio schedules reward a response after a number of responses have occurred since the last reinforced response. The number of responses required for reward may be fixed or variable, which gives rise to *fixed-ratio* (FR) and *variable-ratio* (VR) schedules. An FR schedule is one in which a response is rewarded upon completion of a fixed number of responses counted from the preceding reinforcement. An FR10, for example, is a schedule in which reward is contingent on the tenth response emitted since the last reinforcement. In other words, the subject is rewarded only after making ten responses. In contrast, with the VR schedule, the number of responses required before reinforcement is given varies ran-

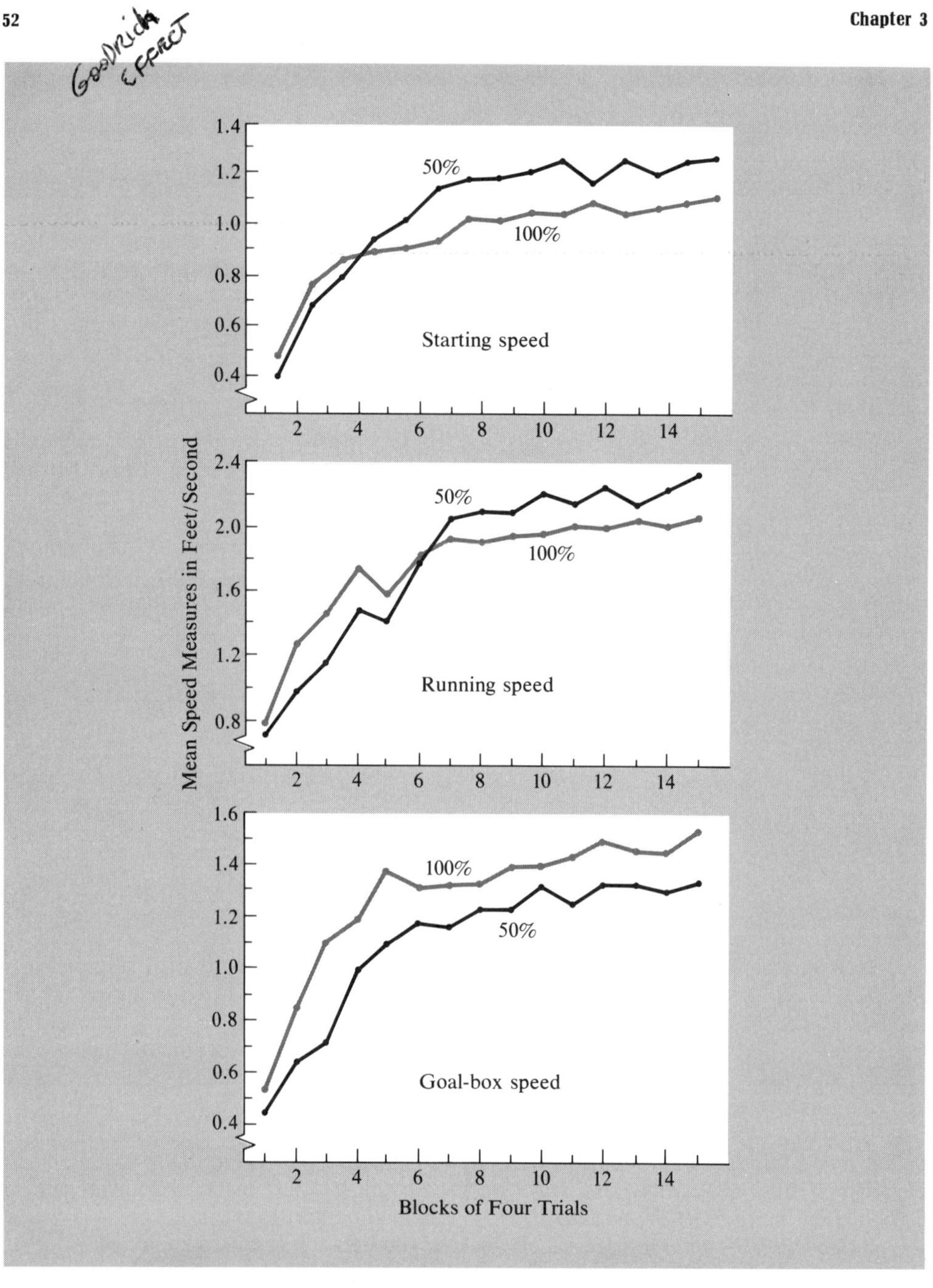

Figure 3–9. Speed of running in partially and continuously rewarded rats for three segments of the alley runway. (From "Performance in Different Segments of an Instrumental Response Chain as a Function of Reinforcement Schedule," by K. P. Goodrich, *Journal of Experimental Psychology,* 1959, *57,* 57–63. Copyright 1959 by the American Psychological Association. Reprinted by permission.)

domly. For instance, only three responses may be required for reinforcement at first, and then 20 responses, and then ten responses, and so on. A VR15 refers to a requirement that, on the *average,* reinforcement is presented after the 15th response, but reward can occur after one, two, or more responses. High rates of responding are obtained on these schedules. Since rewards are contingent on the number of responses, they can be received more quickly as the time between responses shortens. In brief, ratio schedules differentially reinforce short interresponse times (IRTs), and this feature is reflected in high rates of responding.

Human analogs of these schedules are fairly obvious. For example, the piecework system of payment results in behavior typical of FR reinforcement. Consider a migrant worker who receives a dollar for every ten bushels of fruit picked (FR10). Under this system the person works rapidly while working, but there is usually a pause before beginning each new block of work. Slot machines are usually cited as examples of VR scheduling. Suppose a machine has been programmed to pay off on the average of every 100 pulls of the lever. As any casual observer in Las Vegas or Lake Tahoe would attest, behavior generated under this type of scheduling produces a high, steady rate of responding.

Interval schedules reward responses after a period of time has elapsed, usually since the last reinforcement. Reward may be programmed after a fixed period of time between the onset of the interval and the next reward, producing a *fixed-interval* (FI) schedule; or the time between successive reinforcements may be variable, giving rise to a *variable-interval* (VI) schedule.

Figure 3–10 presents typical, relatively stable levels of terminal performance (asymptote) generated by these four types of schedules. Note that FI performance in the lower-left figure is characterized by a scallop; no responding is observed after the last reinforcement, but as the availability of the next reinforcer nears, the response rate begins to accelerate rapidly. The graph showing VI performance (lower right) shows no scalloping; instead, VI scheduling produces a constant and consistent response rate. Bait or "still" fishing is an example of VI responding. Consider a fisherman who catches a catfish every hour on the average. If we were to measure his response rate by counting the number of casts he makes per unit of time, a slow but relatively stable casting rate, typical of "lazy" fishing, would be observed.

Another example will help to clarify the effects of reward scheduling on behavior. Consider a teacher administering an arithmetic test of 30 items of equal difficulty. Suppose that the test can be completed in 15 minutes, with each item taking 30 seconds. The reinforcement contingency can be programmed in one of two ways: the class can be told that they have 30 minutes to complete the test, which will be followed by recess (FI30), or they can be told that recess will begin as soon as the 30 items are completed (FR30). Under the first contingency the children will begin slowly, so that when 15 minutes have expired, few items will be completed. However, as the time for recess approaches, the rate of responding will accelerate; all the children will be busy working just before the recess begins. In contrast, the fixed-ratio schedule makes the availability of recess contingent on completing the 30 items. If this schedule is adopted, a high response rate will be apparent early in the session, with most children completing the test in 15 minutes.

These examples illustrate the sensitivity of behavior to the prevailing conditions of reinforcement and suggest that rules for presenting or terminating rewards can exercise a high degree of control over behavior. In addition, performance differences generated by the different schedules suggest that subjects learn correlations between responses and their outcomes; that is, subjects learn that certain features of their own behavior influence the quality and quantity of reinforcement. Consider the ratio schedules. Apparently, part of what gets learned is a quantitative property of the preceding response—that is, interresponse time. The shorter the time between responses, the more immediate the reward. Thus, a positive correlation exists between response rate and immediacy of reward with ratio schedules.

Subjects are equally adept at acquiring negative correlations. A reinforcement schedule that differentially reinforces *low rates of responding* (DRL) makes the availability

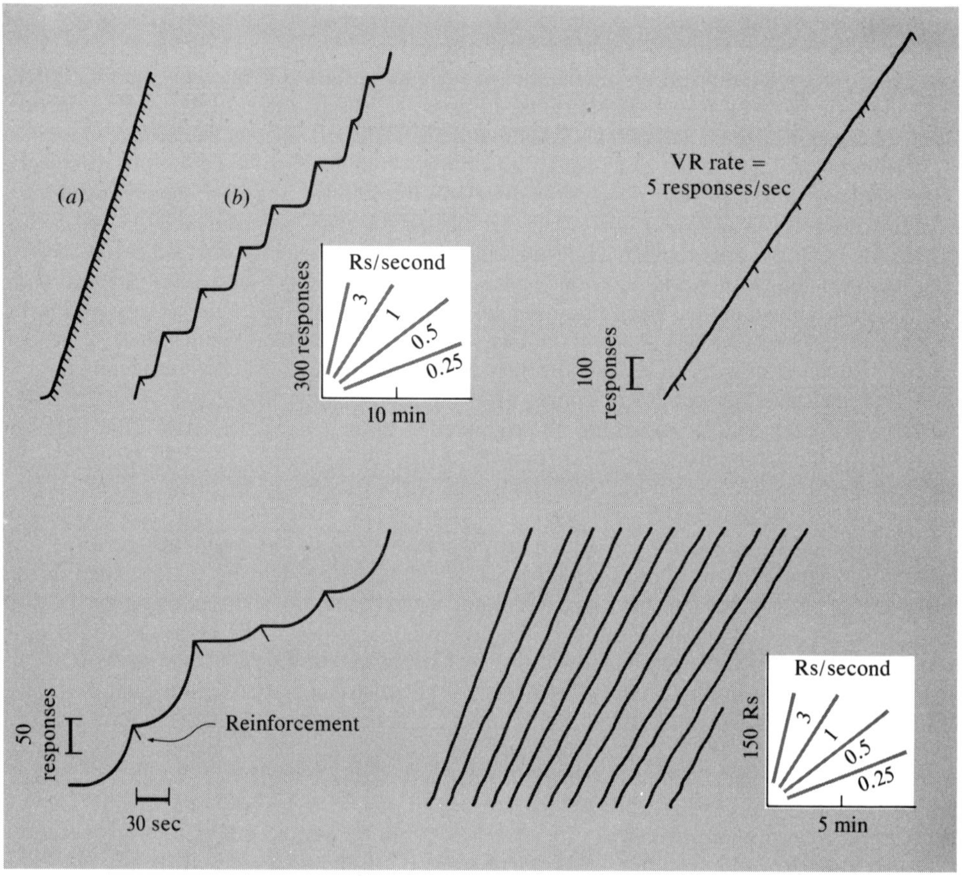

Figure 3–10. Schedules of reinforcement. Upper left: performance under fixed-ratio (FR) schedules. Record (a) shows a high, constant rate of responding on an FR20. The oblique markings (pips) on the curve indicate the delivery of reinforcement. Record (b) demonstrates the postreinforcement pause characteristic of long ratios—in this instance an FR120. Upper right: performance on a variable-ratio (VR) schedule. Note the absence of the postreinforcement pause. Lower left: illustration of fixed-interval (FI) performance. The record shows the characteristic pause after reinforcement followed by accelerated responding. Lower right: performance generated under a variable-interval (VI) schedule. Overall responding is fairly constant, and, in contrast to FI schedules, there is a tendency for response rates to increase after reinforcement. (From *Schedules of Reinforcement,* by C.S. Ferster and B.F. Skinner. Copyright © 1957 by Prentice-Hall, Inc. Reprinted by permission of Prentice-Hall, Inc., Englewood Cliffs, New Jersey.)

of reward contingent on the time elapsing since the last response. For example, a DRL20 schedule programs reward so that 20 seconds must intervene between the last response and the next one if reward is to occur. Interresponse times of fewer than 20 seconds result in nonreinforcement. Here a negative correlation is learned between response rate and reward: slow rates of responding yield more reinforcement.

Another question that is of interest is whether subjects can learn that no correlation exists between behavior and its consequences. Can individuals learn that rewards or punishers occur independently of their actions? If so, what influence does the absence of any correlation have on subsequent behavior? Some of the autoshaping studies suggest that animals may in fact acquire information that the reinforcer is scheduled independently from their behavior. Animals shifted from a condition in which reinforcement is independent from their behavior to one in which reinforcement is dependent perform more poorly than animals that have not experienced the absence of a contingency between this behavior and reward.

Negative Reinforcement

We indicated earlier that response probability may increase following the presentation of pleasurable stimuli or the termination of aversive ones. This symmetry between reward and escape learning suggests that the properties of positive and negative reinforcement affect behavior in similar ways. If negative reinforcement produces behavioral effects similar to those observed with positive reinforcement, we might suspect that positive and negative reinforcers obey the same laws. For stimuli to function as positive reinforcers, the subject must be motivated; that is, to ensure that a stimulus has a positive reinforcing value, an item must be withdrawn to induce motivation and presented to provide reward. For stimuli to qualify as negative reinforcers, the order of presentation is reversed. The application of aversive stimuli produces the motivational state, and the removal of these stimuli provides reward.

Viewed in this way, the analog of reward magnitude would be a reduction in the intensity of the aversive stimulus; that is, the greater the reduction in aversiveness, the greater the reward value. We saw that, in general, asymptotic performance varies directly with larger amounts of reward. Similarly, asymptotic performance is related directly to the magnitude of the reduction in aversive stimulation (see, for example, G.H. Bower, Fowler, & Trapold, 1959; B.A. Campbell & Kraeling, 1953; Woods, Davidson, & Peters, 1964).

In addition, delay of reward can, as was true for positive reinforcement, affect the outcome of negative reinforcement. To determine the effects of delayed negative reward, Fowler and Trapold (1962) ran six groups of rats in an alley runway with start and run segments electrified with 250 volts. Shock was terminated in the goal box after a delay of 0, 1, 2, 4, 8, or 16 seconds. Consistent with results in appetitive-conditioning experiments, they found performance to be inferior with increasing delays; asymptotic performance of the groups varied inversely with the delay of negative reinforcement. Penny (1967) found that delaying the termination of a loud tone produced comparable effects in escape responding by children.

Finally, the frequency of reward affects the outcome of negative reinforcement. Subjects who receive intermittent negative reward during training are more resistant to extinction (exhibit the PRE) than those getting continuous negative reward, regardless of the extinction procedure used (see, for example, G.H. Bower, 1960; Woods, Markman, Lynch, & Stokely, 1972). A further parallel with instrumental appetitive learning is that rats on a single-alternating negative-reward schedule learn to pattern their response speed by slower running on nonrewarded trials and faster running on rewarded trials (Seybert, Mellgren, Jobe, & Eckert, 1974, Experiment 5). What conclusions can be drawn from these studies? The results best suggest that the processes underlying the operation of positive and negative reward are similar; that is, they generally obey the same behavioral laws. However, this conclusion must be tempered with a little caution because some anomalous findings exist between reward and escape learning.

Interactions between the Conditions of Reinforcement

The preceding discussion of reinforcement and motivation suggests that antagonistic motivational systems may be responsible for the reciprocal effects of reinforcement and punishment. The similarity of behavioral outcomes noted with positive and negative reinforcement indicates that reinforcement may reflect an anticipated increase in appetitive or a decrease in aversive stimulation. In contrast, the suppressive effects of punishment and nonreward may result from increasing aversive or decreasing anticipated appetitive states. The behavioral change that occurs as a consequence of the transition from one source of stimulation to another, which may produce an opposing state, is referred to as *induction* or *behavioral contrast.*

Positive and Negative Induction

Pavlov (1927) was the first to report that unusual reciprocal effects were observed under certain conditions following the formation of a classically conditioned discrimination. After discrimination training between a stimulus paired with reinforcement (CS+) and one signaling nonreinforcement (CS−) had occurred, responding to CS+ was enhanced if CS− shortly preceded CS+. The unusually high magnitude of the conditioned response to the positive stimulus following the presentation of CS− was called *positive induction.*

To observe *negative induction,* a discrimination is formed between a compound stimulus (for example, a tone and a light) signaling nonreinforcement and a stimulus consisting of one element of the compound (for example, the tone alone) paired with reinforcement. The compound stimulus is known as a *conditioned inhibitor* because responding to it is inhibited after it has been contrasted with the rewarded stimulus. After the subject learns to respond to the tone but not to the conditioned inhibitor, the tone/light compound is reinforced, but its presentation is alternated with the still reinforced tone. Negative induction is found if the conditioned response remains suppressed to the compound stimulus.

Pavlov explained these phenomena by appealing to complementary processes activated by reinforcement and nonreinforcement. He suggested that an excitatory process results from reinforcement and an inhibitory process from nonreinforcement. In contrast, removal of a stimulus signaling reinforcement or nonreinforcement activates the opposing process. For instance, inhibition replaces excitation following the termination of a positive stimulus. In a reciprocal fashion, terminating a negative stimulus transforms an inhibitory state into an excitatory one. According to Pavlov, positive induction occurs because excitation resulting from terminating the negative stimulus sums with the excitation produced by the positive CS; negative induction is observed when the inhibitory aftereffects following the removal of the old positive stimulus competes with the newly acquired excitation of the previously nonreinforced stimulus. A more complete treatment of Pavlov's theory appears in Chapter 6.

Behavioral Contrast

Successive Contrast. Interactions between conditions of reinforcement of the sort described with Pavlovian conditioning are also found in instrumental learning. Interactions are observed when exposure to more than one condition of reinforcement produces a performance change that exceeds what would normally be found with a single condition of reinforcement. In the context of instrumental learning, changes in behavior that arise as a consequence of interactions between reinforcement conditions are called behavioral contrast.

Since discrete-trial and free-responding procedures reflect different research traditions and protocols, contrast phenomena are studied in different ways. Typically, in discrete-trial settings animals are reinforced in a particular context, usually in alley runways, and are then shifted to either a more or a less favorable condition of reinforcement in the same context. The condition for observing *successive positive contrast* is present when performance to the now more favorable reinforcer, such as a larger reward, is enhanced by the animals' prior experience with the less favorable reinforcer; that is, an animal shifted to a larger reward runs faster than animals that have always received the large reward. *Successive negative contrast* occurs when the animal is shifted from a large to a small reward. In this case, behavior is suppressed relative to a group that has always received the smaller reward.

Although successive negative contrast is readily observable in cases involving a shift in reward magnitude, there are no unequivocal instances of successive positive contrast. Early research findings were thought to demonstrate successive positive contrast, but it was later shown that studies by Crespi (1942) and Zeaman (1949) did not include proper controls. In neither of these studies were animals trained sufficiently long on the preshift amount of reward to determine clearly whether performance had stabilized before the shift occurred. If performance was below its asymptotic level when reward magnitude was increased, subsequent changes in performance may have been due to the additional practice animals received rather than to an increase in reward magnitude.

An experiment by Franchina and Brown (1971), the results of which are shown in Figure 3–11, nicely demonstrates the presence of successive negative contrast and the absence of successive positive contrast. As the figure shows, rats initially trained on a large

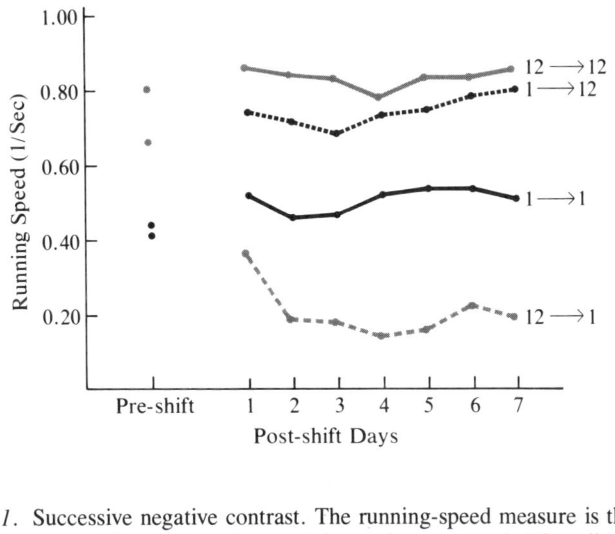

Figure 3–11. Successive negative contrast. The running-speed measure is the reciprocal of time. The group (12→1) initially receiving a large reward (12 pellets) ran more slowly for a small reward than a control group (1→1) experiencing a small reward throughout training. Note that the group shifted from a small to a large reward (1→12) ran no faster than a control group (12→12) that always received a large reward. (From "Reward Magnitude Shift Effects in Rats with Hippocampal Lesions," by J.J. Franchina and T.S. Brown, *Journal of Comparative and Physiological Psychology,* 1971, *76,* 365–370. Copyright 1971 by the American Psychological Association. Reprinted by permission.)

reward ran more slowly following a shift to a small reward than a control group whose experience was confined to the small reward. However, rats shifted from a small to a large reward (Group 1→12) did not run faster than rats whose exposure was limited solely to the large reward.

One possible explanation for the absence of positive contrast may be the insensitivity of the response measure; if rats are running almost as fast as they are able before being shifted to the large reward, increases in the value of the reward would not increase their speed. They just wouldn't be able to run any faster. However, when this problem is controlled, researchers have still not been successful in demonstrating positive contrast. Rats shifted to a larger reward before attaining full speed still fail to show a positive-contrast effect. Furthermore, no successive positive contrast is found when rats are trained under low levels of deprivation, a condition that causes them to run well below any physical limit of their running speed (E.D. Capaldi, 1971).

Simultaneous Contrast. Simultaneous contrast involves the correlation of two separate conditions of reinforcement to two distinctive stimuli. If responding increases to S_1 when the reinforcement predicted by S_2 has become less favorable than the condition prevailing in S_1, *simultaneous positive contrast* is said to occur. *Simultaneous negative contrast* refers to a decrease in responding to S_1 when S_2 now signals a more favorable reinforcement condition than S_1. Simultaneous positive contrast is usually studied using operant procedures, while simultaneous negative contrast is investigated in discrete-trial settings that employ separate alley runways.

A basic experiment for demonstrating simultaneous positive contrast was conducted by Reynolds (1961). Pigeons were trained to peck red or green lights projected on a translucent response key. Initially, the reinforcement condition to the stimuli (both red and green) was the same; each one signaled a VI 3-minute schedule of reinforcement. This was done to ensure that a baseline was established with which to compare later changes in responding. After responding had stabilized, the reinforcement condition was changed on only one of the two keys. Specifically, reinforcement to, say, the green key was changed from a VI 3-minute schedule to extinction, while reinforcement remained unchanged on the red key. Contrast was inferred from the increase in response rate to the red light relative to its initial baseline.

Reynolds suggested that contrast occurred in this situation because the frequency of reinforcement to the red stimulus, relative to the frequency of reinforcement to all other stimuli controlling responding, determined the response rate with which any particular stimulus controls. During the first phase of the experiment, responding was reinforced on a VI 3-minute schedule to both stimuli, so that the relative frequency of reinforcement to red was .5. Although the absolute number of reinforcements remained the same in the unchanged component following a change in the other, the relative frequency of reinforcement increased from .5 to 1.0. According to Reynolds, this increase in the relative frequency of reinforcement was responsible for the contrast effect observed.

Of course, when reinforcement is made less favorable in one schedule component, there is a decrease in responding to the stimulus (S_2) signaling that component. Although a considerable amount of research has been devoted to determining whether positive contrast results from a decrease in the probability of reinforcement or simply a reduction in responding, neither condition appears solely adequate to account for this phenomenon. It appears most likely that simultaneous positive contrast will occur when decreasing the probability of reinforcement to S_2 produces an aversive emotional reaction that strengthens responding to S_1, the stimulus predicting the more favorable reinforcement condition (Amsel, 1971).

Although simultaneous positive contrast is a highly reliable and readily obtained phenomenon when operant procedures are employed, simultaneous negative contrast does not normally occur; that is, increasing the reinforcement value in one schedule component does not decrease responding in the other component. Hence, when the reinforcement schedule associated with S_2 is made more favorable, no decrease in responding occurs to S_1. Usually, in order to obtain simultaneous negative contrast, discrete-trial procedures that vary reward magnitude rather than reinforcement schedule must be employed. G.H. Bower (1961) was the first to present data showing the presence of simultaneous negative contrast in a discrete-trial procedure. One group of rats (differential group) was trained to run down two alley runways of differential brightness. In one runway they received an eight-pellet reward, while in the other they received only one pellet. Two independent control groups were trained to constant reinforcement, one of them receiving an eight-pellet reward and the other group receiving one pellet.

Bower's results appear in Figure 3–12. The crucial feature of his findings lies in the terminal performance of the differential group and the independent control on the one-pellet condition. The slower running speed of the differential group was apparently due to

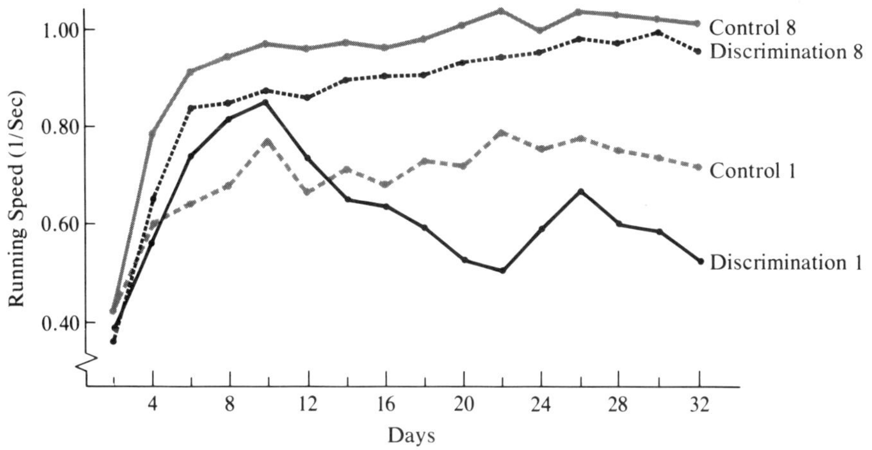

Figure 3–12. Simultaneous negative contrast. The group exposed to both a large and a small reward in the two alley runways ran more slowly for the small reward than a control that received only a small reward. However, the performance of the differential group to the large reward was not reliably different from that of the control trained throughout to the large reward. (From "A Contrast Effect in Differential Conditioning," by G.H. Bower, *Journal of Experimental Psychology,* 1961, *62,* 196–199. Copyright 1961 by the American Psychological Association. Reprinted by permission.)

its exposure to the eight-pellet reward. As the curves show, its performance to the smaller reward was contrasted downward (in a negative direction) relative to the group receiving only one pellet on every trial. The figure also reveals that no difference in performance was present between the other control and the differential group receiving the eight-pellet reward. Bower suggested that the failure to find simultaneous positive contrast with discrete trials was due to the limitation of the response measure. We suggested this possibility when discussing successive positive contrast. In any event, when rewards are contrasted in a discrete-trial procedure, negative contrast is observed, whereas contrasting-reward conditions in free-responding situations result in positive rather than negative contrast.

Although the preceding discussion suggests that different principles govern positive and negative contrast, another explanation, equally plausible, is that the observed effects on behavior are different because of the different experimental procedures. To test the possibility that procedural differences determine the extent to which contrast appears, A.M. Padilla (1971) developed an alley analog of a free-responding situation. Rats were trained to shuttle in a double-alley runway of discriminable brightness where one of two variable-interval schedules and one of two reward magnitudes were correlated with each alley. Padilla defined responses as a shuttle that broke a photobeam 3 feet from the food cup and then a photobeam within the food cup. To initiate another response, the rats were required to go back to the photobeam 3 feet away, break it, and then return to the cup. The advantage of this procedure over traditional runway studies was that rate as well as speed could be recorded. During one phase of the experiment, rats assigned initially to VI 1.5-minute schedules in each runway, but subsequently exposed to a less favorable schedule (VI 3.75-minute) in one of the alleys, showed positive contrast, a phenomenon normally observed only in free-responding situations. Response rates increased in the runway in which reward remained constant following a shift to a lower probability of reinforcement in the other runway. Since latency measures were less sensitive to this manipulation, Bower's suggestion that speed is an insensitive scale for measuring positive contrast gains support.

More recently, Gonzalez and Champlin (1974) found simultaneous negative contrast in a free-responding situation. In their experiment, pigeons receiving differential reinforcement (one versus ten pellets) on VI 1-minute schedules, which were correlated to a red or a green response key, responded more slowly to the stimulus signaling the smaller reward than did an independent control group exposed only to the one-pellet reward on the same reinforcement schedule. Simultaneous positive contrast was not observed in this situation. This finding is comparable to Bower's (1961) discrete-trial results. Taken together, the Padilla and Gonzalez and Champlin experiments support the notion that asymmetrical contrast effects result from procedural differences in discrete-trial and free-responding situations rather than reflecting the operation of different laws.

The Significance of Contrast

Induction and behavioral contrast have attracted the attention of psychologists because the several variations of the phenomena appear to be exceptions to the principles of learning. The empirical basis of many theories of learning is the countless demonstrations that reinforcement facilitates and nonreinforcement weakens behaviors that precede them (law of effect) and that similar changes in related behaviors result to the extent of the similarity of other stimuli to the stimuli signaling reinforcement or nonreinforcement (law of generalization). If, for example, after responding to two stimuli signaling the same conditions of reward, the reinforcement to one of them is diminished, then responding should decline to the nonreinforcement stimulus, and, depending on the extent to which the two stimuli are related, responding to the second stimulus should be reduced as well. Conversely, improving the reinforcement condition to one of the stimuli should enhance performance to that stimulus, and, again, depending on the similarity of the stimuli, responding to the second stimulus should also increase. But each of the varieties of contrast demonstrates a paradoxical effect of nonreinforcement in that one stimulus facilitates responding to the other stimulus and that reinforcement to one stimulus can decrease the rate of responding to the other stimulus. The question of whether the explanatory mechanisms of the existing learning theories can be extended to accommodate contrast or whether the framework of the theories requires radical alteration with a different set of explanatory mechanisms is still open.

Summary

The law of effect is an empirical generalization that specifies how the consequences of a response affect response selection. Initially, the law was treated as though it were generally applicable; it was thought that any arbitrary operant response immediately preceding a reinforcer was strengthened. Behavioral observations of a variety of species, the autoshaping phenomenon, and the Garcia effect suggest, however, that the biological characteristics of a species place constraints on what can be learned. In particular, the Garcia effect suggests that the neurophysiological substrate that mediates behavior must be known before the operation of reinforcement can be clarified.

In avoiding the logical problems inherent in an empirical definition of reinforcement, psychologists have attempted to identify the source of reinforcement by indicating what characteristics of the stimulus, the response, or the subject's motivational state are responsible for the effect of reinforcement. Although a logical division between these sources of reward is possible, it is difficult to isolate them in practice. The evidence indicates that stimulation itself is a necessary but not sufficient condition of reinforcement, and though various properties of consummatory responses or altered arousal level appear sufficient, these are not necessary conditions for reinforcement. A closely related issue is whether reinforcement has a direct effect on learning by strengthening S–R associations or whether reinforcement excites preexisting response tendencies. Most modern theories of learning favor a motivational interpretation of reinforcement even though the evidence remains equivocal.

Organisms are extremely sensitive to the prevailing conditions of reinforcement. Aspects of reward on which considerable research has been conducted are amount, delay, and frequency of reinforcement. In general, performance improves with increasing amounts of reward and deteriorates with long delays of reinforcement. The behavioral effects of reward patterning are more complex. If reward/nonreward sequences are arranged so that the stimulus consequences of these events can be used reliably to predict subsequent outcomes, response patterning develops. On the other hand, if the cues of reward or nonreward are not reliable in predicting the occurrence of impending reinforcement, response-produced stimuli and stimuli resulting from the emotional consequences of nonreward guide selection of ensuing responses. With complex patterns of reinforcement, animals learn contingencies that reflect the prevailing relationship between response and reinforcer, and they adjust their behavior accordingly.

Whether positive and negative reinforcement obey the same laws is an issue that is still unresolved. Although anomalies exist, negative reward produces behavioral effects similar to those found with positive reward when intensity of the aversive stimuli is reduced, when the termination of aversive stimuli is delayed, and when single-alternating schedules of negative reward and nonreward are used.

Pavlovian induction and behavioral contrast have attracted interest because the behavioral anomalies resulting from these interactions between the conditions of reinforcement appear contrary to the widely accepted principles of learning. The crucial issue of whether these phenomena can be subsumed under the general laws of learning or whether theories require conceptual revision to account for them is still open.

Chapter 4

Punishment

Punishment can be defined as the application of an aversive or unpleasant event to behavior in order to suppress or eliminate that behavior. Humans have undoubtedly always used punishment to influence the behavior of other individuals under the assumption that punishment has effects opposite to those produced by reinforcement or reward. As noted in Chapter 3, this view was given scientific respectability by Thorndike (1913) in his early writings on the law of effect. In its general form the law of effect refers to the strengthening or weakening of a stimulus–response bond as a result of its consequences. When a modifiable S–R connection is made and is followed by reinforcement, the strength of the connection is increased. In contrast, according to the law of effect, punishment reduces the tendency to repeat behavior it immediately follows; that is, punishment weakens the S–R association. Thorndike (1922) later modified this view and concluded that punishment really has no inherent weakening effects upon behaviors it follows. Thus, beliefs about the effectiveness of punishment have ranged from one extreme to the other.

As we shall see in this chapter, the effects of punishment are specialized, indirect, and depend upon what type of behavior is emitted once this event is introduced. In some instances, punishment may actually strengthen rather than weaken a response pattern. In light of the widespread use of punishment by our society in attempts to eliminate undesirable behaviors and to teach acceptable behaviors, it is extremely important for all of us to learn under what conditions punishment works and how effective it is.

Thorndike's assertion that punishment is not necessarily effective in eliminating undesirable behaviors was further explored by Skinner (1938) and Estes (1944). Using an operant-conditioning procedure, Skinner examined the effects of punishment on a previously acquired bar-press response. Initially, the rats learned to press a bar to obtain a food reward. After this training two extinction sessions were administered during which lever presses were no longer reinforced. The extinction sessions were each 2 hours in length and occurred on successive days. For one group of rats, each bar press in the first 10 minutes of extinction was followed by a sharp slap to the paw used in pressing the bar. This punishment was delivered by the lever itself. No further punishment was administered during the remaining 3 hours and 50 minutes of extinction. The second group was never punished.

The results of this experiment are depicted in Figure 4–1, which is a cumulative record of the number of bar presses emitted during extinction. There are several interesting things to note in this figure. First, punishment did depress responding during the 10-minute punishment interval. The more interesting finding, however, is that after the punishment period ended, the *rate* of responding of the punished animals became greater than that of the nonpunished animals. This phenomenon continued, so that by the end of extinction the punished rats had caught up with the nonpunished animals in terms of the total number of bar presses emitted. Skinner interpreted these findings as indicating that the effects of punishment on behavior are only temporary, a conclusion that we shall later see has not been invariably substantiated. It is now recognized that under certain conditions punishment can lastingly suppress behavior. But before examining the more recent findings, let us return to these early studies.

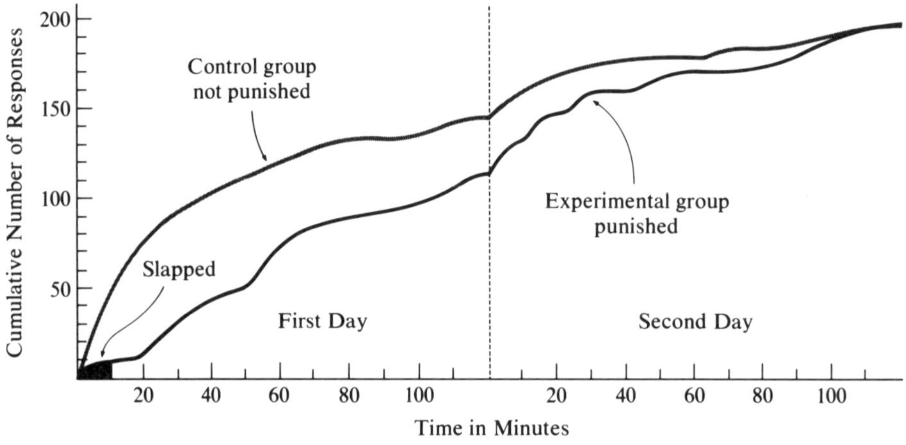

Figure 4–1. Effect of negative reinforcement upon extinction. The two curves are from groups of four rats each, with the same experimental history. All responses made by one group during the first 10 minutes of extinction were slapped. The rate of responding was depressed for some time, but complete recovery eventually ensued. (From *The Behavior of Organisms,* by B. F. Skinner. Copyright © 1938. Renewed 1965. Reprinted by permission of Prentice-Hall, Inc., Englewood Cliffs, New Jersey.)

Estes followed Skinner's research with an extensive investigation of the effects of punishment (shock delivered through the lever) on the operant bar-pressing response in rats. Using mild punishment, Estes found results much like those reported by Skinner. There was a temporary depression in the rate of responding followed by an increase in rate, so that the total number of responses emitted by the punished animals was equal to that of a group experiencing normal extinction procedures. In contrast, with more intense electric shock, a far more pronounced effect on responding occurred. Bar pressing was eliminated within a few minutes after initiating extinction and severe-punishment procedures. During three successive nonpunishment extinction sessions, responding remained at a very low level; however, during four additional extinction sessions, the rate of responding for the previously punished animals was as high as that exhibited by the nonpunished subjects. The contrast between these results and those obtained with less intense shock is very important. Unlike the case with mild punishment, in which an immediate, marked increase in responding occurs following cessation of the aversive stimulus, more intense punishment produces a more permanent suppression of responding. This was the first experimental demonstration of the finding that the duration of the suppression of responding is directly related to punishment severity. This phenomenon has been the subject of a great deal of subsequent research, which will be reviewed later in this chapter.

Another interesting finding of Estes's investigation concerns the effects of intermittent or partial versus continuous punishment of the bar-pressing response on the course of extinction. His results indicate that although continuous punishment produces a greater initial depression in response rate, intermittent punishment results in a more persistent inhibitory effect. This finding suggests that the effects of partial punishment are very much like the effects of partial reinforcement, a fact that was to be well substantiated by later investigators (for example, Azrin, 1956; Azrin, Holz, & Hake, 1963). Much of the research on punishment has attempted to clarify the factors influencing the effectiveness of punishment. It is to these investigations that we now turn.

Factors Influencing the Outcome of Punishment

In this section we will review the major factors that affect the outcome of punishment. Some experiments have examined the effects of punishment on consummatory responses, whereas others have looked at the effects of punishment on behaviors established as the result of positive reinforcement. We will review both kinds of situations in some detail.

The Effects of Punishment on Consummatory Responses

Some of the earliest studies examining the effects of punishment on behavior investigated consummatory behaviors, such as eating, drinking, and copulating. One would expect that because of their biological significance for survival of the organism and the species, consummatory responses should be highly resistant to suppression by punishment (see Solomon, 1964). In fact, however, the opposite is true; indeed, the most devastating effects of punishment seem to occur when punishment is applied to consummatory responses. The copulatory behavior of male rodents can be seriously suppressed by punishment (Beach, Conovitz, Steinberg, & Goldstein, 1956), as can feeding behavior in a variety of species tested, including frogs (Schaeffer, 1911); goldfish (Myer & Ricci, 1968); rats (Klee, 1944); cats (Masserman, 1943); dogs (Lichtenstein, 1950); and monkeys (Masserman & Pechtel, 1953).

A study by Beach and his associates (Beach et al., 1956) examined the effects of punishment on the copulatory behavior of male rats. Each male, placed in an arena with a receptive female, wore a light harness that held an electrode against the skin of its back. This electrode was in turn connected to a current source. The metal floor of the observation cage served as the other point of contact. Via this method the male could be exposed to an electric shock that did not reach the female. The male received a shock of 380 volts for .75 seconds when it attempted to copulate with the receptive female. This procedure produced sexual inhibition in all of the subjects tested, in the sense that they no longer attempted to copulate with receptive females. The effect persisted in some of the rats when tested nearly 2 months later, although the majority of the males recovered from their inhibited state and resumed mating within 12 to 30 days.

This finding has implications for human sexuality. If individuals' initial sexual experiences are highly aversive, it is likely that their subsequent attempts to engage in sexual behavior will be suppressed. Further, if the properties of the aversive stimulus become associated with the opposite sex itself rather than with sexual-approach responses in general, repeated experiences of this sort might ultimately lead to homosexual behavior.

Another example of the effects of punishment on consummatory behavior is provided by Schaeffer's (1911) classic investigations of habit formation in frogs. Specifically, he examined the effects of punishment via electric shock on feeding behavior. Schaeffer connected one electrode to a pan holding wet sand in which his subjects sat. The other electrode was attached to a very thin copper wire, the end of which was attached to the body of a target animal (a cockroach or a worm). In the case of the cockroach, the wire was wrapped so as not to interfere with the normal crawling movements of the roach. As soon as the frog grasped the target, the tongue of the frog touched the wire, the circuit was thus closed, and the shock was delivered to the frog. Immediately upon grasping the bait, the subjects executed a series of hops until the roach or worm was ejected from their mouths. Other foods were then offered, but none was accepted. The inhibition of feeding behavior persisted for 5 days.

Similar results were reported by Myer and Ricci (1968), who studied the effects of electric-shock punishment on feeding behavior in goldfish. The fish were initially trained to eat in the experimental apparatus by presenting them with ten clusters of worms each day. Then a 10-day series of punishment sessions began. Ten clusters of worms were presented each day with a 90-second intertrial interval. Shock was administered for 1 second via electrodes located in the water of the experimental chamber when the subject ingested the worm. The punishment had a pronounced suppressive effect, lasting for several days, on the feeding behavior of the goldfish. The feeding response in the experimental apparatus did gradually recover during subsequent nonpunishment training sessions, and the rate of recovery was closely related to the degree of suppression that occurred during the punishment sessions.

The effects of punishment on feeding behavior in the studies thus far examined were marked but did dissipate after several days. The studies we will next examine illustrate that the effects of punishing feeding behavior can be much more devastating and can actually lead to self-starvation in certain instances. A classic example of this fact is provided by the research of Klee (1944). Using a Lashley jumping stand, illustrated in Figure 4–2, Klee investigated the effects on behavior of exposure to an insolvable problem. With this apparatus a rat is placed on a platform in front of the discriminanda and taught to jump from the platform to the stimuli in order to secure a food reward. The correct stimulus panel is supported by a light spring, which allows the card to fall as soon as the animal jumps against it. The animal can then obtain a food reinforcement located behind the positive stimulus. On the other hand, the negative stimulus is latched from behind. Thus, when the rat jumps against this latter panel, it falls into the net below.

In Klee's study, rats were trained to jump to one of the two visual patterns, but in the insolvable problem the visual-stimulus panel that was locked was randomly varied independently of the pattern and the side of presentation. Hence, any consistent response strategy that the subject used was successful only 50% of the time. The rest of the time, the rat bumped its head against the locked stimulus panel and fell into the net below. Successful jumps were rewarded by food, and at the end of the daily session of ten trials, the subjects were allowed to finish their day's rations on the rear feeding platform of the apparatus. The effects of exposure to this testing situation on feeding behavior were dramatic. Eight of the 15 rats refused to continue responding after training. One subject actually starved to death, and five others would undoubtedly have met a similar fate if this experimental procedure had been continued. In effect, the rats' behavior indicated that they would rather starve to death than attempt the insolvable problem.

In a frequently cited study Lichtenstein (1950) produced feeding inhibition in normal dogs by applying shock (85 volts delivered to the right forepaw) while the animals were eating. The effect was produced in one to four shock trials. On the other hand, feeding inhibitions were not effectively established if the shock was applied prior to eating or while the food was being put into the food box. Once the inhibition of feeding was established, the effect was found to be relatively stable, lasting for weeks or even months in the testing

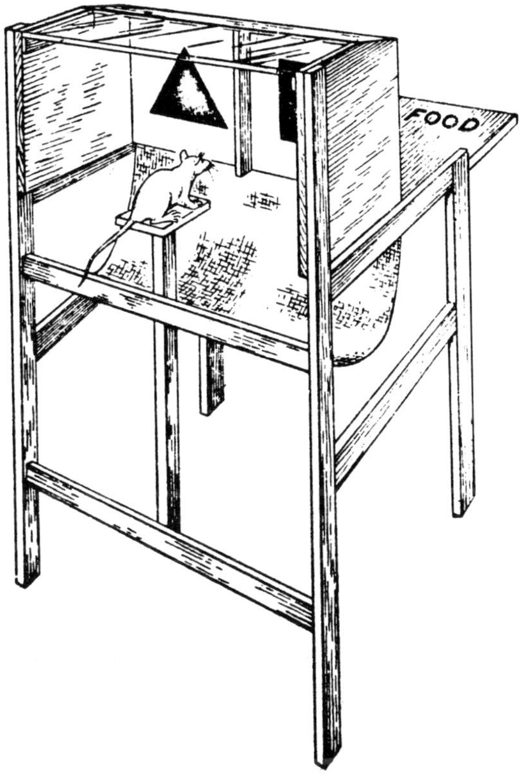

Figure 4–2. One form of Lashley's apparatus for testing the vision of rats. Two cards containing figures serve both as stimuli and as coverings for the apertures by means of which the rat reaches the food platform. The negative stimulus is locked from behind, so that when the rat jumps, it is repelled and falls into the net below. (From "The Mechanism of Vision. XV: Preliminary Studies of the Rat's Capacity for Detail Vision," by K. S. Lashley, *Journal of General Psychology,* 1938, *18,* 123–193. Reprinted by permission of The Journal Press.)

situation without further pairings of shock with the feeding response. In two of the dogs, aversions to food were also observed outside the testing situation. In one of these subjects, the aversion was only temporary, and feeding quickly recovered when the experimenter encouraged the dog to eat. The other dog, however, refused to eat the food pellets until they were ground and mixed with water to make a mash. This avoidance of food pellets, the food item that had been paired with shock in the training situation, continued in this dog in all situations until after a bilateral frontal lobotomy had been performed. Masserman (1943) has reported similar inhibition of feeding behavior in cats that received a brief air blast or electric shock while eating. Most of the cats refused to eat in the apparatus for months without further punishment, even though they were severely deprived of food.

Masserman has also reported that punishment can inhibit feeding in subhuman primates (Masserman & Pechtel, 1953). Monkeys were trained to press a bar to obtain a food reward. After this response was well established, the subjects were presented with the front of a 14-inch toy rubber snake, a terrifying stimulus for a monkey, through a curtained aperture at the back of the food-delivery box just as they reached for the food reward. After two to five such presentations, earned food rewards were refused. Further training resulted in the animals' even refusing to take free fruit placed on the floor of the chamber. For two of the monkeys, additional presentations of the rubber snake were made at various locations in the experimental chamber. The effects were devastating. The animals thereafter refused to eat in any location in the laboratory, resulting in self-starvation. These results provide dramatic evidence against Skinner's (1938) notion that the effects of punishment on behavior are only temporary.

In general, the studies presented so far all suggest that punishment is especially potent in upsetting consummatory behaviors. This situation thus presents a paradox: Why would responses that are so intimately related to the survival of an organism and its species have such a low resistance to the disruptive effects of punishment? Does the aversive event "kill the appetite" of the subject? Probably not, because Masserman (1943) reported contrasting effects of the application of shock to his cats when the temporal order of the food and the shock was reversed. In this case, when the shock was a discriminative stimulus to signal the availability of food, the shock led to very rapid eating. This finding is just one example of the now well-substantiated finding that the effects of punishment are at least partly determined by the events directly preceding and following the punishment. As Solomon (1964) has written, "a punishment is not just a punishment. It is an event in a temporal and spatial flow of stimulation and behavior, and its effects will be produced by its temporal and spatial point of insertion in that flow" (p. 242).

Recent experiments on the effects of punishment on consummatory behavior have been devoted to the question of whether consummatory responses, such as eating, are more sensitive to punishment than instrumental behaviors, such as bar pressing. Church (1969) was one of the first investigators to conduct this type of inquiry. Rats were trained to press a bar for food in a modified operant chamber. The box was modified in that the food cup was located on the wall opposite the lever in order to separate clearly the instrumental and consummatory components of the behavior sequence. A photocell and a source of light were mounted on the sides of the food cup to define operationally the occurrence of a consummatory response. After preliminary training on the task, half of the rats were shocked following each bar press that delivered food to the cup, and the remaining subjects were punished when they broke the beam of light in the food cup. As illustrated in Figure 4–3, Church found that greater response suppression resulted from punishing the instrumental response than the consummatory response. In this study, however, one cannot be certain whether the actual consummatory response or approaches to or entries into the food cup were being punished. Church cited this methodological problem with his study and indicated that typically the subjects actually did have the pellet in their mouths at the time the shock began.

Bertsch (1972) has reexamined the effects of punishment on instrumental versus consummatory responses while attempting to circumvent the methodological problem encountered by Church. Rats were trained to press a bar to obtain a water reinforcement on a VI 30-second schedule. As you should recall, during performance on a VI schedule, the first bar press is rewarded that occurs after a predetermined, variable length of time. On a VI 30-second schedule, the duration averages 30 seconds. To compare directly the effects of instrumental-response and consummatory-response punishment, the subjects were assigned to one of two groups. The rats in the instrumental (bar-pressing) group were shocked for making a reinforced bar press, and the rats in the consummatory (licking) group were punished for the first lick following emission of the reinforced bar press. There were 15 punishment sessions followed by five recovery sessions, and the effects of the two punishment procedures on the rate of licking and bar pressing were assessed after both sets of sessions. The decrements on these response measures were expressed as *suppression ratios.*

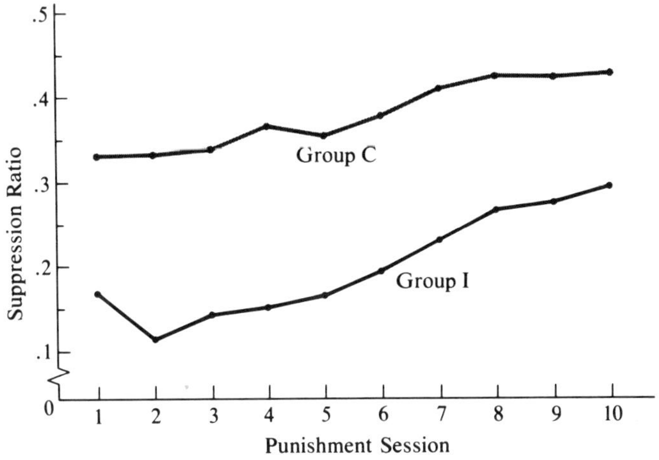

Figure 4–3. Mean suppression ratio as a result of punishment of an instrumental response (I) or punishment of a consummatory response (C). A lower suppression ratio indicates a greater amount of response suppression. (From "Response Suppression," by R. M. Church. In B. A. Campbell and R. M. Church (Eds.), *Punishment and Aversive Behavior*. Copyright © 1969. Reprinted by permission of Prentice-Hall, Inc., Englewood Cliffs, New Jersey.)

Suppression ratios are commonly used in the punishment literature to index the degree of reduction in response rate following introduction of an aversive stimulus. They provide a sensitive comparison of the level of responding during or after the punishment treatment with the response rate prior to the treatment. In Bertsch's investigation suppression ratios were computed by dividing the total number of responses during a given punishment session (A) by the average of the last two baseline prepunishment sessions (B). As noted in Figure 4–3, a lower suppression ratio indicates a greater amount of response suppression.

Figure 4–4 shows the suppression ratios for both behaviors in the two groups. As can be seen from this graph, punishment of the consummatory (licking) response produced more suppression of bar-pressing and licking responses than did punishing the instrumental (bar-pressing) response. Another interesting finding that can be seen from this figure is that the subjects recovered from the effects of instrumental-response punishment during successive punishment sessions, while the effects of punishing the consummatory response appeared to be more lasting. Figure 4–5 shows recovery after the punishment sessions were completed. During the 5 days of recovery, the instrumental group showed a higher overall rate of responding, and within this group, bar pressing occurred at a significantly higher rate than licking. Bar pressing and licking did not differ significantly in the consummatory group, except during the final recovery session.

Bertsch's findings strongly support the view that consummatory responses are much more sensitive to the deleterious effects of punishment than are instrumental responses. This is an interesting finding, but again it seems very incongruous that high-survival-value responses would have a relatively low resistance to the disruptive effects of punishment. Hopefully, future research will clarify this enigma. Perhaps if researchers investigated the effects of punishment on instrumental and consummatory behaviors that occur naturally in an animal's behavior repertoire, this finding would not appear.

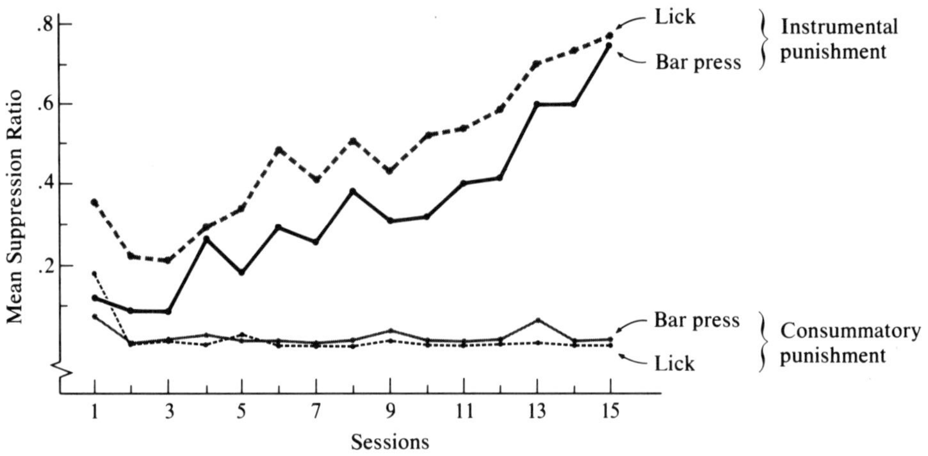

Figure 4–4. Mean suppression ratios for licking and bar pressing during punishment. (From "Punishment of Consummatory and Instrumental Behavior: Effects on Licking and Bar Pressing in Rats," by G. J. Bertsch, *Journal of Comparative and Physiological Psychology,* 1972, *78,* 478–484. Copyright 1972 by the American Psychological Association. Reprinted by permission.)

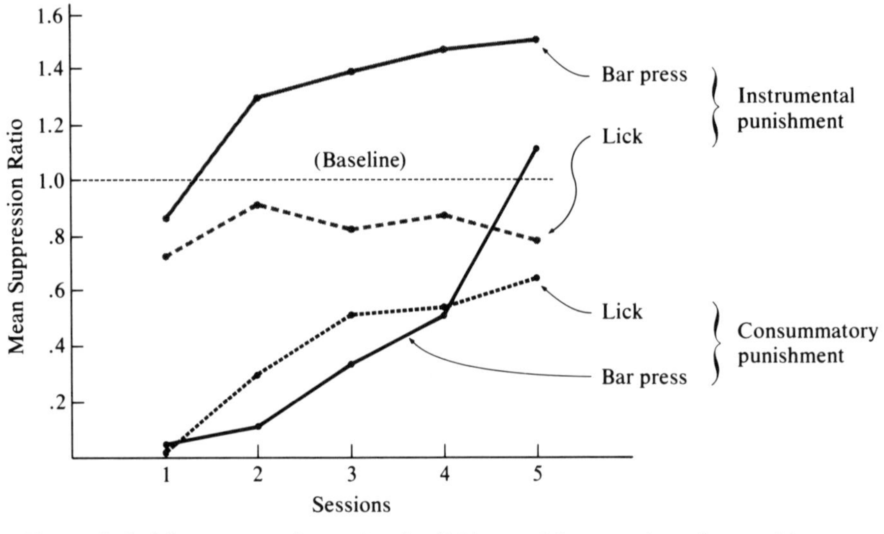

Figure 4–5. Mean suppression ratios for licking and bar pressing after punishment. (From "Punishment of Consummatory and Instrumental Behavior: Effects on Licking and Bar Pressing in Rats," by G. J. Bertsch, *Journal of Comparative and Physiological Psychology,* 1972, *78,* 478–484. Copyright 1972 by the American Psychological Association. Reprinted by permission.)

The Effects of Punishment on Behaviors Established through Positive Reinforcement

In examinations of the effects of punishment on consummatory responses, the behaviors investigated, such as eating, drinking, and copulating, have been relatively simple, stereotyped, innate responses. However, the majority of punishment experiments have concerned the effects of applying aversive stimuli on the emission of relatively complex, learned patterns of responding, and most of these studies have examined the effects of punishment on behaviors previously established through positive reinforcement. The results of these inquiries are presented in this section. The findings indicate that the effects of punishment are variable and depend on such factors as (1) the severity of the punishing stimulus, (2) the proximity of the punishment to the punished response, and (3) the subject's prior experience with aversive events. A fourth factor, the availability of alternative responses that allow the individual to avoid punishment, will be discussed in the next section.

Severity of Punishment: Punishment Intensity. Many aversive events have been used to clarify the effectiveness of the punishment procedure. They have been as diverse as a slap from the bar-press lever, a bump on the nose and a fall into a net, a blast of air, a toy snake, a loud noise, and a blow from a rolled-up newspaper. By far the most popular stimulus, however, has been the application of electric shock. Because the characteristics of this punishing event are relatively easy to quantify and control, experimenters can closely replicate the methods used by other researchers in other laboratories.

One of the most important determinants of the effectiveness of punishment is severity. The severity of a punisher is determined by two factors: the *intensity* and the *duration* of the aversive event. Church (1963) has indicated that, as the severity of punishment increases, the following sequence of behaviors usually occurs:

1. *Detection.* Although the subject can detect the presence of the aversive event and could use the stimulus as a cue to guide ensuing behavior, the punishing stimulus has no detectable effect.
2. *Temporary suppression.* Application of the punishing stimulus results in a temporary suppression of responding followed by a complete recovery.
3. *Partial suppression.* The punishment yields response suppression without complete recovery.
4. *Total suppression.* Recovery of responding does not occur following punishment-produced suppression of the response.

To clarify further the effects of punishment severity on behavior, some of the experimental literature devoted to this topic will next be surveyed.

Probably the most thoroughly documented finding in the punishment literature is that the degree of response suppression varies directly as a function of punishment intensity. An experiment by Karsh (1962) will illustrate this point. Rats were trained to traverse an 8-foot-long straight-alley runway to secure a food reward. After 76 such acquisition trials, each rat was given one shock trial per day for 40 days. During the punishment sessions both food and shock were delivered at the goal box. The animals received one of five shock levels—0, 75, 150, 300, or 600 volts for a duration of 100 milliseconds—and the effects on running speed were assessed. Rats that failed to run down the length of the alley in a maximum time of 300 seconds were assigned a speed of 0, placed in the goal box, and shocked.

The results of this inquiry are depicted in Figure 4–6. First, the running speed of the subjects had reached a stable level during the last 30 acquisition trials. Second, the 75-volt group exhibited little change in running speed and did not appreciably differ from the control group, which was not administered shock during the punishment sessions and whose running speed remained essentially constant for the 40 experimental trials. Third, the speed of the 150-volt group declined during the first ten shock trials and then leveled off at a speed below that exhibited by the control and 75-volt groups. Finally, the 300-volt and 600-volt groups both dropped sharply in running speed and soon failed to complete the alley in the maximum time allowed. The most interesting performance was that shown by the moderately punished group (150 volts). Unlike the mild-shock group, the subjects in this group slowed down, but they did not decrease their response speed precipitously and cease responding as did the rats receiving severe shock.

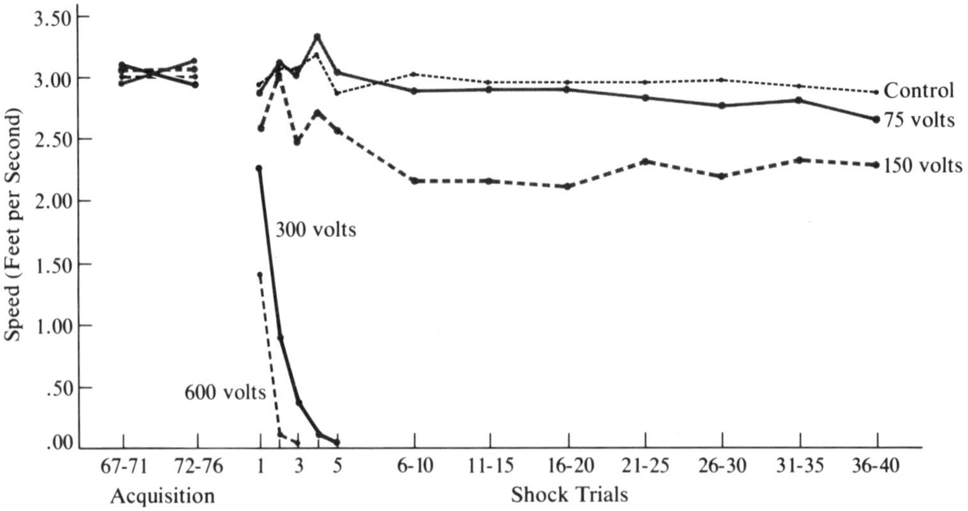

Figure 4–6. The effect of strength of shock on running speed as a function of the number of shock trials. (From "Effects of Number of Rewarded Trials and Intensity of Punishment on Running Speed," by E. B. Karsh, *Journal of Comparative Physiological Psychology,* 1962, *55,* 44–51. Copyright 1962 by the American Psychological Association. Reprinted by permission.)

A similar demonstration of the importance of punishment intensity in the degree of response suppression is available in research conducted by Azrin and his associates (for example, Azrin, 1960; Azrin et al., 1963; W. C. Holz, Azrin, & Ulrich, 1963). In these studies, pigeons were trained to peck a key to obtain a food reward under some reinforcement schedule (for example, VI, DRL). Punishment procedures that tested the effects of variations in punishment intensity were then instituted. Shock for key pecking was administered through electrodes that were permanently implanted in the pigeon's back. Mild shock produced little permanent effect on the rate of responding, whereas moderate-punishment intensities produced a complete suppression of responding for approximately the first 5 minutes of an experimental session. The response rate in this group gradually recovered during the hour-long punishment session, but at the end of the session it was still suppressed below the unpunished rate. Recovery was, in contrast to the mild-punishment group, still incomplete. Finally, in the case of the intense-punishment conditions, the rate of responding typically did not recover either during a single session or between sessions.

Although the procedures employed by Karsh were quite different from those employed by Azrin and his associates, both sets of findings generally support Church's (1963) view that as the intensity of punishment increases, its effect proceeds from temporary suppression to partial suppression to total suppression of the punished behavior. Other studies that have used rats or monkeys as experimental subjects have similarly demonstrated that the rate of emitting a previously reinforced bar press is suppressed according to an inverse function of the severity of punishment (Appel, 1963, 1968; Appel & Peterson,

1965; Camp, Raymond, & Church, 1967; Hake, Azrin, & Oxford, 1967). Hake and his colleagues have also demonstrated that the absolute rate of responding at a given intensity can be altered by the preceding intensities. Using squirrel monkeys as their subjects, they found more suppression of bar pressing at a given punishment intensity when that intensity was preceded by higher intensities of shock than when it was preceded by lower intensities.

After the cessation of punishment for emission of an operant response, two kinds of effects have been reported. In most investigations the behavior returned to normal—that is, to prepunishment levels—as soon as shock was discontinued (for example, Appel, 1963; Azrin, 1960). On the other hand, under certain conditions, when very intense shocks were used and when level of responding was suppressed rapidly and totally, the suppressed behavior remained suppressed for very long periods after punishment had been discontinued. Irreversibilities of this latter kind have been reported for both squirrel monkeys (Hake et al., 1967) and rats (Storms, Boroczi, & Broen, 1963).

Hake and his associates have reported that the chief determinant of the permanence of suppression in an operant situation seems to be the level of responding during the last punishment session. Whenever responses were completely suppressed during the last punishment session, responding did not resume until reshaping of the operant response or several nonpunishment sessions had occurred. On the other hand, if responding had not been completely suppressed during the final punishment session, recovery to prepunishment levels of responding occurred during the first nonpunishment session. The implication of these results is clear. If one is going to use punishment to suppress behavior, and if one desires to have a long-term effect on the punished response, then the punishment used must be sufficiently severe to suppress totally the undesirable behavior.

Let us now return to the generalization that punishment intensity is related to the degree of decrease in responding and look at its applicability in other kinds of experimental paradigms. Azrin (1970), for example, has examined the effects of variations in the intensity of punishment on suppression of shock-elicited aggression. Many animals will attack a partner following application of severe shock to the paw (for example, Ulrich, Hutchinson, & Azrin, 1965). Such fighting after an aversive event will also occur between animals of different species (Ulrich, Wolff, & Azrin, 1964).

In Azrin's study, aggression in squirrel monkeys was elicited by electric shock applied to the tail while the animals sat in restraining chairs, and the aggression was directed toward a bite tube located in front of the subject's face. A shock delivered every 30 seconds elicited a high level of biting attacks on the tube. The number of shock-elicited attacks was later used as a no-punishment baseline. When punishment was instituted, a shock was delivered immediately after each bite. The intensity of the punishment was either 25, 50, 100, or 200 volts, roughly corresponding to 1, 2.5, 5, and 10 milliamps (mA), for each of the three monkeys. A shock of 10 mA is about the same as the shock received from sticking your finger into a light socket. No punishment sessions were employed between successive punishment sessions, thus allowing the effect of each punishment intensity to be evaluated against an immediately preceding baseline session of no punishment.

Figure 4–7 shows the effects of the different punishment intensities on the incidence of biting attacks. The figure indicates that the lowest punishment intensity (1 mA) increased the incidence of biting attacks slightly for one of the monkeys but not for the other two. The incidence of biting attacks decreased for all of the subjects as the intensity of the punishment increased. With the most severe shock, 10 mA, which was equal in strength to the shock used to elicit the biting attacks, biting was reduced by more than 90%.

The results clearly demonstrate that shock-elicited aggression can be suppressed by applying punishment and that the degree of suppression is a direct function of the intensity of the punishment. This finding is similar to those reported earlier about the effects of variations in punishment intensity on learned, nonaggressive responses. Suppression of attack behavior by punishment has also been observed in rats during punishment of an

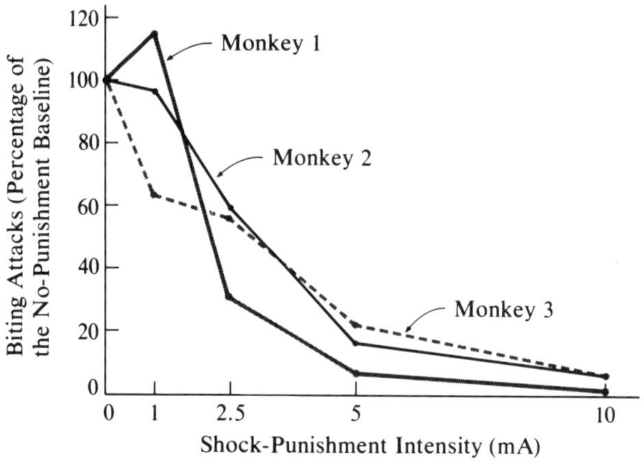

Figure 4–7. The number of biting attacks on a pneumatic tube as a function of the intensity of shock punishment of the bites for each of three monkeys. At the 0-mA value no punishment was delivered for biting. At all values the biting was being produced by shocks (10 mA) delivered every 30 seconds. (From "Punishment of Elicited Aggression," by N. H. Azrin, *Journal of the Experimental Analysis of Behavior,* 1970, *14,* 7–10. Copyright 1970 by the Society for the Experimental Analysis of Behavior, Inc. Reprinted by permission.)

instinctive response, mouse killing (Myer, 1966, 1967, 1968; Myer & Baenninger, 1966), and during attacks elicited by a tail pinch (Baenninger & Grossman, 1969). In addition, punishment has been found to be effective in suppressing the natural aggressive display between male Siamese fighting fish (Adler & Hogan, 1963; Melvin & Ervey, 1973).

Severity of Punishment: Punishment Duration. As indicated earlier in this chapter, the severity of a punisher is determined by the intensity and the duration of the noxious stimulus. We have seen how the intensity of the punishment influences behavior; we next turn to an examination of some of the studies that have investigated how the duration of punishment alters responding. In general, increases in the duration of punishment have been found to have effects on response suppression similar to those produced by increases in the intensity of punishment.

In one series of experiments examining the effects of variations in punishment duration on response suppression, intermittently reinforced responses were continuously punished (Boroczi, Storms, & Broen, 1964; Storms et al., 1963, 1965). It was found that as the duration of the punishment increased (for example, durations of .2, .5, .8, and 1.1 seconds), fewer punishments were required to produce cessation of responding. Similarly, in experiments investigating the effects of administering punishment during extinction, it has been shown that the number of responses emitted during extinction is inversely related to the duration of the punishment (Boe, 1966; Seligman & Campbell, 1965). Finally, Wischner and Fowler (1964) have reported that as the duration of the punishment for incorrect responses increases, the average number of errors on a discrimination task decreases.

The most comprehensive investigation of the effects of punishment duration on response suppression was published by Church, Raymond, and Beauchamp (1967). Albino rats were trained to press a bar for a food reward on a VI 1-minute schedule. After five 30-minute sessions of 1-minute VI responding, punishment-training sessions were begun. During the punishment sessions a 2-minute VI response-contingent shock schedule was superimposed on the reinforcement schedule. There were ten such punishment sessions. A punishment was never delivered to the animal within 7.5 seconds of a reinforcement. The degree of response suppression produced by the punishment was assessed by calculating a suppression ratio. This ratio was $B/(A+B)$, where A was the number of responses emitted during the last session of reinforcement training and B was the number of bar presses made during a particular punishment session. The smaller the suppression ratio, the fewer were the responses emitted by the subject. A subject that continued to respond during punishment treatment (B) at the same rate that it did prior to punishment (A) would have a ratio of .5.

In the first experiment conducted by Church and his associates, the effects of a wide range of punishment durations were assessed. The punishing stimulus (350 volts, or 16mA) lasted either 0, .15, .30, .50, 1.00, or 3.00 seconds. The results, as can be seen in Figure 4–8, were clear-cut. The mean suppression ratio decreased significantly with increasing durations of the punishment, just as we saw happens with increases in punishment intensity. The figure also shows another similar effect between increases in punishment duration and intensity. As the duration of the punishment increased, there was at first no suppressive effect, then partial suppression with complete recovery, next partial suppression without complete recovery, and, finally, with very long shocks (for example, 1.00 and 3.00 seconds), total suppression without recovery.

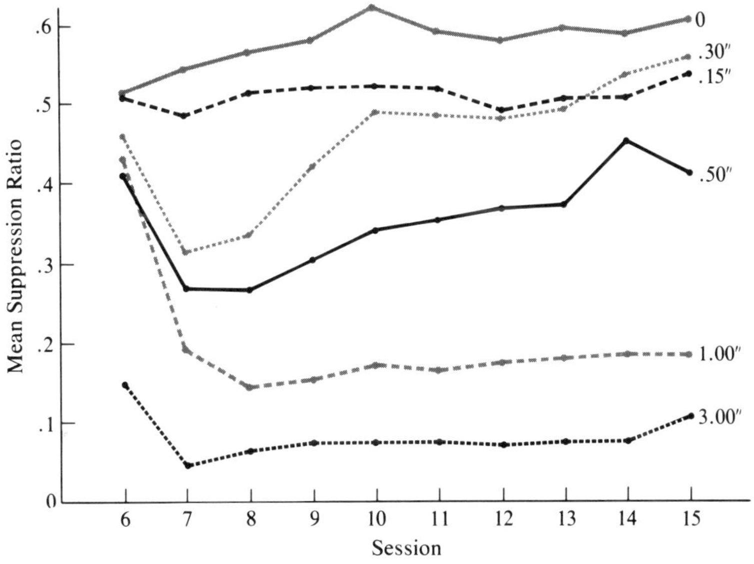

Figure 4–8. Mean suppression ratio as a function of sessions of punishment training for groups with punishment durations of 0, .15, .30, .50, 1.00, and 3.00 seconds. (From "Response Suppression as a Function of Intensity and Duration of a Punishment," by R. M. Church, G. A. Raymond, and R. D. Beauchamp, *Journal of Comparative and Physiological Psychology,* 1967, *63,* 39–44. Copyright 1967 by the American Psychological Association. Reprinted by permission.)

If variations in the intensity and duration of punishers produce similar effects, might they combine in some manner to determine the severity of a punisher? We suggested earlier that this is indeed the case, and a second experiment in the paper by Church and his colleagues clearly demonstrates it. This experiment assessed the joint effects of punishment intensity and duration on degree of response suppression. The subjects were 13 groups of rats. One of these groups was a nonpunished control group, and the other 12 groups received various punishment combinations of intensities of .05, .15, or .25 mA for durations of .25, .50, 1.00, or 2.00 seconds. As in the first experiment, the subjects underwent five nonpunishment sessions during which they were rewarded for pressing a bar on a 1-minute VI schedule followed by ten sessions in which a 2-minute VI response-contingent punishment schedule was superimposed on the reinforcement schedule.

To assess the joint effects of intensity and duration of punishment on response suppression, the following analysis was employed. The product of intensity (in mA) and duration (in seconds) was determined for each experimental group's combination. This gave a value for punishment severity (intensity multiplied by duration). The suppression ratio was then plotted against the logarithm of this value. These data, shown in Figure 4–9, indicate that the mean suppression ratio during the punishment-training sessions was a decreasing linear function of the log value of severity. Thus, in summary, we see that duration and intensity combine in a simple fashion to determine the severity of an aversive event and that the magnitude of response suppression produced by punishment is directly related to its severity.

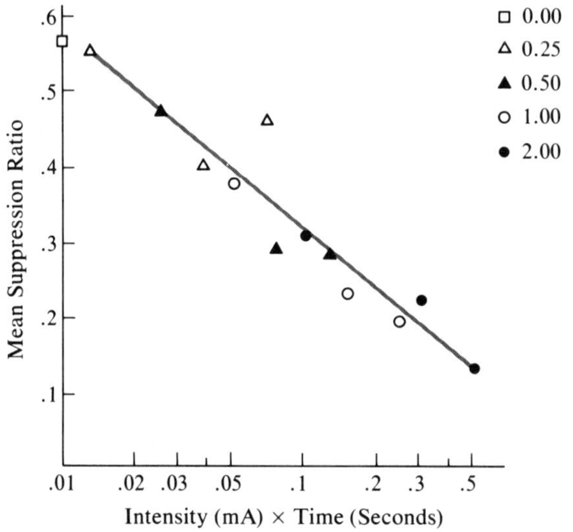

Figure 4–9. Mean suppression ratio during the ten sessions of punishment training as a function of the product of intensity (in mA) and duration (in seconds) of punishment. (From "Response Suppression as a Function of Intensity and Duration of a Punishment," by R. M. Church, G. A. Raymond, and R. D. Beauchamp, *Journal of Comparative and Physiological Psychology,* 1967, *63,* 39–44. Copyright 1967 by the American Psychological Association. Reprinted by permission.)

Proximity of Punishment to the Punished Response. Must punishment be presented almost immediately after the occurrence of a response to exert a suppressive effect on the response? Estes (1944), in his very influential monograph on punishment, proposed that the answer to this question is no. Extrapolating the results from two of the experiments in his paper, Estes suggested that contingent and noncontingent shock will produce similar degrees of response suppression. This finding led him to suggest that in many cases the suppressive effects of punishment can be explained in terms of the increase in the subject's emotionality that results from application of the shock or some other aversive event rather than in terms of the proximity of the aversive stimulus to the response. Estes's proposition served as an impetus for a number of subsequent investigations attempting to determine whether contiguity between response and aversive stimulus is necessary to produce the response suppression generally reported in punishment studies.

One of the early studies shedding light on this question was published by Azrin (1956). Pigeons were trained on a VI 3-minute schedule of food reinforcement until a stable rate of responding was obtained (approximately 100 hours). Azrin then alternated an orange and a blue light on the response key at 2-minute intervals. The VI 3-minute food-reinforcement schedule continued regardless of key color, with the exception that shock was never presented during delivery of food. As we saw earlier in this chapter, such a contingency might have severely disrupted feeding behavior. Shocks were delivered only during the presentation of the orange key.

Either the aversive stimulus was contingent upon the emission of a key peck (programmed to follow the first response after a fixed or variable interval following presentation of the orange light), or the shock was not contingent upon a response and was simply scheduled to occur at a fixed or variable period of time after the onset of the orange light, regardless of the subject's response pattern.

The results were unambiguous. In both the fixed-interval and variable-interval punishment situations, contingent punishment produced a much greater degree of response suppression than did noncontingent punishment. Similar findings on the relative effectiveness of contingent and noncontingent shock were reported at about this same time by H. F. Hunt and Brady (1955).

Azrin suggested that Estes's failure to uncover differences between the effects of response-contingent and noncontingent shock may have resulted from the brevity of his punishment-training procedures. Estes employed only a 10-minute shock period, which probably was not enough time for differences in the two shock-presentation methods to emerge. Azrin, on the other hand, subjected his subjects to an average of 21 daily 3-hour sessions under each condition. On the basis of his findings, Azrin concluded that "it is unnecessary to appeal to an emotional state to explain the effects of punishment; rather, the temporal relationship between the response and the aversive stimulus seems to be the critical factor" (p. 19). Azrin's basic finding that the magnitude of response suppression is greater if the punishment is contingent upon the response has been replicated by Church and his associates (Camp et al., 1967; Church, Wooten, & Matthews, 1970).

In the contingent-punishment versus noncontingent-punishment procedures, either the aversive event occurs immediately after the response is emitted or it is uncorrelated with responding. We have seen that the contiguity between the response and punishment is an important factor in determining the degree of response suppression. For this reason, several researchers have examined the effects of delay of punishment on response strength with the hope of finding evidence for a *delay-of-punishment gradient.* Such a gradient would describe a process such that as the delay between a punished response and an aversive event increased, the effectiveness of the punishment in producing response suppression would decrease. A similar type of gradient occurs with positive reinforcement; that is, as the response/reward interval increases, the effectiveness of reinforcements decreases.

One of the first clear demonstrations of a delay-of-punishment gradient was conducted by Kamin (1959). In his experiment six groups of rats were given avoidance training in which they could avoid shock (US) if they moved to the other side of a shuttle box within 10 seconds after presentation of a signal (CS). A shuttle box is a chamber that is divided into two compartments by a hurdle. The subject must run or jump from one compartment into the other to escape from or avoid an aversive stimulus. Kamin's subjects were run to an acquisition criterion of 11 consecutive avoidance responses. A punishment extinction procedure was then instituted for five of the groups in which the subjects were shocked *only* if they moved to the other side of the shuttle box in the 10-second US interval. During the punishment trials the interval between the punished response and the onset of a shock was either 0, 10, 20, 30, or 40 seconds. The punishment trials were continued until the rats met a criterion of ten consecutive failures to respond or for a maximum of 50 trials.

The delay-of-punishment gradient obtained in this study, in terms of median number of responses made during punishment, is shown in Figure 4–10. As the graph clearly illustrates, there was a tendency for responding to persist longer as the delay of punishment increased. The sixth group, the control group, was subjected to extinction of the avoidance response without punishment, and its rate of extinction was compared to that exhibited by the longest-delay-of-punishment group (40 seconds). The control animals showed much greater resistance to extinction. Thus, even with the longest delays of punishment used in this research, responding was greatly inhibited.

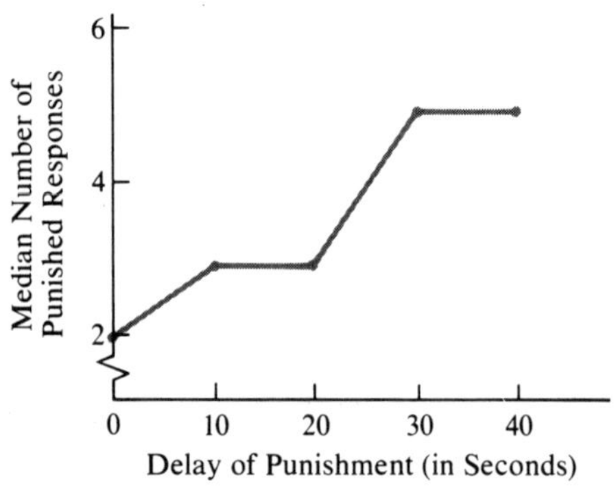

Figure 4–10. Median number of extinction responses as a function of delay of punishment. (From "The Delay-of-Punishment Gradient," by L. J. Kamin, *Journal of Comparative and Physiological Psychology,* 1959, *52,* 434–437. Copyright 1959 by the American Psychological Association. Reprinted by permission.)

A study by Baron (1965) extended the generality of the delay-of-punishment gradient to punishment of positively reinforced behavior. His investigations involved punishing water-reinforced runway behavior of rats by application of fairly intense electric shock at different times after the animals had entered the goal box. In a second phase of his study, punishment of the runway response was discontinued and the rate of recovery from the effects of punishment was assessed. After runway training the rats were assigned to either a control group or five other groups for punishment training. During the punishment trials water reinforcement was still provided for traversing the runway, but, in addition, the animals received a shock (.7 mA for .5 seconds) either 0, 5, 10, 20, or 30 seconds after entering the goal box. The control group was not punished. There were 18 punishment trials, and after punishment training was completed, the rats were run for 72 additional trials without punishment. This procedure provided information on the permanence of the extinction accomplished by punishments of varying degrees, a factor that was not examined in Kamin's investigation.

Baron replicated Kamin's finding on delay of punishment. He found that running speed during the punishment trials varied as a function of the extent to which punishment was delayed following entry into the goal box. The greater the delay, the faster the rats traversed the runway. The effects of the response/punishment interval were also present during recovery, after punishment had been discontinued. The animals receiving longer punishment delays tended to recover their prepunishment running speed more rapidly, and the delay condition differentiated the groups during the first 2 weeks of recovery training (36 trials).

Other investigators have provided additional data in support of the existence of delay-of-punishment gradients when positively reinforced behaviors are punished. For example, Banks and Vogel-Sprout (1965), using human subjects, demonstrated that immediate punishment produced greater response suppression than did punishment delayed for 30 seconds or longer. Myer and Ricci (1968), in a study described previously in this chapter, extended the generality of this phenomenon by investigating the effects of delay of punishment on suppression of feeding in goldfish. As illustrated in Figure 4–11, these researchers found that in addition to varying significantly with shock intensity (10 or 25 volts), suppression of feeding varied significantly with delay of punishment (0, 5, or 10 seconds).

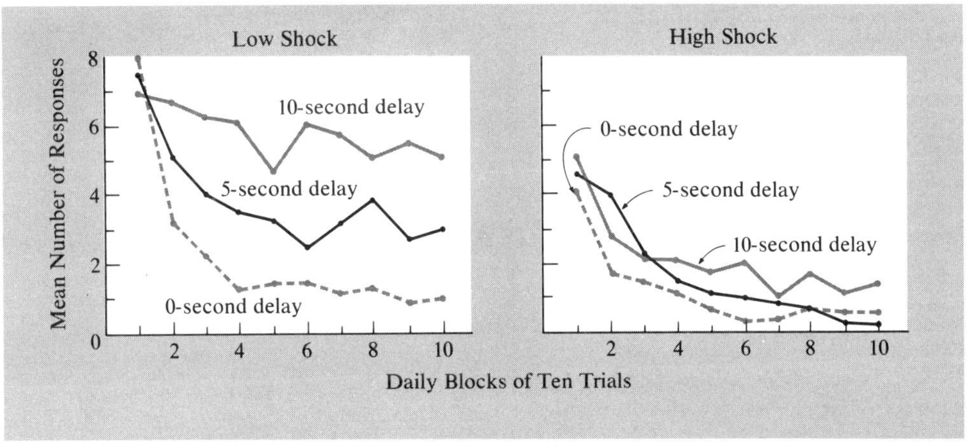

Figure 4–11. Suppression of feeding in goldfish during immediate and delayed punishment with 10-volt and 25-volt shock. (From "Delay of Punishment Gradients for the Goldfish," by J. S. Myer and D. Ricci, *Journal of Comparative and Physiological Psychology,* 1968, *66,* 417–421. Copyright 1968 by the American Psychological Association. Reprinted by permission.)

An interesting collation of the effects of proximity of the punishment to the punished response appears in an article by Camp and his associates (1967). In this experiment not only were the effects of delay of punishment examined, but the effects of long-delay punishment were contrasted with noncontingent shock and no punishment. Rats were taught to press a bar following presentation of a clicking sound (positive stimulus) to secure a food reward. After ten discrimination-training sessions, 12 punishment sessions were administered. An average of 50% of the bar presses were rewarded during the punishment sessions, and the remaining responses were treated differently according to the experimental group. For the response-contingent punishment groups, the rats were shocked either immediately after emission of the punished response or, in the delay groups, 2.0, 7.5, or 30 seconds after the bar press. The control (no shock) and noncontingent-shock groups were not punished during these trials. However, the noncontingent group received a shock on the average of once every 2 minutes in the absence of the positive stimulus regardless of whether the animals responded during presentation of the positive stimulus.

Figure 4–12 shows the average number of positive stimuli to which a bar press was made during the punishment sessions for the six groups. Statistical analysis of the observed differences indicated, first, that the control group made significantly more responses than any other group. Second, although the noncontingent and 30-second-delay groups made significantly more responses than any of the other punishment groups, they did not differ significantly from each other. Finally, the group that was immediately punished made significantly fewer responses during the punishment sessions than did any other group. In addition to demonstrating the effects of delay of punishment on response suppression, the results suggest that under the conditions employed, the relatively long delay of 30 seconds can be considered equivalent to a noncontingent procedure.

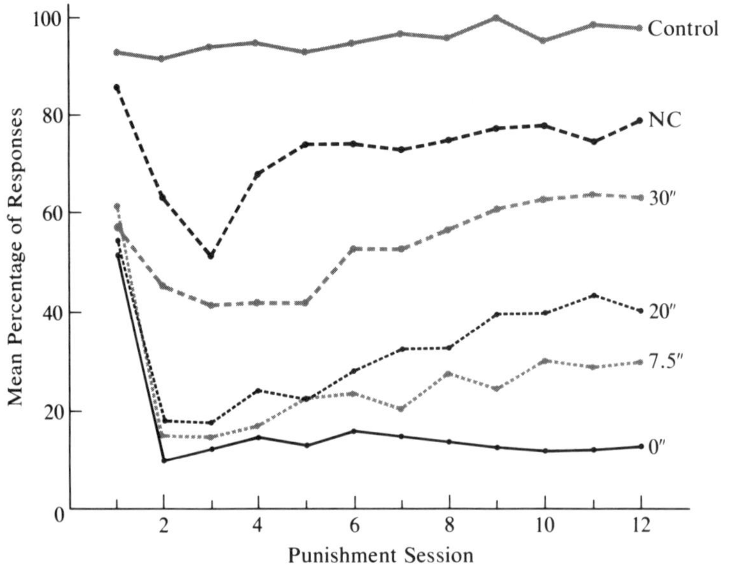

Figure 4–12. Mean percentage of responses as a function of sessions for groups with punishment delays of 0, 2.0, 7.5, and 30 seconds, noncontingent shock, and no punishment. (Failure to press the lever within 10 seconds of the stimulus onset was defined as nonresponse.) (From "Temporal Relationships between Response and Punishment," by D. S. Camp, G. H. Raymond, and R. M. Church, *Journal of Experimental Psychology,* 1967, *74,* 114–123. Copyright 1967 by the American Psychological Association. Reprinted by permission.)

Why do such gradients occur? As Myer (1971) has suggested, they probably result from the interaction of two effects produced by punishment. The first of these effects is a specific suppression of the punished response due to the association of the punishment with the behavior emitted. The second is a nonspecific suppression of behavior that probably reflects an increase in the emotionality of the subject in the experimental situation. The second factor, the nonspecific suppressive effect, is relatively independent of the interval between the response and the punishment. If a response/punishment interval is short, response suppression arises from and reflects the interaction of these two effects. If the punishment follows the response by a very long period of time—that is, a longer interval than associative-learning processes can easily bridge—the effects of punishment are due almost entirely to the nonspecific effects of the aversive stimulus. This explains why the effects of punishment after very long delays are similar to those produced by noncontingent punishment, as observed in the study by Camp and his associates.

Prior Exposure to Aversive Stimuli. Another factor influencing the degree of response suppression produced by punishment is the subject's prior experience with aversive events. Two contrary findings have been reported in studies that examined the effects of prior exposure to shock on the degree of response suppression. On the one hand, it has been found that prior exposure to an aversive stimulus *decreases* the effectiveness of punishment (for example, Feirstein & Miller, 1963; Karsh, 1963; N.E. Miller, 1960) and that this learned resistance to punishment is not limited to the original aversive stimulus but includes novel punishments as well (Terris & Barnes, 1969; Terris & Rahhal, 1969; Terris & Wechkin, 1967). On the other hand, some researchers have reported that prior exposure to a noxious event *increases* the effectiveness of a punishment (for example, Pearl, 1963; Pearl, Walters, & Anderson, 1964). Church (1969) has described a series of experiments he and his colleagues conducted that clarify the conditions under which exposure to an aversive stimulus may either decrease or enhance the effectiveness of a subsequent punishment. The most noteworthy of these investigations was conducted by Raymond (1968), and we will discuss three of his experiments here.

The same procedure was used in all three of Raymond's experiments. First, rats were trained to press a bar for a food reward on an FR 22-second schedule. They received ten 30-minute sessions under these conditions, and the reinforcement schedule remained in effect for the duration of the experiment. Next, half of the subjects were assigned to an experimental group that received noncontingent shock on the average of every 2 minutes independently of responding; the other half, serving as a control group, were not shocked during these preexposure sessions. After completion of this phase, all the subjects were given further training with punishment suspended in order to equate their rates of responding before the punishment sessions began. During the punishment sessions, response-contingent shock was administered on a VI 2-minute schedule. The suppression ratios were calculated in the same way as in the previous studies by Church and his colleagues.

Figure 4–13 shows the results of the first experiment. In this study the noncontingent shock used during Sessions 11 through 15 was relatively mild (110 volts for .2 seconds) and yielded only minimal response suppression. Retraining equated the levels of the groups before the punishment sessions began. Introduction of the shock (145 volts for .1 seconds) produced no measurable effect, as compared to the retraining level of responding, in the experimental group. On the other hand, bar pressing in the group that had not received previous exposure to shock was almost totally suppressed. Such a finding is normally referred to as adaptation in the literature.

In the second experiment the noncontingent shock used during the prior-exposure sessions was relatively severe (220 volts for .2 seconds). As can be seen in Figure 4–14, this procedure resulted in almost total response suppression during the prior exposure and also during the actual punishment sessions. In this latter instance prior exposure to shock strengthened the effects of a later mild punishment. This enhancing effect is dramatic, and such research findings are normally explained by stating that the intense shock produced sensitization.

The major difference between the two experiments examined thus far was the intensity of the shock used for prior exposure. It might appear that the weak shock produced adaptation and the intense shock produced sensitization. However, Church (1969) has suggested that this is probably not the case. Raymond's third experiment provided data on which Church could build an alternative explanation for the effects of prior exposure to shock.

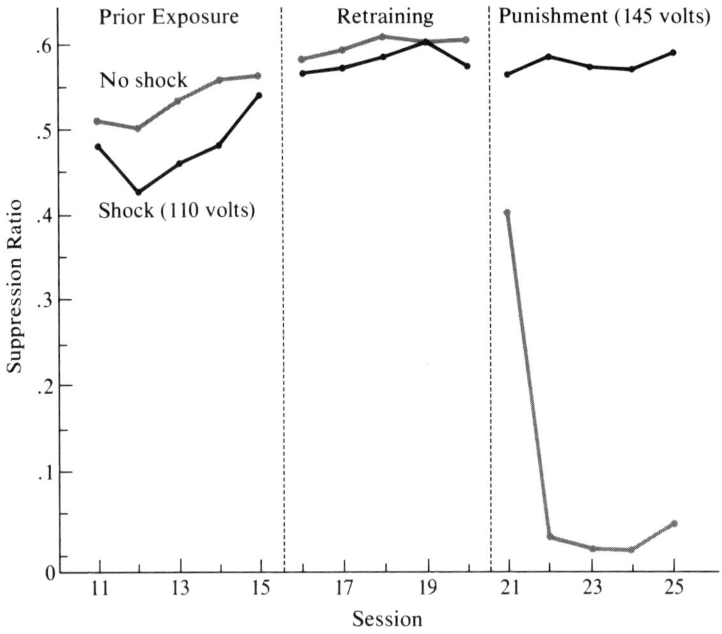

Figure 4–13. Median suppression ratio to a punishment of 145 volts as a function of prior exposure to noncontingent shock of 110 volts. (From "Response Suppression," by R. M. Church. In B. A. Campbell and R. M. Church (Eds.), *Punishment and Aversive Behavior*. Copyright © 1969. Reprinted by permission of Prentice-Hall, Inc., Englewood Cliffs, New Jersey.)

In this very clever study Raymond showed that exposure to identical levels of shock can produce either facilitation or reduction of the effects of subsequent punishment. In this investigation the experimental rats were preexposed to shock, the strength of which was varied so as to yield a suppression ratio in each animal of approximately .30. Again no shock was administered during retraining, so that all experimental and control animals were responding at about the same level before punishment began. But in this last experiment two different shock intensities were used during the punishment sessions, and half of the experimental and half of the control subjects were tested using each punishment intensity.

The results are portrayed in Figure 4–15. These data show that prior exposure to shock enhanced the effects of mild punishment (110 volts) and decreased the effects of intense punishment (180 volts). These findings would seem to disprove the notion that a given intensity of exposure simply either adapts or sensitizes a subject to subsequent shock. Why, then, do these different effects occur?

A plausible alternative explanation for the differences is posited by Church (1969); he calls it the *incomplete-shift hypothesis*. During actual punishment sessions, according to this view, the subject responds in a manner "intermediate between that appropriate to the punishment (as determined by control subjects without prior exposure to shock) and the rate it had previously adopted during the prior exposure condition" (pp.130–131). In other words, when the rat is presented with the second intensity of shock during actual punishment, it tends to persevere with behavior appropriate to the initial aversive stimulus. This incomplete-shift process is apparently an example of stimulus generalization. Since this generalization process seems to occur from one shock intensity to another, it would be of interest to determine whether this phenomenon also occurs from one duration to another or, more generally, from one degree of punishment severity to another.

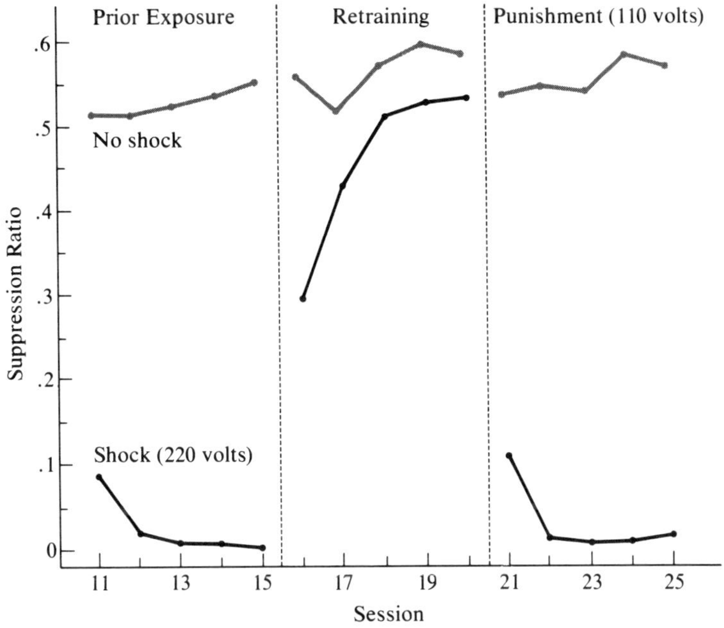

Figure 4–14. Median suppression ratio to a punishment of 110 volts as a function of prior exposure to noncontingent shock of 220 volts. (From "Response Suppression," by R. M. Church. In B. A. Campbell and R. M. Church (Eds.), *Punishment and Aversive Behavior*. Copyright © 1969. Reprinted by permission of Prentice-Hall, Inc., Englewood Cliffs, New Jersey.)

Availability of Alternative Responses and Learned Helplessness

Punishment is an extremely effective tool to use in modifying behavior if the response-suppression period is used to teach the subject new responses that are incompatible with the old ones. In fact, in these sorts of situations a punishment of very low intensity can have enduring suppressive effects on the initial, undesirable response (Azrin & Holz, 1966; Whiting & Mowrer, 1943). Similarly, punishment will produce more response suppression if an additional response is available to the subjects that is not food reinforced but permits the animals to gain "time out" from the punishment schedule (Azrin, Hake, Holz, Hutchinson, 1965). The point is that punishment seems to be most effective in modifying behavior if the subjects can somehow modify their response pattern to avoid future punishments. But what if the animals cannot control the onset of aversive events? What if all their responses prove futile in their attempts to terminate a noxious stimulus? What effects do these sorts of experiences have on subsequent behavior?

The Phenomenon of "Learned Helplessness"

In an intriguing series of experiments, Solomon and his associates have attempted to answer these questions. Their basic finding has been that if subjects are exposed to a series of uncontrollable and inescapable aversive events, their subsequent ability to solve problems leading to escape from or avoidance of these noxious events will be severely impaired. This phenomenon is called *learned helplessness,* and a great deal of recent research has been devoted to clarifying the basis for this effect. Excellent summaries of the findings can

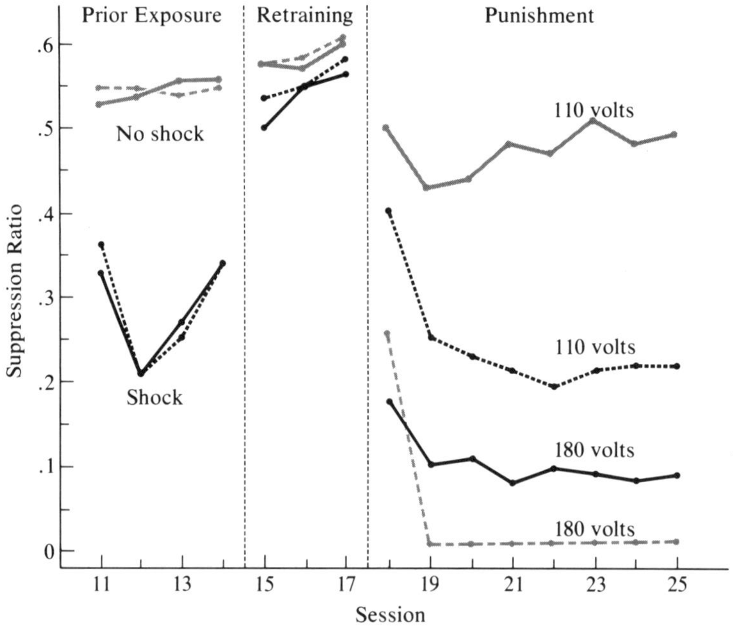

Figure 4–15. Mean suppression ratio to punishment of 110 volts and 180 volts as a function of prior exposure to shock. (From "Response Suppression," by R. M. Church. In B. A. Campbell and R. M. Church (Eds.), *Punishment and Aversive Behavior.* Copyright © 1969. Reprinted by permission of Prentice-Hall, Inc., Englewood Cliffs, New Jersey.)

be found in articles by S. F. Maier, Seligman, and Solomon (1969) and Seligman, Maier, and Solomon (1971).

In the majority of experiments conducted by these researchers, dogs received inescapable shock while they were suspended in a Pavlov harness (see Figure 4–16). Shock was applied through brass-plate electrodes attached to the dogs' hind paws. The shock was painful and traumatic. In experiments conducted by Overmier and Seligman (1967) and by Seligman and Maier (1967), animals strapped into the Pavlov harness were given 64 unsignaled, inescapable shocks. Each shock was 6.0 mA in intensity and 5.0 seconds in duration. The dogs could neither control the onset of these aversive events nor bring about their termination. A control group of dogs was placed in the harness for the same length of time but received no shocks.

The dogs were tested 24 hours after the completion of this phase of the procedure for acquisition of an avoidance habit in a two-way shuttle box. All the subjects were given ten escape/avoidance trials. In the shuttle box used by Solomon and his associates, each dog had 10 seconds to jump the hurdle and move into the next compartment following presentation of a signal. If the dog had not jumped by the end of the 10-second interval, a 4.5 mA shock came on and remained on until the animal jumped into the next compartment. If the dog did not jump within 60 seconds after the signal had come on, the trial ended and the shock was terminated. Note that in this experiment the Pavlov harness and the shuttle box gave the subjects very different degrees of control over the aversive events. In the harness the dog could do nothing to alter the aversive situation, but in the shuttle box the dog could eliminate the aversive experience altogether if it responded to the warning signal.

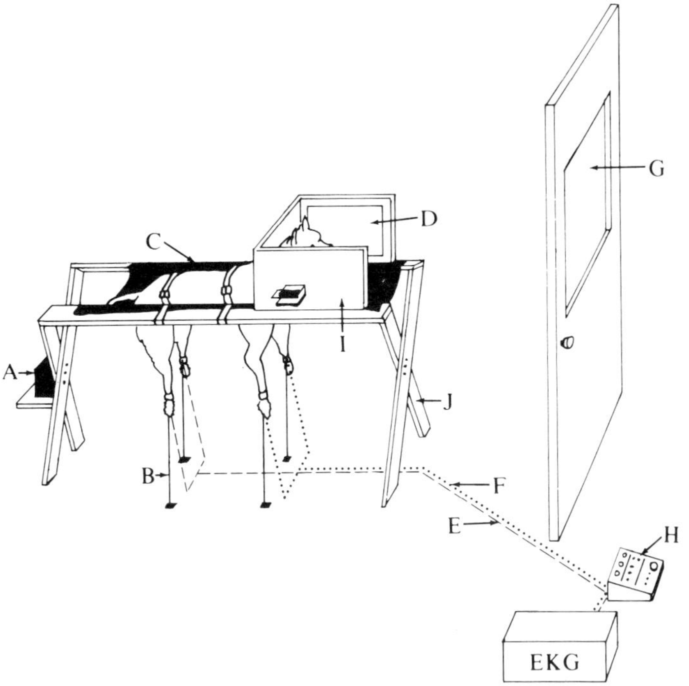

A	Sound generator	F	EKG electrodes
B	Leg ties	G	One-way glass
C	Hammock	H	Control box
D	Contact plate	I	Headpiece
E	Shock electrodes	J	Frame

Figure 4–16. Pavlov harness used either for fear conditioning or for escape and avoidance training. The contact plate (D) is the manipulandum for instrumental training. Shock electrodes are attached to the hind paws. CSs are presented by a tone generator (A). (From "Pavlovian Conditioning and Learned Helplessness," by M. E. P. Seligman, S. F. Maier, and R. L. Solomon. In B. A. Campbell and R. M. Church (Eds.), *Punishment and Aversive Behavior*. Copyright © 1969. Reprinted by permission of Prentice-Hall, Inc., Englewood Cliffs, New Jersey.)

The effects of exposure to shock on subsequent escape and avoidance behavior were pronounced. The dogs that received prior unavoidable shock were severely retarded in solving the escape/avoidance problem. In the Seligman and Maier (1967) study, seven of the eight subjects in this group failed to escape during nine of the ten trials. The no-prior-shock control group, on the other hand, learned to escape and avoid very efficiently. Hence, prior exposure to shock in this instance was debilitating. Seligman and his co-authors (1971) described the behavior of the experimental animals as follows:

> The behavior of the preshocked dogs was bizarre. When they received the first shock in the shuttle box, they initially looked like the naïve dogs: they ran about frantically, howled, defecated and urinated. However, unlike naïve dogs, they soon stopped running around and quietly whimpered until the trial terminated. After a few trials, they seemed to "give up" and passively "accept" the shock. On later trials, these dogs failed to make any escape movements at

> all. A few dogs would get up and jump the barrier, escaping or avoiding shock; yet surprisingly, on the next trial such a dog would go back to taking shock. It did not seem to learn that barrier-jumping produced shock termination [p. 355].

The occurrence of learned helplessness does not seem to depend on the use of any special shock factors in the preexposure phase. Overmier and Seligman (1967) and Seligman and Maier (1967) found this phenomenon with a wide variety of frequencies, densities, durations, and temporal distributions of intense, uncontrollable shock. Similar effects have been found in the dog by Carlson and Black (1960), Overmier (1968), Overmier and Leaf (1965), and Seligman and Groves (1970); in rats by Mullin and Mogerson (1963) and Weiss, Kriekhaus, and Conte (1968); and in goldfish by Behrend and Bitterman (1963) and Pinckney (1967). In dogs, as we have seen, the effect is very dramatic; the subject sits and takes the shocks. In rats and goldfish, on the other hand, the effect is less pronounced; the subjects given prior treatment with inescapable shock are usually simply slower in terminating the shock than are nonpreexposed control animals. An extensive inquiry into the learned-helplessness phenomenon in rats can be found in a paper by Maier, Albin, and Testa (1973).

An explanation of the mechanisms underlying the effects of prior exposure to uncontrollable shock has been offered by Seligman and Maier (1967) and Maier and his colleagues (1969). Central to this view is that during inescapable shocks, what the dog does and what happens to it are uncorrelated. Regardless of the responses that the animal emits, neither the onset, the duration, nor the termination of the aversive stimulus is affected. As a result, the dog probably learns that its responses are independent of the shock termination. In effect, the dog learns "Nothing I do matters." Solomon and his associates have hypothesized that when the dog is later tested with the shuttle-box active-avoidance problem, the occurrence of shock probably elicits the same set of expectations as did the inescapable-shock situation. Therefore, they suggest that the incentive for initiating and maintaining active escape or avoidance responses in the shuttle-box situation is quite low.

Whenever a group of researchers finds as pronounced an effect as that reported following prior exposure to shock in dogs, one always ponders the question of how they discovered the phenomenon. We wrote Dr. Solomon and asked him to share his recollections of how the studies on learned helplessness evolved. The following is his account:

> In the late 1950s at Harvard, Dr. Abraham H. Black and I noticed that, in a panel-pressing avoidance situation, dogs either learned quickly or failed completely to learn. Those which failed completely eventually went limp and made no more panel-press responses. Later, after I moved to the University of Pennsylvania, Russell C. Leaf ran into the same difficulty in studying the interaction between Pavlovian fear conditioning and instrumental avoidance training. He noticed that when Pavlovian fear conditioning was carried out first and then later avoidance training was pursued, very few animals learned. They went limp and looked like the nonlearners which Black and I had noticed. We considered this phenomenon to be a necessary nuisance.
>
> It remained for Dr. J. Bruce Overmier and his collaborator, Dr. Martin E.P. Seligman, to realize that the phenomenon should be studied in its own right. Overmier had previously collaborated with Leaf in some of the studies of the interaction of Pavlovian fear conditioning and instrumental avoidance training. After the collaboration between Overmier and Seligman on the learned-helplessness phenomenon, Seligman really carried the ball, acquired a new collaborator, Steven F. Maier, and elucidated many of the necessary and sufficient conditions for the production of the phenomenon. I believe that Seligman invented the word *helplessness* as a general descriptive term for the behavioral phenomenon. The importance of the phenomenon probably dawned on me during the Overmier and Seligman collaboration, and, of course, I pushed and encouraged the later work by Seligman and Maier.[1]

[1] Personal communication, February 1972.

In addition to accounting for the effects of uncontrollable or inescapable shock, the helplessness hypothesis has generated several predictions that Seligman, Maier, and others have attempted to test. To begin with, the hypothesis implies that it is the animal's lack of control rather than the noxious stimulation itself that yields the subsequent interference with avoidance learning. This proposition was tested in the Seligman and Maier (1967) paper.

Seligman and Maier had two groups of dogs receive shock in the Pavlovian harness. However, one group could escape the shock by pressing a panel located on either side of the head (escape group), while the dogs in the second group (yoked group) received the same number of equal shocks and at the same time as a partner in the escape group but had no control over them. A third group received no shocks in the harness (naïve group). All the subjects 24 hours later received ten trials in the shuttle-box task previously described. As can be seen in Figure 4–17, which shows the median latency of barrier jumping on each of the ten trials for each of the three groups, the escape group exhibited normal escape/avoidance behavior, while the performance of the dogs receiving inescapable shock was severely deficient compared to the naïve control animals. Hence, these data support the helplessness view in that failure to escape during escape/avoidance training was not produced by the prior shock itself; rather, the helplessness apparently resulted from lack of control over the prior shock.

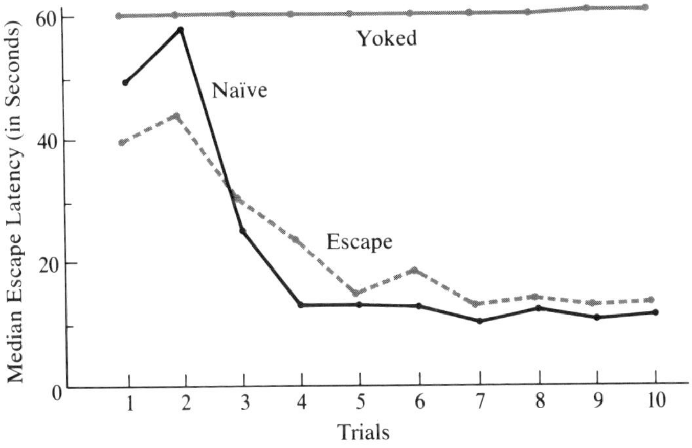

Figure 4–17. The effects of matched escapable and inescapable shocks in the harness on later escape learning in the shuttle box. The arbitrary criterion of failure to escape was 50 seconds of shock (a latency of 60 seconds from the onset of the shock). (From "Unpredictable and Uncontrollable Aversive Events," by M. E. P. Seligman, S. F. Maier, and R. L. Solomon. In F. R. Bush (Ed), *Aversive Conditioning and Learning*. Copyright 1971 by Academic Press. Reprinted by permission.)

Data confirming these findings were later reported by Maier (1970). Maier additionally ruled out the possibility that failure in the avoidance situation on the part of the dogs receiving prior exposure to traumatic shock might be due to their having learned during the inescapable-shock phase some motor-response pattern (for example, freezing) that was incompatible with avoidance performance. On the basis of all these findings taken together, Seligman and his associates (1971) concluded that "it is not trauma *per se* that produces failure to escape but having learned that no response at all can control trauma" (p. 372).

Another deduction from the learned-helplessness hypothesis is that prior experience with *controllable* shocks should proactively interfere with an animal's learning that shock cannot be controlled; that is, it should be possible to immunize subjects against the interference effects normally produced by prior exposure to inescapable shock. Seligman and Maier (1967) verified this possibility. A group of dogs was given ten trials of escape/avoidance training in the shuttle box *before* being exposed to inescapable shocks in the Pavlov harness. After being administered the uncontrollable shocks, the animals were returned to the shuttle box, where they demonstrated normal escape and avoidance behavior. In other words, the passivity-producing effects of uncontrollable shock were eliminated when the dogs had experienced previous success in controlling noxious stimulation. A similar immunizing effect has been produced in rats (Seligman & Beagley, 1975; Seligman, Rosellini, & Kozak, 1975).

A last prediction of the learned-helplessness hypothesis was tested by Seligman, Maier, and Geer (1968) when they demonstrated a "therapy technique" by which learned helplessness can be overcome.They reasoned that if dogs preexposed to inescapable shock fail to escape in the shuttle box because they do not expect their active responding to produce a cessation of shock, then forcibly exposing them to the response that will terminate the noxious event (that is, crossing the barrier and moving into the adjacent compartment) should alleviate the interference. Three dogs that had received prior exposure to inescapable shock and had repeatedly failed to escape were used to test this proposition. The barrier between the sections of the shuttle box was removed, and with leashes attached to the dogs' collars, the experimenters pulled their subjects over to the "safe" side of the apparatus during signaled shock trials. The three dogs had to be pulled across the apparatus on 20, 35, and 50 such trials before they began to respond on their own. The shuttle-box barrier was then replaced, and all of the animals continued responding appropriately.

Urban Stress and "Learned Helplessness"

In research examining human adaptation to urban stresses, such as noise pollution, Glass and Singer and their colleagues have described phenomena that appear to be analogous to learned helplessness (Glass & Singer, 1972a, 1972b). In an initial aspect of their research, they investigated the aftereffects of unpredictable versus predictable noise. Sounds were delivered at either random (unpredictable) or fixed (predictable) intervals throughout a 25-minute period. In the predictable condition the noise was presented at the end of every minute for a duration of 9 seconds. In the unpredictable condition the noise was random in both duration and interval between successive presentations. The noise was a good replication of urban cacophony; it was produced by playback of a tape recording of the following sounds superimposed on one another: (1) two people conversing in Spanish, (2) a person speaking Armenian, (3) a mimeograph machine, (4) a desk calculator, and (5) a typewriter.

Following termination of the exposure to noise, tasks to measure the aftereffects of the exposure were administered to the subjects. It was found that unpredictable noise yielded greater reductions in tolerance for postnoise frustration as measured by the number of attempts the subjects made to solve insoluble puzzles. In addition, the unpredictable noise produced greater impairments of performance on a task requiring care and attention, a proofreading task.

Additional research by Glass and Singer attempted to determine why prior exposure to unpredictable noise produces adverse aftereffects. In an explanation similar to the learned-helplessness view, Glass and Singer (1972a) proposed that unpredictable noise produces more adverse effects on subsequent behavior than predictable noise because "exposure to an unpredictable stressor induces feelings in the individual that he cannot control his environment—or at least certain stressful aspects of it" (p.461).

In a study testing this notion, two groups of human subjects listened to the unpredictable noise tape at an intensity of approximately 110 decibels, which is roughly equivalent to the noise level produced by a riveting machine or a four-engine airplane flying approximately a mile over your head. One group (perceived control) was given control over the noise, while the other group did not have this option (no perceived control). During the preexposure period, the perceived-control group had switches attached to the sides of the chairs in which they were seated; depression of this switch would terminate the noise for the duration of the session. They were informed, however, that the experimenter would prefer that they not press the switch, but that the decision was theirs to make. As a result of these instructions, few subjects ever used the switch. The interesting thing about this experiment is that the two groups differed only in whether they *thought* they controlled the aversive event.

This perceived control had a dramatic effect on the aftereffect measures, as can be seen in Figures 4–18 and 4–19. Perceived control yielded a significant increase in tolerance

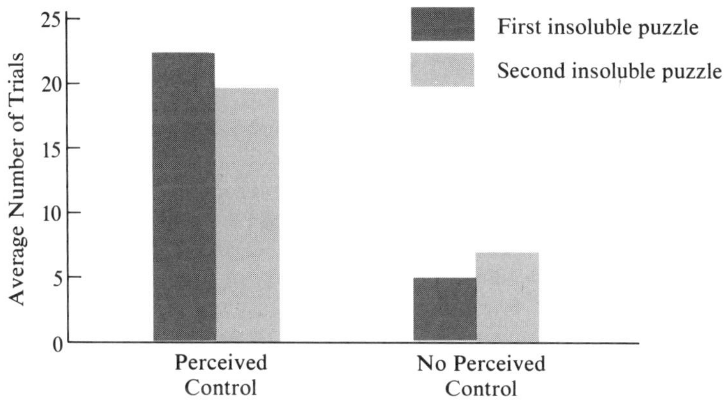

Figure 4–18. Average number of trials on the first and second insoluble puzzles. (From "Behavioral Aftereffects of Unpredictable and Uncontrollable Aversive Events," by D. C. Glass and J. E. Singer, *American Scientist,* 1972, *60*(4), 457–465. Reprinted by permission of *American Scientist.*)

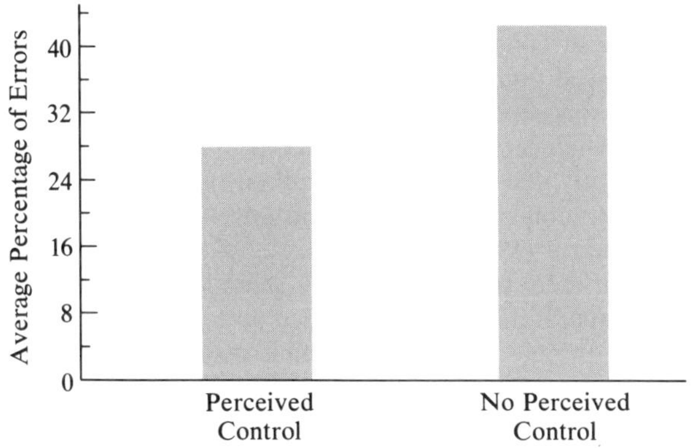

Figure 4–19. Average percentage of errors missed on the proofreading task. (From "Behavioral Aftereffects of Unpredictable and Uncontrollable Aversive Events," by D. C. Glass and J. E. Singer, *American Scientist,* 1972, *60*(4), 457–465. Reprinted by permission of *American Scientist.*)

for postnoise frustration as measured by the number of attempts to solve the insoluble puzzles (Figure 4–18), and proofreading errors were greatly reduced (Figure 4–19). The results of the research by Glass and Singer thus suggest that perceived control of noxious events reduces their deleterious aftereffects. On the basis of these findings, Glass and Singer (1972a) concluded that "unpredictable noise produces adverse aftereffects because it is more aversive than predictable noise, its greater aversiveness being a function of the sense of helplessness induced in an individual who is unable to control and/or predict its onset and offset" (p. 462). Thus, exposure to uncontrollable noise can have effects on humans similar to those produced by uncontrollable shock in lower animals. Uncontrollability produces an organism that is less capable of coping with and performing adaptive responses in its environment. Perceived control over aversive events in our environment appears to be a central determinant of the way in which we respond to these stimuli (Lefcourt, 1973).

Some Paradoxical Effects of Punishment

Thus far in this chapter we have been examining the ways in which punishment can suppress behavior. However, in some instances punishment can actually strengthen behavior and facilitate learning. These findings suggest that punishment as a process is quite complex. Most instances in which punishment facilitates rather than suppresses behavior fall into one of two categories. Punishment will facilitate responding if (1) punishment (an aversive stimulus) is used as a signal for the availability of food reinforcement in an operant situation or (2) punishment is employed to suppress responses established by noxious stimuli. An excellent discussion of the response-facilitation effects of punishment is provided by Fowler (1971).

Punishment as a Cue

The first investigators to demonstrate clearly that punishment can serve as a discriminative stimulus to guide ensuing behavior, just as a buzzer or a light can, were W. C. Holz and Azrin (1961). They trained pigeons on a VI 2-minute schedule of food reinforcement until they were responding at a steady rate. Holz and Azrin then introduced moderate electric shock to reduce the response rate about 50%. After the rate of responding had stabilized under these conditions, nonreinforcement periods were introduced during which the subjects received punishment for responding or nothing at all. A discriminative control by punishment was demonstrated by these conditions. The pigeons continued to peck the key at a fairly high rate when punished but responded very little during periods of no punishment. Apparently, the punishment acquired conditioned reinforcing properties.

A similar demonstration of the use of punishment as a discriminative stimulus is also provided by Holz and Azrin (1962). In this investigation, punishment (electric shock) was selectively applied to different portions of an FI schdule. As you will remember, a subject is confronted with a temporal discrimination when an FI schedule is imposed. For example, in the case of an FI 1-minute schedule, the first response occurring after the 1-minute interval has elapsed is reinforced. In this situation, responding at the beginning of the interval is not associated with reinforcement, while responding at the end of the time period is. One would expect that if a shock was used to signal either the beginning or the end of the interval, it would make it clearer to the animal when to respond. Holz and Azrin found that such was indeed the case. Compared to the rate of responding in the absence of shock, punishment of responses in the first three-quarters of the FI interval (mild shock) suppressed the rate of key pecking. In contrast, the same punishment applied to responses emitted during the final quarter of the interval actually increased the rate of responding, again demonstrating the potential discriminative properties of punishment. This cue function of punishment can be invoked to account for Muenzinger's (1934) finding that punishment of correct, food-reinforced responses in a visual-discrimination task facilitates rather than impairs the learning of this task.

Punishment of Avoidance Responses

The second situation in which application of an aversive stimulus will often facilitate rather than suppress behavior arises when punishment is employed to suppress responses established through aversive events. This situation would most often occur when one used punishment in an attempt to suppress avoidance behavior. The observed increase in responding in this situation probably also reflects the discriminative properties of punishment. A study by A. H. Black and Morse (1961) will illustrate this position.

Using a shuttle-box active-avoidance task, Black and Morse trained dogs to avoid shock. After this response was acquired, the researchers imposed punishment for making the jumping response. The result was a temporary increase in the occurrence of these punished responses, as would be predicted if one takes into account the discriminative properties that had been acquired by the shock. The jumping response was, of course, eventually extinguished following repeated applications of punishment. A similar increase in responding was reported by Migler (1963) when shocks were administered if his rat subjects pressed a bar that had provided escape from or avoidance of a shock. Again, in this sort of paradigm (that is, avoidance learning), we see that the normally occurring suppressive effects of punishment can be reversed if the subjects have had a previous history that allowed the punishment (shock) to acquire discriminative properties.

This general effect has also been confirmed by Sandler and his associates (Sandler & Davidson, 1967; Sandler, Davidson, Greene, & Holzschuh, 1966a, 1966b; Sandler, Davidson, & Malagodi, 1966). In addition, they have reported that although the increase in avoidance responding is often short-lived, this effect can be strengthened if the punishment is gradually introduced during original avoidance learning so as to decrease the distinctiveness of the punishment-versus-avoidance contingencies (Sandler et al., 1966). Also, they have reported that the response-facilitating effects of punishment will often persist for a relatively long time despite the availability of an unpunished alternative response (Sandler & Davidson, 1967).

Punishment of Human Behavior

Taken together, the materials discussed in this chapter regarding the outcomes of various punishment procedures allow us to derive some general rules on the use of punishment in determining human behavior. In so doing, we are not advocating the use of punishment as an alternative to positive reinforcement, but since punishment is so widely used in our society, it is important for us to know how it influences behavior and how to use it effectively if we are going to use it at all. Excellent discussions of the use of punishment in controlling human behavior are provided by Azrin and Holz (1966) and Logan (1976). The effectiveness and usefulness of punishment in human therapy are discussed by Johnston (1972). The following statements provide a summary of some generalized findings of the research described in this chapter and also provide some guidelines for the use of punishment.

First, the intensity of the punishment should be at high levels, and continued exposures to the noxious event should be at the highest reasonable levels (Logan, 1976). It is important that the aversive event not be gradually increased. Rather, it should be introduced at its maximum strength. As Logan suggests, inadequate punishments should be avoided.

Second, the punishment should be delivered promptly after the response. Immediate punishment is far more effective than delayed punishment.

Third, extended periods of punishment should be avoided, especially if mild punishments are used. Extended periods of punishment will often lead to a recovery of the punished response in the presence of the aversive stimulus.

Fourth, avoid rewards after punishments. If you punish your child, do not lavish love on the child immediately afterward. If you do so, the punishment may acquire conditioned reinforcing properties. Logan has suggested that in its extreme form such a procedure might produce a masochistic individual, a person who enjoys experiencing pain. Using psychotic female patients, Ayllon and Azrin (1966) demonstrated how punishment can attain secondary reinforcing properties. In this study, when noise that had been shown to have punishing properties was paired with positive reinforcement, the subjects responded in order to obtain the noxious stimulus.

Fifth, acceptable alternative responses should be made available. Specifically, an alternative response should be available that will lead to the same reinforcement as the punished response but will not produce the aversive event. As Azrin and Holz suggest, punishment of socially unacceptable behaviors (for example, criminal acts) will be more effective if socially acceptable behaviors in which the individual can engage are available. This, of course, underlines the need for rehabilitation and job-training programs in our prisons. Punishment of criminal acts will be most effective if noncriminal behaviors can be learned that will yield the same advantages as criminal behavior.

Sixth, as Azrin and Holz suggest, an alternative that can be used if physical punishment cannot be used because of practical, ethical, or legal considerations is a reduction of positive reinforcement (time out from the reinforcement period). This view has been substantiated in several laboratory studies (see Azrin & Holz, 1966). The use of time-out periods from reinforcement requires that the subject has a substantial prior history of positive reinforcement. Otherwise, there would be nothing to withhold.

Finally, the most important psychological principle regarding punishment, and one that is too often ignored by parents who wish to modify their children's behavior, is that punishment is most effective when it is combined with positive reinforcement of desirable habits. Too often, children hear what not to do without ever being praised or reinforced for doing what they should do. Punish children for engaging in unacceptable behaviors, but reward them lavishly when they do the correct thing.

It has often been suggested that punishment should not be used to modify human behavior. A common criticism of the use of punishment is that it is not very effective. However, as we have seen in this chapter, when properly employed, punishment can be quite effective in suppressing behavior. This effect can be of very long duration, thus allowing for the conditioning of alternative nonpunished responses that will provide for the individual all of the advantages of the punished response. It must be emphasized, however, that punishment is ineffective if inappropriately used. For example, if children are starved for attention, they may misbehave to attract their parents' attention even if the end result is being punished. In this situation, punishment administered by the parents is actually reinforcing misbehavior. A moral: if you don't understand how to use punishment, don't.

A second criticism of punishment is that its use will reinforce escape responses from the punishing situation. This becomes a problem when one considers that such escape might disrupt social relations between the punished individual and others. Johnston (1972) reviews literature suggesting that this negative outcome is rarely realized. For example, he points out that Zeilberger, Sampen, and Sloane (1968) found that there was no tendency for a punished child to avoid either the punished situation or the mother who delivered the punishment. In addition, Lovaas and Simmons (1969) have reported that the amount of time punished children spent avoiding adults decreased, as did the frequency of self-destructive behaviors, when more shocks were given. Lovaas and Simmons also reported that the children did not appear to be fearful of the experimenters who delivered the shocks. These findings, however, need to be further explored before we can be sure of their generality.

A last area of concern regarding the use of punishment in controlling human behavior is that punishment might lead to the development of aggressive responses in the subject's behavior repertoire (Azrin & Holz, 1966). This concern has arisen in light of reports of animal studies, reviewed earlier in this chapter, that demonstrated that prolonged exposure to intense shock will elicit aggressive attacks on and reflexive fighting with nearby animals (for example, Ulrich, Wolff, & Azrin, 1964). Johnston (1972) reports that this does not seem to be a problem with human subjects because "in applied settings the duration of stimulus presentation is usually quite brief, the frequency of stimulus delivery is likely quite low, and most punishing stimuli used with humans are not physically painful" (p. 1050).

Let us close this chapter by stating that there are differences in opinion over whether punishment should ever be used in controlling human behavior, but it always has been used and probably always will be. Receiving punishment as a consequence of our behavior is as much a part of our lives as is receiving reinforcement. It thus behooves us to understand clearly the results of punishment and the factors influencing its outcome.

Summary

Punishment involves the presentation of an aversive stimulus following a response. In general, the behavior that immediately preceded the punishment is thereafter less likely to occur, although in some instances punishment will strengthen the behaviors it follows. Punishment will facilitate rather than suppress behavior if punishment signals the availability of food reinforcement in an operant situation or if punishment is employed to suppress responses that were previously conditioned using aversive stimuli.

In those cases in which punishment suppresses behavior, the extent of behavior suppression is apparently related to the severity of the punishing stimulus, the proximity of the punishment to the punished response, the subject's prior experience of aversive events, and the availability of alternative responses that provide the subject with a means of avoiding the punishment. The extent of behavior suppression also depends upon the type of behavior punished; application of aversive stimulation appears to produce much more dramatic effects on consummatory behaviors than on instrumental responses.

In 1913, Thorndike suggested that positive reinforcers and punishers are events that act equally but in opposite directions on behavior. He later rejected that view, but in all likelihood he should not have. It appears that the view of the effects of punishment has gone full circle and is returning to Thorndike's original position. However, in making such a statement, one must be aware that there are apparently two effects on behavior of aversive stimulation. The first of these, a nonspecific suppressive effect, probably reflects an increase in the emotiality of the subject in the experimental situation. The second, a specific suppressive effect, represents a specific suppression of the punished response due to an association arising between the punishment and the behavior it follows. It is this second effect of punishment that is analogous but opposite in sign to the effects of positive reinforcement.

The chapter concluded with some guidelines on the use of punishment in the management of human behavior. Punishment in conjunction with positive reinforcement can be used in shaping human behavior. However, it must be emphasized that punishment is ineffective if inappropriately used.

Chapter 5

Extinction and Partial Reinforcement

What happens when learned responses are no longer reinforced? When children learn that the act of crying no longer produces a cookie or a piece of candy, the children begin to cease crying. Similarly, when bullies learn that their threats are consistently ignored, regardless of the consequences, they begin to cease bullying. More generally, the withdrawal of reinforcement for some previously reinforced response begins the process of extinction. The response will gradually weaken in the sense that it will occur less frequently or with less vigor.

Extinction is not, however, a simple weakening of a learned response. If, for instance, a rest interval is given after extinction trials, the behavior may spontaneously recover. Thus, although a subject is not responding at the end of extinction, some representation of the habit is still present in the organism because the response does reappear. In addition, it is quite possible that during extinction new responses will be strengthened, which further indicates the dynamic and complex nature of the extinction process.

Extinction and punishment share some features, but they are also quite different. Both extinction and punishment involve a weakening or suppression of learned responses. However, extinction is a weakening of responses by the *removal of reinforcement,* whereas punishment results in a weakening of responses by the *application of noxious stimulation.* Punishment involves the presentation of an undesirable event, whereas extinction involves the removal of a desirable event. Yet despite this difference, extinction and punishment may reflect the same basic processes. This issue is of both theoretical and practical interest. On the practical side, consider the case of a child who has hurt a younger sibling. Given that our concern is the elimination of this undesirable behavior, which approach would be more effective in eliminating this behavior: spanking the child (punishment) or preventing the behavior from being followed by some reinforcing consequence (extinction)? As you can see, the answer to this question depends upon both an understanding of extinction and punishment and the details of the specific case. The theoretical issues will be considered later in this chapter.

Extinction is commonly measured by what is called *resistance* to extinction. When reinforcement is withheld, the behavior does not come to an immediate halt; rather, the response typically weakens in a gradual fashion. Thus, we speak of a response as being more or less resistant to extinction. Normally, an experimenter establishes in advance of the experiment some criterion for indicating resistance to extinction. Then the experimenter counts the responses during extinction and decides that extinction has occurred after some arbitrary number of *trials* has occurred or the rate of responding has been reduced to some arbitrary low level.

Some Factors Influencing Extinction

In order to better understand the extinction process, it is useful to examine several major factors which affect it. In this section we will briefly examine four important factors: number of reinforcements, amount of reinforcement, stimulus and response variability, and partial versus continuous reinforcement.

Number of Reinforcements

An obvious factor that affects resistance to extinction is the number of reinforcements given during training. S. B. Williams conducted one of the early studies examining the effect of number of reinforcements during acquisition on resistance to extinction. His subjects received reinforcement for either 5, 10, 30, or 90 bar presses in a Skinner box prior to extinction. Every correct response brought a constant amount of reward. The results indicated that resistance to extinction increased as a function of the number of reinforcements. With only a few reinforcements, only a few responses were emitted during extinction, whereas with many reinforcements a much larger number of responses was emitted. This finding was consistent with a major assumption of most theories of learning at that time, that the greater the number of reinforcements the stronger was the learned association between a stimulus and a response.

Most recent evidence indicates that the relationship between number of reinforcements and resistance to extinction is not always a clear, simple one. In some cases, for example, resistance to extinction first increases and then decreases as a function of number of reinforcements (see, for example, Ison, 1962). Thus, repeated reinforcements, as such, do not necessarily continue to build up response strength. Indeed, Bunch (1963) has pointed out that there are serious problems in assuming that resistance to extinction is a simple measure of learning.

Amount of Reinforcement

Another factor that influences resistance to extinction is the amount of reinforcement given during acquisition. Although large rewards lead to better performance during acquisition, the opposite is true during extinction. In other words, extinction is faster for subjects who received larger rewards during acquisition (Hulse, 1958; Wagner, 1961). One possible explanation for this finding relates to the emotional properties of frustration. It is conceivable that a subject placed on extinction following large amounts of reinforcement suffers substantially more frustration than a subject that received small amounts of reward. For example, suppose that an adolescent is suddenly told by his parents that he will not receive his allowance for the next month. Presumably, if the allowance was $5 a week, greater frustration will result than if the allowance was only $1 a week. Thus, the shift from a large amount of reward could be sufficiently disruptive to lead to much more rapid extinction.

Stimulus and Response Variability

As a general rule, resistance to extinction is greater if the conditions are more variable during acquisition (compare Logan, 1976). Variability can involve the stimulus, the response, or the reinforcement condition, although we will focus on only the first two aspects in this section. Stimulus variability refers to the degree of variation in the stimulus conditions during training. Consider the situation in which animals learn to run in a simple maze in order to obtain food. In one case an animal may run repeatedly in the same maze, whereas in another case an animal may run in several mazes that vary in length, brightness, and other features. In general, animals running under varied conditions will show much greater resistance to extinction. Logan (1976) suggests that one way to understand the effect of stimulus variability is to consider the number of habits involved. A subject trained under one stimulus condition will acquire some generalized tendency to respond, but the tendency will not be so great as it would be under conditions of varied stimuli. In effect, varied-stimulus training produces more habits in that the response becomes associated with a larger number of stimuli. Therefore, resistance to extinction is greater because more habits must be extinguished.

In a similar vein, the greater the number of ways of making a response, the more resistant to extinction it will be. For example, the more ways in which an animal is trained to press a lever—with its paw, its nose, the side of its face—the more persistent will be the behavior (compare Ferraro & Branch, 1968). The effects of response variability can also be understood in terms of the number of habits involved. If we view each variant of the bar-pressing response as a different habit, then the more habits that have been learned, the greater the resistance to extinction. Even if one or two variants are extinguished, other variants still remain and persist during extinction trials. In summary, as a general rule, if you wish habits to persist, they should be inculcated under conditions of stimulus and response variability.

Partial versus Continuous Reinforcement

An extremely important factor influencing resistance to extinction is reinforcement variability. In operant conditioning the reinforcement can be varied by varying the schedule of reinforcement. As we saw in Chapter 3, reinforcement can be scheduled according to ratio or interval and can be fixed or varied. The general rule is that responses that are only occasionally reinforced during acquisition are more persistent during extinction. This finding is so pervasive that it is called the *partial-reinforcement effect.* We discussed this effect in Chapter 3 and will return to it later in this chapter.

Theories of Extinction

There are a variety of theories of extinction. In this section we will examine two representative theories, *inhibition theory* and *frustration theory.*

Inhibition Theory

An early interpretation of extinction was advanced by Hull (1943), who proposed that a hypothetical process called *inhibition* is responsible for extinction. This classical theory had an elegant reasonableness in its original form but has been largely superseded by new theories. Nevertheless, it is important that we take a brief look at this theory because it represents an instance of a "good" theory—that is, a testable theory.

According to this theory, the course of learning is accompanied by inhibition and another hypothetical process called *excitation.* Excitation is the basic process underlying the strengthening of a response, and inhibition is the process underlying the weakening of a response. The hypothetical process of inhibition is something like the build-up of fatigue. Just as fatigue is built up as a result of the expenditure of effort, an inhibitory process is strengthened as a result of responding. Regardless of whether responses are reinforced, they require effort; therefore, inhibition occurs with both reinforced and nonreinforced responses. At a behavioral level, inhibition is measured by an increase in a tendency *not* to respond. In contrast, the process of excitation occurs only with reinforced responses. Thus, if a response is reinforced, inhibition is offset by the opposing process of excitation. Behaviorally, excitation is reflected in an increased tendency to respond. The basic approach of the theory, then, is to assume two opposing processes, excitation and inhibition, and to use the processes to explain extinction. Hull further assumed that inhibition develops at a slower rate than excitation and that as long as reinforcement continues the subject will continue to respond.

Figure 5–1 is a graph of these hypothetical processes during acquisiton and extinction. During acquisition, inhibition develops at a slower rate than excitation; both processes reach a certain level at the end of acquisition. With the onset of extinction, the curve for excitation remains stable (flat), but the curve for inhibition continues to grow. The reason, of course, is that all responses are now nonreinforced. Because the inhibitory tendency continues to increase, it eventually equals and even surpasses the excitatory tendency. When this occurs, responding declines and eventually ceases. The last part of the figure shows the effect of a rest interval on spontaneous recovery. Inhibition decays during a rest interval, whereas excitation remains at the same level. Thus, if a test is made after a rest interval, there will be some spontaneous recovery because inhibition has decayed below the level of excitation.

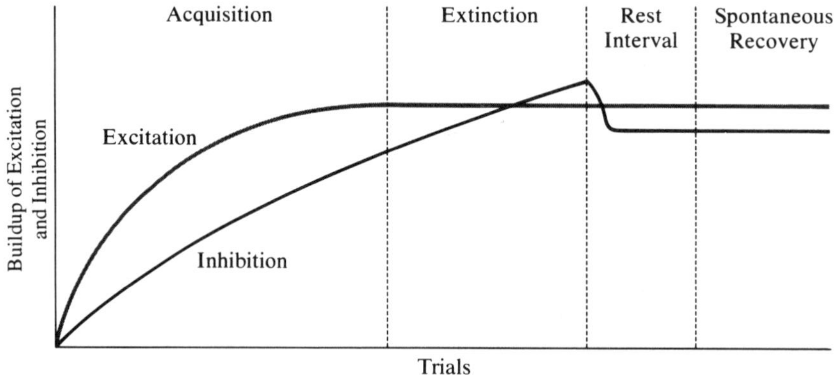

Figure 5–1. Theoretical analysis depicting the formation of excitation and inhibition during acquisition, extinction, and spontaneous recovery.

Despite the reasonableness of inhibition theory, several problems with it developed. For example, it has been found that massing extinction trials—that is, closely bunching the trials—increases resistance to extinction (W. Wilson, Weiss, & Amsel, 1955). This procedure appears to produce greater effort than does distributing the extinction trials over a longer time period and hence theoretically produces a greater amount of inhibition. But the most difficult problem with inhibition theory stems from the partial-reinforcement effect. Indeed, even before inhibition theory was advanced, Skinner (1938) and Humphreys (1939) had found greater resistance to extinction with partial than with continuous reinforcement, despite the fact that partial reinforcement results in fewer total reinforcements during acquisition than continuous reinforcement. This finding was damaging to the inhibition theory because, given the assumption that inhibition occurs after every response, the difference between excitation and inhibition should be less after partial reinforcement. Since continuous reinforcement results in a larger number of reinforcements, inhibition theory must predict greater resistance to extinction under continuous reinforcement, a prediction exactly opposite to the findings. Because of these and other difficulties with inhibition theory, new theories have arisen. One of the most important is frustration theory.

Frustration Theory

The frustration theory of extinction calls attention to the motivational/frustrative effects of nonreinforcement. Put simply, the theory emphasizes that being suddenly cut off from reward induces a state of frustration that, in turn, will affect the course of extinction. Several researchers have advocated the importance of frustration, but the most systematic treatment stems from the work of Amsel (1958, 1967, 1972). A basic assumption of frustration theory is that not receiving reinforcement following reinforced trials produces a state of frustration that serves to motivate the organism. If we are able to escape from the frustrating circumstances, we are reinforced. Accordingly, frustration is viewed as a drive state that can energize behavior.

The idea that frustration has drivelike properties first grew out of an experiment by Amsel and Roussel (1952). Rats were trained to run down a straight-alley runway to obtain food. The apparatus might be best thought of as a two-stage, straight-alley runway. The first stage led to the first goal box, and the second stage led to the second goal box. The runway consisted of a start box, an alley, and a goal box, plus a second alley and a second goal box. The rats were run for a number of days with food available in both goal boxes. On completion of the training, the rats were running rapidly at a stable rate. Then the rats were given additional training with food available in the first goal box for only a random half of the trials; in contrast, food was always available in the second goal box. The measure we are interested in was a comparison of the running times in the second alley following those trials in which the rats had just eaten in the first goal box with the running times when they had not eaten.

The results are shown in Figure 5–2. On those trials in which the rats had been rewarded in the first goal box (reward condition), they ran down the second alley at about the same speed as during initial training. The rats ran faster in the second alley following those trials in which they found no food in the first goal box (frustration condition). Amsel and Roussel interpreted these findings as clear evidence for the motivational effects of frustration. The drivelike or motivational effects were reflected in the rats' increased running speeds following nonreward.

A second feature of the theory is the assumption that the decrement in responding during extinction is due to competing responses produced by frustration (Estes, 1959; Guthrie, 1935). The general idea is that during extinction the animal may be learning a response of nonresponding or may be learning new responses that compete with the response learned during acquisition. (You might note the similarity between this idea and the points made in Chapter 4 about allowing an acceptable alternative response to be made following punishment.) Finally, since frustration produces competing responses, it is assumed that these responses become strengthened through the mechanism of learning by contiguity. The competing responses become associated via contiguity with stimuli that produced the responses learned during acquisition.

The frustration theory, with its assumptions about competing responses, has been nicely supported in an experiment by Adelman and Maatsch (1955). They first trained rats to traverse a straight-alley runway to obtain food. Then they extinguished the behavior under one of three different conditions. One group underwent a standard extinction procedure in which the animals were confined in the goal box for a period of time following a run down the alley. A second group of rats was encouraged to make a response that was

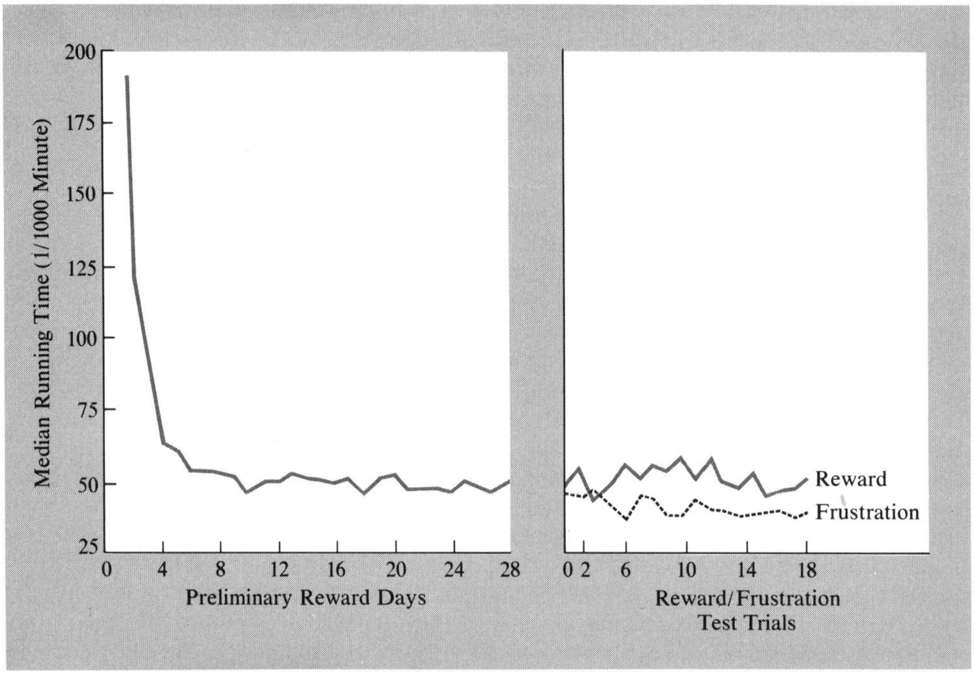

Figure 5–2. Running times following frustration and reward. (From "Motivational Properties of Frustration: I. Effect on a Running Response of the Addition of Frustration to the Motivational Complex," by A. Amsel and J. Roussel, *Journal of Experimental Psychology,* 1952, *43,* 363–368. Copyright 1952 by the American Psychological Association. Reprinted by permission.)

compatible with running; with this procedure the lid of the goal box was raised, and the animals were encouraged to jump from the goal box onto a platform. The third group was led to make a response incompatible with running down the alley; they were allowed to "recoil" from the empty goal box and to make the incompatible response of retracing the alley, that is, running all the way back to the start box.

The results were quite striking and are shown in Figure 5–3. The figure clearly supports the researchers' prediction that extinction would be most pronounced for the recoil group, which made an incompatible response. This group reached the extinction criterion within five blocks of trials, whereas the "jump" group continued to traverse the alley rapidly over the same blocks of trials.

In summary, the frustration theory does a good job of accounting for extinction. When the assumption of response competition is added to the idea of frustration, a comprehensive and powerful theory emerges. In addition, the theory can account for the partial-reinforcement effect, which increases the generality of the theory. Now let us turn our attention to this important effect.

Some Factors Influencing the Partial-Reinforcement Effect

We have already noted that a major factor influencing extinction is the schedule of reinforcement under which the subjects are trained. We further noted that resistance to extinction is greater following partial reinforcement that continuous reinforcement. A

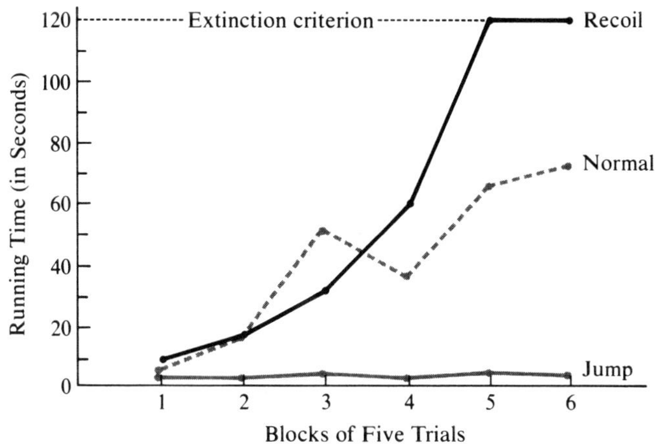

Figure 5–3. Running times in extinction following three experimental conditions. (From "Resistance to Extinction as a Type of Response Elicited by Frustration," by H. M. Adelman and J. L. Maatsch, *Journal of Experimental Psychology,* 1955, *50,* 61–65. Copyright 1955 by the American Psychological Association. Reprinted by permission.)

number of variables are known to influence the partial-reinforcement effect. For example, one factor is the magnitude of reinforcement. In general, the partial-reinforcement effect is enhanced when large rather than small rewards are used (Hulse, 1958). Large rewards given on a partial schedule increase resistance to extinction; on the other hand, large rewards given on a continuous schedule decrease resistance to extinction. Another factor is the degree of training. As a general rule, increased training under partial reinforcement enhances the partial-reinforcement effect (Wagner, 1961). A major factor which affects the partial-reinforcement effect is the percentage of rewarded trials during acquisition. In general, animals show greater resistance to extinction as the percentage of reinforced trials is decreased. A more detailed summary of these and other important factors can be found in the reviews of this research area by Lewis (1960) and Robbins (1971).

Theories of the Partial-Reinforcement Effect

The tendency of organisms to persevere in the face of only occasional reinforcement has posed an interesting theoretical problem. Why do responses by rats and humans persist longer in extinction when they have been trained under partial reinforcement? Several theories of the partial-reinforcement effect have been offered. In this section we will examine three of these: *discrimination theory, sequential theory,* and *frustration theory.*

Discrimination Theory

An early account of the partial-reinforcement effect, proposed by Humphreys (1939), is a discrimination explanation. Humphreys noted that when a continuously rewarded animal is shifted from acquisition to extinction, there is an abrupt change in the stimulus situation. In contrast, for a partially rewarded animal the shift is less obvious and dramatic; extinction does not represent a completely novel situation for an animal that has already experienced nonreinforcement. Since the stimulus situation in acquisition and extinction is more similar for subjects receiving partial reinforcement, they are less readily able to discriminate when acquisition ends and extinction begins. Hence, they are more likely to respond longer during extinction. Although this discrimination theory provided a plausible, commonsense account of the partial-reinforcement effect, it has been superseded by newer theories that can explain a wider range of extinction phenomena.

One problem with a straightforward or *simple* discrimination theory is that it does not easily handle the results of studies in which blocks of continuous and partial reinforcement are used. Suppose, for example, that rats are trained on partial reinforcement for a while and then are shifted to continuous reinforcement for a number of trials before being placed on extinction. Would the usual partial-reinforcement effect still appear? Or would the animals now behave as though they had been on continuous reinforcement throughout training? A simple discrimination theory must predict the latter because the subjects should easily be able to discriminate when they are shifted from continuous reinforcement during acquisition to no reinforcement during extinction. But that is not what happens. For example, Theios (1962) found that rats first trained on partial and then on continuous reinforcement behaved as though they had *not* received continuous reinforcement when given extinction trials. In other words, the effect of prior partial-reinforcement training persisted through a block of training with continuous reinforcements.

A simple discrimination theory cannot handle these data. But if we add an assumption about *memory* and the permanence of memory traces, we have a new kind of theory that begins to handle much of the data. A theory beginning with this assumption has been developed by E. J. Capaldi (1966, 1970) and is called sequential theory.

Sequential Theory

Sequential theory is a sophisticated extension of another type of theory called the *stimulus-aftereffects theory.* The aftereffects theory was proposed by V. F. Sheffield (1949) and Hull (1952) and treats the occurrence of reward and nonreward as stimulus events. The stimulus events of reward and nonreward are thought to be quite distinctive and to generate stimulus traces that persist for some period of time. Thus, on the next trial the response will occur in the presence of a stimulus complex consisting of both the current stimuli impinging on the organism's receptors and the stimulus trace associated with prior reward and nonreward.

Building on the general assumption that there are distinctive stimuli associated with reward and nonreward, sequential theory emphasizes the subject's memory for prior reward/nonreward outcomes in explaining the partial-reinforcement effect. The theory assumes that trials besides the immediately preceding one affect what is learned on the present trial. More generally, the theory assumes that the memory of all previous outcomes enters into an association with the response. In addition, the subject's memory of nonreward outcomes is assumed to show little loss through any decaylike process.

According to Capaldi, three important factors influence the partial-reinforcement effect. One of these is *N* length, where *N* is the number of *successive* nonrewarded trials that precede a rewarded trial. Thus, an *N* length of 1 means that one nonrewarded trial has preceded a rewarded trial, while an *N* length of 2 indicates that two successive nonrewarded trials have preceded a rewarded trial. The theory assumes that different *N* lengths produce different memories and that the memory of nonreward is being modified continuously by the successive occurrences of nonreward.

In Capaldi's theory a rewarded trial has two functions. One function is to replace the memory of nonreward with a memory of reward. This *replacement function* prevents the memory of nonreward from being further changed. The second function of reward is to establish an association between an instrumental response and the memory of previous nonrewards. This *reinforcement function* of reward implies that subjects experiencing different N lengths are learning different things because different memories of nonreward are associated with the same instrumental response. Capaldi points out that although subjects experiencing different N lengths may show no performance differences during acquisition, they may behave differently during extinction.

Sequential theory treats extinction as an indefinitely long series of nonrewards—that is, as an N length of infinity. The extent to which differences in performance are found in extinction depends on the degree of similarity between the N length during training and the N length during extinction. Since longer N lengths during training are more similar to those in extinction, the response of subjects exposed to them will be more resistant to extinction. This assumption rests upon a second factor of the theory, the concept of generalization decrement. The right-hand panel of Figure 5–4 will help clarify this part of the theory. The panel displays the extent to which a response acquired under two training conditions generalizes in extinction. The figure plots the strength of the response against the similarity of acquisition and extinction conditions. As can be seen, an N length of 3 is more similar to extinction than an N length of 1, so there is more generalized response strength in extinction from an N length of 3 than an N length of 1. The longer N length displays *less* generalization decrement than the shorter N length. Thus, the figure suggests that longer N lengths produce *greater* resistance to extinction.

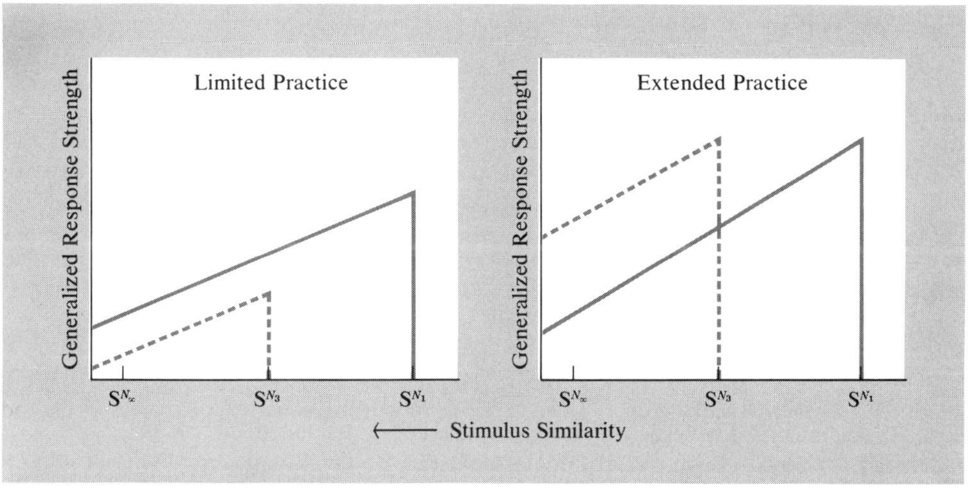

Figure 5–4. Hypothetical generalization decrements for reward schedules differing in N length. (From "Partial Reinforcement: A Hypothesis of Sequential Effects," by E. J. Capaldi, *Psychological Review,* 1966, *73,* 459–477. Copyright 1966 by the American Psychological Association. Reprinted by permission.)

However, this assumption of the theory is restricted to circumstances in which the habits developed with the different N lengths are about the same. In the right-hand panel of Figure 5–4, the height of the vertical lines above the two N lengths indicates that the strength of the habit for these two conditions is equal. The third factor that determines the strength of the association between a response and the different memories of nonreward is called an N–R transition. An N–R transition refers to the number of times a particular N length is followed by reward (R). To see the importance of this factor in resistance to extinction, consider the following schedules of reward: NNNRRR and NRNRNR. The first schedule has an *N* length of 3, the second an *N* length of 1. If just *N* length is considered, you might conclude that the first schedule would produce more resistance to extinction. But this conclusion depends on the number of N–R transitions. The first schedule has only one N–R transition, while the second has three N–R transitions. Since only one N–R transition is available with the first schedule, only one conditioning trial is available for associating the memory of nonreward with the instrumental response. In the second schedule three conditioning trials are available to strengthen the association between the memory of nonreward and behavior. Thus, the theory predicts that with limited practice behavior under the second sequence (NRNRNR) will be more resistant to extinction than behavior under the sequence with the longer *N* length (NNNRRR). However, as training progresses, the habit strengths accruing with the two reward schedules become more nearly the same, and the longer *N* length results in more resistance to extinction.

The left-hand panel of Figure 5–4 illustrates the generalization of habit strength with the two schedules following a *limited* number of training trials. The panel shows that more habit strength generalizes in extinction with the shorter *N* length. Capaldi and his associates have confirmed these predictions of the theory. When different groups of animals received just a few training trials with different *N* lengths, the shorter *N* lengths produced more resistance to extinction (Bacon, 1962; Spivey, 1964). However, following extended training, more resistance to extinction was found with longer *N* lengths (Capaldi, 1966).

A more detailed treatment of sequential theory is beyond the scope of this chapter. But even our brief description of the theory would be incomplete if we did not point out that sequential theory is quite successful in accounting for a wide variety of extinction phenomena. It can better explain the partial-reinforcement effect following a few conditioning trials than frustration theory (see, for example, Capaldi & Waters, 1970; McCain, 1966; Ziff & Capaldi, 1971). The theory has been used to account for the finding that resistance to extinction is greater if partially rewarded subjects receive large rather than small rewards during training (Capaldi & Capaldi, 1970). Finally, the work of Mellgren and his associates (Dyck, Mellgren, & Seybert, 1973; Mellgren & Dyck, 1972), which was done in the framework of sequential theory, provides a more convincing explanation of the *within-subject partial-reinforcement effect* than frustration theory, discussed in the next section.

The within-subject partial-reinforcement effect refers to a situation in which the *same* individual is trained to two stimuli, one associated with continuous reinforcement and the other with partial reinforcement. Experiments conducted before Mellgren reported his work did not show any differences in the extinction of responses to the two stimuli. Capaldi's theory indicates that this inability to find differences in extinction was due to ignoring the *sequence* of reward and nonreward; that is, when the partially rewarded stimulus is nonrewarded, finding a within-subject partial-reinforcement effect depends on whether the subject is then rewarded when responding to the continuously rewarded stimulus, to the partially rewarded stimulus, or to each of them 50% of the time.

Despite the success of the theory in dealing with these phenomena, motivational factors also regulate behavioral persistence. Indeed, Capaldi (1972) acknowledges that emotional or frustrative stimuli must be considered before a complete explanation of the partial-reinforcement effect is possible. In a later section of the chapter, we shall see that nonreward produces an unpleasant emotional state similar to that found with punishment.

Frustration Theory

The view that stimulus traces determine the partial-reinforcement effect under short intertrial intervals while other factors are responsible for the partial-reinforcement effect under longer intertrial intervals (see, for example, Amsel, 1967; Lawrence & Festinger,

1962; Logan, 1968) rests upon one of the properties of the stimulus trace, its dissipation with the passage of time. During acquisition the trace is thought to become part of the stimulus complex to which the next response is made. Since the stimulus complex in extinction contains more components that were present during acquisition for partially rewarded subjects, the strength of the response is greater than for subjects receiving continuous reinforcement. If, however, the stimulus traces of reward and nonreward *persist only briefly*, another process is required to account for the partial-reinforcement effect when the intertrial intervals are long.

There are two contemporary theories that have dealt extensively with this distinction. One theory is a cognitive or *memory* theory, which we have already discussed (sequential theory). The other theory is a *motivational* theory emphasizing the role of frustration. We have seen how frustration theory explains extinction; now let us see how it accounts for the partial-reinforcement effect. Frustration theory emphasizes events that occur *within* a reinforced or nonreinforced trial. When a considerable amount of time elapses between trials, processes that are activated within the trial take on greater importance and thus can account for the effects of partial reinforcement.

Frustration theory points out that a subject trained under partial reinforcement—say, in a straight-alley runway—is learning to run under conditions that signal two kinds of goal events and their respective stimulus traces. The animal is both "frustrated" by nonreward and "excited" by reward. Thus, although the partially reinforced subject is sometimes frustrated by nonreward, it is *learning to persist* in running because it also is rewarded and has the concomitant pleasant emotional experience. The partially reinforced subject, then, is learning to persist in the face of frustrating stimuli. In contrast, the continuously reinforced subject does not experience this frustration and learns to run only to the stimuli that signal reinforcement. When both subjects are given extinction trials, the partially reinforced subject will run longer because it has learned to maintain its behavior in the face of events that produce frustration. The continuously reinforced subject has not been trained to persist in the face of frustration, so it experiences frustration as soon as extinction begins. The frustration leads to competing responses and hence to more rapid extinction.

The Aversiveness of Nonreward

Throughout our discussion of extinction, we have referred to the aversiveness of nonreward. We have indicated that the emotionality produced by nonreward following anticipation of reward is quite unpleasant. Indeed, in our own experiences we are aware of the aversiveness of nonreward. Such events as no job following graduation from college, refusal of a partner to engage in sexual intercourse, and refusal of your parents to let you use the family car are typical instances of nonreward's occurring when reward may be expected. Although we may personally regard these events as punishing, keep in mind that they are operations of extinction (nonreward) rather than punishment. Extinction involves the removal of a benevolent stimulus; punishment involves the application of a stimulus producing pain or injury. Even the language describing the operations of extinction and punishment is different: behavior is *weakened* by nonreward, but it is *suppressed* by punishment. However, if the behavioral effects of these procedures are similar, it is conceivable that the process responsible for the extinction of a response may be the same as the process responsible for the inhibition of a punished response.

Several theories of punishment (for example, Estes, 1944; N. E. Miller, 1959) argue that the response suppression associated with punishment occurs because stimuli signaling the appearance of the punisher acquire fear-producing properties. Fear elicits responses that compete with the punished response. Miller (1961) has reported experimental results consistent with this idea. He found that when previously punished rats were injected with alcohol or sodium amytal (drugs that reduce fear), the punished response recurred. It was then reasoned that if nonreward produces an emotional reaction similar to fear, those drugs should also result in the recovery of an extinguished response. Barry, Wagner, and Miller (1962) tested this hypothesis. Rats were first trained in a straight-alley runway on a continuous schedule of reward. They then received four days of extinction trials. On the last two days, half of the animals were injected with alcohol or sodium amytal. The investigators found that the rats receiving the drugs ran faster than the other rats, which had received only saline solution as a control. These results are consistent with the hypothesis that nonreward produces an aversive emotional state.

We have seen that the responses of partially rewarded subjects show more persistence during extinction than those of continuously rewarded subjects. An analogous situation exists with punishment. Rats receiving gradually increasing levels of electric shock persist with the punished response when exposed to higher shock intensities than rats that have received only reward (Miller, 1960). Miller's data suggest that the fixation of a punished response may be similar to the persistence of a frustrated response.

R. T. Brown and Wagner (1964) have provided additional support for this idea. They trained three groups of rats in a straight-alley runway. Group C (continuous reinforcement) received a food reward on 100% of the trials. Group N encountered nonreward on 50% of the trials. The third group, Group P, received continuous reinforcement on all trials but, in addition, received a random schedule of shock on 50% of the trials after eating the food. To prevent complete suppression of responding, the shock intensity was increased gradually from 75 to 235 volts. The three groups were then divided into two subgroups. One of the subgroups was placed on extinction; the other received a food reward with a 235-volt shock.

The performance of the several groups during extinction or punishment appears in Figure 5–5. The figure shows that the rats previously exposed to either punishment or nonreward continued to respond in the face of their training condition; that is, Group P showed a greater resistance to the suppressive effects of punishment, and Group N showed a greater resistance to the decremental effects of nonreward. Another interesting finding shown in the figure is the transfer that occurred when the nonrewarded and punished groups were shifted to the other aversive condition. Group P persisted longer in extinction than Group C. Similarly, Group N showed more resistance to punishment than the control group. These results provide strong support for the hypothesis that the processes mediating behavior under nonreward and punishment are the same.

More recently, Daly (1969a, 1969b; Daly & McCroskery, 1973) found that rats will learn a response to escape cues previously associated with nonreward. Her results are similar to earlier findings that animals will learn to escape from stimuli signaling impending shock (J. S. Brown & Jacobs, 1949; McAllister & McAllister, 1965; N. E. Miller, 1948). 1948).

Taken together, these results indicate that the emotional reaction from nonreward produces effects similar to those found with punishment. This evidence, considered in conjunction with sequential theory, suggests that frustrative stimuli and the sequencing of nonreward and reward are crucial in understanding behavioral persistence. An adequate theory of partial reinforcement must incorporate elements of both frustration theory and sequential theory in order to explain why "rats and people come to love things for which they have suffered" (Festinger, 1961).

Summary

The term *extinction* refers to a decrease in responding following withdrawal of a reinforcer. Extinction is not, however, a simple weakening of a response, as shown by the spontaneous recovery of a response following extinction and by the finding that competing responses can be acquired during extinction. Extinction and punishment have some

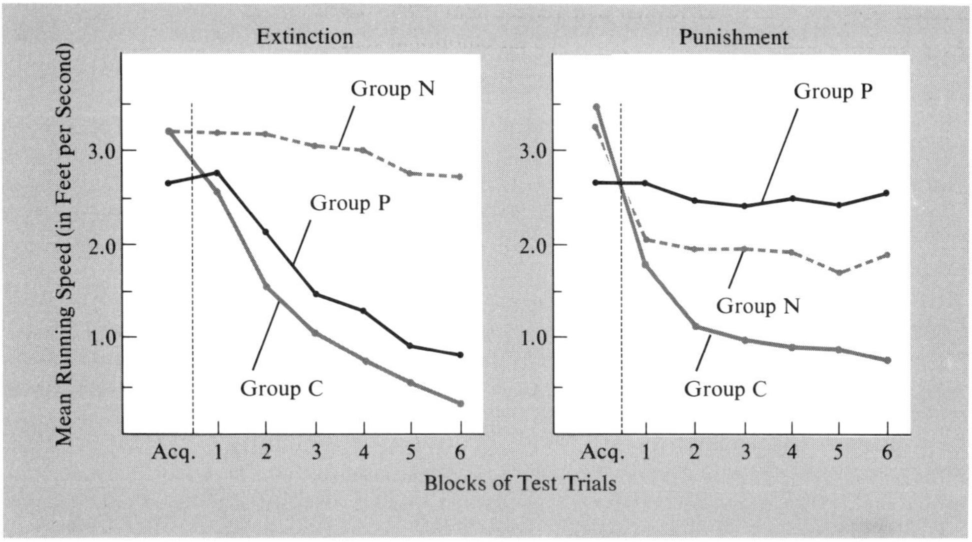

Figure 5–5. Speed of running to nonreward or punishment for groups trained in different ways. Group C was rewarded continuously, Group P was trained with reward and gradually increasing punishment, and Group N was trained with nonreward on a partial random schedule. (From "Resistance to Punishment and Extinction Following Training with Shock or Nonreinforcement," by R. T. Brown and A. R. Wagner, *Journal of Experimental Psychology,* 1964, *68,* 503–507. Copyright 1964 by the American Psychological Association. Reprinted by permission.)

similarities, but they are also quite different. Extinction is a weakening of responses by removal of reinforcement, whereas punishment results in a weakening of responses by the application of noxious stimulation. A number of factors are known to influence resistance to extinction. Some of the more important ones are number of reinforcements, amount of reinforcement, stimulus and response variability, and partial versus continuous reinforcement.

Two theories of extinction were described. The classical inhibition theory accounts for extinction in terms of the build-up of two opposing processes, inhibition and excitation. Extinction occurs when the inhibitory process is greater than the excitatory process. Difficulties with the inhibition theory include the partial-reinforcement effect and the effects of massed extinction trials. The contemporary frustration theory of extinction is a generally adequate theory. Frustration theory makes the assumption that nonreinforcement, following reinforced trials, produces a state of frustration that acts to energize behavior. When this idea is combined with the idea that frustration produces competing responses, the theory can explain the results of extinction.

A longstanding enigma among learning theorists has been the partial-reinforcement effect. Why do responses of both rats and humans show greater resistance to extinction following partial reinforcement than continuous reinforcement? Three theories accounting for the partial-reinforcement effect were described. An early theory emphasizing the difficulty in discriminating between the conditions of partial reinforcement and extinction has been found unsatisfactory. Two modern theories are sequential theory and frustration theory. Sequential theory is a memory theory and assumes that subjects retain the memory traces associated with reward and nonreward. Frustration theory assumes that a subject is actually learning to persist in responding when under partial reinforcement. It may be necessary to combine both theories in order to have a comprehensive theory of partial reinforcement.

Chapter 6

Discrimination and Generalization

Perhaps the most characteristic property of behavior is its selectivity. We respond differently to different features of our physical and social environment. The selective nature of behavior results in responses appropriate to an ever-changing world and thus increases our chances of survival. The selective nature of responding also indicates that we have somehow acquired knowledge or information about the world. In the contemporary psychology of learning, the investigation of how this information is acquired falls within the domain of *discrimination learning*. Considered in this way, discrimination is a fundamental process of all learning.

The questions of what is learned (known) and how it is acquired have intrigued philosophers for centuries. An early philosophical account of the nature of knowledge was developed by the British empiricists, particularly John Locke and David Hume. Although they differed on many matters, they shared the view that knowledge can be accounted for by the association of ideas or sensations. Anticipating the distinction between nominal and functional stimuli (discussed in Chapter 1), Locke proposed that thinking somehow changes sensations. Sensations are further modified when they are combined by associative processes. Thus, knowledge develops gradually by mental operations that somehow alter elementary sensations and then combine them through the laws of association to form more complex ideas.

In their early treatment of discrimination learning, psychologists assumed that associative processes are necessary for the development of knowledge and that in some instances a person's mental or muscular activities somehow supplement sensory input (see, for example, W. James, 1890). It remained for the behaviorists to treat different sensory experiences as different responses and to view thinking as implicit or covert responding (Sechenov, 1965; Watson, 1914). Thus, behaviorism retained the mechanisms of association as the vehicle for the acquisition of knowledge, but the elements of association were stimuli and responses rather than ideas.

Most modern theories of discrimination learning reflect their historical ties to empiricism by retaining the assumption that associative processes provide the necessary structure for learning. However, they differ on how the organism's mental or muscular activities may change incoming stimulation. For example, the classical theories of discrimination learning assume that either all the attributes of the nominal stimulus enter into association with a response or that, in scanning the stimulus, an organism selectively attends to one feature and ignores others. In both cases, Locke's notion that sensory input must be supplemented is absent. It was not until experiments demonstrated that cues can acquire salience (distinctiveness) as a result of our experience with them that later theories proposed an additive process that enriches sensory input (Lawrence, 1949; N. E. Miller & Dollard, 1941).

In any event, two contrasting positions emerged early in theoretical accounts of discrimination learning. One position states that we learn to respond differently to different stimuli because we have acquired information about the absolute properties of the stimulus; that is, all the features of the stimulus striking the receptors, when a response is made, will be associated with that response. The other view regards differential responding as reflecting the selection of the relevant dimension of the stimulus while ignoring its other features. The first position has come to be known as *continuity theory,* while the second view, which emphasizes a selective process resulting in the isolation of stimulus dimensions, is referred to as *noncontinuity theory.* Before examining how contemporary theory deals with this issue, let us look at the classical theories.

Classical Theories of Discrimination Learning

The controversy about how stimuli gain control over responses centers around how to conceptualize the learning process. Continuity theory treats learning as a continuous process; stimulus control is achieved through a cumulative learning process that involves the build-up of approach tendencies for stimuli predicting reinforcement and the development of avoidance tendencies for stimuli signaling nonreinforcement. The summation of these opposing tendencies eventually results in the selection of the cue associated with reward. Noncontinuity theory, in contrast, assumes that animals use hypotheses or cognitions to solve a discrimination problem. Hypotheses are reflected in the display of systematic response tendencies before a discrimination problem is solved. For example, in a discrimination-learning problem involving black and white stimuli, a rat may initially use a position hypothesis, such as always selecting the stimulus on its right, before switching to an appropriate strategy, such as selecting the black cue regardless of its position. When the rat is attending to position rather than brightness, it apparently learns nothing about the relevant cue.

A number of issues are embedded in these different ways of viewing the learning process. One issue, already mentioned, is whether animals use hypotheses in learning a discrimination or whether the correct selection of the stimulus results from an approach tendency that exceeds the avoidance tendency. A second, closely related issue concerns the rate at which a discrimination is mastered. Noncontinuity theory supposes that learning can occur quite rapidly as soon as the animal discovers the correct hypothesis; in brief, an animal may exhibit insight by suddenly solving the problem. The notion that an animal learns nothing about the relevant cue when the incorrect dimension of the stimulus is being sampled, and the possibility of rapid learning, suggest that in some instances learning may be all or none; that is, learning may occur on a single trial.

A final difference between these positions is how the stimulus is conceptualized: do animals respond to the relationship between positive and negative cues, or do they respond to their *absolute properties*? In continuity theory, all the elements of the stimulus complex—position, size, shape, and so on—enter into an association with a response, provided, of course, that the response is followed by reinforcement. Noncontinuity theory views the animal as selecting one component of the cue, such as size, while ignoring its other properties. Central to this controversy is the role assigned to the process of *attention.* Since noncontinuity theory emphasizes that animals use hypotheses in acquiring a discrimination and also suggests that they learn nothing of the relevant cue when an inappropriate hypothesis is employed, attention is postulated as a central mechanism to account for behavioral selectivity. On the other hand, continuity theory suggests that stimulus control over responding is achieved by increasing or decreasing response tendencies to stimuli through differentially reinforcing one cue rather than another. Selection of the correct cue occurs because that cue has acquired a stronger approach tendency. The operation of differential reinforcement is a necessary condition for stimulus discrimination. Now let us take a more detailed look at these theories.

Continuity Theory

The notion that all the properties of the stimulus are associated with the response originated in the work of Pavlov (1927). Pavlov's behavioral investigations stemmed from his view of conditioning as a procedure that clarifies brain function. His primary interest was in brain function; the behavioral research was a means for studying these physiological processes objectively.

Pavlov postulated two opposing processes at work in the brain. One process, excitation, was responsible for the occurrence of the response; the other, inhibition, for its absence. When two perceptibly different stimuli were presented successively to an animal, one predicting reinforcement (the US) and the other nonreinforcement, excitation was presumed to increase to the CS associated with reward and inhibition to the CS predicting nonreward. In short, behavioral selectivity was thought to be established by the reciprocal processes of excitation and inhibition becoming concentrated in different regions of the brain.

Another property that Pavlov attributed to excitation and inhibition was that these physiological processes spread or "irradiated" throughout the brain. He used the term *irradiation* to explain the finding that animals respond to stimuli similar to the one associated with reinforcement and tend not to respond to stimuli that predict nonreinforcement. The irradiation of excitation and inhibition depended on many factors, including prior experience with excitatory or inhibitory CSs, the physical distance and the time interval between them, and the number of presentations of each. Discriminations among stimuli were presumably formed by the degree of excitation and inhibition in specific brain regions. In a similar vein, the wave-like irradiation of neural activity was reflected behaviorally in stimulus generalization, that is, in a tendency to respond to stimuli similar to those previously associated with reinforcement.

Despite the fact that neurophysiological and behavioral studies have not generally supported Pavlov's speculations, many psychologists regarded the facts of conditioning as fruitful sources for explanatory principles that might be used to account for more complex behavior. Without attributing physiological properties to excitation and inhibition, they have used these concepts to make statements about the functional properties of organisms. For example, by ascribing various hypothetical properties to excitation and inhibition, Hull and Spence tried to account for complex maze discrimination learning as well as the facts of simple conditioning. (Recall that the processes of excitation and inhibition were part of Hull's theory of extinction described in Chapter 5. This theory did not, however, assume any physiological processes underlying inhibition.)

In a classic paper, Spence (1936) used excitatory and inhibitory concepts in his analysis of the nature of discrimination learning. The theory was a limited one having application only to simultaneous and simple, successive ("go/no go") stimulus presentations. In a simultaneous discrimination two stimuli are presented together, and the subject chooses between them. The stimuli typically have many common elements, but there are some features unique to the stimulus signaling reinforcement (S+) and some unique to the stimulus predicting nonreinforcement (S−). In the successive, or go/no go, paradigm, S+ and S− are presented singly, one per trial, in an irregular and unpredictable sequence. To obtain reward, the subject must respond appropriately in the presence of S+ and refrain from responding to S−. Another variation of the successive-discrimination paradigm allows the subject to use two distinct responses. Consider a rat in a *T* maze. If a tone (S_1) is present at the beginning of the trial, the rat must turn right (R_1) to obtain reinforcement. In the absence of the tone (S_2), the appropriate response is turning left (R_2). Thus, reinforcement is available when R_1 is made to S_1 or when R_2 occurs in the presence of S_2.

Another constraint on Spence's theory is its application to go/no go discriminations using what is termed a *noncorrection procedure.* With a noncorrection procedure the trial terminates following the occurrence of a correct or an incorrect response; that is, if the first response made is an error, the subject does not have an opportunity to correct it by making another response. In contrast, a *correction procedure* permits the subject to continue responding until the correct response is made; the trial ends with the correct response. These restrictions are important because some critics, by ignoring the constraints of the theory, have evaluated it improperly.

Spence attempted to account for a variety of animal discrimination phenomena by using a few explicitly stated assumptions. As indicated previously, he retained the excitation and inhibition concepts but did not give them neurophysiological properties. The theory assumed that if an organism selects a stimulus and is reinforced, all the components of the stimulus "sensed" during response initiation receive an increase in their association with that response. The stimulus is said to have acquired a tendency to excite that response. Conversely, if the response is not reinforced, all the components of the stimulus complex receive a decrease in the association between stimulus and response. Accordingly, the stimulus acquires a tendency to inhibit that response. Thus, the tendency to approach a stimulus complex is determined by the summation of excitation and inhibition of each feature of the stimulus complex. The selection of one stimulus complex over another results from a higher net excitatory tendency associated with the stimulus chosen.

Spence expanded his basic assumptions by specifying how reinforcement and nonreinforcement affect the strengthening or weakening of associations during training. Specifically, excitation increases with reinforcement according to an *S*-shaped function; that is, reinforcement produces smaller increments of excitation at the beginning and end of training and larger increments on intermediate trials. The increment in excitation will be large when moderately strong habits are reinforced, but reinforcement of very weak or very strong reaction tendencies results in small amounts of excitation. On the other hand, the decremental effects of nonreward are a function of the strength of the preexisting habit. The inhibitory effects of nonreward are assumed to be greater the stronger the habit; that is, nonreward produces substantially more weakening of a strong excitatory tendency, whereas less inhibition develops when the excitatory tendency is weak.

With these assumptions Spence could account for systematic response tendencies before a discrimination problem is solved and for the way in which these tendencies are suddenly abandoned. Consider, for example, one of Spence's own illustrations in which a rat is faced with a simultaneous discrimination involving four stimulus components: black, white, right, and left. The black and white cues are presented in an irregular and unpredictable manner on the right or the left. Although black may be the component associated with reward, the animal may show a position preference—that is, have a stronger excitatory tendency to go to the right. Early in training, then, a systematic response tendency will be shown for the right position. Suppose that on the first trial black appears to the right and that the rat selects the black/right stimulus. Excitation to each will be increased by a small amount because reward results in a small increment of habit to components that are weak (black) or strong (right). On the next trial suppose that white is on the right and black is on the left. Again the rat selects the right side. Nonreward will produce a large decrement in the tendency to go right because it is a strong habit. A much smaller inhibitory tendency will accrue to white because the excitatory tendency of that cue is small. Eventually, the excitatory tendency to the two positions will become equal, whereas the tendency to approach black will gradually increase until the animal always selects it. In this way Spence was able to explain the appearance of, and subsequent abandonment of, the systematic hypothesis behavior that is typically observed early in training.

In his later writings Spence (1937, 1942) added assumptions of generalization of excitation and of inhibition to explain complex relational responding (transposition). Before reviewing this application of the theory and the tests made to assess it, a detailed treatment of noncontinuity theory is in order.

Noncontinuity Theory

Modern attention theories of discrimination learning originated in the ideas of Lashley (see Lashley & Wade, 1946) and Krechevsky (1937, 1938). A crucial aspect of their theories is that a feature of the stimulus complex is selectively abstracted from the complex. It is to this feature that the response is made. Another of their assumptions is that other features of the stimulus complex are disregarded when the animal is attending to one property of the complex. This theoretical position has been characterized as subtractive because it assumes that the functional stimulus has been "subtracted," or removed, from the total stimulation available (Tighe & Tighe, 1966).

Despite the insistence of Krechevsky and Lashley that attention is somehow involved in discrimination learning, their choice of different procedures necessarily emphasized different ways in which the effects of selective attending would be reflected behaviorally. Krechevsky's observations focused on behaviors occurring during what is known as the *presolution phase* of learning—that is, during the period prior to the time the animal begins attending to the relevant feature of the stimulus. The presence of systematic response tendencies during the presolution phase suggested to Krechevsky that the animal was indeed attending to an irrelevant cue. Moreover, if attention to an irrelevant dimension prevents learning anything about the relevant dimension, then reversing the reinforcement contingencies to the stimuli on the relevant dimension during the presolution phase should not impair the performance of animals experiencing the reversal. Consider, for example, a rat that must eventually select the white cue, regardless of its position, in order to solve the problem. At first the rat attends to the irrelevant dimension of position, and black rather than white is associated with reinforcement. Noncontinuity theory predicts that as long as the rat attends to position, it will learn nothing about which cue on the brightness dimension is associated with reward. Consequently, no performance deficit will be found if the reinforcement contingencies for the cues on the relevant dimension are reversed before the rat attends to this dimension. This assumption expresses the strong form of the noncontinuity theory. In contrast, continuity theory would predict a performance deficit after a reversal in cue value, since all the features of each stimulus complex are assumed to acquire excitatory or inhibitory tendencies.

The assumption that attending to one component of the stimulus prevents learning about its other properties was put to an early experimental test by McCulloch and Pratt (1934). They trained five groups of rats to solve a weight-lifting discrimination. S+ was a 75-gram weight, and S− was a 25-gram weight; the final solution of the problem for all of the groups was to choose the heavier of the two weights. The rats in four of the groups were pretrained with the stimulus–reward relation arranged in the *reverse* of that in the final problem; that is, the lighter weight was S+. The difference among these groups was in the amount of prior training on the reverse discrimination—that is, the number of trials during which the lighter weight signaled reward. The fifth group served as a control, with the 75-gram weight reinforced throughout training. McCulloch and Pratt found that errors made on the final problem were proportional to the amount of reversal pretraining. The data provided clear evidence against the strong form of noncontinuity theory.

Krechevsky (1937) criticized McCulloch and Pratt's results by pointing out that the rats may have been attending to more than one dimension during the presolution period; consequently, they could have learned something about the relevant cue while responding solely to position. Later, Krechevsky (1938) reported results consistent with the noncontinuity position. Rats trained on a reversal of a visual discrimination after varying amounts of pretraining (zero, 20, or 40 trials) did not show a performance decrement following cue reversal. In reply to Krechevsky's results, Spence (1940) noted that the stimuli Krechevsky used may have been so located that they were not perceived by the rats unless their receptors were oriented in certain ways. This point emphasizes that only those features of the stimulus complex that impinge on receptors enter into an association with the response. This notion provided behaviorists with a conceptual basis for distinguishing between nominal and functional stimuli. Accordingly, *orienting responses served as an alternative to a central-processing attentional mechanism*. Since orienting responses were peripheral, they had the advantage of permitting direct measurement. Moreover, orienting reactions were apparently subject to the same laws governing other overt instrumental responses.

A more telling criticism of Krechevsky's experiment has been made on logical grounds (Mackintosh, 1965). Noncontinuity theory predicts no performance difference between reversed and nonreversed animals. Thus, the experiments must demonstrate the absence of learning. Even in conditions in which no differences were found, an insensitive measure of learning might have been used or insufficient numbers of subjects might have been run. In brief, evidence for noncontinuity theory using the presolution design can prove only the *null hypothesis*—that is, show no difference between the experimental and control conditions. In general, most experimenters have found that subjects pretrained with stimulus values reversed during the presolution phase learn more slowly than control subjects (for example, Ehrenfreund, 1948; McCulloch & Pratt, 1934; Spence, 1945). The results provide clear evidence against the noncontinuity position—more specifically, against the assumption that attention to one component of a stimulus complex prevents learning about the other components.

Lashley and Wade (1946) have elaborated on another important aspect of noncontinuity theory. They proposed that a stimulus acquires control over behavior only when *it is contrasted with another stimulus on the same dimension*. This hypothesis has important implications for stimulus generalization; it implies that gradients of generalization are obtained only to the extent that the organism has failed to discriminate between two stimuli on the same continuum. Lashley and Wade's *failure-to-discriminate hypothesis* stands in contrast to Pavlov's and Hull's treatment of generalization. For Pavlov and Hull, the empirical phenomenon of stimulus generalization resulted because the conditioning of excitation to the training stimulus ensured that other stimuli physically similar to the training stimulus would acquire excitatory properties. Elicitation of responses by stimuli other than the stimulus associated with reward reflected a process of the generalization of excitation along the stimulus continuum. On the other hand, Lashley and Wade proposed that generalization of responding from training to test stimuli occurs because the animal has failed to discriminate between them. Attention to the particular dimension of the stimulus that is varied by the experimenter in the generalization test is thought to be necessary in order to obtain a progressive decline in responding as the physical distance between test and training stimuli increases—that is, in order to produce a sloping gradient of generalization. The physical dimension of the stimulus varied in the generalization test does not exist for the animal until discrimination training has occurred. Attention to the relevant dimension will not occur until the animal has been given training involving more than one point on the stimulus continuum. Unless the animal attends to this feature of the stimulus, generalization will be complete, because the animal will be unable to associate the relevant dimension of the stimulus with the response.

If the training stimulus is not classified as a point on a physical dimension, then variation along this dimension will not be detected by the animal unless something is done to direct its attention to it. One way to test the failure-to-discriminate hypothesis is to determine whether training on a single stimulus affects the learning of a subsequent discrimination along the same physical continuum. Since presentation of a single stimulus does not permit a comparison of points along the stimulus continuum, the failure-to-discriminate hypothesis predicts no effect on the learning of a subsequent discrimination. The Lashley/Wade position can be clarified by considering a young child whose sole acquaintance with men is his father. The failure-to-discriminate hypothesis implies that if the child is now introduced to another man, generalization will be complete and the child will respond with "Daddy." A further prediction is that exposure to the father alone will not facilitate the child's learning to tell the difference between his father and his uncle.

A single-stimulus training paradigm was designed to test the prediction that training on only one point on a stimulus continuum will not facilitate discrimination between that stimulus and another on the same dimension. The design entails training an animal to a single stimulus, Cue A. Later the subject is required to discriminate between Cue A and another cue (B) from the same dimension. Since noncontinuity theory predicts that prior experience with A alone does not permit any learning about that dimension, no difference in learning the test discrimination between A and B should occur if A is positive (nonreversal) or if A is negative (reversal). Lashley and Wade reported a number of experiments using rats, monkeys, and chimpanzees that confirm this prediction. They found no difference between the reversal and nonreversal conditions. If uncontradicted, their results would provide strong evidence for noncontinuity theory. Later experiments, however, had just the opposite results (Grandine & Harlow, 1948; Grice, 1948a; Warren & Brookshire, 1959). For example, with a different apparatus, and a *noncorrection* procedure rather than the correction procedure used by Lashley and Wade, Grice found that rats learned the nonreversal condition more rapidly.

The strongest evidence against the failure-to-discriminate hypothesis was reported by Pavlov in 1927 (compare Riley, 1968, p. 28). With classical conditioning of the salivary response, Pavlov noted that when a new stimulus was first presented during the generalization test, no CR was elicited. Repeated nonreinforced presentations of the test CS eventually resulted in salivation. Pavlov pointed out that the initial failure to respond was similar to external inhibition. The term *external inhibition* refers to the finding that responding is disrupted when a novel stimulus is introduced together with the CS during acquisition. In a parallel fashion, if a similar but novel test stimulus disrupts responding on the first trial of the generalization test, it is only because the dog has discriminated between the test and training stimuli.

Although much of the evidence contradicts the failure-to-discriminate hypothesis, Prokasy and Hall (1963) emphasize that the stimulus manipulated by the experimenter during the generalization test may not be the stimulus actually associated with reward. At issue here is the extent to which the functional stimulus coincides with the stimulus manipulated by the experimenter. If contextual cues present during training enter into an association with responding, variation in the values of the stimulus associated with reinforcement may not alter the context that much. In this sense, generalization would represent a failure to discriminate between the training and testing situations. Mackintosh (1974) has suggested that the distinction between nominal and functional stimuli may reconcile the apparent differences between Pavlov's spread-of-excitation and Lashley and Wade's failure-to-discriminate theories. If animals respond to stimuli in a generalization test to the extent that the stimuli contain elements that overlap with those controlling responding in the test situation, then generalization occurs to test stimuli because of elements common to the training and testing situation. However, generalization is incomplete because the overlap is less than perfect (Mackintosh, 1974, p. 498).

In any event, if discriminations are formed by the interaction of excitatory and inhibitory gradients of generalization, then the properties of the gradient and the variables affecting them must be specified before definitive tests of the theory can be made. Although this venture is far from complete, sufficient evidence exists to provide at least some tentative answers about the processes underlying discrimination. Now let us turn to the process of generalization.

Stimulus Generalization

In this section we turn our attention to the process of stimulus generalization. We will consider four major topics: methodological issues, factors affecting the slope of generalization gradients, inhibition and gradients of generalization, and the interaction of excitatory and inhibitory gradients.

Methodological Problems of Stimulus Generalization

Methodological issues are important in the study of generalization. In this section we shall examine four specific methodological issues: the use of absolute and relative gradients, the effects of averaging generalization gradients, the use of between and within-subject designs, and the question of a general law of generalization.

Absolute and Relative Gradients. Gradients of generalization are defined by a progressive decline in responding as the similarity between training and test stimuli decreases.[1] Similarity is usually defined in terms of the physical properties of the stimulus; variations in wavelength, size, intensity, or frequency of stimuli are commonly used. Another way in which the difference (or similarity) between stimuli can be expressed is in psychophysical units, or *just-noticeable differences (jnds).* A jnd expresses the number of "psychological steps" between stimuli. Stimuli only 10 jnds apart are perceived as more similar than stimuli separated by, say, 25 jnds.

Just as different physical and psychological scales can be used to measure stimulus similarity, there are different scales for expressing the differential strength of responding to stimuli in the generalization test. One approach is simply to plot the total number of responses given to the training and test stimuli; a gradient so obtained is called an *absolute gradient.* Absolute gradients can be transformed into *relative gradients* by expressing responding to the test stimulus as a proportion of responses to the training stimulus or as a proportion of the total number of responses to all stimuli presented during the generalization test.

Relative gradients possess the advantage of permitting comparisons among subjects exhibiting wide variations in responding. Consider, for example, four pigeons in a generalization experiment. Figure 6–1 illustrates the hypothetical absolute and relative gradients of

[1] The slope of the generalization gradient reflects the extent to which the training stimulus controls responding. A flat gradient implies an absence of stimulus control or, conversely, almost complete generalization. A steep gradient, on the other hand, implies that the training stimulus has exercised considerable control over responding—that is, almost no generalization to similar stimuli.

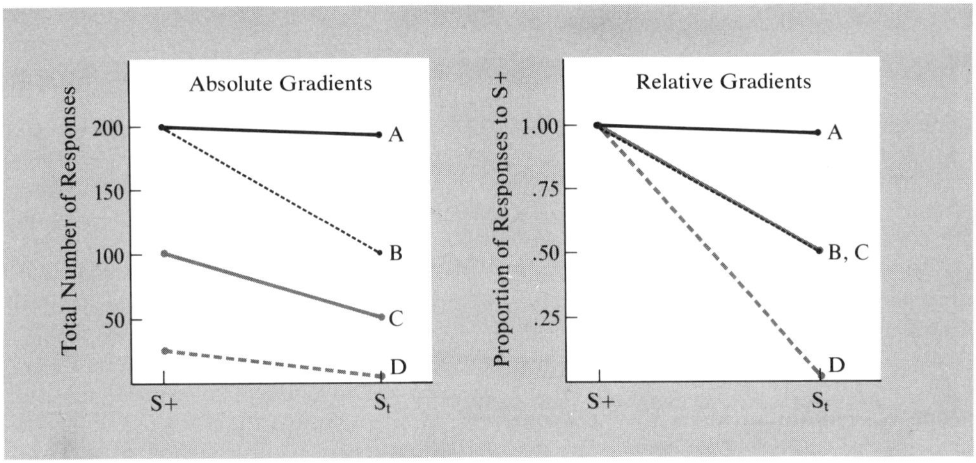

Figure 6–1. Hypothetical absolute and relative gradients of generalization for four pigeons.

generalization of the four birds. One pigeon (A) emitted 200 responses to the training stimulus (S+) and nearly an identical number (195) to the test stimulus (S_t). A second pigeon (B), made 200 responses to S+ but only 100 responses to S_t. Bird C made only 100 responses to the original stimulus and 50 responses to S_t during the generalization test. In absolute terms Pigeon B made twice as many responses to S_t as Bird C.

Further inspection of the absolute gradients shows that the gradients for A and D are shallow and that the gradients generated by B and C are steeper. On the basis of these gradients, one might conclude that A and D show more generalization than B and C. However, examination of the relative gradients produces a much different interpretation. The slopes of the gradients for B and C are now equal, and though A's relative gradient appears similar to its absolute gradient, D exhibits the steepest gradient of generalization. Since Bird D responded at a low rate, its absolute gradient may have been shallow because of a *floor effect*. In other words, responding to S_t cannot fall below zero. Since the relative gradients correct for both the wide differences in responding and the apparent floor effect observed with D, it might be concluded that relative rather than absolute gradients should be used. Unfortunately, the matter is not that simple. Consider the absolute and relative gradients of Bird A. The absolute gradient of this subject may have been artificially flattened because of its high rate of responding. Transforming these data to a relative scale ignores the possibility that the flat gradient may have resulted from a *ceiling effect;* that is, the response measure may not have permitted a difference to emerge between S+ and S_t. The training stimulus may have more response strength than the test stimulus, but the response measure cannot reflect this difference because the subject may be responding maximally. Ceiling effects may also occur because limited exposure to S+ and S_t during the test phase may restrict the number of responses to S+.

Obviously, the question of which transformation to use depends on the response measure and the presence of floor or ceiling effects. However, the most important consideration in expressing the data in absolute or relative terms depends on the scale that renders the data consistent with the results of other generalization experiments and on whether the gradients remain unchanged when a variable that presumably does not affect them is manipulated. When in doubt, some researchers report both absolute and relative gradients.

Averaging Effects on Generalization Gradients. In many instances, gradients of generalization are based on the mean value for all subjects. A single gradient based on an average of the four pigeons presented in Figure 6–1 would appear quite different from the individual gradients. Accordingly, a conclusion drawn from the averaged gradient may be different from an interpretation gleaned from individual gradients.

A question raised early about averaged generalization gradients is whether the smooth, orderly decline in responding reflects a decrease in excitation as the physical or psychological distance between training and test stimuli increases or whether the smooth decline is simply an artifact of the averaging procedure. In reviewing Hovland's (1937a, 1937b) now-classic experiments on generalization along different auditory continua, Razran (1949) pointed out that not one of Hovland's subjects revealed a consistent gradient of generalization. Although the averaged gradient showed a progressive decline in responding as the similarity among training and test stimuli decreased, individual gradients were highly irregular. Razran concluded on the basis of the individual-subject data that the grouped data were an artifact of averaging. We now know, however, that the irregular gradients for individual subjects were due to the experimental procedure that Hovland employed. To balance for the effects of extinction among test stimuli, Hovland presented them in a different order for each subject. This procedure resulted in larger CRs' being recorded to a *remote stimulus*—that is, one dissimilar to the CS—*if* it was presented earlier in the test phase. Since the test phase required presentations of different stimuli without reinforcement, early presentations of remote (dissimilar) stimuli should show less extinction than more similar test stimuli presented later in the generalization test. Thus, the irregular gradients observed for individual subjects are seen as artifacts of the experimental procedure.

Although Razran's objections to averaged data were confined to generalization gradients, Sidman (1952) and Hayes (1953) have raised a more general issue that is not so easily handled. This issue concerns the cogency of any inference about individuals based on group data. These two researchers have demonstrated mathematically that the forms of individual curves are not uniquely specified by the mean curve. Conclusions about individual functions made from group data are permissible only to the extent that the averaged data are a faithful representation of the individual curves. And it is indeed possible that a group-average curve can fail to represent the performance of individual subjects (compare Migler, 1964). For this reason, some researchers report both individual and group curves.

Between-Subject and Within-Subject Designs. We have encountered between-subject and within-subject designs in the previous chapters. Recall that different values of a variable are applied to different groups of subjects in between-subject designs, whereas in within-subject designs every subject receives each value of the variable. In the context of a generalization experiment, a between-subject design entails testing each group with different values of the test stimulus (compare Grice & Saltz, 1950; Wickens, Schroder, & Snide, 1954). The Hovland experiments (1937a, 1937b), on the other hand, used the within-subject design, since each subject was tested with each value of the test stimuli. Since each subject is exposed to all of the test stimuli with this design, it has the advantage of being less time consuming because it uses fewer subjects than the between-subject design. A further advantage of the within-subject design is that it holds systematic differences among individual subjects constant, thereby increasing the likelihood of finding reliable differences among test stimuli.

However, within-subject designs are particularly susceptible to the effects of context. Contextual effects are due to the sequence or order of presentation of the variable—in the case of generalization experiments, to the sequencing and ordering of test stimuli. An *order effect* occurs when performance varies from one trial to another even when the same test stimulus is used on both trials. In a *sequence effect,* responding to a test stimulus is affected by the test stimuli that have preceded it. Since most generalization tests employ extinction trials during the test series, both order and sequence effects are likely to occur. Although various statistical procedures, such as counterbalancing and randomization, can be used to remove or minimize these effects, there is evidence indicating that this sort of testing, especially when many test stimuli are employed, may affect the slope of the generalization gradient.

An experiment bearing on this issue was conducted by Guttman and Kalish (1956). They investigated the relationship between the discriminability of the wavelength continuum and the generalization process.[2] Previous work had indicated that the discriminability function of hue in the pigeon corresponds closely to that found for human subjects (W. F. Hamilton & Coleman, 1933). Wavelength-discriminability functions for both humans and pigeons appear in Figure 6–2. The forms of the functions indicate more sensitivity to change in wavelength in some regions of the color spectrum than in others. For example, humans and pigeons can detect changes in wavelength more readily in the yellow region of the spectrum (570 nanometers) than in the green range (530 nanometers). Guttman and Kalish reasoned that if the subject generalizes to the extent that it cannot discriminate, then the slope of the gradient should reflect the characteristics of the hue-discriminability function. Thus, a generalization gradient in the yellow range should be steeper than a gradient generated by training to a green CS. To test this prediction, they trained four groups of pigeons to a CS of 530, 550, 580, or 600 nanometers (wavelengths that correspond roughly for human observers to green, yellow/green, yellow/orange, and orange). During generalization testing the groups were presented with the training stimulus appropriate to each and with ten test stimuli that varied in 10-nanometer increments above and below the

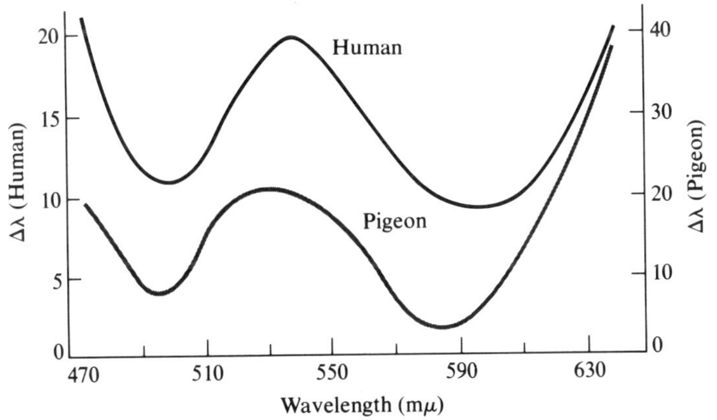

Figure 6–2. Wavelength-discriminability functions in humans and pigeons. (From "Discriminability and Stimulus Generalization," by N. Guttman and H. I. Kalish, *Journal of Experimental Psychology,* 1956, *51,* 79–88. Copyright 1956 by the American Psychological Association. Reprinted by permission.)

[2] Wavelength and tonal frequency are physical dimensions that are often used in generalization experiments. Wavelength is measured in terms of nanometers (nm); 1 nanometer is 1 billionth of a meter (10^{-9} meters). Because this convention was adopted only recently, older books and articles may specify wavelength in millimicrons (mμ) or in angstroms (Å). One nanometer equals 1 millimicron or 10 angstroms. Auditory frequency is measured in cycles per second. One cycle per second is called 1 hertz (hz). The unit is named after the German physicist Heinrich R. Hertz (1857–1894).

training stimulus. The results appear in Figure 6–3, in which the mean total number of responses for each test stimulus is plotted against wavelength. The most interesting feature of the gradients is that their slopes are relatively uniform throughout the color spectrum. There is no correspondence between the discriminability function of hue and the slope of the gradients.

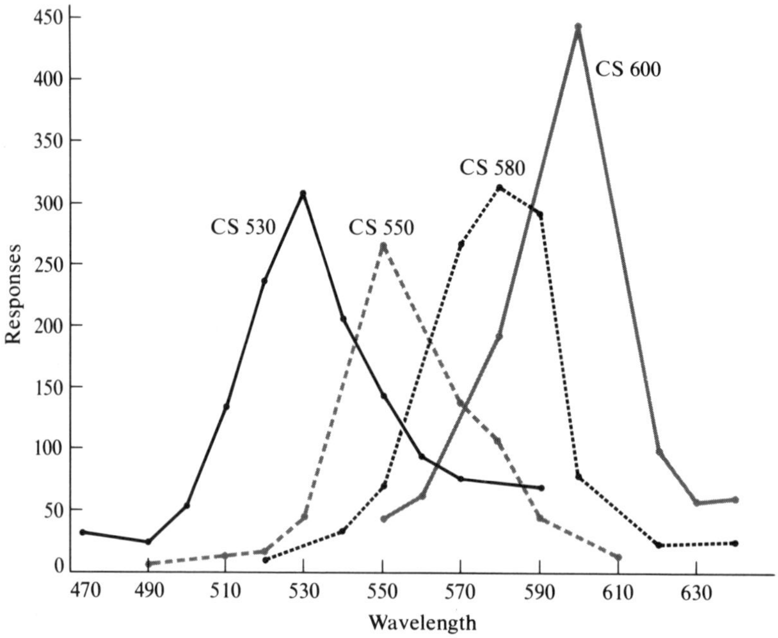

Figure 6–3. Absolute stimulus-generalization gradients for four groups of pigeons. (From "Discriminability and Stimulus Generalization," by N. Guttman and H. I. Kalish, *Journal of Experimental Psychology,* 1956, *51,* 79–88. Copyright 1956 by the American Psychological Association. Reprinted by permission.)

At first glance the data provide evidence against the failure-to-discriminate hypothesis; that is, if generalization gradients reflect a failure to discriminate between training and test stimuli, the slope of the gradients in the yellow region of the spectrum, for example, should be steeper than the gradients in the green range. However, the invariance of the slopes may reflect the use of the multiple-stimulus testing procedure. For example, Marsh (1967) trained pigeons in groups with two, three, or four stimuli. When different groups of birds were trained with an S+ of 520 or 590 nanometers and then tested to a single test stimulus displaced 10 nanometers from S+, a close correspondence between the slope of the gradient and discriminability was found. Figure 6–4 shows that the gradient between 590 and 580 nanometers was reliably steeper than the gradient between 520 and 530 nanometers. However, when two or three test stimuli were used in the generalization test, the difference between the slopes of the gradients disappeared. Presumably, the more remote test stimuli produced more inhibition, which generalized to test stimuli more similar to S+ during the test phase, thereby reducing the difference in excitation between test stimuli displaced only 10 nanometers from the two training stimuli.

A General Law of Generalization? Continuity theorists have used generalization to account for complex discrimination learning. The notion that generalization is somehow basic to discrimination has led to a considerable amount of research to discover the funda-

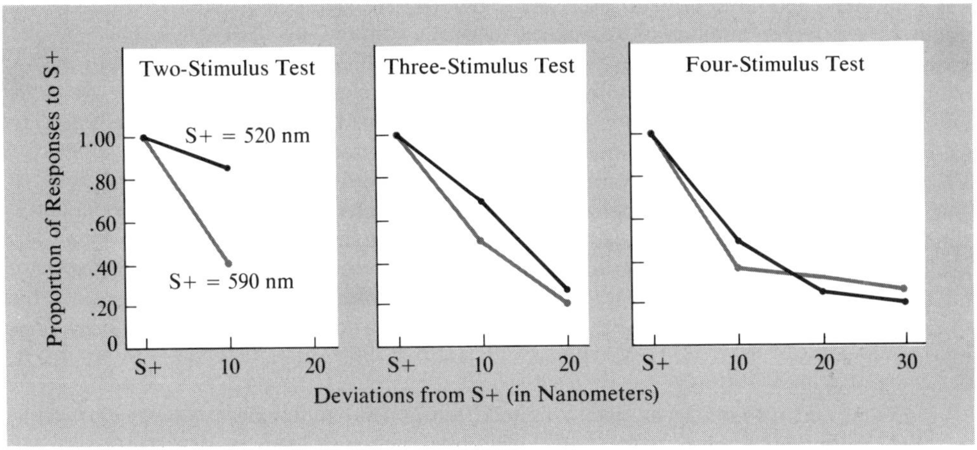

Figure 6-4. The relationship between the slope of a generalization gradient and the discriminability of training and test stimuli. The first panel shows that pigeons had a flatter gradient to a test stimulus displaced 10 nanometers from a training stimulus of low discriminability (520 nanometers) than did pigeons trained to a wavelength of 590 nanometers (a region of good discriminability). The other two panels show that the addition of further test stimuli abolished differences in the slope of the gradients. (From "Inverse Relationship between Discriminability and Stimulus Generalization as a Function of Number of Test Stimuli," by G. D. Marsh, *Journal of Comparative and Physiological Psychology,* 1967, *64,* 284–289. Copyright 1967 by the American Psychological Association. Reprinted by permission.)

mental law of generalization. If an exact *quantitative* law of generalization could be found, the shape of the gradient could be specified. Specifying the slope of the generalization gradient would then permit predictions about the discrimination process.

Attempts to discover this quantitative law of generalization have been unsuccessful. This failure is not surprising if one considers the methodological problems in measuring generalization. As we have seen, the various response measures used to index learning reflect only indirectly what is learned. The problem is complicated further by ceiling or floor effects and by controversy over the appropriateness of absolute or relative scales of measurement. Indeed, even the number of test stimuli employed in the generalization test may affect the slope of generalization gradients. In addition to these methodological issues, the slope of a generalization gradient is affected by a number of different variables. It is to these factors that we now turn.

Variables Affecting the Slope of Gradients

In this section we shall describe three principal factors that influence the slope of generalization gradients. These factors are the schedule of reinforcement under which the subject is trained, the motivational level of the subject, and the amount of practice.

Schedule of Reinforcement. In early generalization experiments the CS was reinforced continuously during training. This procedure has the disadvantage of limiting responding to test stimuli during the generalization test. Consequently, to ensure greater resistance to extinction for test stimuli during the generalization test, the training stimulus was reinforced intermittently in later investigations. Although intermittent reinforcement resulted in a larger number of responses made to stimuli during the test phase of the generalization experiment, it soon became apparent that different values of the same schedule, or different schedules of reinforcement, affect the slope of generalization gradients.

Hearst, Koresko, and Poppen (1964) trained pigeons to peck a key on which a vertical line was projected during training. The stimulus was reinforced for different groups on VI schedules of reinforcement averaging .5, 1, 2, 3, and 4 minutes between food reward. During generalization testing, lines differing in orientation to the vertical were used as test stimuli, and generalization gradients were obtained for each of the VI schedules. The results showed that as the average interval between reinforcements increased, the slopes of the gradients became progressively flattened. In other words, more generalization occurred to test stimuli more remote from the training stimulus when the average interval between reinforcements was increased. A. Haber and Kalish (1963) have reported similar results using wavelengths as stimuli.

Hearst and his colleagues also examined the generalization performance of pigeons on DRL (differential reinforcement of low rates) schedules. (For a discussion of DRL schedule of reinforcement, see Chapter 3.) The pigeons received training on DRL 6-second or 10-second schedules and were then tested for generalization. Although the response rates generated under DRL are low, the short time intervals used in this study resulted in frequent reinforcement. However, the gradients produced under DRL schedules were flatter than the gradients obtained under VI schedule even when the schedules were equated to yield the same frequency of reward. Hearst and his associates suggest that the shallow gradients found after DRL training may have resulted from DRL responding's being controlled by proprioceptive as well as external cues; that is, selection of the next response on DRL schedules may require the use of proprioceptive stimulation arising from the preceding response. In short, the functional stimulus controlling behavior under DRL schedules is presumably different from the effective stimulus guiding performance with VI schedules. If this is the case, changing the external stimulus would result in a smaller response decrement for behavior controlled by DRL contingencies.

D.R. Thomas and Switalski (1966) have advanced a similar argument to account for the relatively shallow absolute and relative gradients found with VR schedules. They trained pairs of pigeons to peck a key in the presence of a 550-nanometer light. One member of the pair received a food reward on a VR 40-second schedule; the second bird got a reward on the basis of a time interval determined by the first bird's behavior. In effect, the second bird was rewarded on a VI schedule under circumstances in which the number of reinforcements for it was identical to that for the first bird. After the pair had achieved stable levels of responding, a standard generalization test was introduced by presenting different wavelengths during extinction. The slopes of the VR gradients were less steep than the slopes of the VI gradients. Thomas and Switalski suggest that the VR gradients were flatter because the proprioceptive stimuli arising from short interresponse times (rapid responding) served as a discriminative cue for additional responding.

Although it is unlikely that animals would rely on proprioceptive cues to mediate responding on schedules in which timing is not essential for reinforcement to the extent suggested by Thomas and Switalski, their data emphasize the importance of schedule contingencies in the stimulus control of behavior. The degree of control exercised by the stimulus manipulated by the experimenter is influenced by the contingencies of reinforcement. The schedule of reinforcement determines the extent to which incidental contextual stimuli control responding. The behavioral effects produced by different reward contingencies further emphasize the distinction between nominal and functional stimuli. The data suggest that prediction of behavior will be possible only when the properties of functional stimuli are clarified.

Motivational Effects. Interest in how drive level affects the slope of generalization gradients stemmed largely from efforts to test the Hullian hypothesis that drive and habit combine multiplicatively to determine performance. Hull's (1943) hypothesis, applied to generalization, predicts higher and steeper absolute gradients with increases in drive level, but no change in the slope of relative gradients. Common sense might suggest that an individual under high drive would make more responses to stimuli similar to those on which the individual was originally trained. Assuming discrimination and generalization to be reciprocal processes, Hull's hypothesis implies that discrimination learning improves with increasing motivation.

Newman and Grice (1965), using rats in a size-generalization task, have reported results consistent with Hull's hypothesis. They found higher absolute responding and steeper gradients of generalization with rats under the higher drive condition. Using pigeons, Kalish and Haber (1965) also found steeper absolute gradients with conditions of high deprivation. They trained different groups of pigeons under varying degrees of motivation (70%, 80%, and 90% of their normal body weight) to peck a 550-nanometer key light on a VI 1-minute reinforcement schedule. After responding had stabilized, generalization tests were instituted by presenting test stimuli differing from the standard stimulus in 10-nanometer steps. Figure 6–5 summarizes the principal findings of their experiment; it shows that the slope of the gradient became steeper the higher the level of deprivation.

Unfortunately, the evidence on motivational influences is far from conclusive. Experimenters comparing the performances of normal and clinical populations on generalization tasks have found shallower generalization gradients among clinical populations (for example, Broen, Stroms, & Goldberg, 1963). These data are usually explained by assuming that psychiatric patients experience more anxiety than normals, partly because of ineffectual coping behavior; anxiety is thought to have motivational properties. If the flatter gradients imply poorer discrimination, these findings are contrary to the implications of Hull's hypothesis. In short, it appears that high drive impairs rather than facilitates discrimination learning.

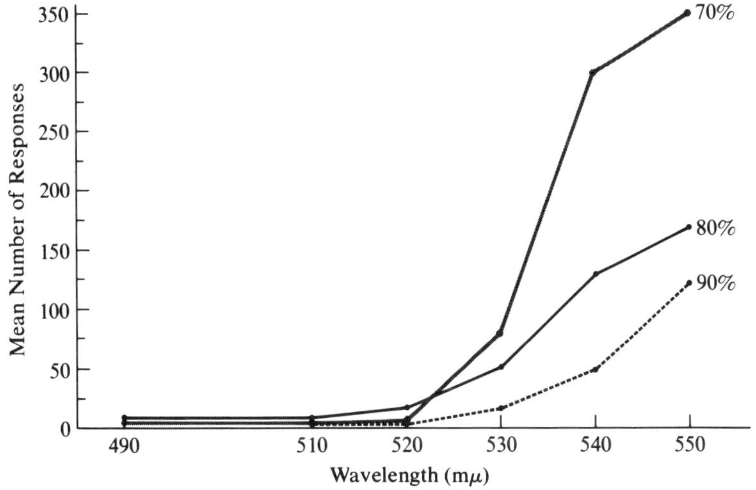

Figure 6–5. Generalization gradients obtained with different deprivation levels following training to a 550-nanometer wavelength. (From "The Prediction of Discrimination from Generalization Following Variations in Deprivation Level," by H. I. Kalish and A. Haber, *Journal of Comparative and Physiological Psychology,* 1965, *60,* 125–128. Copyright 1965 by the American Psychological Association. Reprinted by permission.)

One possible explanation of these discrepant findings concerning the effects of motivation on stimulus generalization relates to the difficulty in discriminating between training and test stimuli. To test this idea, Kalish and Haber trained six additional groups of pigeons on a go/no go discrimination under the three conditions of deprivation mentioned earlier. One-half of the birds were trained to 550-nanometer (S+) and 540-nanometer (S−) key lights. The stimuli for the other groups were 540 nanometers (S+) and 530 nanometers (S−). A comparison of the slopes between 550 and 540 nanometers and 540 and 530 nanometers revealed that the slopes were much steeper in the 540/530-nanometer region for the 70% and 80% group (see Figure 6–5). If slope differences between these points on the stimulus continuum reflect differences in discriminability, learning to discriminate between the 540/530 key lights should be more rapid than between the 550/540 condition. Moreover, if higher levels of motivation facilitate the learning of a discrimination, the 70%-body-weight group should learn the discrimination more rapidly than the 80% and 90% groups. Consistent with this prediction, the pigeons with the highest level of drive acquired the 540/530 discrimination faster than the pigeons with lower motivational levels. However, the birds with the highest drive level (70%-body-weight condition) were the slowest in learning the 550/540-nanometer discrimination. In short, *high drive may facilitate the learning of easy discriminations but impair the acquisition of difficult discriminations.*

This interaction between motivation and problem difficulty is known as the *Yerkes / Dodson law.* The law states that the more difficult the discrimination, the lower the level of motivation required for solution of the problem. The law has been supported in many experiments that used aversive stimuli (for example, Broadhurst, 1957; Dodson, 1915; Hammes, 1956), but the evidence is less conclusive in the case of deprivation drives. In summary, the notion that high drive facilitates learning easy but not difficult discriminations helps to resolve some of the conflicting findings.

Practice Effects. If there is an inverse relation between generalization and discrimination, the slope of the generalization gradient should indicate the ease of learning a discrimination. A flat gradient implies that distinguishing between stimuli would be difficult. A steep gradient, on the other hand, suggests more rapid learning to discriminate between stimuli. In a review of the Russian classical-conditioning literature on stimulus generalization, Razran (1949) concluded that increased training to S+ results in a steeper gradient of generalization. Hearst and Koresko (1968) provided additional support for this conclusion in a free-responding situation. They trained pigeons to key peck a vertical line and then gave independent groups of subjects 2, 4, 7, or 14 practice sessions with the line on VI reinforcement. The generalization test consisted of angular displacement of the line for the different groups. The slope of both absolute and relative gradients increased with increasing practice.

On the other hand, experimenters using discrete-trial procedures in an alley runway have found that extended practice produces either no change or a flattening in the slope of the gradient (Margolius, 1955; McCain & Garrett, 1964). In an earlier chapter we saw that the external environment is relatively uniform in the discrete-trial situation and that behavior in this situation is probably mediated by proprioceptive stimuli. If anything, extended training probably increases the extent to which proprioceptive cues control responding. As a result, changes in exteroceptive stimulation in discrete-trial situations probably exercise limited control over responding following prolonged training.

In any event, how practice affects the slope of the gradient, and by implication the ease of learning a discrimination, may depend on the extent to which differential reinforcement is present. In the classical-conditioning experiments reviewed by Razran (1949), background stimulation is always present with the training stimulus. The CS together with the incidental stimulation predict reinforcement, but the background stimuli without the CS are always followed by periods of nonreinforcement. Conceivably, the slope of the gradient depends not only on the amount of practice but on whether the CS is absent during nonreinforcement. H. M. Jenkins and Harrison (1960) have reported an experiment germane to this issue. They trained two groups of pigeons to peck a key in the presence of a 1000-hertz tone on a VI schedule of reinforcement. For one group the tone was present throughout each session. The other group's experience with the tone was limited to periods during which reinforcement might occur. The pigeons in the nondifferential condition—that is, tone always present—got from ten to 40 practice sessions. The pigeons in the differential condition were trained until differential responding was established between the tone and nontone periods. During the test phase tonal stimuli ranging from 250 to 4000 hertz were presented to each bird. The generalization gradients obtained under the two conditions appear in Figure 6–6. The differential condition produced the gradients shown in the bottom panel. The steepness of the gradients indicates that the 1000-hertz tone acquired considerable control over responding. The top panel depicts the generalization gradients of the pigeons in the nondifferential condition and reveals uniformly flat gradients and an absence of stimulus control. Simply increasing exposure to S+ is apparently insufficient to produce a change in the slope of the gradient. The data suggest that a feature of a stimulus complex acquires control over responding only when its absence is correlated with nonreward (compare H. M. Jenkins & Sainsbury, 1969).

Inhibition and Gradients of Generalization

Thus far, we have examined the effects of several variables on the slopes of excitatory gradients—that is, on the extent to which stimuli similar to the training stimulus control responding. Equally important, however, was the role assigned inhibition by the continuity theorists in discrimination learning. Much of their theorizing was based on Pavlov's observations indicating that an active process was somehow producing behavioral effects opposite to excitation. Pavlov was aware that not responding to a stimulus was insufficient for inferring the presence of inhibition; a failure to respond could result simply from an absence of excitation. Although there was an obvious conceptual parallel between excitation and inhibition, that inhibition was difficult to detect retarded experimental investigations of its properties for many years. Psychologists were content either to assign hypothetical properties to it (for example, K. W. Spence, 1942) or to argue that it is a redundant concept indicating an absence of or a decrease in excitation rather than an opposing process that may produce a decrease in responding (Skinner, 1938).

To determine whether a stimulus is inhibitory, Pavlov developed a technique known as *summation*. The procedure involves presenting a possible inhibitory stimulus in combination with another stimulus that reliably produces a response. Inhibition is inferred when a response decrement occurs to the compound stimulus. The summation procedure assumes that excitation and inhibition are algebraically additive. Unfortunately, the logical basis of the technique is questionable. A response decrement observed after the introduction of another cue to the stimulus complex obviously alters that complex; consequently, the decrease in responding may reflect generalization decrement rather than inhibition. In short, the addition of any novel stimulus may produce a response decrement. Furthermore, if the assumption of algebraic summation of excitation and inhibition is correct, the summation technique provides only an indirect measure of inhibition; that is, inhibition must be inferred from a change in responding.

To circumvent this difficulty, H. M. Jenkins and Harrison (1962) developed a more direct method of measuring inhibition. They reasoned that if these processes are additive, then tests of excitatory and inhibitory control can be made by reinforcing and nonreinforcing responses to stimuli on dimensions independent of each other. The assumption is that

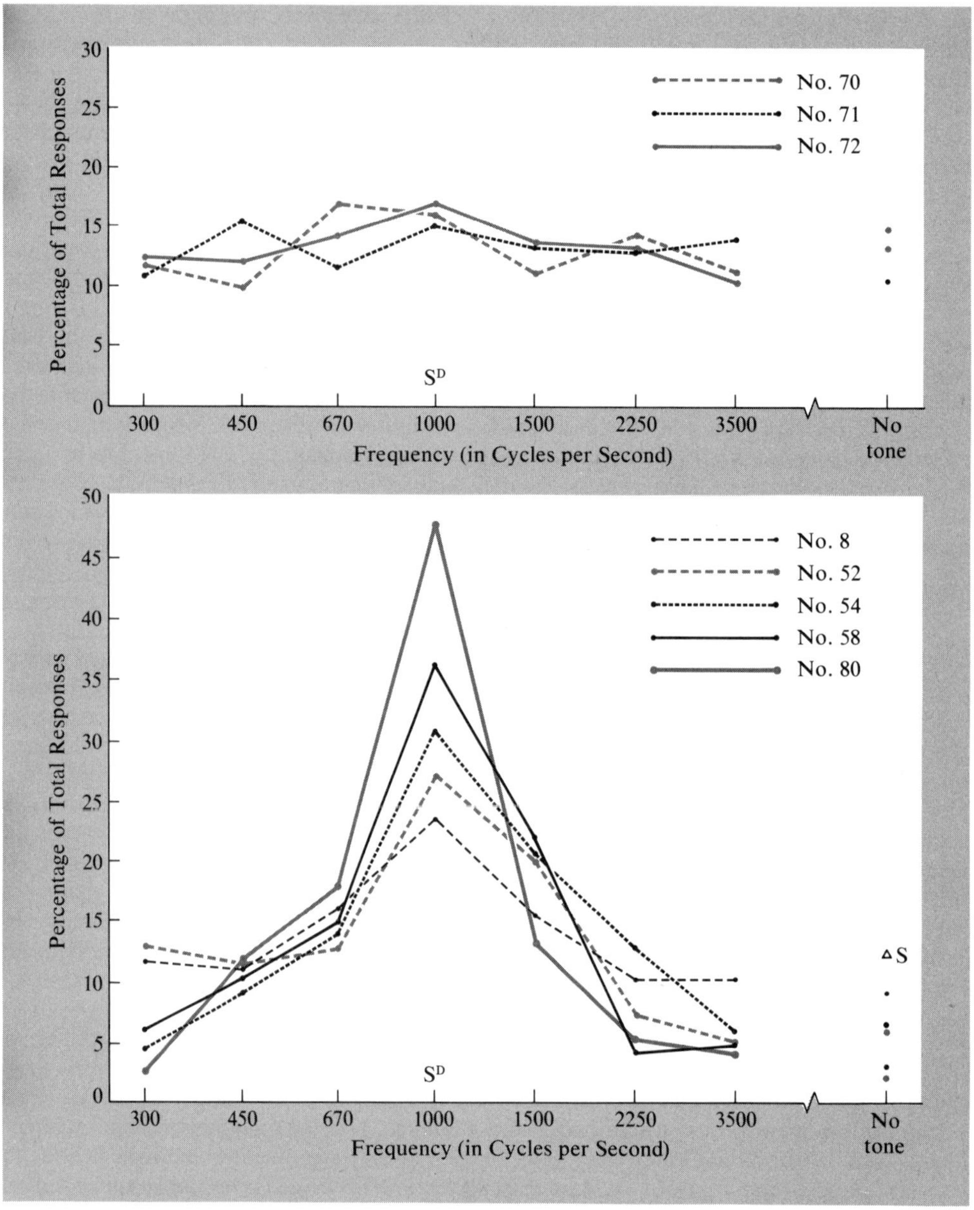

Figure 6–6. Generalization gradients following nondifferential (top panel) and differential (bottom panel) training with a 1000-hertz tone as S+. Individual gradients are based on the means of three generalization tests. (From "Effect of Discrimination Training on Auditory Generalization," by H. M. Jenkins and R. H. Harrison, *Journal of Experimental Psychology,* 1960, *59,* 246–253. Copyright 1960 by the American Psychological Association. Reprinted by permission.)

stimulus variation on one dimension will be equidistant from stimuli on the other dimension. During the generalization test, responding to a particular test stimulus will be determined by the distance between that stimulus and the training stimulus. And since the reinforced and nonreinforced training stimuli are located on independent dimensions, no interaction between the test stimulus on one dimension and the training stimulus on the other dimension will occur.

The logic of this approach is illustrated in an experiment by Jenkins and Harrison (1962, Experiment III), who trained pigeons to respond to white noise on VI reinforcement and to refrain from responding to a 1000-hertz tone. Since the white noise is correlated with reward, it should acquire excitatory properties. On the other hand, the 1000-hertz tone should become inhibitory because it predicts nonreward. After a discrimination was established between the noise and the tone, pure tones varying between 300 and 3500 hertz and white noise were introduced in the generalization test. Since white noise is a mixture of all pure tones on the frequency spectrum, it should be the same distance from each of the test stimuli as it is from the inhibitory training stimulus. Therefore, varying the distance between the 1000-hertz tone and the other tones should change the degree of inhibitory control. As the distance between the training and test stimuli on the frequency continuum is increased, there should be a decrease in nonresponding. In other words, responding should increase to test stimuli as the distance between them and the training stimuli increases. This should produce a *U*-shaped inhibitory gradient around the 1000-hertz tone.

Figure 6–7 presents the results of the Jenkins and Harrison experiment and a later experiment by Honig, Boneau, Burstein, and Pennypacker (1963). In the latter experiment the degree of angular tilt of a line was used to measure the extent of inhibitory control. The figure shows the *U*-shaped inhibitory generalization gradients that were found in each experiment.

The importance of these experiments is that they demonstrate that inhibition can be measured and that the concept may be useful in describing the formation of a discrimination. Note, however, the difference in emphasis in measuring inhibition by a generalization test versus the summation technique. The generalization test draws attention to the slope of the inhibitory gradient; the steeper the slope of the gradient around S−, the stronger the degree of inhibitory control. In contrast, the summation technique focuses on behavioral decrement as the crucial feature of inhibitory stimuli. In 1965 Jenkins argued that a stimulus is inhibitory to the extent that it controls not responding. In the context of the generalization test, Jenkins's argument implies that responding will increase the more remote the test stimulus from S−.

A difficulty with measuring inhibition by the generalization test is how to interpret a flat gradient around S−. One inference, drawn by analogy from a flat gradient around S+, which suggests an absence of excitation, is that a flat gradient around S− indicates a similar absence of inhibition (Terrace, 1966c). The other interpretation of a flat inhibitory gradient is that the response measure used in the generalization test is not sensitive enough to detect whether responding was any weaker at S− than to the test stimuli. Since responding cannot fall below zero, any differences between S− and the test stimuli can be obscured by a floor effect (Hearst, Besley, & Farthing, 1970).

To support the idea that a flat gradient implies an absence of inhibitory control, Terrace (1966b) used a unique *errorless-discrimination procedure* to train pigeons without errors to S− and then compared this group to one trained in the conventional manner (a group that responds to S− during training; responses to S− are recorded as errors). An inhibitory gradient similar to that reported by Jenkins and Harrison (1962) and Honig and his colleagues (1963) was found for the error group, but the errorless-discrimination procedure resulted in gradients along the inhibitory continuum.

Since the errorless-discrimination procedure figures prominently in other by-products of discrimination learning, the technique will be described briefly. Early in training, pigeons are exposed to S+ alone. As training progresses, S+ alternates with a brief exposure to a dark key. Since pigeons tend not to peck dark keys, no responses occur. Next, the duration of the dark key is gradually increased until finally the pigeons are exposed to it for

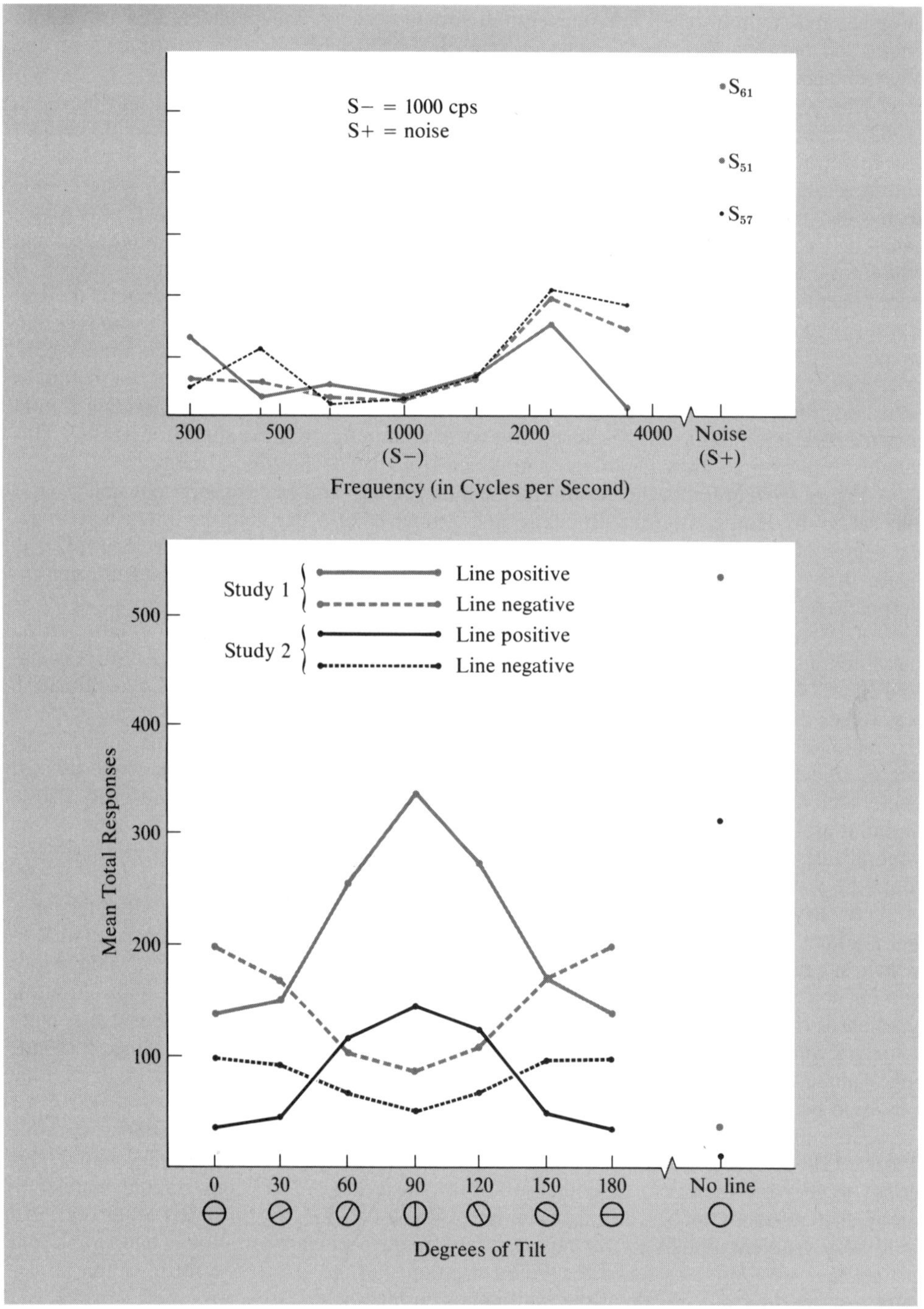

Figure 6–7. Relative and absolute inhibitory gradients of generalization. The upper graph shows the gradient obtained following interdimensional training on an auditory continuum. The lower graph shows the gradient obtained following interdimensional training on a line-orientation dimension. (The lower graph is from "Positive

as long a period of time as S+. Then exposure to the dark key is reduced to its original, brief level. At this point a wavelength different from S+ is projected through the translucent key and, over subsequent sessions, is gradually increased until it is as bright as S+. Finally, the duration of S− is progressively increased until by the end of training exposures to S+ and S− are equivalent. Birds trained under these conditions emit few responses to S−, and occasionally the discrimination is established without any errors to the negative stimulus. Hence, it is called errorless discrimination.

Karpicke and Hearst (1975) have reported data contradicting Terrace's interpretation. Their results support the argument that flat inhibitory gradients reflect a floor effect. The design of their experiment was similar to Terrace's 1966 experiment. They trained pigeons under error and errorless conditions, but to eliminate the possibility of a floor effect, they used a *resistance-to-reinforcement procedure* during generalization testing (compare Hearst et al., 1970, pp. 292–293). Instead of using the standard method of extinguishing responding to test stimuli during the generalization test, they provided VI reinforcement for responding at all values of the test stimuli. This procedure ensured that responding would occur along the entire S− dimension. If some values along the continuum are more inhibitory than others, they should be less susceptible to the effects of reinforcement.The possibility of floor effects should be precluded by the elevation of responding above zero.

Contrary to Terrace's (1966b) findings, Karpicke and Hearst found clear-cut evidence of inhibitory gradients for birds trained under either condition. Figure 6–8 presents relative and absolute gradients of generalization obtained under the error and errorless training procedures. As can be seen, both training procedures produced relatively steep inhibitory gradients along the S− dimension. The data emphasize the importance of heeding the methodological problems described in an earlier section of the chapter. Furthermore, since an inhibitory gradient was obtained with the errorless-discrimination procedure, the conclusion that responding to S− is necessary to produce inhibitory gradients is incorrect. As Karpicke and Hearst point out, the stimulus/reinforcer contingency is as important in operant as in classical conditioning. Apparently, experiencing a negative contingency between stimulus and reinforcer is sufficient for that stimulus to acquire inhibitory properties.

Interaction of Excitatory and Inhibitory Gradients

The previous section described several procedures for measuring inhibition. Although they differ in many ways, both the summation and generalization procedures require discrimination training between stimuli to ensure that the stimulus associated with nonreward acquires inhibitory properties. In experiments that obtained inhibitory gradients of generalization, discrimination training preceded generalization testing. To prevent the algebraic summation of excitation and inhibition, discrimination training was between stimuli from independent, or orthogonal, dimensions. For example, Jenkins and Harrison (1962) used a pure tone as S− and white noise as S+. Honig and his colleagues (1963) used a vertical line for S−; the absence of a line served as S+. This type of discrimination

---

and Negative Generalization Gradients Obtained under Equivalent Training Conditions," by W. K. Honig, C. A. Boneau, K. R. Burstein, and H. S. Pennypacker, *Journal of Comparative and Physiological Psychology,* 1963, *56,* 111–116. Copyright 1963 by the American Psychological Association. Reprinted by permission. The upper graph is from "Generalization Gradients of Inhibition Following Auditory Discrimination Learning," by H. M. Jenkins and R. H. Harrison, *Journal of Experimental Analysis of Behavior,* 1962, *5,* 435–441. Copyright 1962 by the Society for the Experimental Analysis of Behavior. Reprinted by permission.)

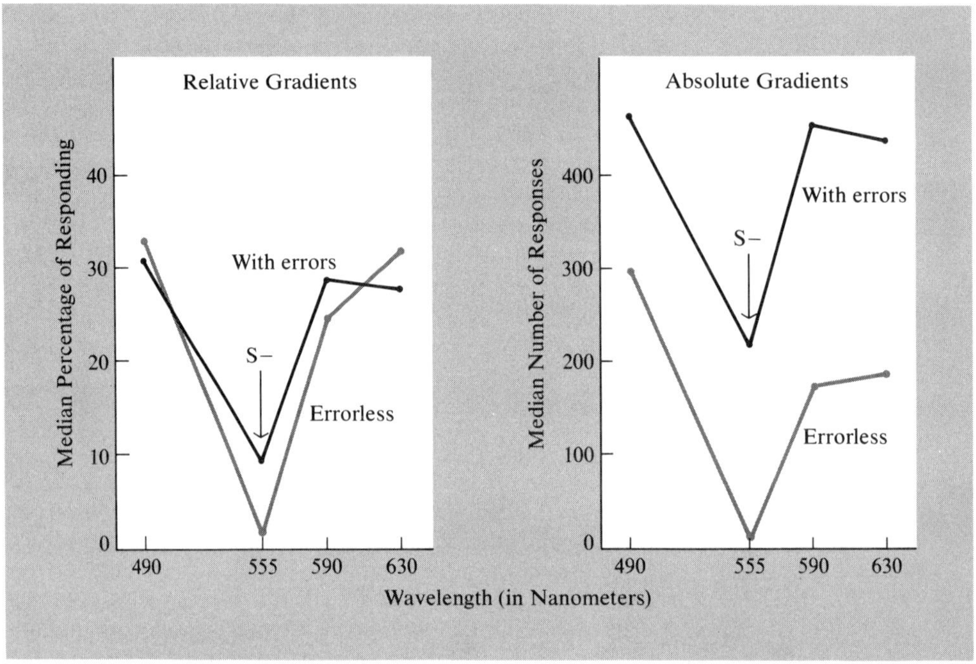

Figure 6–8. Relative and absolute inhibitory gradients of generalization obtained under error and errorless conditions following discrimination training with a white S+ and a 555-nanometer (green) S−. (From "Inhibitory Control and Errorless Discrimination Learning," by J. Karpicke and E. Hearst, *Journal of the Experimental Analysis of Behavior,* 1975, *23,*159–166. Reprinted by permission of the Society for the Experimental Analysis of Behavior.)

training is *interdimensional* because S+ and S− are stimuli that lie on different dimensions.

In this section we will examine the effects of discrimination training between stimuli on the same dimension. Generalization gradients obtained following *intradimensional*-discrimination training are called *postdiscrimination gradients.* The shape and slope of postdiscrimination gradients have important implications for theories of discrimination learning.

In K. W. Spence's (1936) theory of discrimination learning, the formation of a discrimination results from the algebraic summation of excitation and inhibition that occurs to different features of the stimulus complex. According to Spence, the organism approaches one feature of a stimulus rather than another because the net excitation (excitation minus inhibition) to that feature is greater than the net excitation to another feature. Spence's subsequent papers (1937, 1942) elaborated on this formulation. Briefly, in his later work he assumed that when a response to a stimulus is reinforced, a gradient of excitation will develop about that stimulus. Second, when a response to another stimulus on the same dimension is nonreinforced, a gradient of inhibition will develop. Finally, the gradients of excitation and inhibition sum algebraically, so that a tendency to respond to any stimulus along that dimension is obtained by subtracting the inhibitory gradient from the gradient of excitation.

A graphic representation of Spence's model appears in Figure 6–9. Note that the net excitation (the difference between excitation and inhibition, represented by the vertical

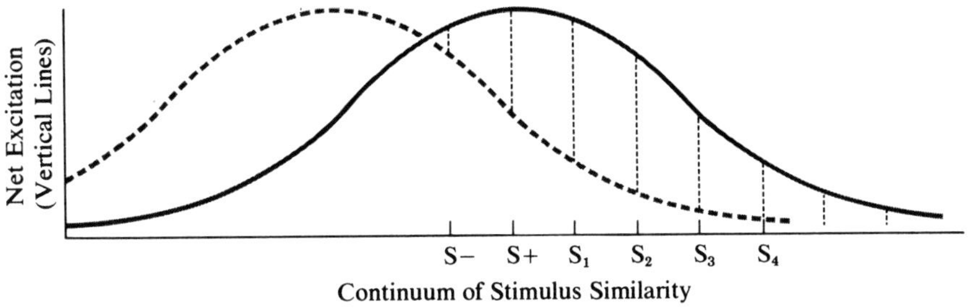

Figure 6–9. Spence's analysis of transposition based on gradients of excitation (solid line) and inhibition (dotted line). S+ denotes the stimulus predicting reinforcement, while S− represents the stimulus predicting nonreinforcement. (From "The Differentiated Responses in Animals to Stimuli Varying within a Single Dimension," by K. W. Spence, *Psychological Review,* 1937, *44,* 430–444. Copyright 1937 by the American Psychological Association. Reprinted by permission.)

lines in the figure) for some stimuli never directly associated with reward is greater than the net excitation for S+ itself. This implies that an animal trained to select the larger of the two stimuli represented by S+ in the figure would, however, if presented with S+ and an even larger stimulus (S_1), select the larger of the two, S_1. The figure indicates, however, that this sort of relational responding decreases as the physical distance between S+ and other stimuli increases. This type of relational responding is called *transposition.* We will examine data bearing on these deductions of the theory in a later section.

In the context of Spence's theory, the postdiscrimination gradient represents the residual, or net, excitation occurring to stimuli along the stimulus continuum. If Spence's theory is correct, the postdiscrimination gradient should exhibit properties that differ from generalization gradients obtained without intradimensional-discrimination training. As Figure 6–9 implies, the highest level of responding during the generalization test should be displaced away from S+ in a direction opposite that of S−. In short, there should be a shift in the peak of the postdiscrimination gradient. Furthermore, if the postdiscrimination gradient represents the summation between excitation and inhibition, the peak shift should increase as the difference between S+ and S− is reduced.

In a classic experiment Hanson (1959) tested these predictions by training pigeons to discriminate between two monochromatic wavelengths. Four groups of birds received discrimination training between 550 nanometers as S+ and a negative stimulus of 555, 560, 570, or 590 nanometers. Each group was assigned to a value of the negative stimuli. A fifth group received no intradimensional-discrimination training. Since it was exposed only to 550 nanometers, this group served as a control. Figure 6–10 shows the principal results of Hanson's study. As can be seen, the peak of each postdiscrimination gradient is shifted away from S+ and in a direction opposite from the negative stimuli. Moreover, the magnitude of the peak shift varies inversely with the distance between S+ and S−; the further removed S+ and S−, the smaller the displacement in the peak of the gradient.

Although Hanson's results confirm several predictions of Spence's theory, other features of the data indicate that processes in addition to simple summation of excitation and inhibition may be present. If postdiscrimination gradients are simply a residual of excitation and inhibition, then the height of these gradients should be lower than the height of the gradient of the control group because that gradient reflects only excitation. But Figure 6–10 shows that the postdiscrimination gradients are higher than the excitatory gradient of the control group. The usual explanation advanced for this result is to attribute the increased responding to contrast effects. In Chapter 3 we saw that one of the conditions responsible

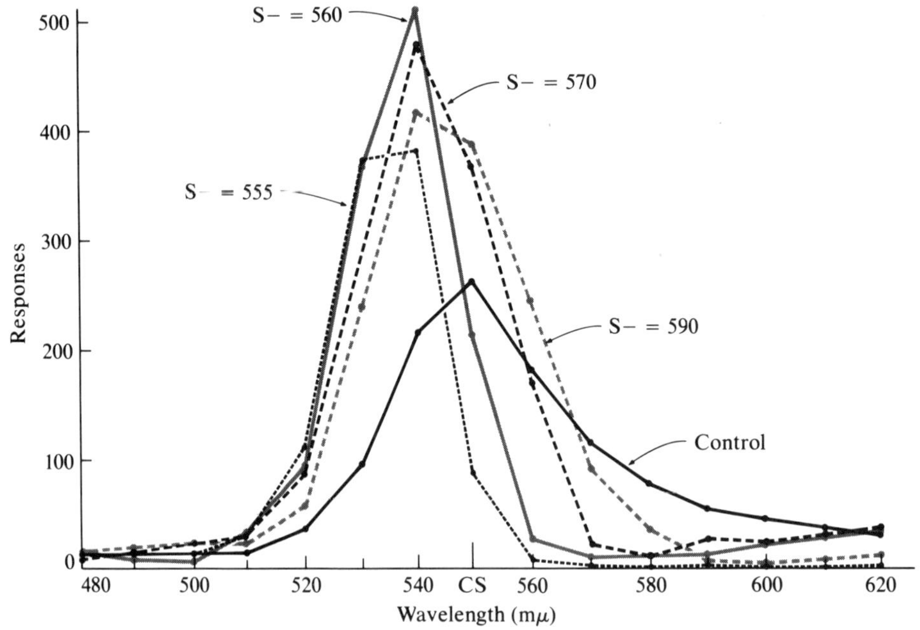

Figure 6–10. The effect of variations in the value of the negative stimulus on the post-discrimination gradient following intradimensional-discrimination training. (From "Effects of Discrimination Training on Stimulus Generalization," by H. M. Hanson, *Journal of Experimental Psychology,* 1959, *58,* 321–333. Copyright 1959 by the American Psychological Association. Reprinted by permission.)

for behavioral contrast is alternating periods of reward and nonreward in the presence of explicit exteroceptive cues. Alternating S+ and S− in this fashion often results in enhanced responding to S+ and a corresponding reduction in responding to S−.

Since behavioral contrast is present in the postdiscrimination gradient, Terrace (1966a) has suggested that the conditions necessary to produce either phenomenon are identical. He argues that contrast and the peak shift are by-products of frustration that results from responding to S−. His hypothesis is based on several sorts of observations. First, the peak shift is not found following extended discrimination training (Terrace, 1966c), a condition that presumably parallels the finding that contrast is attenuated by extended practice. Second, animals receiving errorless-discrimination training do not exhibit a peak shift (Terrace, 1964).

Despite the evidence marshalled in support of the hypothesis that behavioral contrast and peak shift result from the emotional aftereffects of nonreward, Terrace's suggestion is probably premature (Purtle, 1973). As we saw in a previous section, gradients of generalization steepen with extended training (Hearst & Koresko, 1968). Consequently, no peak shift should be found if no overlap occurred between gradients of excitation and inhibition. Terrace's (1964) finding that the postdiscrimination gradient following errorless-discrimination training shows no peak shift led to the conclusion that establishing an S− by the errorless procedure results in an absence of aversive or inhibitory properties for that stimulus. However, Karpicke and Hearst (1975) have demonstrated that an S− established by errorless training is an inhibitory stimulus. Conceivably, the slope and shape of an inhibitory gradient generated about an errorless S− are quite unlike those of a similar gradient around an S− established by conventional training procedures.

In conclusion, it appears that postdiscrimination gradients reflect the operation of both behavioral contrast and the simple algebraic summation of excitation and inhibition. Specifying the relative contribution of each must await a clarification of the conditions in which contrast occurs.

Transfer Effects in Discrimination Learning

The effects of discrimination learning transfer or carry over to new learning situations. Four kinds of transfer effects which are of interest are transposition, the transfer of discrimination, the acquired distinctiveness of cues, and learning sets.

Transposition

Although Spence's theory accounts for several important properties of the postdiscrimination gradient, the theory was actually developed to provide an alternative interpretation of *transposition,* the tendency to respond in a relation fashion. In 1918 Köhler (1939), a Gestalt psychologist, reported an experiment in which chickens were exposed to two intermediate-gray stimuli and rewarded for choosing the lighter of the two. After learning the discrimination, they were presented with the previously reinforced stimulus and one yet lighter. The new stimulus was separated by the same ratio that separated the original training stimuli. He found that the chickens tended to select the new stimulus in preference to the original S+. Köhler explained this result by contending that the chickens were responding to the *relationship* between the two stimuli—that is, the relationship of "lighter than" rather than the absolute properties of the stimuli. Köhler likened relational responding to the transposition of a melody: if music is played in a new key, it is still recognizable as the same melody.

Köhler's interpretation of transposition and of discrimination learning in general was damaging to a continuity-theory account of the discrimination process. In continuity theory a discrimination is formed by the gradual build-up of excitation and inhibition to the absolute values of each stimulus, and stimulus selection results from the algebraic summation of the opposing processes.

A continuity interpretation of transposition was provided by Spence's (1937) extension of his theory of discrimination learning. As we have seen, Spence assumed that gradients of excitation and inhibition develop around S+ and S−, and as a consequence test stimuli never associated with reinforcement may acquire a larger net excitatory tendency than S+ (see Figure 6–9). More important, the theory makes stronger predictions than the interpretation provided by Köhler. For example, it predicts that the incidence of transposition will vary with the distance between S+ and the test stimulus. As Figure 6–9 shows, a larger amount of transposition will be observed in the "near" test—that is, when the test stimulus is highly similar to S+ (see, for example, S+ and S_1 in Figure 6–9). However, as the distance increases between S+ and the test stimulus—for example, S+ and S_4—, transposition declines. The prediction of greater transposition in the "near" rather than "far" test has been confirmed many times (for example, T. S. Kendler, 1950; Spence, 1937).

Subsequent experiments have constrained Spence's theory in at least two ways. First, considerable evidence exists for a relational basis of transposition. D.T. Campbell and Krael (1958), Lawrence and DeRivera (1954), and Riley (1958) have demonstrated that choice behavior during transposition is controlled by the relationship between stimuli or the relationship between the stimulus and its surround. For example, Lawrence and DeRivera trained rats on a successive discrimination to seven stimulus cards. During the training the bottom half of each card was a medium gray. The top half was any of three shades of lighter gray or any of three shades of darker gray. The rats were rewarded for jumping to the right whenever the top half was lighter than the bottom, and for jumping to the left whenever the top half was darker than the bottom. In the transposition-test phase 24 new cards were used that varied the shade of gray for the bottom half of the card. According to continuity theory, since the same gray was present on the bottom of the seven training cards, its associative value should be the same throughout the transposition test. Therefore, the effective stimulus would be the top half of the test card. Consider now a test card with a black bottom half and a top half only a shade lighter. If the rats are responding to the absolute properties of the stimulus, they should jump left. A relational interpretation, on the other hand, predicts that the rats will jump right because the top half of the card is lighter than the bottom half. The majority of the tests revealed that the animals had learned the relationship between the stimuli.

A second limitation of continuity theory applied to transposition is that it is restricted to nonarticulate organisms. Criticism of the theory on these grounds is probably unwarranted, since Spence himself acknowledged this limitation (see Spence, 1956). Indeed, the necessity of some sort of mediational process to complement the assumptions of the theory was demonstrated in Spence's laboratory by Kuenne (1946). Kuenne tested four groups of children with mental ages of 3, 4, 5, and 6 years on a size-discrimination problem. After learning the discrimination, they were given transposition tests with stimuli similar to or very different from the training stimulus. The children's performances on the "near" test were quite similar, but relational responding on the "far" test varied directly with their mental age. Children with a mental age of 3 behaved like nonarticulate organisms, showing only chance responding on the "far" test. Contrary to the prediction of the theory, children with a mental age of 6 showed perfect transposition on the "far" test.

Subsequent experiments provide strong support for the notion that language may mediate responding on a variety of complex discrimination tasks (for example, Alberts & Ehrenfreund, 1951; H.H. Kendler & Kendler, 1962). These data suggest that processes in addition to excitation and inhibition govern relational responding and that they are relied upon to an increasing extent as symbolic modes of representation come to predominate.

Transfer of Discrimination

Transfer of discrimination is closely related to transposition. As in transposition, animals are trained initially to discriminate between two points on a stimulus continuum, but unlike transposition the transfer task involves exposing the animals to a more difficult discrimination along the same continuum. The question raised by transfer of discrimination is whether prior acquaintance with a dimension increases the "salience" of that dimension. As adults we have no difficulty distinguishing between *b* and *d,* yet young children readily confuse them. Has our experience with the alphabet somehow facilitated our ability to discriminate between letters that are physically and phonically highly similar? Or consider learning the differences between the mixed economies of the United States and Sweden. Would learning to distinguish between classical capitalistic and socialistic economic models facilitate learning about the two countries' present economies? The evidence suggests that it would.

Transfer of discrimination refers to the fact that training on an easy discrimination facilitates the learning of a more difficult discrimination along the same stimulus continuum. Although reported long ago (Pavlov, 1927), this phenomenon captured little attention until the controlled investigations of Lawrence (1952). Lawrence trained four groups of rats on a brightness discrimination. The stimuli were graded from a very light (1) to a very dark (7) gray. One of the groups was trained to discriminate between two highly similar, intermediate shades of gray (3 and 4) from the outset of training (hard-discrimination group). The other three groups were trained initially on easier discriminations and then transferred gradually or abruptly to the difficult problem. The gradual group spent the first ten trials on 1 and 7, the next ten on 2 and 6, the next ten on 3 and 5, and the last 50 trials on the difficult discrimination (3 and 4). One of the abrupt groups (abrupt–1) spent the first 30 trials on 1 and 7 and was then shifted to 3 and 4 for the last 50 trials. The second abrupt group (abrupt–2) was first trained on a discrimination only slightly easier than the difficult problem (3 and 5) for 50 trials before being transferred to the 3 and 4 problem.

The results of the Lawrence experiment appear in Figure 6–11. The figure indicates that the rate of learning, reflected by the slopes of the curves, varied directly with the difficulty of the discrimination. Moreover, the performance of the gradual and abrupt groups on the difficult problem was clearly superior to that of the hard-discrimination group. This finding indicates that *prior experience with the easier discrimination facilitated learning the more difficult discrimination.* Another interesting feature of the data is that after the shift to the more difficult problem the curves of the various groups were essentially parallel. This finding suggests that experience on the easier tasks resulted in the generalization of reaction tendencies to the more difficult problem rather than increasing the discriminability of the two cues. If the stimuli had been more finely differentiated by exposure to the easy discrimination, the slopes of the learning curves for the transfer groups on the difficult discrimination would have been steeper than the slope for the hard-discrimination group.

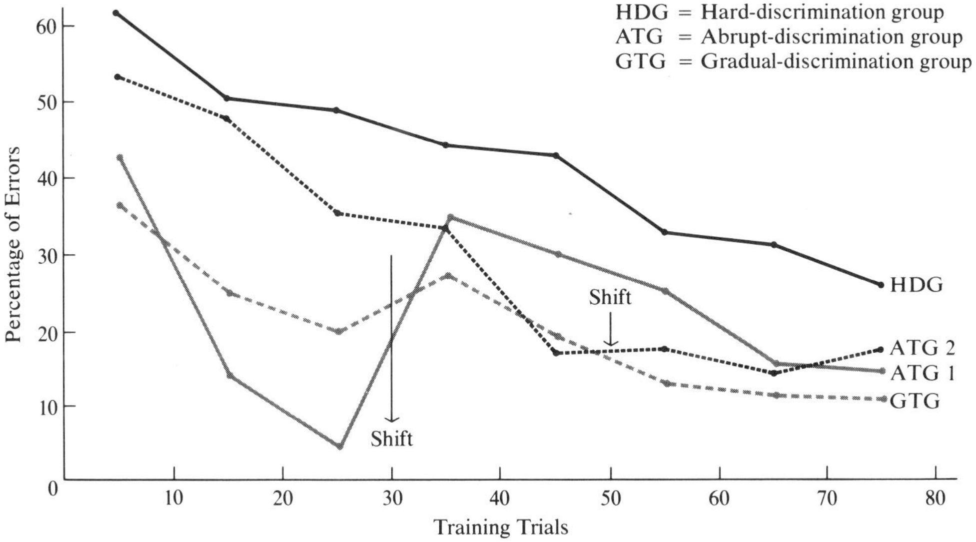

Figure 6–11. The effects of prior training with an easier discrimination on the learning of a more difficult discrimination along the same stimulus continuum. (From "The Transfer of a Discrimination along a Continuum," by D. H. Lawrence, *Journal of Comparative and Physiological Psychology,* 1952, *45,* 511–516. Copyright 1952 by the American Psychological Association. Reprinted by permission.)

Although the parallel form of the learning curves provided evidence for a continuity interpretation of transfer of discrimination, Lawrence (1955) argued that Spence's theory cannot account for the difference in performance between the abrupt–1 group (animals shifted from the easy to the difficult discrimination on the 31st trial) and the hard-discrimination group. Lawrence demonstrated that in order for Spence's theory to predict the performance of the abrupt group on the difficult task, the relative slopes of the gradients must increase with additional training. A characteristic of the form of gradients used by Spence, however, is that the relative slopes of the gradients are independent of response strength. Consequently, a necessary assumption for a theory of discrimination learning based on gradients of excitation and inhibition is that additional training must steepen the slopes of the gradients.

The problems encountered by continuity theorists in dealing with transfer of discrimination and related phenomena helped bring about renewed interest in noncontinuity theory. In its modified form noncontinuity theory assumes that there is a hierarchy of *stimulus-analyzing mechanisms* that selectively abstracts a particular dimension from the potential stimulus (Lawrence, 1963; Sutherland, Mackintosh, & Mackintosh, 1963). An analyzing mechanism is a hypothetical device used to explain a wide range of learning phenomena. The operation of an analyzer on the dimension extracted by the subject produces a centrally located output that functions as the effective stimulus. Responses are then associated with the output of the analyzing mechanism. The theory involves two stages of processes because the organism must first learn to switch in an analyzer, which yields maximal differences in output for the two points on the stimulus continuum, and only then learns to attach responses to the different outputs—that is, to the encoded stimuli.

Figure 6–12 is a diagram of a set of analyzers that select dimensions of a potential stimulus varying in shape, color, orientation, and location. If the shape analyzer is selected, the output, or encoded stimulus, is one of two values correlated with whether the nominal stimulus is a triangle or a square. If a triangle is present, the triangle output is active. A response probability occurs when the corresponding output is present. Reinforcement or nonreinforcement of the response to a particular output increases or decreases the probability of response to that output. If shape is the relevant dimension and "yes" and "no" are the response classes, the probability of saying "yes" to the encoded triangle would approach unity when followed by reward, whereas the probability of saying "yes" to the square output, which is followed by nonreward, would approach zero. Reinforcement also affects the extent to which a particular analyzer will be selected. If reward follows the selection of a particular analyzer, the probability of remaining with that analyzer increases. Staying with the correct analyzer also increases if a different analyzer is nonreinforced.

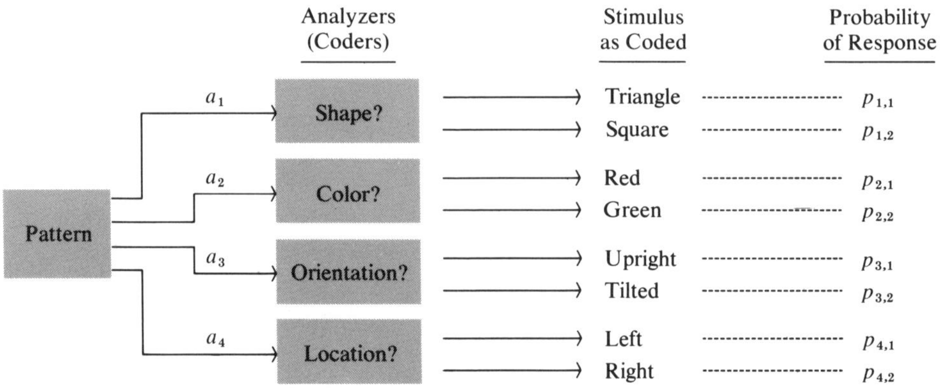

Figure 6–12. Pattern analyzers in discrimination learning. (From *Attention in Learning: Theory and Research,* by T. Trabasso and G. H. Bower. Copyright 1968 by John Wiley & Sons, Inc. Reprinted by permission.)

Attention theories of discrimination learning differ in the number of analyzers that can be sampled from trial to trial. For example, so-called *one-look models* assume that only a single analyzer is active on any given trial (see, for example, Zeaman & House, 1963), whereas *multiple-look* models propose that multiple analyzers can be selected on a particular trial, so that a response can be associated with the weighted output of the separate analzyers (Trabasso & Bower, 1968). A complete discussion of these different formulations is beyond the scope of this chapter. For our purposes the crucial distinction between attention (noncontinuity) and continuity interpretations of transfer of discrimination is whether prior training on the easy discrimination increases the salience of the relevant dimension over the irrelevant ones or whether learning the difficult discrimination is facilitated by the transfer of the habit of responding differently to the two stimuli.

A modified noncontinuity theory accounts for transfer of discrimination by assuming that when the organism is trained initially on the easy discrimination there is a high probability of attending to the relevant dimension and of selecting S+ because the outputs of the analyzer do not overlap. In contrast, animals confined to the difficult task throughout training make more errors, since there is an overlap between the outputs. Errors weaken the correct analyzer and allow for the selection of a different one. Switching from one analyzer to another produces inconsistent attention to the relevant dimension. *Transfer of discrimination occurs because the correct analyzer is strengthened by prior training on the easy task.* Since this produces more consistent attention to the relevant dimension, learning the difficult discrimination will be facilitated because the dimension selected has acquired dominance over the other dimensions of stimulation.

Acquired Distinctiveness of Cues

That learning can modify our perceptions has long been known. In 1890 William James discussed two closely related phenomena that illustrate how we learn to respond to small differences as though they were large. These phenomena are now known as transfer of discrimination and the *acquired distinctiveness of cues*. Although similar, they differ in the way each is assessed. Transfer of discrimination refers, as we have seen, to the fact that previous experience with dissimilar stimuli facilitates our learning to distinguish between similar stimuli along the same continuum. On the other hand, evidence of the acquired distinctiveness of cues is determined by learning to respond differently to stimuli that originally produce difficult-to-distinguish perceptions.

According to James, initially confusable stimuli become more distinctive as a result of the *addition* of more distinctive cues, or associations, to each stimulus. Stimuli that are hard to discriminate become more distinctive if they are initially experienced in different contexts. As an example, James considered learning to distinguish between burgundy and claret. When the two wines are sampled for the first time, their tastes might be different but not very distinguishable. However, as the flavors of the two wines are experienced repeatedly in future situations, each flavor comes to evoke its own particular associations. Thus, the associations come to influence the tastes of the two wines. If the associations are sufficiently different from each other, the initially subtle differences in their tastes become more distinct, and they are thus more readily discriminated.

The interpretations later offered by continuity and noncontinuity theorists for the phenomenon James described obviously differed. Since continuity theorists were committed to the view that learning consists of the formation of associations between stimuli and responses, the mechanism evoked to account for the acquired distinctiveness of cues must share the functional properties of these basic analytical units. Continuity theorists argued that cues acquire distinctiveness when different responses are made to them. Since responses are assumed to have stimulus consequences, the differential proprioceptive, or feedback, stimuli produced by them would become part of each of the two similar stimuli. The addition of these response-produced stimuli to the two cues would serve to enhance the distinctiveness between them. For example, we might eventually come to distinguish between burgundy and claret because we assign different labels to them. Each naming response would produce its own characteristic feedback, which becomes part of the sensation whenever one of the wines is resampled. Thus, the different names assigned to the wines serve to increase the difference between them. In contrast, noncontinuity theory treats learning as a two-stage affair: the individual must first learn to attend to the relevant dimension and only then make a response appropriate to that dimension. Reinforcement of a particular dimension enhances that dimension's salience independently of the responses made to it.

Lawrence (1949, 1950) tested these opposing interpretations by determining whether rats showed positive transfer from one discrimination to another, but under conditions in which the responses required for solving the second problem were unrelated to the responses used during the first discrimination. If learning involves two distinct processes, attention to the relevant dimension on the first problem will produce faster learning on the second, provided, of course, that the same dimension is relevant to the second task. Lawrence found support for the noncontinuity interpretation of acquired distinctiveness of cues: rats trained to a simultaneous brightness discrimination learned a successive discrimination with brightness relevant more rapidly than rats trained on a texture or width discrimination and then shifted to the brightness problem. We will examine these issues again in the chapter on perceptual learning and memory.

Learning Sets

The final class of transfer phenomena deals with an individual's ability to learn new problems more efficiently as a result of sustained practice on similar or related problems. This form of learning is exemplified by performance becoming increasingly independent of incidental cues present on each successive problem. Since the subject exhibits behavior suggesting that it has acquired a class of abstract habits that enable it to identify contextual structures or sequences of one type rather than another, this class of transfer phenomena is referred to as learning to learn or as learning-set phenomena.

Although several early investigators observed that positive transfer progressively increased from one related problem to another (for example, Bunch, 1944; Melton & Von Lackum, 1941; Ward, 1937), learning to learn attracted little attention until Harlow (1949) reported several experiments with monkeys. Harlow trained monkeys on a series of simple discriminations in which reward, such as a raisin, was arbitrarily associated with one of two objects. For example, the monkeys might be presented with a large and a small square. Reward was associated with one object but never with the other. The position of the objects was randomized, so that in order to maximize reward the monkeys had to attend to the object rather than its position. Usually, after six trials on this problem, the monkeys were presented with another discrimination, which might be a cube and a triangle, and again reward was arbitrarily correlated with one of the two objects. Successive problems involving novel discriminations continued to be presented, and the monkeys became progressively more efficient in solving the new problems.

Figure 6–13 shows the performance of Harlow's monkeys over the six trials on blocks of successive problems. As can be seen, initial learning was extremely slow; mastery of this type of discriminative task was evident only after hundreds of trials on the successive-discrimination problems. Eventually, however, the monkeys acquired a learning set that could be applied to the solution of similar problems. More specifically, the monkeys may have learned a win/stay, lose/shift strategy for this type of task.

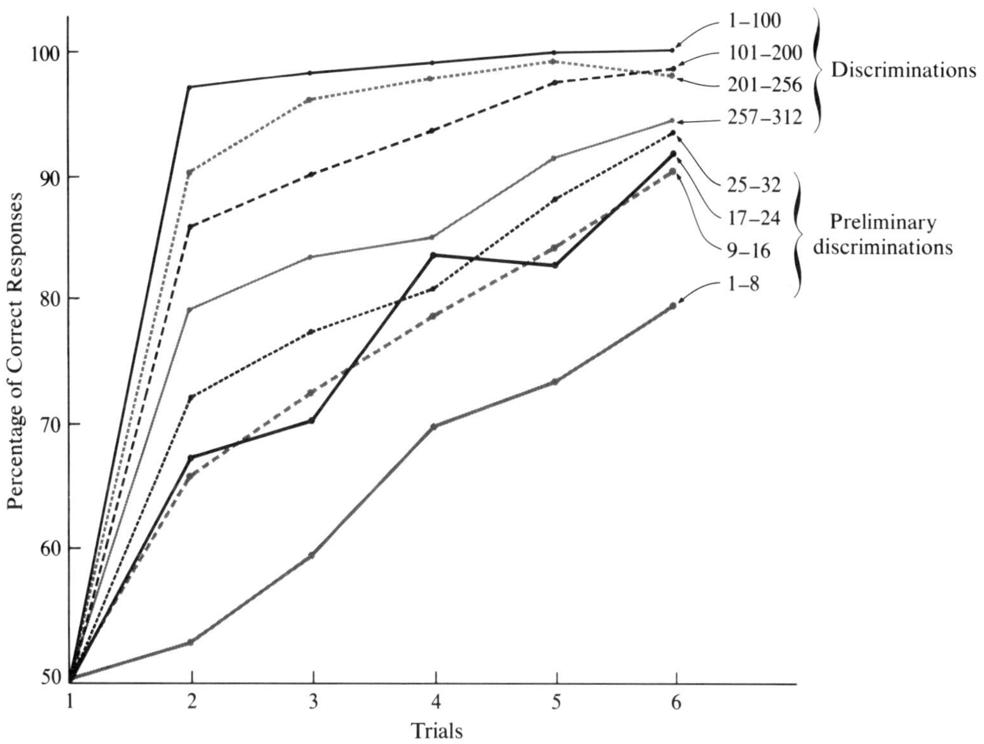

Figure 6–13. Discrimination-learning curves on successive blocks of problems. (From "The Formation of Learning Sets," by H. F. Harlow, *Psychological Review,* 1949, *56,* 51–65. Copyright 1949 by the American Psychological Association. Reprinted by permission.)

Consider again the cube/triangle problem, with the cube correlated with reward. Assume further that the animal has learned how to learn the problem. Of course, on the first trial the monkey does not know which of the two objects predicts reward, so the probability of selecting the correct cue is at a chance level. If the cube is selected on Trial 1, the monkey stays with that cue for the remaining trials; on the other hand, selection of the triangle on the first trial would result in the monkey's shifting to the cube for the next five trials. Once the win/stay, lose/shift strategy is learned, performance is nearly perfect on Trials 2 through 6.

The formation of learning sets is not limited to a simple discrimination between two objects. Harlow (1949) also showed that monkeys become proficient in learning how to learn discrimination-reversal problems. After the subjects had received seven, nine, or 11 trials on a discrimination problem, the reward contingencies of the stimuli were reversed for the next eight trials. To solve the reversal, the monkeys had to abandon a response pattern that was correct for seven to 11 trials and to initiate a response in opposition to the one originally used. The performance of the monkeys on the last 42 reversals of a series of 112 reversal problems was as efficient as their performance on the original simple-discrimination problem.

The win/stay, lose/shift strategy of the object-type discrimination is probably used for the formation of learning-set reversal as well. When the originally correct cue is no longer rewarded (that is, the monkey loses), a shift to the previously incorrect cue results in reward and the monkey's staying with it. Although the rule may be the same for solution of discrimination and discrimination-reversal problems, the information required to master the reversal is contained on the "informing" trial—that is, the trial on which the cues are reversed. Solution of the discrimination reversal requires a finer discrimination; attention must be focused on the outcome of the immediately preceding trial.

The formation of learning sets and learning-set reversal seems to rely on the informational value of reward or nonreward from previous trials; that is, the outcomes from preceding trials convey information about whether the rule has been correctly applied. Bessemer and Stollnitz (1971) have presented evidence indicating that the memory of prior outcomes mediates a win/stay, lose/shift strategy. By varying the time between trials in a series of experiments, they found that increasing the intertrial interval retarded the formation of learning sets. However, performance remains unimpaired over long retention intervals once the learning set is well established (Strong, 1959). This result implies that, once learned, strategies are stored in long-term memory. In any case, the evidence suggests that short-term memory mediates performance during the development of learning sets, but once they are learned, the cognitive structure is readily available for subsequent retrieval, since the information has been transferred to long-term store. Since solution of discrimination reversals demands using information from the immediately preceding trial, different memory mechanisms may be implicated in learning sets and learning-set reversal even though their solution entails the application of the same strategy. This hypothesis may explain why rats learn discrimination reversals but demonstrate more limited evidence of learning to learn. Perhaps their capacity to store or use previously stored information is limited.

The learning-set data provide some of the strongest empirical evidence for discontinuities in learning. That monkeys abandon reaction tendencies associated with reinforcement and adopt a response previously nonreinforced after only one trial on the discrimination-reversal problem severely restricts the application of a continuity interpretation of learning. Further experiments demonstrating that animals learn to ignore the similarity of features between objects—that is, learn not to generalize from one problem to another despite the similarity between them—provide additional evidence for a process other than a generalization mechanism (Riopelle, 1953).

Response Generalization and Differentiation

Phenomena analogous to stimulus generalization and discrimination have been found for responses. Response generalization is demonstrated when responses similar to the reinforced response are emitted in the presence of an unchanging stimulus complex. For example, if a criterion of 21 grams of pressure is imposed to produce reward for a bar-pressing response, rats emit responses which vary about this value (Hull, 1943). On the other hand, response differentiation is usually indexed by a change in the relative frequency of some quantitative property of a response. If, for example, a bar-press duration of .4 to .6 seconds is correlated with reward, the frequency of this duration will increase relative to other response durations (Notterman & Mintz, 1965).

Response differentiation is such a pervasive phenomenon that we tend to be unaware of it. However, variations in any qualitative or quantitative feature of the response that are correlated with reward are instances of response differentiation. We learn, for example, to speak softly on some occasions and loudly on others. All motor skills, from shooting a basketball to driving a car, require finely tuned response selection.

Response differentiation, although as commonplace as discrimination, has received far less attention, in part because of the difficulty in controlling the events that regulate it. Since procedural differences exist between the establishment of stimulus and response selection, Skinner (1938, p. 308) suggested that the mechanisms responsible for stimulus discrimination and response differentiation are not functionally equivalent; they obey different laws. However, after an extensive series of experiments on response differentiation, Notterman and Mintz (1965) concluded that the distinction "between discrimination and differentiation is not any difference in 'process' but rather in the difference between the classes of discriminative stimuli cueing the organism's behavior" (p. 83). In short, the crucial distinction between these phenomena appears to be the locus of the cue (external or internal) controlling behavior.

Since proprioceptive stimuli are difficult to control and measure, there is little evidence bearing on this point. Insofar as comparable work has been done, the evidence suggests that response differentiation is a subset of stimulus discrimination and that the difference between them resides in the nature of the cue controlling responding. Rickert (1969) has reported data consistent with this hypothesis. He investigated two roles commonly assigned response-produced stimuli by a variety of learning theories. One role of these inferred events is to guide ensuing behavior; the organism selects what to do next on the basis of what it has already done. The second role of response-produced stimuli is to guide ongoing behavior; the organism selects what to do now on the basis of what it is going to do later. The difference between these roles resides in the temporal sequencing of potential response-produced stimuli. Rickert showed that when the temporal sequencing of response-produced stimuli was controlled, both ensuing and coincident response selection could be mediated by response-produced stimuli. In addition, his results demonstrated that proprioceptive stimuli have functional properties similar to exteroceptive stimuli, that training on an easy task facilitates learning a difficult task. In other words, response-produced stimuli obey the laws of exteroceptive stimuli in the sense that they share the property of facilitating transfer of discrimination.

Summary

This chapter summarized some of the topics in discrimination learning. Theories of discrimination learning were classified into continuity and noncontinuity interpretations. Continuity theory accounts for the formation of discriminations by the algebraic summation of excitatory and inhibitory tendencies. In contrast, noncontinuity theory dissociates learning from performance; before engaging in appropriate behavior, the organism must first learn to attend to the relevant dimension.

A variety of generalization and discrimination phenomena were described that have implications for the theoretical accounts of discrimination learning. We noted that the measurement of stimulus generalization involves methodological problems. One involves the use of absolute versus relative gradients, another involves the issue of averaging gradients, and a third involves the use of between-subject and within-subject designs. Factors that significantly affect the slope of the generalization gradient are schedule of reinforcement, motivational level, and degree of training.

Gradients of inhibition as well as excitatory tendencies have been measured. However, the explanatory power of the concepts of inhibition and excitation in accounting for discrimination learning appears to be limited. Although several important features of post-discrimination gradients are handled by continuity theory, problems arise with the theory in accounting for other phenomena such as transposition, transfer of discrimination, and the acquired distinctiveness of cues. In contrast, noncontinuity theory fares better in clarifying more complex discriminative phenomena, but many of its details are yet to be developed. Currently, neither theory adequately accounts for the full range of the data.

Response generalization and differentiation are thought to be analogous to the processes of stimulus generalization and discrimination. In addition, there is some evidence that the major difference between response differentiation and stimulus discrimination centers on whether the cue that controls behavior is an external or an internal one.

Chapter 7

Early Experience and the Development of Learning

The ways in which experiences early in life affect adult behavior are of interest to us all. Freud and others have emphasized the importance of early experience in the development of personality. Parents are concerned about early experience, as were their parents, who made up sayings such as "Spare the rod and spoil the child." Unfortunately, much of what is done to control the sorts of early experiences that individuals encounter is guided by adages such as this one rather than by a rationale based upon research findings. This chapter reviews the effects of early experience on learning and related behaviors. Initially, some examples will be provided. Next, we will examine some specific early-experience variables affecting behavior. Finally, we will present a survey of an area of research that has recently received a great deal of attention, the development of visual-discrimination abilities in the human infant.

Excellent examples of the importance of early experience can be found in the behavioral repertoire of lower animals. Many behaviors exhibited by infrahuman species appear so exceedingly simple that they are often thought to be totally unlearned. However, research has demonstrated that many of these behaviors are indeed largely learned and that their development is inseparably linked to certain early environmental encounters. Unless the opportunity for learning these behaviors occurs at a very early age, the animal will at best be retarded in performing these responses. Since these behaviors have obvious survival value for the organism, the development of these response patterns is of crucial importance. Such is the case with both the pecking and the imprinting response of fowl such as ducks, geese, chickens, and quail.

The normally reared chicken is quite skillful in obtaining food from the ground by pecking at it. This behavior is quickly established and appears almost reflexive in very young chickens. However, in a classic study S. G. Padilla (1935) demonstrated that a period of practice is required before this feeding response reaches full efficiency and that this practice must occur within about 14 days after hatching. If it does not, chickens can never learn to make the pecking response. They can learn to maintain themselves only if they are laboriously taught to employ the drinking response to scoop up grain.

Many fowl, mostly ground nesting, tend to follow their parents almost as soon as they are hatched. This phenomenon was well known to William James (1890), who cited the early experimental work on this response by Douglas Spalding (1873). The European ethologist and Nobel Laureate Konrad Lorenz (1935) later "rediscovered" this behavior and named it *imprinting*. Since sticking close to its mother has obvious survival value for the young bird, it was tempting for early researchers to speculate that the bird has some innately determined image of its mother. Numerous investigators have demonstrated, however, that the young bird will simply follow any moving object initially experienced. There are many anecdotal reports in the literature of young birds' becoming imprinted to their human caretaker. Although there are species differences, it has generally been found that the opportunity for imprinting must occur during approximately the first day of life. If the initial experience with a moving object is delayed, the bird's reaction will be fear rather than following. Since Lorenz's investigations of this behavior in the 1930s, imprinting has been the target of many laboratory studies, which have, to a great extent, clarified the nature of and the mechanisms underlying this behavior. An excellent comprehensive review of imprinting has been presented by Sluckin (1965).

The influence of early experience on the pecking and imprinting responses of fowl serves to illustrate the importance of early environmental encounters in the development of adaptive responding. In the following section we will look at specific research programs, involving subjects from rats to people, that have attempted to clarify the role of early experience in learning and associated behaviors. Most of the research to be considered was conducted on lower animals rather than human subjects, often because the degree of experimental control required in these investigations could not be attained using humans.

The Effects of Early Handling and Social Contact

A factor that can clearly affect both the initial rate of acquisition and later performance is the degree of emotionality of the subject, and numerous experimenters have attempted to clarify the effects of early experience on the development of adult emotionality. One cannot assess the emotionality of a rat or another lower animal in terms of "feelings" or some other verbal report normally used by humans. Rather, we say that the animal is emotional if it exhibits certain behaviors characteristic of lower animals when confronted with a situation that apparently elicits a state of emotional excitement.

This chapter will use a definition of emotional behavior developed by Denenberg, a psychologist whose research has done much to clarify the role of early experience in adult emotionality. According to Denenberg (1967), an emotional animal, behaviorally speaking, is one that exhibits "little or no movement and defecates or urinates in response to certain stimuli" (p. 163). These types of emotional indexes can be observed in an *open field test,* during consummatory behavior, and in other structured or relatively unstructured behavior-assessment situations. By far the most frequently used index of emotional behavior is performance in the open-field test. Thus, before we examine some of the specific experiments in this area of research, it will be helpful to describe how this test operates.

The Behavioral Assessment of Emotionality

An open-field apparatus is a square arena with the floor marked off into smaller squares. The size of the apparatus depends upon the size of the subject being run. For rats an apparatus of approximately 3 to 5 feet square is used. The behavior of the animal is observed for a given period of time, usually several minutes. At the beginning of testing, the animal is placed in one of the corners facing into the center of the chamber. During the testing session the path of the animal is recorded with a quantification of the number of squares entered and the degree to which the animal ventures away from the perimeter of the arena into the center. The number of rearings, defecations, and urinations is also recorded.

One animal is said to be more emotional than another if it crosses fewer squares, tends to venture less frequently into the center squares, rears up less often on its hind legs, and has a higher occurrence of defecations and urinations. As can be seen, then, this testing procedure allows the experimenter to quantify empirically the emotionality of a subject.

The Effects of Prenatal Stimulation

As indicated, a number of investigators have examined the effects of early stimulation on later emotionality. For purposes of organization, these experiments will be divided into prenatal and preweaning stimulation, where *preweaning* refers to stimulation between birth and weaning.

Any discussion of prenatal stimulation must begin with a classic study by W. R. Thompson (1957). His work represents the first experimental attempt to examine the effects of maternal stress during pregnancy on the emotionality of the offspring. In this experiment the prospective mothers (rats) learned an avoidance task in which shock could be prevented if the animal opened a door and ran to the "safe" side of a shuttle box following presentation of a buzzer. After reaching a criterion level of responding, the experimental animals, together with control animals, were mated with a common group of males. The pregnant experimental females were then exposed to the buzzer three times every day in the shock side of the shuttle box with the shock turned off, but they were not allowed to make the anxiety-reducing response—that is, opening the door and moving to the "safe" compartment. This procedure terminated at the birth of the infants. To control for possible postnatal influences, the rat pups were cross-fostered at birth between the experimental and the control mothers. The offspring were later tested at either 30 to 40 days or 130 to 140 days of age in an open-field apparatus to assess their degree of emotionality. As measured by the amount of activity in the open field, the offspring of the experimental mothers were much more emotional than those of the control mothers. These findings point out that prenatal stimulation can affect the emotionality of the offspring and that these differences persist into adulthood (a rat is considered to be an adult at about 60 days of age). They do not, however, indicate how the stress had its effects. We will look at some possible explanations later in the chapter.

Since the publication of his research, Thompson's basic findings have been verified by a number of independent investigators (see, for example, Ader & Belfer, 1962; Doyle & Yule, 1959; Morra, 1965). In contrast, Ader and Conklin (1963), in a rigorously controlled study, found that if prospective mothers were gentled by being handled for 10 minutes three times daily throughout pregnancy, their offspring were generally less emotional than the offspring of nonhandled mothers.

The Effects of Preweaning Stimulation

In this section, we will examine the effects of preweaning stimulation on emotional behavior, learning and performance, and the physiology of the animal. Possible mechanisms underlying the early-stimulation effect will also be described.

Emotionality. The majority of the studies on the relationship between stimulation and later emotionality have examined the effects of stimulation between birth and weaning, and handling has been the most widely used procedure for manipulating the young animals. Research using this technique includes studies by Denenberg and his associates (for example, Denenberg & Morton, 1964; Denenberg & Smith, 1963).

As an illustration, Denenberg and Morton examined the effects of infantile handling on open-field performance. Beginning on the day following birth, infant rats were handled by being removed from their cage and placed for 3 minutes in a 1-gallon can containing shavings. They were then returned to the home cage, where their mother had remained during their treatment. This procedure was continued daily until the subjects were 24 days of age. At 70 days of age, the animals were tested in the open field, and it was found that the handled subjects, as indexed by their open-field scores, were significantly less emotional than nonhandled control animals.

Similar decreases in adult emotionality following infant handling have been noted in tests that used consummatory behavior as the dependent variable. S. Levine (1957, 1958) has reported that rats not handled in infancy consumed significantly less water following deprivation than did animals handled prior to weaning. He interpreted his results as indicating that the nonhandled rats were more susceptible to emotional disturbance. Similar effects of early handling on adult emotionality have been reported in other species, such as the cat (M. Wilson, Warren, & Abbott, 1965) and the rabbit (C. O. Anderson, Denenberg, & Zarrow, 1972; Denenberg, Wyly, Burns, & Zarrow, 1973). Thus, the early-stimulation effect is apparently a very broad phenomenon.

Learning and Performance. In addition to examining the effects of early manipulation on adult emotionality, related research has examined the effects of manipulation-produced stimulation on learning and performance. Supporting his notion that infant stimulation makes subjects more tolerant of later stressful events, Levine and his associates (Levine, 1956; Levine, Chevalier, & Korchin, 1956) demonstrated that rats handled for the first 20 days of life were significantly better avoidance learners than nonhandled controls. However, not all investigators have replicated this finding. For instance, Denenberg and Karas (1960) found that although rats handled on days 11–20 were superior to controls in learning a one-way active avoidance, animals handled for 20 days, as in the studies by Levine and his co-workers, did not differ significantly from the controls and, in fact, were slightly inferior. Since no clear methodological reasons for this discrepancy were immediately apparent, Denenberg and Karas suggested that the different findings may have been a function of genetic factors arising from the different strains of rats employed in the two studies. If such an interpretation is correct, one would have to assume that for the strain of rats used in the experiments by Denenberg and his associates, 20 days of handling in infancy reduced the animals' emotionality to such a low level that avoidance-learning behavior was impaired (Denenberg & Smith, 1963). Levine and Wetzel (1963) have published data supporting such an interpretation.

In another study Denenberg (1962) attempted to isolate critical periods during which early stimulation would yield later changes in emotionality. Infant rats were handled on days 1–3, 3–5, 1–5, 6–8, 8–10, or 6–10. Next, the avoidance-learning abilities of these experimental groups were compared to those of two reference groups, a group handled on days 1–10 and a nonhandled control group. Prior work had shown that animals receiving early stimulation on days 1–10 were superior to control rats in avoidance learning. The results indicated that Group 6–10 was significantly superior in avoidance learning to all the other experimental groups; the remaining five experimental groups did not differ significantly among themselves. When compared to the two reference groups, Group 6–10 did not differ from Group 1–10 but was significantly better at learning the avoidance task than the nonhandled control animals. On the basis of these findings, the authors concluded that later behavior is critically influenced by both the number of days of handling and the age of the subject when this stimulation occurs.

Additional experiments on the effects of early handling on learning and performance have used tasks other than active avoidance. In one study Karas and Denenberg (1961) examined the effects of early handling on learning by using an underwater *Y* maze. This task required the subject to swim to the brighter arm of the maze to reach dry ground via a wooden ramp. No differences emerged among the groups as measured by the percentage of errorless trials during testing. Analysis of the swimming times, on the other hand, did indicate an effect of early stimulation on behavior. Less emotional rats tended to exhibit shorter swimming times during the performance phase of training.

In the experiments we have looked at thus far, the learning situation involved noxious or stressful components (shock-avoidance learning, underwater swimming). A final study we will consider, by Denenberg and Morton (1962), was an attempt to determine whether early handling would affect performance in a nonnoxious testing situation, the Hebb/Williams test of problem-solving behavior. This is something of a rat intelligence test comprised of detour problems of varying complexity that must be solved to obtain food. Rats that had been handled once a day from 1 to 24 days of age began testing on the sequence of 12 test problems when they were 66 days old. The results were unambiguous; as compared to nonmanipulated subjects, early handling did not affect problem-solving behavior. Similar findings have been reported by Schaefer (1957). In light of their findings, Denenberg and Morton concluded that such preweaning stimulation as handling affects emotional processes but does not have any direct effect upon problem-solving behavior. Hence, the stimulation affects performance variables but not the learning process itself.

Physiological Effects. In addition to behavioral data, physiological indexes of decreased emotionality in early-handled rats have been reported. It has been well documented that an adult rat, when confronted with a stressful situation, will react physiologically by releasing the hormone corticosterone from the adrenal cortex into the bloodstream. The function of corticosterone is to reduce blood-sugar use by the tissues with which it comes in contact. However, corticosterone does not cross the blood/brain barrier and hence does not depress brain usage of blood sugar. The net effect is that more blood sugar is available to the brain during stressful situations, when a great deal of incoming information must be quickly processed. Levine, Haltmeyer, Karas, and Denenberg (1967) reasoned that handled animals demonstrating less emotionality than nonhandled animals in the open-field test should exhibit decreased plasma corticosteroid levels. To test this possibility, male rats were either handled for 20 days during infancy or left undisturbed in their rearing cages. As adults these animals were tested in the open field for 1, 2, 3, or 4 days; then their plasma corticosteroid levels were assessed immediately, 5 minutes, or 15 minutes following testing.

The results indicated that the animals receiving early stimulation were more active in the open field, defecated less in the apparatus, and exhibited a lesser corticosterone response. The plasma corticosterone levels for the handled and nonhandled rats are shown in Figure 7–1. Two aspects of the data depicted in this figure are important. First, the handled animals exhibited a lower adrenal response during all 4 days of testing than did the nonhandled subjects. Second, both groups exhibited a significant linear decrease in plasma steroid output as a function of the number of testing days. On the basis of these findings, the authors concluded that "stimulation in infancy results in an animal which is less responsive to stimuli (that is, less emotional) as measured at both the behavioral and the physiological level" (p. 58).

The Mechanisms Underlying the Early-Stimulation Effect. On the basis of the research findings thus far reported, one might be tempted to postulate that being "gentle" to the animals produced the decreased emotionality or was in some way a critical feature of the treatment. However, such is not the case. Similar effects on adult emotionality have been demonstrated in experiments in which the preweaning stimulation consisted of shaking or moving the living cages of the animals (Levine, 1959) or administering electric shock (Denenberg & Smith, 1963; Levine, 1957, 1958; Lindholm, 1962; Salama & Hunt, 1964) In Lindholm's experiment, for example, infant rats were removed from their mother

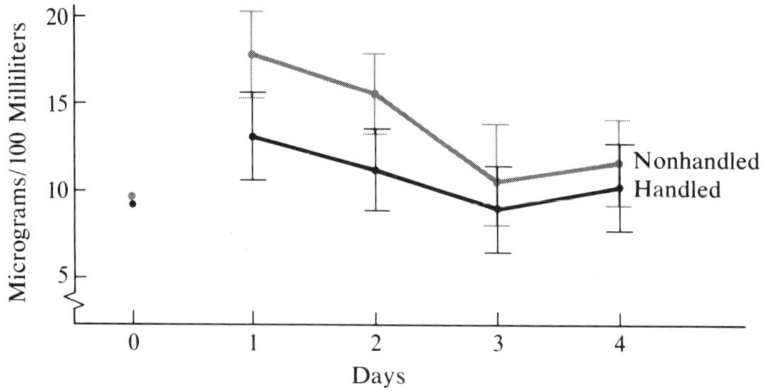

Figure 7–1. Plasma corticoid levels for handled (black line) and nonhandled (gray line) rats over days following 3 minutes in the open field. The points represent the mean value, and the bars represent the standard error of the mean. The two points at zero days are the base levels of corticosteroids for handled (open circle) and nonhandled (closed circle) rats. (From "Physiological and Behavioral Effects of Infantile Stimulation," by S. Levine, G. C. Haltmeyer, G. G. Karas, and V. H. Denenberg, *Physiology and Behavior,* 1967, *2,* 55–59. Reprinted by permission of Brain Research Publications.)

daily, placed in a cubicle, and shocked for 3 minutes. When tested as adults, the rats stimulated (shocked) during infancy exhibited shorter latencies than did nonstimulated control subjects in approaching water in a testing chamber following 24 hours of water deprivation. These differences indicate that infant shock, like handling, will reduce susceptibility to emotional disturbances occurring later in life.

Taken together, the data obtained from studies of early stimulation have been used to support the view that the primary effect of the early stimulation is to provide additional tactual/kinesthetic stimulation, which then acts directly on the organism to bring about some change in the physiological systems mediating the observed differences in adult behavior. There have been several challenges of this assumption, and an excellent review of these alternative interpretations is provided in an article by P.A. Russell (1971). Of these, the one best supported by empirical data is the "cooling" hypothesis of Schaefer, Weingarten, and Towne (1962).

Schaefer and his colleagues have argued that nontreated subjects in the early-stimulation studies normally receive frequent tactile stimulation during maternal care. Hence, they suggest that it is unlikely that the extra stimulation provided by handling would be great enough to yield the large differences observed in adult emotionality between handled and nonhandled animals. These researchers assert that the effect may have arisen from the incidental cooling of the handled animals during the time when they were removed from their nest and stimulated. Such an interpretation seems plausible when one considers that the lack of fur and the high ratio of surface area to body volume in the neonate rat permit rapid heat loss. In support of this interpretation of the mechanism underlying the early-stimulation effect, Schaefer and his associates have reported that handled animals and those whose body temperature was lowered by refrigeration without handling during the first week of life showed significant depletion of adrenal ascorbic acid when later subjected to stress, while control animals did not. Levine, Alpert, and Lewis (1958) previously determined that adrenal ascorbic-acid depletion provides a physiological index of handling that is comparable to behavioral measures.

Support for the cooling hypothesis using behavioral measures has been provided in research conducted by Hutchings (1965) and McIver and Camp (1966). These investigators found that handled noncooled rats performed similarly to nonhandled subjects on tests of emotionality. On the other hand, additional data are not entirely consistent with the cooling hypothesis. McIver, Jeffrey, Stevenson, and Nielson (1968) have reported that handled cooled rats and handled noncooled subjects were both less emotional than nonhandled subjects as indexed by open-field behavior. Future research will have to resolve these conflicting findings. If it is found that handled noncooled rats do indeed demonstrate some degree of decreased emotionality, it would suggest that at least some of the effect arising from early stimulation is due to factors other than cooling. In addition, such findings would support the view relating the effects of early stimulation to the total amount of stimulation impinging upon the infant organism.

Regardless of what event or events yield the later observed differences in emotionality between handled and nonhandled animals, the question remains of why the handled subject is different from the nonhandled one. Levine (1956) has asserted that the essential feature of all the various treatments used in the early-stimulation studies is that the infant animal is subjected to stimulation that is in some way noxious or stressful. In adulthood the end result of this stress is to make the subject more tolerant of stress. Levine's hypothesis is consistent with most of the data obtained in the early-stimulation investigations, assuming, of course, that the treatments are indeed in some way stressful. Unfortunately, we can consider a treatment stressful only if it alters the behavior of an adult. As a result, Levine's notion suffers from its circularity (P.A. Russell, 1971). Future research on the effects of early stimulation on emotionality and associated indexes of learning and performance needs to clarify whether such diverse treatments as cooling, handling, shaking, and shocking neonates do indeed yield similar response systems in adults. Before this can be accomplished, a better definition of our dependent variable of emotion must be obtained and its critical components delineated.

Early Affectional Bonds and Behavior

No discussion of the effects of early experience would be complete without a mention of the very influential work on the affectional systems of primates conducted by Harry F. and Margaret K. Harlow and their many associates at the Wisconsin Primate Laboratory. Harry Harlow joined the staff of the University of Wisconsin as an assistant professor of psychology in 1930 after receiving his Ph.D. at Stanford University and immediately set out to create a primate-research facility.

In the beginning his task was arduous. There was not even space available on the campus to house his facility. Never one to be easily thwarted, Harlow accepted the challenge, and late one night, as the story goes, with cinder blocks and graduate students in hand but without authorization from the superintendent of buildings and grounds, he constructed a building on a vacant spot of land on the campus near the railroad tracks. Since the building was unauthorized, as the sun rose in the east the crew put the final touch on the building's exterior—camouflage, consisting of a stand of honeysuckle bushes. Alas, their skulduggery was uncovered, and a few days later Professor Harlow received the following message from the superintendent of buildings and grounds: "Dr. Harlow—We are aware of your illegal building." The next day a letter arrived on the superintendent's desk that read: "Dear Superintendent—Thank you for acknowledging our primate laboratory. Harry F. Harlow." The building survived, and over the years the Wisconsin Primate Laboratory has developed into one of the leading facilities of its kind. A delightful account of the research conducted at the laboratory appears in an article by Harlow, Harlow, and Suomi (1971).

The most famous of the research programs conducted at the facility investigated the effects of early social experience on the development of infant/parent affectional bonds. Prior to Harlow's work the view was widely held that an infant's "affection or love" for its parents is entirely derived from the parents' association with the reduction of primary drives, particularly hunger, thirst, and pain. Unfortunately, though, no direct experimental analysis of the relative importance of various environmental stimuli in producing affectional bonds had been attempted. Harlow and his associates embarked on such a program.

A major impetus for their research was the incidental observation that laboratory-raised infant monkeys showed strong attachment to the diapers used to cover the floors of their cages. Not only did the parentless monkeys cling to these pads, but they also had violent temper tantrums when the pads were changed for cleaning. This observation suggested that "contact comfort" might be an important variable in the development of neonate/parent affectional bonds. To examine this possibility, the famous surrogate mother was born.

The Surrogate Mother. The original surrogate mother was made from a block of wood covered with sponge rubber and sheathed in tan cotton terry cloth. A light bulb behind her radiated heat, and a single breast (a milk bottle) was situated in the upper thoracic region. Harlow (1958) described her as a mother who was

> soft, warm and tender, a mother with infinite patience, a mother available 24 hours a day, a mother that never scolded her infant and never struck or bit her baby in anger. It is our opinion that we engineered a very superior monkey mother, although this position is not held universally by monkey fathers [p. 676].

To test the relative importance of feeding and contact comfort, a second substitute mother was born—the wire surrogate. She was made from wire mesh but differed in no essential way from the cloth mother surrogate other than in the amount of contact comfort she could supply.

In the initial experiment a cloth mother and a wire mother were both placed in the living cages of individually housed newborn monkeys. For four of the neonates, the cloth mother provided milk and the wire mother did not; this condition was reversed for an additional four infant monkeys. The results of this procedure were unambiguous. As indicated by a wide variety of behavioral tests, the cloth mother was by far the more effective surrogate, even if the wire mother supplied the infant's milk. In addition, the infants developed very strong affection for the cloth mothers but showed little toward the wire mothers. In light of these findings, Harlow (1958) concluded that "contact comfort is a variable of overwhelming importance in the development of affectional responses, whereas lactation is a variable of negligible importance" (p.676). Thus, a fatal blow was struck to the notion that primary-drive reduction underlies the development of infant/parent affectional bonds.

The Importance of Peer Contact. Although contact comfort proved to be an important variable in the establishment of mother/infant bonds, contact comfort in itself was not a sufficient condition to lead to normal adult-monkey behavior. Rather, a more important love system for adaptive adult social behaviors was found to be peer interaction (Harlow, 1962). Harlow and his associates discovered that surrogate-raised monkeys were inadequate as sexual partners and parents. On the other hand, infants raised on cloth mothers and given only 20 minutes per day of experience with other young monkeys in a playroom developed normal patterns of sexual and social behavior. Even neonates reared by their own mothers were retarded in their adult behavior patterns if they were denied some contact with their peers. Thus, even a good mother may not be enough for the normal development of adult social and sexual behaviors. The same is probably true for humans.

Early Social Experience and Adult Learning Ability. To assess further the effects of early social experience on behavior, Harlow and his associates (Harlow, Harlow, Schlitz, &

Mohr, 1971) examined how early social conditions affect learning and performance. Three groups of rhesus monkeys were used: a socially deprived group, a socially enriched group, and a control group. The socially deprived monkeys were reared under conditions of 6, 9, or 12 months of total social isolation. Because of the existing features of the laboratory environment, the "normal" control animals were actually reared under conditions of partial social isolation. The socially enriched animals, on the other hand, were reared in a "nuclear-family environment" (see Harlow, Harlow, & Suomi, 1971). In this enriched environment, all the infants had access to four adult females (one of which was its mother), four adult males, four age-mate infants, and in some cases other, younger infants.

All tests of learning and performance were administered using the Wisconsin General Test Apparatus (WGTA), pictured in Figure 7–2 (see also Harlow, 1959). With this apparatus the monkey, confined in either a restraining cage or its home cage, responds by displacing one of the stimulus objects that cover the food wells on the test tray. If the correct stimulus object is displaced, the animal secures a food reward located in the food well. Between trials an opaque screen is lowered in front of the monkey to prevent it from seeing which stimulus will be associated with reinforcement on the subsequent trial. A one-way vision screen prevents the monkey from seeing the experimenter during trials.

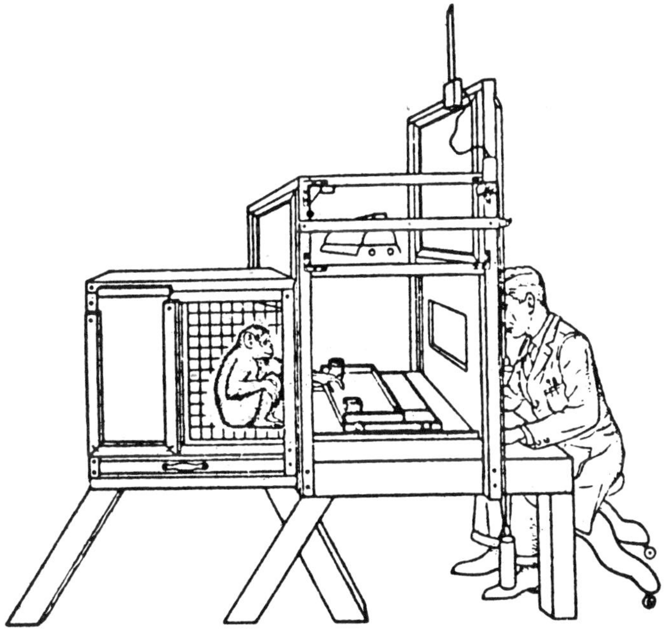

Figure 7–2. The Wisconsin General Test Apparatus. (From "The Formation of Learning Sets," by H. F. Harlow, *Psychological Review,* 1949, *56,* 51–65. Copyright 1949 by the American Psychological Association. Reprinted by permission.)

Prior to the tests Harlow's monkeys received extensive adaptation experience with the testing situation. The animals were then given the following problems: object discrimination; delayed response, including short, long, and multiple delays; discrimination-learning set; and oddity-learning set. Details of these testing procedures can be found in Harlow (1959).

Through the testing it was found that rearing conditions had no significant effects on any of the tasks except for the oddity-learning set. In the case of this task, which was the most complex problem administered to the monkeys, the socially enriched animals proved to be substantially superior to the socially isolated and control monkeys. These latter groups did not differ from each other. On the basis of these results, one might conclude that being reared in the socially enriched environment allowed the monkeys to attain higher levels of intellectual performance than those achieved by socially isolated or normally reared subjects. However, the reason for this difference is not quite so obvious. The difference might just as easily have been due to nonintellectual factors. Animals reared in the enriched environments are, according to Harlow, Harlow, and Suomi (1971), "the most self-confident, self-assured, fearless animals we have ever tested. They are more relaxed in the test situation than other subjects and could well be more persistent, thus persevering after normal subjects give up" (p. 543). Hence, the results might have been due more to emotion or personality variables than to intellectual attributes.

Early Social Restriction and the Adult Behavior of the Chimpanzee

Researchers at the Yerkes Regional Primate Research Center, now located at Emory University, have examined the long-term effects of early social and perceptual restrictions on the development of social, sexual, and learning behavior in chimpanzees (Davenport & Menzel, 1963; Davenport & Rogers, 1968; Davenport, Rogers, & Menzel, 1969; Menzel, Davenport, & Rogers, 1970; C.M. Rogers & Davenport, 1969; Turner, Davenport, & Rogers, 1969). The chimpanzee is, of course, an excellent model to use if one wants to determine what effects such restrictions may have on human behavior because chimpanzees are the species most closely related to people (Simpson, 1966). The isolates (five males and seven females) were removed from their mothers within 12 hours after birth and reared in individual cages for 3 years. The cages, measuring 48 by 24 by 28 inches, were illuminated, covered cribs constructed so that care could be provided without the chimpanzees' seeing or coming into contact with their caretakers. Noise was minimized. After this initial deprivation they were housed in caging similar to that of wild-born chimps used as comparison subjects.

Even when approximately 10 years had elapsed since their isolation, many of these animals persisted in abnormal social interactions across a wide range of activities. They tended to be withdrawn, fearful animals and spent much of their time engaged in unnatural, prolonged posturing or repetitive, stereotyped movements resembling the behavior patterns exhibited by Harlow's monkeys and by autistic children. These behaviors included swaying, rocking, eye poking, lying prone, and pushing the shoulders up and down (Davenport & Menzel, 1963; Turner et al., 1969). Although both the males and the females were successful in copulating with wild-born mates, male intromissions were often interrupted by these stereotyped, repetitive behaviors (Rogers & Davenport, 1969; Turner et al., 1969).

To test the effects of early restriction on learning ability, the chimpanzees were administered delayed-response and discrimination-learning-set problems, and their ability to use "tools" to obtain a food reward was assessed (Davenport & Rogers, 1968; Davenport et al., 1969; Menzel et al., 1970). In contrast to Harlow's monkeys, the performance of the chimps on all of the tasks was inferior to that of the wild-born chimps. At least part of the poor performance was due to nontask-oriented behaviors on the part of the deprived subjects, but it was also partly due to a higher incidence of stimulus-perseverance errors—that is, the persistence of inappropriate or incorrect responses—by the deprived animals. Hence, the results of these inquiries seem to suggest that early deprivation can adversely affect intellectual capabilities, a conclusion that at least partly conflicts with Harlow's monkey data.

The findings reported for chimpanzees corroborate the view that the characteristics of the early environment have a profound effect on the learning ability and intellectual level of humans. Children reared in relatively deprived environments are often found to be poorer learners, and they score lower on IQ tests than children raised in more stimulating environments (Kessler, 1966). Deprived children may even show, to some degree, the blunted responsiveness and ritualistic mannerisms characteristic of deprived chimpanzees (Spitz & Wolf, 1946). These apparent similarities underscore the importance of providing human infants with varied and enriched environmental and social experiences.

The Effects of Early Stimulus Deprivation on Learning and Performance

The purpose of the experiments that we will examine in this section and the next was to evaluate the effects of early experience on discrimination-learning ability. In general, in these studies the subjects' contact with their environment was carefully controlled. For purposes of organization, these investigations will be divided into two groups by the type of methodology employed. With the *stimulus-deprivation method* experimental subjects are deprived from a very early age of some of the normal environmental encounters of their species. In contrast, with the *extra-experience method* experimental subjects receive some sort of extra stimulus experience that control subjects do not get. The effect of either the extra experience or the deprivation is later assessed in a learning situation by comparing the learning ability and performance of the experimental subjects with those of the controls.

Visual Form Deprivation in Humans

Although it is clearly not feasible to deprive human subjects experimentally of early sensory experience for prolonged periods, data from clinical cases do provide some relevant information. These data came from the study of human adults who were blind from birth due to cataracts (a clouding of the lens) and whose vision was surgically restored in adulthood. After removal of the cataracts, these individuals were visually naïve but otherwise normal. Dember (1960) has described such patients as "visual infants, but infants who can talk and whose other sense modalities are fully developed" (p. 237).

In 1932 Max von Senden (1960) published a monograph describing several case histories of such individuals that had been reported by a number of independent investigators. Even at that time surgically removing cataracts was not new. William Cheselden (1728a, 1728b), one of the most famous surgeons of the 18th century, published articles in the *Philosophical Transactions of the Royal Society* on this surgical method and described a case history on what a cataract-induced blind individual sees following removal of the cataracts. Senden's monograph was neglected by psychologists until Hebb incorporated this work into his theory of perception as presented in his book *The Organization of Behavior* (1949).

In describing the visual abilities of the patients about whom Senden reported, Hebb distinguished between two skills, figural unity and figural identity. He used the term *figural unity* to refer to the ability to separate a figure from its background—that is, to detect the presence of an object. In contrast, figural identity also requires recognizing that an object belongs to a class of figures; that is, the subject must be able to discriminate between two classes of forms that are shaped differently. Figural identity involves such processes as object discrimination, recognition, and identification.

The distinction between figural unity and figural identity provides an excellent means of delineating the basic difference between the visually naïve and the visually sophisticated individual. The patients about whom Senden reported were at once able to make figural-unity discriminations, but a long and arduous period of training was required before their figural-identity discriminations approached those of normal persons. These observations suggest that the visual ability of figural unity is innate, or unlearned, while the development of figural-identity capabilities requires experience, or learning.

Visual Deprivation in Subhuman Primates

Although the findings incorporated into Senden's monograph provide important information about the development of human visual-discrimination skills, these data were not obtained from a carefully designed and controlled experiment. As a result, Riesen (1950) attempted to reproduce experimentally the conditions under which Senden's human patients had developed. He used three chimpanzees as his subjects. One chimp, Debi, was reared in complete darkness for 7 months. Another, Kora, was also raised in complete darkness except for 1.5 hours per day, when she experienced diffuse illumination. The third chimp, Lad, was allowed 1.5 hours of normal visual experience each day. The conditions imposed on Kora were most like those of cataract patients, since the effect of cataracts is to prevent pattern experience; cataracts do not eliminate all light stimulation of the retina.

The physical results of the study were clear. Debi, the dark-reared chimpanzee, suffered structural defects of the retina, indicating that normal development of the primate retina requires light stimulation. Kora exhibited no such physical problems. Apparently, 1.5 hours per day of diffuse light are sufficient for normal development of the retina. The behavioral results were also clear-cut. Lad, the chimpanzee allowed 1.5 hours per day of normal visual experience, did not differ in visual skills from normally reared chimps. Therefore, these data indicated that 1.5 hours each day of exposure to patterned visual stimulation, over a 7-month period, were sufficient for normal pattern vision to develop.

In contrast, both Debi and Kora were markedly deficient in even very simple visual/motor skills. These included the ability to fixate on the image of a stationary person and the ability to pursue a moving object visually. When the latter skill was acquired by Kora 13 days following her removal from darkness and by Debi at 30 days, it was acquired by a series of refixations on the moving object instead of by following it smoothly, as do normal chimps of comparable age. Riesen's findings fit in nicely with and add some phylogenetic generality to the Senden data. Further, Siegel (1953) has similarly demonstrated the importance of early patterned stimulation in the development of visual form discrimination in ring doves, as P. D. Wilson and Riesen (1966) have done for the rhesus monkey.

Taken together, these findings have been convincingly used to argue for the view that the observed effects arose from a lack of early visual experience and that early form experience is crucially related to the development of visual object-discrimination skills. A word of caution must be inserted, however, against a wholesale acceptance of this view. Using a similar method, in which form experience was prevented by covering the eyes of newborn kittens with translucent contact lenses, Hubel and Wiesel (for a review, see Hubel, 1967) found a resultant impairment of visual abilities. In addition—and this is the important point for our present discussion—they found that cells in the lateral geniculate body of the thalamus and in the visual cortex failed to respond normally to visual stimulation. Hence, gross abnormalities in the neural systems mediating the behaviors under study probably at least partially underlie the observed abnormalities following early stimulus deprivation. This finding would indicate that, in general, defects induced by stimulus deprivation reflect an inability of the machinery of the brain to process information as well as a lack of early experience, or learning.

Tactual/Kinesthetic Deprivation in the Chimpanzee

The role of early experience in tactual/kinesthetic perception and motor coordination was examined in a study by Nissen, Chow, and Semmes (1951). A young chimpanzee named Rob served as the subject. Beginning at the age of 4 weeks and continuing for 30 months, use of the hands and feet in climbing, grasping, and other manipulative skills was prevented, and sensory feedback from these parts was greatly reduced.

Initially, Rob's limbs were covered with bandages held in place with adhesive tape. This technique proved unsatisfactory because it prevented almost all movement of the fingers and toes and because the exclusion of air by the adhesive tape resulted in a peeling of the skin from the palms of the hands and the soles of the feet. As a result, the mode of restriction was changed, and from 15 weeks of age until the end of the deprivation period his limbs, from elbow to fingertips and from knee to toes, were encased in cardboard tubes.

At 31 months of age, Rob was freed from his cardboard confines and administered a tactual-discrimination task. To obtain a food reward, Rob simply had to indicate by proper head movement which of his hands had just been stimulated. If his right index finger was squeezed, he was reinforced if he turned his head to the right; if his left index finger was squeezed, turning his head to the left was rewarded. Despite the simplicity of the task, Rob never demonstrated evidence of having learned the problem, and so, after more than 2000 trials in which Rob had made more than 1000 errors, training was discontinued. A nondeprived control chimpanzee reached a level of almost perfect responding in slightly over 200 trials. It is important to note that Rob was not suffering from a general perceptual deficit; he demonstrated normal performance on a series of visual-discrimination problems. Nissen and his associates were hesitant to generalize from results obtained on only one animal. They tentatively concluded that tactual/kinesthetic and manipulative experiences play an important role in the development of tactual/motor skills. However, we do not know what neural effects were produced by this procedure.

Movement-Produced Feedback in the Development of Visually Guided Behavior

The studies we have examined thus far have assessed the effects of deprivation in a specific modality on the acquisition of skills that employ the deprived modality. An interesting extension of this type of research is found in an often-cited experiment by Held and Hein (1963). These investigators examined the effects of restricting experience in one modality (movement-produced stimulation) on the development of behaviors that involve both the restricted modality and another modality. Specifically, they have examined the effects of depriving animals of movement-produced feedback on the development of visually guided movement skills. The subjects were kittens, and they were reared in the dark except for a daily stimulus-exposure period for a few weeks before testing. The kittens were assigned to pairs; their daily exposure took place in a circular arena whose sides were painted with vertical stripes. Inside the arena one member of each pair was free to walk about as it desired. The kitten was, however, attached to a lever by a harness it wore. The lever had a center pivot, and from its other end was suspended a gondola in which the other kitten rode. The second kitten was restrained in the gondola by a neck yoke and a body clamp and was passively moved around in the arena as the active kitten walked about (see Figure 7–3). The procedure resulted in both animals' receiving equivalent early visual experience. However, the restrained kitten's visual experience was uncorrelated with any movements of its own.

The effects of these variations in early experience were assessed by tests of visually guided behavior. These tests included visual placing of the paws on approach to a surface, the visual cliff (see Walk & Gibson, 1961), and the eye-blink response to an approaching object. Although the active kittens performed normally on all of these tests, the passively exposed kittens were severely deficient. However, an interesting discovery was that the deficiency could be reversed. The experimenters reported that following 48 hours of free-

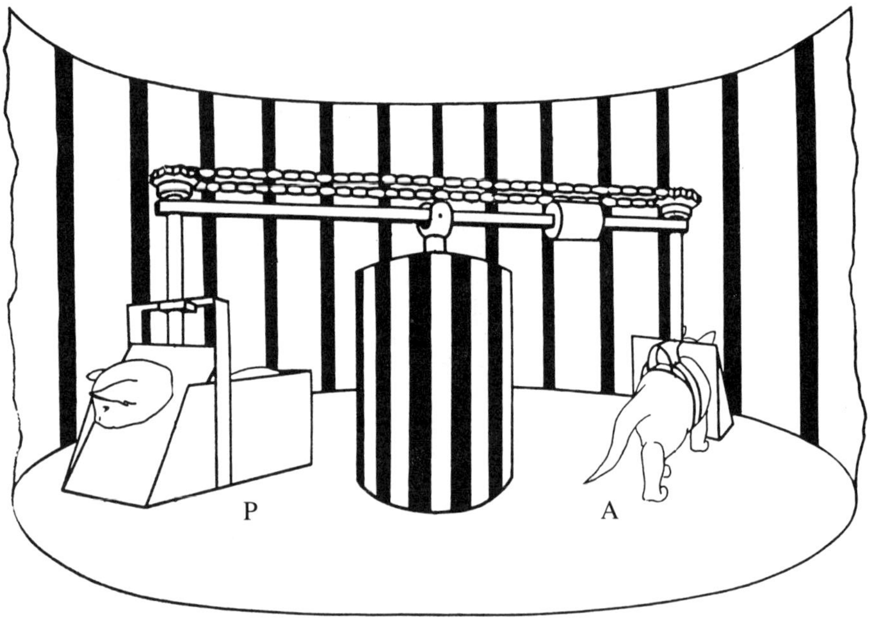

Figure 7–3. Apparatus for equating motion and consequent visual feedback for an actively moving (A) and a passively moved (P) subject. (From "Movement-Produced Stimulation in the Development of Visually Guided Behavior," by R. Held and A. Hein, *Journal of Comparative and Physiological Psychology,* 1963, *56,* 872–876. Copyright 1963 by the American Psychological Association. Reprinted by permission.)

dom in an illuminated room, the passively exposed kittens displayed normal visually guided paw placement and performed all descents to the shallow side of the visual cliff. The results were consistent with the thesis of the authors that self-produced movement, with its concurrent visual feedback, is a requisite for the development of visually guided behavior. The speedy recovery of their deprived animals rules out the possibility that the deprivation produced permanent neural defects. More recently, their findings have been confirmed and extended in several experiments (for example, Hein & Diamond, 1971; Hein, Gower, & Diamond, 1970).

An alternative explanation for the findings that deprivation of movement-produced stimulation during early visual experience results in impaired visual/motor performance is that any sensory-restriction procedure will produce an organism that interacts differently with its sensory world. It is possible that during deprivation the animal learns that the restricted modality is ineffective in extracting relevant information from the impinging stimulation. If so, this phenomenon would be almost like learned helplessness, described in Chapter 4, in which the animal learns "Nothing I do matters." For this reason the deprived animal ceases to attend to information involving the restricted modality. Such an interpretation of Held and Hein's data seems plausible when we consider that two of the tests they used were reflexes (blink response and paw placement) and the third (visual-cliff performance) apparently innately programmed, or unlearned (Walk & Gibson, 1961). Thus, early stimulus deprivation may alter behavioral processes. However, the effects may arise not because the animal has lacked the opportunity to learn adaptive response patterns using the affected modality but because the animal has learned to respond differently to its environment.

The Effects of Early Stimulus Enrichment on Learning and Performance

As noted earlier, a second approach employed by researchers attempting to clarify the role of early experience in the development of learning is the extra-experience method. This procedure involves giving experimental animals some sort of extra experience that control subjects do not receive. As with the stimulus-deprivation procedure, the effects of the experimental manipulation are later assessed in mature animals by the use of some sort of learning task. This approach, which depends on controlling the complexity of the organism's early environment, avoids the disadvantages of drastic sensory deprivation inherent in the stimulus-deprivation method.

Free-Environment Experiments

In *The Organization of Behavior* (1949), Hebb described an informal experiment that was to provide an impetus for a number of subsequent investigations. At a very early age a group of rats was moved from the laboratory to Hebb's home, where they were placed in the care of his two young daughters. Henceforth, the life of the rats was plush compared to the dull existence of their little mates, who remained in cages back at the lab. The experimental rats had toys to play with and spent a lot of time outside their cages cavorting about the house. After several weeks of this royal treatment, the rats were returned to the lab and administered the rat intelligence test of Hebb and Williams (1946). The performance of the experimental animals on this series of detour/maze problems was consistently superior to that of the cage-reared control animals. More important, the pets improved their standing during the final days of testing, indicating that their superior performance was not entirely due to receiving extra handling. The results demonstrated, in effect, that the extra experience of the pets during development made them more capable of profiting from new experiences at maturity. This is, of course, an attribute usually assigned to an "intelligent" human.

Several experiments of the same general sort have since been conducted using more rigorously controlled procedures. These investigations have, in general, replicated Hebb's original findings. In addition, Hymovich (1952) and Forgays and Read (1962) have demonstrated that postweaning environmental enrichment occurring early in life is more effective in enhancing maze performance than when given later in life.

In the Forgays and Read study, rats were placed in an enriched environment for a 3-week period at different ages. The complex environment was a large living box containing several wooden and metal playthings. One group lived in this free-environment box from birth until 21 days of age. The other groups were housed in small laboratory cages during this part of their lives. At 21 days of age, the initial group was transferred to laboratory cages and a second group placed in the enriched environment, where it also remained for 21 days before being transferred back to the laboratory cages. This procedure was repeated in successive 3-week periods for three remaining experimental groups. At approximately 120 days of age, all the rats began training on the Hebb/Williams maze.

The results indicated that the animals that had had free-environment exposure from 22 to 43 days of age made the fewest errors, while a control group with no early experience in the complex environment made the most errors; the remaining four groups had error scores between these extremes. The control group made significantly more errors than all the other groups with the exception of a group that had been placed in the complex environment between 88 and 109 days of age, an age when a rat is considered to be a mature animal. In addition, the group placed in the free environment immediately after weaning (at 21 days of age) performed better than did the group exposed during the first 3 weeks of life and the group exposed between 88 and 109 days of age. It is, of course, not surprising that the group placed in the free environment during the first 3 weeks of life did not benefit from it, since during much of this time their eyes were closed and they were not mobile as a result of their lack of neurological development. Similar results on the effects of preweaning versus postweaning enriched experience on later problem-solving ability have been reported by Denenberg, Woodcock, and Rosenberg (1968).

The results of these inquiries appear to indicate that it is important for young humans to be exposed to as enriched a perceptual environment as possible during their early rather than late rearing. This proposition received empirical support in research conducted by Heber, Garber, Harrington, and Hoffman (1972), who provided dramatic evidence that preschool environmental enrichment, instituted very early, can improve a child's intellectual abilities. Working in a ghetto, an area characterized by a high incidence of mental retardation in children, Heber and his associates isolated a group of potentially retarded infants on the basis of the fact that their mothers scored 75 or below on the Wechsler Adult Intelligence Scale (100 is average). The children of these 40 mothers were assigned to either an experimental environmental enrichment condition or a control group. The infants in the experimental group were assigned to a teacher when they were only 3 months old; the teacher was in charge of the infant for most of its waking day 5 days a week. This continued until the child was 12–15 months old, at which time the child was gradually introduced to other teachers and children. Initially, for 6 to 8 weeks, the teacher worked with the child in its own home. Later the child was worked with at a teaching center. The general program was to provide the child with an intellectually enriched, stimulating environment in an affectionate setting. When the child was old enough (24 months), the program gradually became more structured and promoted skills in language, reading readiness, and mathematics/problem solving.

The Gesell Developmental Schedule, an infant-intelligence test, was administered to the experimental and control children at the ages of 6, 10, 14, 18, and 22 months. Other intelligence tests were administered every 3 months between the ages of 24 and 48 months and at 6-month intervals thereafter. Up to about 14 months of age, both groups performed at a level fairly comparable to the test norms. At 18 months, however, the two groups began to diverge; the experimental group showed superior test performance. By the age of 22 months, the experimental group began to be clearly above the group norms, while the control subjects fell slightly below normal levels. The IQ scores of the groups diverged more and more as the children grew older. By the time the children had reached the age of 5 years, the experimental children had a mean IQ of 118, while the control children's mean was 92. These intriguing findings suggest that with an early, intensive infant-stimulation program, later problem-solving ability, as measured by intelligence-test scores, can be improved. Long-term follow-up studies of these children will eventually evaluate the significance of these findings as indexed by academic achievement.

Exposure to Specific Stimuli

As with the studies just described, the following experiments have, with few exceptions, used the rat as the experimental subject. In general, this type of experiment exposed rats to a few stimuli and later tested the ability of the subjects to distinguish between these or similar stimuli. The first experiment on the effects of specific-form exposure on later discrimination learning was conducted by E. J. Gibson and Walk (1956). Basically, these researchers found that exposure to specific forms during rearing facilitated the later discriminability of these shapes. All subsequent studies have been attempts to clarify the nature of the mechanisms underlying their results. Several of these investigations have examined the theoretical basis of their findings. Therefore, before we examine the empirical findings, it will be helpful to look at the two major theories of discrimination learning that have been applied to these data.

Theories of Perceptual Learning. J. J. Gibson and Gibson (1955), in support of the *differentiation theory,* hold that in order for positive transfer to result from stimulus exposure, *experience* with the to-be-discriminated stimuli is all that is necessary. To an opposing view, which uses associative processes, reinforcement, and drive-reduction theories to explain perceptual learning, the Gibsons have given the name *enrichment theory.* This theory should be distinguished from the methodology of placing animals in an enriched environment. According to the enrichment view, perceptual experience in itself is not always sufficient for discrimination of the critical features of stimuli to occur; rather, perceptual learning requires that this experience be associated with reinforcement, drive reduction, or attachment of relevant labels to the forms. Through such associative processes the reinforcement or labeling practice produces cues that become added to the to-be-discriminated stimuli, thereby making these stimuli more distinctive.

In general, according to differentiation theory, perceptual learning consists simply of learning to respond to various stimulus aspects not previously responded to; on the other hand, according to enrichment theory, perceptual learning may be facilitated as a result of associative processes arising from labeling practice, reinforcement, or drive reduction, factors that influence discrimination learning over and above mere responding to an increasing number of critical features of the stimuli. The results of several human and animal studies have been used as evidence for either the differentiation or the enrichment view. The experiments that we will next examine investigated stimulus-discrimination learning in animal subjects.

The Early-Experience Paradigm and Experimental Findings. As previously indicated, several animal studies conducted by Gibson, Walk, and their associates have in general demonstrated that early experience with stimuli enhances their later discriminability. In the first of their experiments, E. J. Gibson and Walk (1956) attempted to determine the effects of early and continued exposure to stimuli on the later ease with which an animal learned to discriminate between them. The methodology used in this experiment has served as a prototype for all subsequent investigations of this sort. Two groups of albino rats were raised from birth in well-illuminated cages situated in white compartments, thereby placing the rats in a visually sparse environment. The experimental rats had black circle and triangle cutouts hanging in their cages from birth throughout the duration of the experiment. At 90 days of age, the experimental and control subjects learned a circle/triangle discrimination in a two-choice discrimination apparatus as a test of the effects of the preexposure conditions. The animals were run until they attained a criterion of 18 out of 20 correct responses, with the last ten consecutive responses correct.

As indicated by Figure 7–4, the experimental animals attained the criterion in significantly fewer trials than did the nonexposed control animals. Gibson and Walk concluded, on the basis of this finding, that visual experience with the to-be-discriminated shapes, even in the absence of differential reinforcement, enhanced the subjects' later ability to discriminate between them. As a result, they cited their data as supporting differentiation theory.

This conclusion has not gone unchallenged. There were powerful reinforcers, such as food, water, and social contact, in the early environment of the experimental animals. Although the animals' ability to obtain these reinforcers did not depend on the emission of a specific response, such as an attention or investigatory response directed toward the shapes, these nondifferential reinforcers may nevertheless have become associated with the preexposure stimuli and thus have made them more distinctive.

To determine whether the early-experience effect was indeed mediated by nondifferential reinforcement of the cage stimuli, Kerpelman (1965), in an impeccably controlled experiment, reared albino rats from birth under conditions closely replicating those of Gib-

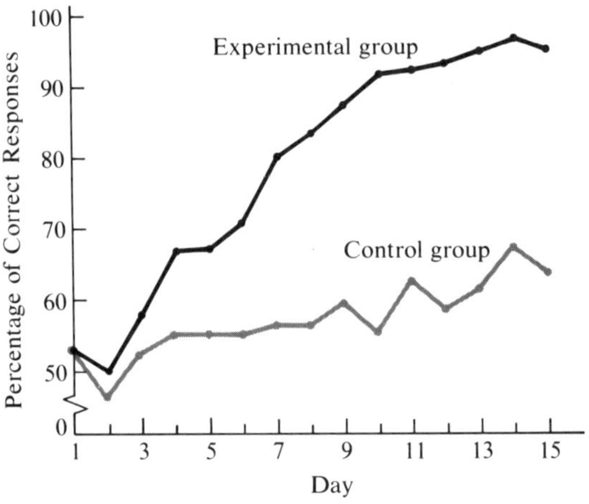

Figure 7–4. Learning curves, in percentage of correct responses per day, for the experimental and control groups. (From "The Effect of Prolonged Exposure to Visually Presented Patterns on Learning to Discriminate Them," by E. J. Gibson and R. D. Walk, *Journal of Comparative and Physiological Psychology,* 1956, *49,* 239–242. Copyright 1956 by the American Psychological Association. Reprinted by permission.)

son and Walk, except that nondifferential reinforcement in the presence of the preexposed stimuli was regulated. One group was exposed to the stimuli, cutout circles and triangles, for 22 hours per day, the stimuli being removed during the two 1-hour daily feeding periods (the no-nondifferential-reinforcement group). A second group, the nondifferential-food-reinforcement group, was exposed to the stimuli for an equal amount of time, but the stimuli were removed for two 1-hour nonfeeding periods. Thus, this group had the shapes present during feeding. A third group was a no-stimulus-preexposure control group. Kerpelman found that the group that had received nondifferential food reinforcement in the presence of the forms performed significantly better on the circle/triangle problem than did the group that had not received food in the presence of the stimuli. In addition, the latter group did not perform any better on the discrimination task than did the control group, which had received no experience with the shapes prior to the discrimination task.

In this experimental situation, differentiation theory would have predicted no effect on later discrimination performance as a function of whether or not the shapes were nondifferentially reinforced during the early-experience period. Differentiation theory would also have predicted better performance of the nonreinforced group compared to the control group. Neither prediction was supported by the results. Kerpelman's basic findings were replicated by T. L. Bennett and Ellis (1968). Since both of these investigations demonstrated a very real effect arising from nondifferential reinforcement of the cage stimuli, the differentiation viewpoint appears incomplete, and the enrichment theory gains support as a strong contender in explaining the positive transfer that results following early experience with the to-be-discriminated stimuli.

In the research examined thus far, the training and test stimuli were identical. To determine the necessity of this feature in producing the early-experience effect, T. L. Bennett, Anton, and Levitt (1971) investigated the effects on later discrimination learning of varying the similarity of the early-experienced forms to the to-be-discriminated shapes.

Group I received early experience with forms that were identical to the to-be-discriminated stimuli, a circle and an equilateral triangle. A second group, Group R, received experience with isosceles triangles and ellipses, stimuli that were relevant to and of the same family as the to-be-discriminated shapes. Group NR (nonrelevant preexposure) received early experience with a struniform (curved shape) and an irregularly shaped cross. There were two of each stimulus per cage. These stimuli were not of the same general class as the to-be-discriminated stimuli but were constructed from the same elements (curved and straight lines). A no-early-exposure control group (Group C) was also employed.

The results indicated that the performances of Groups I and R on the discrimination task were similar and that both groups mastered the problem at a significantly faster rate than did Group C. In addition, Group NR did not differ from Group C in rate of task mastery. These findings suggest that early stimulus preexposure must be with stimuli of the same general class as the to-be-discriminated forms if the positive-transfer effects are to occur. Similarly, E. J. Gibson, Walk, Pick, and Tighe (1958) demonstrated that early experience with circles and equilateral triangles produced a similar degree of facilitation on an equilateral-triangle versus circle discrimination as on an isosceles-triangle versus ellipse problem.

Another common feature of the experiments presented is that they gave albino rats early experience with cutout stimuli. This is an important feature, as demonstrated by Walk, Gibson, Pick, and Tighe (1959). These investigators found that if two-dimensional (painted) stimuli were used in the early rearing environment, the rats' later ability to discriminate between the preexposed forms was not enhanced even though the to-be-discriminated shapes were themselves painted ones. In contrast, if three-dimensional forms (cutouts) were used as the preexposed stimuli, their subsequent discriminability was facilitated. To account for this difference, Walk and his associates postulated an "attention-getting" hypothesis. Presumably, exposure to three-dimensional stimuli enables the animal to sort salient attributes as cues from the total stimulus influx because they physically stand out from their background.

An alternative interpretation of these findings emphasizes the possible role of tactual/kinesthetic feedback in learning about the environment. T. L. Bennett and Ellis (1968) tested this interpretation by employing three-dimensional forms as stimuli during preexposure. However, they allowed one group of albino rats to manipulate the forms, while they prevented a second group from doing so by enclosing the shapes in a wire-mesh box. The forms were still quite visible. The animals allowed to manipulate the forms would be expected to perform better if a tactual/kinesthetic-feedback account was reasonable. In addition, nondifferential reinforcement of the cage stimuli was covaried with the ability to manipulate the shapes. This procedure was undertaken to examine the possibility that for greatest facilitation to result from early experience with the to-be-discriminated stimuli, nondifferential reinforcement of the cage stimuli must be paired with tactual/kinesthetic feedback from the preexposed shapes.

As indicated by Figure 7–5, the subjects allowed to manipulate the forms performed better on the subsequent discrimination-learning task than those not allowed to manipulate when both groups had received concurrent nondifferential reinforcement. Manipulation of the forms in the absence of nondifferential reinforcement produced no differential effect. Finally, subjects receiving nondifferential reinforcement performed better than subjects who received experience alone. In addition to substantiating Kerpelman's (1965) assertion that differentiation theory is not an adequate explanation of the early-experience effect, these findings question the adequacy of an "attention-getting" hypothesis in accounting for differences in transfer effects in studies using two-dimensional versus three-dimensional forms as the preexposure shapes.

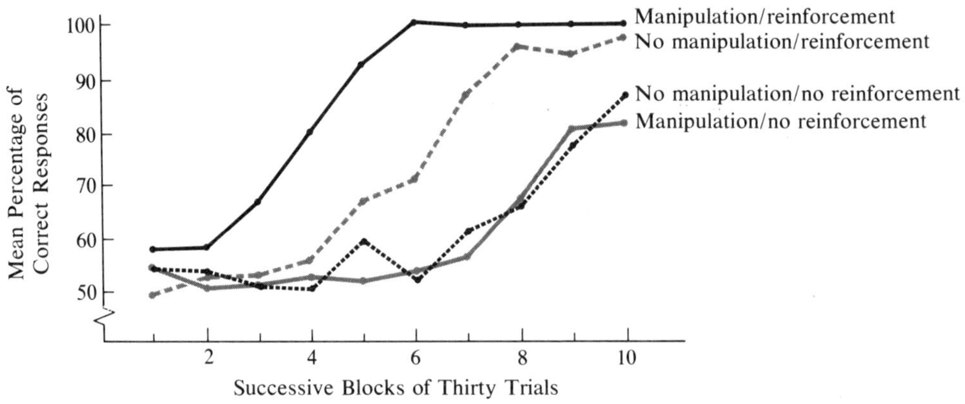

Figure 7–5. Discrimination-learning curves as a function of preexposure conditions. (From "Tactual–Kinesthetic Feedback from Manipulation of Visual Forms and Nondifferential Reinforcement in Transfer of Perceptual Learning," by T. L. Bennett and H. C. Ellis, *Journal of Experimental Psychology*, 1968, *77*, 495–500. Copyright 1968 by the American Psychological Association. Reprinted by permission.)

Early Experience and Adult Stimulus Preferences

We will conclude our review of the effects of early environmental enrichment on later behavior with an examination of two research efforts involving the effects of early experience on adult stimulus preferences. One of these research programs investigated the effects of early olfactory experience on later social behavior in the rat, and the second examined the effect of early auditory stimulation, in the form of music, on later music "preference" in rats.

A series of studies by Marr and his associates have demonstrated that specific social patterns in the adult rodent are a function of early olfactory experience with the species (Marr & Gardner, 1965; Marr & Lilliston, 1969). These investigators have found that rearing rodents with mothers and litter mates characterized by nonnatural odor results in modification of later social behaviors. To demonstrate this, Marr and his fellow researchers exposed infant rats to an unnatural odor on the mother and litter mates from 3 to 29 days of age. To produce the experimental odor, the mother and members of the litter were rubbed on the back, belly, and sides with a cloth containing the experimental odor, either ethyl benzoate or acetophenone. Both of these substances were nontoxic as employed in this research, and rats show no natural aversion to their odors. The subjects were housed individually from day 30 until preference testing began at 45 to 60 days of age. It was found that the experimental subjects preferred nonnatural-odor rats to natural-odor rats. In addition, these animals were less sexually responsive to natural-odor animals and reared young that were more emotional than offspring raised by normally reared animals.

The second example of the ways in which early stimulus exposure can influence adult stimulus preferences is provided in a clever investigation by Cross, Halcomb, and Matter (1967). In this study, rats were exposed early in life to music by either Mozart or Schönberg. In adulthood the animals' preference for different works by the same composers was examined. While on one side of a testing chamber, the rats received Mozart music. If the subject shifted to the other side of the chamber, it received music by Schönberg. Analysis of the results indicated that Mozart-reared rats showed a definite preference for the Mozart music, but Schönberg rats showed no preference. The authors attributed the latter effect to the complexity of the Schönberg music. Perhaps, they suggested, his music is "too complex to be an appropriate 'object' of attachment for the lowly rat" (p. 234).

Perceptual Development in Human Infants

Although newborn humans are helpless, even casual observation suggests that they are receptive to sensory stimulation. Consequently, in recent years great interest has evolved in examining the development of infant perceptual abilities. In the past, researchers had assumed that infants do not have the neurological maturity to react differentially to discrete changes in incoming stimulation, but such is not the case. With respect to form perception, for example, much research literature indicates that from a very early age are present the prerequisite muscular skills for eye coordination and the receptor processes for receiving and analyzing information. Excellent reviews of infant perceptual development can be found in articles by Bond (1972) and Hershenson (1967).

Methods of Study

Assuming that infants have the potential to discriminate between forms, we next have to determine that they indeed make such discriminations. This is hard to do for several reasons. Discrimination-training techniques cannot be used with very young infants; thus, special experimental procedures are necessary. These methodologies, which we will shortly examine, generally involve presenting the subject with a pair of stimuli and determining whether the child attends to one stimulus more than the other. If the infant does exhibit a preference, the experimenter can conclude that the subject is discriminating between the forms. Unfortunately, if the infant does not exhibit a preference, this does not necessarily indicate an inability to discriminate. Such a finding may simply indicate no preference. Finally, to conclude that a subject is responding to a form, an experimenter should demonstrate that the child is indeed responding to the entire stimulus rather than to just a border or an angle (Hershenson, 1967). Hence, one should attempt to isolate what attributes of a stimulus are guiding an infant's observing or investigatory responses. With these problems in mind, let us next look at the methodology used to assess infant form perception.

Fantz (1958) began his work in this area by examining infant preferences for different visual patterns. In his studies he measured the fixation time on each of a pair of patterns that were simultaneously presented in the infant's visual field. An example of one of his apparatuses is shown in Figure 7–6. The patterns were presented to an infant seated in a semiupright infant seat while an observer watching through a small hole in the back of the chamber recorded on which of the two stimuli the infant's eyes fixated. The total amount of fixation time on each stimulus was used to assess the subject's degree of preference for that stimulus. The criterion for looking was the appearance of a tiny corneal reflection of the pattern on the pupil.

Kagan and his colleagues (Henker, Asano, & Kagan, 1968) have altered Fantz's visual-preference apparatus without changing the basic methodology. By using a polarized, partially reflective mirror and videotape equipment, these researchers record the subject's eye movements for later judging. Also, their apparatus was designed to present stimuli projected onto a screen, thereby allowing the immediate change of stimuli without disturbing the infant. With the use of these methods, the following findings have been reported.

Figure 7–6. Visual-preference-testing apparatus with a doll serving as the subject. (From "Visual Abilities and Pattern Preferences of Premature Infants and Full-Term Neonates," by S. B. Miranda, *Journal of Experimental Child Psychology,* 1970, *10,* 189–205. Reprinted by permission of Academic Press, Inc., and R. L. Fantz, photographer.)

Research Findings

From an early age, infants prefer (in terms of looking time) pattern stimuli to homogeneous stimuli, and they generally prefer more complex patterns to more simple ones. Fantz (1963) has shown preferences for black-and-white patterns (schematic face, bull's-eye, and newsprint) over plain stimuli (colored or achromatic) in infants under 5 days of age. Even infants less than 24 hours old fixated on ⅛-inch stripes longer than gray at a distance of 9 inches (Fantz, 1965). Preference for the more complex of two patterns probably appears no later than the age of 2 months (Fantz, 1958). In general, these results have been reliably replicated (Berlyne, 1958; Munsinger & Weir, 1967; Spears, 1964). Brennan, Ames, and Moore (1966), using checkerboard stimuli, have further reported that the observed preference for complexity is age related. Although 3-week-old infants looked longer at 2-by-2 checks, 8-week-old subjects preferred 8-by-8 checks, and the oldest subjects (14 weeks of age) preferred the most complex pattern (24-by-24 checks). In general, there appears to be a developmental shift in preference for complexity, with older children preferring more complex stimuli (Hershenson, Munsinger, & Kessen, 1965).

As a result of his findings, Fantz (1961) has argued that form perception is, to some degree, innate. Is he justified in drawing this conclusion? Earlier it was indicated that an operational definition of form perception is that the subject attends to the entire stimulus. The available data do indicate that infants respond differentially to form stimuli—that is, show a preference for patterns such as a bull's-eye over stripes or a checkerboard over a square—but to say that they possess form perception on the basis of these data may not be warranted. These findings demonstrate only that the infant is sensitive to some difference between stimuli, and it might be the brightness, number of lines, number of angles, or some dimension other than form to which the subject is reacting.

Eye-movement recordings indicate that although newborn infants do indeed fixate on salient features of a stimulus, other features of the pattern may be ignored (Salapatek, 1968; Salapatek & Kessen, 1966). This tendency is maintained for several years. Kerpelman and Pollack (1964) have reported that preschool, first-grade, and second-grade children showed a tendency to be guided by cues at the bottom part of the stimulus when attempting to discriminate among five irregular pentagons. A more equal distribution of attention responses over the entire figure apparently occurs with increasing age and is correlated with improved discrimination performance. In a related study Ghent (1964) found that the tendency to scan the entire figure beings to occur at about 4 to 5 years of age. Taken together, these findings indicate that from birth infants respond selectively to elements of a form rather than to the total form. As children mature, they examine a more extensive portion of the entire stimulus through active scanning of the shape, and true form perception gradually develops.

A very interesting aspect of the research on infant perceptual development is studies of perception of the human face. Discrimination between adult individuals probably develops early in infants. It is probably based on multidimensional or multisensory cues such as olfaction, audition, touch, and vision. In the visual realm facial pattern is the most distinctive attribute of an individual, and the available evidence suggests that infants can visually discriminate their mothers from strangers sometime between the ages of 1 and 3 months (Ainsworth, 1967; Ambrose, 1961; Yarrow, 1967). Fantz (1961) hypothesized that a facelike pattern might be an especially potent stimulus in eliciting selective perception in infants.

To examine this notion, infants were tested with three flat objects the size and shape of a head, as depicted in Figure 7–7. A schematic face in black on a pink background was painted on the first of these ovals; on a second, the features were rearranged in a scrambled pattern; on the third, a solid patch of black with an area equal to that covered by all the facial features was painted at the top of the pink oval. The features were large enough so that visual acuity was not a problem, and the three objects, paired in all possible combinations, were shown to 49 infants ranging in age from 4 days to 6 months. All the subjects looked somewhat more at the "real" face than at the scrambled face and largely ignored the control pattern. However, the preference difference between the "real" and the scrambled face was not significant.

Other investigations using scrambled faces have also demonstrated that preferences for the scrambled and unscrambled faces are about equal (Fantz, 1963; Hershenson, 1965). The differences observed in many investigations between scrambled and unscrambled faces and control forms may simply be reflecting the infant's preference for more complex stimuli. Consistent with this interpretation is H. Thomas's (1965) finding that infants fixated on a checkerboard more than on a schematic oval drawing of a face. On the other hand, Silbiger (1968) has shown that when faces and abstractions of equal complexity are paired, faces elicit more attention in infants. Moreover, some research has suggested that older infants, those 4 to 6 months old, prefer correct to scrambled schematic faces (Fantz & Nevis, 1967; Kagan, 1970).

After even a very brief review of the information available on infant perceptual development, one must question the widely held notion that infants play a passive role in their environment and that their behavior is based solely on the gratification of basic needs. Newborns to some extent investigate their environment and actively seek stimulation from their surroundings. The sophistication of their perceptual and response systems has only

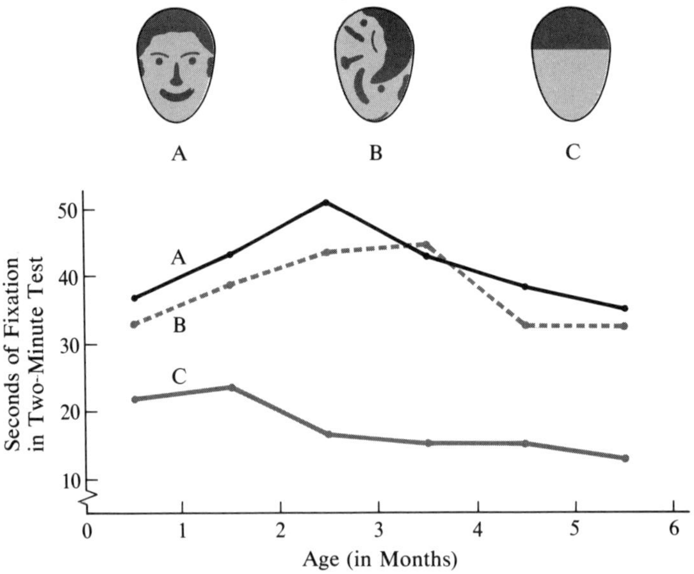

Figure 7–7. Adaptive significance of form perception as indicated by the preference of infants for a "real" face A over a scrambled face B, and for both over a control C. (From "The Origin of Form Perception," by R. L. Fantz. Copyright © 1961 by Scientific American, Inc. All rights reserved.)

recently begun to become apparent. As our methods for examining infant behavior improve, our knowledge of this intriguing area of psychology will increase.

Summary

In this chapter we reviewed some of the many effects exerted by early experience on adult learning and performance. First, early handling apparently produces taming effects, which in turn can influence adult performance, but the learning process itself does not appear to be affected. Although some researchers have argued that the observed changes in emotionality are produced by the extra stimulation itself, there have been several challenges of an uncritical acceptance of this view.

The effects of early social contacts on later behavior were next examined. Research using the rhesus monkey and the chimpanzee indicates that extreme social handicaps result from early social restriction. The effects on learning and performance are less clear-cut. Although research using monkeys does not indicate any definitive learning deficits following early social deprivation, data obtained with chimpanzees suggest that early restrictions cause intellectual impairment in this species, a syndrome similar to that observed in human children reared in an impoverished environment.

Two research methods, the stimulus-deprivation and extra-experience techniques, use variations in amount of early stimulus experience to determine the influence of these differences on later discrimination-learning ability. With the stimulus-deprivation method experimental subjects are deprived from a very early age of some of the normal encounters (for example, visual) of their species. With the extra-experience method experimental animals receive some sort of extra stimulus experience that control subjects do not.

Results obtained with the stimulus-deprivation method are strong evidence for the importance of early stimulation experience in the development of adult discrimination abilities. However, it is often difficult to determine the mechanisms underlying the effects of stimulus deprivation because one cannot necessarily ascertain what structural changes at the neural level may have been caused by the deprivation procedure. These changes may permanently impair the ability of the subject to process information involving the formerly deprived stimulus modality.

Researchers using the extra-experience method have generally shown that animals reared in enriched environments from birth are better problem solvers as adults than are animals that did not receive such treatment. Other researchers have subjected animals to more specific sorts of stimulus preexposure to clarify the mechanisms underlying discrimination learning. Basically, these investigators have reported that exposure to specific forms during rearing facilitates the subsequent discriminability of these shapes. The processes by which this early-experience effect occurs have been enthusiastically debated.

The perceptual development of human infants was the last topic considered. The findings suggest that from birth, or very soon thereafter, infants can discriminate between two patterns that vary in complexity. When very young infants react to a shape, they seem to react only to selected features of the stimulus while ignoring its other features. This finding has led some researchers to conclude that true form perception is learned.

Early experience exerts pervasive effects on adult learning and performance. It affects motivational and emotional states, which in turn influence performance. Early experience appears to determine, to some extent, adult discrimination abilities and general intelligence. Research has generally indicated that experience at a very early age has the most profound effects. This finding underscores the importance of enriched environments for human infants if they are to attain their full capabilities as adults.

Chapter 8

The Physiological Bases of Learning and Memory

We can predict much of an organism's behavior from its history of reinforcement and from the stimuli currently impinging on, and the responses available to, the organism. However, understanding behavior also requires a knowledge of its physiological substrates—of how the brain operates and of how its functions mediate learning and memory.

The human brain consists of an exceedingly complex labyrinth of 10 billion cells. It is pinkish gray, has the consistency of oatmeal, and weighs about 3.5 pounds. Galen (129–199 A.D.) was one of the first to realize the importance of the functions exercised by this master-control organ. He decided that the mind is in the brain; Aristotle had placed it in the heart. Everything that humans have ever been, are now, and ever will be is the product of the brain, but many, if not most, of its functions are still a secret.

In this chapter we will look at some of the methods and findings of researchers who have attempted to understand this structure. Specifically, we will examine the anatomical substrates of learning and memory, the electrophysiological correlates of information processing and memory consolidation, the effects of electroconvulsive shock on memory consolidation, and the possible biochemical bases of memory. Before we delve into these topics, however, a brief overview of neuroanatomy is in order. For a more detailed discussion of the topics described in this chapter the reader should refer to T. L. Bennett (1977).

The Anatomy of the Mammalian Brain

The great raveled knot, as Sir Charles Sherrington once called the brain, is an incredibly intricate network of neurons. So tightly packed are they that one nerve cell is probably never active without influencing some of its neighbors. With maturation of the human embryo, the nervous system develops from a tubelike structure into the central nervous system, which is comprised of the spinal cord and the brain. The spinal cord has two main functions: it mediates reflex actions, and it conducts neural impulses to and from the brain. Early in the development of the embryo, three enlargements appear in the head region of the neural tube. These enlargements further develop into the major subdivisions of the mammalian brain: the *hindbrain*, the *midbrain*, and the *forebrain*.

Within the hindbrain are the *medulla,* the *pons,* and the *cerebellum.* The medulla is essentially a continuation of the spinal cord and contains ascending sensory tracts that carry information to higher regions of the brain and descending pathways that carry motor information to the spinal cord. The medulla also contains several so-called "vital" autonomic nuclei that are concerned with such functions as heart rate and respiration.

Located just above and behind the medulla are the two lobes of the cerebellum, a phylogenetically old structure that was the first brain structure to become specialized for sensorimotor coordination. Even slight damage to this structure can at times seriously disrupt motor responses that require a good deal of coordination. The pons, which lies above the medulla and in front of the cerebellum, contains fibers that connect the two hemispheres of the cerebellum and also fibers that carry ascending and descending information within the central nervous system.

The most recently evolved portion of the central nervous system that still maintains the basic tubular structure of the spinal cord is the midbrain. The midbrain forms a bridge between the hindbrain and the forebrain by merging anteriorly into the *hypothalamus* and the *thalamus.* The dorsal portion of the midbrain contains two pairs of important sensory centers that appear as four small bumps on the surface. One pair, which is a primitive center for vision, is called the *superior colliculi,* and the pair situated just below it is referred to as the *inferior colliculi.* The inferior colliculi are lower centers for audition. The floor of the midbrain is a passageway between higher and lower regions of the nervous system. Sensory tracts ascend and motor tracts descend. The major structures of the hindbrain and the midbrain are shown in Figure 8–1.

A number of important structures and regions comprise the forebrain. Among these are the thalamus, the structures of the *limbic system,* the *basal ganglia,* and the *cerebral hemispheres,* or *cerebrum.* The thalamus is a large grouping of nuclei just above the midbrain. It is shaped somewhat like two small footballs lying side by side, one in each hemisphere. Although some information processing appears to occur at thalamic levels, the thalamus can be conceived of as a relay station for sensory and motor information. It carries information between the cerebral hemispheres and subcortical regions and connects various subcortical areas.

The basal ganglia are a large group of nuclei situated in the central region of the cerebrum. This structure overlies the thalamus and is in turn encapsulated by the cerebral hemispheres. The nuclear groups of the basal ganglia, the *caudate nucleus,* the *putamen,* and the *globus pallidus,* perform important functions in mediating movement. The relation of the basal ganglia to other structures is depicted in Figure 8–2.

A number of forebrain structures appear to comprise an integrated network and are collectively referred to as the limbic system. Although many of the regions of the limbic system were originally thought to be concerned with processing olfactory information, the consensus now is that they are involved in mediating behaviors such as emotion, motivation, and learning. We will examine the functions of limbic-system structures in learning and memory later in this chapter. Within the limbic system are the *hippocampus,* the *cingulate gyrus,* the *septal area,* the *amygdala,* and the hypothalamus. The hippocampus and the amygdala lie in the temporal lobe of the cerebrum, while the other limbic-system structures straddle the midline of the cerebrum. The hypothalamus, a piece of tissue that is about the size of the head of a pin in rats and about the size of a lump of sugar in humans, lies at the base of the cerebral hemispheres, just below the thalamus. In front of and above the hypothalamus is the septal area. The cingulate gyrus, an evolutionary older part of the *cortex,* lies just above the *corpus callosum.* The corpus callosum is the major pathway linking the two halves of the cerebral cortex and is particularly well developed in humans, with their extremely well-developed cortex. The major relationships of the limbic-system structures are shown in Figure 8–3.

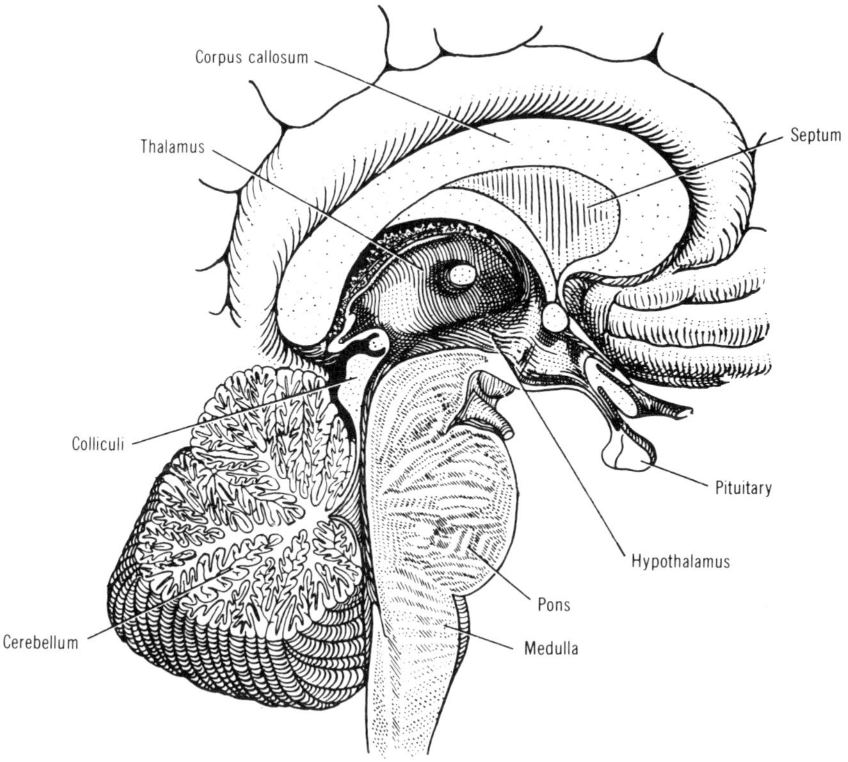

Figure 8–1. Midline section through the human brain stem. (From *A Functional Approach to Neuroanatomy,* by E. L. House and B. Pansky. Copyright 1967 by McGraw-Hill Book Company. Reprinted by permission.)

About 75% of the mass of the human brain is contained in the cerebral hemispheres. The cerebral cortex was the last neural system to develop in the course of evolution and is divided into two halves, the left and right cerebral hemispheres. For convenience, each hemisphere is subdivided into *lobes: frontal, parietal, temporal,* and *occipital.* All incoming sensory systems project to specific regions of the cortex, and motor-control systems arise in other areas. Many of the functions of the cortex in mediating behavior have been delineated, but as with other regions of the brain, many of its specific functions remain an enigma.

Three-fourths of the human cortex is comprised of *association cortex* as opposed to sensory and motor cortex. Presumably, association areas perform vital functions in mediating higher-order behaviors, such as thinking, memory, and verbal processes. Association cortex is what makes humans unique in their behavior repertoire. The basic organization of cortical sensory and motor regions does not change much from rats to humans. However, as one ascends the phylogenetic scale, the proportion of cortex that is association cortex increases markedly. Humans, by the way, do not have the largest brain in the animal kingdom. Porpoises, whales, and elephants have larger brains, but the density of the cells in their brains may be less (R.F. Thompson, 1967).

No description of the brain would be complete without mentioning the *reticular formation,* a structure that extends from the top of the spinal cord, or base of the medulla, to the posterior of the hypothalamus. Anatomically, it is a complex network of cell bodies,

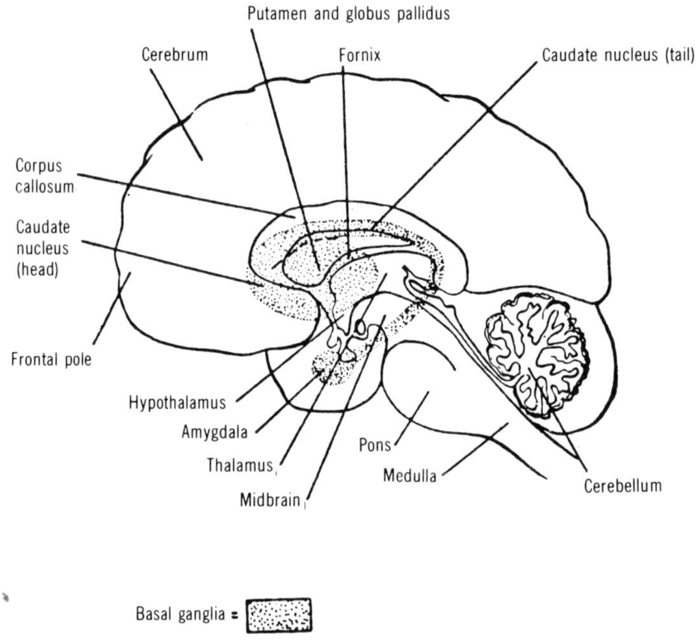

Figure 8–2. Outline drawing of the brain showing the approximate internal locations of the basal ganglia within the cerebral hemisphere. (From *Foundations of Physiological Psychology,* by R. F. Thompson. Copyright 1967 by Harper & Row, Publishers, Inc. Reprinted by permission.)

fibers, and nuclei. There are two major aspects of reticular-formation function. Its descending influences modulate movement. Stimulating different descending pathways can result in either facilitation or inhibition of skeletal movement. The reticular formation's ascending influences are often called the *ascending reticular activating system* in light of this region's demonstrated importance in behavioral arousal. Stimulation of this system will arouse a sleeping animal (Moruzzi & Magoun, 1949), while destruction of these ascending influences will produce a comatose state (Lindsley, Bowden, & Magoun, 1949).

This brief overview of the brain probably suggests to you that the brain, like other organs of the body, is organized into discrete parts with specialized functions. Guided by this supposition, many brain researchers have examined the effects on behavior of removing various parts of the brain. We will summarize the results of these types of inquiries with respect to learning and memory in the next section. However, this view has not always proved fruitful in brain research. Rather than having centers with specific functions, the brain apparently mediates behavior through the action of systems. Sometimes these systems are comprised of specific structures or parts of structures. At other times the systems seem to have no distinct anatomical boundaries. It is problems such as these that make an analysis of brain functions so difficult and perplexing on the one hand but so challenging and exciting on the other.

The Anatomical Substrates of Learning and Memory

The oldest and still most widely used technique for studying neural functions is the lesion, ablation, or extirpation method, in which all the cells in one region are destroyed

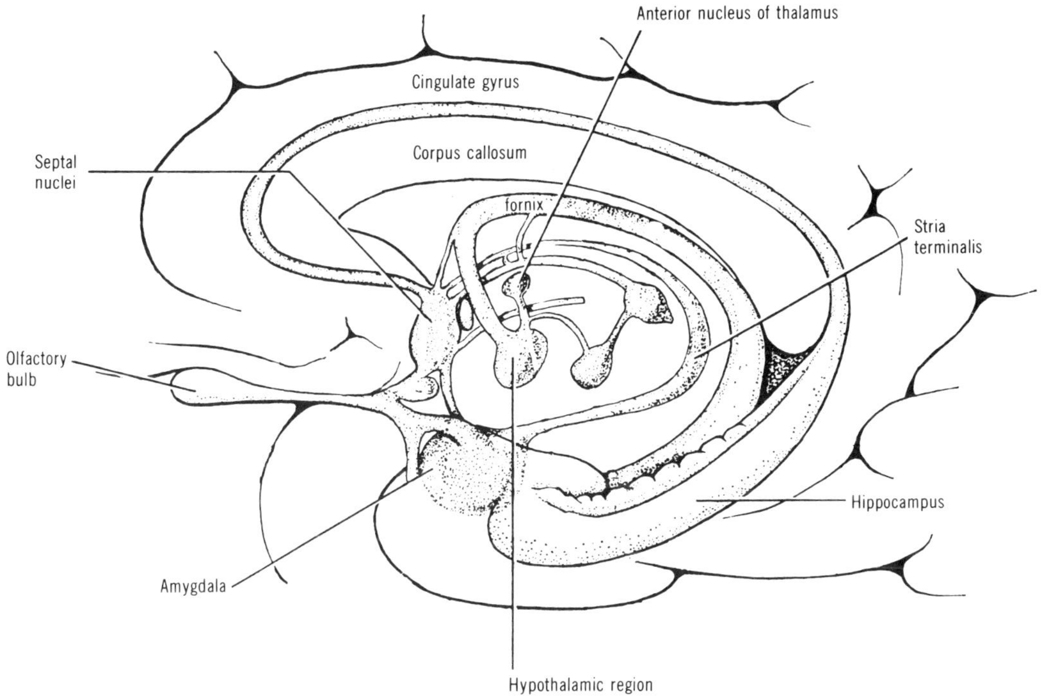

Figure 8–3. Semischematic drawing of limbic-system relationships as seen in a medial view of the right hemisphere. Both deep and superficial structures are indicated. (From *A Functional Approach to Neuroanatomy,* by E. L. House and B. Pansky. Copyright 1967 by McGraw-Hill Book Company. Reprinted by permission.)

and the resultant effects on behavior are examined. Pioneered by Pierre Flourens in the early 19th century, this technique was, with few exceptions, the only method available for studying neural aspects of learning and memory until the 1930s.

Victor Horsley (1857–1916) must be credited with laying the foundations for modern neurosurgical techniques in both clinical and research settings. His first brain operation was performed in 1886, and during his career he contributed many innovations in operative techniques. His development of the stereotaxic method, with R. H. Clarke, made possible the destruction of small areas in the depths of the brain without causing injury to overlying tissue.

A number of different procedures are used to ablate neural tissue. Ablation of the cortex forming the surface of the cerebral hemispheres is probably best accomplished via aspiration using weak suction and small pipettes. Deep lesions are usually accomplished by Horsley and Clarke's stereotaxic technique. A stereotaxic instrument (see Figure 8–4) holds an animal's head in a fixed position and enables the researcher to insert electrodes into the brain at locations having a known relation to skull landmarks or the *intraaural plane* (an imaginary line connecting the right and left ear canals). Although this technique is quite accurate, the placement of the electrodes must later be verified histologically.

The electrodes inserted into the brain are usually stainless-steel wires that are insulated except for the tip. They may be either monopolar (single) or bipolar (double) electrodes. Similar electrodes are employed for studies involving electrical stimulation or recording of subcortical structures. In the case of lesioning electrodes, when a continuous

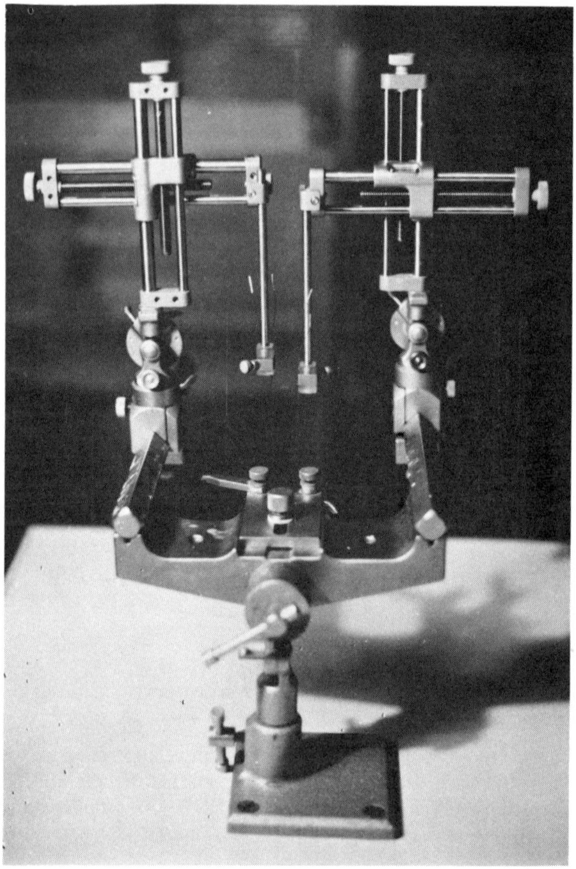

Figure 8–4. A modern stereotaxic device. (From *Brain and Behavior,* by T. L. Bennett. Copyright © 1977 by Wadsworth Publishing Company, Inc. Reprinted by permission of the publisher, Brooks/Cole Publishing Company, Monterey, California.)

flow of electrical current is applied to the electrode, tissue is destroyed in the region of the uninsulated tip, thereby yielding a discrete and localized lesion. Although this lesion technique is widely used, it does have several disadvantages. The most obvious problem is controlling the exact position and size of the ablation. Another problem is that the shape of the lesion is roughly spherical, which is really only desirable if one wishes to destroy a spherical area. Finally, the extent of the lesion does not have clearly distinct borders.

The brain-lesion technique has been used by researchers in the neurosciences in attempts to determine structures or pathways responsible for learning and memory functions. For example, Hebb (1949) and others have suggested that memories in humans are stored in sensory-association areas that border specific sensory-projection regions of the cortex. Such a view certainly appears reasonable in light of findings from some lesion studies indicating that modality-specific deficits result following damage to cortical association areas (for example, visual-discrimination abilities are disrupted by lesions in the visual-association cortex). There is a problem in interpreting these data, however. It is often difficult to discern whether a deficit in learning or performance actually reflects a disruption of mechanisms specifically related to memory or whether the deficit has arisen because of a disruption of complex sensory, motor, and/or motivational functions that are essential for the integration of behavior.

In the case of the complex behavior repertoire of humans, higher-order associations may involve the neocortex. Stimulation of the temporal-lobe neocortex can at times elicit complex memories from the patient's past (Penfield, 1965). However, the cortex does not appear to be essential for the recall of past events, since these memories can still be experimentally elicited after the cortex has been removed (Penfield, 1965; Penfield & Perot, 1963). Simple conditioning does not appear to require the cortex, and even very difficult discrimination problems can often be relearned following damage to cortical association areas.

Results such as these have led many researchers to conclude that the actual formation of stimulus–response associations occurs at the subcortical level. As a consequence, many brain investigators have examined the effects of lesions in various subcortical structures on learning and retention. Attention to the role of subcortical structures in learning and memory processes has also been dictated by the availability of subjects for neural research. The rat seems to have been the most popular subject for experiments, and although this animal's subcortex is fairly well differentiated, its cortex is not too highly developed. The rat has virtually no association cortex; its cortex is almost entirely devoted to sensory and motor functions.

The Hippocampus

The possibility that the hippocampus is involved in learning and memory was first suggested by human clinical observations. Its functions were later at least partially clarified by studies using nonhuman species.

Human Clinical Observations. Over the past 20 years the subcortical structure most widely investigated for its posited role in memory storage and retrieval has been the hippocampus. The interest in this structure and its possible functions in associative processes was first generated by human clinical observations. Case studies indicated that bilateral damage to the hippocampal formation in humans as a result of tumor growth or vascular disturbances resulted in severe defects in recent memory—that is, in the ability to add new information to long-term memory. This type of memory loss is called anterograde amnesia. The damage appeared to affect only the consolidation mechanism. General intelligence was not disrupted, and the ability to recall information acquired prior to the damage was generally unaffected. In other words, retrograde amnesia did not occur.

A similar disturbance of memory-consolidation processes has been noted in clinical cases in which bilateral temporal-lobe excisions were performed for the relief of epileptic seizures and psychotic personality disorders. Such radical treatment methods were undertaken only after more conservative types of treatment had failed. In these surgical procedures, in addition to removing approximately the anterior two-thirds of the temporal-lobe neocortex, the hippocampus and the amygdala were destroyed. It was found that in all patients having bilateral hippocampal damage, a recent-memory deficit developed. Furthermore, the extent of this disruption roughly bore a direct relationship to the volume of hippocampus bilaterally removed. These observations led Penfield and Milner (1958) to propose that initial recording of memory traces may be accomplished by hippocampal mechanisms, an observation that was to precipitate a flood of investigations on the role of the hippocampus in learning and memory in lower animals. We will look at these animal experiments shortly, but before we do, let us examine the postsurgical behavior of the most famous of the human hippocampal patients, H. M.

An example of the drastic effects on memory consolidation resulting from hippocampal lesions is provided by the case of this patient, whose hippocampus was bilaterally destroyed in 1954 to stop intractable seizures associated with temporal-lobe epilepsy. H. M.'s postoperative memory disturbance was immediately apparent. Scoville and Milner (1957) wrote that

> after the operation this young man could no longer recognize the hospital staff, nor find his way to the bathroom, and he seemed to recall nothing of the day-to-day events of his hospital life. There was also a partial retrograde amnesia, but his early memories were apparently vivid and intact [p. 14].

The loss of memory-consolidation processes was apparently permanent. In 1966, 12 years after H. M. had had the surgery, Milner wrote that "the remarkable memory defect persists, and it is clear that H. M. can remember extremely little of the experiences of the past twelve years" (p. 7). These observations are strong evidence that the hippocampus is crucially involved in the transfer of new information into permanent memory.

These clinical reports were based on relatively few subjects, and the exact locus and extent of the lesions were rarely confirmed histologically. Nevertheless, the findings have provided a strong impetus for research attempting to define the role of thc hippocampus in behavior. As with any type of neurological research involving human patients, this research has had severe limitations. To examine further the functions of the hippocampus in learning and memory, investigators have turned to lower animals for their subjects.

That human patients with hippocampal lesions were severely impaired in the acquisition of new skills suggests that recent memory may not be clearly distinguishable from learning ability. Operationally, both of these constructs imply an ability to consolidate new material into memory and to recall this stored information when necessary. For this reason, tests of the recent-memory hypothesis of hippocampal functioning using infrahuman subjects have usually investigated the effects of hippocampal ablations on the mastery of novel learning tasks.

Animal-Lesion Studies. Much to the surprise of early researchers, clear support for the recent-memory hypothesis did not emerge from studies of animal hippocampal lesions. The lesions did not produce a general memory-consolidation defect, as they appeared to in humans; rather, the lesioned animals could learn some fairly complex problems. Rats, cats, and monkeys were found to be normal in their learning and retention of a simultaneous-discrimination problem regardless of whether they learned to discriminate between tactual stimuli (for example, Webster & Voneida, 1964); spatial cues (D.P. Kimble & Kimble, 1965); or visual stimuli that varied in brightness, size, or shape (for example, R.J. Douglas & Pribram, 1966; D.P. Kimble, 1963). Hippocampal lesions actually facilitated performance on a two-way active-avoidance problem (for example, Isaacson, Douglas, & Moore, 1961). On the other hand, hippocampectomized rats have generally been found to be deficient in learning complex mazes (for example, D.P. Kimble, 1963; Spiegel, Hostetter, & Thomas, 1966). Once they master the maze, however, they remember it as well as do normal rats.

Overall, experiments on animal lesions have neither proved nor disproved the recent-memory hypothesis of hippocampal functioning. The reason could be evolutionary differences in the role performed by the hippocampus in mediating the behavior of humans and lower animals. It seems more plausible, however, that the lack of conclusive evidence has resulted from the use of relatively simple testing procedures, usually two-choice, in the animal studies; in human experiments the testing involved recall of chains of verbal items or complex events from the patient's daily life.

A human verbal response is often one out of thousands of possibilities, the majority of which are incorrect. R.J. Douglas (1967) has suggested that the animal analog of a recent-memory defect should be found in excessive stimulus generalization; that is, hippocampectomized animals should have a flatter generalization gradient. Wild and Blampied (1972) have published findings that seem to confirm this prediction. However, instead of reflecting an increased degree of stimulus generalization, their results may have resulted from response perseverance, a behavior pattern common in hippocampally lesioned animals.

One rather consistent effect of hippocampal lesions on learning and performance has been reported. In general, hippocampally lesioned animals are less likely than control subjects to stop doing something that brings either punishment or nonreward; that is, they seem to be deficient in the ability to inhibit previously reinforced responses and make different, opposing ones. In other words, acquisition of information appears to interfere *proactively* with learning new information at some later time. On the basis of some carefully conducted experiments, Warrington and Weiskrantz (1973) have suggested that the phenomenon of proactive interference is the basis for the recent-memory defects observed in human clinical patients.

One sign of a hippocampally lesioned animal's perseverance defect is the greater resistance to extinction of a variety of responses in operant situations. Such animals are also deficient in coping with passive-avoidance and discrimination-reversal problems. Finally, they overrespond when shifted from an operant continuous-reinforcement schedule to an intermittent schedule. Reviews of the studies demonstrating this defect are provided by Douglas (1967) and D. P. Kimble (1968). The defects in learning and performance following hippocampal lesions suggest that the hippocampus is responsible for the matching of expected and obtained consequences of responding. Again, the animals seem to exhibit learning disabilities when old information proactively interferes with the acquisition of new information.

The defects in learning and performance due to response perseverance in hippocampectomized animals have led several researchers (for example, Kimble, 1968; Schmaltz & Isaacson, 1966) to suggest that an important role of the hippocampus in mediating behavior is to inhibit previously reinforced response patterns when a mismatch occurs between the expected and the obtained consequences of responding. A variation of this theme is the suggestion that the basis for the perseverance defect lies in the inability of hippocampectomized animals to make an "attention shift" when reinforcement contingencies are altered (see, for example, D.P. Kimble & Kimble, 1970). Finally, Isaacson and Kimble (1972) have suggested that the defect occurs because hippocampally lesioned animals tend to show longer runs of presolution-behavior strategies in determining the correct behavior pattern for task mastery.

There are data, on the other hand, that do not support a simple response-inhibition, attention-shift, or hypothesis-shift explanation of the effects of hippocampal lesions on behavior. In agreement with previously reported data, Pellegrino and Clapp (1971) and Rickert, Bennett, Anderson, Corbett, and Smith (1973) found that hippocampally lesioned rats exhibited performance deficiencies when shifted from a continuous to an intermittent DRL operant schedule. As you will recall, with a DRL schedule the animal must wait a relatively long time between bar presses if it is to obtain reinforcement; pressing before the "time out" has elapsed results in a resetting of the interval, and reinforcement is thus postponed. These researchers further demonstrated that if the DRL task was modified so that the end of the time out and the availability of reinforcement were signaled by the onset of a light, the experimental animals learned the DRL schedule at a normal rate. These observations led Rickert and his colleagues to suggest that the role of the hippocampus is to process information derived from response-produced or proprioceptive feedback when a mismatch occurs between the expected and the obtained consequences of responding (see also Rickert & Bennett, 1972).

However, an alternative interpretation of these findings is that the addition of the light cue may have altered the conditions of training to such an extent that proactive interference did not occur or made the conditions of reinforcement so distinctive for the lesioned animals that their perseverance tendency was negated. Regardless of its basis, proactive interference appears to be the most reliable effect produced by hippocampal lesions. In light of Warrington and Weiskrantz's (1973) reinterpretation of the effects of human hippocampal lesions and in light of the kinds of defects that infrahuman species exhibit following such lesions, it might be profitable to conceive of the hippocampus's function in learning and memory as being involved in the process of "stamping out" previously acquired but inappropriate information rather than "stamping in" memory traces.

Projections of the Hippocampus

Several structures to which the hippocampus projects have also been implicated in learning. The *fornix* (see Figures 8–2 and 8–3) is the major efferent pathway from the hippocampus and links this structure with other regions of the subcortex. Fibers from the hippocampus course downward via the fornix to join the septal area or septum, the mammillary region of the hypothalamus, and the anterior nuclear complex and the medial nuclear group (dorsomedial nucleus) of the thalamus. All of these connections are reciprocal.

The mammillary bodies of the hypothalamus and the medial regions of the thalamus have been implicated in memory because they (but not the hippocampus) are destroyed in the human clinical syndrome called Korsakoff's psychosis. This disorder, which is characterized by severe memory defects, results from continuous overindulgence in alcohol for many years. Lesions in lower animals have generally confirmed these observations (see, for example, R. Thompson, 1969; Vanderwolf, 1971), but the effects are often not as pronounced as they are in humans. Unfortunately, lesions in the mammillary region or the medial thalamus may also produce hyperemotionality in animals. Hence, it is often difficult to determine whether defects in learning and performance reflect an inability to consolidate and/or recall information or reflect a heightened emotional state that interferes with adaptive responding.

This confounding effect was eliminated in work by Means, Huntley, Anderson, and Harrell (1973). These researchers reported deficient learning and retention of a two-choice discrimination in rats with medial-thalamus lesions in the absence of lesion-induced changes in emotionality, motor activity, food consumption, or visual-placing responses. These results appear to corroborate the findings from the human clinical cases suggesting that medial-thalamus lesions yield memory defects. The basis for the defects will have to be clarified by future research.

There are very few data, of either a clinical or animal-lesion type, to suggest that other structures in the brain are intimately related to basic processes of memory consolidation or recall. Nevertheless, let us review some of the proposed functions in learning and performance that are exerted by some of the other major brain regions. As indicated, the hippocampus is directly connected, via the fornix, to the septal region. It is also connected to the cingulate gyrus. The septum and the cingulate gyrus will be considered together because they often appear to exert opposite influences in mediating behavior.

From experiments on the role of these structures in learning and performance, it appears that they exert equivalent but opposite effects on the initiation of movement. A number of researchers (see McCleary, 1966) have posited that the role of the septum is response suppression while the cingulate gyrus has a response-initiation function. In some species, such as the rat, this entails resolving a conflict between "freezing," which the septum presumably initiates, and "fleeing," which is under the control of the cingulate gyrus (G.J. Thomas, Hostetter, & Barker, 1968; Trafton, 1967).

The functions of these structures in learning and performance apparently do not involve laying down or recalling memory traces. Cingulectomized animals are deficient in learning tasks that require response initiation (for example, two-way active avoidance; see G.J. Thomas & Slotnik, 1963) but superior to normal animals in tasks that require response suppression (for example, passive avoidance; see Lubar, 1964). In contrast, septally lesioned animals are superior in mastering tasks that require response initiation, such as a two-way active avoidance (see, for example, L.W. Hamilton, 1972; D.A. Johnson, 1972; Trafton, 1967), but retarded on tasks that require response suppression (for conditioned suppression of activity, see Trafton, 1967; for passive avoidance, see Fried, 1969, 1971; Zucker, 1965).

Although the available data indicate that the cingulate gyrus and the septal region appear to exert equivalent but opposite influences on responding or movement, more work needs to be done on this question. Lubar (1964) analyzed the learning ability of cats with lesions that overlapped both the septal and the cingulate region to determine whether the lesions would cancel each other. His subjects learned a passive-avoidance problem at a normal rate. Thus, the cingulate lesion appeared to offset the defect caused by the septal lesion that normally occurs in passive-avoidance learning. No one has ever conducted the complementary study; that is, it has not been determined whether septal damage would offset the cingulate damage normally observed during two-way active-avoidance learning. It is possible that such compensatory action would occur, and if it did, it would strengthen the view that the influences of these two regions are roughly equivalent.

The loss of inhibition in septally lesioned animals is in many ways similar to the perseverance defects seen in hippocampally lesioned subjects. As with these and also cingulectomized subjects (Schwartzbaum, Kellicutt, Spieth, & Thompson, 1964), performance defects induced by septal lesions occur in both aversive and appetitively motivated situations. A task that has been widely used to assess the effects of septal lesions is DRL performance following continuous reinforcement. As do hippocampectomized animals, septally lesioned subjects overrespond on DRL schedules, seeming to persist with patterns of responding that are appropriate to the continuous-reinforcement contingencies (Ellen & Aitken, 1973; Ellen & Braggio, 1973; Ellen, Wilson, & Powell, 1964). Septally lesioned rats also learn to respond normally on a DRL schedule if the end of the time-out interval and the availability of reinforcement are signaled by an external cue (Ellen & Butter, 1969). Finally, in animals with selective septal lesions, overresponding on DRL schedules is most pronounced for those subjects whose lesions involve the regions of the septum that directly project to the hippocampus (MacDougall, Van Hoesen, & Mitchell, 1969). These findings support the existence of a septohippocampal system or subsystem mediating response inhibition or attention processes.

In addition to reciprocal connections with the hippocampus via the fornix, the septum has reciprocal connections via the *stria terminalis* (see Figure 8–3) to the amygdala, a structure to which we now turn our attention. The amygdala has long been implicated in the mediation of affective behavior (Fuller, Rosvold, & Pribram, 1957; Klüver & Bucy, 1937, 1939; Schreiner & Kling, 1953). For this reason, examinations of this structure's role in learning have centered around the learning and performance of various types of avoidance responses. Numerous investigations have not produced any evidence of a simple memory defect or an inability to acquire new behaviors following amygdala lesions.

As with the cingulate gyrus and the septum, the amygdala seems to be involved in the initiation and suppression of responding. However, in the case of the amygdala, these opposing functions appear to be organized in different regions of the same structure. A number of years ago, Kaada (1951), on the basis of experiments investigating the effects of amygdala stimulation on movement in cats, reported that the lateral portions of the amygdala facilitate movement while the medial amygdala appears to inhibit movement. In light of this finding, that opposing motor functions are organized in different parts of the same structure, the wisdom of making total-amygdala lesions must be questioned. We will confine our discussion to experiments using a discrete-lesion approach in which the effects of lesions in different amygdala areas were compared.

One of the most carefully conducted and comprehensive investigations of the role of the amygdala in avoidance behavior was published by Ursin (1965), who examined the effects of variously placed lesions in the amygdala complex. His data are of particular interest because he was able to separate the behavioral effects of laterally from medially placed amygdala ablations. The avoidance defects that Ursin observed correspond nicely with Kaada's findings on motor facilitory and inhibitory effects of amygdala stimulation. Ursin found that defects in active avoidance occurred when the lesions were confined to the lateral, or motor-facilitation, region of the amygdala complex and that passive-avoidance defects occurred when the lesions were in the motor-inhibitory regions of the medial amygdala. Passive-avoidance defects also occurred when the fibers of the stria terminalis, the pathway connecting the medial amygdala to the septum, were severed.

These data, when added to the results previously reported in this chapter, provide evidence for the existence of discretely organized neural response-initiation and response-inhibition systems that mediate behavior. In the same paper Ursin also provided evidence to support the view that amygdala lesions do not have a general deleterious effect on learning processes. He found no impairment in visual-discrimination learning (brightness or pattern discrimination) in any of the amygdala-lesioned cats.

The results of studies examining the effects of discrete amygdala lesions on passive-avoidance or conditioned-suppression responses in the rat directly conflict with Ursin's cat data. In the rat the ability to inhibit a previously conditioned response appears to be mediated by the lateral amygdala rather than by the medial amygdala, as is the case with the cat (Kemble & Tapp, 1968; Pellegrino, 1968; Pellegrino & Clapp, 1971; J.B. Thompson & Schwartzbaum, 1964). One explanation for these conflicting results is the possibility that species differences exist in the functional organization of the amygdala. Another possibility, suggested by Kemble and Tapp, is a difference in the characteristics of complex intraamygdala connections between these species. Future research will have to answer this question.

Another feature of the behavioral-inhibition defect observed in amygdala-lesioned animals bears mentioning. Just as we saw to be the case with inhibition defects associated with septal and hippocampal ablations, the amygdala-produced impairment will disappear if a visual cue is added to guide behavior. Although rats with bilateral lesions of the lateral regions of the amygdala show defects in DRL performance and spatial alternation without cues, this impairment disappears when the rats learn either a cued-DRL or a visually cued spatial-alternation problem (Pellegrino, 1968; Pellegrino & Clapp, 1971).

Overview

Experimental attempts to discover a structure or pathway that is crucial for the consolidation of memory and its subsequent recall have been somewhat discouraging. Of all the structures examined, probably the hippocampus performs the most pervasive functions in memory, particularly in light of human clinical investigations that evaluated the effects of ablations and electrical stimulation on the consolidation and recall of complex memories. But even if the hippocampus is required for higher memory processes in humans, it apparently is not essential for basic memory functions in lower animals. They are able to master a variety of tasks in the absence of an intact hippocampus.

The findings reported in this chapter have led many researchers in the neurosciences to conclude that memory is not localized in any particular brain region or identifiable pathway (John, 1967, 1971; Lashley, 1958). As an alternative, John has suggested that memories reflect unique spatiotemporal patterns of discharge of electrical activity in neural systems that encompass most, if not all, of the brain. This view is based on the finding that most brain cells are always active. Alterations in the average temporal pattern of firing may serve as the basis for information coding. Hence, different bits of information would not need to be coded as activity in different cells, as a localization-of-function view might contend. Rather, different items of newly acquired information may be represented by the same group of cells that are firing in different patterns of electrical activity (John, 1971).

The next section of this chapter investigates this possibility by examining research on the electrophysiological correlates of learning and memory. Such research allows investigators to determine whether changes in the spatiotemporal pattern of electrical activity in neural systems do indeed occur and whether these changes reflect, and are necessary for, the processing, consolidation, and recall of information.

The Electrophysiological Correlates of Learning and Memory

As previously indicated, brain-lesion experiments have demonstrated that no specific structure is required for basic learning and memory processes. Guided by the supposition that memory is diffusely organized, many brain researchers have investigated the electrical activity of the brain in the hope that they might be able to discover changes in neural electrical activity that are correlated with information processing, memory consolidation, and recall. It has been shown that such changes do occur. The problem that next confronts researchers is to determine whether the alterations in the electrophysiology of the brain do indeed reflect learning and memory processes. If the answer to this question is yes, then the investigators must determine whether the physiological changes are necessary for the processes they seem to accompany.

Modern electroencephalography began in 1929, when Hans Berger, a German psychiatrist, reported a method for recording the electrical activity of the brain from an intact skull. His findings were based on research he had conducted in relative seclusion; Berger had made electroencephalograms (EEGs) from the brains of animals since 1902 and from humans since 1924. However, much earlier, in 1875, Richard Caton in England had made the original discovery that the brain continuously emits very low-voltage electrical waves that are rarely more than several hundred microvolts in amplitude; their frequencies range from one wave approximately every half-second to 50 or more per second. A *brain wave* is an undulation in the electrical activity of the brain, and an *electroencephalogram* (EEG) is a record of these waves. EEG records obtained from the hippocampus are shown in Figure 8–5. Only in death do these regular oscillations cease.

In the 1930s Berger's findings were developed into a clinical tool for the study of brain pathology. In 1935 Gibbs, Davis, and Lennox discovered the EEG pattern typical of petit-mal epilepsy, and in 1936 Walter demonstrated that tumors can be located through an unopened skull by abnormal EEG responses recorded from the tissue adjacent to the tumor. Other scientists, such as R. Jung and Kornmüller (1938), set the stage for later experiments on the physiological significance of specific EEG patterns recorded from discrete areas of the brain. Their inquiries served as a basis for the current interest in uncovering EEG patterns related to learning and memory.

Today a large number of neuroscientists are attempting to make significant correlations between the bioelectric rhythms of the brain and behavior in the hope that the functions of a structure are signaled by its electrical activity. The methodology used ranges from examining the electrical activity of single brain cells to investigating the combined pattern emitted by neurons in a relatively large region of the brain. Analyses of the data range from visual inspection to highly sophisticated computer analysis of the brain's rhythms. Only computer analysis can isolate minute changes in wave patterns over time as well as the relationship of the electrical activity of one brain region to that of another.

The Electrical Activity of the Hippocampus

Because of the role in memory processes posited for the hippocampus from human clinical observations and its easily distinguished EEG patterns, the hippocampus has been a favorite target in research on the electrophysiological correlates of learning and memory. Changes in the bioelectric rhythms of the hippocampus have been found to accompany memory consolidation as reflected by improved performance of certain learned responses. However, researchers are still debating whether these changes indeed reflect the role of this structure, or a system of which it is a part, in memory processes.

A number of experimenters have attempted to determine the behavior conditions associated with specific brain-wave patterns. For example, it has been found that recordings from the dorsal hippocampus of permanently implanted, freely moving, unanesthetized cats normally show fast, low-amplitude, desynchronized activity, which is similar in appearance to the EEG arousal pattern of the neocortex. But when the cats move about or make a learned response, the bioelectric rhythm shifts and the desynchronized pattern is replaced by a much slower (4–7 hertz, meaning 4–7 peaks, or waves, per second), high-amplitude, synchronized EEG response called *hippocampal theta activity.* Samples of these two wave patterns are shown in Figure 8–5.

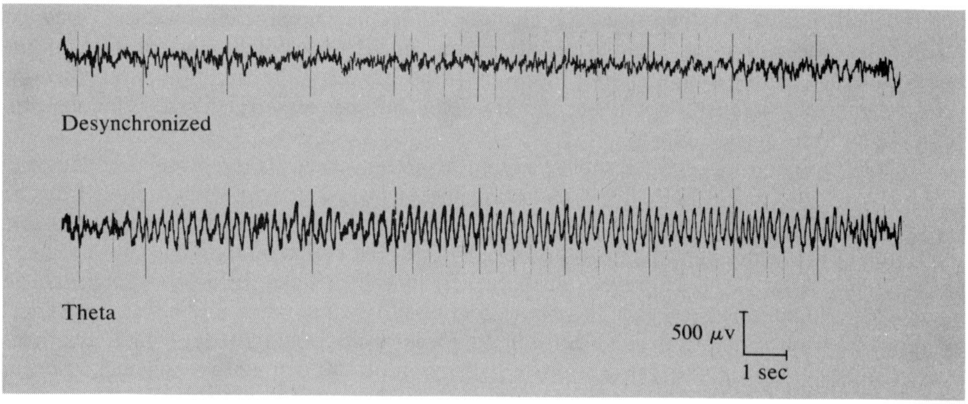

Figure 8–5. Patterns of electrical activity recorded from the dorsal hippocampus of the cat (μV = microvolts). (From *Brain and Behavior,* by T. L. Bennett. Copyright © 1977 by Wadsworth Publishing Company, Inc. Reprinted by permission of the publisher, Brooks/Cole Publishing Company, Monterey, California.)

There are species differences in both the frequency of the theta rhythm and the ease with which it can be recorded. In the cat the frequency of the theta rhythm is 4–7 hertz, while in the rat theta is slightly faster, averaging 6–10 hertz. Theta is very easy to observe in the rat's hippocampogram; it is actually the dominant EEG pattern from the hippocampus. On the other hand, theta is much more difficult to observe in the cat, where there appears to be a balance between the neural systems producing theta and desynchronized activity. Finally, in the primate EEG, desynchronized activity dominates records obtained from the hippocampus, and it is almost impossible to record a train of theta activity. However, it is unlikely that these differences signify that the functions of the hippocampus are different in different species. These observations probably indicate that the EEG correlates of hippocampal functions vary in different species. These differences undoubtedly underlie some of the controversies over the significance of the theta EEG pattern (Winson, 1972).

Several theories have been proposed on the possible significance of the theta pattern as a correlate of functions being performed by the hippocampus and other regions to which this structure relates. The appearance of this slow-wave EEG response has been linked by different theorists to possible functions performed by this structure in mediating such processes as arousal, attention to environmental cues, voluntary movement, and memory. The desynchronized pattern, on the other hand, has been correlated with functions performed by the hippocampus in mediating "automatic" behaviors, inhibiting attention responses to environmental stimuli, and processing information derived from response-produced feedback. A more detailed examination of these theories than is possible in this book is presented by T. L. Bennett and his associates (Bennett, 1971; Bennett, Hébert, & Moss, 1973) and by Vanderwolf (1971).

Hippocampal Theta and Memory. Adey and his associates have suggested that theta reflects the role of the hippocampus in the processing, consolidation, and recall of information (see, for example, Adey, Dunlop, & Hendrix, 1960; Adey & Walter, 1963; Elazar & Adey, 1967; Holmes & Adey, 1960). This conclusion was based on data from a number of studies of the electrical activity of the cat hippocampal system during learning and performance of a visual-discrimination or a delayed-response task. Their findings were similar regardless of the task. Since the majority of the experiments used a two-choice simultaneous-visual-discrimination problem in a straight-alley runway, only these results will be examined.

In the 1960 experiment by Adey and his colleagues, each trial was begun when the cat was placed in the start box at one end of the alley. After presentation of a 500-hertz tone, the door opened and the cat was able to see the opposite end of the apparatus, where there were two translucent plexiglass windows separated by a divider, with a metal dish under each window. One of these windows was illuminated during each trial. Approaching directly to the lighted window was the correct response and was rewarded with food.

The researchers found that with every training trial, a very regular, rhythmic train of theta at 5–6 hertz appeared in the hippocampus and the adjacent *entorhinal cortex* (cortex of the temporal lobe that surrounds the ventral hippocampus) as the animal approached the food reward. Computer analysis of these data uncovered some interesting findings. Cross-correlation analyses were computed between the electrical activity of the hippocampus and that of the entorhinal cortex to determine the time relations between these two regions at different levels of training. It was found that in early training the electrical activity of the hippocampus led that of the entorhinal cortex by 20 to 35 milliseconds. In contrast, this time relationship in the same animals was reversed once the behavioral response was well established. In this case the EEG activity of the entorhinal cortex led that of the hippocampus by as much as 65 milliseconds.

These observations led Adey and his associates to postulate that theta may signal the active involvement of the hippocampus in the processing, storage, and recall of information. More specifically, Adey (1966) wrote that "deposition of a memory trace in extrahippocampal systems may depend on such wave trains [theta] and subsequent recall on the stochastic reestablishment of similar wave patterns" (p. 25). Substantiation of such a view would support the general theory that consolidation of memory results from alterations in the spatiotemporal firing patterns of brain cells. As indicated earlier in this chapter, Penfield and Milner (1958), on the basis of human clinical observations, suggested that the initial recording of memory traces is accomplished by hippocampal mechanisms. In his formulation Adey suggested a neurophysiological correlate of this function.

In subsequent research Elazar and Adey (1967) examined subtle shifts in hippocampal electrical activity as a function of trial segments and amount of training. The trial segments were (1) the prestimulus period before the tone, (2) the stimulus period between the tone and the opening of the start-box door, (3) the approach period, and (4) the postapproach period. It was found that the dominant frequency (spectral peak) in the theta range was 4 hertz for the prestimulus period, 5 hertz for the stimulus period, 6 hertz for the approach period, and 4–5 hertz for the postapproach period. These shifts became more pronounced and regular as training progressed. In addition, no shift of the theta peak of activity to 6 hertz during approach occurred on trials when the animal made an incorrect response. As a result, Elazar and Adey proposed that it is this 6-hertz theta activity that is the essential electrophysiological correlate of functions performed by the hippocampus in information processing, memory consolidation, and recall.

Hippocampal Electrical Activity and Processes of Attention. Adey and his associates have clearly demonstrated that changes in the electrical activity of the brain accompany the learning process. However, their data do not necessarily imply that the observed alterations in patterns of hippocampal electrical activity reflect general learning and memory processes themselves. Investigations of the electrical activity of the hippocampal complex by Grastyán and his co-workers (Grastyán, Karmos, Vereczkey, & Kellényi, 1966; Grastyán, Lissák, Madarász, & Donhoffer, 1959) and by T. L. Bennett and his associates (Bennett, 1969, 1970, 1971, 1973; Bennett & Gottfried, 1970; Bennett et al., 1973; Bennett, Nunn, & Inman, 1971) have led to an alternative view of the significance of hippocampal EEG patterns. They have proposed that theta in the cat reflects the role of the hippocampus in analyzing information derived from exteroceptive stimulation; that is, theta is a correlate of attention to environmental cues. This bioelectric rhythm does not reflect a general processing/consolidation/recall function of the hippocampus.

In summarizing his findings, Bennett (1973) reported that the most apparent factor determining whether learning and performance will be accompanied by hippocampal theta or desynchronization is whether successful performance requires attention to environmental cues. In tasks that can be learned by attending to exteroceptive stimuli, original learning and performance are accompanied by theta activity (for example, successive or simultaneous auditory or brightness discriminations in an operant chamber, light-cued DRL schedules in an operant chamber, and simultaneous brightness discriminations in a straight-alley runway). Learning and performance of tasks that cannot be mastered by attending to environmental cues (for example, continuous reinforcement schedules and noncued DRL schedules in an operant chamber) and instead require attention to proprioceptive feedback (response-produced cues) for their solution are accompanied by hippocampal desynchronization.

According to Bennett, the appearance of theta in cats does not seem to be related to general memory processes but to specific processes of attention. Shifts in the characteristics of the theta response occur during the course of learning, as Elazar and Adey reported, possibly because the nature of task-oriented attention responses changes as the cats learn to attend to only those stimuli that will help guide their ensuing behavior. As the components of their attention responses become more directed, one would predict that the EEG correlates of these responses would also change.

The data thus far reviewed have been derived from cat subjects. As indicated earlier, species differences exist in the hippocampograms. In the rat the occurrence of theta is apparently uncorrelated with attention. Rather, the occurrence of theta appears to accompany the execution of phasic patterns of voluntary movement (Vanderwolf, 1971). In contrast, hippocampal desynchronization in the rat appears to accompany the making of relatively stereotyped or automatic response patterns.

Is Theta Necessary? Even if theta did accompany and reflect general learning and memory processes, we would have to ask whether theta is necessary for the occurrence of these processes. A more general question is whether theta is necessary for the occurrence of behaviors with which it is correlated. In two studies Bennett and his associates (Bennett, 1973; Bennett et al., 1971) examined this issue.

Bennett (1973) investigated the effects of centrally blocking hippocampal theta on learning and retention of a simultaneous brightness discrimination (Adey task), a task whose performance is normally accompanied by theta on 90%–95% of the approach trials. Theta blocking was accomplished by injecting 2 microliters of the anticholinergic agent scopolamine hydrobromide into the medial septal nucleus of cats via a permanently implanted tube. The septum was chosen for the site of injection because the activity of some of the cells in the medial nucleus acts as a pacemaker for the hippocampal theta response. The blocking procedure resulted in theta's occurring on only 6%–8% of the approach responses as compared to 92%–93% of the trials in the nondrugged state. The electrical activity recorded from the hippocampus of the same cat during nondrugged and drugged approach performance is shown in Figure 8–6.

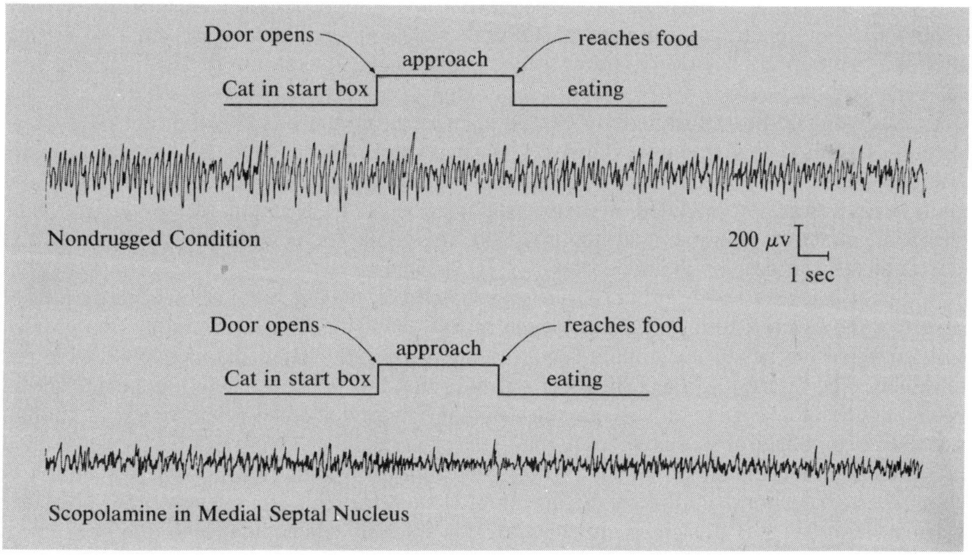

Figure 8–6. Effects of centrally injecting scopolamine hydrobromide on the electrical activity of the hippocampus during correct-approach performance. (From "The Effects of Centrally Blocking Hippocampal Theta Activity on Learning and Retention," by T. L. Bennett, *Behavioral Biology,* 1973, *9,* 541–552. Reprinted by permission of Academic Press, Inc.)

The cats were administered the drug during either original-learning or retention-test sessions. Analysis of the results indicated that neither the rate of original learning nor the amount retained was affected by theta blocking. On the basis of these findings, one would have to conclude that theta is not necessary for the occurrence, during learning, of behaviors with which it is normally correlated and that hippocampal theta is clearly not required for either the laying down of memory traces or the subsequent recall of information. Whether the same can be said for the desynchronized pattern will have to be ascertained by future research.

Fast (High-Frequency) EEG Rhythms

What is normally referred to as fast rhythmic activity has also generated a great deal of interest among neuroscientists. Often at a frequency of approximately 40 hertz, bursts of fast rhythmic activity have been recorded from many regions of the subcortex and the neocortex during arousal, attention, and learning. In the neocortex 40 hertz bears an interesting relationship to overt behavior that has led Sheer (1970) to refer to this bioelectric pattern as the consolidation rhythm. Lesse (1960), using cats, was one of the first to study the 40-hertz burst of activity of the basolateral amygdala. The amygdala fast is apparently evoked by meaningful or noxious stimuli, such as the presence of food, water, a mouse or a dog, loud noises, and so on. It appears before avoidance learning has become apparent and persists long after it is established.

Sheer (1970) has indicated that the amygdala fast is a concomitant of olfactory orienting responses (see also Delgado, Johnston, Wallace, & Bradley, 1970). Its occurrence seems to be highly correlated with sniffing and the movement of air through the nasal passages (Gault & Leaton, 1963). Bilateral ablation of the olfactory bulb abolishes the amygdala fast (Sheer, 1970). As Sheer suggests, the ecological significance of this rhythm is obvious. For quadruped animals particularly, processing olfactory information during attention or orienting behaviors is an essential component in exploratory, feeding, and sexual behaviors.

A similar 40-hertz fast activity can be recorded from the visual and motor neocortex. Sheer has studied this rhythm extensively during learning and performance of a visual-discrimination task. It is important to note that the occurrence of 40 hertz in the visual and motor cortex was uncorrelated with the appearance of 40 hertz in the amygdala. Furthermore, olfactory ablations that abolished the amygdala fast activity had no effect on the electrical fast patterns of the neocortex.

Sheer had cats learn an operant task in which bar presses were reinforced by a milk reward if they were emitted in the presence of a 7-per-second flickering light. Bar presses emitted when the negative stimulus was presented, a 3-per-second flashing light, were not rewarded. The interesting facet of Sheer's data is that the 40-hertz rhythm appeared in the visual and motor cortex only when the animal made the correct bar press, a finding suggesting to Sheer that this rhythm may reflect consolidation processes. It would also presumably reflect recall processes during performance. Additionally, there was an EEG correlate of behavioral inhibition during periods of refraining from responding when the negative stimulus was presented. In this case the interval when a nonreinforced bar press would normally have occurred was dominated by 20-hertz activity in the visual and motor cortex.

Sheer's findings are intriguing, and more work on the behavior correlates of these neocortical EEG patterns needs to be conducted. It would be interesting to investigate the necessity of the 20-hertz and 40-hertz rhythms for the occurrence of behaviors with which they are correlated. Finally, it would be of great interest to determine the relationship of these patterns to the theta and desynchronized activities of the hippocampus.

Microelectrode Investigations of the Electrophysiological Correlates of Learning and Memory

Some researchers have argued that since macroelectrodes (such as those used in the experiments already described) record regional EEG patterns and since neurons that are functionally related are not necessarily regionally located, it is hard, if not impossible, to obtain meaningful correlations between summed EEG patterns and brain functions. Such an argument is considerably weakened by findings published by Ranck (1973b). In an elegant series of experiments, he demonstrated that there are cells in the septum and the hippocampus whose individual firing patterns invariably correlate with the appearance of hippocampal theta activity. Ranck reported that these "theta cells" increase their firing rate if and only if a regular theta rhythm occurs in the hippocampus. In terms of behavior correlates, either an increase in the rate of firing of theta cells or the occurrence of hippocampal theta activity accompanies the same behavior patterns.

Until relatively recently, microelectrode studies were confined to immobilizing surgical preparations. Technological advances have made it possible to record the firing pattern of a single cell for several hours in an unrestrained, vigorously moving animal with almost no distortion of the record due to a movement artifact (see Ranck, 1973a). Experiments investigating changes in the rate of firing of single cells in the mammalian nervous system can be divided into two types: attempts to alter the discharge rate of single cells by applying reinforcement and examinations of alterations in firing patterns in single cells during learning and performance.

The first published account of conditioning the firing rate of single cells was by Olds and Olds (1961). In this study, which used rats as subjects, individual cells were found that were spontaneously active, and increases in their rate of discharge were reinforced by rewarding electrical brain stimulation. Particularly in the hippocampus, cells were found that responded to this treatment procedure. After only ten to 20 reinforcements, cells that normally responded at a rate of once or twice per second increased their firing rate to levels of up to 30 discharges per second. Unfortunately, it soon became evident that overt postural or receptor adjustments were being reinforced and that what was being recorded were the central correlates of these behavior alterations. For example, a neuron would increase its firing rate if the rat sniffed or moved a limb. Reinforcement would then be administered, and the subject would repeat the response that led to reinforcement. Fetz (1969) has demonstrated similar changes in the rate of firing of neurons when food was used as the reinforcer, but again his results are probably best explained as a correlation of the changes with alterations in patterns of gross movement.

To circumvent this problem, Olds and his associates (Olds, 1965; Olds & Hirano, 1969) repeated their investigations but conditioned cells only when the animals remained motionless. In some of these cases, some slight motor responses occurred, but even if they had not, the data would still be ambiguous. Olds and his associates may have been recording from cells that increase their firing rate directly with the degree of inhibition of movement, or they may have been recording from cells that increase their firing rate in response to alterations in heart rate, respiration, or some other vegetative response.

Other researchers studying single cells have observed changes in cellular activity during learning and behavior. One of the most comprehensive investigations of this kind was conducted by Ranck and his associates (Feder & Ranck, 1973; Ranck, 1973b). Ranck differentiated two types of neurons in the hippocampus: theta cells, which were mentioned earlier, and "complex spike cells," so named because of the complex impulse they exhibited during discharge. Theta cells increased their rate of firing when theta was recorded by macroelectrodes in the hippocampus. Increases in their rate of firing were correlated with the appearance of voluntary motor responses (for example, walking, orienting, postural adjustments, jumping, exploring). Decreases in their firing rate accompanied the onset of hippocampal desynchronization and the performance of relatively stereotyped or automatic behaviors (for example, eating, drinking, grooming, teeth chattering, and performance on continuous and FR 50-second reinforcement schedules).

The firing rate of complex spike cells was also correlated with alterations in overt behavior but bore no relation to the presence or absence of theta. Ranck identified several types of different complex spike cells on the basis of their concomitant overt behavior. For example, an approach/consummate cell fired most rapidly during certain consummatory behaviors and the successful appetitive behavior associated with them. One type of cell increased its rate of firing during approach to, exploration of, and eating of a food pellet. An approach/consummate/mismatch cell fired when an approach/consummate cell fired but also discharged if the rat's approach behavior was not consummated. Such a cell would fire during a rat's approach to water and during drinking but also during exploration of the water-bottle hole after the bottle had been removed.

Other researchers have observed changes in the rate of firing of single cells during learning (for a review, see Leiman & Christian, 1973). For example, Woody, Vassilevsky, and Engle (1970) studied the rate of firing of single cells to a conditioned stimulus (a click) during classical conditioning of an eye-blink response in cats. The cells studied were in the coronal-precruciate area, one of the cortical regions that mediate the eye-blink response. After conditioning the CS was followed by more frequent and longer discharges of cells in this area, and their latency of firing to the CS decreased.

Changes in the activity of single cells have also been observed when operant-conditioning paradigms were employed. Travis and his associates (Travis, Hooten, & Sparks, 1968; Travis & Sparks, 1967; Travis, Sparks, & Hooten, 1968) examined the responsiveness of cells in the globus pallidus of monkeys trained to press a bar for food. They found that during a response sequence in which an animal obtained and consumed a familiar reward, the firing of about 30% of the cells sampled was inhibited. However, the firing of these cells was not inhibited when the monkey was grasping unfamiliar or inedible objects or when it was eating an unfamiliar food. It is possible that these cells mediate the chaining of stimulus–response sequences. Future research should clarify the behavior correlates of these very interesting cells.

Fuster and Uyeda (1971) were able to isolate, particularly in the amygdala but also in the hippocampus and the *piriform cortex* (a cortical region adjacent to the amygdala), cells that differentially responded with changes in firing to visual stimuli associated with food reward and electric shock. After these researchers' primates had learned to press two separate levers in response to two different visual stimuli, the firing patterns of these neurons were assessed. Correctly pressing one of the levers led to food reinforcement, while correct responses on the adjacent lever yielded avoidance of an electric shock. Although a number of the cells studied increased their rate of firing to both signals, some cells selectively responded to either the food signal or the shock signal. The authors concluded that their results support the view that an essential role of the amygdala is to identify reinforcing stimuli.

With regard to appetitive signals alone, Olds and his associates (Olds, Mink, & Best, 1969; Phillips & Olds, 1969) have reported finding cells, most frequently located in the hippocampus and the hypothalamus, that seem to be specifically related to either feeding or drinking behaviors. Ranck (1973b) has also located such cells in the hippocampus. In Olds's investigations, rats were trained to press a bar and remain motionless for 2 seconds. After the first second had elapsed, one of three tones was presented. The tones signaled that food, water, or nothing would be delivered for a subsequent bar press. Some cells were found to increase their firing rate if the tone signaled the availability of food and if the rat was hungry. On the other hand, certain cells increased their rate of firing if the tone signaled the availability of water for thirsty rats. Hence, the cells responded if and only if the signal indicated the occurrence of a reward that was relevant to the animal's current motivational state.

The results obtained with cell recordings are certainly intriguing. They seem to indicate changes in the firing pattern of cells that are concomitant with the learning process. Unfortunately, we do not know whether these changes reflect memory processes or whether, as seems more likely, they signal the occurrence of motor and sensory components of learned-behavior sequences.

Steady (DC) Potentials

Earlier in this chapter, we indicated that Caton had discovered the EEG in 1875. At the time he was investigating the effects of inducing, with various stimuli, negative deflections, or variations, in the steady cortical "current" of awake animals. During his experiments Caton also noted small, continuous current fluctuations that were activating his Thompson galvinometer in the absence of stimulation. These fluctuations were no less than the discovery of the EEG. He was really interested, however, in the DC, or *steady potentials (SP),* of the brain. Brazier (1961) suggests that his emphasis on the SP phenomena actually obscured the investigation of the EEG. As Rowland (1968) points out, the vast amount of literature on the EEG now obscures what little has been learned since Caton's investigations on stimulus-induced changes in SP.

It is interesting to note that Caton considered the EEG to be "noise." Investigators of EEG phenomena consider SP and shifts that occur in this electrophysiological response to be a nuisance or "noise." Modern EEG amplifiers are AC coupled and so lose this DC information, but EEG researchers, fascinated with their fluctuating rhythms, do not seem to mind that the SP is not preserved. Special amplifiers and electrodes have been developed and must be used to study SP phenomena.

The term *steady potential,* as it pertains to the cortex, denotes "the maintained or nonrhythmic difference of potential between the surface of the cortex and the immediately subjacent white matter" (Rowland, 1968, p. 5). It ranges from .5 to 5 millivolts and exhibits a slow shift as a function of time, but rarely changes by more than about .5 millivolts over several hours when an animal is left undisturbed. The steady potentials are apparently generated by the depolarization of *glia cells* and the massed activity of neurons (Castellucci & Goldring, 1970). Glia cells constitute 90% of the cells in the brain, leaving only 10% of the cells to be neurons (Nurnberger, 1958). Glia cells, which seem to surround nerve cells and their branches, have often been considered to be a type of connective tissue. More recently, evidence has suggested that they perform important nutritive and regulatory roles in nerve-cell function.

Current interest in SP phenomena has followed Caton's lead and centered around the relationship between SP shifts and behavior. Excellent reviews regarding SP are provided by Rowland (1968) and Rowland and Anderson (1971). In the following examples the SP shift appears as a shift in the baseline of the EEG.

All novel stimuli (for example, visual, auditory) evoke SP shifts that weaken rapidly with further repetitions of the stimulus. The SP shift appears most prominently in the cortical sensory-projection area associated with the modality of the presented stimulus (Gumnit, 1961; Köhler & Wegener, 1955; Lickey & Fox, 1966). Figure 8–7 shows this phenomenon in the rat cortex during repeated presentations of a moderately intense light stimulus in a darkened chamber. Note that the SP shift apparently is correlated with the orienting response; diminution of the orienting response as the animal becomes used to the stimulus is reflected by a disappearance of the SP shift.

In contrast to decrements in the magnitude of SP shifts following repeated presentation of neutral stimuli, SP shifts accompanying stimuli having biological significance do not decrease in amplitude simply as a function of repeated presentations (Rowland, 1968). Rowland and his associates have demonstrated this finding with respect to the following stimuli: food, perineal stimulation in the estrous cat and rat, peripheral electric shock, and positively and negatively reinforcing electrical hypothalamic stimulation.

In the case of these biologically significant stimuli, decrements in the SP shift seem to be related to decreases in drive state. For example, if hungry cats are presented with food, they will exhibit an SP shift as large as 1 to 2 millivolts over the first 5 to 10 minutes of eating. The slope of the shift is steepest at the onset of feeding and gradually declines as the total magnitude of the SP shift reaches its maximum amplitude when the cat approaches satiety. After cessation of feeding, the SP reverses its direction and returns to the baseline level (Rowland, Bradley, School, & Deutschman, 1967). Taken together, these data suggest that the occurrence and maintenance of SP shifts are related to the arousal, attention, and drive level of an organism and may provide us with an additional physiological index of these processes.

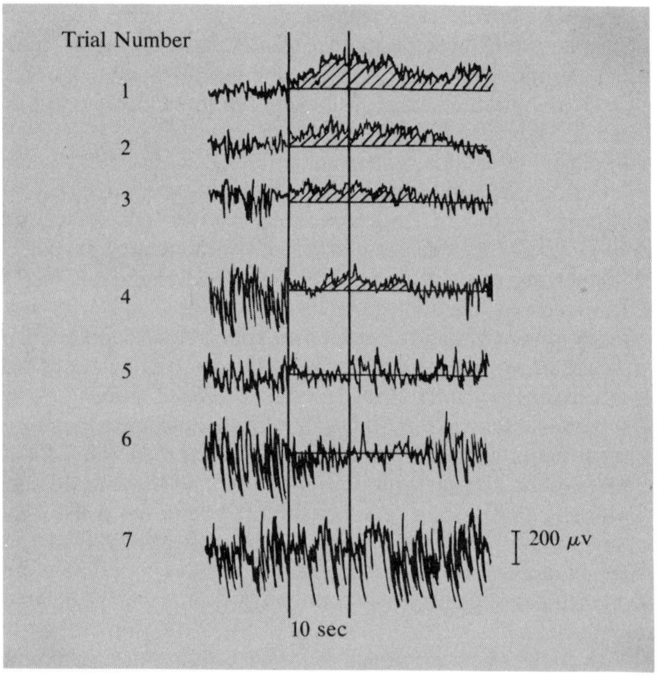

Figure 8–7. Progressive loss of SP shift with subsidence of orienting response, followed by loss of desynchronization response in the rat. The recording is across the depth of the anteromedial portion of the frontal-pole cortex. (From "Cortical Steady Potential [Direct Current Potential] in Reinforcement and Learning," by V. Rowland. In E. Stellar and J. M. Sprague [Eds.], *Progress in Physiological Psychology* [Vol. 2]. Copyright 1968 by Academic Press, Inc. Reprinted by permission.)

Evidence that SP shifts are related to attention is provided by the work of Walter and his associates (see, for example, Walter, 1964). They have described an SP shift in humans that occurs during the interval between presentation of a meaningful stimulus and the reaction to it. Called the *expectancy wave* or *E* wave, it appears in situations in which conditional stimuli are paired. In a typical experimental paradigm the subject learns, "If there is a click (conditional stimulus), there will be flashes of light (imperative stimulus), so press the button (imperative response)." Under these conditions an *E* wave appears in the frontal cortex immediately after the onset of the conditional stimulus and endures until the imperative response is emitted. Thereafter, the response declines to the baseline. This SP shift is elicited by attention to the conditional stimulus and occurs during sensorimotor associations.

Other researchers have studied SP shifts during operant learning in lower animals. For example, Rowland and Anderson (1971) examined SP shifts during FR 50-second performance. As illustrated in Figure 8–8, an SP shift developed prior to each reinforced bar press, a larger shift accompanied food delivery, and a slow return to the baseline accompanied the cessation of eating and a return to bar pressing. Wisenfeld (1969) recorded SP shifts from the cortical surface of rats performing a food-reinforced turning in a *T* maze. Opening the start-box door elicited a large SP shift, which diminished in amplitude as the animal crossed the choice point and entered the goal box. Subsequent eating was accompanied by an SP shift in the opposite direction. Extinction of the behavioral response was accompanied by marked reductions in the amplitude of the shifts. An examination of SP shifts during learning and performance provides additional support for the view that SP shifts, at least in part, reflect central processes related to arousal, attention, and drive level. Whether these responses also reflect associative mechanisms is still open to question.

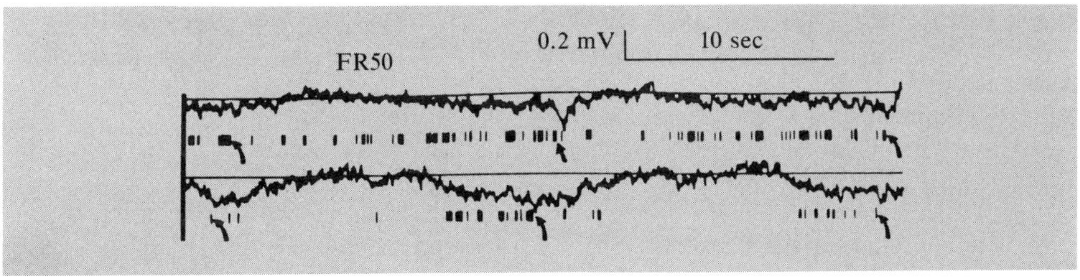

Figure 8–8. SP shifts from a rat in FR 50 performance. The arrows indicate reinforcement. (Adapted from "Brain Steady Potential Shifts," by V. Rowland and R. Anderson. In E. Stellar and J. M. Sprague [Eds.], *Progress in Physiological Psychology* [Vol. 4]. Copyright 1971 by Academic Press, Inc. Reprinted by permission.)

Overview

In this section we have examined electrophysiological correlates of learning. Interest in these phenomena has been partially generated by the view that memory processes may be reflected by alterations in the spatiotemporal pattern of electrical activity in the brain. Such a view was postulated because of the lack of good evidence for the existence of centers or regions of neural tissue that are intimately related to basic learning and memory processes.

Several approaches to studying the electrophysiological correlates of learning were presented, and we saw that certain electrophysiological changes appear to be unique to specific stages of learning and performance. The main problem with this approach, as illustrated by the hippocampal theta research, is determining whether the observed electrophysiological changes reflect actual information processing, memory consolidation, and recall rather than such processes as attention, drive level, movement, or other behaviors that are correlated with the acquisition, storage, and recall of information.

Memory Consolidation

Most contemporary theories of learning assert that the consolidation of new information into long-term, more or less permanent memory takes place in two stages. Immediately after an experience has occurred, memory traces are in a very unstable form. They become "permanent," "fixed," or "consolidated" after some period of time. Present-day anatomical theories of learning also include a two-stage concept of memory consolidation, a tradition that was initiated by Hebb's (1949) very influential two-factor learning theory. In general, the anatomical theories contend that memory traces are initially represented by reverberatory circuits of cells that process the incoming information. This reverberatory activity continues until anatomical changes occur in the nerve tissue. Two anatomical changes that have been proposed as possible substrates for long-term memory are an enlargement of existing presynaptic terminals between adjacent nerve cells (Eccles, 1953) and the development of additional end feet containing neurotransmitters in the presynaptic nerve endings (Hebb, 1949).

The notion of reverberatory circuits has been supported by the results of several experiments. For example, Burns (1958) reported that a single electrical stimulus train can initiate bursts of electrical activity in isolated slabs of cortex that may persist for 30 minutes or longer. However, it is not clear whether such electrical activity has a specific role in memory consolidation. It is also unclear whether reverberatory circuits could persist long enough to maintain memories so that structural change could occur.

Experimental investigations of memory consolidation became possible following the introduction of electroconvulsive shock (ECS) by Cerletti and Bini in 1938 as a treatment for psychiatric patients. ECS treatments consist of passing brief but very intense electric currents through the subject's head via electrodes placed on opposite sides of the head. ECS may produce brief periods of unconsciousness, convulsions, and EEG seizures. It soon became apparent that human patients treated with ECS experienced retrograde amnesia (see, for example, Flescher, 1941). This observation precipitated a flood of experiments. A comprehensive review of the use of ECS in studying memory-consolidation processes is provided by McGaugh and Herz (1972).

In a classic study published in 1949, Duncan brought the ECS technique from the psychiatric setting to the animal laboratory, where ECS could be systematically employed in carefully controlled studies to elucidate the consolidation process. His initial inquiry was to serve as the major impetus for hundreds of subsequent investigations. In this experiment, rats were administered one trial per day on an active-avoidance task. Different groups of rats were subjected to ECS either 20 seconds, 40 seconds, 60 seconds, 4 minutes, 15 minutes, 1 hour, 4 hours, or 14 hours after each trial. As can be seen in Figure 8–9, learning was significantly retarded in those rats that received ECS shortly after the trials. In addition, it was found that the longer the delay between training and ECS administration, the smaller was the retardation produced. These findings seemed to support the view that memory traces need a period of undisturbed gestation before they become permanently consolidated.

Such an interpretation of these data has not, however, been uncritically accepted. Many subsequent investigations were conducted in an attempt to clarify the basis for

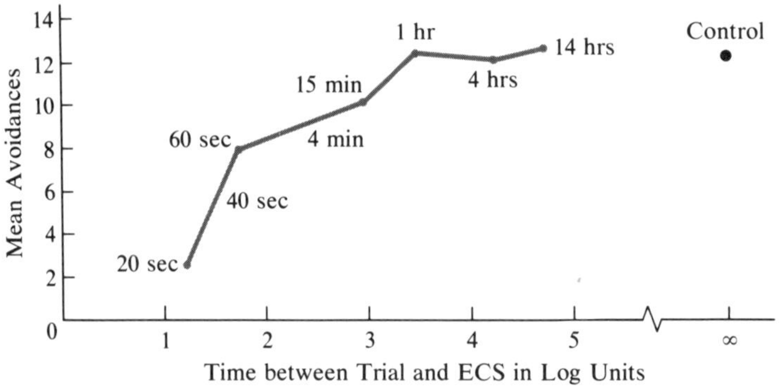

Figure 8–9. Mean avoidance responses by rats on 18 daily trials in an active-avoidance task as a function of the trial/ECS interval (expressed in log units). (From "The Retroactive Effect of Electroshock on Learning," by C. P. Duncan, *Journal of Comparative and Physiological Psychology,* 1949, *42,* 32–44. Copyright 1949 by the American Psychological Association. Reprinted by permission.)

the observed behavior defects, and several alternative interpretations of the findings have been proposed. These alternative views suggest that instead of interrupting memory-consolidation processes, ECS treatments yield other behavior changes that are mistaken for evidence of a memory impairment. Two of these postulated changes are the development of fear and the conditioning of incompatible responses.

Alternative Interpretations of the ECS Effects

Coons and Miller (1960) have suggested that ECS may have aversive properties for the subject and that, therefore, an ECS-induced fear of the goal may develop. In the type of learning paradigm used by Duncan, the subject has a choice of not responding and receiving a shock to the paws or of responding and receiving a shock to the head. If the animal chooses the former alternative over the latter, it does not necessarily mean that memory of the avoidance response has not been consolidated. This is a critical issue, because if the ECS effects simply reflect a punishment phenomenon, data collected with this method are irrelevant to the problem of memory storage.

To test this interpretation, Coons and Miller taught rats to solve various avoidance-response problems. In their experiments they replicated Duncan's findings but added a further condition in which rats that had originally learned to make an active-avoidance response were now required to withhold this response to avoid shock to the paws. Under these conditions the sooner ECS followed each trial, the faster was the acquisition rate. In addition, the rats that received ECS after short delays appeared to show increased emotion as indexed by urination and defecation scores. These results clearly supported the theory that ECS can have aversive effects. However, subsequent research has suggested that the acquired-fear hypothesis cannot totally account for the ECS effects. Because of the potential aversive effects of ECS when applied over a series of daily learning trials, recent investigations have generally employed one-trial learning tasks and one application of ECS.

Numerous researchers have demonstrated that a single application of ECS will disrupt subsequent behavior. For example, Bureš and Burešová (1963) found such effects in a passive-avoidance situation. If rats are placed in an apparatus that has two adjacent compartments, one small and the other large, the animals will spend most of their time in the small compartment. If they are shocked in the small compartment and put back in the apparatus the next day, they will avoid the small compartment. Bureš and Burešová reported that if rats were given ECS treatments up to 6 hours after they had received shock in the small compartment, they would return to the small compartment on the next day more often than animals not given ECS. In a one-trial, one-ECS-treatment procedure such as that employed by Bureš and Burešová, the possibility that the effects of ECS are due to learned fear responses is minimized.

Another way of minimizing the possibility that the animal is learning fear responses that interfere with performance is to administer ECS in a relatively nonaversive manner. This can be accomplished in several ways. In one of the early ECS studies, Friedman (1953) found that no aversion to ECS developed in rats subjected to ECS treatments twice a day for four successive days if the convulsions were prevented by anesthetizing the animals with ether prior to applying the ECS. This finding, which has been replicated by McGaugh and Alpern (1966), suggests that the aversive component is intimately linked to the occurrence of seizures rather than simply resulting from the passage of electricity through the brain. Similarly, Kesner, Gibson, and LeClair (1970) have reported that if ECS is delivered through cortical electrodes rather than the commonly used ear clips, no aversion will develop. They suggest that the ears of the rats become sensitive to the ear clips following repeated treatments. A third way of separating the aversive and amnestic effects of ECS is to administer ECS in the home cage rather than in the training apparatus. This procedure reduces the possibility that ECS will become associated with the response being measured.

When this procedure is followed, a performance defect will still occur in the convulsed subjects (Leonard & Zavala, 1964; Quartermain, Paolino, & Miller, 1965).

There are data that are simply inconsistent with a view that the observed effects on behavior result from aversive effects of the ECS. If ECS produces its effects because of its aversive properties, it should increase the rate of extinction if administered after each extinction trial. This has not been found to be the case. Several investigators (for example, Gerbrandt & Thomson, 1964; Greenough & Schwitzgebel, 1966; Madsen & Luttges, 1963) have reported that ECS yields increased resistance to extinction of both aversively and appetitively motivated behaviors.

A second alternative interpretation of the basis for the ECS effects centers on the notion that ECS may lead to the development of responses that are incompatible with performance of the learned operant response (M. Black & Suboski, 1971; Lewis & Maher, 1965). More specifically, this view contends that ECS interferes with performance by causing the animal to be less active in the testing chamber. Such an interpretation must be questioned, however, in light of the finding that ECS produces learning defects in passive-avoidance as well as active-avoidance situations. Since passive-avoidance learning is assessed by increases in the latency of approach, one would expect ECS to facilitate learning, but this has not been found to be true (see, for example, Bureš & Burešová, 1963; McGaugh & Alpern, 1966). Also inconsistent with this proposal is that, as discussed earlier, animals given ECS in their home cages still show retrograde amnesia. The conditioned-inhibition view assumes that the behavioral inhibition is conditioned to the environmental cues of the training chamber in which the ECS is administered. The data reviewed thus far suggest that the effects of ECS on behavior arise primarily from a disruption of memory-consolidation processes.

Other recent investigations of ECS have been attempts to determine (1) the maximally effective training/ECS interval, (2) the factors affecting the ECS-induced retrograde amnesia, and (3) the permanence of the ECS-produced retrograde amnesia. The rest of this section is devoted to these three research directions.

The Duration of the Training/ECS Interval

Experiments on ECS have generally shown that the treatment must be administered fairly soon after training. Just how soon has been the subject of some disagreement. Some researchers (for example, Kopp, Bohdanecky, & Jarvik, 1968; McGaugh, 1966; Paolino & Hine, 1973) have reported that significant amnestic effects will occur if ECS treatment is delayed for up to several hours after training, but other experimenters (Chorover & Schiller, 1965; Lee-Teng & Sherman, 1966; Schiller & Chorover, 1967) have reported the occurrence of amnesia following ECS treatment only if the subjects were treated within a few seconds after training. Reports of such contradictions in the retrograde-amnesia gradient following administration of ECS are common, but, as McGaugh and Herz (1972) point out, no simple explanation of these divergent findings has been offered.

In light of these discrepancies, some researchers (Chorover & Schiller, 1966; Spevack and Suboski, 1969) have argued that the actual amnestic gradient is quite short (1 minute or less); impairments in performance observed with longer training/ECS intervals probably indicate effects on behavior other than a "loss of memory." Other experimenters (Paolino & Levy, 1971; Paolino, Quartermain, & Levy, 1969) have claimed that the observed effects on performance with long training/ECS intervals still represent defects in memory consolidation, but the effects are on other phases of the consolidation process.

The Factors Affecting the ECS-Induced Retrograde Amnesia

A number of researchers have shown that certain features of an experiment may affect the ECS-produced retrograde-amnesia gradient. These factors include the characteristics of the ECS treatment, training variables, the criterion used for retention, and subject differences.

In research on the first of these factors, the characteristics of the ECS treatment, a number of experimenters (for example, Buckholtz & Bowman, 1972; Haycock & McGaugh, 1973; R. A. Hughes, Barrett, & Ray, 1970a; Zornetzer & McGaugh, 1971a, 1971b) have shown that the degree of amnesia produced by ECS varies directly with the intensity of the current. Researchers (Alpern & McGaugh, 1968; Buckholtz & Bowman, 1972) have also demonstrated that the same relationship occurs with respect to the duration of the ECS, with greater amnesia being produced by ECS treatments of longer duration. However, conflicting data on this factor have been reported (see, for example, Paolino et al., 1969). It appears that the effects of ECS treatments on memory depend on the interaction of ECS intensity and the training/treatment interval. For a constant interval a lower intensity of ECS will produce less amnesia. On the other hand, for a given ECS intensity a longer interval will produce less amnesia (Haycock & McGaugh, 1973).

In research on the characteristics of the training situation, R. Thompson (1958) demonstrated that the degree of amnesia produced by ECS varies inversely with the degree of training prior to the ECS treatment (also see Keyes, 1973) and directly with task difficulty. O. S. Ray and Bivens (1968) found that another task variable affecting the degree of amnesia is the intensity of shock to the paws that is used in the avoidance training, and Peeke, McCoy, and Herz (1969) reported that the degree of amnesia for an appetitively motivated problem produced by ECS depends upon the length of deprivation.

The characteristics of an ECS-produced retention gradient also depend on the criterion (Schneider, Kapp, Aron, & Jarvik, 1969) as well as on the response measure (H. E. Adams & Calhoun, 1972; Hine & Paolino, 1970; Mendoza & Adams, 1969) employed to assess the degree of retention. In the Hine and Paolino experiment, rats given ECS immediately after one-trial passive-avoidance training showed amnesia for the punished response. However, changes in heart rate indicated that the rats exhibited heightened arousal in the testing situation, suggesting retention of a fear response associated with the passive-avoidance paradigm. The authors postulated that these findings may indicate that consolidation was faster for the generalized fear response than for the overt-behavior index of retention. More recently, Caul and Barrett (1972) have shown that under certain conditions ECS will attenuate heart-rate changes normally associated with passive-avoidance training as well as produce an amnesia of the learned-avoidance response.

Subject differences are the fourth factor affecting the ECS-produced amnesia gradient. McGaugh, Landfield, and Dawson (1972) have reported that the gradient may vary as a function of the strain of mice used. Heinze (1970) has similarly reported that the degree of amnesia produced by ECS treatment varies as a function of the strain of rats employed.

The Permanence of the ECS-Produced Retrograde Amnesia

It is generally assumed that ECS treatments interfere with memory consolidation by upsetting neural processes and thereby exert permanent effects on recall. For some time, most researchers assumed that the amnesia produced by ECS is permanent. Consequently, few experiments were conducted on this matter. Later experiments on the permanence of the ECS effects have produced somewhat divergent results. Luttges and McGaugh (1967) have reported that the amnestic effect lasts a month or more. Their results are shown in Figure 8–10. Mice were given one trial in a step-through passive-avoidance problem (in which they were punished for moving from one compartment into the adjacent one). They were treated with shock to the paws and ECS as indicated in the graph. Independent groups were tested for retention 14 hours, 1 week, or 1 month after their original treatment. Similar findings on the permanence of ECS effects have been reported by Chevalier (1965), King and Glasser (1970), O. L. Ray and Barrett (1969), and others. R. A. Hughes and his associates (Hughes et al., 1970a, 1970b) have reported that the degree of amnesia in rats may actually be strengthened with the passage of time.

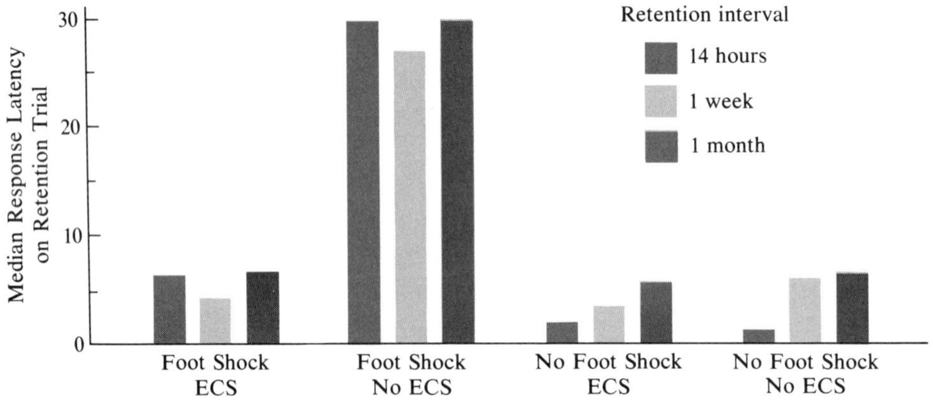

Figure 8–10. Permanence of ECS-induced retrograde amnesia. Mice were given a single trial in a step-through inhibitory-avoidance task and treated with shock and ECS as indicated. Independent groups were given retention tests 14 hours, 1 week, or 1 month later. (From "Permanence of Retrograde Amnesia Produced by Electroconvulsive Shock," by M. W. Luttges and J. L. McGaugh, *Science,* 1967, *156,* 408–410. Copyright 1967 by the American Association for the Advancement of Science. Reprinted by permission.)

In contrast, some researchers have reported recovery from the ECS-produced amnesia with the passage of time when either repeated (Zinkin & Miller, 1967) or single (Kohlenberg & Trabasso, 1968; Koppenall, Jagoda, & Cruce, 1967) tests were administered. McGaugh and Herz (1972) point out that these conflicting results have not yet been accounted for satisfactorily. However, they suggest, on the basis of data published by Pagano, Bush, Martin, and Hunt (1969), that incomplete amnesia may result when the ECS treatment used is not sufficient to disrupt the consolidation process. Hence, incomplete interference with memory storage may provide a basis for at least some recovery. They suggest that when recovery occurs, it will most likely do so when interference is incomplete, a view supported by data published by Cherkin (1969) and by Haycock, Gold, Macri, and McGaugh (1973).

Overview

The results of investigations using ECS to study memory-consolidation processes seem to indicate that memories of our experiences do not become fixed at the time the experiences occur. The ECS technique has been a valuable tool in uncovering the course of and the many factors affecting memory consolidation. Several hypotheses have been offered to account for the observed effects of ECS on performance. However, none of them accounts for all the available evidence as well as does the view that ECS produces its effects on behavior by disrupting memory-consolidation processes.

Many questions in this area of inquiry need to be answered, not the least of which is the elucidation of the mechanisms that are affected by the ECS treatment to produce the amnestic effect. ECS may produce its effects on memory by altering the electrical activity of the brain, which, as we have seen, some researchers contend may serve as a basis for memory storage, or ECS may produce its effects by disrupting the production of macromolecules, which many investigators contend may serve as a template for permanent memory. In recent years much attention has been given to trying to understand the possible role of macromolecules in various memory processes.

The Biochemistry of Learning and Memory

Memory must ultimately be related to the cellular level, since changes in neural cellular activities undoubtedly mediate both memory-consolidation processes and changes in the spatiotemporal firing patterns of neurons that reflect these processes. When discussing cellular processes, one must relate them to protein molecules because the metabolic functions of cells and their structural features are determined by the nature and quantities of the proteins the cells manufacture. In light of the crucial role performed by protein molecules in cellular physiology, it seems logical to assume that the protein-synthesis mechanism plays a major role in the neurophysiological substrates of memory consolidation.

Several different approaches have been used by researchers attempting to clarify the biochemical basis of learning and memory. Among these are investigations of the effects of experience and learning on brain chemistry and investigations of the effects of certain drugs on acquisition and recall.

The Effects of Experience and Learning on Brain Chemistry

Environmental-Enrichment Studies. One of the first major attempts to relate protein synthesis and other neural activities to experience or learning was conducted in a series of studies begun in the early 1960s by E. L. Bennett, Diamond, Krech, and Rosenzweig at Berkeley. Excellent reviews of this very comprehensive work are provided by Bennett, Rosenzweig, and Diamond (1969) and by Rosenzweig (1971).

In most of the experiments conducted by this group, litter-mate rats were assigned to either an enriched condition (EC) or a nonenriched condition. The animals in the EC condition were housed in a group of 10–12 in a large cage containing a variety of stimulus objects or toys, such as ladders, wheels, boxes, platforms, and so on. Nonenriched environments were of two types, both of which produced similar outcomes. In the standard-colony condition (SC) the rats were raised three to a cage; in the isolated condition (IC) the rats were raised one to a cage. After the rats were maintained in the different conditions for the experimental period, generally 80 days, they were destroyed and various anatomical and biochemical measures were made of their brains.

Upon analysis of their findings, these researchers found a number of differences in the cerebral cortex between animals raised in the EC versus SC and IC conditions. These differences included changes in tissue weight, in the amounts of certain enzymes, and in a number of anatomical indexes. The most consistent finding, which emerged in 13 replications (Bennett et al., 1969), was that rats reared in the EC condition had a heavier cerebral cortex than did litter mates reared in the SC or IC condition. This increase was not due to variations in the fluid content of the brains obtained from the animals in the various rearing conditions (Bennett, Rosenzweig, & Diamond, 1968). In general, the effects of different rearing conditions were especially prominent in the occipital, or visual, cortex. However, several experiments (for example, Krech, Rosenzweig, & Bennett, 1963) have shown that visual experience itself is not necessary for the observed effects. Other indexes of cortical bulk differ according to the conditions of early experience.

Animals reared in the enriched environment had thicker cerebral cortexes, and there was more total protein in their brains. At a more molecular level there was a significant difference in the number of glia cells, which support the activities of the neurons (Altman & Das, 1964; Diamond, Law, Rhodes, Lindner, Rosenzweig, Krech, & Bennett, 1966). Although the number of neurons did not increase significantly for the EC animals, the cross-section area of their neural cell bodies—that is, the perikaryon cross-section—was greater by about 13% (Diamond, 1967). Changes in brain enzymes were also noted in the

Table 8–1. Effects of differential experience on the occipital cortex of rats kept in enriched or impoverished conditions from 25 to 105 days of age

Measure	*Percentage differences (EC/IC)*	P	*EC > IC (No.)*
Weight	6.2	<0.001	114/151
Total protein	7.8[a]	<0.001	25/32
Thickness	6.3	<0.001	47/52
Total AChE	2.6	<0.01	90/150
Total ChE	10.2	<0.001	86.5/108
Total hexokinase	6.9[b]	<0.01	17/21
Neurons (No.)	−3.1	NS	7/17
Glia (No.)	14.0	<0.01	12/17
Perikaryon cross-section	13.4	<0.001	11.5/13

[a]Weight difference 7.0% in these experiments.
[b]Weight difference 5.5% in these experiments.
From "Effects of Environment on Development of Brain and Behavior," by M. R. Rosenzweig. In E. Tobach, L. R. Aronson, and E. Shaw (Eds.), *The Biopsychology of Development*. Copyright 1971 by Academic Press, Inc. Reprinted by permission.

EC animals. Increases were found to occur in the amounts of acetylcholinesterase (AChE) and cholinesterase (ChE), two substances concerned with transmission at many brain synapses because they inactivate the synaptic transmitter acetylcholine. Increases were also noted in hexokinase, an enzyme important in energy transformation. These differences are summarized in Table 8–1.

Earlier we showed that many researchers have hypothesized that the hippocampus is intimately related to learning and memory. For this reason, Diamond, Rosenzweig, and Bennett (1971) undertook an examination of hippocampal thickness in litter mates reared under either EC or IC conditions. It was found that the hippocampus of the EC rats was thicker than that of their IC litter mates, although the observed differences were smaller and less reliable than the EC/IC differences in cortical thickness. Other subcortical changes have been assessed (see Bennett et al., 1969), but, in general, the differences in the subcortex have been small.

In the previous chapter, devoted to early experience, we reviewed the work of Hymovich (1952) and Forgays and Read (1962), which suggested that rearing animals in an enriched environment such as that used by the Berkeley researchers led to superior problem-solving ability in adults. It would be nice if one could directly relate differences in cerebral measures to problem-solving scores. Unfortunately, this has not been the case. Rosenzweig (1971) writes that "while we have been able to demonstrate both significant cerebral effects and significant behavioral effects of prior environmental manipulations, we have not found any simple way of relating these two sets of observations" (p. 327).

This failure may have occurred because these researchers have attempted to measure transfer effects from a generally enriched environment to quite different task situations. A more fruitful approach might be to examine possible cerebral changes arising from exposure to discrete stimuli in an early environment. More specifically, one could employ the early-experience paradigm used by T. L. Bennett and his associates and by Gibson, Walk, and their co-workers. As pointed out in Chapter 7, in research using this paradigm, animals are exposed to specific stimuli (for example, circles and triangles), and later tested to determine whether they have learned something about these stimuli. Studies of this type have generally found that animals preexposed to specific stimuli can learn to differentiate between them more rapidly than can animals not receiving this early experience. It would be interesting to determine whether preexposure to specific forms produces changes in cerebral indexes, and if such changes do occur, whether they are directly related to discrimination-learning ability. If such a relationship occurs, it might suggest a neural substrate for the early-experience effect.

The research of the Berkeley group has examined the effects of general environmental enrichment on brain physiology. A different approach, one taken by a number of researchers in recent years, is to examine changes in brain chemistry following the learning of a specific response or problem.

Changes in Brain Chemistry with Training. Researchers using this approach have often attempted to relate their findings to possible changes in the genetic materials of brain cells, RNA (ribonucleic acid) and DNA (deoxyribonucleic acid). DNA controls cellular processes because it directs protein synthesis via its management of messenger RNA. One of the many important functions of RNA is the synthesis of transmitter substances, such as acetylcholine, that mediate neural transmission. It has long been known that increased activity of neurons is correlated with an increase in the amount of RNA in the cytoplasm of the brain cells (see, for example, Brattgård, 1952). For this reason, several researchers have postulated that learning results in the formation of novel RNA or protein molecules. One of the first to suggest such a possibility was Monné (1948), but most of the current interest in biochemical models of memory can be directly traced to the work of Hydén (1959).

The basic methodology for examining the role of nucleic acids and protein in learning and memory—one that has been used by Hydén and his associates—is to assess possible quantitative or qualitative changes in these substances in the nervous system following training. In principle this is a simple procedure, but in practice it is not always easy. Chapouthier (1973) indicates that a major difficulty in interpreting such experiments is that it is not always possible to distinguish between chemical changes occurring in the brain after training and changes occurring after stimulation without learning. Increases in RNA and protein synthesis occur in the nervous system after various types of stimulation without learning (Debold, Firshein, Carrier, & Leaf, 1967; Rappoport & Daginawala, 1968; Ungar, 1970).

Another problem for molecular theories of learning occurs at the conceptual level. This problem concerns the mechanisms involved in the formation of novel RNA and ultimately protein molecules that presumably serve as a template for the memory traces. The type of protein produced by a cell is dictated by the DNA found in the genes of the cell. The RNA manufactured, and in turn the protein produced, are a faithful replica of the DNA template of the gene. This is a necessary condition for survival of the cell and the organism. Hydén emphasizes that the RNA produced during learning is different from that made by the same cells during nonlearning. This supposition requires that neurons manufacture RNA different from that dictated by their DNA, a notion that runs counter to all our understanding of cell processes.

However, there is a way to circumvent this problem. Bonner (1966) suggests that electrical input to a nerve cell may "derepress" parts of a gene that were previously repressed or not maximally active. Hence, learning may not change the basic structure of the DNA; rather, it may yield a derepression or activation of parts of the gene that already exist. Derepression of such a gene would yield an increase in RNA synthesis, which has been reported in several investigations. The gene, once derepressed, may maintain this state forever, thereby causing a permanent change in the total protein-synthesis characteristics of the brain cell and presumably allowing for the encoding of a unit of permanent memory.

In the late 1950s Hydén developed a technique for measuring the composition of minute quantities of RNA. With this methodology, experimenters could directly assess the notion that learning results in the formation of unique RNA. In his initial investigations (Hydén & Egyházi, 1962, 1963), rats learned to obtain food by balancing on and climbing up a long narrow wire that was set at an angle of 45 degrees. The composition of the RNA extracted from neurons in their vestibular nucleus (a structure important in balance) was then compared to that obtained from control rats, which had not learned the task but had been swung around for an equivalent amount of time to stimulate their vestibular nucleus. The RNA extracted from the two groups of rats was different, apparently supporting Hydén's theory. This finding has been criticized on several grounds, the most important of which has to do with the appropriateness of the control group. It is possible that the different treatments—balancing versus swinging—stimulated different aspects of the complex vestibular system. Hence, the observed difference in RNA may have reflected this variation rather than a neural substrate in memory in the trained animals.

In other investigations Hydén and his associates (Hydén & Egyházi, 1964; Hydén & Lange, 1965) examined changes in the composition of RNA extracted from the motor cortex of rats that had been forced to reach with their nonpreferred paw for food at the end of a tube. The observed change in "handedness" (rats have distinct handedness preferences, just as people do) was regarded as learning. Control neurons for RNA analysis were taken from the contralateral cortex of the same rats. The researchers found that the RNA taken from the two sides of the cortex differed in both concentration and composition. No interhemispheric differences in the quantity and composition of the RNA were seen in animals allowed to use their preferred paw to obtain food. Using similar behavior-assessment techniques, Hydén and Lange (1971a, 1971b) have shown that differences in protein concentration can be obtained from samples of hippocampal tissue in rats allowed to use their preferred versus nonpreferred paw to obtain food. In spite of the elegance of these experiments, we cannot conclude that the observed changes in brain chemistry necessarily reflected memory encoding. Instead, the changes in RNA and protein may have resulted from massive activation of previously relatively inactive regions of the motor system.

The Effects of RNA and Protein-Synthesis Inhibitors on Memory

Inhibition of RNA Synthesis. An alternative approach to detecting changes in RNA and/or protein following training is to examine the effects on learning and retention of drugs that interfere with the synthesis of these proposed substrates of memory consolidation. Dingman and Sporn (1961) were the first researchers to conduct this type of inquiry. RNA synthesis was inhibited by administering the substance 8-azaguanine either before or after training on a maze. It was found that the rats injected before training showed a significant acquisition impairment. However, the animals injected after training showed no impairment of responding. The results appeared to indicate that RNA is important for original learning but not for retention. Unfortunately, a clear interpretation of these findings was confounded by the fact that the drug had severe side effects on the subjects. The rats were made sick by the drug, and it is well-known that almost any treatment that makes an animal sick will have a more profound effect on original learning than on retention or performance. For this reason, the authors wrote in 1964 that their original findings were inconclusive. Nevertheless, their original research was important in that it represented the first attempt to affect learning by using a substance that alters RNA synthesis. The problem of whether the observed changes in behavior following administration of certain drugs arise from altered brain metabolism or from side effects of the drugs is central to many of the experiments in this area of research.

Another RNA-synthesis inhibitor that has been used in studies of learning and memory is actinomycin-D. This drug is a more potent RNA-synthesis inhibitor than is

8-azaguanine, but researchers have not consistently demonstrated memory defects following its administration. For example, actinomycin-D was not found to affect original learning or retention of either a passive-avoidance task (Barondes & Jarvik, 1964) or a maze-learning problem (Cohen & Barondes, 1966). On the other hand, actinomycin-D was found to inhibit acquisition of an avoidance response in cockroaches (Glassman, Henderson, Cordle, Moon, & Wilson, 1970) and the acquisition of an olfactory discrimination in homing salmon (Oshima, Gorbman, & Shimada, 1969).

Inhibition of Protein Synthesis. Another popular agent in the study of the biochemical basis of memory is the protein-synthesis-blocking substance puromycin. Intracranial injections of this drug result in amnesia for a previously learned avoidance response in mice (J. B. Flexner, Flexner, & Stellar, 1963; L. B. Flexner, Flexner, Roberts, & De la Haba, 1964) and in goldfish (Agranoff & Klinger, 1964) and amnesia for a learned reversal response in mice (J. B. Flexner et al., 1963) and in rats (Moss, 1973). On the basis of the majority of these findings, it has been concluded that the puromycin-induced amnesia resulted from temporarily reducing protein synthesis in the central nervous system. These results have been taken as evidence for the view that protein metabolism serves as a template for long-term memory. This view is certainly a reasonable one in light of our current knowledge of cellular processes. On the other hand, it is not clear whether puromycin-induced amnesia results from a disruption of protein synthesis or from other effects of this drug on the physiology of the organism. For example, a basic premise of the puromycin research is that this agent prevents long-term memory consolidation. It follows that the observed performance defects should be irreversible. However, this is not the case. Flexner and Flexner (J. B. Flexner & Flexner, 1967; L. B. Flexner & Flexner, 1968) have reported that intracerebral injections of isotonic saline solution brought about a recovery of a conditioned avoidance response as long as 60 days after the response had been eliminated by puromycin administrations. J. B. Flexner and Flexner (1970) later found that other solutions, including an ultrafiltrate of blood and water alone, also produced the same effect. This was a surprising finding and has not yet been satisfactorily explained.

Another problem with the puromycin research is that other drugs, such as acetoxycyclohexamide or the related cyclohexamide, which are more potent protein-synthesis inhibitors than puromycin, do not always yield amnesia for a previously learned habit, even in those tasks in which puromycin usually has a very potent effect (L. B. Flexner & Flexner, 1966). Further, the disruptive effects of puromycin can be circumvented by the addition of acetoxycyclohexamide or cyclohexamide to the puromycin injections (Barondes & Cohen, 1967; Flexner & Flexner, 1966). This latter finding is inconsistent with the view that the maintenance of memory depends upon the synthesis of cerebral protein. One would have expected that the addition of a second protein-synthesis inhibitor would have increased, not decreased, the amnestic effects of the puromycin treatment.

Why, then, does puromycin yield such a marked performance defect even weeks after its administration? A possible explanation comes from some work by Cohen, Ervin, and Barondes (1966). They recorded hippocampal EEG patterns from mice that had been injected with puromycin, cyclohexamide, or saline. They found that the puromycin-injected animals, but not the animals treated with cyclohexamide or saline, showed EEG abnormalities, a finding that was replicated by Macrides and Chorover (1968). Thus, puromycin may yield a functional lesion of the hippocampus that causes the observed changes in behavior.

In light of these observations on the effects of puromycin on hippocampal EEG patterns, an interesting series of experiments presented itself to Carlton and his associates (for a review of their work, see Carlton & Markiewicz, 1973). They wondered whether it might be possible to produce consolidation and recall defects, in the absence of significant decreases in protein synthesis, by inducing electrical silence in the hippocampus. A simple learning task was employed in these investigations. During the first session thirsty rats were allowed to lap water from a drinking tube. On the subsequent day the animals were given a training session in which a tone was presented several times. The termination of this tone was accompanied by a brief, inescapable, painful shock delivered to the grid floor of the chamber. The next day the rats were given intrahippocampal injections of potassium chloride (KCl), a drug known to induce reversible electrical silence in brain tissue. The control animals were injected with isotonic saline.

The rats were returned three days later to the testing chamber in a water-deprived state. After an animal had licked the drinking tube 100 times, the tone that had been paired with shock was presented. The tone remained on until the animal had licked an additional ten times or for a maximum of 300 seconds. Although normal, saline-injected rats showed complete suppression of licking during the presentation of the tone, the animals given KCl showed essentially no suppression of licking. In addition, these researchers found that the magnitude of the retention defect bore a direct relationship to the duration of the electrical silence produced by the KCl injections. These findings provide further evidence in support of the view that puromycin-induced memory defects result from the effects of puromycin on factors other than protein synthesis. Similar effects of intrahippocampal KCl injections on conditioned suppression have been reported by R. A. Hughes (1969) and Kapp and Schneider (1971).

Although the puromycin data do not provide unambiguous evidence for the view that protein macromolecules form a template for memory, data from experiments using other protein-synthesis-blocking agents do provide more compelling support. Flood, Rosenzweig, Bennett, and Orme (1973) examined the effects of duration of protein-synthesis inhibition on memory processes. For their amnestic agent these researchers used anisomycin, which is an effective blocker of cerebral-protein synthesis but does not have many of the adverse side effects of the other amnestic agents we have discussed. Most important, anisomycin does not have toxic side effects, so that successive doses of it can be used to vary the length of protein-synthesis inhibition following training.

The most important finding of this inquiry had to do with the effects of varying the length of protein-synthesis inhibition on retention of a previously acquired passive-avoidance response. If protein synthesis does indeed underlie the formation of memory traces, one would predict that the longer protein synthesis is inhibited, up to some maximally effective length of time, the greater would be the memory loss. The results of this experiment confirmed such an expectation. These findings, that longer inhibition of protein synthesis yielded greater amnesia, provide the strongest support to date for the view that protein is required for long-term memory to become established.

Overview

For a number of years, researchers of memory consolidation have asserted that changes at the molecular level must serve as a template for the memory trace, but only fairly recently has evidence been emerging that supports this position. We have examined some of these findings in this last major section of the chapter. Unfortunately, this field of inquiry is so new that in many instances more questions than answers have emerged from the research. Nevertheless, this research area has already established itself as a most promising one for unraveling the mystery of the brain's operation.

Summary

This chapter examined several approaches to clarifying the physiological basis of learning and memory. Results obtained from the lesion technique have been somewhat discouraging in that no single structure has been found to be crucially involved in memory processes. The hippocampus has been the most strongly implicated structure in memory functions, particularly in light of the severe memory defects noted to occur following hippocampal ablations in human clinical patients. However, its integrity is not essential for basic memory processes, since lower animals can learn a variety of tasks after its removal.

The inability to discover a structure or pathway that is crucial to memory processes had led many researchers to suggest that memory is not the product of any anatomically distinct structure or pathway. As an alternative, it has been suggested that memory is diffusely organized throughout the brain and is represented by unique spatiotemporal patterns of electrical activity in neural systems. Several proposed electrophysiological correlates of learning and memory were considered. These included EEG recordings, the activity of single nerve cells, and steady (DC) potentials. Data were presented that indicate that specific electrophysiological changes accompany discrete stages of learning and performance. The chief problem with this type of research is in determining the actual correlates of electrophysiological variations. Often these alterations reflect changes in attention, drive level, movement, or other behaviors that are correlates of the learning and memory process but do not represent memory functions themselves.

The effects of electroconvulsive shock on memory consolidation were next examined. We concluded that although many interpretations have been posited to account for decrements in performance following ECS treatments, none of these views explains the results as well as does a view that ECS produces its effects by disrupting memory-consolidation processes. The basis of the ECS effects is unclear. ECS may produce amnesia by severely disrupting the electrical activity of the brain or by interfering with the production of macromolecules that serve as a template for memory.

The substrates of memory must ultimately be related to the cellular level, since some change in the characteristics of brain cells must serve as the basis for alterations in the electrical activity of cells that convey information either into or out of memory. Researchers have examined changes in the amounts or types of macromolecules such as RNA or protein, but it is often unclear whether the observed changes were specifically related to the encoding of information. More recently, researchers have examined the effects on learning and retention of drugs that supposedly interfere with the synthesis of these proposed memory substrates. Data obtained in these investigations have been far from conclusive, and relatively unambiguous information on the biochemical basis of learning and memory is only just beginning to emerge.

Chapter 9

Memory: The Processing of Information

So far in this book, our emphasis has been on principles of learning derived largely from animal-learning research and on physiological and developmental aspects of learning and memory. With this chapter we turn to the study of complex processes in human learning and memory. Our approach in this second half of the book is to begin with an overview of human memory as an information-processing system. We will then look at language and the organization of long-term memory as a semantic-memory system. Subsequent chapters, covering a wide range of traditional and contemporary topics, will fill in many details of the human-memory system.

Until about 1960, psychologists studying human memory were primarily concerned with explaining how learned associations between stimuli and responses are forgotten. There was virtually complete agreement that stimulus–response associations are forgotten because of the *interference* effects of different S–R associations learned at another time. Typical experiments required subjects to learn several lists of paired words (or "nonsense" syllables). After some delay the subjects were given one of the items of a pair and asked to recall the other. Failure to recall items correctly from one of the lists was generally attributed to interference from associations learned in previous or subsequent lists. The general associative/interference account had consistently been supported by a wide variety of laboratory experiments and by our everyday experience with forgetting. When we forget the telephone number of a friend, for example, the reason is often confusion (interference) with the many other numbers we have learned before and after having learned that friend's number.

Psychologists currently approach the study of human memory in a different way. This change in memory research is consistent with a general trend toward more *cognitive* conceptualizations of behavior and is usually labeled the information-processing approach. This approach has greatly influenced many different areas of psychology and has essentially replaced the stimulus–response associationism that guided the study of human memory from the turn of the century.

Although a number of factors have played a role in the development of the information-processing approach, perhaps the most important has been the rapid increase in the sophistication of computer technology. The computer has become an increasingly important tool in the conduct and analysis of research in psychology. It has served as a medium for the expression of theories and as an instrument for testing them. But most important, the modern computer, with its highly sophisticated processing capabilities and greatly increased capacity for storing and using information, has come to be used as a *model* of human perception, learning, and memory. Thus, humans are viewed as though they were a highly sophisticated information-processing system.

For any information processor, inputs from the outside world must first be translated into a form that can be managed by the rest of the processing system. Second, if these inputs are to have any influence beyond the present moment, some representation of them must be retained by the system. Finally, whenever more than one representation is retained, there must be some means of identifying and recovering the required representation. As an information-processing system, then, human memory must involve these same three basic processing stages, referred to as *encoding, storage,* and *retrieval.* Their relationship in the information-processing system is schematically indicated in Figure 9–1.

Figure 9–1. General information-processing model.

In the remainder of this chapter, we will extend and elaborate upon this basic information-processing model of human memory. We will first consider the processes that transform sound, light, and other components of our environment into useful information about that environment. Then we will look at how this information is represented in the system, how it is retained over time, and how it is located and retrieved from storage. Finally, we will consider how all these stages interact to form the enormously sophisticated information-processing system that is human memory.

Encoding

We do not experience our environment directly. Our awareness of the world around us is based upon the information that is encoded from it. Aspects of the external environment that are not encoded are not available for subsequent processing and thus are not a part of our experience or memory. A great many aspects of the environment do not find their way into our experience. We are constantly surrounded by events of which we are unaware. We do not have appropriate receptors for some energy events, such as radio waves, ultraviolet light, and TV signals, or if we do have the appropriate receptors, they are not keen enough to detect the events. Other events give rise to changes in energy to which we are sensitive, but the changes are not of sufficient magnitude to produce a reaction. Finally, on some occasions a stimulus that would normally be noticed is missed because we are not "paying attention." The first two reasons for missing environmental events have been studied primarily by psychologists interested in the processes of sensation and perception. The last instance, failure to attend, has been of considerable interest to researchers investigating human memory.

Selective Attention

Failing to attend to events in our environment can be disastrous, as when we fail to notice the car stopped on the freeway ahead of us. For the most part, however, the ability to ignore some events is extremely beneficial. Consider trying to carry on a conversation with a friend in the student-union cafeteria at noon. The ability to focus attention on a subset of our environment at the expense of the rest of it is an important part of the encoding process.

If we were able to process effectively all the information in our environment, there might be little need for selective attention (Montague, 1972). There is, however, considerable evidence that the amount of information that can be processed at any one time is limited. The information available in the environment virtually always exceeds our processing capacity. The system, then, must constantly be selecting which information will be processed and which will not.

An experimental approach to studying information-processing capacity and selective attention is suggested by the example of conversing in the cafeteria. How are we able to listen to one conversation in the midst of many other conversations? This problem has been addressed directly in a series of *selective-listening experiments*. In one early experiment (Cherry, 1953) two messages were recorded, one on top of the other, on magnetic tape. This combined message, described by the experimenter as babble, was presented to subjects, and they were asked to unravel the two messages. Even though both messages were spoken by the same person and had rather similar content, the subjects were eventually able to interpret the two messages. The task was quite difficult, however, and the subjects required many repetitions of the superimposed messages. Because we do not generally experience this much difficulty in dealing with multiple conversations, the procedure used in this first experiment does not seem to represent the situation in the cafeteria.

Other experiments using slightly different procedures have produced results that seem more consistent with our apparent ability to focus on one message in spite of the presence of a number of others. In some of these experiments, the two messages were separated and presented one to each ear of the listener. Subjects in these *dichotic-listening experiments* had little difficulty in understanding one or the other of the messages and were able to switch their attention from one to the other rapidly. Apparently, presenting the two messages separately (one to each ear) allowed the subjects to use their ability to attend selectively to one of the messages.

Investigators have continued to use the dichotic-listening technique together with several other multiple-message techniques to study information-processing capacity and selective attention. In general, human subjects show an excellent ability to focus their attention on one of several simultaneous messages. When attention to one message is assured by requiring subjects to *shadow* (repeat verbatim) the message, they seem to encode very little information from another, simultaneously presented message. Moreover, they generally do not notice changes in the content of the other message, changes from English to a foreign language, or shifts from meaningful material to nonsense.

Nonattended messages are nevertheless encoded to some extent. Subjects are able to tell whether an unattended message was human speech and whether it was spoken by a male or a female. There is also evidence of more extensive encoding of the rejected material. If a particularly relevant word, such as the listener's name, is spoken, the listener's attention to the selected message will be disrupted, and he or she will encode and retain the word. If a subject is shadowing a message being presented to the left ear while "ignoring" a message in the right ear and if the content of the messages is suddenly reversed in the middle of a sentence or a word, the subject will often shift to shadowing the message being presented to the previously ignored ear.

Although the first experiments discussed seemed to indicate that only rather gross characteristics of the unattended message are encoded, these later findings suggest much more extensive encoding of the rejected message. That subjects are affected by unattended words that have special meaning (one's own name), or that complete the meaning of the preceding parts of the attended message, suggests that the unattended message is encoded sufficiently for the subjects to abstract the meaning or significance of the information presented.

These findings have important implications for our conceptualization of the role of selective attention in information processing. It seems obvious that unattended information does get encoded and that it is processed to a considerable extent. How, then, can selective attention be said to reduce the information-processing load?

Theories of selective attention have generally dealt with this problem in one of two basic ways. One approach is to extend the encoding stage of information processing so that it involves several substages. A "preattentive" or "presensitizing" stage is postulated to operate very early in the encoding process to set or prepare the later encoding stages for receiving specific types of information. The later stages may, then, be predisposed further to process information having certain physical (for example, male voice), grammatical (a verb may be expected in the middle of a sentence), or semantically relevant (as determined by the previous content) characteristics. The later encoding processes may, in addition, be biased against information having characteristics associated with the unattended message.

The other theoretical approach is to assume that selective attention is postponed until after the encoding stage of processing. By this account, all of the information in both the attended and the unattended message is completely encoded. The encoded information is held (stored) very briefly, rapidly analyzed, and then either dumped out or further processed and stored in permanent memory.

These two analyses of selective attention differ somewhat conceptually, but both require a rather brief but very large processing capacity at some point in the encoding of information. By either account, the principal limitations on our information-processing capacity are not established by the amount of information that can be taken into the system. Rather, the limitations are introduced later by our inability to process and/or retain effectively all the information that was initially encoded. Although there is general agreement on the importance of attention in memory, we do not yet have a detailed account of how selective-attention mechanisms operate in the information-processing system (Norman, 1976).

Serial and Parallel Processing

From our brief discussion of selective attention, it is clear that at some point in the encoding process there is the capacity for handling large amounts of information presented essentially simultaneously. We must exercise some caution, however, before concluding that this information is encoded all at once. For example, a time-sharing computer seems to deal simultaneously with many inputs, but it accomplishes this task by very rapidly switching back and forth, processing only one of the inputs at any given instant. The human information-processing system may also sequentially encode several simultaneously presented messages. Such sequential encoding is referred to as *serial processing*. Alternatively, all messages may be encoded at the same time. Simultaneous encoding of several sources or types of information is termed *parallel processing*. Which of these two models best represents human information processing is the subject of theoretical controversy and experimental investigation.

One technique that has been used to investigate serial and parallel processing is the *visual-search task*. There are many kinds of visual-search tasks, but all of them involve the scanning of some array of stimuli to locate some specific target stimulus or stimuli. Proofreading a theme or paper for typographical errors is a good example of a visual-search task. The stimulus array consists of a large number of letter sequences, spaces, and punctuation marks. The target stimuli are missing or misspelled words, misplaced punctuation marks, and so on. Proofreading is a very complex visual-search task, but the human information processor can learn to perform it rapidly and with few errors. That an apparently simultaneous search for many different kinds of target stimuli is involved suggests that several types of information may be processed in parallel. Of course, as indicated earlier, a rapidly alternating serial-processing strategy may also be employed. A much more detailed analysis of the search task is required if we are to determine which processing strategy best describes the human information-processing system's approach to visual search.

Systematic experimental analysis of a laboratory task that is very similar to the proofreading task has provided a considerable amount of information about how the human processing system accomplishes visual-search tasks. The laboratory task, studied most extensively by Neisser and his associates (Neisser, 1963, 1967; Neisser & Beller, 1965; Neisser, Novick, & Lazar, 1963), requires subjects to scan a list of letters or words in search of a designated letter or set of letters. The amount of time taken to find the target is the datum that is usually of greatest interest.

You can try this type of visual-search task for yourself with the following lists:

A		*B*	
ODQGRU	RGDQUO	IVMXEW	EVXWMI
RGUODQ	UQODGR	MXEWVI	VXIWEM
CUDQOR	ORGQDU	EMXVWI	XIWEMV
DCUROQ	QURDOG	XIEVMW	IWEMVX
URCQOD	QOUDRG	WWEVIM	WEMXIV
QCDURO	RGUQRO	VMVWXI	MMIXEW
DCURCO	GUDQOR	IEWVMX	IEVWMX
CDRCOU	OGORUD	MWVIXE	VXEMWW
URCOCD	ODRUGQ	WVEXMV	MIWVXE
DQZROG	DRUGOQ	VIXWME	WMIWVX
ODGQRU	OQDGUR	IEXIVV	XWEIVM
RGQDOG	UGDQRO	XVEVIW	EVWMXI
UQDROG	OGDRQR	XVIMWX	MIXVEW
QROUDG	DGQRUO	EVIWME	IVWMEX
QDOUGR	URGDOG	MEVZXI	WEMXVI

First search through List A and find the letter Z as quickly as you can. Not a difficult task. How long did it take you? Now find the *Z* in List B. Did it take you longer than in List A? Probably so.

There are several things to be learned from this simple experiment. One reason for your finding the *Z* faster in List A than in List B is that the *Z* occurred earlier in List A. Fewer lines of letters had to be searched (from the top of each column) before the target, *Z*, appeared. Thus, the number of items to be searched seems to affect the amount of time needed to find the target; the more items searched, the longer the time required. The number of items searched does not account for all of the difference in search times between the two lists, however. List B is also much more difficult to search than List A. The *Z* shows up much more easily in the latter, where the nontarget letters (*O, D, Q, G, R, C,* and *U*) are all rounded or curved. That the letters in the other list (*I, V, M, X, E,* and *W*) are frequently straight and angular, as is the target letter *Z*, makes the search task more difficult and increases the search time. Thus, the similarity of the nontarget letters to the target letter influences search time; the more similar the letters, the longer the search time.

That increasing the number of lines that must be searched prior to finding the target letter leads to longer search times might be interpreted as indicating a serial-processing strategy, in which each letter is encoded separately. If the letter is not a *Z*, it is rejected and the next letter encoded and so on, until the target letter is found. Search time, then, would simply be the number of letters searched multiplied by the amount of time taken to encode each letter. This analysis is too simple, however, because it fails to explain why an *M* (List B) takes longer to encode and reject than the letter *O* (List A).

Experiments have shown that when the nontarget letters are very dissimilar to the target letter, subjects encode hardly any information at all about the nontarget letters. After some practice with search lists such as List A, subjects report that the target letter seems to jump out at them. There is little awareness of the nontarget letters; they seem to be a blur. Did you notice, for example, that there are *two* *C*s in line 7 of List A? Probably not. These results indicate a need for some modification of the serial-processing account of visual search. Perhaps only those aspects of nontarget letters that are sufficient to distinguish them from the target letter are encoded. This would mean that serial search of letter lists does not proceed letter by letter but by separate *features* of the letters. This possibility would explain why the *C* was not distinguished from a *G*. In List A it was only necessary to determine whether a given letter had a curved line.

That more search time was required for List B than for List A would also be consistent with the feature-processing account. All of the letters in List B were rather similar to the target letter, *Z*, so more features of each letter had to be encoded before the letter could be rejected as a nontarget. All of the letters had straight lines and acute angles, for example, so some additional feature or features (say, the absence of a horizontal line across the top and bottom of the letter) had to be encoded before the letter could be rejected. By the serial-processing account these additional features would be encoded and processed sequentially, thus increasing the total search time.

The serial-feature-processing account seems to explain the most important differences in search times and other aspects of our experiment with the two lists. There are some findings from more complex search tasks, however, that seem to require a parallel-processing interpretation. For example, search times are not appreciably increased by adding more letters to each line of the search list. More important, search times do not seem to be affected when subjects are required to search for more than one target at the same time (for example, a *Z* or a *K*). With practice, subjects can search for as many as ten different targets about as rapidly as they can search for one (Neisser et al., 1963). Neisser (1967) notes that experienced readers at a news-clipping agency can scan newspapers at a very rapid rate, simultaneously searching for and finding references to any of several hundred clients of the agency.

If we now reconsider the proofreading example discussed earlier, a parallel-processing model would seem to be required there also. A great many targets are involved in this search task. Further, many of the targets are rather complex, and some are defined only by exclusion; that is, the absence of letters, words, punctuation marks, and spaces must all be sought and discovered. Using a serial-processing strategy here would require the reader to consider every letter or space and sequentially determine whether it represents one or another of the many types of errors that are being sought. Although such a strategy cannot be ruled out entirely, especially if we allow for very high-speed processing, the speed and accuracy with which the proofreading task can be accomplished would seem to strain the serial-processing account.

Even though the visual search involved in proofreading may be accomplished by a parallel process of some kind, the processing system does not have an unlimited capacity. If you attempt to proof your paper for typographical errors while at the same time reading for "meaning" and proper grammatical structure, you will probably overlook a number of errors. On the other hand, a person unfamiliar with your subject may proof the manuscript and find all of the misplaced commas and misspelled words but completely overlook the fact that an entire paragraph has been omitted or a page duplicated.[1]

[1] The personal experience of one of the authors supports the notion that the capacity of the system is limited in proofreading. After numerous readings of his master's thesis had convinced several typists and the author that the manuscript was error free, the page numbers were carefully typed on each page, and xerox copies were made. All the copies were bound and distributed to the library and elsewhere to be preserved for posterity. To his knowledge, all the copies still contain two identical pages numbered 37 and 38, respectively.

Researchers continue to investigate the processes involved in visual search and other tasks. In some instances the data indicate that a serial process is employed; at other times a parallel-processing strategy is used. Some experiments have led researchers to postulate a third alternative, *integral processing*. In some information-processing tasks several separate stimulus dimensions (color, shape, size) seem to be integrated into a single compound feature that is processed as a unit. Part of the difficulty in distinguishing between these different accounts is that any outcome of a parallel-processing system (or an integral one) can be duplicated by a sufficiently rapid, time-sharing, serial-processing system.

For most purposes, any of these accounts would suffice to explain the empirical facts of visual search. Indeed, there is some reason to believe that the way we process information depends upon the nature of the information to be processed and the circumstances and requirements of the processing task. In some situations, information may be processed serially; in other circumstances, processing may be parallel or integral. Accordingly, theorists have turned from attempting to decide whether information processing is serial, parallel, or integral and have concentrated more on determining under what conditions one or another processing strategy is employed.

Information Codes

In our visual-search experiment the similarity of the target and nontarget letters was found to have an important influence on the difficulty of the task. The effect of physical similarity suggests that at some point the letters are encoded in terms of lines, angles, and other figural characteristics. There are, however, several indications that this is only part of the encoded representation of a letter in the human information processing system. The letter *A*, for example, comes in a great many forms, but all seem to be essentially equally acceptable. For most purposes, *A*, *a*, ɑ, **A**, and 𝒜 will all serve very well to represent the letter *A* in *CAT* or *bat* or *sat*. Indeed, a great variety of letter *A*s differing in color, size, or other characteristics are all tolerated by the human information-processing system. Though we are all aware that these several forms of the letter *A* are different in some respects, they are at the same time alike. This observation suggests the need for a distinction between *physical identity* and *functional* or *name identity.*

The relationship between figural (physical) characteristics and name characteristics of letters has been used by Posner and his associates (Poster, 1969; Posner & Keele, 1968; Posner & Mitchell, 1967) to investigate the encoding process. One procedure involves the simultaneous presentation of letter pairs to subjects, who are instructed to indicate whether the two letters are the same or different. In some experiments the subjects are told to respond "same" only when the letters are physically identical (*AA*); in others they are instructed to respond "same" whenever the letters have the same name (either *AA* or *Aa*). As in the visual-search task, emphasis is on the amount of time required for making the correct judgment. The subjects are provided with two response buttons, one for "same" judgments and one for "different." When a letter pair is exposed, the subjects press the appropriate button as quickly as they can. The reaction time (RT), or latency, the time between the onset of the letters and the pressing of the appropriate button, is then recorded.

It has generally been found that "same" reaction times for simultaneously presented letters are faster for physically identical pairs (*AA*) than for name-match pairs (*Aa*). This advantage for physical matches persists even when a name-match task is employed; if the subjects are instructed to respond "same" when letters have the same name, RTs are still faster for *AA* pairs than for *Aa* pairs. The extra time required for name matches has been attributed to the *additional encoding operations* needed to match the two different letter configurations. The implication is that physical features are encoded first (or more quickly) and that additional processing time is required to determine whether two physically dissimilar letters have the same name. If the two letters are found to be physically identical, there is no need for any further processing because they must also have the same name. This analysis receives additional support in the physical-match experiment in which the subjects respond "same" only if the letters are identical (*AA* or *aa*). "Different" RTs are equal in the physical-identity task for name-match pairs (*Aa* or *Bb*) and nonname-match pairs (*Ab* or *Ba*). If name codes occur later in the processing sequence than physical codes, name identity would not be expected to interfere with physical-match performance.

The distinction between physical and name codes is useful, but there are indications that more complex encoding processes are involved in matching tasks. It has been found, for example, that RTs are not appreciably increased when some of the letters are turned upside down. Also, name matches for some letter pairs—for example, *Cc* or *Ss*—while slower than physical matches (*CC* or *AA*), are faster than *Aa* matches. Posner (1969) concludes from these findings that less encoding is required for these *analog matches* than for name matches. Apparently, transformations of figural properties of the letter stimuli, such as size and orientation, can be accomplished in the encoding process without the need for a name code.

Other variations of the letter-matching experiment have produced results that even further complicate the analysis of encoding processes. When the members of a letter pair are separated and presented one after the other, there is a progressive decline in the time superiority of physical matches over name matches. As illustrated in Figure 9–2, if the two letters are separated by as much as 1.5 seconds, name matches are as fast as physical matches. The indication is that once the name code is established, physical identity of the two letters no longer offers any advantage for "same"/"different" judgments.

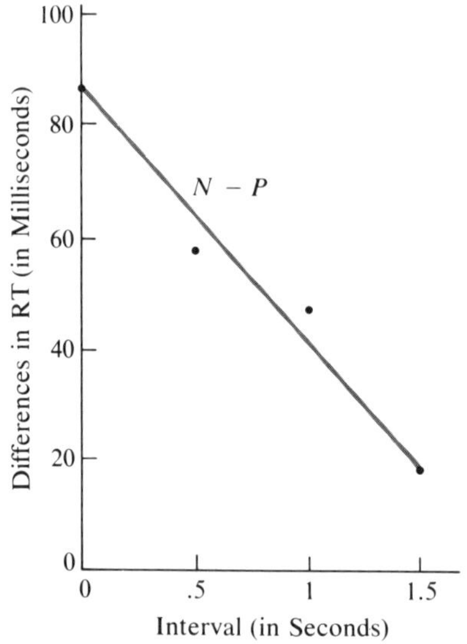

Figure 9–2. Difference in reaction time between name match, *N*, and physical match, *P*, as the delay between the target and the test letter is increased. (From "Decay of Visual Information from a Single Letter," by M. I. Posner and S. W. Keele, *Science*, 1967, *158*, 137–139. Reprinted by permission of the American Association for the Advancement of Science.)

There is some evidence that letter stimuli are processed as something other than figural (physical) or name codes. In several experiments the first letter of a pair was presented auditorily, and after a brief delay the other letter was presented visually. This change in the task would seem to present little difficulty if there were sufficient time between the letters for the production of a name code. However, when intervals of up to 1 second were allowed between the letters, "same" RTs were significantly faster for auditory-to-visual matches than for visual-to-visual name matches. In fact, auditory/visual matches were as fast as physical matches in which both letters were presented visually. These results might indicate that, rather than a name code, the auditorily presented letter is translated to a visual code, allowing for the more rapid physical match with the visually presented test letter. However, no differences in "same" RTs were found between upper-case (*A*) and lower-case (*a*) test items after auditory presentation of the initial letter.

If a visual code were generated from the auditorily presented letter, it would seem to be a code that is equally similar to upper-case and lower-case forms of the letter. Thus, both name codes and visual codes, at least as discussed to this point, appear to be ruled out by these data. What type of code, then, is used to mediate auditory-to-visual letter matches?

The answer to this question is not yet fully formulated. Posner (1969) has suggested, however, that a higher-order visual code, an abstract code, may be employed in this context. This code, though still essentially visual, does not represent the letter in any specific form. Rather, the abstract code involves only general characteristics of the letter, characteristics common to all forms of the letter *A*, for example. A generalized representation of several related but different visual patterns has been referred to as a *schema*. In some sense the schema is the "average" or central tendency of the whole set of specific patterns that are included in the same category, such as all letter *A*s. The auditory letter *A*, then, produces an abstract code (or schema) against which any specific form of the letter presented visually can readily be compared.

An abstract-code concept seems to be required by the findings of the auditory-to-visual letter-match experiments. However, as Posner (1969) points out, it does leave some important questions unanswered. For example, why should auditorily presented letters produce abstract codes more readily than visually presented letters? (Recall that name matches take longer for *Aa* pairs than for *AA* pairs when both letters are presented visually.) Also, the exact nature of the abstract code is not entirely clear. Both name codes and abstract codes apparently share the essential property of transcending differences in specific features of letter patterns (size, orientation, color, and so forth), yet they are proposed as different codes.

Research continues into these and other questions about the processes that transform external stimulus figures or patterns into functional representations that can be recognized and compared. Although many laboratory experiments have focused upon rather simple types of stimuli (such as letters), the encoding processes that seem to be required appear to be very complex. More recent research has extended the investigation of encoding processes to more complex stimuli. An increasing number of studies are devoted to discovering and analyzing the processes involved in the encoding of words, pictures, sentences, and stories. Future research should provide us with more and more detailed analyses of the complex processes that encode environmental stimuli into the human information-processing system.

Storage

In many respects, storage is at the core of our conceptualization of memory. Because events are remembered for days or even years, some representation of those events must be retained during that period. In the general information-processing account of memory, the storage stage of the processing sequence is responsible for the maintenance of encoded information over time.

In early research on human retention, memory (storage) was generally viewed as a single process. The memory of an event was thought to be best or strongest soon after the occurrence of the event and then to weaken over time. The results of later experiments, however, suggested that memory over very short time intervals might be qualitatively as well as quantitatively different, in several ways, from memory over longer intervals. Thus, a distinction was made between *short-term memory (STM)* and *long-term memory (LTM)*.

The contemporary conceptualization of memory goes further than this distinction and suggests at least three different substages of storage, each having different properties. But many investigators argue that it is not necessary to view memory as segmented into qualitatively different components. They favor a conceptualization including a single well-integrated memory system that adopts different modes or processing strategies depending upon the nature of the material and/or memory task. The substages of memory discussed in the following pages, whether essential to a model of memory processes or not, do provide a useful framework for viewing many of the more important features of memory. These substages have been differentiated by the length of time they hold the encoded information (the substages do seem to overlap somewhat in this regard, however) and by the nature and the amount of information that is retained in each store. The first and generally shortest-lived storage stage is sensory-information storage *(SIS)*. The second stage is usually termed short-term memory, and the final stage is long-term memory or permanent memory.

Sensory-Information Storage

As you look around a room and notice a window, a door, or another person, your perception of these environmental events seems to be continuous and essentially instantaneous. You are not aware of taking time to integrate a constellation of separate features into your perception of a friend's face. There is no conscious effort to note and remember the eyes, so that they can be added to the perception of the nose, so that memory for both the eyes and the nose can in turn be combined with the perception of the mouth, and so on. The face seems to be immediately perceived as a face, intact and complete at a single glance. In spite of our own introspective impressions, however, the perception of a face or any other event typically involves the integration of information from many different "snapshots" (fixations) separated by measurable intervals of time. Thus, storage is involved even at the very earliest stages of information processing.

One very convincing demonstration of the temporal integration involved in perception is the camel-through-the-eye-of-a-needle experiment. In this demonstration a line drawing of a camel is exposed to observers one small segment at a time. One way to do so is to cover the figure with an opaque screen that has a small vertical slit in it. As indicated in Figure 9–3, only a small segment (a 1/64-inch slit was used in one experiment) of the underlying figure can be exposed through the slit at any one time. Nonetheless, if the figure is moved behind the slit at the proper speed (fast enough to expose the whole figure within about 250 to 500 milliseconds), the observers will be able to identify the figure. Further, they will report that they see a complete camel. This integrative capacity of the information-processing system is responsible for our ability to see motion in cartoons, to see intact moving images on our TV screens, and, in the auditory sense, to piece together strings of sound into comprehensible words and sentences.

We do not yet know how these individually encoded "snapshots" of information are retained and finally put together to form the integrated, continuous perception of the world that characterizes our experience. However, we do have considerable systematic knowledge about some aspects of this complex process. One very important component of the process is a storage system that can retain the very large amounts of information contained in a single input, at least until the next input can be further encoded. A large capacity is re-

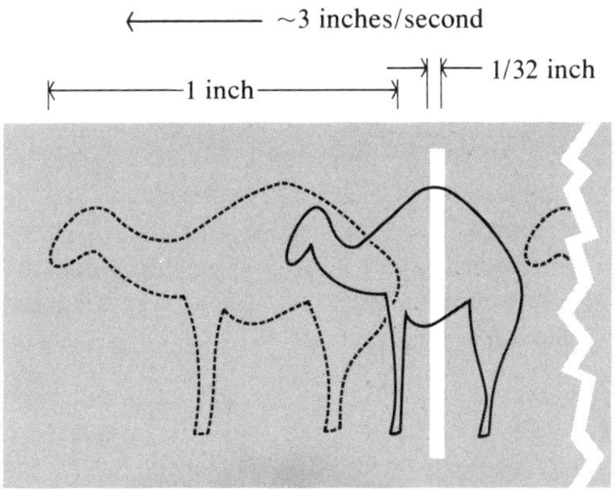

Figure 9–3. Passing a camel through the eye of a needle. A simple outline figure (dashed line) is passed behind a slit in an opaque screen. If it passes in approximately 250–500 milliseconds, it will be seen to move slightly and to be foreshortened (solid line). The foreshortening increases with the speed of its passage until only a blur is seen. At slow speeds the figure can be identified but will not be seen as a whole. (From "Post-retinal Visual Storage," by T. E. Parks, *American Journal of Psychology*, 1965, *78*, 145–147. Reprinted by permission of the University of Illinois Press.)

quired because there is little or no basis for leaving out any of the information available in the first input until after the complete "percept" begins to be formed. This storage component is related to the "preattentive" encoding process described in the discussion of selective-attention phenomena. This initial storage system must briefly hold large amounts of information without regard to its subsequent usefulness or its relationship to as-yet-unencoded information. It is this rather short-term, nonselective, large-capacity system that is referred to as sensory-information storage.

The capacity and other characteristics of sensory-information storage were most clearly revealed in a series of very clever experiments by Sperling (1960, 1963). He found that after a set of 12 letters (three rows of four letters each) was exposed very briefly (50 milliseconds), subjects were generally able to name no more than four of the 12 letters. Usually the letters they recalled were in the first row of the array and were reported in left-to-right order.

From these data it would appear that the subjects encoded letters serially from left to right. With the very brief exposure time they were able to encode only the first few letters of the array. However, Sperling varied the experiment by using a *partial-report procedure* and made an important discovery. He presented a tone either immediately or after a short delay following the termination of the visual array. The tone signaled which row of letters the subject was to report; a high tone indicated that the top row was to be reported, a medium tone the middle row, and a low tone the bottom row. Thus, the number of items the subject had to report was always held to just four of the 12 letters. Even when the tone was delayed for as much as 250 milliseconds after the termination of the visual array, subjects were able to recall accurately most of the letters regardless of which row was to be reported. Because the subject could not know in advance which row would be cued, these data indicate that all three rows of letters must have been available at the time the tone was presented. Thus, although the first experiments indicated that subjects could encode only about four of the letters, these data indicate that all 12 letters were encoded and retained in the processing system for at least a quarter of a second.

Sperling's data, together with the results of a number of related experiments, indicate that memory for briefly presented visual stimuli (for example, letter arrays) is initially held in a large-capacity, very short-term storage system. Sperling referred to this earliest storage stage as *visual-information storage* (*VIS*). There is evidence that a similar sensory-information storage is involved in the processing of other types of stimuli as well. Most notably, auditory stimuli appear to be retained initially in an "echoic" storage system. Similar short-term storage of tactile, kinesthetic, and chemical (taste and smell) stimulation probably occurs, but to date less research has been done in this area. Most of our systematic knowledge of the characteristics of sensory-information storage derives from research employing visually presented stimuli.

The Iconic Image. In Sperling's experiments it appeared that so long as visual-information storage lasted, subjects were able essentially to "read" information from its contents. Some rather complete, internal replica of the visual stimulus seemed to have been retained that represented most or all of the information contained in the original stimulus. This internal replica has been labeled the *iconic image* (Neisser, 1967), a term that emphasizes the visual, spatially arranged representation of information at this point in the processing sequence.

The duration of the iconic image varies depending upon a number of factors, but the best overall estimate of its duration is about 250 milliseconds. This time is consistent with the period that separates the individual "snapshots" from which our perception of most stimuli is composed. Also, recall that 250 to 500 milliseconds was the best "sweep time" for producing the camel-through-the-eye-of-the-needle phenomenon.

The iconic image has generally been considered to be a visual, spatially arranged, large-capacity (but with a relatively brief duration) information store. The visual character of the icon is indicated by the importance of the brightness of the originating stimulus as a factor influencing the duration and clarity of the iconic image. Moreover, subsequent visual inputs generally interfere with iconic memory, while auditory inputs, for example, do not. Subjects will retain visually presented letters in the iconic image even though the names of other letters are being very loudly presented auditorily at the same time.

The spatial organization of the icon is indicated by the fact that Sperling's subjects tended to "read" letters in order from the image. Also, in several experiments (for example, Eriksen & Collins, 1968), subjects were able to retain random dot patterns in iconic memory. In the Eriksen and Collins study, several pairs of apparently random dot arrays were constructed so that if one member of a pair was superimposed over the other, a three-letter nonsense syllable was readable. A sample of these arrays is presented in Figure 9–4. Note that either dot array, by itself, gives no clue to the letters of the syllable.

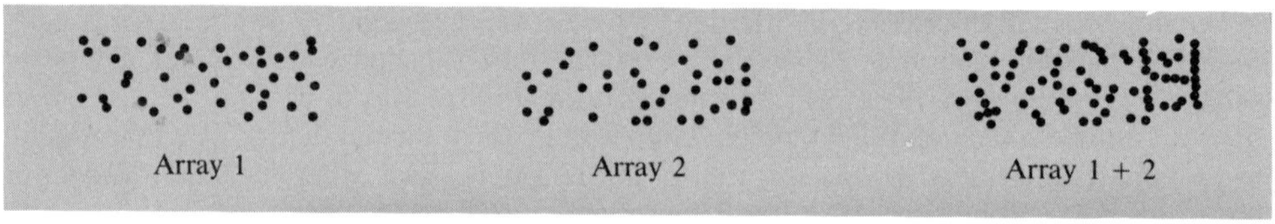

Figure 9–4. Random dot arrays and the nonsense syllable formed by their superimposition. (From "Sensory Tracts versus the Psychological Moment in the Temporal Organization of Form," by C. W. Eriksen and J. F. Collins, *Journal of Experimental Psychology,* 1968, *77,* 376–382. Copyright 1968 by the American Psychological Association. Reprinted by permission.)

The subjects in this experiment were shown two members of a dot-array pair, one after the other, with separations between the two arrays varying from no separation up to 500 milliseconds. About 90% of the syllables were correctly identified when the arrays were presented simultaneously, and just over half of the syllables were identified when the arrays were presented 100 milliseconds apart. Even when the arrays were presented 500 milliseconds apart, 30% of the syllables were correctly identified. A spatially arranged store of some kind seems to be required by these results. Apparently, the iconic image contains sufficient information for the dots in the first array to be precisely located so that they can be superimposed over the second array to produce the nonsense syllable.

Central versus Peripheral Interpretations. It is tempting at this point to think of sensory-information storage as an unanalyzed, internal replica of the external stimulus. That large amounts of information are held and can be "read" after the external stimulus has been absent for a quarter of a second, and sometimes longer, provides compelling evidence for this interpretation. In some experiments, subjects have even had difficulty distinguishing between the iconic image of an external stimulus and the stimulus itself. This can occur because the iconic image has a very clear visual character. However, this interpretation raises a number of important questions about the early stages of information processing. To date we do not know how such a replica of an external stimulus could be encoded and stored in the human sensory-information-processing system. One hypothesis that has appealed to some investigators is that some effect of the external-stimulus energy persists in the peripheral components of the visual system—for example, in the retina of the eye. Alternatively, the iconic image has been viewed as a more central development that requires much more extensive information processing.

A moderate amount of information has been developed that supports the view of the iconic image as a peripheral, sensory phenomenon. By this analysis the icon would be related to the class of visual aftereffects that are generally referred to as *retinal afterimages*. The existence of afterimages has been known for some time, and their characteristics have been studied by sensory/perceptual psychologists. Afterimages almost invariably follow brief exposure to a bright stimulus. If you stare at a light bulb or the sun, for example, and then look away, you will "see" a spot for up to several minutes afterward. Usually the afterimage will appear as the *negative* of the original stimulus, a bright stimulus producing a dark afterimage on a lighter background. This phenomenon has generally been attributed to fatigue of the rods and cones of the retina that were stimulated most extensively by the original stimulus. When you subsequently look away at a homogeneously illuminated area, these fatigued retinal cells underreact, relative to those cells that were less affected by the original stimulus, producing the impression of a darker area corresponding to the original stimulus.

The iconic image does seem to share a number of characteristics with retinal afterimages. Both types of visual aftereffects will be stronger and will persist longer if the original stimulus is much brighter than the prior and subsequent levels of illumination. Very brief exposures, reducing the possibility of eye movements, tend to produce better images in both cases. Also, both iconic images and retinal afterimages are disrupted or "masked" when the original stimulus is followed quickly by a second stimulus. The second, *masking stimulus* may simply be a bright flash of light or a visual array consisting of a meaningless pattern of lines or squiggles or, in some experiments, fragments of letters (see Figure 9–5). A patterned masking stimulus is usually referred to as a *visual-noise field*.

In spite of these similarities, some important differences between iconic images and retinal afterimages have been reported. Retinal afterimages are almost always negative with respect to the original stimulus, and they seem to move with the eyes. Iconic images are

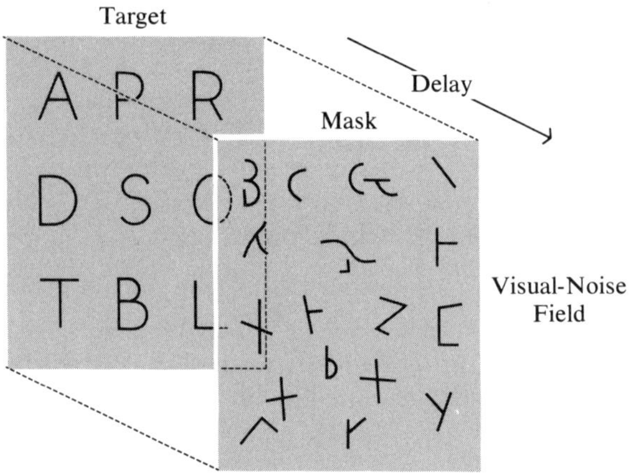

Figure 9–5. Target stimulus and visual-noise-field mask for testing sensory-information storage.

generally reported to be positive and more stable. Although both images tend to be lessened by subsequent masking stimuli, there are differences in the specific effects of the mask. The most disruption of the iconic image is accomplished by delaying the masking stimulus briefly (approximately 10 to 25 milliseconds) after the original stimulus. Apparently, the icon is not formed immediately but must be constructed. This construction time has been attributed to the more extensive information processing or encoding involved in the iconic image and suggests that the icon is not a peripheral, retinal phenomenon. Moreover, it has been found that some types of masking stimuli are equally effective even though the original stimulus is presented to one eye and the mask to the other eye. This *dichoptic-masking effect* strongly indicates that some more central information processing is involved in the construction of the iconic image.

These arguments suggest that iconic-memory images and retinal afterimages can be differentiated by the degree of central encoding or information processing required for each. Retinal afterimages seem to involve primarily peripheral components of the visual sensory system. It should be noted, however, that some evidently retinal-afterimage phenomena strongly suggest information processing of a much higher order of complexity than would usually be ascribed to the retina. Afterimages of patterns or forms, for example, generally do not appear to fade away en masse. Rather, components of the image seem to disappear quite systematically. The afterimage of a word may seem to disappear one letter or part of a letter at a time, often so as to leave a meaningful word at each point. R. N. Haber (1969) offers the example *BEER BEEP BEE BE*. Similar effects have been observed when the projection of a visual stimulus onto the retina, the retinal image of the stimulus, is stabilized or stopped. Stabilization of the retinal image is usually accomplished by means of a system of lenses and mirrors, one mirror being attached to a contact lens worn by the subject. Stopping the retinal image results in the loss or fading (presumably due to habituation of affected retinal cells) of the image. Again, this loss of the image tends to progress by meaningful units rather than by a generalized (or random) decay process (Pritchard, 1961). These data are somewhat difficult to account for in terms of simple fatigue or habituation of the retinal cells.

Perhaps the most intriguing visual aftereffects involve afterimages of chromatic (colored) stimuli. Typically, a chromatic afterimage is produced by staring at a brightly colored stimulus such as a red-striped pattern. After staring at a red pattern briefly, if you then look at a plain white surface, you will "see" a green-striped pattern. Green is the "negative," or complement, of red. As with black-and-white afterimages, the complementary-colored afterimage has generally been attributed to fatigue of the affected retinal cells, in this example the cones that are most sensitive to red light.[2] When a white field (white light is composed of all the spectral colors) is subsequently viewed, the fatigued red-sensitive cones will underreact relative to the blue-sensitive and yellow-sensitive cones, and the result will be a green (blue + yellow = green) afterimage.

A variety of procedures and stimulus patterns have been shown to produce color-pattern dependence in the afterimage. Two differently colored dot patterns, one having large dots and the other small, work very well, as do a variety of curved lines and other patterns. Perhaps the most striking demonstration is that the same pattern (for example, a horizontal-stripe pattern) can be presented, alternately being red and moving upward and then green and moving downward. Subsequently, a black-and-white horizontally striped test pattern will appear green when moving upward and red when moving downward (Stromeyer, 1969; Stromeyer & Mansfield, 1970).

If the phenomena just described do represent peripheral (retinal) processes, the processes must be far more complex than the simple fatigued-receptor explanation indicates. Probably the best conclusion to draw from these observations is that the very earliest stages of visual-information processing are very complex and involve many interacting components. Any attempt to distinguish iconic images from retinal afterimages simply on the basis of the extent of central information processing involved will probably prove futile.

Regardless of the peripheral/central distinction, iconic imagery remains as an important component in visual-information processing and memory. Although our general conceptualization of iconic memory continues to be of a spatially arranged, visual store from which information can be "read," some recent experiments (for example, Estes, 1973; Parkinson, Kroll, & Parks, 1973) do cast some doubt on this view. Strings of letters were presented visually to subjects, and they were required to recall one (or more) of the letters as indicated by a partial-report marker presented after the letters were no longer present. When all of the letters were presented either simultaneously or sequentially across the subject's visual field, recall of the designated letter indicated that essentially all of the letters were retained. These data, like Sperling's (1960) discussed earlier, suggest an iconic-memory image. However, when the same letters were presented sequentially, one after the other *in the same place* in the visual field (that is, one on top of the other), the subjects still showed memory by an iconic image. These latter data are somewhat difficult to explain in terms of iconic-memory images as they have been considered to date. Certainly the notion of iconic memory as a two-dimensional array or image seems to be questionable.

The final implications of these research findings have not yet been determined, but the indications are that our conception of iconic-memory images will need revision. Nonetheless, some form of very short-term visual-information storage will probably remain as an important component of visual-information processing. Some early storage system seems to be required to extend our processing time, allowing for additional encoding of information from stimuli that are available only very briefly. Most important, our ability to perceive the visual world as a continuous and integrated whole depends greatly on our ability to hold large amounts of visual/spatial information between eye fixations.

[2] The generally accepted theory of color vision recognizes three differentially sensitive color-receptor cells (cones) in the retina of the eye. These cones are maximally sensitive to either the red range, the blue range, or the yellow range of the electromagnetic (light) spectrum. Normal color perception depends upon the proportions of these three types of cones that are stimulated by a given source of light.

Short-Term Memory

The initial representation of an input to the human information-processing system involves the retention of a large amount of information, at least briefly, in the sensory-information store. During the short period that information is available in SIS, some, but not nearly all, of the information may be "read" and reported. Alternatively, information may be transferred for retention in a longer-lasting storage system. Information that is not transferred from SIS is lost from the information-processing system and is no longer available in memory. In this section we will discuss the processes involved in the extraction of selected information from SIS and the transfer of that information to a longer-lasting storage component. This slightly more durable storage stage is generally referred to as short-term memory. It not only holds information longer than does SIS but also represents it differently.

An everyday experience that illustrates the operation of STM is looking up a telephone number in the directory. Suppose that you want to call a department store to inquire about an item you wish to purchase. You may turn to the Yellow Pages of your directory, scan the list of department stores (a visual-search task), and locate the desired store. Printed next to the name of the store will be a seven-digit telephone number. After looking at the number, thus encoding it into SIS, you must then turn to the telephone and dial the number. Information in SIS will, of course, have faded before you can dial the first number. You need to hold the number much longer than 250–500 milliseconds to complete the task of dialing successfully. Close observation of how you perform this task reveals several aspects of how the information is retained. Usually, immediately after looking up the number, you will repeat the number to yourself, silently, several times. Frequently you will repeat the numbers to yourself again as you dial the number.[3]

If your call goes through and you get the information you want you will probably not be able to remember the number without looking it up again. On the other hand, should you get a busy signal, you may retain the number for several minutes and then dial it again. Usually, in this latter instance, you will have to repeat the number to yourself several more times in order to retain it until you next attempt to complete the call. This repeating of the number to yourself is *rehearsal,* and it seems to be very important in the process of extracting information from SIS and establishing it in STM.

Rehearsal and STM Capacity. Psychologists have used tasks very similar to the telephone-number example to investigate the characteristics of STM. In an important study reported by Peterson and Peterson (1959), subjects were presented with a series of three consonants to remember. As one might suspect, the task proved very easy, and the subjects were generally able to recall all three letters. The really important finding in this study, however, was produced when the subjects were required to perform a rehearsal-preventing task during the brief delay before recall. If immediately after hearing the three consonants the subjects were required to count out loud backward from some number by 3s (for example, 537, 534, 531, . . .), their recall performance was markedly impaired. On the average, the subjects in this condition were unable to recall one of the three consonants after 15 to 18 seconds. In fact, recall performance declined very rapidly, frequently falling to less than half of the immediate-test performance within 5 or 6 seconds. Virtually identical results have been obtained using words or three-letter nonsense syllables instead of consonants.

The outcome of the Peterson and Peterson experiments indicates that, barring the opportunity for continued rehearsal, STM has a rather small capacity for storing informa-

[3] Sometimes when you are trying to dial an unfamiliar number in the context of a lot of interference—for example, on the pay phone in a noisy bar—you may catch yourself actually saying the number out loud.

tion. Further, the information in STM may be lost in a very short time. The critical factor determining whether information will be retained or lost in STM seems to be the extent to which the information can be actively attended to and rehearsed. If rehearsal is prevented or interfered with shortly after information is entered into STM, either by some task (for example, counting backward) or by the introduction of new information, the contents of STM are lost very quickly. In terms of the telephone-number example, if your call is completed and you engage in conversation even briefly (for example, you get a wrong number), you probably will not be able to recall the number. If you get a busy signal and plan to place the call again, you will have little difficulty remembering the number provided nothing interrupts your rehearsal.

We may conclude, then, that the capacity of STM is quite limited and that the duration of storage in STM depends primarily on rehearsal. There are, however, some aspects of STM that suggest a need for reconsideration of this conclusion. For example, in the Peterson and Peterson type of experiment, the number of items retained in STM is essentially the same regardless of whether three consonants or three words are employed (see Figure 9–6, which summarizes the work of Murdock, 1961, and Peterson and Peterson, 1959). This indicates that it is the number of chunks or units of information that is important and not the type of item.

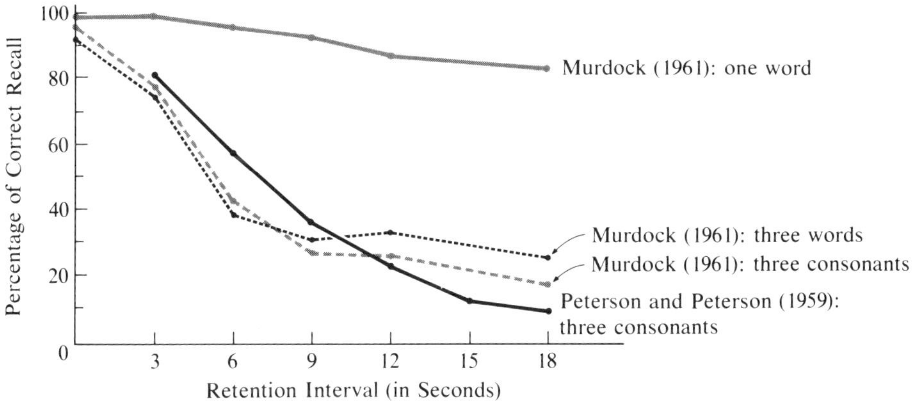

Figure 9–6. Chunking in short-term memory. (From "Implications of Short-Term Memory for a General Theory of Memory," by A. W. Melton, *Journal of Verbal Learning and Verbal Behavior,* 1963, *2,* 1–21. Reprinted by permission of Academic Press, Inc., and the author.)

Chunking in STM. In light of the relative insensitivity of STM to the "size" of the items to be stored, in what sense is the information capacity of STM limited? The answer seems to be that the limitation resides in the number of units of information, not in the amount of information in a unit. This finding has been most clearly stated in a landmark paper by G. A. Miller (1956) entitled "The Magic Number Seven, Plus or Minus Two." According to this paper and several subsequent papers by other authors (for example, G. Mandler, 1967), we are generally able to retain between five and nine items in STM. These items may, however, each represent rather large organized units of information that Miller calls *chunks*.

Miller offers several examples of how this chunking of information can increase memory capacity. In learning the Morse code, for instance, each *dit* and *dah* may initially represent a separate unit of information, so that only a few (7 ± 2) *dits* and *dahs* may be retained in STM. Eventually, however, these elements are organized into larger units, such as letters, words, and finally phrases or sentences, so that very large numbers of the elementary units are included in a single chunk. Thus, although STM capacity may appear to increase from seven elements (*dits* and *dahs*) to perhaps several hundred elements, a constant number of chunks of information is being retained in each case. Through this organization of elements into chunks, STM is able to hold large amounts of information in spite of having a rather limited capacity.

Several processes besides chunking seem to be employed to increase the efficiency of the information storage in STM. One important process concerns the selection of information to be rehearsed. Subjects may select especially important materials in STM to be rehearsed and retained. This selection may be based on the judged relevance or value of the information to the subject. Selection in STM may be related to the selective-attention processes that were found to be so important in the initial encoding of information (compare Montague, 1972). Selection of information in STM, however, can be delayed for a much longer time after the initial input has been encoded and seems to be accomplished primarily by variations in rehearsal. More highly valued information can be rehearsed more often, and its rehearsal can be initiated sooner.

As with selective attention, selective memory is achieved at the cost of nonselected information. Research indicates that, in general, information in STM that is not rehearsed is lost completely. Subjects may in some circumstances choose not to rehearse and thus do not retain certain information related to a specific stimulus input. In other words, they may use *selective forgetting*. Whether through selective memory or selective forgetting, the efficiency of STM can be greatly improved by establishing rehearsal strategies that favor retention of more valued information.

By organizing information into larger and larger chunks and by selecting the most relevant or important information for rehearsal, we apparently can retain relatively large amounts of information in a storage system with a rather limited capacity. Nonetheless, STM is generally restricted to storing information for only short periods. There is some argument about how long information can be retained in STM, but a few minutes is usually considered the maximum extent. Some researchers argue that after that time the information decays or fades; others favor the view that new inputs to the system supplant (perhaps via interference) the old information in STM storage. In either case, information in STM seems to be either transferred to permanent memory or lost entirely from the system within a few minutes.

The Characteristics of the STM Code. To this point in our discussion of STM, we have emphasized its capacity and duration and have not dealt with the form of the information stored in STM. Recall that information stored in SIS seems to be a rather direct, sensory representation of the original input. For visual inputs, we characterized SIS as an iconic image, for example. How is information represented in STM? The importance of rehearsal in establishing information in STM provides a clue to the form of the information stored there. Rehearsal seems to involve subvocal (usually) "speaking" of the material to be stored. If in rehearsal subjects are "speaking" to themselves, it seems reasonable to assume that they are also "listening" to what they are saying. Information in STM, then, must be in some form that permits speaking and hearing. A likely candidate would be a representation analogous to spoken words.

Most investigators currently favor the hypothesis that information in STM is stored as an *auditory/verbal representation* or *acoustic code*. A visually presented word, initially stored in SIS as an iconic image, is transformed or translated via rehearsal into a (subvocally) spoken word, and some representation of the sound of that word is stored in STM. This acoustic-code conceptualization is consistent with most observations about STM. In the telephone-dialing example, you may "hear" yourself rehearsing the number while you dial. As was noted, under high-stress or interfering-noise conditions, you may find yourself actually saying the number out loud.

Although this example is suggestive, the best evidence for a verbal/acoustic representation of STM storage has been obtained from systematic experiments. One of the most important of these studies was reported by R. Conrad (1964). Conrad began his memory experiment by doing a perception experiment. He had subjects listen to and attempt to identify auditorily presented (spoken) letters of the alphabet in the presence of rather high levels of white noise (random, static-like sounds). Conrad determined the degree to which each letter was confused with the others. For example, the letter *T* was often erroneously identified as *P* or *B* but was rarely confused with *F* or *J*.

After establishing the acoustic confusability of the letters in the perceptual-identification task, Conrad presented the same letters to a new group of subjects in an STM experiment. This time six letters were presented visually on a screen one after the other. Immediately after the last letter was shown, the subjects were required to write down, in order, all of the letters they could recall. It was found that when the subjects made errors in *serial recall* of the letters, they most frequently erroneously recalled (and wrote down) a letter that had been found to be perceptually (acoustically) confused with the correct letter. For example, if the third letter was *T*, the subjects tended to write down *P* or *B* in the third position on the test more often than any other wrong letter.

Recalling visually presented letters from STM, then, was closely related to identifying spoken letters in noise. These data support the view that information is represented acoustically in STM. A number of subsequent experiments have generally substantiated Conrad's findings. Errors in STM for letters, words, or digits usually involve items that sound like the correct item. Similar-sounding items are more difficult to retain and differentiate in STM than are items that are less confusable auditorily. Further, requiring subjects to do verbal, vocalizing tasks during delay intervals retards STM performance regardless of whether the to-be-remembered items are initially presented visually or auditorily.

The evidence for an acoustic/verbal representation of information in STM is quite strong, but there is another conceptualization that accounts for the findings equally well. It is possible that information in STM involves an *articulatory code*. This account, rather than referring to the way words sound, emphasizes the way they are spoken; for example, the pattern of speech-related muscle movements associated with pronouncing a word is important. To date, however, it has proved impossible to distinguish empirically between acoustic and articulatory conceptions of STM codes. The most important reason for this difficulty is that words or letters that sound alike also require very similar movements for pronunciation. Future research will no doubt focus more intently on the problem of distinguishing between these two STM representations, but for now this issue remains unresolved.

Some verbal representation of information in STM, whether acoustic or articulatory, seems to be supported by the majority of research findings in this area. However, a verbal code may not be sufficient to account for all of STM. We are quite capable of remembering a wide variety of nonverbal visual stimuli, such as unfamiliar shapes and very complex or abstract pictures, auditory stimuli ranging from bird calls to symphonies, and a wide assortment of tastes, smells, and tactile inputs. All of these stimuli are retained well beyond the time intervals that are typically covered by SIS. Presumably, then, these stimuli must somehow be represented in STM. Verbal codes, either acoustic or articulatory, may not be suited to represent any of these forms of information.

The dilemma presented by the diverse forms of information that apparently are retained in STM might be resolved if there were not one but many STM systems. Perhaps verbal stimuli, whether presented visually or auditorily, are encoded and retained in a verbal STM in which information is represented in an acoustic or articulatory form. Visually presented form or shape stimuli, on the other hand, might be encoded differently, perhaps being retained in a nonverbal, "image" STM system. Similarly, other kinds of environmental stimuli (sounds, tastes, smells, and so forth) might each be assigned to a different STM in which information is represented in some appropriate form. Although this multiple-STM conceptualization cannot be ruled out, it certainly is not a very elegant solution to the problem. A theoretical model that requires as many types of memories as there are classes of stimuli to be remembered fails the test of parsimony.

If we are to have a single STM system in which all stimuli are encoded into the same representational form, the code will almost certainly have to be very abstract. Shapes, sounds, words, smells, tastes, and so on must all be represented and stored. Posner's (1969) suggestion that letter stimuli presented visually or auditorily are coded in memory as an abstract schema may be a step in the direction of a suitably flexible mode of representing information in storage.

The idea that specific environmental stimuli are encoded in terms of a general schema is not a new one; Bartlett (1932) used the concept extensively in his book *Remembering*. Unfortunately, our knowledge about general schemata and how they may relate and represent large numbers of individual stimulus characteristics or how these schemata, once formed, may be represented in the human information-processing system is very limited. Thus, although the data are relatively clear regarding the duration and capacity of STM, we still have much to discover about how the information in STM is represented. Future research, especially that employing nonverbal stimuli and using other than verbal reports to assess memory, will hopefully begin to unscramble the mysteries of how information encoded from the great variety of environmental stimuli is represented and stored in STM.

Long-Term Memory

The preceding sections were primarily concerned with the storage of encoded information for very short intervals, so short that we do not typically associate them with "memory." This section will consider the storage system that holds very large amounts of information for much longer periods. The amount of information that can be stored in long-term memory is indefinite, and the duration of LTM storage is generally measured in hours, days, years, or decades. Many psychologists explicitly recognize this durability by labeling LTM permanent memory.

LTM can be differentiated from SIS and STM by the length of time that information is stored in each system. However, there are several other important differences between LTM and these earlier storage systems. Although SIS is characterized by essentially direct representations of encoded stimuli, LTM generally involves a great deal of transformation, elaboration, and organization of the initially encoded information. STM has a rather limited capacity for storing information and is quite fragile, new inputs tending to obliterate and replace previously stored information. LTM, on the other hand, appears to have an unlimited capacity for information storage and continually absorbs new inputs at rather minimal costs to previously stored information. In general, LTM can be characterized as a highly organized storage system capable of retaining an essentially unlimited amount of information for an indefinite period.

The emphasis given to the performance of LTM storage may appear to be inconsistent with the obvious fact that we frequently forget information that was at one time available in LTM. Even though forgetting often seems to be the most important, or at least the most frustrating, aspect of LTM, it is actually only indirectly related to LTM storage. By far the most prominent characteristics of LTM are its large capacity and great durability.

With a little effort you are generally able to recall in rather vivid detail information about events that was originally encoded many years ago, events that you have had little or no occasion to think about for a very long time. For example, what was the name of your first-grade teacher? You will probably not have too much trouble recalling your teacher's name (mine was Mrs. Wells). After recalling the name, you may also be able to remember many other details about the first grade. What did your teacher look like? What about the school building? Who were some of your classmates? What did they look like? Remember the time when. . . .

Clearly, LTM can store large quantities of information for very long periods. We must, however, view such memory performances with a certain amount of caution. Whenever very long retention intervals are involved, it is almost impossible to verify the accuracy of the recalled information in any detail. Recall from LTM may be accurate in many details, but often material is fabricated by the information-processing system at the time of the report. Missing information is often filled in so that a reasonably complete and consistent "memory" will be produced. Nonetheless, there is little reason to doubt that a great many rather arbitrary details of events that occurred years or decades ago can be recalled with substantial accuracy.[4]

Classical Views of Forgetting

In spite of the capacity and durability of LTM, we are sometimes unable to recollect previously encoded information. After only a few hours in a theater, for example, you may be unable to remember where you parked your car. An important—and sometimes all too obvious—characteristic of memory is that we do forget. In this section we will examine some classical views of forgetting, *decay theory, interference theory, Gestalt theory,* and *consolidation theory.* The first two are the most important.

Decay Theory. The decay theory of forgetting assumes that memory *traces* are established during learning. The trace concept is some hypothetical event that may or may not have a physiological basis, depending on the particular version of decay theory. The trace gradually fades away, or decays, with the passage of time unless we rehearse the to-be-remembered information and thus keep the trace activated. The critical assumption of decay theory is that the memory trace will automatically weaken with time as the result of autonomous processes. Thus, according to this view, forgetting occurs because of the progressive weakening of the trace itself. Decay theory assumes that the loss is due to something actually happening in storage; neither encoding nor retrieval is implicated.

One problem with decay theory is that it does not provide a clear explanation of the mechanisms that presumably underlie decay. Certainly time itself does not constitute an explanation, for events do not change merely because of the passage of time but rather because of what goes on during time (McGeoch, 1932). For example, iron does not rust because of the passage of time but because of certain chemical processes such as oxidation. Similarly, forgetting does not occur simply because of the passage of time but because of some processes that occur over time. These arguments clearly apply to long-term memory.

[4]For a further demonstration of the capacity and durability of LTM, you might do a couple of simple memory exercises. For example, list all of the people's names that you can remember. You might list family members, friends, classmates, celebrities, politicians, teachers, and so forth. The list will be extensive and will include many names that are recalled from a very long time ago. Other essentially arbitrary bits of information that you can recall in staggering quantities include telephone numbers, addresses, names of towns you have visited, and so on.

However, studies of short-term memory have raised the prospect of a simple decay process in the STM system.

Interference Theory. A second view of forgetting contends that forgetting occurs because of the interference of prior and/or subsequent learning. According to classical interference theory (McGeoch, 1932), once something is learned it remains permanently in memory and does not decay. New learning, especially if it is similar to previously learned materials, tends to interfere with the older learning. One way this interference occurs is through the process of *response competition,* in which the learning of new responses acts to block the recall of old responses. Consider the A/B, A/D transfer paradigm in which new responses are associated with the same stimuli. (In this paradigm A/B represents a paired-associate list in which A stands for the stimuli and B for the response terms. Thus, when you learn A/D, the stimuli remain the same, but the responses are new.) If, after learning the A/D associations, you attempt to recall the B responses, you may experience difficulty because of competition from the D responses. Thus, one reason for forgetting is competition between responses at the time of recall.

Very early in the development of this theory, Melton and Irwin (1940) noted that response competition alone was insufficient to account for all of the interference seen in experiments using this paradigm. They proposed that a second mechanism, *unlearning,* is necessary for a more complete account of forgetting. The basic idea is that during A/D learning, the A/B associations actually become weakened. As the subject learns the second (A/D) list, the B responses may be given, or at least thought of, by the subject. These responses are incorrect during second-list learning and hence go unreinforced, or are extinguished. Therefore, a later test for retention of the A/B association will show forgetting of the B responses to the extent that they have been extinguished. Such unlearning has been shown in several experiments (for example, Barnes & Underwood, 1959). The analogy of unlearning with extinction has not, however, received strong support.

The notion of unlearning emphasizes the extinction of specific stimulus–response associations. More recently, Postman and Stark (1969) have emphasized that unlearning, as reflected in the relative unavailability of the first-list associations, represents a "set" to respond in terms of the list more recently learned. In effect, subjects restrict themselves to the responses of the more recently learned list. Thus, the first-list responses are not actually unlearned but decline in availability because of a *suppression* of first-list responses at the time of recall. In the Postman and Stark study, subjects were given two kinds of retention tests. One was a typical recall test in which subjects recalled responses when presented with the stimuli. The other was a stimulus–response matching test designed to eliminate the necessity for recall; subjects simply matched the appropriate stimulus–response pairs. The results indicated much less interference with the matching test than with the recall test, and in some cases there was no reliable amount of interference in the matching test. What is critical here is that the matching test cannot be completed if the stimulus–response association has been unlearned. Consequently, the results strongly suggest that the associations were not weakened as such but that the associations were simply unavailable in the recall test.

This shift from extinction of associations to suppression of associations represents an important change in interference theory. Other modifications have also occurred, so that the once-elegant theory has faced increased difficulty. Although Postman's efforts to incorporate necessary changes in the theory have been ingenious, other problems have arisen that have not been resolved within the context of the theory (Tulving & Madigan, 1970). Yet despite the difficulties in interference *theory,* the concept of interference is very important in accounting for forgetting in LTM.

Gestalt Theory. The Gestalt theory of forgetting is primarily concerned with qualitative rather than quantitative aspects of memory. According to this theory, forgetting is not simply a weakening or decaying of traces as reflected in ordinary forgetting; memory processes involve a qualitative distortion or modification over time. The dynamic changes in memory over time are reflected in our tendency to ignore certain details, emphasize other details, and actively reconstruct our memories so that events are remembered in ways more suitable for convenient organization. For example, our memory of visual patterns is thought to change over time such that the patterns approximate a "good" figure. If shown a circular line drawing with a gap, an individual may, according to Gestalt theory, remember it as a closed circle.

Another feature of Gestalt theory that has received considerable attention in current conceptions of memory is the emphasis on organization. The early stress on organization in memory can be seen in the work of Katona (1940), who showed the importance of understanding a general rule as a factor in long-term memory of information. The organizational viewpoint has been reemphasized in recent years (see, for example, G. H. Bower, 1970b; G. Mandler, 1968; Tulving & Donaldson, 1972).

Consolidation Theory. The last theory of forgetting we shall consider emphasizes that the events occurring after learning, in the form of consolidation of neural traces, are essential for long-term memory. This theory was discussed in detail in Chapter 8, so we will only briefly review it here.

An early version of consolidation theory was outlined by Müller and Pilzecker (1900). They proposed that the neural activity produced by some learning experience tends to persist some time after the experience itself and that this persistence allows for the consolidation of long-term structural changes essential for memory. If the neural activity is not allowed sufficient time to consolidate, retention of the learning experience will be poor. Thus, if the neural activity is interfered with by some new learning before consolidation has occurred, memory of the previous learning experience will be impaired.

The Müller/Pilzecker version of consolidation theory was originally designed to account for the facts of interference in the recall of verbal materials. It is well-known that retention of verbal materials is affected by the nature of the activity that is interpolated between learning and the test of retention. For example, if one group of subjects is allowed to rest or even sleep during the retention interval while another group is required to learn some new material or is engaged in some kind of activity, the subjects who rested during the interval will show substantially better recall (Ekstrand, 1972; J. G. Jenkins & Dallenbach, 1924). This type of finding has, however, been more efficiently handled by interference theory than by consolidation theory. Nevertheless, there has been a sustained interest in consolidation theory, especially in animal studies of memory (compare Glickman, 1961; McGaugh & Herz, 1972).

Current Conceptions of Forgetting

It may well be that most forgetting has little to do with storage. For the most part, our inability to remember some past events can be attributed to either a failure to encode them well in the first place or a failure of retrieval. If the desired information was not attended to sufficiently to be encoded into the information-processing system, it will not be available for remembering at a later date. You are most likely to forget where you parked your car if you were a little late getting to the theater or were otherwise distracted at the time you parked it. If you wish to remember something, then, you must pay careful attention and be sure to encode the relevant information at the time the event occurs.

As noted, the other most common reason for forgetting is the inability to retrieve the desired information from storage. The inability to locate appropriate information becomes particularly apparent when you attempt to recall some information under stress, as on an important examination or as in the lost-car example, when you are anxious to impress your companion. Frequently in such situations you cannot recall the desired information even though you know that it is in storage. As soon as the tension is reduced, however, the information may be remembered. The answer to the question that stumped you during the exam may "come to you" as soon as you walk out the door of the classroom. The processes of retrieval will be dealt with more extensively in the next section of this chapter. For now, it is sufficient to note that much forgetting is the result of a failure to retrieve information that is in storage.

Is information, once encoded into LTM, ever lost or erased from storage? It does seem that, once the forgetting that can be attributed to failures of encoding or retrieval is eliminated, there is little information loss from long-term storage. Perhaps the most dramatic research evidence favoring a permanent status for information stored in LTM derives from the work of Wilder Penfield, a Canadian surgeon. Penfield's observations have generally been made in the context of clinical operations in which a locally anesthetized patient's brain is exposed. Because such patients are conscious during the operation, they can converse with the surgeon and report their experiences.

Penfield has reported in several papers (for example, Penfield, 1959) that direct electrical stimulation of certain parts of the brain produces reports of "memories." These memories often involve extensive amounts of information, apparently recalled in response to this open-brain stimulation, that the patients seemed completely unaware were in memory and that they almost certainly would not have recalled under normal circumstances. The following case studies provide examples:

> The patient S. Be. observed, when the electrode touched the temporal lobe (right superior temporal convolution), "There was a piano over there and someone playing. I could hear the song you know." When the cortex was stimulated again without warning, at approximately the same point, the patient had a different experience. He said: "Someone speaking to another, and he mentioned a name but I could not understand it. . . . It was like a dream." Again the point was stimulated without his knowledge. He said quietly: "Yes, 'Oh Marie, Oh Marie'! Someone is singing it." When the point was stimulated a fourth time he heard the same song again and said it was the "theme song of a radio program."
>
> The electrode was then applied to a point 4 centimeters farther forward on the first temporal convolution. While the electrode was still in place, S. Be. said: "Something brings back a memory. I can see Seven-Up Bottling Company—Harrison Bakery." He was evidently seeing two of Montreal's large illuminated advertisements.
>
> The surgeon then warned him that he was about to apply the electrode again. Then after a pause, the surgeon said "Now," but he did not stimulate. (The patient has no means of knowing when the electrode is applied, unless he is told, since the cortex itself is without sensation.) The patient replied promptly, "Nothing."
>
> A woman (D. F.) heard an orchestra playing an air while the electrode was held in place. The music stopped when the electrode was removed. It came again when the electrode was reapplied. On request, she hummed the tune, while the electrode was held in place, accompanying the orchestra. It was a popular song. Over and over again, restimulation at the same spot produced the same song. The music seemed always to begin at the same place and to progress at the normally expected tempo. All efforts to mislead her failed. She believed that a gramophone was being turned on in the operating room on each occasion, and she asserted her belief stoutly in a conversation some days after the operation.
>
> A boy (R. W.) heard his mother talking to someone on the telephone when an electrode was applied to his right temporal cortex. When the stimulus was repeated without warning, he

heard his mother again in the same conversation. When the stimulus was repeated after a lapse of time, he said, "My mother is telling my brother he has got his coat on backwards. I can just hear them."

The surgeon then asked the boy whether he remembered this happening. "Oh yes," he said, "just before I came here." Asked again whether this seemed like a dream, he replied: "No, it is like I go into a daze."

J. T. cried out in astonishment when the electrode was applied to the temporal cortex: "Yes doctor, yes doctor. Now I hear people laughing—my friends in South Africa!"

When asked about this, he explained the reason for his surprise. He seemed to be laughing with his cousins, Bessie and Ann Wheliow, whom he had left behind him on a farm in South Africa, although he knew he was now on the operating table in Montreal.[5]

Penfield's work strongly indicates that LTM storage is very extensive, detailed, and permanent. His observations also support the view that much forgetting is actually produced by a failure to retrieve information from storage. However, we cannot draw completely unequivocal conclusions from Penfield's research because there has been little effort to verify objectively the events recalled by the subjects, at least not in the same detail that the memories have been reported. There is a strong tendency for recalled events to be reported in an organized and coherent manner whether there is sufficient information in storage or not. Further, there is a danger in believing the verbal reports of the subjects in this type of experiment. Although it may seem to the subjects that the electrical stimulus is producing a delayed replay or flashback of a previously occurring event, there is no guarantee that this is in fact what occurs. But whatever the final explanation of Penfield's findings, they do lend support to the view that LTM storage is very extensive and essentially permanent.

The contention that LTM is permanent does not rest on Penfield's data alone. It has already been noted that events encoded decades in the past can be recalled in substantial detail under very normal circumstances. Further, it has been demonstrated that by providing clues or memory aids or by arranging special contexts, as by hypnotic suggestion, dreaming, or simply returning to the scene of the original event, information that has apparently been forgotten can be recalled. In each of these circumstances, it would seem that retrieval is affected and that the "forgotten" information was in LTM storage from the beginning.

To demonstrate losses of information from LTM storage, the effects of both encoding and retrieval must be eliminated. This probably cannot be accomplished completely, but it may be possible to demonstrate changes in memory under conditions that minimize the contributions of either encoding or retrieval. A demonstration of changes in LTM storage would also require that the conditions of initial stimulus input and subsequent memory output be held essentially constant. At the same time, the amount of time between input and output must be systematically varied. On the surface, conducting such an experiment does not appear to be overly difficult. However, time is always filled with events and activities, and these constitute new demands on the information-processing system and new inputs to LTM. New inputs can compete with already stored information at the time of retrieval. Generally, the greater the time interval between encoding and retrieval, the more opportunity for encoding new, potentially interfering events. Thus, simply testing memory after different periods of time does not ensure that "pure" storage effects will be shown. The simple fact that errors in memory tend to be greater after longer retention intervals does not necessarily indicate losses or changes in *stored* information.

[5] From "The Interpretative Cortex," by W. Penfield, *Science,* 1959, *129,* 1719–1725. Reprinted by permission of the American Association for the Advancement of Science.

One experimental approach to the time/activity confounding in memory has been to vary systematically the nature of activities that subjects engage in between stimulus input and the memory test. Following the lead of an early experiment by J. G. Jenkins and Dallenbach (1924), Ekstrand (1972) and his colleagues have compared memory performance following periods of sleeping or wakefulness. In these experiments the subjects are usually given some material to learn and then either go to sleep or engage in their usual waking activities for the same period of time. Then both groups are tested to determine how well they retained the material. The subjects who sleep during the retention period generally have better recall than those who remain awake.

Interestingly, the time that sleep occurs after original learning, either very soon or following some delay, and the depth of sleep during the retention interval differentially affect recall performance. Sleep immediately after learning is better than the same amount of sleep immediately before the retention test. Also, the deeper the sleep during the memory interval, the better the retention. In any event, although there is some forgetting over retention intervals filled by sleep, there is much less forgetting than occurs when the subject remains awake during the interval.

Ekstrand offers two tentative conclusions from these sleep/memory experiments. First, the effects of sleep during the retention interval, especially when occurring soon after learning, suggest that sleep facilitates *consolidation* of the material in memory. In other words, the relatively quiet period, free of interfering activities, that is provided by sleep (or presleep) immediately after learning aids the subject in organizing, rehearsing, and otherwise establishing the learned material in LTM. In addition, Ekstrand suggests that sleep aids LTM by its effects on physiological, metabolic activities that occur during the retention interval. Metabolic rates are generally lower during sleep than during wakefulness, and the deeper the sleep the lower the metabolic activity. A possible implication of this relationship is that information in LTM storage is subject to some physiological erosion and that sleep, by slowing down this process, results in greater information retention. (See Chapter 8 for some ideas on how this metabolic erosion may take place.)

No firm conclusions are possible at this point, but investigations of the effects of sleep on memory do suggest that some information is lost from storage. Even when the retention interval is largely filled with deep sleep, there is some reduction in the ability to recall the learned material. These losses, however, are extremely small when compared to the tremendous amount of information retained in LTM. Further, though the effects of encoding and retrieval appear to have been minimized in the sleep/memory experiments, they cannot be ruled out entirely as a reason for the small amount of forgetting that was typically observed. The view that LTM storage is permanent, then, continues to be a viable conceptualization of its function in the human information-processing system.

The Dynamics of LTM Storage

In the preceding discussion of forgetting, the general conclusion was that there is little loss of information from LTM storage. Once information is encoded into LTM, it remains there permanently, awaiting proper conditions for its retrieval. In light of this stability, it is tempting to view LTM storage as a static component in the information-processing system, in effect a filing cabinet wherein memories are stored.[6] Most of the errors that we have observed in LTM appear to be consistent with the static model of storage. As in any filing system, failures occur when desired information has not been properly filed or recorded (encoding), or when information has been filed but cannot be located (retrieval), or when the wrong file is inadvertently retrieved (interference).

[6] A storage tape or disk would be more appropriate to the computer analogy we have been using than a filing cabinet. The results of Penfield's brain-stimulation experiments seem to suggest such a model of LTM storage.

Although the static, filing-cabinet model does seem to fit rather well, there are some indications that it is not entirely adequate as a conceptualization of LTM storage. Though information does not typically erode away from LTM on a large scale, often there does appear to be rather extensive alteration, elaboration, and reorganization of the stored information (compare Cofer, Chmielewski, & Brockway, 1975). Witnesses' recollections of an accident, for example, are notoriously inconsistent, and descriptions provided months after an accident may differ systematically and sometimes rather dramatically from the original depositions taken at the scene. There are numerous examples of memories changing over time. You need only ask your mother and father to recall their childhood ("the good old days") or have recent graduates tell how tough it was when they were in school if you wish additional indications of how memory can be distorted by time. Although most of these changes in memory can be attributed to encoding and/or retrieval processes, some of the variation may be introduced by dynamic processes associated with the storage component of LTM.

The nature of changes in stored information can be seen more clearly by considering some experiments on the temporal course of LTM. The Gestalt psychologists were among the first to investigate systematically the dynamics of memory on a large scale. They argued, as noted earlier, that the internal (encoded) representation, or memory trace, changes in a qualitative fashion over time. More specifically, asymmetrical or incongruent inputs to memory were thought to *assimilate,* or become more symmetrical, congruent, and complete.

Illustrative of the Gestalt approach is an experiment investigating memory for form stimuli originally reported by Wulf in 1922 and more recently summarized by Riley (1962). Wulf showed subjects a number of ambiguous line drawings, line segments, dot patterns, and squiggles. The stimuli were generally quite asymmetrical and incomplete in appearance; they lacked *closure* (in Gestalt terminology). The subjects were required to draw the figures from memory 30 seconds, 1 day, and 1 week after seeing them. Wulf inspected the drawings and found evidence, in his judgment, of progressive changes toward "better" figures, figures that were more symmetrical and complete.

Although Wulf's experimental procedures leave something to be desired (a more objective procedure for determining that progressive changes had occurred, for example), the results of subsequent, more sophisticated experiments have tended to confirm that such changes do occur in subjects' reproductions of ambiguous shapes from memory. These results, however, have been interpreted somewhat differently from the original Gestalt conceptualization. Several investigators have noted that the changes in subjects' reproductions tend to be in the direction of more familiar figures suggested by the ambiguous shapes. For example, a squiggle that resembled a spiral might tend to be reproduced from memory so as to appear even more like a spiral.

An important experiment by Carmichael, Hogan, and Walter (1932) investigated the familiarity hypothesis more directly by providing explicit verbal interpretations (labels) for the ambiguous figures at the time they were initially shown to subjects. Some of the drawings and their labels are shown in Figure 9–7. As you will note, there were two experimental groups, one seeing the shapes with one set of labels and the other group with the second set of labels. The experimenters reported that when changes in reproductions did occur in the memory test, the change tended to be toward a figure suggested by the assigned label. For example, the subjects having the label *pine tree* assigned to the first form tended to draw something more similar to a pine tree, while the subjects having the label *trowel* tended to reproduce the figure as more like a trowel.

The procedures employed in this experiment do not permit us to attribute the observed changes in reproduction solely to the storage component of LTM. Encoding and retrieval effects would be very important, if not entirely adequate, in accounting for the changes. Similar results have, however, been obtained in a more recent experiment by

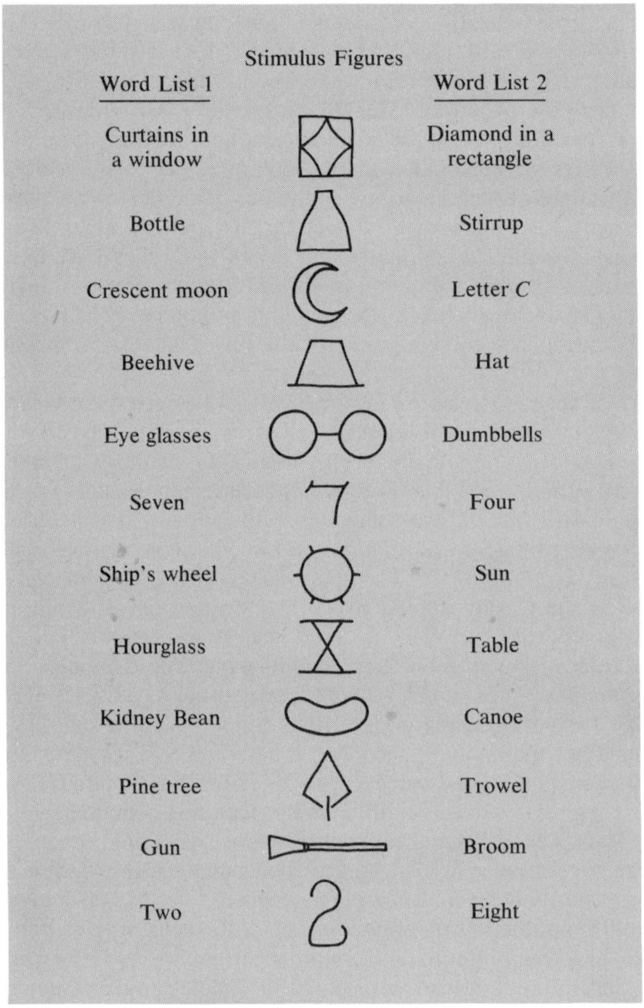

Figure 9–7. Ambiguous figures and labels. (From "An Experimental Study of the Effect of Language on the Reproduction of Visually Perceived Form," by L. Carmichael, H. P. Hogan, and A. A. Walter, *Journal of Experimental Psychology,* 1932, *15*, 73–86.)

Daniel (1972), who essentially replicated the experiment but used a more sophisticated, recognition-memory, testing procedure. In this later experiment, memory for an ambiguous form showed progressive changes toward a more familiar shape suggested by a verbal label. The shift in memory was found to increase substantially over a 1-week delay between presentation of the ambiguous form and recognition-memory testing. Because the effects of encoding and retrieval processes were essentially the same in all of the tests, the increased shifts at the longer delay could be attributed to changes in the stored representations of the originally encoded figure.

Similar changes in stored information have been observed for materials other than forms. Bartlett (1932), for example, conducted experiments with a variety of materials, including visual forms, and found evidence of systematic distortion in memory. Bartlett's studies (discussed further in Chapter 12) indicate, for example, that memory for passages of text (stories) often shifts over time to become more consistent with events familiar to the subject. More recent research has produced similar findings; a subject's memory for verbal passages often shows changes that make the meaning of the passage more "reasonable."

In general, then, although it appears that information is not lost from LTM storage, there is some indication that considerable changes in the character of the retained information will occur. Our knowledge of the processes responsible for changes in stored information is far from complete. It does, however, appear that a static, filing-cabinet conceptualization of the storage component of information processing is not entirely adequate. Systematic organization and elaboration of information in LTM seem to be the rule, and some of this alteration of information apparently occurs during the storage stage of the memory process.

LTM Codes

How is information represented in LTM storage? Recall that we characterized SIS as a rather direct representation of the encoded environmental event (for example, the iconic image for visual stimuli). STM was characterized as involving a recoding to an acoustic/verbal representation. The immense quantity and variety of information that is retained in LTM would seem to argue against any one simple memory code. Some of the contents of LTM seem to be largely verbal—for example, names, telephone numbers, and rote-learned rhymes or poems. Other memories have a distinctly sensory quality, such as your memory of melodies, the smell of fresh coffee, and your mother's face.

Our own introspections about how we remember things produce persuasive evidence for the distinction between verbal and sensory/perceptual aspects of memory. As an example of visual memory, or *imagery,* consider a question originally suggested by Roger Shepard: How many windows are there in the house you lived in before your present residence? This query to LTM usually results in what introspectively appears to be the retrieval of an image (mental picture?). You seem to "take a walk" through the indicated house and "count the windows." The memory image is not as sharp or as short-lived as the iconic image of SIS, but it does seem to have a definite visual, spatially arranged quality.

Similar examples of memory imagery abound. Recall the figure presented earlier in this chapter of the camel through the eye of the needle. Where was it located on the page? Top? Bottom? Right or left page? Which direction was the camel facing, left or right? Check your answer by turning back to the illustration. The chances are good that you were able to place the figure correctly even though, at the time it was presented, there was no need to take note of where it was located on the page. It seems, then, that sensory/perceptual information routinely finds its way into LTM storage.

In the past decade a great deal of experimental evidence has accumulated that also strongly supports the distinction between verbal-memory and perceptual-memory modes. Although the number of researchers adhering to the stricter forms of this conceptualization has recently been declining, the *dual-code view* has been very influential in the development of our current understanding of how information is coded in LTM storage.

The dual-code conceptualization has been most extensively studied by Paivio and his associates. The most comprehensive statement of this approach appears in Paivio's 1971 book *Imagery and Verbal Processes.* Generally, he argues for making a distinction between two memory modalities, a verbal-coding system and an image-coding system. *Verbal codes* are more important in circumstances in which abstract materials are involved and sequential processing or serial-order information is emphasized. The *image code* generally refers to a visual/spatial process of some sort, but Paivio also acknowledges auditory and other sensory-based codes. Image codes are more important in remembering relatively concrete stimuli, especially when parallel processing of spatially arrayed information (for example, pictures) is of primary concern. Paivio reviews a large number of experiments that generally support the dual-code view. He also attempts to develop a systematic theoretical account of the relationship between verbal and image codes in memory, learning, and language.

Imagery continues to be an important and useful construct in theoretical accounts of LTM. In addition to the very compelling subjective experiences of imagery in memory, there are several important experimental findings that seem to require the construct. For example, pictures are generally remembered better than words or sentences. This is true even when very complex pictures containing a great deal of information are used, such as color pictures clipped from magazines. Memory for very complex, unfamiliar, random-shape stimuli is also generally very accurate; in one study (Ellis & Daniel, 1971, Experiment III), retention was found to be essentially unaffected by as much as 28 days of delay between learning and memory testing.

Another consistent finding is that concrete words (for example, *apple, car, lawyer*) are remembered better than abstract words (for example, *truth, wealth, hate*), especially when the subjects are instructed to imagine the referents of the concrete words. Also, in paired-associate learning tasks, subjects perform better if instructed to imagine the two referents of the paired words in some form of interaction. The pair *lawyer/apple,* for example, can be learned and remembered better if the subject imagines a lawyer eating an apple.

Although the importance of a nonverbal, perceptual component in LTM is generally agreed upon, conceptualizations differ on how this information is represented in memory. J. R. Anderson and Bower (1973), in presenting their model of Human Associative Memory, HAM, summarize the accounts that have been offered for the imagery effects just reviewed:

> There have been essentially three theoretical postures taken in interpreting such results. We wil! call them the "radical imagery" hypothesis, the "conceptual–propositional" hypothesis, and the "dual-coding" hypothesis. The radical imagery hypothesis (e.g., Bugelski, 1970) supposes that subjects convert the verbal materials to mental pictures, store these pictures away in memory, then revive and describe these pictures at the time of the retention test for learning. At the other extreme is the conceptual–propositional hypothesis of *HAM* which supposes that knowledge—even knowledge that is derived from pictures or that is used in generating images—is always represented in the form of abstract propositions about properties of objects and relations between objects. . . .
>
> Finally, there is the dual-coding hypothesis that was advocated vigorously by Paivio (1969, 1971) and was subscribed to earlier by the second author (G. H. Bower, 1972b). In rough outline, the hypothesis supposes that there are two distinct representational and storage systems—the verbal and the imaginal [p. 452].[7]

Although our own introspections about our memory processes might seem to support the *radical-imagery hypothesis*—that is, mental pictures—this view is not very widely held among research psychologists. There are a number of reasons for this, but perhaps the most important is that our contemporary conception of the brain and of human information processing does not seem to provide any way that pictures, mental or otherwise, could be processed or stored. Also, having pictures in storage would seem to require some inner perceiver or "mind's eye" to view and interpret them for memory.

The dual-coding hypothesis has probably motivated the most extensive discussion of the imagery concept in experimental psychology. Although this approach distinguishes quite

[7] From *Human Associative Memory,* by J. R. Anderson and G. H. Bower. Copyright 1973 by Hemisphere Publishing Company. Reprinted by permission.

systematically between verbal and image codes, details of the nature of these codes have not been fully developed. The more recent *conceptual/propositional hypothesis* offered by Anderson and Bower goes farther toward specifying the characteristics of the perceptual-memory code. Their HAM model does retain a distinction between verbal-memory and perceptual-memory components, represented in the model by a *linguistic parser* and a *perceptual parser*. Rather than viewing these as two separate memory codes, however, these authors argue that both are represented by propositional structures. These structures can be represented graphically by a "tree" diagram, as in Figure 9–8.

Anderson and Bower have concentrated their efforts on linguistic/sentential materials and admittedly have done little more than assert that nonverbal, perceptual information can be represented by the same type of propositional structure. An important problem that prevents a more detailed description of the nonverbal structures is the lack of a sufficient "grammar" of perceptual events. Neither the elements nor the rules that relate the elements of perceptual events have been specified.

Conceptualizations of how information is represented in LTM storage are very much in a state of flux at present. New empirical findings and theoretical developments are continually being added to the literature. Currently, the conceptual/propositional approach (for example, Anderson and Bower's model, HAM), seems to offer considerable promise. The most significant gains have come in the development of representational systems for verbal, linguistic information (see Chapter 10). The main impetus for these developments

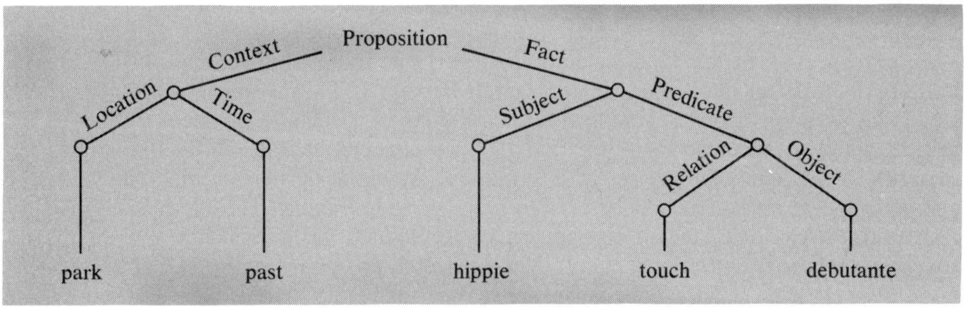

Figure 9–8. The HAM propositional structure for the sentence "In a park a hippie touched a debutante." (From *Human Associative Memory,* by J. R. Anderson and G. H. Bower. Copyright 1973 by Hemisphere Publishing Corporation. Reprinted by permission.)

seems to have come from advances in computer technology, programming, and artificial intelligence. (Artificial intelligence involves the design of efficient programs that perform complex tasks.) The largest gaps in our understanding of how information is represented in LTM storage are in the area of nonverbal, perceptual inputs. The sights, sounds, and tastes that make up our perceptual environment have traditionally been difficult for psychologists to conceptualize and explain.

Retrieval

The human information-processing system has a tremendous capacity for encoding and storing information. At any given moment there is a vast amount of information in memory, and there appears to be no appreciable forgetting of that information over very long intervals. Nonetheless, we never have command of all of this information at any one time, and often a vital piece of stored information is not available when we need it. Though memory is in principle unlimited, for practical purposes it is restricted by our ability to locate and recover desired information from storage. *Retrieval* refers to the processes of searching through storage, locating, and making available specific information that is required by the processing system.

When a question is posed to memory, several different but interrelated processes may be involved before an overt reply can be made. The earliest stage of the retrieval process is a search through storage to locate information relevant to the query. In some instances this search seems to be rather direct and immediate. On other occasions it assumes a more complex, problem-solving type of character. As relevant information is located, it is collected together and held in a *working memory*. Here the relevant information is organized, and in many cases missing information is "filled in" to compose a coherent, intelligible memory. In the final stages of the retrieval process, the information in working memory directs an appropriate verbal and/or motor response.

To observe these processes in action, think about the stages of retrieval as you try the following memory exercise:

> What did you have for breakfast 3 days ago?
> Can you itemize what you ate?
> Could you draw a picture of the table setting? The food on your plate?
> Did you eat alone?
> What time was it?

Introspection of this kind generally confirms that retrieval is accomplished in stages. Initially, there is an intelligent, guided search through LTM storage (for example, "Let's see, today I had ________ for breakfast; yesterday . . .). Thus, we seem to "get in the neighborhood" of the desired information and then begin to make more specific queries and searches of this more limited set of information. After the desired information is located and collected, it must somehow be used to program and produce some appropriate memory response (for example, recall, recognition, or reproduction). This component of the retrieval process is less well understood than the search components. When highly practiced response modes are required, such as verbally reported recall, there is little indication of an active response-programming process. When a less familiar response mode is required, as when you attempt to draw a picture of what you have retrieved from memory, the response-programming component may be more apparent. Somehow the information collected into working memory must direct your drawing responses, sometimes approving and encouraging and sometimes rejecting your efforts.

Retrieval does not always seem to require this elaborate, multistage process. If the query to memory is your home address, the answer seems to be almost immediately available. Your reply is direct and automatic. For such highly practiced memory performance, some or all of the retrieval stages may be circumvented in favor of a conditioned, reflexive reaction. It is possible that the retrieval processes may occur so quickly and effortlessly that they are not noticed by our introspecting "mind's eye." Many of our everyday memory performances do, however, seem to require distinct search, recovery, and response-programming components.

Searching SIS

The characteristics of the search process may vary depending upon which storage stage contains the desired information. If the desired information is in SIS, it is already highly available, and the initial search process is presumably unnecessary; the information is apparently "read" directly from the store. For the visual-information store, search is a matter of *scanning* the available iconic image, in effect a visual-search task.

Sperling (1963) has estimated that iconic images produced by random arrays of visually presented letters are scanned at the rate of approximately 10 milliseconds per letter. Further, the scan seems to follow a left-to-right order. These results have been confirmed in other experiments. In addition, it has been found that more familiar letter sequences—that is, those that approximate familiar words—can be scanned at even higher rates than random letters.

Most of the data are consistent with the view that retrieval from SIS involves "reading" the desired information from an available store. Nevertheless, the interpretation of the "reading" involved in searching an iconic image should be approached with some caution. Your reading of the words on this page involves a sequence of directed eye movements and fixations—that is, visual scanning. The nature of the scan involved in memory search, however, is very unclear at this time. For example, what scans the iconic image? Most psychologists find reference here to the "mind's eye" unpalatable. That apparently iconic images can be produced by successive presentations of superimposed items (see, for example, Estes, 1973; Parkinson, Kroll, & Parks, 1973) and that these memory images can also be "read" mean an additional vote for caution. Still, a search or scan process, however abstract, is strongly indicated for SIS.

Searching STM

Search of STM storage is also generally referred to as a memory scan. In our previous discussion of STM storage, however, we concluded that information in STM is generally coded in a verbal/acoustic form and is maintained by rehearsal. This would seem to argue against any scan operations, at least to the extent that they imply a visual-search process of any kind. On the other hand, if the STM scan is an acoustic/auditory process, the memory search would be indistinguishable from what we have called rehearsal.

In spite of the conceptual difficulties, empirical data suggest a distinction between rehearsal and search or memory scan in STM. S. Sternberg (1966), for example, has argued that digits stored in STM can be scanned at a rate of 25 to 30 items per second. That is about four times as fast as the same items can be subvocally spoken (rehearsed). His estimate of scan time was derived from experiments in which he systematically varied the number of items in STM and then observed the time required (reaction time) to decide correctly whether a particular test item was in the set.

In these experiments Sternberg showed 1, 2, 3, 4, 5, or 6 random digits to subjects one at a time. After a 2-second delay he then showed them a single test digit. The subjects were required to indicate, as quickly as they could, whether the test digit was among the set they had been asked to remember. Some results from these experiments are presented in Figure 9–9. Note that as the number of digits in memory increased, the time required to find one of them and correctly respond (reaction time) also increased. In fact, each item added to memory increased reaction time by about 38 milliseconds. Sternberg interpreted these results as showing that following presentation of the test item, the subjects serially searched (scanned) STM to determine whether that item was in the memory set.

Thus, although the nature of the process is still unclear, some search of stored information seems to be involved in STM tasks. As with SIS, however, an initial organized search is probably not necessary. The contents of STM storage are rather limited and are generally quite readily available.

Searching LTM

LTM presents by far the most interesting and complex problems for retrieval. Unlike that in SIS or STM, information is neither normally directly available nor limited to a few items. As a consequence, a search of LTM storage generally involves several distinct levels.

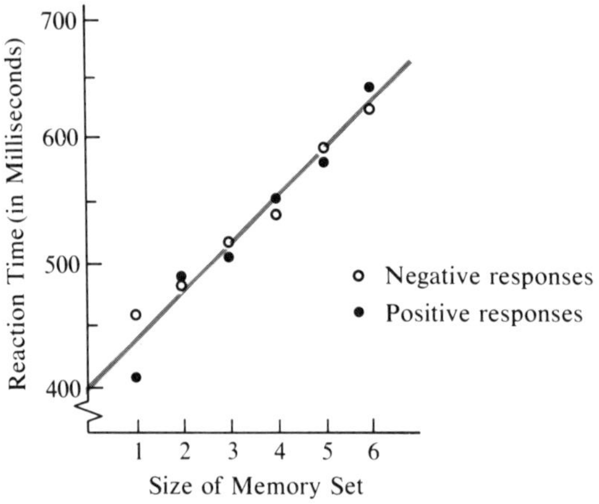

Figure 9–9. Search time for digits in short-term memory. (From "High-Speed Scanning in Human Memory," by S. Sternberg, *Science,* 1966, *153,* 652–654. Reprinted by permission of the American Association for the Advancement of Science.)

The first level seems to be a wide-ranging search for general information related to the specific query. In the example of what you had for breakfast 3 days ago, one approach is to begin with the most recent breakfast and work backward to the day in question. The first level of search is generally an intelligent search. It is not a random sorting through the contents of LTM but an orderly tracing of a series of clues that eventually leads to the desired information.

The first level of search may be preceded by an even more general verification process. When a query is posed, search may not begin immediately. A preliminary decision may be made on whether even to search for the information in LTM. For example, consider the query "What did George Washington have for breakfast 3 days ago?" This query does not lead to the usual LTM search. Instead, you seem to know immediately that the requested information is not in memory, and you can respond forthwith that the query is not legitimate. No one knows for sure how this preliminary verification process is accomplished. Norman (1973) has presented a fairly comprehensive discussion of what the relevant theoretical questions are, but the answers have not yet been formulated. Some of Norman's points are illustrated in the following discussion.

With some queries, such as the one about George Washington's breakfast, an analysis of the query itself reveals an inconsistency signaling that it is not a valid question for memory. The query can be rejected essentially without reference to LTM. We must, however, make use of some stored information, such as that Washington has been dead for longer than 3 days and that dead people don't eat breakfast. Other queries may be reasonable and valid but may be rejected without an extensive search of LTM. An example is the question "What did Jimmy Carter have for breakfast 3 days ago?" The query itself would appear to be legitimate, but you are unlikely to respond to it by initiating an extensive search of your LTM store. You know that this information is not in storage (at least not for most of us). Similarly, if a query seems to demand a very difficult and extensive search, it may be rejected as not worth the effort. This phenomenon is frequently observed by teachers. Many queries initially produce an "I don't know," but if a sufficient incentive (or threat) is provided, the requested information can often be dredged up. The basic characteristics of the preliminary verification or screening process are not known, but it is a very pervasive and important aspect of human memory and will no doubt be the object of increasing experimental and theoretical effort.

If the preliminary verification process results in a "go" decision, the first level of search is begun. The search does not proceed willy-nilly to rummaging around in the vast storehouse of LTM but seems to be guided by an intelligent strategy. A search for the menu of a 3-day-old breakfast may proceed by a backward tracing through related information. Such organized-search strategies would, of course, be rather fruitless if the contents of LTM were not systematically organized. The selection of a search strategy, then, must depend on both the nature of the information requested and the arrangement of that information in storage.

There was a time, for example, when my response to the query would probably have been something like "Let's see, three days ago. Today is Friday, so that would be Wednesday. Wednesday we had stewed prunes, baked powdered eggs (ugh![8]), two link sausages, cold toast, and milk." Thus, the search strategy selected will vary depending upon the context in which the query is presented, and it may be quite unique to the individual answering the query. Normally, though, the initial search tends to be rather generalized, a search for a conceptually related information set. The result of the search, if it is successful, is a package of information, or a scenario, that contains the specific information required by the query. In the breakfast example the first-level search serves to locate the designated breakfast. Once that general scenario is located, a more detailed search for specific aspects of the scene (for example, what food was eaten) is possible.

Interestingly, once the general scenario has been located, a great deal of specific information may become more available. Often this information is only remotely related to the query that motivated the initial search. In our example the query that leads to the breakfast scene is what food was eaten. Nonetheless, once the appropriate scene is located, other questions, unrelated to the food, may also be readily answered (for example, who was at the table and what time it was). It is as though the first level of search is accomplished by a wide-angle but rather low-power telescope. When the general package of desired information is found, a second search process zooms in on the scene, focusing with increased magnification and resolution on a much smaller field.

The speed and accuracy with which the human information processor can search the vast store of information in LTM is unmatched by our most sophisticated computers. Information storage and search processes in LTM probably pose the most challenging of all research questions currently being considered in experimental psychology. The answers to these questions will not be found easily, but they are essential to our understanding of human memory.

Working Memory

Locating the information designated by a query does not complete the retrieval process. More often than not, the stored information is incomplete or not in a form appropriate for answering the query. Information located in LTM storage must be gathered together, translated into an appropriate form, organized, verified, and then retained briefly in a more readily available store until the required response can be programmed and emitted. Further, missing or vague information must be noted and, where necessary, substitute information created to complete a "reasonable" memory. Working memory is the component of the retrieval process where these necessary operations are performed.

Working memory is related to the two stages of LTM search. The information package that is located by the first level of search may be activated or held in a short-term, high-availability store. The second level of the search process can then be restricted to this smaller, more available working memory.

[8] I can still see that pale-yellow cube of congealed matter floating in its compartment on the breakfast tray. The persistence of LTM has its drawbacks.

Often the first-level search produces an information set that is unclear or incomplete. Working memory may then be inadequate for answering the query that was posed. Suppose, for example, you meet a couple who are old acquaintances but you cannot recall their names. You know that you know them, and you may be able to recall many things about them, but their names seem to hang just below consciousness. If, however, someone were to speak their names, you would know them instantly. The names are "right on the tip of your tongue."

The tip-of-the-tongue phenomenon was investigated in a very clever experiment by R. W. Brown and McNeill (1966). Subjects were read dictionary definitions of unfamiliar words and asked to produce the words. For example, the subjects would be read the definition "A navigational instrument used in measuring angular distances, especially the altitude of the sun, moon, and stars at sea." Most of the subjects either knew the word (*sextant*) or knew that they did not know it. Some subjects, however, were sure that they knew the word but could not quite produce it. It was on the tip of the tongue. Sometimes they offered words that sounded like the correct word (for example, *secant, sextent,* or *sexton*) or had related meanings (for example, *compass* or *protractor*). The subjects were often able to report the first letter of the word or how many syllables it had, but they still could not produce the word.

The results of this tip-of-the-tongue experiment tend to confirm the two-level search scheme described earlier. It appears that the first level of search may result in an inadequate information package. In these instances, responses to the memory query may be improvised from whatever information is available in working memory. This improvisation, or *fabrication,* in working memory takes information retrieved from LTM, integrates it, and fills in missing information to achieve a coherent "memory."

The extent and nature of the fabrication depend on a number of factors. The studies by Bartlett referred to earlier in this chapter suggest that fabrications are shaped by expected or familiar patterns. Another important factor is the context of the retrieval and reporting of memories. Recollections of events may be fabricated differently when recounted to our cronies at the friendly neighborhood tavern than when produced in court under oath. Even when we attempt to make our recall as accurate as possible, context can have important effects on our reported memories.

Loftus and her associates (Loftus, 1974; Loftus & Palmer, 1974; Loftus & Zanni, 1975) have shown that the testimony of eye witnesses can be highly unreliable. In one study (Loftus & Palmer, 1974) the subjects were shown a videotaped collision of two cars. Later some of the subjects were asked "How fast were the cars going when they hit each other?" The other subjects were asked "How fast were the cars going when they smashed into each other?" The subjects who were asked the second question recalled the speed as having been much faster than did the subjects hearing the first question. Also, when asked "Did you see any broken glass?" the subjects who had heard the "smashed into" question said yes twice as often as the subjects who had heard the "hit" question. *No* broken glass was present in the videotape of the accident. Fabrication, whether motivated by immediate context or expected, familiar patterns, has important effects on working memory and thus on the "memory" that is finally reported.

Although there is general agreement on the need for a working-memory component in retrieval, there is some disagreement over its representation in conceptual models of memory. Some researchers (for example, Greeno, 1973) have postulated that working memory is a separate short-term store that, unlike STM storage, which accepts inputs from the environment via SIS, accepts inputs from LTM storage. Others (for example, Lindsay & Norman, 1972; Shiffrin & Geisler, 1973) postulate that working memory employs the same structures and processes as STM storage, in effect recycling information from LTM back to STM. Anderson and Bower (1973) prefer to view working memory as a part of LTM storage, a "currently active" section of the LTM store. But regardless of how working memory is represented conceptually, its function is to organize, elaborate, and retain information accumulated from LTM until an appropriate response to the original memory query can be formulated.

Response Programming

The last stage of the retrieval process is the programming of an overt response. The response required by a memory query may vary from a simple yes or no to a detailed reconstruction or reproduction of the information requested. Responses may be motor or verbal. Verbal responses may be complex grammatical text, either spoken or written, a simple word or two, or perhaps only a grunt. Motor responses may be a simple pointing or button-pushing response, a detailed drawing, or a complete reproduction of a complex action. Sometimes no overt response is required by a query.

Even though the overt responses resulting from a query may vary greatly, any or all of them may be directed by essentially identical information in working memory. Thus, there seems to be a need for some additional processes to produce a response after search is completed and a working memory is established. Most formal models of memory do acknowledge that some output processes are required. Anderson and Bower (1973), for example, include a "language generator" for speech or writing outputs in their model of sentence memory and question answering. However, they do not elaborate on the specific properties of this component of the model. There has, in general, been little detailed analysis of the output components of the memory system in information-processing models. Most models are concerned only with how previously encoded and stored information can be retrieved to the point of an available working memory.

Perhaps the most that can be done at this point is briefly to consider two possible approaches to the output component of retrieval. One approach can be called the feedback model. Working memory would serve as the basis for guiding overt responses by a system much like that used to guide a heat-seeking missile to its target. Motor or verbal responses could be monitored and either encouraged ("You're getting warm") or discouraged ("You're getting cold") depending upon how well they matched the information in working memory. There are, of course, many difficult problems to be dealt with in working out the details of such a system. How, for example, is the information in working memory translated into a form that would allow matching to the overt response (or vice versa)? Also, who (what) does the matching and decides upon the appropriate feedback? These and other questions would all have to be dealt with in developing a systematic model of output or response programming for a general memory system.

The other approach can be termed behavioristic. In effect, the information in working memory could assume the same status as an external environmental stimulus. The behavioral laws and processes of learning and motivation could be called upon to account for the responses that are emitted as a reaction to the "stimulus" of working memory. Many questions must be answered in developing this type of model as well. For one, there is less than general agreement on the behavioral laws of responses to environmental stimuli, much less how these might be applied to account for responses to "internal" working memories. The internal, cognitive character of the information-processing model that we have followed in this chapter may be completely incompatible with the stimulus–response behavioral model. At least, a marriage of the two models could prove to be a turbulent one.

The emphasis in information-processing and memory research has been on encoding, storage, and memory-search processes. The response/output components have been put aside, for the most part, and experiments and theories have generally dealt with very simple response modes. As the earlier stages of memory become better understood, perhaps more attention will be directed to the response-programming and output components of information retrieval. In the meantime these processes will have to remain unspecified.

A Brief Overview of the Information-Processing Approach

There is no single information-processing model of human memory. The information-processing approach encompasses dozens of individual formal models and less formal conceptualizations of memory and mental processes. These models vary greatly in their theoretical constructs and modes of expression. Though most adhere to the general encoding/storage/retrieval format, the specific hypothetical structures and functions of these processing components may vary from model to model. Computer-programming concepts and terminology are ubiquitous, but the degree to which individual models adhere to a computer analogy varies. Some models are formally expressed as actual computer programs. Others use computer terminology rather informally to describe characteristics of their conceptualization of memory.

Without exception the individual models deal only with specific subsets of the total memory/information-processing system. There are areas of overlap between the models, but there often appears to be little or no relationship between one model and another. As a result, there are gaps in our understanding of the total memory system.

Research and theoretical development are proceeding at a vigorous pace, and areas of agreement between information-processing models are expanding. There is an encouraging trend toward the development of more comprehensive models that attempt to integrate more of the components of the information-processing system into one consistent theoretical structure. The information-processing approach apparently will continue to evolve toward a comprehensive, cohesive theory of human memory.

Single or Dual Memory Systems?

The last question we will address in this chapter is the continuity/discontinuity of short-term and long-term memory. The basic issue is whether STM and LTM represent essentially two different systems governed by different principles or whether they represent a continuum governed by largely the same principles. We have discussed these systems as though they were different, but it is not necessary to treat them in this fashion. Until quite recently this issue attracted considerable debate.

A distinction frequently made between STM and LTM is that STM is regarded as subject to rapid decay whereas LTM is stable. Experiments (for example, J. Brown, 1958; Peterson & Peterson, 1959) demonstrating rapid forgetting in the absence of rehearsal have been viewed as supporting this distinction. According to the dual-process view, the different storage systems operate in accordance with different processes. For example, Broadbent (1957, 1963, 1971) has argued for a dual process in which the initial, or primary, memory trace declines in accordance with decay-theory principles, whereas a consolidated trace is prevented from decaying and is transferred into long-term storage, where it is then governed by principles of interference. In a similar vein, Hebb (1949) has argued for a dual system of memory based on physiological assumptions. It is his contention that two stages of physiological activity underlie the development of memory. In the first stage a cluster of neurons recurrently excite one another; this phase accounts for events during STM. In contrast, LTM is due to structural changes in the nerve networks that are the result of repeated stimulation.

In contrast to dual-process views, other psychologists have argued that memory is best thought of as a continuous set of processes. In an important paper Melton (1963) argued that STM and LTM are points along some continuum. His position is that the process of interference operates in both STM and LTM, and he uses this as the basis on which to treat STM and LTM as continuous; he sees no need for postulating a decay process as outlined by Hebb or Broadbent. Murdock (1974) has proposed a similar view emphasizing the continuity of human memory.

Decay and interference principles are not the only ones proposed to account for different stages of memory. Waugh and Norman (1965) have suggested the principle of STM *displacement,* in which an item is retained until it is displaced by another item. In addition, theorists (for example, Posner & Konick, 1966) may assume that both decay and interference principles interact. Finally, Craik and Lockhart (1972) have suggested that differences in the two memory stores may be due to differences in the depth or level at which the information is processed. Let us now examine some of the evidence for dual and single conceptions of memory storage.

Capacity Differences

Earlier we noted the difference in storage capacity between STM and LTM. The capacity of LTM seems virtually unlimited, whereas STM is a limited-capacity system. Moreover, we noted that humans are limited to about seven items or chunks of information in STM. The items may be numbers, letters, words, or chunks (groups) of these, but we are still restricted to about seven. Some psychologists (for example, J. A. Adams, 1967) have argued that the huge discrepancy between STM and LTM capacity is one reason for believing in a dual memory system. Granted this difference in capacity, it can still be argued that this difference does not necessarily reflect two different storage systems.

Decay and Interference

Another approach to the distinction between STM and LTM taken by some memory theorists has been to assign different processes to the two systems. In his classic study of STM, J. Brown (1958) argued that the forgetting occurring during STM can be attributed to a decay process. In his first experiment, subjects were required to recall consonants following conditions in which the subjects were free to rehearse the items if they wished or in which they were given a rehearsal-prevention task of naming digits. As expected, the subjects who were free to rehearse recalled more items than the subjects who named digits. Brown assumed that the digit-naming task prevented rehearsal but argued that it was unlikely to produce interference because the items were from a different category than the letters. Since the forgetting in the digit-naming group was presumably not due to interference, Brown attributed forgetting in STM to a decay process. Peterson and Peterson (1959) described a similar procedure for measuring STM for single items that yielded comparable results. Forgetting was rapid with retention less than 10% after an 18-second interval.

These early studies of STM seemed to implicate decay as a major factor in forgetting in STM. Nevertheless, psychologists operating from the base of interference theory were quick to argue that the rapid forgetting in STM is attributable to *proactive interference* (*PI*). This term refers to forgetting that is due to the effects of prior learning. Since it was known that PI increases as a function of the number of prior lists learned in LTM (Underwood, 1957), Keppel and Underwood (1962) devised an experiment in which they varied the number of prior items. Using two retention intervals, 3 and 18 seconds, they demonstrated that forgetting of nonsense syllables in STM increased as a function of the number of prior tests, thus indicating the operation of PI in STM. The importance of this finding is that it supports the view that STM and LTM are basically continuous processes in that they both are affected by PI.

Experimental Factors Differentiating STM and LTM

Another approach to distinguishing STM from LTM is to determine whether experimental variables influence one system but not the other. It has been argued on the basis of data from studies of the serial-position curve in *free recall* that the two systems are distinct.

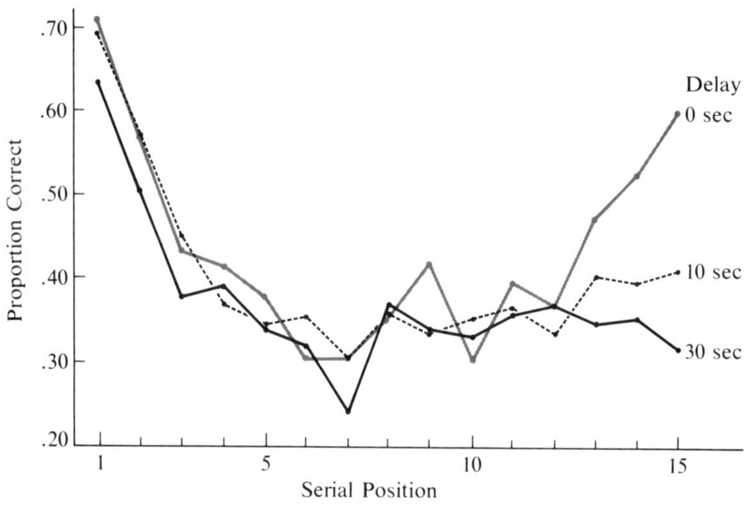

Figure 9–10. The proportion of words correctly recalled from a 15-word list as a function of a serial (input) position on the list. The curves show the effect of a delay of 0, 10, or 30 seconds in recall. The recency effect is eliminated at the 30-second delay. (From "Two Storage Mechanisms in Free Recall," by M. Glanzer and A. R. Cunitz, *Journal of Verbal Learning and Verbal Behavior,* 1966, *5,* 351–360. Reprinted by permission of Academic Press, Inc.)

Free recall allows the subject to recall a list of items in any order. However, the accuracy of free recall is dependent upon the *order* in which the items are recalled. Subjects tend to recall the last items first, and recall is typically greatest with these items; then they recall the early items next, and finally the items from the middle of the list. The high recall of the last items is referred to as the *recency effect,* whereas the high recall of the early items is called the *primacy effect.* The recency effect can be interpreted as due to the last items' still being in STM, whereas the primacy effect can be regarded as the result of greater opportunity for rehearsal of the first-presented items.

If it is true that the recency effect is due to STM, it should be possible to eliminate or reduce this effect by varying the delay interval after presentation of the items while not producing any change in the primacy effect. By having delay intervals of 0, 10, or 30 seconds in which subjects counted, Glanzer and Cunitz (1966) showed that the recency effect is weakened after a 10-second interval and eliminated after a 30-second interval. Figure 9–10 shows the results of this experiment.

Postman and Phillips (1965) found essentially the same results but interpreted them differently. They proposed that during the delay interval there is an increase in PI that acts to interfere with the items learned last. Again, we see that although psychologists may agree on the findings of experiments, they may hold quite different interpretations of them.

Support for the Glanzer and Cunitz interpretation comes from a study on free recall by Rundus (1971). Adopting a clever procedure, Rundus had his subjects rehearse aloud during presentation of a list of 20 words rather than covertly rehearse, as is typically the case. The subjects were allowed to rehearse overtly at any time during the presentation of the list and as often as they wished. Rundus then related the frequency of rehearsal to free recall and the serial-position curve. The results are shown in Figure 9–11. One curve shows the proportion of words correctly recalled, and the other shows the number of rehearsals given each item as a function of the serial position of the words. The number of rehearsals is clearly closely related to the items in primacy positions, but the relation between recall

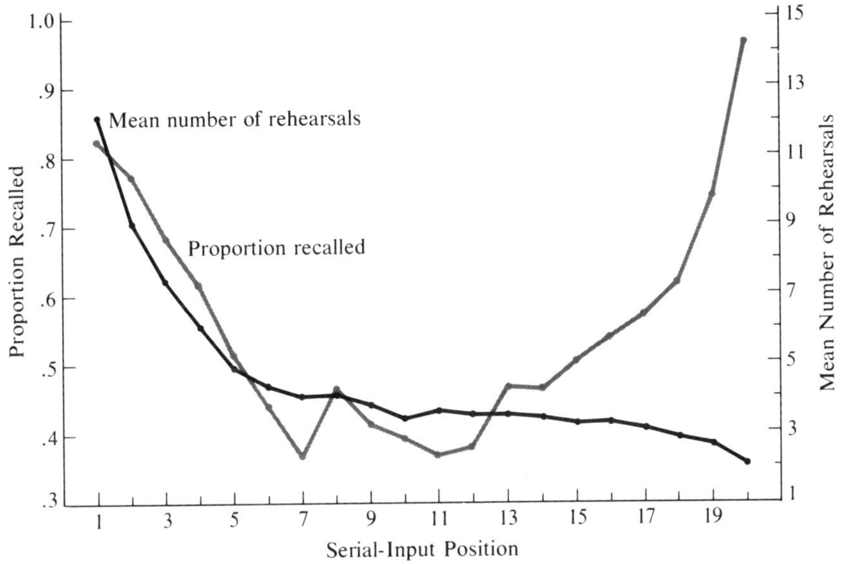

Figure 9–11. Comparison of correct recall with number of overt rehearsals given each word in a 20-word list. (From "Analysis of Rehearsal Processes in Free Recall," by D. Rundus, *Journal of Experimental Psychology,* 1971, *89,* 63–77. Copyright 1971 by the American Psychological Association. Reprinted by permission.)

and rehearsal is eliminated in the recency portion of the curve. The point to note is that the items in the recency part of the curve are recalled quite well without much rehearsal, suggesting that the brief retention in STM can occur in the absence of rehearsal, whereas rehearsal is important in the primacy portion of the curve, which involves LTM. In a review of this research, Glanzer (1972) argues that variables that affect LTM affect the primacy portion of the curve.

Another line of research on the STM/LTM distinction has focused on the *type* of interference in STM and LTM. It has been proposed that interference in STM is due to the *acoustic* (phonological) similarity of the items whereas interference in LTM is due to the semantic similarity of the items (R. Conrad, 1964). These experiments suggest that STM is essentially an auditory storage system in which acoustic information is stored but no interpretation of the information is made. Meaning develops in LTM; hence, semantic similarity provides the basis of interference. In one experiment Baddeley (1966) had subjects immediately recall a serial list of acoustically similar words (*mad, man, mat, cap, cad, can,* and so on) or semantically similar words (*big, long, broad, great, high, tall,* and so on). When compared with the performance of appropriate controls, recall was much poorer for the acoustically similar list. To test this proposition further, Baddeley and Dale (1966) had subjects learn two successive paired-associate lists in which the stimulus terms (adjectives) were similar in meaning but were not acoustically similar. The subjects were required to recall the first list after learning the semantically similar second list, and the usual interference results were found. In a second experiment they used the same pairs, constructed lists of two, four, or six pairs, and presented them only once. The subjects were then given the stimulus items and required to recall the appropriate response. Here they found equal forgetting for groups having semantically similar stimuli compared with control stimuli. As you probably have anticipated, they interpreted their findings as indicating that semantic memory plays an important role in LTM but none in STM.

This interpretation has, however, been criticized by both Shulman (1972) and Cermak (1972). Cermak's argument is that the investigations of STM and LTM have used different methods of presentation, which may readily account for the differences. The essence of his argument is that presenting digits and letters in STM experiments will produce acoustic but not semantic interference. In short, the differences in techniques of studying STM and LTM may well be responsible for some of the experimental differences. Moreover, there is some evidence for acoustic effects in LTM (Dale & McGlaughlin, 1971; Nelson & Rothbart, 1972). Consequently, the distinction between STM and LTM in terms of acoustic versus semantic interference has been seriously questioned.

Physiological Evidence

A last line of evidence that has been proposed as favoring dual-process theories of memory comes from physiological studies. It is known that if the hippocampus is destroyed, memory defects will result (Penfield, 1959). Milner (1959) has further shown that if the hippocampus is destroyed, subjects will have great difficulty in learning new information even though they remember information prior to the operation. Moreover, their performance on intelligence tests is unaffected. What is particularly pertinent for dual-process theory is that the patients can retain information in STM if allowed to rehearse it, but they have lost the capacity to process the information in some meaningful fashion and thus transfer it to LTM. If tested for retention of the new information, the patients are unable to recall it. This type of evidence has suggested to Atkinson and Shiffrin (1968) that the hippocampal lesions have affected either the ability to place new information into LTM or the ability to retrieve information from LTM. But how is the issue of single versus dual memory systems to be resolved? Let us look at a more recent approach, which argues for a single memory system.

Levels of Processing

An important approach to dealing with the issue of multiple memory systems comes from the work of Craik and Lockhart (1972), who argue that the data that seemingly support the idea of separate storage systems can just as easily be explained in terms of *levels of processing*. The basic assumption underlying this idea is that the presentation of any stimulus initiates a series of processing stages that vary along a continuum of depth. They begin with the preliminary assumption that perception involves the rapid analysis of stimuli at a number of levels or stages (Selfridge & Neisser, 1960; Treisman, 1964). In the early stages of processing, stimuli are analyzed in terms of physical or sensory features, such as lines, angles, brightness, pitch, loudness, and so forth, whereas later stages focus on matching input against stored representations of previous learning (pattern recognition). After a stimulus has been recognized, it can be further processed by triggering associations, images, stories, and so forth on the basis of past experience with the stimulus. Here elaboration coding and semantic processing can begin to occur. The basic idea is that of a hierarchy of processing stages in which information is processed at progressively greater depths. The notion of greater depth means a greater degree of semantic or cognitive procesing. Memory is thus viewed as a "continuum from the transient products of sensory analysis to the highly durable products of semantic associative operations" (Craik & Lockhart, 1972, p. 676).

The usefulness of such a conception of memory in the argument of single versus dual or multistage stores is that dual and multistage conceptions of memory appear no longer necessary to account for the data on SIS, STM, and LTM. The empirical differences between STM and LTM can now be viewed as differences in levels of processing. The basic factor in how well information will be remembered is the depth at which the information is processed. As Craik and Lockhart note, the levels-of-processing idea does not constitute a theory of memory. What it does do, however, is allow us to view memory as a continuum and thus seriously questions the necessity of postulating separate storage systems.

Support for the levels-of-processing concept also stems from studies of incidental learning by Jenkins and his colleagues (for example, Hyde, 1973; Hyde & Jenkins, 1969, 1973; Walsh & Jenkins, 1973). The term *incidental learning* refers to situations in which subjects are not instructed to learn the materials presented but are told to do something with the materials such as rate them in terms of pleasantness. The basic finding is that the amount of information recalled by subjects is dependent on whether they semantically process the material. For example, Hyde and Jenkins (1969) read subjects a list of words and asked them either to rate each word on a scale of pleasantness (semantic processing) or to indicate whether the word contained the letter *e*. Following this task a recall test was given. The subjects who had semantically processed the words showed much greater recall than the subjects who had identified the letter *e*. Thus, the way in which the subjects had processed the information influenced their recall. In addition, there was no difference in recall between the subjects who had processed the material semantically and were under incidental-learning instructions and the subjects who had expected to be tested for recall. The general conclusion drawn from these results is that the important factor determining recall is the way the information is processed, as required by the orienting task.

Summary

In this chapter we described human memory as though it were a complex information-processing system. This way of looking at memory has proved very useful to psychologists and has had an important influence on temporary conceptualizations of memory processes. Memory phenomena, informally experienced by us all and systematically investigated in psychological experiments, have been related to a general encoding/storage/retrieval model.

Memory of environmental events requires that those events be translated into some form that is compatible with the information-processing system. Encoded representations must be retained for some period of time, and upon request the stored representation must be located and retrieved. It is the retrieved representation of the originally encoded environmental event that guides the final memory response.

The components of the information-processing sequence and the relationship among those components in memory are presented in more detail in Figure 9–12. This diagram will serve as a schematic guide for reviewing the information-processing analysis of memory.

External stimuli have no direct effect on memory. These stimuli are first translated and transformed by an encoding process. Encoding includes sensory/perceptual processes that may work serially or in parallel. The immediate results of the encoding processes (stimulus-as-coded) may be briefly retained in sensory-information storage. Additional processing, including the operation of selective-attention mechanisms, is required if the encoded information is to be retained for more than a very few minutes.

Encoded information selected for retention in short-term memory appears to be translated into a verbal/acoustic (articulatory) code and rehearsed. The functional capacity of STM, though relatively small (perhaps no more than 7 ± 2 stimulus items), can be greatly expanded by chunking. For information to be retained in STM, it must be rehearsed. Blocking of rehearsal by an interfering task (for example, counting backward by 3s) or by the introduction of new material into storage severely disrupts or even eliminates information from STM. Within a few minutes, information in STM must be processed into long-

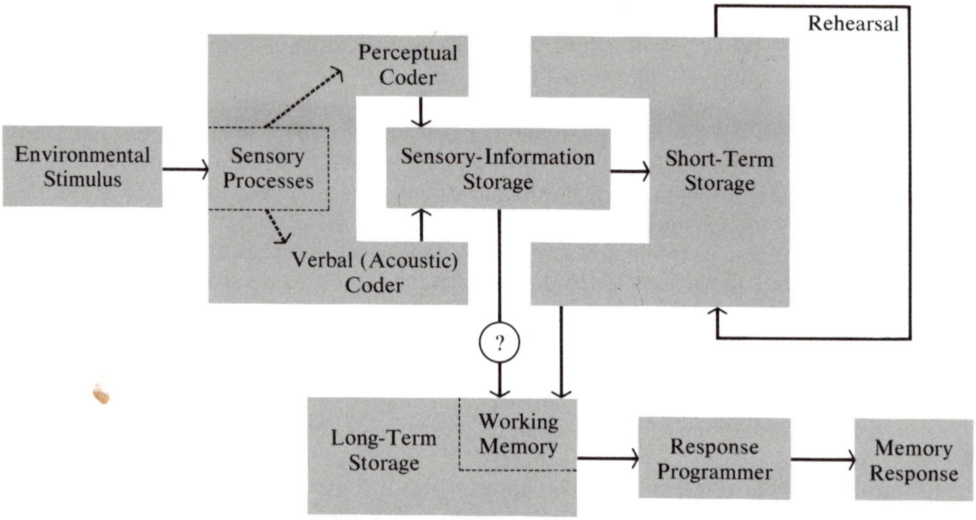

Figure 9–12. An expanded information-processing model of memory.

term storage, or it will be lost from the information-processing system and will no longer be a part of memory.

A theoretically limitless amount of information can be stored in LTM, and, once stored, it becomes a permanent part of the information-processing system. The information in LTM is highly organized and interrelated.

There is some evidence suggesting that two general information forms are represented, a verbally coded system and an image or perceptually coded system. Recent theoretical approaches have tended to favor a single, abstract system of conceptual/propositional structures for representing all information in LTM. The exact nature of the elements in these structures or of the rules by which the elements are related is as yet unspecified. Although important progress has been made in determining how verbal/linguistic information may be stored, less is known about nonverbal, perceptual-information storage.

Even though information is permanently stored in LTM, it is frequently unavailable when it is required. For information in memory to be useful in guiding behavior, it must be retrieved. The first stage of the retrieval process is memory search, in which the required information is located in the vast store of LTM. The search proceeds from an overall organized search for generally pertinent information to a more detailed search for the specific information requested. As relevant information is located, it is collected together and held in working memory. Here the relevant information is organized, and in many cases missing information is filled in to provide a complete and coherent "memory." Information in working memory is used to guide an appropriate verbal and/or motor response.

Also discussed was the topic of single versus dual memory systems. A review of the evidence indicates that we may think of memory as a single system rather than two or more separate systems.

Chapter 10

Language and Semantic Memory

The most unique and most important feature of human behavior is language. Whether written, spoken, or used covertly in thinking, language shapes our knowledge of the world and serves importantly in our efforts to use and communicate that knowledge. Although the ability to communicate is not restricted to *Homo sapiens,* language in the sense of a complex, rule-ordered system capable of symbolically representing, relating, and manipulating the environment seems to be a uniquely human possession. Every human culture has developed some form of language, and any attempt to understand human behavior, past or present, must include a study of language.

There are several possible approaches to the study of language. Anthropologists, for example, have been concerned with differences between various languages and the ways they reflect differences in the cultures in which they were developed. Linguists may focus on structural characteristics, searching for those formal aspects that remain constant from one language to another. The psychological study of language is more concerned with how people use language to manipulate and communicate their basic store of knowledge. Psychologists are primarily interested in language performance, in how language skills are learned, how verbal messages are generated, and how they are understood.

A distinction must be made between the structure of language and its meaning. *Structure* generally refers to the language itself—its basic elements and the rules by which those elements are combined into messages. The meaning of a language, its *semantic* basis, involves the concepts, objects, and relations about which the language user attempts to communicate. The distinction between structure and meaning is perhaps most evident when two different languages are compared:

Ahora vamos a estudiar la lengua.
Now we are going to study language.

Obviously, many aspects of the structure of these two statements are different, but their meanings are essentially the same. As we shall discover, however, the structure of a linguistic statement has important implications for the meaning that the statement conveys. An understanding of the structural characteristics of language is essential to the study of how humans generate and comprehend language.

In this chapter the structure of language will be considered first. Some of the basic elements of language will be defined, and the rules by which those elements are combined to produce comprehensible statements will be described. We will then discuss how language users are able to generate statements about their knowledge of the world and how they are able to comprehend the statements of others. Finally, some interactions between language structure and meaning will be considered.

The Structure of Language

Descriptions of language structure vary depending upon which aspect of the language is being described. The spoken language can be described in terms of its characteristic patterns of sounds, its *phonological structure.* Another aspect is *syntax,* the systematic arrangement of the meaningful elements of a language into phrases and sentences. The set of rules that describes the structure more generally and applies to both its written and its spoken form is referred to as the *grammar* of a language.

You may think of grammar primarily in the context of school. Most of us recall having some difficulties learning grammar in elementary (grammar) school. We were all formally instructed in proper verb tenses ("John was/were a good boy"), in what words are to be capitalized (the word *I* is always capitalized), and in identifying the various classes of words and their function in sentences (a noun names a person, place, or thing). Later you progressed to worrying about split infinitives, dangling participles, and invidious adverbs. Perhaps you have more recently struggled with grammar in the context of learning a foreign language. The type of grammar that emphasizes the official rules for a language is referred to as *prescriptive grammar.* Linguists—and psychologists—are not concerned with prescriptive grammar. Rather, they focus on describing the rules that underlie language as it is used by speakers—that is, on a *descriptive grammar.*

The formal rules of a language are important, but awareness of the rules seems to be rather peripheral to your effective (and even grammatical) use of language. For the most part, you learned the basic grammatical rules of your language before you entered school. Although you could not identify or state the rules, your verbalizations were generally grammatical. Even now, in your everyday conversation as an adult, you are rarely conscious of applying grammatical rules. Nonetheless, your verbalizations are generally consistent with the basic grammatical constraints of the English language.

How you acquired your knowledge of grammar and how that knowledge is used in generating and comprehending language are subjects of much concern to psychologists, and these topics will be discussed later in the chapter. First, however, we will focus principally on the structure of language itself, the basic elements of which language is composed, and the rules by which those elements are combined to produce meaningful, grammatical messages.

The Elements of Language

The simplest unit of language is the *phoneme.* Phonemes are the elementary sounds that are combined to make up words. It has been estimated that humans can utter approximately 100 distinguishable sounds (phonemes). Languages differ in the number of phonemes used and in which particular phonemes are employed, but no language uses all the sounds humans are able to utter. The English language, for example, uses approximately 45 different phonemes.

Phonemes can be indicated in writing by two slashes, / /. For example, the phoneme /b/ refers to the sound of *b,* as in the word *boy.* Phonemes can be differentiated by the way they are produced. Some phonemes are *voiced,* and others are *unvoiced.* Voiced phonemes require the use of the vocal chords, while unvoiced phonemes do not. Both /b/ (as in *boy*) and /v/ (as in *van*) are voiced, while /p/ (as in *pay*) and /f/ (as in *face*) are unvoiced. Phonemes can also be either *stopped* or *fricative.* Stopped phonemes are produced by stopping the outward flow of air briefly, then releasing it in an explosive burst. Fricative phonemes involve a more gradual retardation of the air flow, allowing air to slip through while uttering the sound. Examples of how these two basic forms combine include /b/, a stopped, voiced phoneme; /p/, stopped, unvoiced; /v/, fricative, voiced; and /f/, fricative, unvoiced.

Although phonemes are important and useful in the analysis of the structure of language, they are not particularly useful for understanding the meaning of a language. The simplest meaningful unit of a language is referred to as a *morpheme.* Morphemes are essentially equivalent to simple, one-syllable words (for example, *boy, had, run*). Meaningful suffixes and prefixes are also morphemes (for example, *-ed, -ing, -s, con-, un-, pre-*). All of the legitimate morphemes of a language comprise a vocabulary, or *lexicon,* for that language. *Words,* then, are composed of one or more morphemes. For example, by adding the morpheme *-'s* to the morpheme *boy,* we produce the possessive, *boy's.* Similarly, we can change *bat* to *bats* (plural) or *run* to *running* (progressive). How morphemes combine to produce words is further illustrated in Figure 10–1.

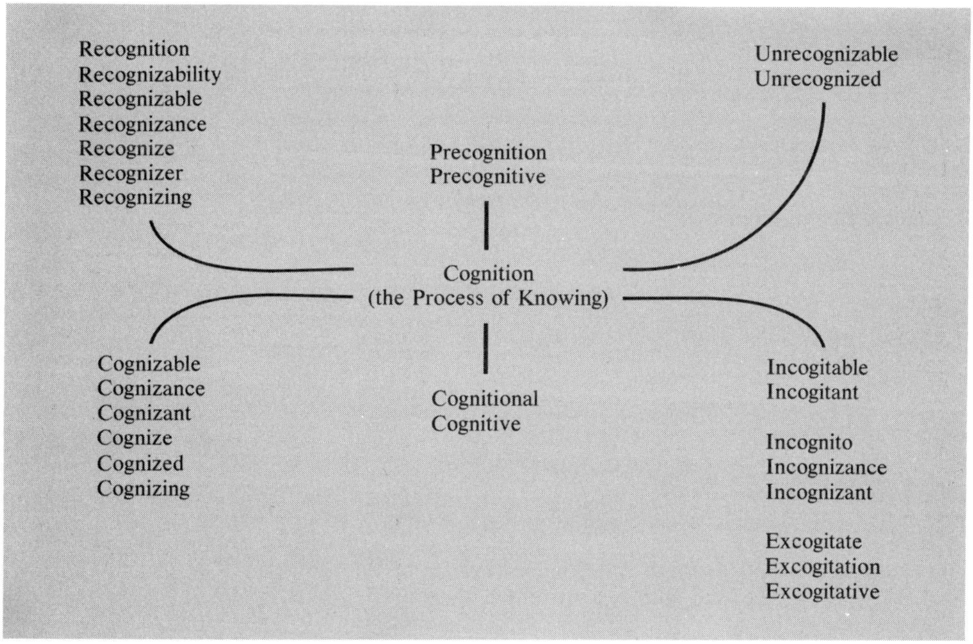

Figure 10–1. Combination of morphemes into words.

Morphemes are generally composed of several phonemes. The rules for combining phonemes into morphemes and for combining morphemes into words are usually quite consistent within a language. The language user is often only marginally aware of these rules. Certain phoneme orders are, however, quickly recognized as illegitimate (for example, *ulcnta*), while others may fit the rules but are not used in the language (for example, *lactun*). These latter, anomalous forms are very apt to show up in Scrabble games and are often vigorously defended.

That not all phonemes are equally likely to follow one another has some important advantages for the language user. In particular, comprehension is made easier, especially in ambiguous circumstances, such as might be provided by unfamiliar handwriting or by speech heard in a noisy environment.

Although morphemes are an important element of language, our use of language cannot be understood solely in terms of morphemes. Very early in a child's learning of a language, morphemes begin to be combined into larger and more complex units. Adult language is almost entirely composed of phrases or sentences, or at least comprehensible morpheme strings that approximate phrases or sentences. Further, the meaning of an individual morpheme or word may vary greatly depending upon its relationship to other elements of the sentence in which it is embedded. An analysis based on morphemes, then, is not adequate if we are to understand the generation and comprehension of language.

Sentence Structure

A sentence is much more than a string of words. There are definite rules that determine the structure of a sentence, a *syntax* that specifies which words can be used together and what their placement should be within the sentence. However, syntax is not just an arbitrary system for ordering words in a sentence. The meaning of words and the interpretation of sentences depend to a large extent upon how the elements of the sentence are ordered.

Small changes in word order can produce very important changes in the meaning conveyed. For example,

John hit Sally

is quite different from

Sally hit John.

However, word order alone does not determine meaning.

John hit Sally

and

Sally was hit by John

are synonymous statements in spite of the reversal of the positions of *John* and *Sally.* We shall have to look beyond simple word order, then, if we are to understand how sentences convey meaning.

It has proved useful in both linguistic and psychological studies of language to analyze sentences as component phrases. Basically, an English *sentence* (*S*) can be broken down into a *noun phrase* (*NP*) and a *verb phrase* (*VP*). The noun phrase contains a *noun* (*N*) and its appended *article* (*Art*) and *modifiers* (*Mod*). For example, the noun phrase

The big black dog

consists of a noun (*dog*), a definite article (*The*), and two modifiers, (*big* and *black*). A verb phrase is composed of a *verb (V)* and a noun or noun phrase. The verb phrase bit the small boy

consists of a verb (*bit*) and a noun phrase (*the small boy*).

The *phrase structure* of a sentence can be represented graphically. The sentence formed by the noun phrase and the verb phrase just described is diagrammed in Figure 10–2. Note that, proceeding from the bottom of the diagram, the elements of the sentence (words) are progressively combined into larger units, or phrases. Proceeding from the top of the diagram, the largest unit, *sentence,* is progressively divided into phrases and finally individual words. This branching structure, or *tree diagram,* can be used to represent the composition of any sentence.

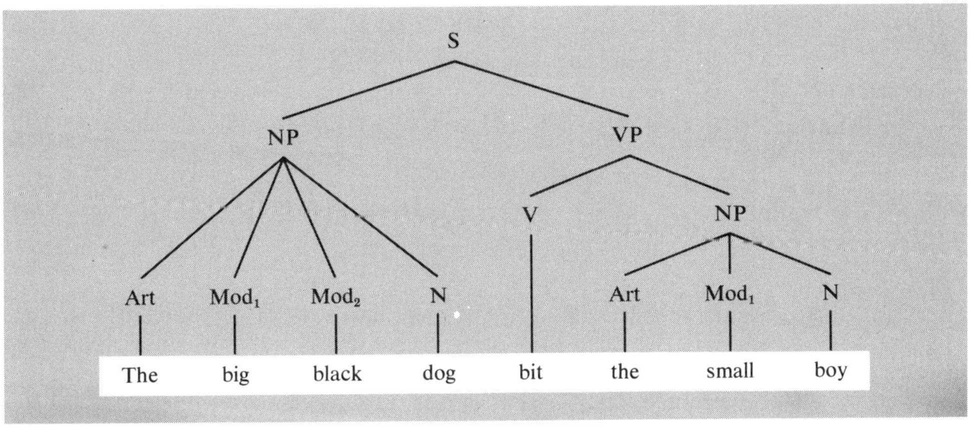

Figure 10–2. A tree diagram for phrase-structure grammar.

An alternative (but equivalent) approach to representing the phrase structure of a sentence is by a set of *rewrite rules*. The first rule might be stated: "A sentence can be rewritten as a noun phrase plus a verb phrase," or in abbreviated form,

$$S \rightarrow NP + VP.$$

Other needed rules can also be derived and added to the set. An example set of phrase-structure rewrite rules is

Rule 1: $S \rightarrow NP + VP$
Rule 2: $VP \rightarrow V + NP$
Rule 3: $NP \rightarrow Art + N$
Rule 4: $N \rightarrow Mod + N$
Rule 5: $Mod \rightarrow Mod_1 + Mod_2 \ldots.$

Applying these rewrite rules to our example sentence produces:

by Rule 1: $S \rightarrow NP + VP$
by Rule 2: $S \rightarrow NP + (V + NP)$
by Rule 3: $S \rightarrow (Art + N) + [V + (Art + N)]$
by Rule 4: $S \rightarrow [Art + (Mod + N)] + \{V + [Art + (Mod + N)]\}$

by Rule 5: $S \rightarrow \{Art + [(Mod_1 + Mod_2) + N]\} + \{V + [Art + (Mod_1 + N)]\}$

The phrase structure of the sentence at this point in the rewrite sequence is *context free;* that is, it is composed of interrelated abstract elements (N, V, Art, and so on) rather than words. To produce the actual sentence, then, we must add rules specifying the relationship between these abstract components and the *terminal elements* (words) of the sentence.

NP	*VP*
Art → The	V → bit
Mod_1 → big	Art → the
Mod_2 → black	Mod_1 → small
N → dog	N → boy

The result is

$S \rightarrow [Art + (Mod_1 + Mod_2) + N] + \{V + [Art + (Mod_1 + N)]\}$
S → The big black dog bit the small boy.

Tree diagrams and rewrite rules are two different ways of representing the same sentence-structure analysis. The example just presented deals with only a very limited set of rules; a great many more rewrite rules would be required to describe the English language adequately (for example, prepositional-phrase rules, negation rules, and so forth). A complete set of rewrite rules sufficient to describe and generate all the sentences in a language would comprise a *phrase-structure grammar* for the language.

Although context-free, phrase-structure grammars are a very useful way to analyze languages, they do fall short of being an ideal system. In the first place, a phrase-structure grammar is not a very efficient system because virtually every sentence in a language would require a separate application of the rewrite rules. A particularly important shortcoming is that synonymous sentences may require entirely different phrase-structure rewrite specifications. For example, the structures of the two sentences

John kissed Marsha [N + (V + N)]

and

Marsha was kissed by John [N + (Aux + V) + (Prep + N)]

are quite different, but both sentences convey the same message. Another problem occurs when a single sentence can convey two entirely different meanings. The interpretation of the sentence

They are kissing fishes

is quite different depending upon whether *kissing* is rewritten as a verb or as a modifier. To resolve these problems, it is necessary to consider more than the structure of the sentence itself; we must look to its underlying structure, or meaning.

Chomsky's Transformational Grammar

The influence of the work of linguist Noam Chomsky (for example, 1957, 1959, 1965, 1968) is evident in virtually every contemporary study of language. His structural-analysis approach dominates much of formal linguistics and, at the same time, has had profound effects on the psychological study of language.

Chomsky's (1959) attack on the behavioristic analysis of language represented by Skinner's *Verbal Behavior* (1957) stimulated and redirected the psychological study of language acquisition and use. The vigorous growth of the field of psycholinguistics and the current interest of psychologists in the complex processes involved in the generation and comprehension of natural language are important examples of the influence of structural linguistics on psychology. Reactions to Chomsky's work have been varied, some being quite critical, and more recent theoretical analyses have moved beyond the structural distinctions made by Chomsky, but the impact of his work is undeniable.

In an effort to overcome some of the shortcomings of the simpler phrase-structure grammars, Chomsky proposed an analysis by a *transformational grammar*. Through making a distinction between the implicit, underlying structure of a sentence and the form of the sentence, transformational grammar provides a way to represent relationships between sentences that on the surface appear to be quite different. For example,

Jack kissed the lady

and

The lady was kissed by Jack

have quite different phrase structures as sentences, but they have a common underlying structure.

Chomsky referred to the underlying structure of sentences as *deep structure*. The deep structure is the basis of the semantic interpretation, or "meaning," of a sentence and is distinguished from the actual sentence, or its *surface structure*. The two sentences just presented have different surface structures that are generated by separate grammatical transformations of the same deep structure. The deep structure is conceptualized as an abstract phrase structure or *base string*. It results from the application of context-free, phrase-structure rewrite rules (for example, S → NP + VP) and word-symbol rewrite rules (for example, NP → *Jack;* V → *kiss*). The common deep structure for the two surface sentences can be represented as in Figure 10–3.

The surface structures of sentences are produced by the application of various transformational rules to the deep structure. The first surface sentence ("Jack kissed the lady")

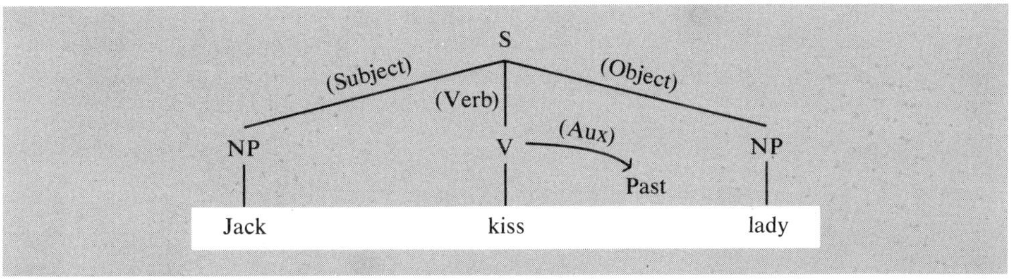

Figure 10–3. Common deep structure for "Jack kissed the lady" and "The lady was kissed by Jack."

is an *active-declarative* transform of the deep structure, and the second sentence ("The lady was kissed by Jack") is a *passive-declarative* transform.

Many different surface structures can be generated from the same deep structure. The following are some examples of different surface structures that can be generated by allowable English-language transforms:

Active declarative: Jack kissed the lady.
Passive declarative: The lady was kissed by Jack.
Negative declarative: Jack did not kiss the lady.
Negative passive: The lady was not kissed by Jack.
Active interrogative: Did Jack kiss the lady?
Passive interrogative: Was the lady kissed by Jack?
Negative active interrogative: Didn't Jack kiss the lady?
Negative passive interrogative: Wasn't the lady kissed by Jack?

It is important to note that although all of these surface sentences can be viewed as transforms of the same deep structure, they do have quite different meanings. The deep structure can be thought of as indicating some relation (*kiss*) between a subject (*Jack*) and an object (*lady*). The first two sentences assert that the relation exists (or existed), the negative transforms deny the relation, and the interrogatives question whether the relation existed.

That these alterations of meaning are allowed, at least in the early version of transformational grammar (Chomsky, 1957), points to an important distinction between the deep structure of a sentence and its semantic meaning. The deep structure is viewed as an abstract phrase structure that can be elaborated into a surface sentence by transformational rules or can be translated by a *semantic interpreter* to find its "meaning." Because the semantic interpreter operates only on the deep structure, and not the surface structure, it should not be possible for different surface sentences generated from the same deep structure to have different meanings. More recent versions of transformational grammar (for example, Chomsky, 1965) recognize this problem and disallow any meaning-changing transformations of the base structure.

A schematic representation of central aspects of Chomsky's transformational grammar is presented in Figure 10–4. The major component in the model is the *linguistic generator*. There are two subcomponents of the linguistic generator, a *base component* and a *transformational component*. In the base component abstract (context-free) phrase-structure rewrite rules and word-symbol rewrite rules are applied to produce a deep structure. The transformational component transforms deep structures into surface structures. A variety of transformation rules, including addition, deletion, substitution, and permutation, are applied in this component to produce one of the several possible surface structures for each deep structure. For example, a passive-declarative surface structure can be produced by (1) permuting the subject noun phrase and object noun phrase and (2) adding an auxiliary to the verb (for example, *was*) and a preposition before the subject noun phrase:

Jack kiss lady → The lady was kissed by Jack.

The transformational component produces a variety of surface structures from any deep structure. The *phonological operator* in turn translates the surface structure into a spoken sentence.

In the meaning component of the model, the deep structure is translated by a semantic interpreter to produce a meaning, or *semantic reading,* for the sentence. Notice that the semantic interpretation is applied after the deep structure has been generated and is a

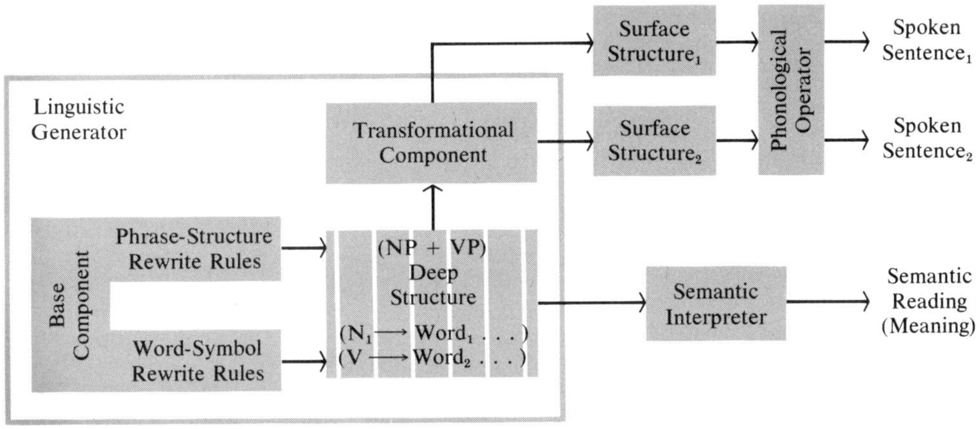

Figure 10–4. Chomsky's transformational grammar.

separate operation from the transformational processes that produce the surface sentence. When the model is applied to the comprehension of a heard sentence, for example, the operations are reversed. In effect, the transformational rules can be applied to the surface structure to derive a deep structure. This deep structure is then interpreted to obtain a semantic meaning. Because meaning is derived from the deep structure, not the surface structure, all surface sentences with the same deep structure must have the same meaning.

Many aspects of Chomsky's structural linguistics have necessarily been omitted from our discussion. The components of the model that have been described have been greatly simplified in comparison to formal presentations of transformational grammar. Even this brief discussion, however, should indicate that Chomsky's system of analysis is a very effective method for describing sentence comprehension and the relationships among apparently different surface sentences.

The major weakness of the Chomsky model has been in the specification of the relationship between deep structures and the underlying semantic representation of a communication. The model gives precedence to the linguistic deep structures. The actual sentences (surface structures) originate from the linguistic generator, and the meaning of the sentence is derived separately from the deep structure by the operation of the semantic interpreter. A psychological analysis of language use would seem to demand that the meaning of a sentence precede the construction of any linguistic structures. In other words, the meaning that a speaker wishes to communicate would seem to determine the linguistic structures (deep or otherwise) that will be used, not the reverse.

Case Grammar

Chomsky's transformational grammar continues to be one of the most useful systems available for analyzing and describing the formal structure of language. This system does, however, leave some questions unanswered. The rewrite rules of transformational grammar emphasize structural (syntactic) relations between lexical surface elements of a sentence and the deep structure. In contrast, a grammar that places more emphasis on meaningful (semantic) relationships would seem to be more germane to understanding the generation and comprehension of language. One such system of analysis is *case grammar* (Fillmore, 1968).

Case grammar is an extension and modification of transformational grammar, differing primarily in its treatment of the relationship between surface structure and deep structure. In Chomsky's transformational grammar a lexical item in a surface sentence is related to its deep-structure representation by its *syntactic* role. For example, in the sentences

The dog bit the boy

and

The boy was bitten by the dog,

the relationship between *the dog* and its abstract representation in the common deep structure of the two sentences might be "noun phrase that is the subject of the sentence." Similarly, the surface elements *bit/bitten* and *the boy* can be related to the deep structure by the functions "main verb of" and "object of." As the first tree diagram in Figure 10–5

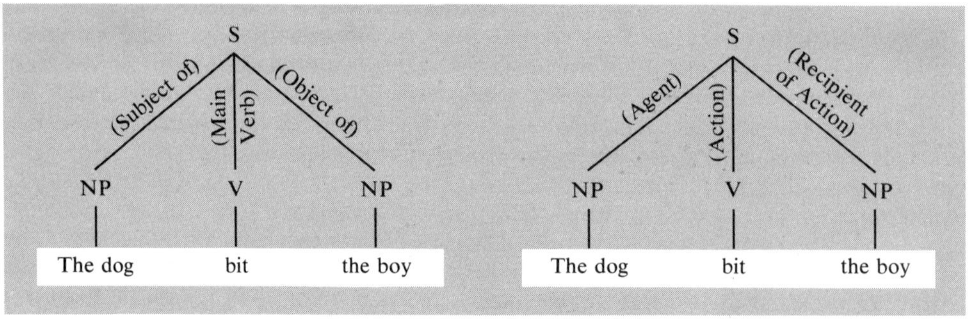

Figure 10–5. Tree diagrams representing transformational grammar (left) and case grammar (right).

illustrates, surface-to-deep-structure relationships are determined by syntax. Case grammars, on the other hand, relate surface elements to their deep structure by their *semantic* functions. As illustrated by the second tree diagram, *the dog* bears the relation "agent causing the action" to the deep structure. The verb, *bit/bitten,* exemplifies the relation "action that occurred," and *the boy* is "recipient of the action."

Case grammars recognize that "subject of the sentence," for example, can play a number of semantic roles. In the sentences

The dog bit the boy

and

The walk circled the park,

both *the dog* and *the walk* are "subject of." However, in the first sentence *the dog* serves the semantic function of "agent" (that is, it is doing the action), and in the second sentence *the walk* is semantically an "instrument" (that is, it implements the action). Similarly, "object of" is in one case a "recipient" of the action (*the boy*) and in the other case a "location" (*the park*).

There are a greater number and variety of surface-to-deep-structure relationships in a case grammar than are expressed in a transformational grammar. The following sentences illustrate some frequently encountered *case relations:*

Action: The girl *hit* the boy.
Agent: The *dog* barked.
Recipient: The cat scratched the *rug*.
Instrument: The *rock* crushed the cabin.
Location: The *park* was cool.
Quality: The city was *crowded*.

Case-grammar relations preserve important semantic distinctions that transformational grammars do not. This distinction is especially evident when *paraphrases* of sentences are considered. For example,

The girl hit the boy

can be paraphrased in a variety of ways. These are only a few:

The boy was hit by the girl.
It was the girl who hit the boy.
It was the boy who was hit by the girl.
The girl was the one who hit the boy.
The girl gave the boy a hit.
A hit is what the girl gave the boy.
What the girl did was hit the boy.

Only the first of these paraphrases is clearly related to the same deep structure as the original sentence by transformational grammar. In contrast, all of the examples, and any others that preserve the basic *girl* (agent)/*hit* (action)/*boy* (recipient) relationships, would stem from the same deep structure in a case-grammar analysis.

Case grammars do share many characteristics with Chomsky's transformational-grammar approach to language analysis. Sentences are analyzed in terms of phrase-structure rewrite rules in both systems. Also, Chomsky's four basic levels of analysis (phonological structure, surface structure, deep structure, and meaning) are used in case-grammar analysis. As in transformational grammar, case grammar assumes that surface structures are derived from transformations of a deep structure. The major difference between the two approaches is that surface and deep structures are related primarily by syntax in transformational grammar (for example, subject, verb, object), but that the relationship is more semantic in case grammar (for example, agent, action, recipient). This variation from Chomsky's approach may appear relatively minor, but it represents an important step toward a more psychologically relevant analysis of language because the role of meaning is more central.

Both the transformational-grammar and the case-grammar analysis of language emphasize the *interpretative* role of semantics. Deep structures can be derived from surface structures, as in language comprehension, or produced by some basic linguistic component, as in language generation. In either event the meaning of the message is derived from an interpretation of the deep structure. Thus, the semantic component of language plays no role in the generation of the deep structure of a message. The incompatibility of these models with psychological analyses of language performance has already been noted; it seems more likely that the meaning of a message is the more basic component and that meaning determines linguistic structure.

Semantic-Marker Theory

Semantic-marker theory (see, for example, J. J. Katz & Fodor, 1963; J. J. Katz & Postal, 1964) is an important extension and elaboration of some aspects of the transformational-grammar analysis of language. All of the central components of transformational grammar are accepted, and attention is focused upon providing a more detailed description of the relationship between deep structure and underlying semantic meaning.

Semantic-marker theory postulates that the meaning of a sentence is derived from a combination of the semantic interpretations of the individual constituents of the sentence and their syntactic interrelationships as specified by the deep structure. The interpretations of the individual terms must be combined and synthesized to determine the overall meaning of the phrases or sentences that they compose.

The semantic interpretation of a lexical item is represented in the theory by *semantic markers*. These markers refer to general conceptual categories to which a word belongs. For example, the words *girl, woman, sister, lady, mother, aunt,* and so forth all have the semantic marker *female*. According to the theory, only a relatively small number of (universal) semantic markers are required to represent the semantic relationships of all of the words in a language.

The relationship between a lexical item and its semantic markers can be represented by a tree diagram. For example, a semantic-marker diagram for the word *bachelor* is presented in Figure 10–6. Recall from the discussion of the tranformational-grammar model (Figure 10–4) that each constituent of the deep structure is labeled by its phrase-structure, syntactic role—N, Mod, V, and so on. Consistent with this notion, the first entry in the semantic-marker tree for *bachelor* is the grammatical designation (or marker) *noun*. The syntactic marking indicates a number of important aspects of a word. For example, words marked *noun* can be made singular or plural, used as the subject of a sentence, replaced by pronouns, and so forth. Further, some words can have more than one syntactic marking, each associated with a different set of semantic meanings—for example, *run* (V), to move rapidly on foot, versus *run* (N), a score in baseball.

Each branch of the tree becomes more specific until a distinct meaning, referred to as a *distinguisher* rather than a marker, is reached. The marker-to-distinguisher sequence

bachelor → *noun* → *human* → *male* →(who has never married)[1]

exemplifies this hierarchical arrangement of semantically relevant characteristics.

As the tree diagram expands, other markers reveal the multiple semantic relationships represented by the term *bachelor*. The sequence

bachelor → *noun* → *human* →(who has the first or lowest academic degree)

presents quite a different interpretation of the word than does the sequence

bachelor → *noun* → *animal* → *male* → (young fur seal when without a mate during the breeding time).

[1] Strictly speaking, a bachelor is someone who is not currently married.

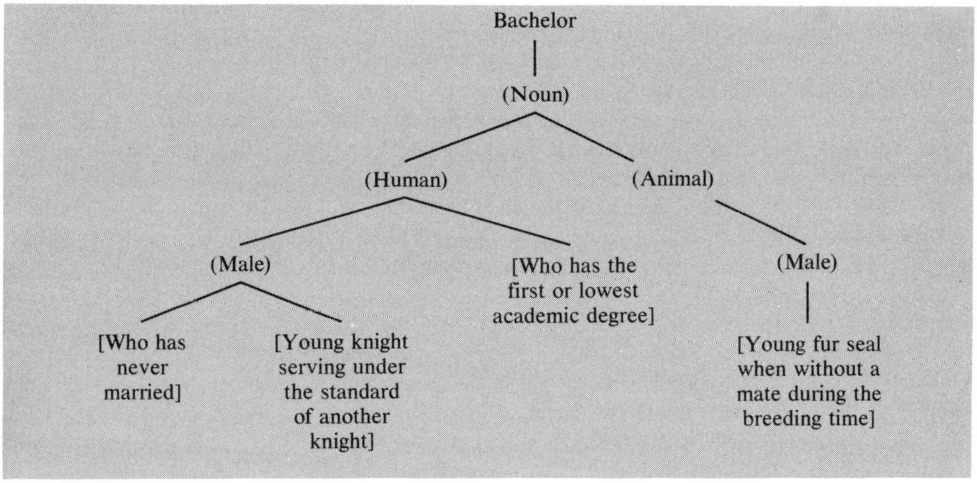

Figure 10–6. Semantic-marker diagram for *bachelor*. (From "The Structure of a Semantic Theory," by J. J. Katz and J. A. Fodor, *Language,* 1963, *39,* 170–210. Reprinted by permission of the Language Society of America.)

Which path will be followed in a particular sentence using the word *bachelor* is determined by the grammatical (deep-structure) role assigned to the word and by the semantic possibilities (marker sequences) of other constituents in the deep structure. For example, in the sentence

The bachelor picked up his date,

there is only one semantic-marker sequence for *bachelor* that is consistent with the word's syntactic function ("subject of") and with the semantic markings of the other constituents of the sentence (*picked up* and *date*):

noun → *human* → *male* → (who has never married).

The semantic interpretation of the sentence, then, is an amalgamation of the mutually consistent semantic markings and grammatical functions of all the lexical constituents of the sentence.

The addition of semantic markers to transformational analysis does help to clarify the role of meaning in language. However, there are several semantic-interpretation problems that are not well explained by the theory. The assumption that the meaning of a sentence is determined by amalgamating the mutually consistent semantic markings of the separate constituents of the deep structure leads to great difficulty, or to failure, in interpreting a number of frequently occurring types of sentences and expressions. Consider the sentences

Let's bury the hatchet.
The country has been had.
The old man finally kicked the bucket.

The meaning of these sentences is quite clear in most contexts, but any attempt to understand them in terms of an amalgamation of the semantic markings of the individual words (for example, *bury* and *hatchet, been* and *had, kicked* and *bucket*) seems doomed to failure, or at least a great deal of confusion.

Further complications arise for the semantic-marker theory when the context of a sentence is considered. The theory focuses upon interpretations of elements within the deep structure of a single phrase or sentence. In actual language use, however, sentences are rarely encountered all by themselves. Preceding sentences and/or other aspects of the context in which a sentence is embedded can have a dramatic influence on the meaning of that sentence and the individual words of which it is composed. For example, the sentence

Visiting professors can be boring

would be interpreted one way when preceded by

Students who attended the guest lecture learned an important lesson,

but it takes on a different meaning in the context of

The annual faculty/student picnic did prove one thing to the students who attended.

There is an even broader sense in which context can influence the interpretation of words and sentences. The general "world knowledge" shared by a speaker and a hearer is crucial to the semantic interpretation of language. Bolinger (1965) offers the example

Our store sells alligator shoes.

This sentence is not likely to be interpreted as meaning

Our store sells shoes for alligators

unless, perhaps, the store is located on Sesame Street. It is clear that language users' world knowledge plays an important role in their semantic interpretation of sentences. However, it is not yet clear how this fact could be incorporated into semantic-marker theory.

One possible avenue for dealing with these problems is to expand the list of markers that can be applied to each constituent in the deep structures. This approach is costly, however, because the assumption of a relatively small set of common semantic markers that apply to all lexical items is an important aspect of the theory. Clearly, if the list of markers were allowed to escalate, the task of choosing mutually consistent semantic markings for all of the words in a sentence would soon achieve proportions that may be unreasonable to expect of a human language user.

Overview

At the beginning of this chapter, a distinction was made between the structure of language and its underlying meaning, or semantic base. To this point in the chapter, we have been primarily concerned with describing the formal structure of language. In that regard we have been emphasizing a *linguistic analysis* of language. Linguists have traditionally been concerned with developing formal models of language *competence*. These are models that ignore language as it is actually used by individuals and focus upon how it might be used by an "ideal" language user. This emphasis has led linguists to focus their attention on formal descriptive analyses of language structure in attempts to determine the rules of a language that are necessary to produce grammatical sentences.

The work of Chomsky has been particularly important in linguistic analysis. He postulated that a linguistic deep structure is the basis of all surface sentences, each resulting from the application of different transformational rules to a syntactically labeled deep phrase structure. The meaning of a sentence, whether it is being spoken or comprehended, is separately derived from a semantic interpretation of the deep structure. It is important to note that in the transformational-grammar model the deep structure of a sentence is a product of the linguistic generator and is only indirectly related to some representation at the semantic level of language.

Later linguistic analysts have become more concerned with actual language use. The increasing concern with the semantic intent of a sentence, exemplified by the case-grammar and semantic-marker extensions of transformational grammar, is one indication of this change in linguistic analyses. Some recent linguistic models have gone even farther toward a semantic orientation.

According to the *generative semantics* approach (Lakoff, 1970, 1971), meaning must be more directly involved in the generation of sentences. The generative-semantics model assumes that an abstract *semantic phrase structure* composed of "atomic predicates" (ideas) forms the basis of linguistic utterances. This basic semantic structure (the intended meaning) is transformed and elaborated on until finally the surface sentence is generated. Thus, the generative-semantics model postulates that a semantic (meaning) structure is the basis of a surface sentence.

This model appears to represent more closely what actual language users must do—that is, formulate a meaning they wish to convey, then generate a linguistic structure that will communicate that meaning. In this regard linguistic analyses seem to be approaching a model that is more consistent with the psychological conceptualization of language and language use.

The Psychological Analysis of Language

Psychologists are more concerned with the meaning of language than with its structure. Language is viewed as a symbol system that is used for communicating some set of ideas, knowledge, or concepts to a listener or reader. The psychological study of language has emphasized actual language use, or *performance*, the language user's ability to create, comprehend, and remember the meaning of verbal messages.

The study of language by psychologists can be divided into several different conceptual approaches. The *stimulus–response* behavioral analysis, primarily identified with Skinner, attempts to explain language acquisition and performance with the same principles of conditioning that have been employed to account for other overt behaviors of humans and lower animals. Other approaches within the general S–R-association analysis have emphasized the role of mediational processes, postulating that various covert events or processes intervene between the observable, verbal S and R events. Most recently, analyses based on what can be termed a cognitive, information-processing model of language performance have been developed. These approaches often employ "computer" models to conceptualize (and simulate) human language generation and comprehension.

The S–R Conditioning Approach

Skinner was among the first psychologists to attempt a comprehensive analysis of the complex set of behaviors encompassed by people's use of language. His conceptualization of human verbal behavior is true to the operant analysis that has been successfully applied to the behavior of rats and pigeons in the Skinner box. Skinner's book *Verbal Behavior* (1957) presents an analysis of human language performance founded on the basic principles of operant conditioning. Attention is focused almost entirely on overt verbal behaviors, although there is some discussion of covert behaviors that may be closely related to verbal behavior.

The operant analysis relies heavily upon the principles of reinforcement to account for language acquisition and use. The application of these principles is most clearly illustrated by the "naming" response, especially as it is acquired and used by children. This class of verbal behaviors includes, for example,

That is a dog.
This is blue.
I have a stomach ache.

These naming responses are referred to as *tacts,* and they are thought to be acquired and shaped by the principles of operant conditioning.

Children frequently produce naming responses as imitations of adult verbal behaviors. When infants produce a tact in the presence of certain appropriate environmental stimuli, as when they utter "ma-ma" in the presence of their mother, they are generally reinforced. This reinforcement is most often the approval and attention of adults, especially the mother and father. Later, when the same or similar stimuli recur, the children will tend to repeat the originally reinforced response (tact).

An obvious and important characteristic of the tacting behavior of even relatively young children is that appropriate naming responses are often applied to stimuli that have never before been encountered. For example, a child is usually able, after some experience, to assign the label *dog* to an unfamiliar dog. The operant analysis of how tacts come to be correctly applied to novel instances of a general class of stimuli involves the basic conditioning processes of generalization and discrimination. Initially, for instance, the label *dog* may be applied and reinforced (for example, by parental attention and approval) only in the presence of the family's poodle. Afterward, when a cow (or a picture of a cow) is encountered, it too may be assigned the label *dog*. This misapplication of the label comes about because of stimulus generalization; that is, the cow has some features in common with the poodle (both are alive, have hair, have four legs, and so on) and, as a result, tends to elicit the verbal label learned for the poodle. This misapplication of the label *dog* will be corrected, or at least not reinforced, and in time the response *dog* will no longer be applied to cows. A further sharpening of the naming response will be required when the neighbors' cat is first encountered. Gradually, the process of discrimination learning will narrow the class of stimuli to which the label *dog* is applied.

The discrimination process can be carried too far. An appropriate but novel instance of the class *dog*—for example, a Dalmation—may not be correctly labeled at first. Eventually, however, with experience and differential reinforcement, the class of stimuli that can correctly be called *dog* will become better defined.

The acquisition and definition of stimulus classes and their appropriate names is a complex process. In our example the poodle may, in many ways, resemble the neighbors' cat more than it does the Dalmation, and neither the poodle nor the Dalmation is very similar to a collie. Further, on some occasions the label *dog* may not be appropriate. Perhaps *animal* or *Coco* or *poodle* or *mine* will be required instead. The generalization and discrimination learning that is required to achieve appropriate verbal naming responses seems much more complex than that required by a pigeon pecking a lighted disk inside a box. The contention of the operant approach is, however, that in principle both types of behavior can be explained by the same basic conditioning processes.

Another important functional category of verbal behaviors primarily involves affecting the behavior of others. These behaviors include requests, demands, and commands, and they are referred to as *mands*. Examples include:

Cookie?
Pass the salt.
Would you please close the door?

The utility of this class of verbal behaviors should be obvious, and the operant analysis of how mands are acquired and maintained can be easily anticipated. The reinforcement for appropriate mands is the compliance of the individual or individuals to whom they are directed and the commensurate changes in the speaker's environment.

The processes of discrimination and generalization again play the central role in shaping this group of verbal behaviors. For example, a child may learn that the mand *cookie,* directed at father or mother, produces a cookie. Similar behaviors are learned and generalized to other situations. The child will learn that the mand *water* produces a glass of water. An important discrimination may be learned when the mand *milk* is denied or ignored. Eventually the child will learn that father or mother may require that additional verbal responses accompany mands if they are to be reinforced—for example,

Milk, please.

Later, even more may be demanded of the child, so that only mands of the general form

May I have a cookie, please?

will produce the desired result.

Further complications with mands arise. Requests for cookies, for example, are generally not complied with unless there are some cookies in the vicinity, and perhaps not even then if it is too near time for dinner. Another important condition signaling that mands may be appropriate is the presence of a (hopefully sympathetic) listener. Children may learn that some mands are better reserved for presenting to mothers if the presence of fathers frequently signals nonreinforcement (extinction). In summary, the mand, like the tact, is a verbal behavior that is presumed to be acquired, maintained, and elaborated by the operation of the principles of reinforcement. Reinforcement of a mand usually takes the form of the compliance of a listener.

The operant analysis of tacts and mands differs greatly from the approach to language taken by the linguists. The structure of language is seen not as a primary determiner of verbal behaviors but as a secondary property that develops because of various demands and rewards presented to speakers by their verbal communities. The treatment of meaning is also quite different. The linguists tend to view meaning as an underlying property of language that is derived from deep base structures (as in transformational grammars). The operant analysis does not postulate any underlying linguistic structures or meanings. Rather, overt verbal behaviors are the result of interactions of speakers with their verbal communities. Statements such as

This car is blue

and

Please open the door

are not viewed as efforts on the part of the speaker to communicate knowledge or meaning to a listener. These statements are made because, in the past, when the same (or similar) verbal statements were made under similar environmental circumstances (blue cars and closed doors) in the presence of similar listeners, some reinforcement generally resulted (people agreed with the speaker or opened the door).

Extensions of the Operant Analysis

The operant analysis has been extended to account for the acquisition and performance of other, more complex verbal behaviors. For example, Skinner (1957) included what he termed *intraverbal behaviors*. These are the learned word-to-word associations that determine the use of abstract terms (for example, *truth, freedom, knowledge*) and events or objects that cannot actually be experienced (for example, historical events, people, and places; projected future events; or remote places and events). Intraverbal responses differ from tacts and mands in that they depend entirely upon language for their acquisition and maintenance. They are verbal responses that are learned and understood only in terms of their association with other verbal responses.

The most troublesome problem for the operant analysis of language has been accounting for the fact that abstract grammatical rules control the production of overt verbal behaviors, that a definite syntax constrains verbal behaviors and is applied quite consistently across sentences. This is the abstract grammatical structure underlying surface sentences that has been one of the principal concerns of the linguists. Ideally, the acquisition and use of these grammatical rules should be explained in terms of reinforcement contingencies operating upon overt verbal behaviors.

There have been several efforts (for example, Braine, 1963; Staats, 1968, 1971) to account for these aspects of language performance within the general S–R analysis of verbal behavior. Very briefly, these theorists have tried to explain the observed order of words in sentences in terms of previously reinforced word-to-word associations. The first word in a sentence serves as a stimulus for the second word (response), which in turn serves as a stimulus for the production of the third word, and so on. Particular word sequences (sentences) occur because they were reinforced in the past.

It is necessary, of course, to extend this analysis further because the same word sequence (sentence) is rarely repeated; that is, novel word sequences are quite routine in normal language performance. What seems to remain constant from one sentence to the next is not the ordering of the overt words but the relationships among the various (grammatical) classes of words. The syntax describes the acceptable relationships among nouns, articles, verbs, prepositions, and so forth. Within these rules, however, an infinite number of actual sentences can be produced.

One approach to these problems has been to postulate that the relevant word classes are formed and their appropriate interrelationships learned by the processes of generalization and discrimination. Because all the words belonging to a given class (for example, nouns) rarely occur together in a single overt sentence, the generalization between words must be based upon (or mediated by) their usual position (or function) in the many different sentences that are encountered; that is, the class of words that can serve as the subject of a sentence (nouns) generally occurs early in a sentence. Verbs, on the other hand, tend to occur later in the sentence, following nouns. By selecting different members of each class and placing them in their appropriate positions, novel but grammatical sentences can be produced.

A great many questions remain to be answered in the S–R analysis of sentence production. Positional generalization and other aspects of the formation of functional word classes have not been adequately described. Further, it is not at all clear how specific members of a given word class are chosen and placed into sentences that are simultaneously grammatical and appropriate to the circumstances surrounding the verbal response.

Perhaps an even greater problem is presented by the fact that a human language user typically pays very little attention to the words that are spoken or heard. In normal conversation it seems that the *meaning* of what is said is the important aspect and that once the meaning has been comprehended, the actual words that were spoken are quickly forgotten. Consider what would happen if a conversation were interrupted without warning and the speaker and hearer were asked to determine which of several alternative sentences had occurred a few minutes earlier in their conversation. Would they be more likely to select a

and word order, but an accurate para-
t was on the surface very similar to one
conveyed? Common sense and the data
iraphrase would be more likely to be

culties for an analysis of language per-
ng elements of surface sentences. We
a sentence can be changed markedly
ces

boy

the dog

words employed. Yet these sentences
sers. On the other hand,

by the dog

will be interpreted quite differently.
n an important part of the trans-
does not appear to be any way that
ig overt words could account for trans-
ot seem plausible that reinforcement of
, identical reactions) between the above
ig to discrimination (that is, different
.
esented by sentences that have embed-

l who lives
e boy.

e girl

and

who lives with the Jones family

intervene between the two components of the main sentence,

The dog . . . bit the boy.

In spite of the embedded clauses, and there can be any number of them, the relationship between the main-subject noun (*dog*) and the main verb (*bit*) is maintained; that is, the sentence will be interpreted as

The dog bit the boy

rather than, for example,

The Jones family bit the boy.

It is not at all clear how sequential, word-to-word associations, even with covert mediating accompaniments, can "jump over" an arbitrarily long set of embedded clauses and exert the appropriate constraints on the selection (production) of the next word in the principal sentence. After considering the problem posed for S–R-association theories of language by such embedded clauses, J. R. Anderson and Bower (1973) concluded:

> The only formal means available to capture dependency between elements separated by arbitrarily many embeddings is by the introduction of nonterminal elements which serve to "keep track of" the dependency commitments and which are only *abstractly* related to the observed output elements.
>
> For this reason alone, we can know that S–R theories of language are inadequate for representing the complexities of natural language [p. 103].

Although problems, and criticisms, are increasing as attempts are made to extend S–R analyses to more complex verbal behaviors, the effort to account for language performance in S–R, behavioral terms persists. In his recent book *About Behaviorism* (1974), Skinner continues to view verbal behavior, in all its complexity, as resulting from the operation of basic operant-conditioning processes on overt verbal responses. The "verbal community," by differentially "reinforcing" acceptable and appropriate verbal responses, "shapes and maintains" verbal behavior. The criticisms with regard to the acquisition and application of the rules of syntax (especially transformation and recursive embedding) remain, for the most part, unanswered.

Information-Processing Approaches: Models of Semantic Memory

As in many other areas of psychological research, information-processing analyses have become increasingly popular and influential in the study of language performance. The information-processing approaches differ in a number of ways from the S–R, behavioral analysis. Generally, there is less concern with the temporal and spatial relationships among overt words and more interest in the cognitive relationships among meanings of words and sentences. Information-processing models tend to view language comprehension and generation in terms of the encoding, storage, and retrieval of semantic information. These models have focused on the structure of semantic memory and are thus concerned with the content of long-term memory. The construction of models of semantic memory has proceeded at a rapid pace since 1969.

Information-processing models are much more linguistically sophisticated than the S–R conditioning analyses because they show more appreciation of the syntactic complexities of language. In this respect these models tend to borrow rather heavily from the linguistic analyses discussed earlier in the chapter. Unlike the linguists, however, psychological information-processing models have focused primarily on the semantic aspects of language rather than on the grammatical aspects. The treatment of meaning in information-processing models places considerable emphasis on the "world knowledge" and environmental circumstances shared by language users. As a result of this concern for knowledge and contextual factors, there is much more concern in the psychological models with perception and memory as components of language performance.

The computer has played an important role in the development of information-processing models of all types (for example, memory and pattern-recognition models) and has certainly had considerable influence on the development of language models. In this section we will look at some of the most comprehensive information-processing models of language performance, the *Teachable Language Comprehender, TLC* (Quillian, 1968, 1969); the language components of J. R. Anderson and Bower's (1973) *Human Associative Memory,* HAM; and the *ELINOR* and *MEMOD* models (Norman, Rumelhart, & LNR Research Group, 1975; Rumelhart, Lindsay, & Norman, 1972). All of these models have been simulated, at least in part, by interactive computer programs that interpret, comprehend, verify, and retain linguistic information.

The Teachable Language Comprehender (TLC). Quillian's Teachable Language Comprehender is a model of language comprehension that emphasizes the role of semantics, particularly *semantic memory.* In this model language inputs are comprehended in terms of their relationship with the general knowledge that readers or hearers already have stored in their semantic memories. Thus, memory plays a central role in language performance. Quillian (1968) assumes that

> humans, in using language, draw upon and interact with the same memory in which their non-linguistic information is stored. Under this assumption semantic memory is simply general memory and hence must be flexible enough to hold anything that can be stated in language, sensed in perception, or otherwise known and remembered. In particular, this includes facts and assertions as well as just objects and properties.
>
> Further, under this assumption the semantic component becomes the primary factor in language rather than a "secondary" one subordinate to a separate syntactic component [p. 232].

Quillian's conceptualization characterizes the psychological approach; meaning is given precedence over structure. In addition, both the immediate perceptual and linguistic context and the memory of previous perceptual and linguistic inputs ("world knowledge") combine with current linguistic inputs to determine semantic interpretations. A schematic diagram representing these general characteristics of the TLC model is presented in Figure 10–7.

An important aspect of this model is that a language input—a sentence, for example—is assumed to occur in some context. In other words, the immediately preceding verbal and perceptual inputs form an intimate surround for any linguistic input. This assumption has important advantages for the interpretation of ambiguous sentences, such as

Visiting professors can be boring

and

They are kissing fishes.

There is no ambiguity if the first sentence is spoken by one student to another at a faculty/student tea, and the second sentence is clear if the speaker is seen pointing at an aquarium

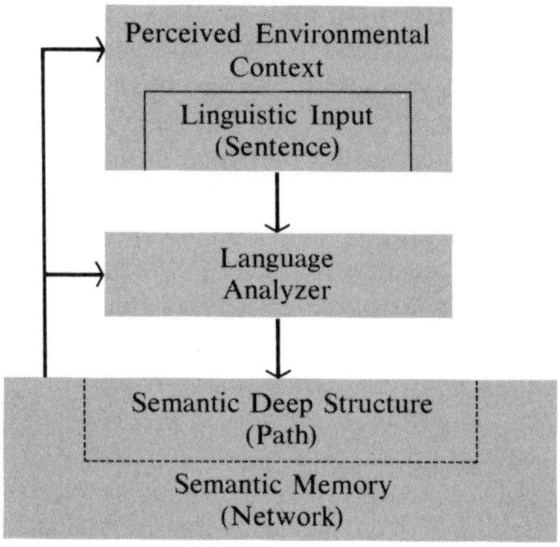

Figure 10–7. Quillian's TLC model for language comprehension.

full of fish. Recognition of the importance of the surrounding context clearly makes the TLC model more psychologically realistic than the primarily structural, linguistic models.

The *language analyzer* in the model serves much the same purpose as Chomsky's tranformational component (see Figure 10–4). Because surface sentences can take a number of forms and because words can be ordered in a variety of ways (for example, active versus passive constructions, embedded clauses, and so on) without changing the meaning of the sentence, some linguistic analysis must be applied to determine the deep structure of the sentence. However, unlike Chomsky's model, in which the deep structure of sentences is determined essentially without reference to meaning, Quillian's linguistic processor employs information from semantic memory. The listener's "world knowledge," knowledge of syntax and the lexicon, and expectations based on the linguistic and perceptural context in which the sentence is presented all combine to determine the *semantic deep structure* of the sentence.

It is important to note the early involvement of the listener's semantic memory in the language-comprehension process. Comprehension of a sentence is represented in TLC by a change (or activation) in the existing structure of semantic memory; that is, new concepts are added to memory or new relationships are established between existing concepts. All language inputs are comprehended in terms of their relationship to the existing semantic memory. An understanding of the structure of semantic memory is essential, then, if we are to understand language comprehension.

Semantic memory is conceptualized in TLC as an interconnected network of concepts related by labeled associations. Concepts form the *nodes* of the network, and the nodes are interconnected by *pointers*. The concept nodes are the basic units of memory in TLC. They represent the semantic conceptualizations of objects, events, ideas, assertions, facts, and so on. These units can be represented by single words or morphemes, but they can also be more complex, requiring something equivalent to whole sentences or even longer texts to represent them. The nodes are interconnected by two classes of pointers. *Superset pointers* relate subordinate concepts to their superordinate categories (for example, *dog* → *mammal, canary* → *bird*); *property pointers* relate concept nodes to their associated properties (such as color, location, sex, and so forth).

A representative segment of the memory structure of TLC is presented in Figure 10–8. Notice that the node *canary* is connected by a superset pointer to the *bird* node, which in turn is connected by a superset pointer to the *animal* node. Each node also has pointers to a list of properties. *Animal,* for example, has the properties *can move around, can eat, can breathe,* and *has skin.* Because *bird* is a subordinate of *animal,* these same properties are also associated with *bird,* but only indirectly. *Bird* does have properties that are not shared by all *animals: has wings, can fly,* and *has feathers.* These properties are connected directly to the *bird* node. In a similar fashion, *canary* is indirectly connected to all of the properties associated with *bird* and *animal* and, in addition, has direct connections to properties of its own: *is yellow* and *can sing.*

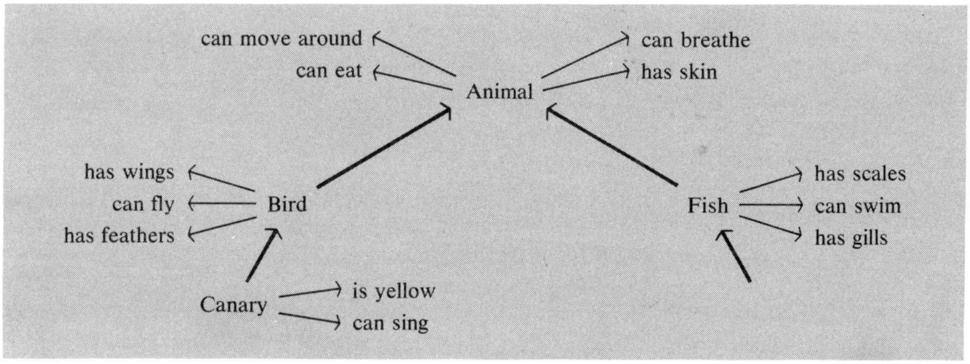

Figure 10–8. Graphic representation of a segment of semantic memory in TLC. (Adapted from "Retrieval Time from Semantic Memory," by A. M. Collins and M. R. Quillian, *Journal of Verbal Learning and Verbal Behavior,* 1969, *8,* 240–247. Reprinted by permission of Academic Press, Inc.)

The segment of the memory structure presented also reveals that *bird* and *fish* are related, but in a more remote way than *bird* and *canary.* Both *bird* and *fish* have connections through superset pointers to *animal* and thus to the property *has skin.* Because both are subordinates of *animal,* however, there is no connection between their specific properties: *birds can fly,* but *fish can swim.* Thus, the hierarchical structure of memory in TLC prevents the misassignment of subordinate-concept properties to superordinate concepts; the superset pointers are one-way.

Semantic memory in TLC, then, is conceived of as a gigantic network interconnecting many, many concept nodes by superset and property pointers. The use of a hierarchical structure wherein properties of superordinate concepts are indirectly associated with subordinate concepts, and thus need not be repeated as properties of the subordinate concept, provides TLC with a highly efficient memory system.

In the TLC model, comprehension of a sentence is represented as a change in the memory structure, or as an activation of a *path* connecting the nodes referred to by the input. For example, the sentence

John's pet is a cute canary named Oliver

could be analyzed and entered into TLC's semantic-memory structure. Comprehension of this sentence would be represented by an appendage to the previously existing memory. Thus, if the semantic memory were as indicated in the top part of Figure 10–9, comprehension of the new language input might be represented by the bottom part of the figure.

This change in the memory structure illustrates several aspects of TLC. First, new inputs are incorporated into the semantic-memory structure by being related to the existing

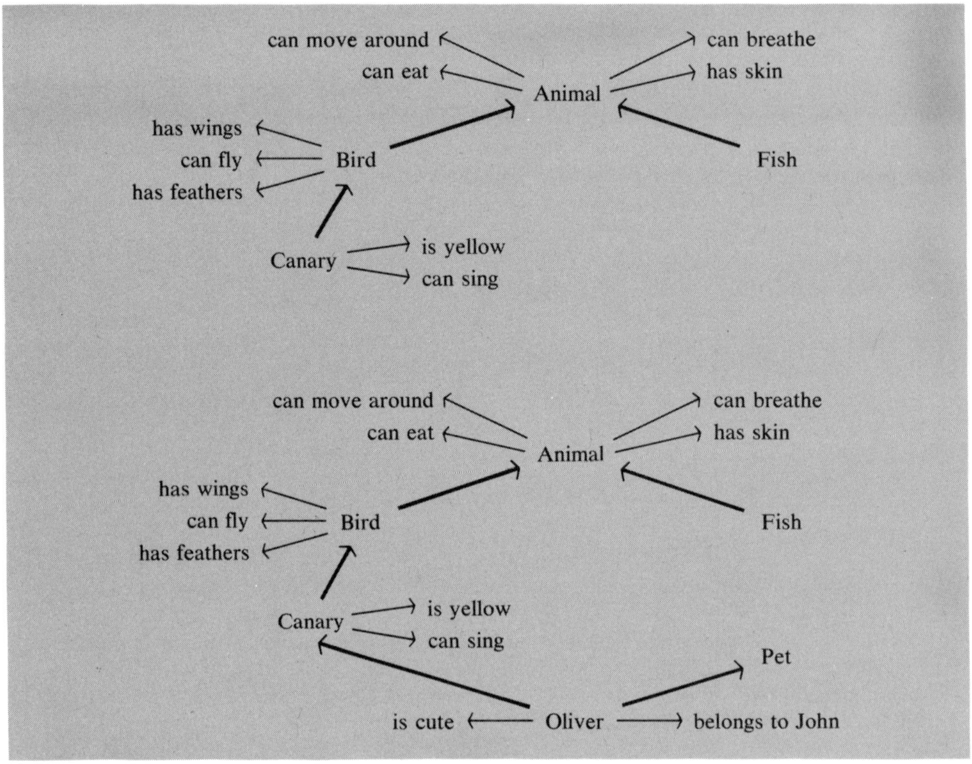

Figure 10–9. Comprehension in TLC of "John's pet is a cute canary named Oliver."

structure. The example sentence added the superset pointer connecting a new node, *Oliver,* to *canary.* Also, a new path was produced:

$$pet \leftarrow Oliver \rightarrow canary \rightarrow bird \rightarrow animal.$$

To determine whether TLC comprehended the sentence, questions might be asked about the new input. For example, questions such as

Can Oliver sing?

should be comprehended and answered. TLC could comprehend this question because there is now a path linking *Oliver* to the property *can sing:*

$$Oliver \rightarrow canary \rightarrow can\ sing.$$

In this case the TLC answer would be in the affirmative. The more complicated question

Does Oliver have skin?

would result in a more expansive *intersection search* extending outward simultaneously (that is, in a parallel search) from the nodes *Oliver* and *has skin.* Because there is a path

Oliver → *canary* → *bird* → *animal* → *has skin*

in TLC's semantic memory that would allow such a relation between *Oliver* and *has skin,* the question would be comprehended and answered in the affirmative.

The validity of the TLC model of language comprehension has been tested directly in a number of psychological experiments. Testing the TLC conceptualization of how verbal inputs are comprehended was approached in much the same way that a teacher might test your comprehension of a set of verbal materials. To determine how well you have understood the material presented in a textbook, for example, your teacher might give you a true/false test; statements about the material in the text are presented, and you must decide whether each is true or false. Your understanding of the material is indicated (no matter how unfairly) by the number of statements that you are able to answer correctly. According to the TLC model, your ability to understand and correctly respond to the statements depends upon whether you have established the appropriate paths, or relationships, in your semantic memory.

If the structure of semantic memory is like the network presented in Figure 10–8, the TLC model would predict that the statement

A canary is a bird

would initiate an intersection search in semantic memory; that is, the statement refers to two existing memory nodes (*canary* and *bird*), and the model postulates that comprehension of the statement involves an outward tracing of all connections from each of those two nodes. If the nodes are found to be interconnected—that is, if any of the paths being traced from each node intersect at some point—then there is a relationship between those two concepts in semantic memory. In the example statement *bird* is related to *canary* by a superset pointer, so the statement would be comprehended and judged to be true. However, because of the direction of the superset relation, *canary* → *bird,* the reverse statement,

All birds are canaries,

would not be accepted as true.

By making some assumptions about the nature of the postulated intersection search, Collins and Quillian (1969) were able to make specific predictions about the speed with which a human subject should be able to comprehend and confirm or deny statements. Basically, they assumed that it takes time to trace a connection from one concept node to another (superset pointer) or to one of its properties (property pointer). Further, they assumed that all pointers from each node are searched in parallel (at the same time). Thus, the more pointers that have to be searched before an intersection is found relating the concept nodes referred to in a statement, the longer it should take to comprehend and confirm or deny the statement.

The statement

A canary is a bird

requires that only one connection be traced, the superset pointer *canary* → *bird* (see Figure 10–8). Thus, a "true" judgment should be made rather quickly—that is, with a short reaction time, or *verification latency.* The statement

A canary has skin

should take more time because at least three pointers must be traced before an intersection will be found:

canary → *bird* → *animal* → *has skin.*

Collins and Quillian presented a number of statements similar to our examples to subjects and recorded the time required to confirm or deny each statement. The statements selected required zero connections for comprehension (for example, "A canary is a canary"), one connection ("A canary is a bird" or "A canary can sing"), or two connections ("A canary is an animal" or "A canary can fly"). Some of the results from this experiment are presented in Figure 10–10.

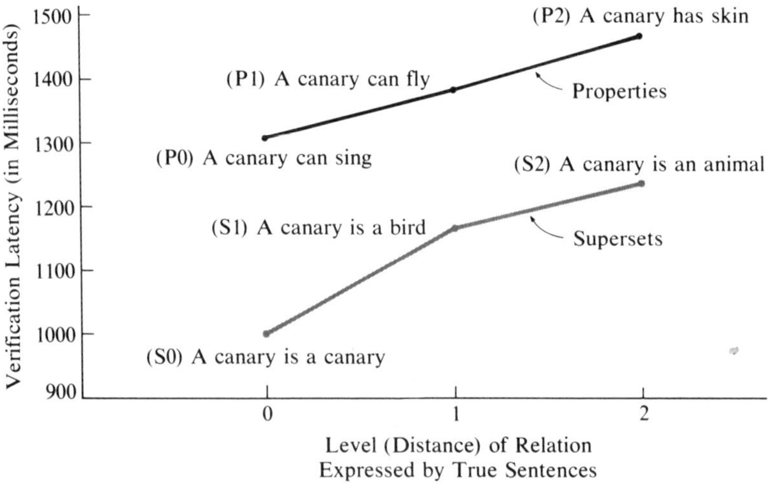

Figure 10–10. Verification latencies for three levels of true statements. (From "Retrieval Time from Semantic Memory," by A. M. Collins and M. R. Quillian, *Journal of Verbal Learning and Verbal Behavior,* 1969, *8,* 240–247. Reprinted by permission of Academic Press, Inc.)

The predictions based on the TLC model were essentially confirmed. Notice that correct "true" judgments took longer (had longer verification latencies) as the number of connecting links (pointers) was extended from zero to one to two. Interestingly, superset pointers seemed to be traced more rapidly than property pointers. For example, verification latencies for statements such as

A canary is a bird (one superset pointer)

were generally about a tenth of a second shorter than those for statements such as

A canary can sing (one property pointer).

These data generally support the TLC model. Findings on correct false statements, such as

A canary is a fish,

may also be consistent with the model. The intersection-search strategy could be used in several ways to negate a false statement. The most direct approach might be to assume that searches proceed along property and superset pointers until a contradicting path is found. For example,

A canary has scales

might be denied because an intersection search extending outward from *canary* would produce

canary → *bird* → *has feathers*.

At the same time, a search from the other direction (from *scales*) would reveal

has scales ← *fish*.

Because feathers are not scales and because fish are not birds, and therefore canaries are not fish, canaries do not have scales. In this way the hierarchical, superset relations among concepts in semantic memory are used inferentially to determine whether acceptable relationships between concepts and their properties are implied by a statement.

Although this intersection-search strategy might work for statements involving concepts that are related in semantic memory, it would not work for statements about totally disjoint concepts—for example,

A canary is a tool.

An intersection search from either node, *canary* or *tool,* would traverse many connections before coming to a contradicting path between the two nodes. It seems unlikely that the intersection search would have to proceed to this point before a judgment about the statement could be made. A more attractive assumption is that some time or effort criterion is set, so that after some limited set of connections is searched and no affirming or denying intersections are found, a "false" judgment is made. One difficulty with this analysis, however, is that such statements relating totally disjoint concepts are typically rejected quite rapidly by subjects.

These and other complications for the TLC model have been discussed at some length by Collins and Quillian (for example, 1972) and others (for example, Collins & Loftus, 1975), and the feasibility of several approaches to dealing with them has been explored. Though many problems remain to be resolved, the TLC model does appear to be a worthwhile beginning approach in our understanding of human language performance. Most important is the recognition given by this conceptualization to the role of the existing content and structure of semantic memory in the comprehension of language inputs. The greater emphasis on semantics (rather than syntax) and the inclusion of "world knowledge" in the semantic base of language would seem to make TLC at least a workable model of human language performance. Tests, modifications, and extensions of the model continue. Although it has undergone changes (see, for example, C. Conrad, 1972), it certainly remains an important landmark in the evolution of psychological conceptualizations of language comprehension.

Human Associative Memory. The information-processing model of language performance considered in this section has been extracted from a more comprehensive model of human verbal learning and memory. Only a brief sketch of Anderson and Bower's

(1973) model Human Associative Memory can be presented here, and the reader is encouraged to refer to the original text for a more detailed presentation.

There are many similarities between HAM and the TLC model. In general, the meaning component is given the central role in language performance. Further, the meaning component is derived from the language user's total world knowledge, both linguistic and perceptual. As a result, memory plays an important part in language comprehension. A schematic summary of the information processes involved in the encoding, storage, and retrieval of linguistic information in HAM is presented in Figure 10–11.

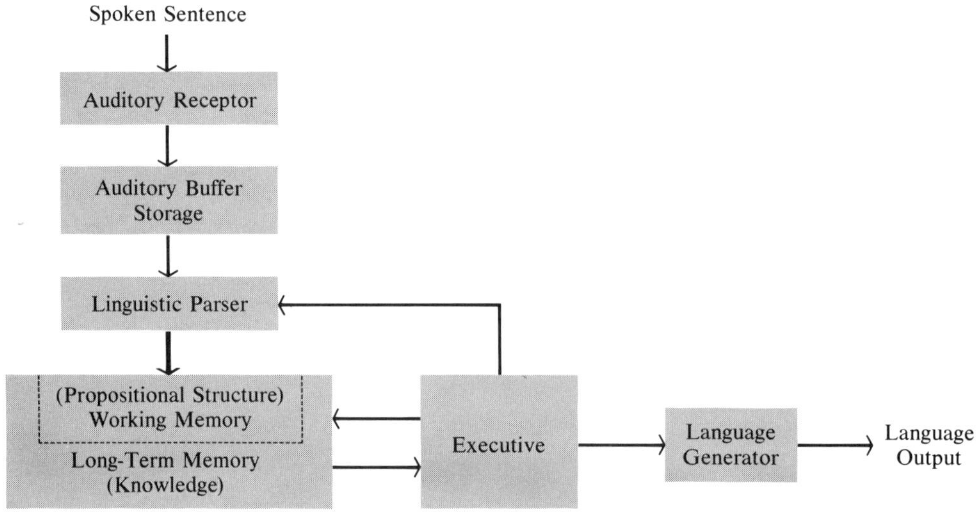

Figure 10–11. Schematic representation of some of the information processes postulated for HAM. (Adapted from *Human Associative Memory,* by J. R. Anderson and G. H. Bower. Copyright 1973 by Hemisphere Publishing Corporation. Reprinted by permission.)

The model recognizes several psychologically relevant aspects of language performance. All inputs must first be encoded by a perceptual/sensory receptor system and stored briefly before being further processed. Because linguistic inputs are sequential (especially when presented as spoken sentences), many elements of the input must be held in storage before being processed and interpreted.

The *linguistic parser,* as in the previously discussed models, serves to translate surface sentences into an appropriate deep structure. These semantic deep structures can be added to memory as new concepts or relations, or, if the input is a query, they can serve to initiate a search for relevant information already stored in memory. In either event, the particular parse, or interpretation, produced by the linguistic parser will be determined to some extent by the nature of the information already in memory.

The *executive* "oversees" the information-processing sequence and, making use of information in memory, guides the operation of the linguistic parser. Thus, as in the TLC model, the language user's memory and "world knowledge" enter into the initial linguistic parsing of sentences. This view can be contrasted with Chomsky's transformational grammar in that his (linguistic) deep structure is derived separately, with no input from the semantic level of the system. The executive in HAM also monitors memory to direct the *language generator,* or output component, of the model.

Many aspects of the HAM model are not yet fully developed, especially some aspects of the executive and its function and the operations involved in the language generator. Anderson and Bower acknowledge these and other incomplete and unspecified elements of the model but choose for the present to concentrate on other components of language and memory processes. In particular, they focus upon a representation of the structure of memory, or knowledge.

In general, HAM's memory, or knowledge, can be represented as a binary treelike structure composed of interconnected concept or idea nodes. The nodes are related by semantically determined associations. In this respect HAM is very similar to TLC, but the particular characteristics of the nodes, and their relationships to one another, are somewhat different.

In HAM a sentence (or any other perceptual input) is composed of one or more *propositions*. These propositions can be represented by binary trees composed of concepts associated by any of a large number of possible semantic relations. HAM uses a much greater variety of associations, or connectors, between concepts than does TLC. Anderson and Bower refer to the possibility of a "just finite" number of semantic relations.

Each propositional tree is composed of a *context branch* and a *fact branch*. An example binary tree for a simple, one-proposition sentence is presented in Figure 10–12. The context branch of the tree indicates where and when the event occurred, or under what circumstances the asserted *fact* is true. In the example sentence the context (b) is specified as a location (d) and a time (e). The context delimits the fact (c). The fact is composed of a *subject* (f) and some *predication* (g), a statement or assertion about the subject. In the example sentence it is predicated of the subject (f) that it bears a relation (h) to an object (i); that is, the proposition (a) is that, at a park somewhere, at some time in the past, it is true that a hippie touched a debutante. The propositional-tree structure represents the input to HAM's memory that would result from hearing or reading the example sentence. Anderson and Bower postulate that essentially this same structure could represent the input to memory that would result from actually witnessing the event perceptually.

Depending upon the nature of the fact, the context branch of a proposition may vary. For example, propositions such as

Scott is a boy

are not restricted to any particular context; they are true regardless of time or place. Other propositions involve facts that need only be constrained by time, such as

Sean was small when he was a baby.

Other facts are constrained by location but not time:

It is humid at the equator.

The fact component of a proposition is represented as a *subject/predicate relation;* that is, a fact is a predication (assertion) that some subject has some property. Simple facts, such as those indicated by the sentences

Caesar is dead

and

Scott is thin,

can be represented in HAM by the subject/predicate binary trees shown in Figure 10–13. In each case the "idea" of the fact is the combined product of the subject and its predicate. Other, more complex facts can be constructed by predicating something of a simple fact. The sentence

It is fortunate that Caesar is dead

produces the two-level tree shown in Figure 10–14. Thus, *fortunate* is predicated as a property of the fact that *Caesar is dead.*

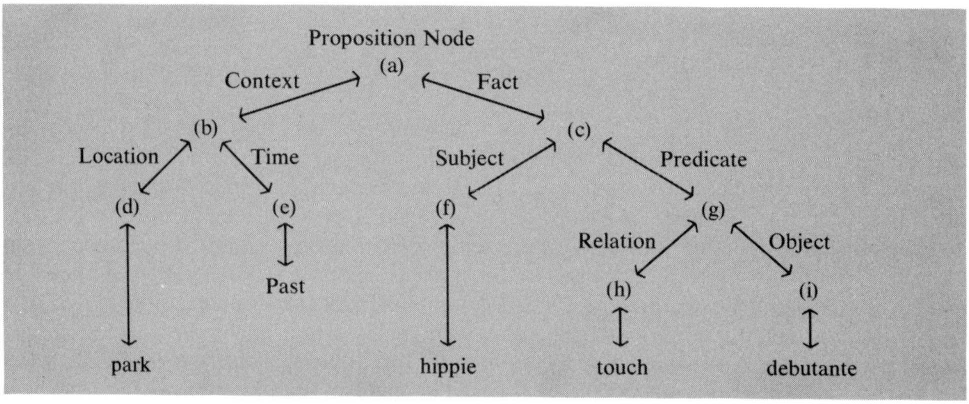

Figure 10–12. HAM's propositional representation of "In a park a hippie touched a debutante." (From *Human Associative Memory,* by J. R. Anderson and G. H. Bower. Copyright 1973 by Hemisphere Publishing Corporation. Reprinted by permission.)

Figure 10–13. Subject-predicate trees in HAM.

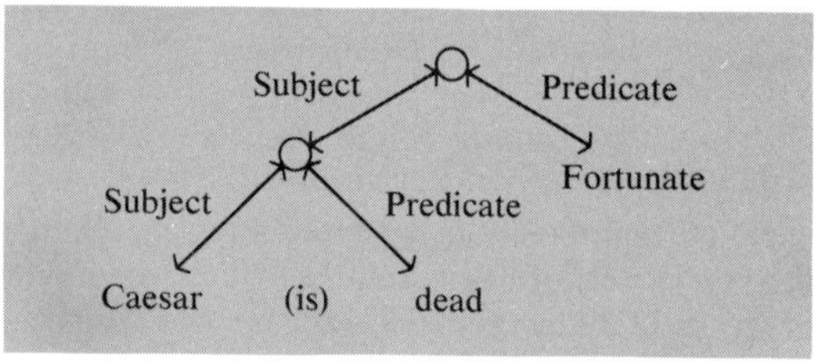

Figure 10–14. Two-level tree from HAM.

More complex predicate forms can be represented in HAM. Facts, in addition to simply predicating some property of a subject (or another fact), can assert that the subject bears some *relation* to some object. The statement

Scott hit Sean

would be represented by the propositional structure in Figure 10–15. As with the simpler property predicate, additional predicates can be assigned to a relation. The sentence

Scott cruelly hit Sean

produces the structure shown in Figure 10–16. Note that this structure makes it clear that it was the relation to Sean (the hitting) that was cruel. Scott may or may not be a cruel person; the proposition is that Scott's action was a cruel one.

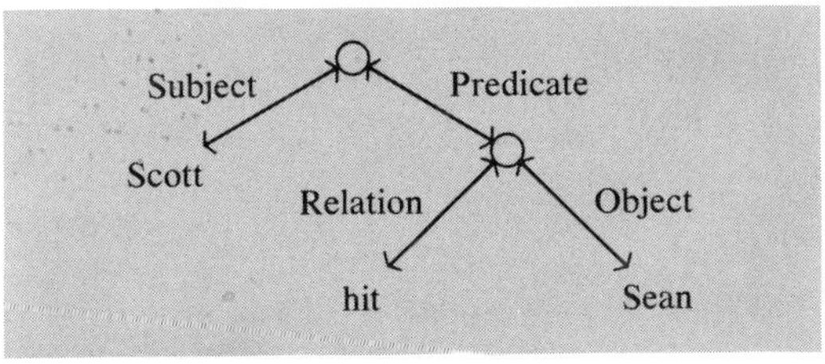

Figure 10–15. Another tree structure from HAM.

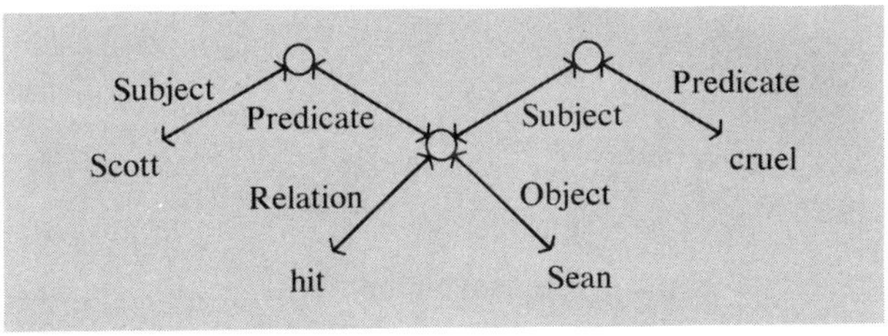

Figure 10–16. Another tree structure from HAM.

These illustrations touch upon only a few of the rules, or "deep grammar," that organize linguistic inputs to HAM's memory. The figures do, however, illustrate several contrasts with the TLC model. First, the principal connectors relating individual ideas, or concept nodes, in HAM's memory are subject/predicate relationships. HAM's propositional structure can be compared to the hierarchical structures postulated for TLC by comparing their respective representations of the assertion

A canary is a yellow bird that sings.

Notice in Figure 10–17 that in TLC *is yellow* and *can sing* are represented as conceptual "packages" that are connected directly by unlabeled property pointers to *canary.* The model relates *canary* to the superordinate category *bird* by means of the superset pointer.

The representation in HAM appears to indicate a somewhat less direct relationship among the concepts. The relationship between *canary* and the properties *yellow* and *sing* is represented as a proposition. Because the asserted relation is universally true, there is no context branch indicated. Thus, the proposition is represented as a subject/predicate relation, or in HAM's terminology, a fact. The fact is composed of two predicates relating the subject (*canary*) separately to two general concepts (*singing* and *yellowness*). These

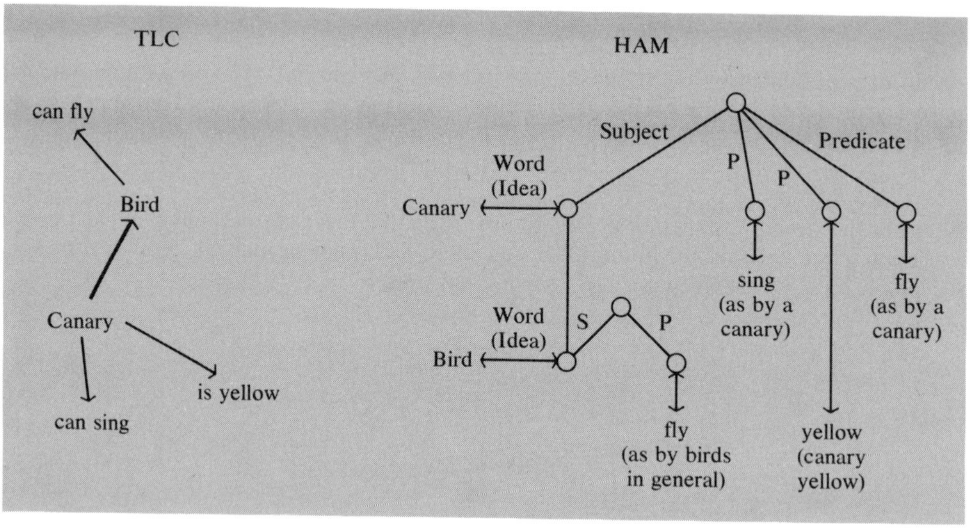

Figure 10–17. Graphic representation of "A canary is a yellow bird that sings" in TLC and HAM.

generic concept nodes can be refined to more specific nodes, *sing* (as by a canary) and *yellow* (canary yellow). The terminal points on the predicate branches are highly specific. The concept *sing* (as by a canary) is different from the *sing* concept that might be employed to represent

Frank Sinatra can sing.

There is a similar refinement of concepts and connections on the *subject* side of the fact relation. There is a generalized concept that can be thought of as "something" that has the properties, via the predicates, of being (canary) yellow and singing. For all instances of this concept, the verbal name is *canary.* Further, these instances ("canaries") are a subset of the concept *bird.*

The memory structure of HAM, then, is in many ways more specific than that of TLC. Although more types of relations and connections among concepts are allowed, these are all represented within the fairly limited format of the propositional tree. Concepts themselves are more precisely defined (*sing,* as by a canary), and the relationship between concepts and their verbal names is explicitly formalized as a word associative link.

There are a number of distinctions between HAM and the TLC model that are not exhibited by Figure 10–17. In the hierarchical semantic-memory structure postulated for TLC, properties of a concept that are also shared by a superordinate concept are directly connected only to the superordinate concept. Thus, the fact that canaries can fly is represented by having the property *can fly* connected directly to the concept *bird* and only indirectly to *canary* via the superset pointer to *bird.* In HAM the assertion that canaries can fly would be represented as a direct subject/predicate relation between *canary* and *fly.* HAM might have a subject/predicate relation between *bird* and *fly* in memory as well.

Although the representation in TLC is more efficient in that it uses less "storage space" than the double representation required in HAM, Anderson and Bower argue that HAM's approach is closer to that employed by the human memory system. They postulate that storage space is abundant and cheap in the human memory system, while inference of the type required to get from *canary* to *bird* and then to the property (of canaries) *can fly,* as required by the TLC model, is difficult and expensive. Inference, they argue, is used only when the required information or relation has never been presented directly with the subordinate concept. A query such as

Does a canary have a liver?

may require inference: a canary is a bird; birds have livers (especially chickens); therefore, canaries must also have livers. Most of the time, however, properties are represented by direct subject/predicate relations between the specific concept and the property.

The verification-latency experiments (Collins & Quillian, 1969) reviewed in our discussion of the TLC model seemed to provide support for the hierarchical-structure/intersection-search model of semantic memory. However, other findings have tended to cast some doubt on the generality of the results and on the TLC interpretation. Such research has indicated that the remoteness of the association, or the frequency of joint occurrences in natural language of the two words (concepts) related in a statement, may account for the time required to verify the statement (C. Conrad, 1972). For example, the word *canary* is more often associated in everyday language with the word *sing* than with the word *skin.* Thus, the finding that the statement

A canary can sing

is verified faster than

A canary has skin

may simply reflect the greater associative frequency of *canary/sing* than *canary/skin.* In any case, the verification-latency findings may not require a hierarchical-search explanation.

In place of the intersection-search procedure postulated for TLC, HAM employs a *match process.* This process is actually a set of interrelated procedures, but it can be represented reasonably well as follows. When a statement or query is presented to HAM, it is first parsed, or translated, into a propositional format. This proposition is held in working memory and compared to any propositional structures already in memory that relate the concepts referred to by the statement or query. The match process matches the propositional structure representing the statement or query with the best-fitting (matching) structure already in memory.

A brief example will illustrate some of the more important aspects of this process. Consider a query to HAM such as

What did the hippie do in the park?

This query would be parsed to produce the proposition indicated in the first part of Figure 10–18. A search would ensue for all facts stored in HAM that involve "the hippie" in the context of "the park" at any time in the past. Recall from Figure 10–12 that HAM's memory contains the proposition represented by the second part of Figure 10–18. Assuming there were no other "hippie in the park" propositions in memory, this would be the best fit for the query. Thus, HAM would formulate a reply by filling in the blank indicated by

What did the hippie do?

in the query with the indicated relation in the retrieved proposition. HAM would reply

The hippie touched a debutante.

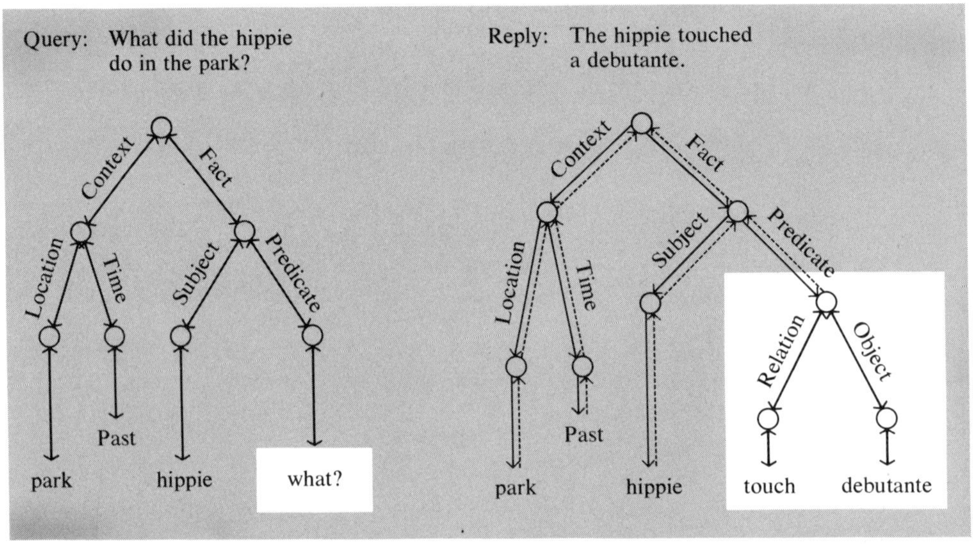

Figure 10–18. Query to HAM and the resulting match to memory enabling a reply.

A great many aspects of the HAM model have been omitted from the preceding discussion. The primary focus here has been on the representation of knowledge in memory, but Anderson and Bower (1973) devote chapters to the description of many other aspects of HAM. The encoding of linguistic and perceptual information and the processes employed by the linguistic parser to transform sentence inputs into the propositional structures suitable for HAM's memory are covered in considerable detail.

As HAM's authors themselves conclude, however, there is still much work to be done. In particular, they cite the need to expand the power of the linguistic parser. At the same time, they hope to specify and formalize further the procedures used by the parser to translate English sentences into HAM-type propositional structures. Only some tentative aspects of the processes that might be employed by the perceptual parser have been developed, and the output component of HAM, the language generator, is not developed as yet.

An Extension of the HAM Model (ACT). More recently, Anderson (1976) has extended and modified the HAM model to produce a model that he calls *ACT*. Very briefly, among the more important changes introduced in the newer model is a distinction in the representation of *declarative knowledge* (essentially facts) and *procedural knowledge* (how to perform certain acts).

Declarative knowledge is represented by propositional structures that are very similar to those used in HAM. Unlike the HAM structure, however, the context branch of the proposition has been dropped, so that all information is represented in the basic subject/predicate format. Further, predicate links to the subject can be differentiated in terms of their strength. The principal feature that distinguishes procedural knowledge from declarative knowledge is that procedural knowledge is not directly reportable. The effort here is to represent the automatic, unconscious responses that humans make, as in well-practiced motor skills (stopping at a red light, hitting a tennis ball, and so on) or cognitive problem-solving skills (adding two numbers together, making a move in chess, and so on). Procedural information is represented by what is termed *production systems*. When the conditions of one of these production systems are met, an action (procedure) is carried out. For example, when the conditions "approach intersection, see red light" occur, the procedure for bringing the car to a stop would be activated. Queries might be made of the system that require reports of factual (declarative) information based on procedural acts, such as Where is the car now? or How did you stop the car? However, the processes involved in answering these queries are different from the processes employed to carry out the acts.

There are other aspects of the ACT model and its relation to the other models discussed here that are important. The match process of HAM, for example, has been replaced by a spreading activation/intersection-search process that is more similar to that used by Quillian's TLC. Because of the newness of the ACT model, it has not yet undergone sufficient scrutiny and analysis by the scientific community to identify its lasting contributions to the understanding of human language-comprehension and memory processes. It is clear, however, that work begun in the context of the HAM model will form an important foundation for future research and theoretical analysis.

ELINOR and MEMOD. Rumelhart and his colleagues (1972; see also Lindsay & Norman, 1972) have developed an information-processing model of language comprehension and memory that they have named ELINOR (or LNR, for *L*indsay, *N*orman, and *R*umelhart). This model has much in common with Quillian's TLC and Anderson and Bower's HAM, especially in the emphasis placed upon semantics and thus memory. ELINOR makes the essential distinction between the surface structure of language, the actual written or spoken sentences, and what is termed the *meaning structure*. Meaning structure is very similar to the semantic deep structure referred to by Quillian and is intimately related to the language user's semantic memory.

Perhaps the major distinction between ELINOR and the TLC model is in the representation of knowledge in memory. Quillian chose to represent semantic memory as a network of concepts, or nodes, interconnected by superset pointers and elaborated by property pointers. ELINOR also has concept or idea nodes but has, in addition, *relation nodes*. The relation nodes can be thought of as representations of verbs (such as *fall, put, go*) and of comparative adjectives (such as *bigger, largest, small*). Unlike concepts, relations are by their nature incomplete. The relation *put* requires a subject, an object, and a location; something must be put somewhere and usually by someone. The relation *larger* requires a subject and an object; what is larger than what?

The distinction between concepts and relations can be clarified by an example. A graphic representation of a concept, *tart,* and a relation, *photograph,* is presented in Figure 10–19. Notice that the concept *tart* is composed of a list of properties (*small, baked, jelly-filled* or *fruit-filled*); a classification (is a member of the class *pastry*); and some specific examples (*cherry tart*). The concept *tart,* then, is defined in terms of other concepts. These concepts must, in turn, be defined in terms of still other concepts, and so on. In short, ELINOR defines concepts in the same way that a dictionary defines concepts.[2]

The graph for the relation, *photograph,* presents a somewhat different picture. As indicated, a relation is incomplete. In this example the missing elements are the implied object, instrument, location, and time. These missing parts (either concepts or other relations) are indicated by labeled pointers. The types of pointers are very similar to the semantic cases discussed earlier in this chapter in the context of case grammars.

[2]*Webster's New World Dictionary* provides the following definition cycle: tart. n., a small shell of *pastry* filled with jam, jelly, etc.; pastry. n., flour, dough, or paste made with shortening and used for the *crust* of pies, tarts, etc.; crust. n., pastry shell of a pie, tart, etc.

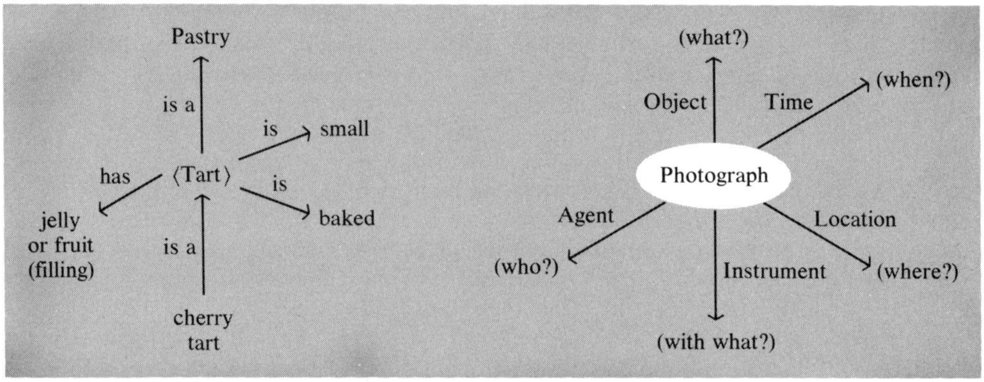

Figure 10–19. Graphic representation of a concept (*tart*) and a relation (*photograph*) in the ELINOR model. (Adapted from *Human Information Processing: An Introduction to Psychology,* by P. H. Lindsay and D. A. Norman. Copyright 1972 by Academic Press, Inc. Used by permission.)

Concepts and relations are assumed to be interrelated in a network similar to that postulated for TLC. In ELINOR, however, the pointers are somewhat more differentiated. There are many types of pointers in ELINOR's memory structure, but the most frequently used pointers are of three types. *Isa pointers,* like TLC's superset pointers, connect concepts with their associated superordinate classes. The reverse of the isa pointer indicates the subordinate concept. Thus, although *tart* is related to *pastry* by an outgoing *isa* pointer, it is connected to *cherry tart* by an incoming *isa* pointer. *Has and is pointers* connect concepts to their properties, as do property pointers in the TLC model. The *has* pointers serve to indicate object properties (a tart *has* jelly), while *is* pointers indicate quality properties (a tart *is* small).

Concepts and relations combine to represent more complex *events* in the memory structure, as is illustrated by the representation of the event indicated by the sentence

Yesterday, at the beach with my new camera, I
photographed the house on Ninth Street.

By combining the relation, *photograph,* with the concepts specified in the sentence, a *scenario,* or event, can be formed. Such a scenario can be represented by a graph, as illustrated in Figure 10–20.

Several events can be combined in ELINOR's memory structure to represent a more complex *episode.* An episode is a sequence of related events and can be characterized as in Figure 10–21.

For comprehension, statement verification, and question answering, ELINOR employs an intersection-search strategy like that used by TLC. To verify the statement

A canary can fly,

ELINOR would search outward along the various pointers extending from the concepts *canary* and *fly.* If an intersection is reached, the statement will be comprehended and, in this case, confirmed. The time needed to confirm or deny the statement would depend upon the number of pointers that have to be traversed before a path relating *canary* and *fly* is found. Because the same intersection-search technique for comprehension and verifica-

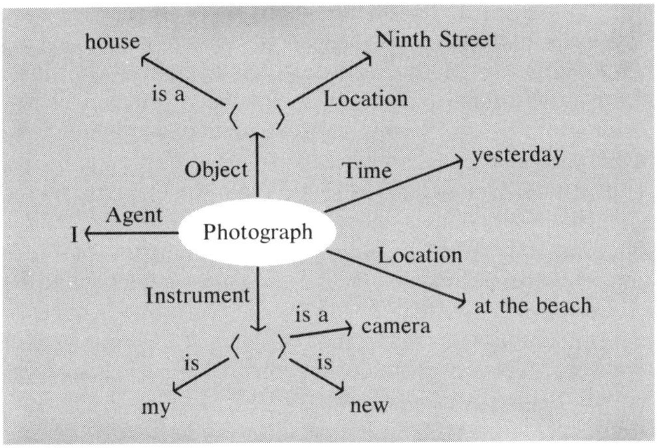

Figure 10–20. Representation of an event in the ELINOR model. (Adapted from *Human Information Processing: An Introduction to Psychology,* by P. H. Lindsay and D. A. Norman. Copyright 1972 by Academic Press, Inc. Used by permission.)

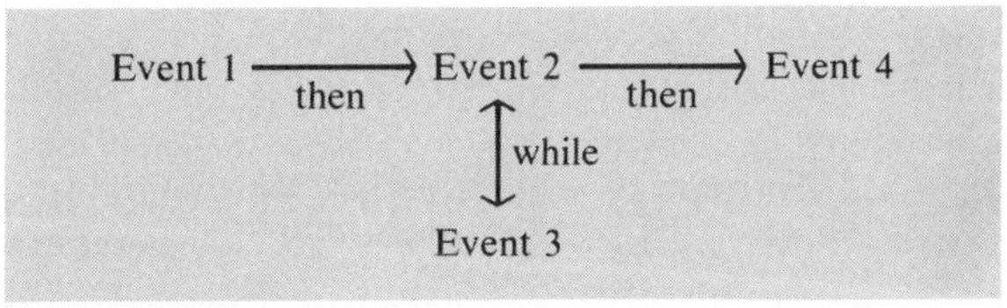

Figure 10–21.

tion is employed, ELINOR finds some comfort in the Collins and Quillian data presented earlier.

In an attempt to deal with some of the unresolved problems with the intersection-search concept, a *multistage search* has been postulated for ELINOR. To deal with false statements that specify some relationship between remote concepts, such as

All canaries are applesauce,

Lindsay and Norman (1972) propose that a preliminary "plausibility" test is applied before a more extensive search is undertaken. This is like the question of whether or not to search, as discussed in the previous chapter. For example, "What did Jimmy Carter eat for breakfast three days ago?" is first given a plausibility test. The above statement should be rejected rather quickly because a preliminary test (perhaps in the form of a quick scan of the memory network) would indicate that there is very little likelihood of an intersection between these two concepts in memory.

The ELINOR model is not complete, and not all of the aspects of the model that have been developed were presented here. A number of generative rules and procedures have been proposed that would enable ELINOR to generalize and divide existing concepts in the memory structure to form new and more precise concepts. ELINOR is, however, an important advance in the psychological analysis of language.

Another model based on the ELINOR model has been presented in *Explorations in Cognition* (1975), by Norman and his colleagues at the University of California, San Diego. This model, MEMOD (for Memory Model), has apparently subsumed ELINOR, but many of the basic features of the older model have been retained. Thus, ELINOR, like Quillian's TLC, represents a significant landmark in the continuing effort to achieve a comprehensive psychological account of human language and memory performance.

MEMOD, like ELINOR, maintains a distinction between concepts (essentially nouns) and events (verbs). The distinction is, however, more quantitative than qualitative. Both nouns and verbs are conceived of as *predicates,* general functions specifying relationships among sets of simpler concepts (nodes). Nouns, and most adjectives, differ from verbs by generally having fewer *arguments*; that is, fewer types of related concepts are allowed (or required) for the specification of a noun predicate than for a verb predicate. A predicate (either a noun or a verb) that has all of its arguments (all designated concepts and their relationships) specified defines a *proposition*.

As an illustration of how MEMOD represents events in memory, consider the sentence used in the discussion of HAM (see Figure 10–12):

In a park a hippie touched a debutante.

The central theme of this sentence (the event referred to) is indicated by the verb *touch. Touch* can be represented as a predicate requiring several arguments. Among the arguments might be an *agent,* some animate object that does the touching; a *recipient,* an object that is touched; *time,* when the touching occurred; and perhaps other arguments (for example, some indication of how long the touching lasted, where it took place, or what part of the agent did the touching of what part of the recipient). The relationship of these concepts forms the basic proposition expressed by the sentence, which is represented graphically in Figure 10–22.

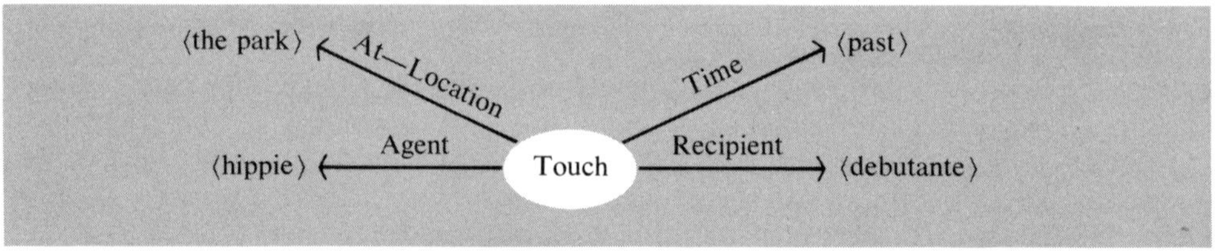

Figure 10–22. Representation of the event "In a park the hippie touched a debutante" in the MEMOD model.

The graph shows an *event node* (labeled *touch*) linked by labeled *relations* (time, agent, recipient) to *concept nodes* (*past, hippie, debutante*) to form a proposition.[3] This representation is generally similar to that employed by the HAM model; both models rely on propositions formed by labeling relationships among concept nodes as the basic *memory units*. In both models semantic memory (knowledge) is a complex network of interrelated concepts.

A principal difference between the HAM and MEMOD models is the relative emphasis on the verb, or action, component of the proposition. Verbs are more central to the

[3] As in TLC and HAM, the concept or event nodes are abstract and must be related to words or descriptions that are stored separately in the vocabulary (or dictionary) portion of the system. The nodes are labeled directly in the graph to simplify the presentation.

MEMOD representation. As a further elaboration in the MEMOD model, verb predicates can be reduced to a limited set of *primitive semantic predicates*. The meaning of any verb can be represented in terms of primitive predicates such as:

Stative, states of the world, such as location or possession.
Change, as from one state to another.
Causative, as when a change is caused by some agent.
Actionals, reflecting how an action occurred, or the manner of performing the action.

A possible analysis into semantic primitives for the event of the hippie's touching a debutante is presented in Figure 10–23.

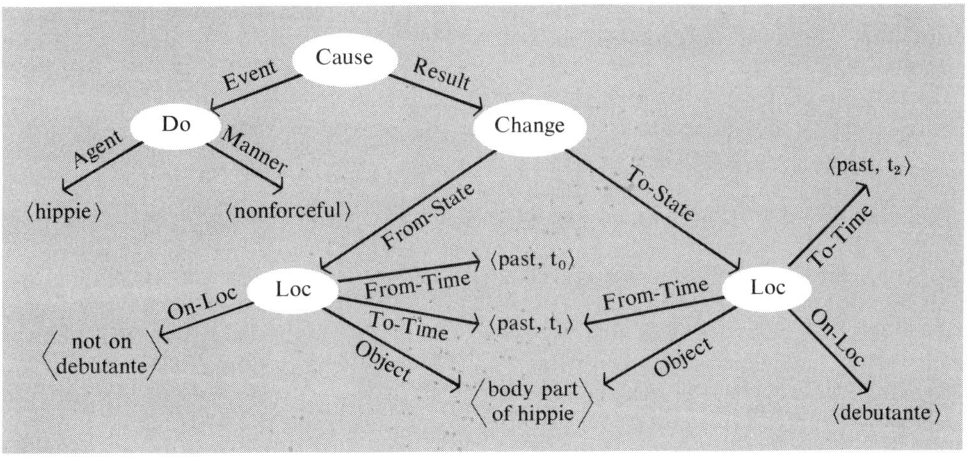

Figure 10–23. Analysis into semantic primitives in MEMOD.

For this illustration the meaning of *touch* has been taken as implying an intentional act on the part of the agent (the hippie). Thus, the primitive causative predicate, *cause,* is employed in the analysis. A complete reading of the graph would be the following. *Touch* is defined as (is when) some agent (a hippie) performs some act (not specified but labeled generally as *Do*), in a relatively nonforceful manner, that causes (*Cause*) a change (*Change*) in the location (from-state *Loc*) of a part of his body (the undetermined object of both *Loc* predicates) from some place (the *On-Loc* known only to be not in contact with the debutante) to a new location (the to-state *Loc*) that is in contact with a debutante. The *time* relations (from-time, to-time) would specify the duration of the touching.

One major advantage of the analysis to semantic primitives is that many different actions (verbs) can be seen to involve very similar primitive components. For example, *bumped, hit, grabbed, socked, patted, brushed, pinched,* and so forth might all involve some *change* in *location* of all or part of an agent's body so as to come in contact with some recipient. Each specific verb would be distinguished in terms of the manner (the forcefulness, for example) of the act and by the degree of intentionality (by the agent) involved. Some data have been presented that attest to the psychological validity of the semantic-primitives analysis. For example, it has been shown (Gentner, 1975) that the correct use of verbs having more complex semantic primitive structures (*buy* and *sell*) is learned later by children than is the use of simpler verbs (*give* and *take*).

Work on MEMOD and related work by the LNR group continues, but some rather impressive accomplishments have already indicated the fruitfulness of the approach.

Among them is a fascinating question-answering program dubbed *LUIGI* (Scragg, 1975). LUIGI is equipped with a variety of processes and bits of knowledge that are appropriate to "his world," which is a kitchen. The program is capable of answering questions such as:

How do you make a baked ham and cheese sandwich?

Correctly answering this question first requires that the question be comprehended. For example, the adjective *baked* must be seen as applying only to *ham* and not to *cheese* or to *ham and cheese sandwich*. If the query had referred to a grilled ham and cheese sandwich, for example, the correct procedure would require that ham (perhaps baked ham) and cheese be combined into a sandwich and then that the whole sandwich be grilled. Proper interpretation of the adjective, then, requires some knowledge about sandwiches. In addition to correct interpretation of the query (that is, sentence comprehension), the procedure for making the sandwich must be known—that is, placing ham and cheese between slices of bread.

Perhaps the most interesting and important capability of the LUIGI simulation program is what can be referred to as introspection. LUIGI can, for example, answer questions like:

If you were to bake a cake, what utensils would you get dirty?

To answer the question, the program "simulates its simulation" of baking a cake (LUIGI does not really make cakes, yet) and (introspectively) observes the process and takes note of the utensils that are used. This ability to "look in on" procedures is an important advance in computer simulations of human memory and language processes and gives the model a great deal of flexibility for answering questions about its "world."

We have presented only a few of the aspects of the recent work by the LNR group. Many very thought-provoking applications and tests of their general approach are presented in *Explorations in Cognition,* and the interested reader will be well rewarded for going to that reference for more details.

Overview

Although the attempt to explain human language performance in traditional S–R, behavioral terms persists, there has been little cause for optimism about the ultimate success of this approach. Analyses that attempt to account for language performance in terms of learned associations between overt words and other environmental events have been relatively successful in explaining simple language phenomena (for example, tacts and mands). On the other hand, they have failed to explain many language-performance phenomena that seem to require semantic, or meaning, relationships. That the human language user reacts identically to a great many linguistic transformations and other paraphrases of a sentence in spite of great differences in the overt words and the word orders employed is difficult for the S–R theory to explain. Yet this lack of concern for the features of the surface sentence is highly characteristic of human language performance.

The introduction of various hypothetical implicit stimulus and response events, as postulated by mediation theories, provides some ability to deal with meaning relations. However, the implicit mediating processes have often been only partially specified, and, more important, they have yet to be shown capable of explaining more complex language phenomena. In particular, none of the S–R or S–R-mediation accounts have convincingly dealt with the transformational relationships emphasized by Chomsky or with the problems introduced by the recursive embedding of clauses within a sentence.

The most promising approach to the development of a comprehensive psychological model of language performance seems to be represented by the information-processing models. They have shown an ability to deal with some of the more complex aspects of language, especially in their treatment of the role of semantics in language comprehension and generation. Because the information-processing models explicitly include the language user's "world knowledge" in the semantic component of language, they have tended to emphasize the importance of memory, both linguistic and perceptual, in language performance.

All of the models reviewed in this chapter, TLC, HAM and ACT, and ELINOR and MEMOD, have been formulated relatively recently, and most are still in developmental stages. Many aspects of these models are not yet fully specified. In particular, there is no clear statement of how the complex, interconnected networks of concepts and relations in memory might initially be acquired by the language user. Also, the output components of these models, the "language generators," are not described except in very general terms. The approach does show much promise, however, and the next few years will no doubt be exciting ones for psychology as the details of these models continue to be developed. Perhaps through elaboration of one of the models reviewed here, or by the development of new models of the same general form, a truly comprehensive psychological model of human language performance and semantic memory will eventually emerge.

Structure and Meaning: Some Interactions

We have now reviewed the linguistic analysis of language structure and several psychological conceptualizations of the role of meaning in language. In some respects the distinction between structure and meaning, though a useful way of thinking about language, is a false dichotomy. Most aspects of human language performance cannot be understood in terms of either structure or meaning but require a consideration of the interaction between both. In this section a few of the more important areas of language performance that exemplify this interaction will be briefly discussed.

Language and Your Perceptual World

All of us have, at one time or another, found our language, the words and the rules for combining them, insufficient for describing some experience or expressing some feeling. In these circumstances it seems clear that some meaning or knowledge exists somehow separate from the words we try to use to convey that meaning.[4] Although occasionally some poet, songwriter, or novelist seems to hit upon a phrase that "says it all," often there seem to be experiences and feelings that cannot be adequately expressed in words.

On the other hand, there are many indications that what we are able to experience (perceive), know, and feel may be determined to a great extent by the characteristics of our language. The relationships between the perceptual world that you construct and live in and the verbal system that you use to communicate about the world are one of the most important areas in which the structure and meaning of language interact.

That the structure of language may have important effects on language users' perceptions of the world they live in has often been recognized. George Orwell, in his popular novel *1984* (1949), recognized the power of language structure to limit and shape experience and thought. "Newspeak" was a language designed to limit thought by eliminating any

[4] This separation is also suggested by the fact that if you were to learn a new language, you would not have to "relearn" everything you now know. You would only be learning a new way of communicating your knowledge.

words that might express thoughts counter to the "Big Brother" philosophy. Such thoughts would eventually be eliminated.

On a similar theme, but in many ways suggesting an opposite problem, Stuart Chase, in *The Tyranny of Words* (1938), offered many examples of how words can shape and influence our perceptual world. Chase was concerned with how words and language not only constrain our thoughts but can also introduce "verbal spooks" into our perceptual world. In this book he expressed concern that the reactions of people to verbal nonentities were leading to legal morass, economic disaster, and even war. Chase argued that verbal statements like

> Communism is stirring up the masses against the mother country

are largely meaningless phrases (composed of "blabs," or semantic blanks) referring to nonexistent verbal spooks. Meaningless as they may be, such phrases have often produced very real reactions from those who hear them.

Similar effects of the structure of language on semantic interpretations are still a matter of much concern. In the mid-1970s in the United States, for example, "the Administration" (a verbal spook created by the news media) was struggling to come up with a suitable verbal label for the current economic situation. Some were urging the use of the technical term *recession,* but this word was apparently politically unpalatable. Besides, its opponents argued, the situation was complicated by a high rate of inflation, so the label *stagflation* was suggested as a more acceptable term.

The Whorfian Hypothesis

One of the most systematic analyses of the interrelationship between the structure and the function of language is that of the linguist Benjamin Whorf (1956). He proposed that our understanding and perception of the world depends to a great extent on the characteristics of our language. The *Whorfian hypothesis* suggests, for example, that the popularity of the "scientific" approach in Western cultures may have derived from the basic subject/predicate form of our languages, which encourages a cause-and-effect view of the universe; that is, the structure of Western languages may have predisposed us to seek "causes" for the events that we observe in our universe. People living in a culture that has a different language structure might not think in terms of cause and effect at all.

As another example of language-structure effects, Whorf noted that the Hopi (American Indian) language has no feature analogous to the time marking, or tense, of the English language; that is, there is no obligatory indication of past, present, or future in Hopi linguistic structure. He speculated that a description of the universe developed by a Hopi culture would be very different from that developed by a culture with an Indo-European language because there would be no reference to time in the Hopi conceptualization. Time, of course, is central to the contemporary, Einsteinian conception of the universe.

Perhaps the most commonly referenced of the Whorfian notions is that the words that a culture has for describing its perceptual world have important influences on the nature of that world. The English language, for example, has only a few words for the object/concept *horse*—for example, *horse, pony, colt,* and so on. In contrast, the Arabic language has a great many words for *horse,* each relating to different aspects of horses—their varieties, health, values, functions, and so on. Similarly, the Eskimos have many words for *snow,* while English-speaking people have essentially only one.

These general cultural language comparisons reported by Whorf are suggestive but somewhat ambiguous. It is not clear whether the structure of the language produces different perceptions, values, and thoughts or vice versa. That Eskimos have many words for *snow* may have led them to perceive snow differently than English-speaking individuals. On the other hand, because snow is more frequently encountered and more important to Eskimos than to most English speakers, Eskimos may be required to differentiate more precisely among the different types and characteristics of snow. Their need for better differentiation might well have led to their having more words for describing snow.

Further evidence in favor of the "reverse" Whorfian hypothesis comes from the fact that English-speaking individuals may develop special vocabularies depending upon their needs. For example, owners, breeders, and others who have a great deal of contact with horses may have and use many more words for *horse* than the average speaker (for example, *gelding, foal, quarterhorse, thoroughbred,* and so forth). As another example, English speakers who frequently come into contact with and need to make distinctions among various types of snow (for example, skiers) may have and use a number of words and phrases to describe it (for example, *powder, glare ice, slush, corn,* and so forth). Whether the availability of these distinctive verbal labels enhances an individual's ability to perceive and respond more appropriately to the different forms of snow is an interesting question, and it will be dealt with at some length in Chapter 14.

Regardless of whether differences in language structures produce differences in perception, or differences in perception produce different language structures, or both, the interaction of language structures and perception seems evident. The structural characteristics of your language, then, may have important effects on how you perceive and think about the world in which you live.

The Language Brain and the Perception Brain

The human brain is divided into two hemispheres. Each hemisphere receives information from the senses, but there is generally a separation in the information received. Information from visual inputs, for example, is divided; that from the left visual field is primarily projected to the right hemisphere, and information about stimuli in the right visual field is projected to the left hemisphere. Normally, there is a great deal of "cross-communication" between the two hemispheres, so that the separate items of information in each half of the brain are coordinated.

Through studies of patients who have had the normal interhemispheric-communication channels disrupted, researchers have begun to discover the different roles played by the two hemispheres in language production and comprehension. The "split-brain" condition has generally resulted from surgery as a therapy for severe and chronic cases of epilepsy. Because the normal communication channels between the hemispheres are severed, it is possible to observe the function of each half of the brain essentially independent of the other half. Important and dramatic differences in how the two hemispheres are involved in language performance have been discovered.

A series of experiments and clinical observations of human subjects with split brains is reported in a fascinating book, *The Bisected Brain,* by Gazzaniga (1970). These studies reveal that there is a definite separation in the way the brain processes language information. The left hemisphere of the brain seems to be the primary language-comprehending and language-generating half of the brain. The right hemisphere does seem to "comprehend" many perceptual inputs, but it has virtually no capacity for language comprehension or generation.

A number of systematic experiments have provided a more detailed analysis of these differences in hemispheric functions. When a printed word is flashed on the far-left side of a screen so that it falls in the extreme-left visual field, the resulting information will be transmitted exclusively to the right hemisphere of the brain. In split-brain subjects the left hemisphere cannot "know" about or aid in the interpretation of the information. If the subjects are asked to say the word that was presented, they are unable to do so. They may report that they saw nothing or that they saw only a flash of light. If further urged to produce the word, they may hazard a guess but show no signs of having comprehended the word. The same subjects will have no difficulty comprehending and producing words presented to the right visual field (and thus to the left hemisphere of the brain).

Although the right hemisphere cannot generally comprehend word inputs, it apparently can "comprehend" pictures. If a picture of an object (for example, a knife) is presented in the left visual field, subjects will not be able to label the object verbally. They can, however, pick out the object from among several other objects or sometimes indicate some aspects of the object's function (for example, by making cutting motions with their hands).[5]

The results of most experiments have indicated that the right hemisphere is "mute," that it cannot generate language. Although the language-comprehension capability of this hemisphere is very limited, there is some indication that it may "understand" some words. If the printed verbal name of a familiar concrete object (for example, *pencil, cut, knife*) is presented to the left visual field, split-brain subjects may be able to select that item (with the left hand) from among several others. Even after selecting the correct item, however, if they are not allowed to look at it in their right visual field or transfer it to their right hands, they will still be unable to produce the word label. More abstract words, such as verbs or nouns derived from verbs (for example, *writer, runner*), are apparently not comprehended by the right hemisphere.

There is some indication that although the right hemisphere cannot comprehend verbs it can "understand" pictures that suggest an action. Gazzaniga reports an experiment in which split-brain subjects were shown verbal commands such as *knock, tap,* and *point.* If these commands were presented to the left hemisphere (right visual field), the subjects could say the word and perform the indicated action. If the commands were presented to the right hemisphere, the subjects could do neither. When a picture of a hand in the act of knocking, tapping, or pointing was presented in the left visual field (right hemisphere), however, the subjects were able to respond appropriately (with their left hands).

These and other studies indicate a separation in function between the two halves of the human brain. The left hemisphere seems to be primarily responsible for language production, both spoken and written, and for comprehension of verbal information. The right hemisphere, though able to comprehend some concrete, familiar object words, has no capacity to generate language. Further, it apparently is unable to comprehend abstract words or verbal commands. The right hemisphere can, however, interpret and respond appropriately to perceptual inputs such as pictures.

This separation between language processes and perceptual processes is not easily noticed in normal individuals because of the characteristically rapid interhemispheric communication in the brain. The separation in hemispheric functions revealed by studies of split-brain subjects may, however, provide some insight into the interrelationship between language structures and (perceptual) concept and meaning relations. Perhaps, when we are unable to express feelings or describe experiences adequately with language, it is because the left hemisphere is not equipped to translate properly the information in the right hemisphere into words. In any event, the observations of the language performance of split-brain subjects suggest some interesting possibilities for the interrelationships between language and our understanding of our perceptual world.

[5] In both cases, selecting the object or indicating its function, the subjects must use their left hands. The motor control of the left hand is primarily centered in the right hemisphere.

Summary

Many aspects of language and of semantic memory have been discussed in this chapter, but the topic has by no means been exhausted by this very brief and rather simplified account. Early in this chapter a distinction was made between the structure of language and its underlying meaning. In the end, language performance was seen to depend greatly on the interaction between both aspects.

The structural characteristics of language, ranging from the simplest phonemic units to the more complex aspects of grammar and syntax, were briefly described and discussed. Relationships between lexical, syntactic, and semantic components of language were discussed in the context of contemporary linguistic theory. Linguistic models of language competence, especially those related to the work of Chomsky, were reviewed.

Psychological analyses of language performance were also considered. The S–R analysis, particularly as represented by the work of Skinner, was found to be reasonably effective for dealing with relatively simple, concrete aspects of language phenomena. When more complex language performance was considered, however, such as the effects of linguistic transformations, semantic paraphrases, and embedded clauses, the S–R conditioning model was generally found to be inadequate. Even with the addition of inferred, covert, mediating elements, there does not seem to be a way to solve all the problems of language performance within the traditional framework of an S–R model.

Several aspects of recently developed information-processing models of language were also briefly described. These models are generally linguistically sophisticated, explicitly including components to deal with the transformational and other complex syntactic aspects of language. More emphasis is placed, however, on the meaning component of language and on its role in the comprehension of verbal stimuli. By including the perceptual surround and the language user's "world knowledge" as central elements, the information-processing models emphasize the importance of perception and memory in language performance.

The particular models that were considered, TLC, HAM and ACT, and ELINOR and MEMOD, all represent rather recent developments in the psychological analysis of language. Many components of these models are still being developed, and many of those elements that have been specified will require modification and elaboration. Nonetheless, the approach taken in these models seems to offer a very promising lead that, if followed, may eventually result in a truly comprehensive psychological account of the many complex aspects of the human ability to develop, comprehend, and generate language.

Chapter 11

Verbal Learning and Memory

The scientific study of human learning began with an analysis of verbal learning and memory, and one issue of concern was how humans form associations between events. Interest in this field was spurred by the publication in 1885 of Ebbinghaus's now-classic monograph on the forgetting of nonsense syllables. Ebbinghaus was strongly influenced by the school of philosophy known as British associationism, represented by Locke, Hume, Berkeley, and others. Two features of British associationism had an important impact on early verbal-learning research. One was the assumption that human knowledge arises out of a person's *experience* with the world; all knowledge comes from experience because there are no innate ideas. The second was the assumption that simple ideas can become linked to form more complex ideas by the process of *association*. Thus, the way to understand how humans acquire knowledge is to begin with the association of simple ideas or events. With these philosophical views as background, the obviously logical approach as perceived by Ebbinghaus was to study the manner in which associations are formed.

Ebbinghaus's approach was continued in the 20th century by psychologists of the functionalist tradition. The early functionalists, such as Harvey Carr and John Dewey, were based mainly at Columbia University and the University of Chicago. Their philosophical descendants, such as Arthur Melton, John McGeoch, and Marion Bunch, helped advance the functionalist tradition during the 1930s and 1940s. Until about 1955 most verbal-learning research was concerned with establishing functional relations between independent and dependent variables. The fundamental aim was to *describe* verbal learning by noting what factors affected it in laboratory settings. Most of the research was atheoretical, and where theory did enter in, the concepts were derived largely from principles of animal learning.

In the late 1950s and early 1960s, the emphasis in the field began to change. First, researchers became increasingly involved with theory, although their emphasis was not on grand, general theories of learning but on restricted classes of phenomena. Examples of this trend are Estes's (1960) one-trial model of learning, McGuire's (1961) multiprocess model of paired-associate learning, and Martin's (1968) encoding-variability hypothesis. Second, researchers became increasingly interested in organizational processes and strategies used by humans in acquiring information. Studies on the role of organizational processes in memory (for example, Tulving & Donaldson, 1972), coding processes in learning and memory (Ellis, 1973; Martin, 1972), mnemonics (G. H. Bower, 1972a), language and elaborative strategies (Montague, 1972), and imagery (Paivio, 1971), to mention only a few, illustrate this major shift in thinking. Related to this change was the increasing tendency to view verbal learning from an information-processing viewpoint (for example, Kausler, 1974; Solso, 1974). Perhaps the most important feature of these changes was the increasing emphasis on the active role of the learner, as reflected, for example, in the trend toward examining how humans organize and reorganize verbal materials in idiosyncratic ways.

Research Procedures in Verbal Learning

The classic procedures in verbal learning usually involve the study of association formation. Subjects are required to learn lists of verbal materials such as words, letters, or nonsense syllables, or they may be required to learn sentences or paragraphs. They may be required to learn lists in serial order, to associate pairs of words or syllables, or to free-recall a list of items. In brief, many different kinds of materials may be used in combination with one or more procedures. To evaluate various processes in verbal learning, researchers may introduce variations in the kind of materials used, in instructions to subjects, and in procedures themselves, or they may examine individual-difference variables as they relate to any of the above factors.

Materials Used in Verbal-Learning Research

The selection of materials is usually based upon the nature of the research issue and the processes the investigator wishes to examine. In this section we will examine several representative examples of materials, but not in great detail. For a detailed description of materials in verbal learning, the reader may consult Cofer (1971) or Kausler (1974).

Syllables. Nonsense syllables may seem to be uninteresting material and certainly unrepresentative of the kinds of information normally experienced by humans. Ebbinghaus, however, developed the nonsense syllable because he wanted materials that were reasonably free of the past experiences of the adult human learner. Obviously, familiar or prose materials were unsatisfactory because he believed that such materials would make it difficult to disentangle the influence of past learning from the processes under investigation in the laboratory. We now know, however, that nonsense syllables are not free from the influence of past experiences and that they vary considerably in such properties as meaningfulness and pronounceableness.

The nonsense syllable is a verbal unit consisting of a consonant/vowel/consonant sequence, such as *zaf,* or a consonant/consonant/consonant sequence, such as *qbx.* Because the items do vary in meaningfulness, it is now regarded as more appropriate to refer to them as *CVC trigrams* or *CCC trigrams,* terms proposed by Archer (1960). These materials have been scaled on a number of dimensions, such as association value, meaningfulness, pronounceableness, and familiarity. A major reason for scaling these various dimensions was to determine what dimension (or dimensions) best predicts learning.

One of the earliest investigations of properties of nonsense syllables was conducted by Glaze (1928), who scaled more than 2000 syllables. He presented each syllable to subjects for 2 or 3 seconds and asked them to indicate in a word or two what, if anything, the item meant to them. The association value of each syllable was determined by computing the percentage of the subjects who had an association with a given syllable. For example, all the subjects had an association for *bal,* which was thus assigned an association value of 100%; in contrast, none of the subjects had an association for *xyj,* which thus received a value of 0%.

Archer (1960) made a thorough reevaluation of all 2480 CVC trigrams using a much larger sample of subjects. He had his subjects view each trigram for 4 seconds and pronounce each item to themselves. Then they were asked the following questions: Is it a word? Does it sound like a word? Does it remind you of a word? Can you use it in a sentence? The subjects responded "yes" if they could answer at least one of the four questions affirmatively; if none could be answered affirmatively, they responded "no." The percentage of subjects who answered "yes" to an item defined the association value of that item. High positive correlations between the Archer and the earlier Glaze values were obtained.

Words. Other scaling studies have used words. For example, C. E. Noble (1952) used 18 artificial two-syllable words and 96 actual two-syllable words. Each item was presented to subjects for 60 seconds, and they were asked to provide as many associations as possible within this period. According to Noble, this procedure defines the meaningfulness of an item, which he views as the relationship between a stimulus item and a response. In this procedure, meaningfulness, or $\bar{m}$, is defined in terms of the average number of associations elicited by an item in a specified arbitrary period of time. Thus, the more associations an item elicits, the greater the meaningfulness of the item. For example, the word *kitchen* has an $\bar{m}$ value of 9.61, whereas the artificial word *gojey* has an $\bar{m}$ value of only .99.

An important characteristic of words is their frequency, defined either as the frequency with which the word appears in print or as the frequency with which the word occurs in the spoken language. A widely used frequency count is the Thorndike and Lorge (1944) count of frequency values for common English words. This count was obtained by calculating the frequency with which words appeared in a wide range of printed materials, including newspapers and magazines. On the assumption that differences in frequency of occurrence of words reflect differences in the ways humans experience words, high-frequency words should be more readily learned. A more recent word-frequency count has been conducted by Kučera and Francis (1967), who restricted their material to prose printed in the United States by American writers.

Frequency counts have been taken from spoken as well as printed English. Howes (1966) has provided a frequency count of spoken English obtained from words in spoken discourse between 1960 and 1965. The materials consisted of interviews of 5000 words each with a number of different subjects. College students and hospital patients were the principal subjects. Each interview was general and open-ended, beginning usually with "Tell me about the field you are majoring in" or "Tell me what brought you to the hospital." These topics easily elicited discourse.

Another important feature of words is the abstractness/concreteness dimension. Concrete words have a relatively direct referent or object, whereas abstract words do not. Using only two judges, Gorman (1961) rated a large number of nouns as either concrete or abstract and demonstrated that this feature is an important factor in recognition memory. Subsequently, Paivio, Yuille, and Madigan (1968) used a seven-point rating scale for judging the concreteness/abstractness of nouns as well as for obtaining imagery ratings.

Relations among Words. So far, we have described measures of characteristics of single items. With these measures the experimenter is usually not interested in relations among the items. Nevertheless, it is clear that human subjects will try to form relations even if none is immediately apparent (Montague, 1972). Moreover, many situations involve words that are related. Therefore, to understand better the learning of related words, psychologists have sought ways to describe the relations among items.

One longstanding method for determining the relations among words is the word-association test. With this procedure a subject is presented with a stimulus word and asked to give the first word that comes to mind. Originally used as a clinical/diagnostic tool, the measure provides a picture of verbal hierarchies of humans and of the relative frequency with which particular responses are given to stimulus words. For example, *cat* is a frequent associate given for *dog,* whereas *desk* is a rare associate. The advantage of free-association norms is that they predict several things about learning and memory. One obvious thing is that a list containing high-frequency associates is easier to learn than one containing low-frequency associates.

Sentences and Prose. We have been examining discrete learning materials, such as trigrams and words, which obviously differ from connected discourse. Many verbal materials are not encountered as single units but are connected, as in sentences, prose, poetry, and spoken discourse. Learning and memory psychologists have been increasingly interested in the context in which verbal information is encoded, and as a result, the study of sentence and prose learning has received considerable attention (see, for example, Perfetti, 1969).

Verbal-Learning Tasks

In this section we will examine five basic procedures used in the study of verbal learning. These are serial learning, paired-associate learning, free recall, recognition learning, and verbal-discrimination learning.

Serial Learning. In serial learning the verbal units are presented in the same order on successive trials, and the subject must recall them in the order presented. A familiar accomplishment is your ability to recite the days of the week or the months of the year. Serial learning thus involves the acquisition and retention of *order* information. Many everyday situations require that information be remembered in its proper order, so interest in serial memory dates from the ancient Greeks and Romans (see Yates, 1966).

In laboratory studies of serial learning, the *anticipation method* is often used. Subjects are shown a list of verbal items, one at a time. The items can be presented manually with, say, index cards, but they are usually presented with a slide projector so as to control the duration of exposure of each item. After presentation of the list once, each item is presented again, and the subjects attempt to anticipate (guess) the next item. When shown the first item, they attempt to anticipate the second item; when shown the second item, they attempt to anticipate the third item; and so on. Thus, each item is said to serve as a stimulus and a response. The list is presented repeatedly until the subject learns it to some arbitrary criterion, such as one perfect recital of the list.

A second method used in serial learning is the *recall method.* Here the material is also presented item by item. However, after presentation of the list, the subjects are required to recall as many items as possible in their correct order. Again the items are presented until the subjects attain criterion-level performance.

Paired-Associate Learning. In paired-associate learning the task is to learn to associate pairs of items. One member of the pair is referred to as the stimulus item, and the second member is designated the response item. Although conventional stimulus–response terminology is used, the task is currently viewed as far more complex than stimulus–response association itself. The paired-associate procedure has been widely used to study such processes as transfer, mediation, and interference effects in retention. Its use as a research tool has been, in part, due to the historical assumption that it provides a way of examining basic associative processes. This procedure was viewed for many years as analogous to methods used in the study of association formation in lower animals or as related to the study of conditioning processes. More recently, however, the procedure has been recognized as far too complex to be easily related to conditioning processes (Battig, 1968) and has come to be regarded as a tool for studying different processes in human learning.

A common method used to investigate paired-associate learning is again an anticipation one. With this method, subjects are shown a stimulus item followed by that item paired with its response term. Then they are shown a second stimulus item followed by a stimulus–response pair. This procedure continues until the list is shown once. Then the list is repeated, with the subjects instructed to say aloud (anticipate) the response when they are shown the stimulus item. After each presentation of the stimulus alone, the subjects see the pair of items and thus can confirm their anticipation. The following list represents a typical paired-associate task:

Stimuli		*Responses*
foz		
foz	→	cat
gik		
gik	→	apple
tal		
tal	→	shoe
zef		
zef	→	pipe
huq		
huq	→	chair
moy		
moy	→	pencil

On the second presentation of the list, the subjects thus attempt to anticipate the response *cat* when they are shown the stimulus item *foz* alone. They continue to do this for the entire list. Usually the order of the pairs is varied on successive presentations to prevent serial learning, and the subjects learn the list to some arbitrary criterion, such as one or two perfect anticipations of the list.

A second method used to investigate paired-associate learning has been the *study/test* (or *study/recall*) *procedure*. Here the pairs are presented successively at a controlled rate, and after being given all the pairs, the subjects are presented with the stimulus terms singly in succession and asked to recall the appropriate responses. This procedure is repeated until the subjects learn to some criterion established by the experimenter.

Free Recall. In free recall the subjects are presented with a series of items, usually one at a time, and asked to recall the items in any order they wish. Usually the list is presented only once. However, multitrial free-recall procedures are also used. In this case the order of presentation of the items is varied from trial to trial. The importance of the free-recall procedure is that it permits a study of the way in which verbal information is organized in memory and the way in which retrieval or output processes operate during recall. The free-recall procedure has been widely used to study a variety of phenomena, and we will note several examples.

One of the striking characteristics of free recall is that recall of individual items is a function of their position on the list. Murdock (1962) presented six groups of subjects with lists of unrelated but common English words. The lists consisted of 10, 15, 20, 30, or 40 words and were presented for either 1 or 2 seconds (all the possible combinations were not used; hence only six groups). Following a single presentation of the list, the subjects were given a free-recall test in which they were instructed to write down as many words as they could remember as they came to mind. The results are shown in Figure 11–1, in which the probability of recall is plotted as a function of position on the list for all six groups.

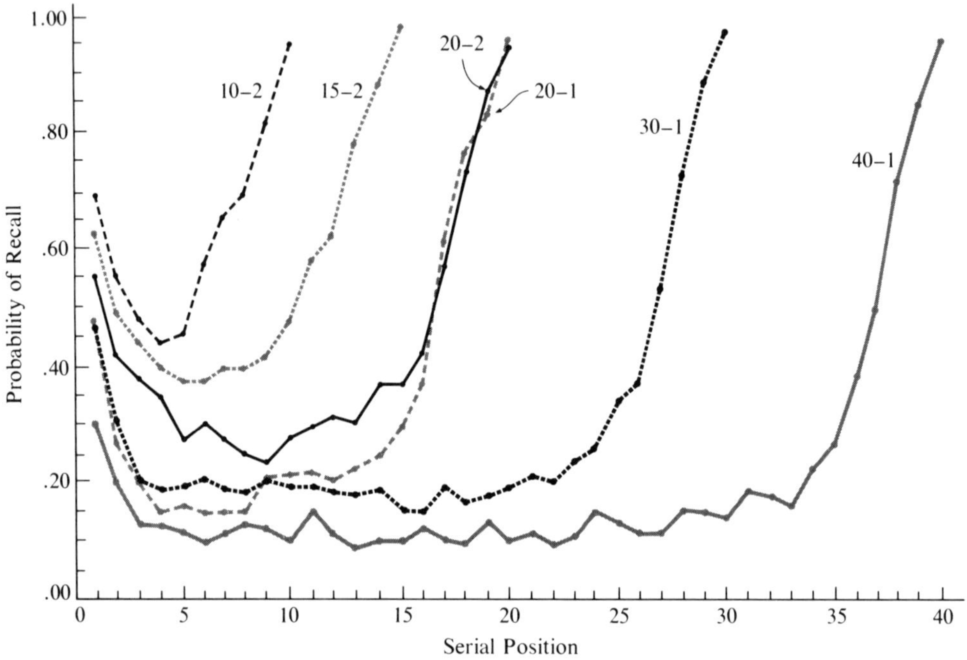

Figure 11–1. The probability of recall in free recall as a function of the serial position of the items on a list. (From "The Serial Position Effect of Free Recall," by B. B. Murdock, Jr., *Journal of Experimental Psychology,* 1962, *64,* 482–488. Copyright 1962 by the American Psychological Association. Reprinted by permission.)

The figure shows that all the groups exhibited characteristic serial-position effect regardless of the length or duration of the list. In addition, they all showed a clear recency effect, the tendency to recall more items on the latter portion of the list. The recency effect can be interpreted as due to these items' still being predominantly in short-term memory, since they were the items most recently presented. As noted in Chapter 9, if recall is delayed, the recency effect will disappear (Glanzer & Cunitz, 1966). Finally, all the curves show a primacy effect as well, which is the tendency for the items early in the list to be recalled at high levels. The primacy effect in free recall can be interpreted in terms of a greater opportunity for the subjects to rehearse the earlier-presented items. This point was also discussed in Chapter 9.

Recognition Learning. In a recognition-learning task, subjects are presented with items during a study phase and then given a recognition test. The study and test are repeated on successive trials, so that improvement in recognition performance can be measured. During recognition testing the subjects are presented with a series of items, one at a time, and asked to recognize the "old" items (ones presented during study) by indicating "old" or "new" when shown each item. The new items serve as lures or distracters. A *forced-choice procedure* may also be used. In this type of test, the subjects must select the old item from among two or more alternatives. New distracter items are introduced on each trial to prevent the subjects from learning the distracters.

Verbal-Discrimination Learning. Although the verbal-discrimination procedure is a type of recognition-learning task, it will be described in its own right. It received little use until recent years (for example, Ekstrand, Wallace, & Underwood, 1966; Kausler, 1974). With this procedure, subjects are presented with pairs of verbal items, one of which is arbitrarily designated as correct. The subjects are required to learn which item of the pair is correct upon repeated presentation of the pairs.

Mixed versus Unmixed Lists. One methodological issue is worthy of note before we turn to an examination of major variables affecting verbal learning. This issue concerns the use of *mixed* versus *unmixed lists.* Suppose, for example, that we were interested in the role of stimulus imagery in paired-associate learning. One procedure would be to have subjects learn a single list containing several levels of stimulus imagery. If, say, the list contained 12 pairs, four pairs might have high stimulus imagery, four might have moderate imagery, and four might have low imagery. The use of several levels of the variable in one list constitutes a mixed-list design. The mixed list has the important advantage of minimizing the variability of the results due to individual differences among subjects. Since the same subjects serve under all conditions, we increase the precision of the experiment.

An unmixed list consists of only one level of the list factor, and different groups of subjects would learn different paired-associate lists varying in stimulus-imagery value. In the example cited, three different groups would be used, each learning only one list of high, moderate, or low stimulus imagery. The distinction between mixed and unmixed lists is, of course, simply an instance of the general distinction between within-subject and between-subject designs.

The important question that must be asked about the two types of experimental designs is whether they produce comparable results. There is no general answer to this question simply because the answer depends upon a variety of experimental conditions. The mixed-list design is used when characteristics of the material itself are the main variable under study. Mixed and unmixed lists are unlikely to produce the same results if subjects notice the heterogeneous nature of the mixed list and adopt a strategy for learning the material that is different from what they would do if they were learning separate lists. If it is unclear whether the two designs produce comparable results, then an unmixed list is preferable. Direct comparison of the two types of lists is desirable particularly if they are expected to yield different results and if the experimenter is interested in the possible interactions or transfer effects in learning different types of material within a single list.

Variables Affecting Verbal Learning

In this section we turn our attention to an examination of some of the major variables that influence verbal learning. Any generalization about the effect of a particular variable on verbal learning may be dependent upon the particular task used—for example, free recall versus paired-associate learning. Thus, our description will focus on particular tasks rather than on verbal learning in general. We will consider both the learning of discrete items and the learning of connected materials.

Discrete Materials

Important variables in the learning of discrete verbal materials include meaningfulness, similarity, frequency, pronounceableness, concreteness/abstractness, and imagery value.

Meaningfulness. We have already described one definition of meaningfulness, the average number of associations a verbal item produces in a fixed time period (C. E. Noble, 1952). The term *meaningfulness* is also used generically to refer to a class of attributes such as rated or judged meaningfulness (C. E. Noble, 1961), association value (Archer, 1960; Glaze, 1928), and other characteristics such as judged ease of learning. In general, the various measures tend to correlate moderately to highly with one another (Cofer, 1971; Runquist, 1966). Moreover, the measures correlate well with how rapidly verbal items are actually learned. The strong relationship between meaningfulness and free recall has been demonstrated by Underwood (1966). He found high correlations between various measures of meaningfulness and free recall, ranging from .91 to .92.

Meaningfulness is also an important variable in paired-associate learning, where the meaningfulness of the stimulus and response terms can be varied independently. Typical findings are shown in Figure 11–2, which are the results of a study by Cieutat, Stockwell, and Noble (1958). The figure shows the acquisition curves for four conditions involving all combinations of low and high stimulus and response meaningfulness using the items from Noble's (1952) scale of meaningfulness. Several features are obvious. First is that learning is easiest when both stimulus and response terms are high in meaningfulness (H/H) and poorest when both terms are low in meaningfulness (L/L). Second, the influence of stimulus meaningfulness is less than that of response meaningfulness. Third, variations in stimulus meaningfulness produce a greater effect on learning when response meaningful-

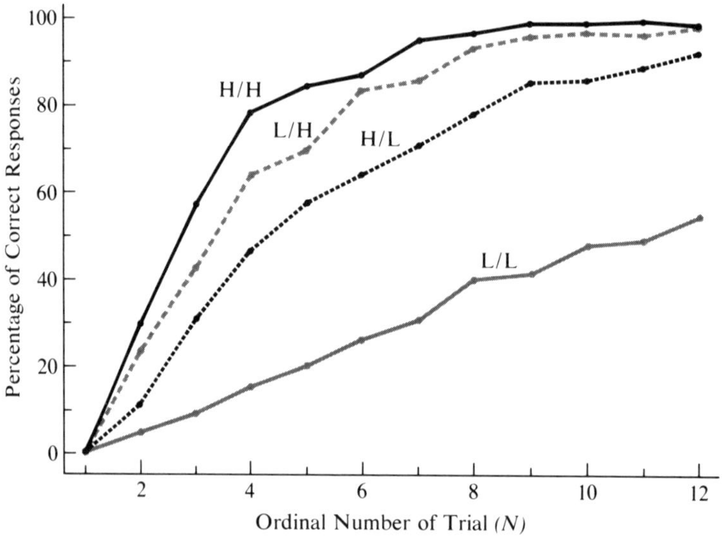

Figure 11–2. Paired-associate learning as a function of stimulus and response meaningfulness. (From "The Interaction of Ability and Amount of Practice with Stimulus and Response Meaningfulness (m, m') in Paired Associate Learning," by V. J. Cieutat, F. E. Stockwell, and C. E. Noble, *Journal of Experimental Psychology,* 1958, *56,* 193–202. Copyright 1958 by the American Psychological Association. Reprinted by permission.)

ness is low as distinct from high, which simply notes an interaction between stimulus and response meaningfulness on learning.

Meaningfulness and Encoding Variability. One approach to understanding the effects of meaningfulness on learning stems from the *encoding-variability hypothesis.* Shepard (1963) has proposed that the fragmented/integrated character of an item underlies the effects of meaningfulness and that more meaningful items are items that are more easily encoded or integrated as an intact unit, whereas less meaningful items are more fragmented, with the subject perceiving and encoding only a portion of the item to be learned on a given presentation. Martin (1968, 1972) has formalized Shepard's conception in terms of an encoding-variability hypothesis, which proposes that variability in encoding a given stimulus is inversely related to its meaningfulness. Stimuli that are high in meaningfulness can be readily encoded as a unit; for example, the word *mop* used as a stimulus term in a paired-associate list will be encoded as *mop*—that is, as an intact unit. In contrast, stimuli that are low in meaningfulness are likely to be variably encoded on successive presentations because the entire unit cannot be readily encoded. For example, the trigram *xfg* is more difficult to encode consistently on successive trials because the unit cannot be easily integrated. On one presentation the subject may encode the item in terms of the first letter alone; on another presentation encoding may be based on the first two letters; and so on.

From the encoding-variability hypothesis it would be expected that low-meaningfulness items would be more difficult to recognize because they are less likely to be consistently encoded as a unit during presentations. Therefore, the encoding would be more fragmented, and recognition performance would be predictably poorer than with items high in meaningfulness. As noted earlier, research results quite clearly indicate that meaningfulness correlates positively with recognition (see, for example, Ellis, 1968; Martin & Melton, 1970).

Similarity. A second major factor that affects verbal learning is intralist similarity. In addition, the effects of similarity depend upon the type of verbal-learning task and upon the way *similarity* is defined. *Formal similarity* is defined by the number of common letters possessed by the verbal items in a list. Thus, *crm* and *crp* are more similar than are *klx* and *fhz*. The role of letter position is also important in *judged similarity,* with the identity of the first letter in a trigram being most important in determining the rated similarity of trigrams (Runquist & Joinson, 1968). Words can also vary in *meaningful similarity,* which usually refers to the degree of synonymity among words. For example, *cheerful, happy,* and *genial* would be regarded as meaningfully similar words. *Conceptual similarity* refers to the degree to which words belong to the same class (for example, *gold, silver, lead*).

A number of experiments have shown that in free recall, learning is facilitated by conceptual and meaningful similarity. Underwood, Ekstrand, and Keppel (1965) found that conceptually similar lists consisting of animals (for example, *fox, rabbit, tiger, sheep*) were more easily learned than conceptually dissimilar lists (for example, *captain, cotton, leg, cow*).

In paired-associate learning the effects of similarity depend upon whether the manipulation is on the stimulus or the response side and upon the type of similarity measure. On the stimulus side, the higher the degree of similarity, the slower is the rate of learning. This relation holds for both conceptual (for example, Underwood et al., 1965) and formal (Runquist & Joinson, 1968) similarity. Moreover, the relationship holds across a wide range of stimuli, such as trigrams, random shapes, and complex letter matrixes (Ellis & Shaffer, 1974).

Frequency and Pronounceableness. The factors of frequency and pronounceableness are related to meaningfulness, and both factors are important predictors of the ease of verbal learning. Postman (1962a) examined the effect of word frequency on paired-associate learning using two-syllable nouns and found that the rate of learning was faster for more frequent words when frequency was varied on the response side. In a classic analysis of the effects of meaningfulness on verbal learning, Underwood and Schulz (1960) initially hypothesized that frequency represents a basic dimension of meaningfulness, a position consistent with findings on the effects of word frequency on learning. However, analyses of the effects of trigram frequency did not support their hypothesis, which led them to conclude that pronounceableness may be more important under certain circumstances. Their emphasis on pronounceableness has led to extensive investigation of this variable in verbal learning.

Concreteness/Abstractness. The concreteness/abstractness dimension is the extent to which a word has object-like properties that can be experienced by one or more of the senses. For instance, the word *apple* is very concrete, whereas *justice* is quite abstract. As you might expect, this dimension is importantly related to learning, with concrete words being more easily learned than abstract words. In an early study on this factor, Gorman (1961) found that concrete words were more easily recognized than abstract ones in a recognition-learning task. Other experiments (for example, Epstein, Rock, & Zuckerman, 1960; Paivio, 1963) have shown that concreteness is an important variable in paired-associate learning. In an effort to explain the effects of concreteness on learning, Paivio and his associates (for example, Lambert & Paivio, 1956; Paivio et al., 1968) hypothesized that imagery is the major psychological attribute underlying the effects of concreteness and abstractness.

Imagery. The emphasis on imagery as a major variable in verbal learning represents an important shift in verbal-learning research. For decades, psychologists were wary of imagery partly on the grounds of its presumed subjectivity—that is, its difficulty in being scientifically studied—and thus for many it was forbidden territory. With the development, however, of techniques for studying imagery in the laboratory, imagery research achieved considerable popularity in the 1960s, and this interest has been maintained (G. H. Bower, 1972a; Paivio, 1969, 1971).

Imagery research has usually proceeded in two ways. One has been to vary the imagery value of words by selecting words from a set of imagery norms. The other has been to instruct subjects to use imagery in learning a task. The performance of the instructed subjects is then compared with that of an uninstructed control group. We will consider the results of both kinds of studies because both provide substantial evidence for the important role of imagery.

The relative contributions of imagery and meaningfulness in paired-associate learning have been examined by Paivio and his colleagues in a series of studies. Smythe and Paivio (1968) found that the effects of imagery were more powerful than meaningfulness and that the effects of meaningfulness were more potent on the stimulus side than on the response side of paired-associate learning. Similar results were reported by Paivio, Smythe, and Yuille (1968) for a study in which subjects learned 16-pair lists of nouns. One of the lists consisted of variations in stimulus and response meaningfulness, with four combinations being used: high/high, high/low, low/high, and low/low. The first term refers to the stimulus and the second term to the response. The meaningfulness values were equated for each combination, so that only variations in imagery occurred. In a second list, meaningfulness was varied, with imagery controlled. Here imagery was held constant across the different conditions. A third condition was used in which imagery and meaningfulness covaried; the nouns were either high or low in both imagery and meaningfulness. The important questions were the role of imagery versus meaningfulness and the effect of covarying the attributes versus imagery alone. The recall results averaged over four trials are shown in Figure 11–3, where the results for the three conditions are compared.

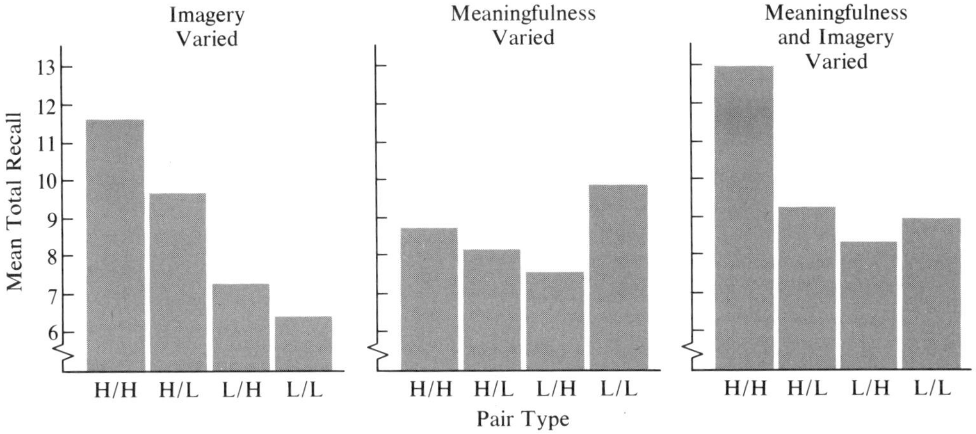

Figure 11–3. Mean total recall for items varying in either imagery or meaningfulness or both. (From "Imagery versus Meaningfulness of Nouns in Paired-Associate Learning," by A. Paivio, P. C. Smythe, and J. C. Yuille, *Canadian Journal of Psychology,* 1968, *22,* 427–441. Reprinted by permission.)

The effects of imagery are quite apparent, with recall being ordered as follows: high/high, high/low, low/high, and low/low. The effects of meaningfulness, in contrast, were small and slightly negative, recall being better for the low/low pairs than for other pair types. Covarying imagery and meaningfulness produced higher recall for the high/high pairs; in contrast with the imagery list, however, variations in the other pairs were negligible, indicating that the pattern of recall was quite different for the two lists. These and other findings have led Paivio (1971, p. 258) to conclude that the effects of imagery cannot be explained in terms of variations in meaningfulness and that the effects of meaningfulness are weak or negligible when imagery values are held constant.

Other approaches to the study of imagery have used instructions on imagery. For example, G. H. Bower (1972a) required subjects to learn a 20-pair list of nouns, with half of the subjects given instructions in using imagery mediation and half instructed simply to learn the pairs. The subjects were presented with the list at a 5-second rate and then tested for recall; five successive lists were presented. The results showed that the imagery-instructed subjects recalled about 1.5 times more items than the control group. Moreover, Bower demonstrated that the effects of imagery instuctions were not due simply to subjects' verbal elaboration of the pairs, such as making sentences out of the pairs.

Connected Discourse

In this section we will briefly examine some of the factors and processes in the learning and retention of connected discourse. This area is of increasing interest to psychologists, and we can anticipate further research on it.

Prose Learning. The early research on prose learning and retention began with the work of Bartlett (1932), where the emphasis was on presumed qualitative rather than quantitative changes in recall. Bartlett's interest was in the change in retention of prose material using the method of successive reproductions. He required his subjects to read passages of prose, such as brief stories, and then reproduce the passages as accurately as possible in repeated sessions. The following is an example of one of his stories, an Indian folktale called "The War of the Ghosts." An initial reproduction by one of the subjects is also provided.

"The War of the Ghosts"

One night two young men from Egulac went down to the river to hunt seals, and while they were there it became foggy and calm. Then they heard war-cries, and they thought: "Maybe this is a war-party." They escaped to the shore, and hid behind a log. Now canoes came up, and they heard the noise of paddles, and saw one canoe coming up to them. There were five men in the canoe, and they said:

"What do you think? We wish to take you along. We are going up the river to make war on the people."

One of the young men said: "I have no arrows."

"Arrows are in the canoe," they said.

"I will not go along. I might be killed. My relatives do not know where I have gone. But you," he said, turning to the other, "may go with them."

So one of the young men went, but the other returned home.

And the warriors went on up the river to a town on the other side of Kalama. The people came down to the water, and they began to fight, and many were killed. But presently the young man heard one of the warriors say: "Quick, let us go home: that Indian has been hit." Now he thought: "Oh, they are ghosts." He did not feel sick, but they said he had been shot.

So the canoes went back to Egulac, and the young man went ashore to his house, and made a fire. And he told everybody and said: "Behold I accompanied the ghosts, and we went to fight. Many of our fellows were killed, and many of those who attacked us were killed. They said I was hit, and I did not feel sick."

He told it all, and then he became quiet. When the sun rose he fell down. Something black came out of his mouth. His face became contorted. The people jumped up and cried.

He was dead.

Subject's Reproduction

Two youths were standing by a river about to start seal-catching, when a boat appeared with five men in it. They were all armed for war.

The youths were at first frightened, but they were asked by the men to come and help them fight some enemies on the other bank. One youth said he could not come as his relations would be anxious about him; the other said he would go, and entered the boat.

In the evening he returned to his hut, and told his friends that he had been in a battle. A great many had been slain, and he had been wounded by an arrow; he had not felt any pain, he said. They told him that he must have been fighting in a battle of ghosts. Then he remembered it had been queer and he became very excited.

In the morning, however, he became ill, and his friends gathered round; he fell down and his face became very pale. Then he writhed and shrieked and his friends were filled with terror. At last he became calm. Something hard and black came out of his mouth, and he lay contorted and dead.[1]

Bartlett stressed the principle that during the reading of prose material, subjects acquire a cognitive structure that he called a schema. A schema is a representation of the story's thematic content and is generally idiosyncratic to the subject. This is simply to say that the subject's values, attitudes, and personality characteristics can influence the way in which the information is encoded and thus influence the pattern of information recalled. The general theme of the story was unfamiliar to most of Bartlett's subjects and was also somewhat mystical. The subject's reproduction indicates that the subject tended to reconstruct the story into a more personally coherent and unified pattern. The core meaning was retained but was highly abstracted, some details of the story were dropped, and other details were exaggerated or emphasized.

[1] From *Remembering, by F. C. Bartlett. Copyright 1932 by Cambridge University Press. Reprinted by permission.*

Bartlett's early work was interpretative and depended upon general impressions received in evaluating the recall protocols. Current research on prose learning and recall has placed much greater emphasis on developing scoring systems for the recall protocols that allow estimates of quantitative changes in retention. Moreover, interest in sentence and prose retention has accelerated with a renewed concern with issues such as the representation of meaning in memory (Kintsch, 1974) and constructive processes in memory that deal with the way we formulate information (Cofer, 1973).

Grammatical Factors. We have already noted the importance of several grammatical factors in the learning of connected discourse. One important factor is semantics, whose role is illustrated in a study by Marks and Miller (1964). In this study they were able to compare the effects of semantic constraint with no constraint and were also able to compare the effects of semantic and syntactic constraints. These variables can be easily understood by examining the conditions of the experiment. Four conditions were used in the study. In the first condition the task consisted of five sentences that were normal in the sense of being fully constrained semantically and syntactically. An example is "Noisy parties wake sleeping neighbors." A second condition consisted of words that formed anomalous sentences; they were syntactically correct but semantically meaningless. An example is "Noisy flashes emit careful floods." A third condition consisted of anagram strings, each string being formed by randomly rearranging the words of one of the real (normal) sentences. An example is "Neighbors sleeping noisy wake parties." Finally, the fourth condition consisted of strings of words constructed by scrambling the anomalous sentences. An example is "Floods careful emit noisy flashes."

In each condition the subjects received five such strings using a study/recall procedure. Five trials were administered. During testing the subjects were instructed to free-recall the sentences (strings) as accurately as possible. The results are shown in Figure 11–4, which is a plot of the median percentage recall of total correct words for the four

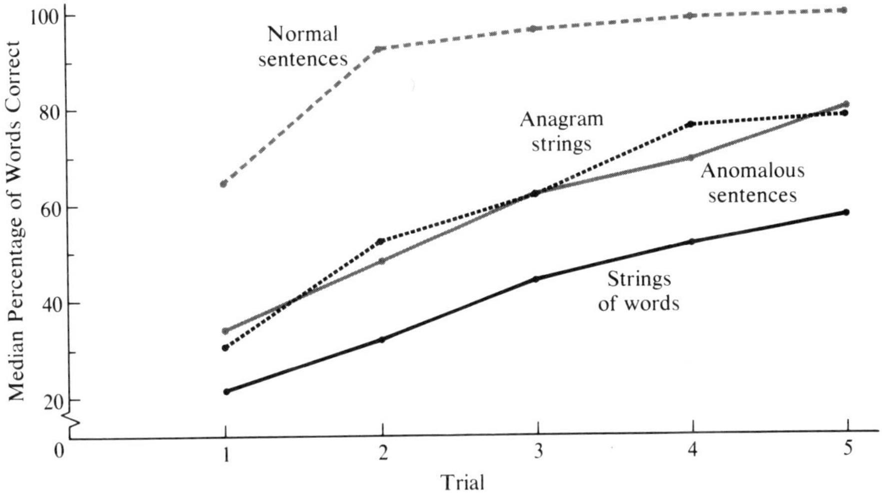

Figure 11-4. Median percentage of recall of total correct words for normal sentences, anagram strings, anomalous sentences, and strings of words. (From "The Role of Semantic and Syntactic Constraints in the Memorization of English Sentences," by L. E. Marks and G. A. Miller, *Journal of Verbal Learning and Verbal Behavior,* 1964, *3,* 1–5. Reprinted by permission of Academic Press, Inc.)

conditions. The figure clearly shows that normal sentences—that is, strings having both semantic and syntactic constraints—were recalled best; the scrambled words (word lists) were recalled poorest. The facilitating effect of semantic constraint was slightly greater than that of syntactic constraint, since recall of words from anagram strings was greater than recall of words from anomalous sentences. Nevertheless, the study shows the clear importance of both semantic and syntactic structure in the memory of sentences.

The Stage Analysis of Verbal Learning

In this section we turn to some basic processes of paired-associate learning. Learning and memory psychologists are not content simply to describe the role of various factors influencing verbal learning. A major objective has been to understand the fundamental processes underlying verbal learning by analyzing the various components of a total learning situation. This process of breaking down learning tasks into their individual component is called *component* or *stage analysis*. The first important breakthrough in stage analysis came with the separation of response learning and associative learning, so we will begin our discussion there.

Response and Associative Learning

In learning a list of paired associates, two processes are apparent. One process is that of response learning, which is learning the responses to the level where they are readily recallable as units. In this stage the responses are said to become available for recall. The second stage involves hooking up particular responses to particular stimuli and is designated the associative stage. The distinction between the two components describes the *two-stage theory* of paired-associate learning formalized by Underwood and Schulz (1960).

These two processes were successfully separated in a study by Underwood, Runquist, and Schulz (1959) by examining the effects of response similarity on paired-associate learning. In postulating two stages in paired-associate learning, they reasoned that meaningful response similarity should facilitate the response-learning stage but should retard the associative-learning stage. In this study, subjects learned a list of ten pairs, with CVCs of low formal similarity as stimuli. However, the response terms were either high or low in meaningful similarity. The high-similarity responses consisted of words similar in meaning (*cheerful, sunny, carefree, pleasant, gleeful, laughing, happy, genial, jolly, smiling*), whereas the low-similarity responses were unrelated (*spicy, rounded, hairy, equal, modern, tiresome, fiery, faithful, plastic, guilty*).

In one case, groups of subjects were stopped after 1, 2, 3, 5, 8, or 13 paired-associate trials and asked to free-recall the responses. In another case, subjects learned the two response-similarity lists by the paired-associate anticipation method. Figure 11–5 shows the free-recall results in the left-hand panel and the paired-associate results in the right-hand panel. The free-recall results show that recall of the high-similarity response was greater particularly during the early trials. In contrast, the paired-associate results show that performance was retarded under conditions of high response similarity. In short, low response similarity facilitates paired-associate learning despite the facilitation of response learning from high response similarity. The confusion generated by similarity during the hookup stage offsets any superiority produced by similarity during the response-learning stage.

A longstanding view of response learning is that of integrating the responses into an available response unit. The basic idea is that unfamiliar responses such as *xug* or *jfl,* must

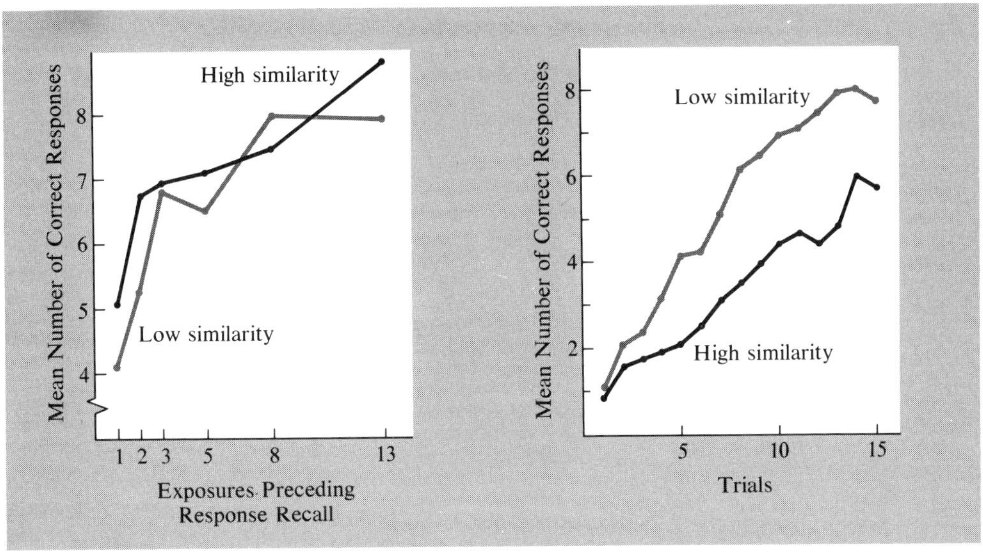

Figure 11–5. Free-recall and paired-associate learning as a function of response similarity. (From "Response Learning in Paired-Associate Lists as a Function of Intralist Similarity," by B. J. Underwood, W. N. Runquist, and R. W. Schulz, *Journal of Experimental Psychology,* 1959, *58,* 70–78. Copyright 1959 by the American Psychological Association. Reprinted by permission.)

be integrated as a functional unit before they can be made fully available for recall. Thus, the letter components must become *chained* or "blended," so they can function as a pronounceable, recallable unit. One approach to the study of response integration has been to provide subjects with familiarization training prior to paired-associate learning. Responses low in meaningfulness are made familiar on the grounds that such training should reduce or eliminate the response-learning component of paired associates.

An alternative to the response-chaining view of response learning has been proposed by N. F. Johnson (1969, 1970). He emphasizes that the process of response integration is basically a *coding* process in which the subject forms a code to represent a sequence of letters. The code represents a chunk, such as *sbj,* in the subject's memory, and the recovery (recall) and decoding of the code will produce the individual letters in the correct order. The code is thus some higher-order representation of the letter sequence. This view is similar to Lashley's (1951) classic conception of serial behavior. Although there is some support for the coding conception of response integration, it is not yet clear whether this view will fully supplant the traditional S–R chaining conception.

Stimulus Learning

Another process observed during paired-associate learning is stimulus learning. Although the first influential theory of verbal learning (E. J. Gibson, 1940) held that the process of stimulus discrimination is of central importance, stimulus-learning processes were, until the 1960s, assigned a subordinate or unimportant role; response and associative learning were regarded as of primary importance. However, it is now recognized that stimulus-learning processes play a significant role in paired-associate learning. There are several identifiable components of stimulus learning, including stimulus discrimination, stimulus selection, stimulus coding, and stimulus recognition.

Stimulus Discrimination. The process of discriminating among the stimuli in a paired-associate task is basic to learning a list. Obviously, a given paired-associate stimulus must be differentiated from others in a list in order for it to produce its appropriate response. As stimuli become more similar or confusable, the process of stimulus discrimination becomes more important. Indeed, many experiments (for example, Ellis & Shaffer, 1974; Runquist, 1968; Underwood & Ekstrand, 1968) have shown that as the similarity among the stimuli increases, paired-associate learning is retarded. Finally, to the extent that stimulus discrimination takes place as a result of selective focusing on certain components of a given stimulus, this process overlaps with a second important stimulus-learning process known as stimulus selection.

Stimulus Selection. We have already noted that subjects do not always "use" stimuli as they are presented by the experimenter. That subjects often use only a part of the experimenter-presented stimulus to cue a response calls attention to the distinction between the nominal and the functional stimulus. As noted in earlier chapters, nominal stimuli are experimenter-defined stimuli, whereas functional stimuli are the components actually used by the subject. The significance of stimulus selection is that it is an active process in which subjects come to focus on only a portion of a stimulus and thus can ignore redundant stimulus information (Richardson, 1971, 1972). More generally, the selection process emphasizes the active, strategy-using characteristics of humans.

The basic procedure for studying stimulus selection requires presenting subjects with a list of paired associates in which each stimulus compound contains two or more components and a different response is consistently paired with each compound. For example, a combination of a word and a color might be used as a stimulus compound, or a word and a trigram, or even a single trigram. Following learning of the paired-associate list, the components of each compound are presented individually, and the subjects are asked to recall the appropriate response. For example, if the stimulus compound consisted of *chair* and *xuj,* for which the subjects learned the response *23,* they are shown *chair* and *xuj* individually and asked to recall the correct response. Similarly, if the subjects learned the response *23,* to the single trigram *zaf,* they are presented with the letters *z, a,* and *f* individually and asked to recall the response.

That recall is stronger to one cue than another is the fundamental evidence for the stimulus-selection process. This assumes, of course, that the recall reflects the direct learning of the response to the component, which may not necessarily be the case, as indicated by Postman and Greenbloom (1967). They noted that associations might be formed among the stimulus components themselves during learning; if so, then recall given to one component might actually be mediated by a component/component association rather than by a direct component/response association. For example, subjects might recall the response *23* used in the above example when presented with *xuj* alone; however, they might first recall an association between *xuj* and *chair,* and thus mediate their recall by the sequence *xuj* → *chair* → *23,* without being able to recall directly *xuj* → *23.* To eliminate the possibility of component/component mediation as the basis for recall, Postman and Greenbloom proposed that cue selection be inferred with trigram stimuli only when the subjects recall the correct response to a single letter *and* correspondingly fail to recall additional letters from the trigram. These complications indicate some of the problems involved in inferring cue selection.

Numerous experiments have examined a wide range of factors influencing selection. Representative factors include component meaningfulness of trigrams (for example, Leicht & Kausler, 1965; Underwood, Ham, & Ekstrand, 1962); meaningfulness of colors (Solso, 1968); instructions (Houston, 1967); item position (Lovelace & Blass, 1968; Postman & Greenbloom, 1967); stimulus distinctiveness (Rabinowitz & Witte, 1967); and degree of learning (Berry, Joubert, & Baumeister, 1971; C. T. James & Greeno, 1967).

Stimulus selection is a dynamic process in that cue selection can change over trials or as the result of extended training. James and Greeno (1967) have shown that in the course of learning, subjects come to select the more meaningful part of a word/trigram compound; this finding has been frequently demonstrated and thus is of no special interest. With extended training beyond a criterion of learning, however, they found that subjects continue to learn the weaker (trigram) component, as shown by the fact that recall continues to improve in the presence of the weaker cue. James and Greeno suggest that subjects actively select the more meaningful stimulus during learning but with overtraining they relax their attention to the more dominant stimulus.

Stimulus Coding. A third stimulus-learning process is stimulus coding. This term refers to the process in which nominal stimuli are transformed into some new representation that is easier to use as a cue. A simple example would be changing the trigram *bol* into *bold,* which would be a more meaningful stimulus. The importance of the stimulus-as-coded was noted by Lawrence (1963), who called attention to the principle that the way a stimulus is *encoded,* as distinct from its nominal properties, determines its function in learning tasks. Ellis (1973) has distinguished stimulus coding from stimulus selection by noting that usually coding is viewed as an *elaborative* or reconstructive process involving either rearrangement of the elements of the nominal stimulus or storage of additional information with the nominal stimulus, whereas selection involves responding to only a portion of the nominal stimulus. The way in which a stimulus is encoded is typically inferred from tests of stimulus recognition or from performance on transfer tests. Interest in stimulus coding stems from the general view that performance on a variety of learning tasks, including paired-associate learning, transfer, memory, and concept learning, cannot be fully understood unless we have some measure of the stimulus-as-coded—that is, an understanding of the nature of the stored representation that serves to cue responses.

Stimulus Coding and "Belongingness." One important feature of stimulus coding in paired-associate learning is that the response terms can affect the manner in which stimuli are encoded. This effect is known as response-dependent stimulus encoding and has been demonstrated in several experiments (for example, Ellis, 1968; Martin, 1972). A principal finding of these experiments is that if a response is in some way representative of the stimulus, the response effectively instructs the subjects in what features of the stimulus to encode. The basic idea is that properties of the response can affect the manner or effectiveness with which the stimulus is encoded, which means that a "belongingness" relationship between a stimulus and a response can affect the encoding of the stimulus. For example, if subjects label random shapes with words representative of the shapes, they recognize the shapes much better than if they label the shapes with nonrepresentative words or nonsense syllables (Ellis, 1968).

In a related experiment Martin (1967a) presented evidence indicating that stimulus recognition was unaffected by the association of responses during paired-associate learning. In this study, subjects learned to associate trigram/digit pairs of two types. In one case the subjects learned consistent pairs, and in the other the digits were re-paired on successive study trials. Martin found that the presence of strong, stable associations, as would be expected with the consistently paired items, did *not* enhance the recognizability of the stimuli. On the surface Martin's and Ellis's results appear contradictory, but the apparent difference was clarified in two experiments (Ellis & Shumate, 1973; Ellis & Tatum, 1973).

Using a slight modification of Martin's procedure, Ellis and Tatum demonstrated that pairing of stimuli and responses consistently had no effect on stimulus recognition over re-pairing the items when the responses were digits, which were assumed to be unrepresentative of the stimuli. In contrast, when the responses were representative of the stimuli, stimulus recognition was facilitated.

Ellis and Shumate demonstrated that the encoding effects due to responses were present with low-meaning but not high-meaning stimuli. According to Ellis and Shumate, a low-meaning stimulus can benefit from a response that suggests an encoding, whereas high-meaning stimuli are readily encoded as such and thus do not benefit from response-context factors. Ellis (1973) has formalized this account in a *conceptual-coding hypothesis,* which proposes that stimuli that are initially difficult to encode are more readily influenced by verbal context. More generally, the fact that response terms can affect the way in which stimuli are encoded should not be too surprising and can be viewed as an instance of the more general phenomena of context effects in memory.

Stimulus Recognition and Association Formation. A final issue concerns the relation between stimulus recognition and association formation. This issue focuses on the relation between recognition of the stimulus and recall of the response during paired-associate learning. The issue can be stated as follows: Is stimulus recognition following associative training a necessary prerequisite for recall of the associated response? It would logically appear that an association between a stimulus and its appropriate response could not be activated unless the subject first recognized the stimulus. Martin (1967b) has argued for this dependency based upon his finding that the probability of correctly recalling the response given stimulus recognition steadily increases with paired-associate trials, whereas the probability of correct recall given nonrecognition of the stimulus was no better than chance. Martin's results are shown in Figure 11–6 for two levels of stimulus meaningfulness. The figure shows that the results are comparable for the two levels.

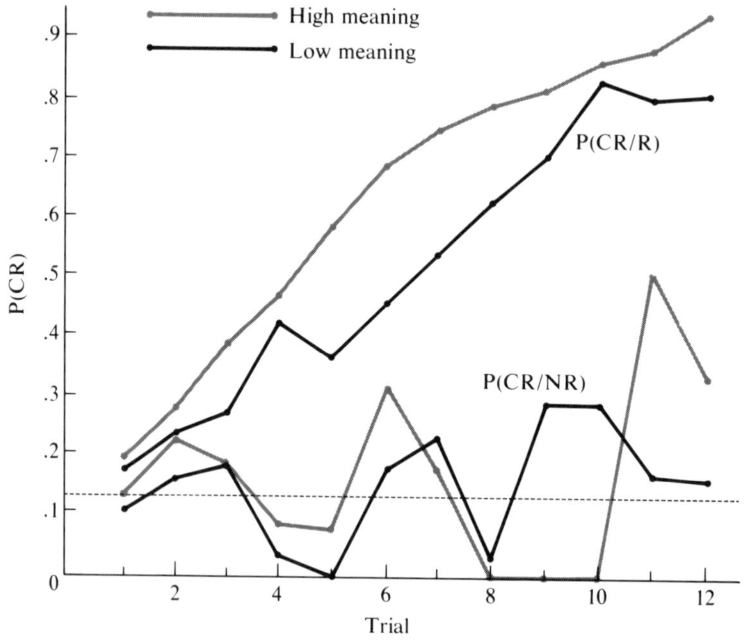

Figure 11–6. Correct recall (CR) of responses as a function of recognition (R) and nonrecognition (NR) of the stimulus terms. (From "Stimulus Recognition in Aural Paired-Associate Learning," by E. Martin, *Journal of Verbal Learning and Verbal Behavior,* 1967, *6,* 272–276. Reprinted by permission of Academic Press, Inc.)

Although these results were replicated by Ellis and Tatum (1973), they also found that the relation between stimulus recognition and response recall depended again upon the "belongingness" relation between the stimuli and responses. Using both single-stimulus and forced-choice methods for stimulus recognition, they found that with representative words as responses, the probabilities of correct response recall given nonrecognition of the stimuli were .53 and .60, respectively; chance recall was .17. In short, subjects could recall the response terms far above the chance level even when they failed to recognize the stimuli! This finding held only with trigram/word pairs, whereas results comparable to Martin's were obtained when trigram/digit pairs were used. Ellis and Tatum account for these findings by assuming that even though a subject may fail to recognize a correct stimulus, the nominal stimulus will allow access to an encoded version of the stimulus that can cue recall of the response.

Associative Learning

In this section we turn our attention directly to several issues in association formation.

Contiguity in Association Formation. The question of contiguity in association formation focuses on the more general issue of how associations are learned. This question is complicated because humans have already learned many associations prior to participating in an experiment. Frequently we use mediating events to help associate two items. Consider learning the association *pipe/sleep*. This is easily learned if you think of *pipe dream* as a common expression and then *dream/sleep*. Thus, the word *dream* enables you to hook up efficiently the words *pipe* and *sleep*. We obviously learn many associations simply by bringing to bear our rich associative networks in linking stimuli and responses. But where do the linkages come from? How are they established in the first place? Can two events be associated simply on the basis of contiguity without any obvious intent to learn? The answer to the last question appears to be yes.

Spear, Ekstrand, and Underwood (1964) have provided evidence indicating that contiguity itself appears to be sufficient for association formation. Subjects were first required to learn a verbal-discrimination task consisting of 12 pairs of low-frequency words to a criterion of two successive perfect trials. Recall that in verbal-discrimination learning the subject has only to recognize which member of each pair of words the experimenter has designated as correct. The task permits the repeated contiguous presentation of two words without requiring that the subject establish an association between them. The research question was whether associations would be established as a result of repeated contiguity under these circumstances. The test of this was to place the words in a paired-associate task after they had been used in the verbal-discrimination task. Three kinds of pairs were formed. For some of the subjects, the pairs were identical to those in the verbal-discrimination list; these constituted *appropriate* pairs. Another group of subjects learned items from the discrimination list that were rearranged into different pairs in the paired-associate list, constituting *inappropriate* pairs. A third group learned a paired-associate list containing words unrelated to those learned in a prior discrimination list; this condition constituted a control for learning-to-learn and warm-up effects.

The experimenters reasoned that if associations between words are being established during verbal-discrimination learning, these associations should transfer to a paired-associate list in which the words are appropriately paired. In contrast, when the words are inappropriately paired in the paired-associate task, the previously acquired associations should generate interference. The basic results, shown in Figure 11–7, fully confirmed the researchers' predictions. The figure clearly shows that more correct responses to the appropriate pairs were made relative to the control condition, whereas fewer correct responses were made to the inappropriate pairs. In brief, these results strongly support the contiguity hypothesis on association formation.

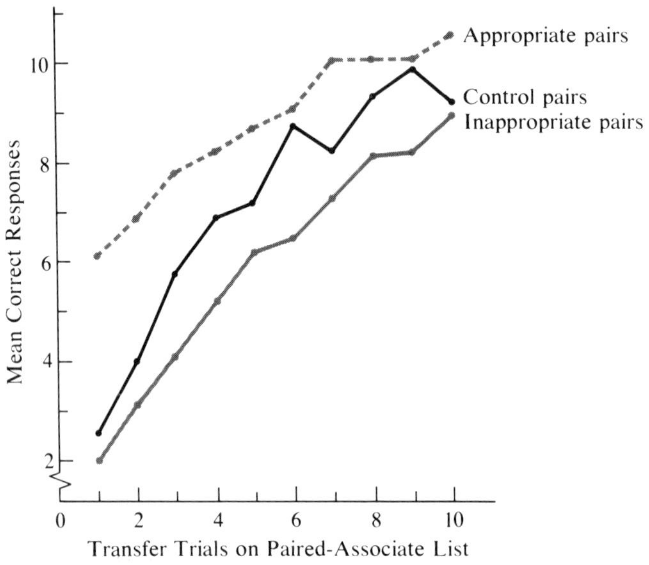

Figure 11–7. Mean correct responses on a paired-associate list as a function of appropriate or inappropriate pairing during verbal-discrimination learning. (From "Association by Contiguity," by N. E. Spear, B. R. Ekstrand, and B. J. Underwood, *Journal of Experimental Psychology,* 1964, *67,* 151–161. Copyright 1964 by the American Psychological Association. Reprinted by permission.)

Backward Associations. The paired-associate task normally requires only the learning of forward (S–R) associations, or associations in which the direction is from stimulus to response. Backward (R–S) associations are also learned; these are inferred when subjects recall the stimulus when presented with the response as a cue. There is substantial evidence that backward associations are readily acquired in paired-associate learning (for example, Ekstrand, 1966; Kanak & Neuner, 1970; Kausler & Kanoti, 1963; Wollen, 1970). Common experiences also attest to the everyday learning of backward associations. For example, in learning the foreign-language equivalents of English words, you learn the pairs not only in a forward direction but also the backward associations to some extent.

The principal theoretical issue regarding backward associations has been the principle of *associative symmetry* espoused by Asch and Ebenholtz (1962). According to this view, the strength of a backward association between *b* and *a* is equal to the strength of the forward association between *a* and *b*. Although empirically the forward association is usually stronger (Ekstrand, 1966), the argument for associative symmetry is based largely on the difference in availability between stimulus and response terms. The stimulus need only be recognized, whereas the response must be recalled. Since the response terms are more available than the stimulus terms, it is argued that if the stimuli were made as available as the responses, associative symmetry would prevail. Attempts to increase the availability of the stimuli have not, however, led to consistent results (Ekstrand, 1966).

Recent work suggests that forward and backward associations are not necessarily equivalent even when stimuli and responses are equally available. Furthermore, Kausler

(1974, pp. 169–176) points out a number of methodological issues that still cloud this question and indicate that the problem is not yet fully resolved. Nevertheless, three features of this research have begun to emerge: (1) the evidence is largely against an associative-symmetry principle; (2) forward and backward associations appear to be separable, contrary to the Asch and Ebenholtz principle; and (3) backward associations tend to be weaker in a number of circumstances despite various elaborate efforts to equate stimulus and response availability.

Incremental versus One-Trial Learning. Psychologists allied with associationistic conceptions of learning have, historically, viewed the process as *incremental.* According to this view, association formation is a gradual and continuous process that develops over repeated trials. In contrast to the incremental view is the belief that associations are formed on an all-or-none basis. This view emphasizes that once an association is formed, it develops full associative strength; hence, this view is a *one-trial* conception of learning.

The difference between the two is illustrated in Figure 11–8, which shows a schematic representation of the learning of a single paired associate as interpreted by an incremental theory and by a one-trial theory. Associative strength is assumed to vary from zero to maximum strength. In the incremental position associative strength grows gradually over trials; in the one-trial theory associative strength goes from zero to maximum on one trial.

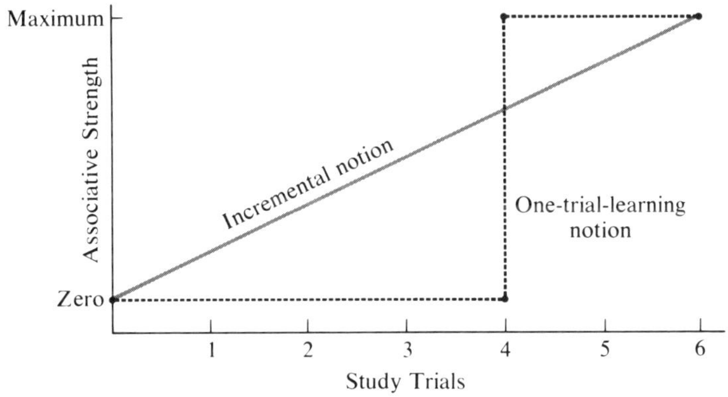

Figure 11–8. Schematic representation of the learning of a single paired-associate list as viewed by incremental theory and one-trial theory. (From "One-Trial Learning?" by B. J. Underwood and G. Keppel, *Journal of Verbal Learning and Verbal Behavior,* 1962, *1,* 1–13. Reprinted by permission of Academic Press, Inc.)

The majority of verbal-learning psychologists viewed association formation as an incremental process, a view having continuity with classical S–R theory (see, for example, Hull, 1943), until provoked into reevaluation of their position by an experiment by Rock (1957). Rock found that paired-associate learning under typical repeated trials was no better than learning with a "drop out" procedure in which pairs were eliminated from the list if they were not learned on the first trial and were replaced with new pairs. Rock concluded that learning is a one-trial process and that repetition is unnecessary for learning. Rock's procedures were quickly criticized, however, especially the use of the dropout procedure, which allowed learning of only the easier items (see, for example, Postman, 1962a).

The upshot of this research is that the controversy between one-trial and incremental theories has quieted down, with little current activity. The positive consequence of this research has been to increase psychologists' attention to the range of processes involved in paired-associate learning. Paired-associate learning is far from being a rote association-formation affair but is highly complex. In a cogent summary of this issue, Kintsch (1970) concludes that it has been improperly posed. As he suggests, the true issue seems to be one of distinguishing between the conditions in which learning might be represented as an all-or-none process or the sum of several all-or-none processes and those in which learning might be represented as an incremental process. At present we do not have clear answers to these questions. However, what is clear is that the widely accepted belief that learning is a gradual, incremental process has been challenged by a new body of research.

Summary

This chapter has described some of the major laboratory procedures, empirical findings, and theoretical interpretations in the study of verbal learning. Although research on verbal learning began with a study of the learning and retention of associations, it has expanded to cover a vast array of human verbal processes. Verbal learning is now seen as a complex, multiprocess affair in which coding and organizational processes, rules and strategies, all of which are part of cognitive psychology, play important roles.

Researchers studying verbal learning use a wide variety of materials, ranging from single items to connected discourse. Syllables, words, phrases, sentences, and paragraphs are still used; which one depends on the particular issue under investigation. Five types of procedures are typically used: serial learning, paired-associate learning, free recall, recognition learning, and verbal-discrimination learning. Each procedure taps somewhat different processes or components of verbal learning, so the choice of procedure depends upon the research problem. Several variations of these procedures are also used.

Several factors affecting verbal learning were described. The meaningfulness of the material is an important factor. Its effect on learning appears to be due to the greater readiness with which more meaningful materials can be encoded as functional units. Frequency and pronounceableness are also important variables and are correlated with meaningfulness. The similarity of materials has a complex effect on learning, both facilitating and retarding learning depending upon the type of similarity and the components of the learning involved. The enhancing effect of concreteness appears to be due to the imagery-evoking capacity of the materials studied. The importance of imagery was documented. The study of prose learning is receiving increasing attention, and the role of grammatical/linguistic factors is now clearly recognized. Semantic factors were seen to be especially important in the learning of prose material.

Stage analysis of verbal learning indicates that paired-associate learning is composed of several processes, including response learning, associative learning, and stimulus learning. Relations between stimulus recognition and association formation were examined. The role of contiguity in association formation and the nature of backward associations were discussed.

Chapter 12

Organization and Coding in Memory

We have already noted that an important characteristic of human memory is that it is organized. Humans are viewed as actively processing information rather than just passively registering it. Moreover, new information stored in long-term memory is thought to be frequently integrated and made congruent with existing information in order to maximize available storage capacity. In this chapter we will discuss coding and organizational processes in memory and look at some of the evidence for these processes.

Organization in Free Recall

Since the items in a free-recall task can be recalled in any order, this method provides insight into the ways in which humans organize and retrieve information. Although the free-recall procedure was described early in the history of psychology, it was not widely used until the 1960s. The popularity of this method in current research is largely due to its flexibility and to the variety of processes that can be studied with it. Indeed, it is one of the most widely used methods in human learning and memory research today.

A distinction between two kinds of organization in memory has been suggested by Tulving (1968). One kind is defined as some consistent discrepancy between input and output orders that is independent of subjects' prior familiarity with the set of input items. Input order is simply the order in which the items are presented for study; output order is the order in which the items are recalled. Organization, as defined in this fashion is labeled *primary organization*. An example can be seen in the recency effect, which is subjects' tendency to recall the last items on a list first, regardless of the characteristics of the items. In contrast, *secondary organization* refers to situations in which subjects' output order is governed by semantic or other characteristics of the items themselves. We noted evidence for primary organization in our earlier discussion of free recall and input order of the list (Murdock, 1962), so we will confine our discussion here to the latter type of organization. We will first consider some examples of organization based on semantic characteristics.

Clustering in Free Recall

One type of secondary organizational process is *clustering* in free recall, which refers to situations in which the output is governed by semantic or phonetic relations among the items. Clustering can be of two types, *associative* and *categorical*. In associative clustering, associatively related words, such as *night* and *day* or *bread* and *butter,* are recalled one after the other even though they were presented in a scrambled order. In categorical clustering the recall order of items is determined by the conceptual relations of items on the list.

Category Clustering. One of the earliest investigations of category clustering in free recall was conducted by W. A. Bousfield (1953). He found that when subjects attempted to recall from a categorized list, they tended to recall words that belonged to a given category in clusters. For example, a subject's recall protocol, or order of output, might be *donkey, zebra, wildcat, carrot, lettuce, Byron, Adam, Howard, Wallace, typist, plumber, dentist, waiter,* even though items had been presented in a quite different order. This example illustrates perfect clustering although this is not typically observed. The identification of a clustered sequence in recall is thus defined objectively in terms of consecutive recalls that are all members of an experimenter-predetermined category.

Bousfield also developed a quantitative index of clustering that he called the *repetition ratio*. This ratio is obtained by dividing, for each subject, the number of consecutive items recalled from the same category by the total number of repetitions possible for the words recalled. This index was compared with an index calculated on the basis of chance; the mean repetition ratio for Bousfield's subjects was .45, whereas chance was .24. Since Bousfield's early work, a number of alternative measures have been proposed (see, for example, A. K. Bousfield & Bousfield, 1966; Roenker, Thompson, & Brown, 1971). In general, these are minor changes based upon assumptions about scoring free recall.

Bousfield's 1953 study did not address the question of whether clustering itself actually aids recall. Clearly, subjects cluster in free recall or categorized lists, but do they actually recall more words from a categorically organized list than from a control list of equal length but without an obvious structure? The results of several experiments (for example, Cofer, 1967; Puff, 1970) suggest that the answer to this question is affirmative. Puff found, for instance, about 55% recall of a list of 30 items divided equally into three categories but only 44% recall from a control list matched for frequency and other characteristics.

As you might suspect, the fundamental question that emerges is whether the greater recall of words in a categorized list *depends* upon clustering. What we have seen so far is a correlation between clustering and recall, but a correlation does not necessarily imply a causal relationship. Puff approached this problem by dividing his subjects into two groups on the basis of their clustering, thus obtaining a group of high clusterers and a group of low clusterers, and then compared them on recall accuracy. Surprisingly, Puff found that the groups were very similar in recall despite differences in clustering. Thus, any causal relationship between clustering and recall was questionable. Puff concluded that something other than clustering must underlie the superior recall of categorized lists. This unexpected finding complicated thinking about clustering and recall.

Insight into Puff's negative results came from a study by C. P. Thompson, Hamlin, and Roenker (1972). They noted that Puff gave his subjects only one trial and that the one trial may not have been sufficient for a relation between clustering and recall to appear. These researchers gave their subjects three trials on each of three categorized lists and used more categories and more items. Each list contained 48 items split into four categories.

When they divided their subjects into high and low clusterers, they found a clear positive relationship between clustering and recall, beginning with the first trial. High clusterers recalled substantially more items throughout practice.

Associative Clustering. Related to Bousfield's work on category clustering is associative clustering, the tendency of subjects to recall items in clusters that are known to have associative connections. An experiment by J. J. Jenkins and Russell (1952) illustrates this type of clustering. They had subjects recall a list of 48 words composed of stimulus–response pairs selected from the Kent and Rosanoff norms of associatively related words, such as *table* and *chair*. The words were presented in a random order, but in recall the subjects showed a clear tendency to recall associates in clusters. Subsequent studies (for example, W.A. Bousfield, Whitmarsh, & Berkowitz, 1960) have shown that the amount of associative clustering in recall correlates positively with the degree of associative relatedness among the words.

Other Factors in Clustering. Psychologists have examined a large number of factors that influence clustering in free recall, and in this section we will discuss the effects of several kinds of factors. One line of research has examined the generality of the clustering effect to other kinds of materials. For example, Cofer and Bruce (1965), using nouns, verbs, and adjectives, found no evidence for clustering based on grammatical categories. Other studies have examined clustering based on acoustic similarity, and the results have been mixed. Both W. A. Bousfield and Wicklund (1969) and Dolinsky (1972) have reported positive results, whereas Forrester and King (1971) have reported negative results.

Another factor is blocked versus random presentation of the items, which has the obvious effect of making the presence of categories more apparent to the subject. In general, the results indicate greater recall and clustering with blocked presentations (see, for example, Cofer, Bruce, & Reicher, 1966; Puff, 1966).

Finally, the number of categories in a list and the size of the categories can influence recall. Larger categories certainly would be expected to yield poorer recall, a result obtained by Slamecka (1967). The role of number of categories, however, is more complicated. For example, Dallett (1964) performed a series of experiments investigating the effects of number of categories on amount of recall. The results depended upon whether the subjects recalled from short lists (12 items) or long lists (24 items). With long lists Dallett found that recall decreased with more categories in the list, using one, two, three, four, or six categories, whereas with short lists the relationship was curvilinear, with the best recall for an intermediate number of categories. Dallett's subjects were not provided with the category names, nor were they cued for recall.

If cues are provided during recall, the relationship between number of categories and recall appears to be the opposite of the findings reported by Dallett. The role of cues versus noncued recall was carefully examined in an experiment by Tulving and Pearlstone (1966). They varied the number of items per category (one, two, or four items) in lists of three different lengths (12, 24, or 48 items). (Note that when the number of items per category is varied in a list of a *fixed* length, the number of categories is automatically varied.) The subjects were given three kinds of recall tests: cued recall, noncued (free) recall, and cued recall following noncued recall. Figure 12–1 shows the mean number of words recalled for the various conditions of the experiment. Regardless of the length of the list, there was a tendency for recall to improve with fewer items per category (hence, more categories) when recall was cued. The reverse was true with noncued (free) recall. These data clearly reveal the importance of retrieval cues in recall: cued recall resulted in the best performance, cued recall following noncued recall resulted in the next best performance, and noncued recall resulted in the poorest performance.

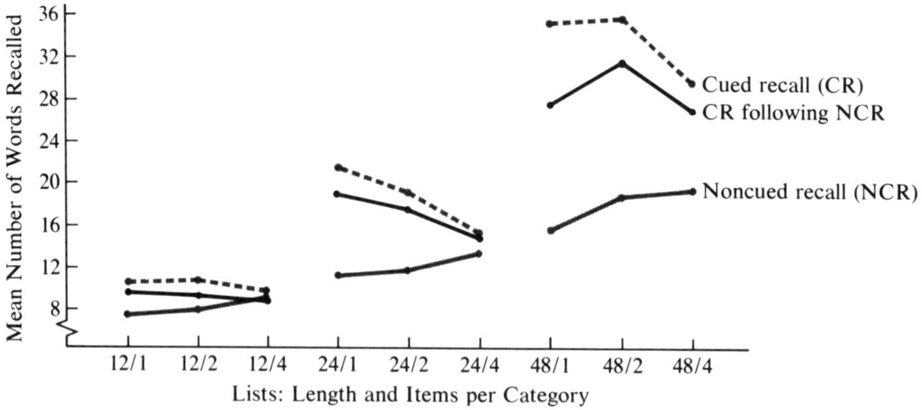

Figure 12–1. Recall as a function of the type of cuing situation. (From "Availability versus Accessibility of Information in Memory for Words," by E. Tulving and Z. Pearlstone, *Journal of Verbal Learning and Verbal Behavior,* 1966, *5,* 381–391. Reprinted by permission of Academic Press, Inc.)

Subjective Organization

So far, we have examined studies in which the materials to be learned are categorized or associated in some way. What happens when subjects are given lists to learn that have no evident categories or structure? Do subjects show evidence for organization of unrelated items? Clear evidence for organization in this type of situation has been shown by Tulving (1962). Tulving believed that evidence for organization of unrelated items would be revealed by subject's tendency to recall a series of unrelated words in much the same order on successive trials.

Basic Findings. Tulving's experiment required subjects to learn a list of 16 unrelated words; the words were arranged in 16 different trial orders such that each word appeared once in a given position. The words were presented at a fairly fast rate (one per second), and following each trial the subjects were given 90 seconds to recall as many words as possible. The mean number of words recalled and an index of the amount of subjective organization as a function of number of trials are shown in Figure 12–2. The index of subjective organization is based upon pairwise dependencies in successive recall, and the interested reader should consult Tulving (1962) for the details of this measure. Basically, the increase in subjective organization simply means that the subject's recall order became more consistent over successive trials. As can be seen in the figure, both recall and the index of subjective organization increased over trials, and the two measures correlated highly. It is clear that even with a series of unrelated words humans impose some kind of organization in free recall.

As in the case of clustering, an important theoretical question in free recall is the nature of the relationship between degree of subjective organization and amount of recall. Does subjective organization actually lead to increases in recall? Tulving's (1962) initial evidence was only correlational (for example, $r = .78$ for subjective organization and recall

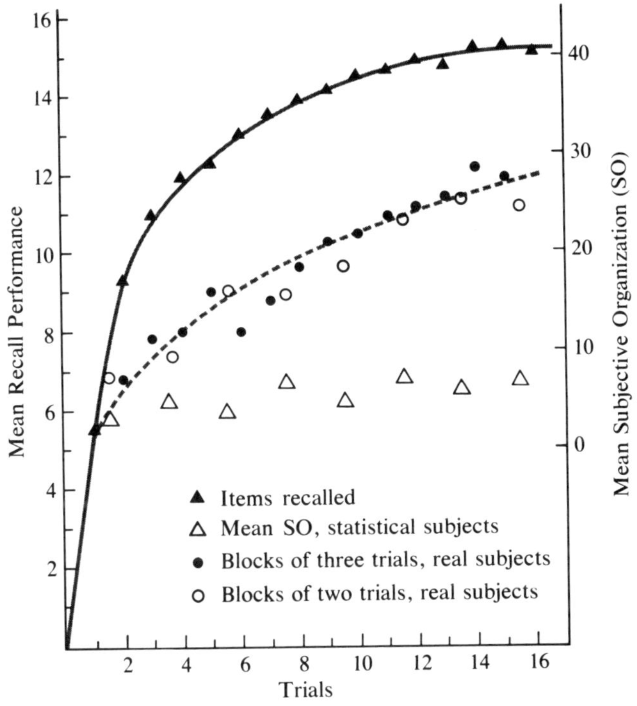

Figure 12–2. Mean recall performance with unrelated words and mean subjective organization as a function of number of trials. (From "Subjective Organization in Free Recall of 'Unrelated' Words," by E. Tulving, *Psychological Review,* 1962, *69,* 344–354. Copyright 1962 by the American Psychological Association. Reprinted by permission.)

for individual subjects over Trials 9 to 16), which does not necessarily imply a causal relationship. However, some indirect evidence in favor of a causal relationship is available (see, for example, Allen, 1968; M. Earhard, 1967). This evidence is generally of the form in which some experimental variable is manipulated, and if the manipulation affects both measures of organization and free recall concomitantly, support is lent to the causal interpretation. On the other hand, other studies have not shown a relationship betwen subjective organization and recall. Indeed, Postman (1971, 1972) has suggested that there are good reasons that organization will not necessarily be reflected in a high degree of output consistency. As he points out, a one-to-one relation between degree of organization and output consistency can be expected only when the groupings are based on a sequential rule, such as an alphabetical schema. For a critical examination of organizational theory and methodology, see papers by Postman (1972) and Wood (1972) and the volume by Tulving and Donaldson (1972).

Part/Whole Transfer. Another line of evidence that initially appeared to support a causal relationship between subjective organization and free recall came from studies of *part/whole transfer* in free recall. The logic of such studies was advanced by Tulving (1966), who hypothesized that having subjects learn part of a free-recall list prior to learning the entire list might actually hinder their learning of the entire list. The argument was that higher-order units established during part learning may not be useful in learning the entire list because they would have to be reorganized during whole-list learning and would thus offset any advantage due to prior learning of single items.

Tulving's hypothesis is of interest in part because it is not what common sense seems to predict. Intuitively we might expect that if we already know half the words on a list, learning the entire list would be easier even though the old and new words are mixed in the complete list. In addition, Tulving's hypothesis is incompatible with any frequency theory of learning because we would expect that subjects who had learned the partial list would show superior performance on the whole list on the basis of differential frequency of experience.

Tulving (1966) required two groups of subjects to learn an entire list of 36 unrelated words. Prior to learning the whole list the experimental subjects received eight trials of learning 18 words selected from the whole list. The control subjects received eight trials in learning 18 unrelated words that did not appear on the whole list. Figure 12–3 shows the free-recall learning curves for the two conditions on the whole list of 36 words. Although the part-list group had an initial advantage over the group starting from scratch, the latter surpassed the part-list group after the fourth trial. Tulving concluded that whatever organization had been acquired during learning of the partial list eventually came to interfere with learning the second list. This finding has been replicated in several experiments (for example, Birnbaum, 1968; G. H. Bower & Lesgold, 1969), so the effect can be regarded as reliable.

Tulving's interpretation was, however, quickly questioned on both theoretical and methodological grounds. As an alternative, Novinski (1972) proposed a hypothesis that is the reverse of Tulving's, arguing that the negative-transfer effect—that is, the poorer performance of the part-list group—is the result of the subjects' failure to retain the organization developed during the learning of the partial list. Both hypotheses are organizational theories, but they are otherwise reversed. Novinski's argument is based on her finding that positive transfer from part learning to whole learning resulted simply from instructing the experimental subjects about the nature of the whole list.

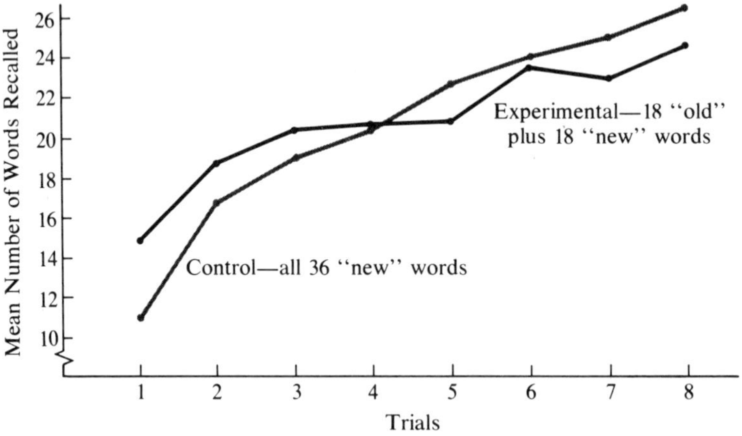

Figure 12–3. Free-recall learning curves for control and experimental groups of subjects. The experimental group learned half of the test-list words before learning the test list; the control group learned an unrelated list of words. (From "Subjective Organization and Effects of Repetition in Multi-trial Free-Recall Learning," by E. Tulving, *Journal of Verbal Learning and Verbal Behavior,* 1966, *5,* 193–197. Reprinted by permission of Academic Press, Inc.)

In addition to these two organizational hypotheses, alternative hypotheses emphasizing list discrimination have been proposed. Slamecka, Moore, and Carey (1972) have suggested that in learning the whole list, some of the subjects in the experimental condition (part-list training) will recognize that some of the part-list items have been included in the whole list; they may not be certain, however, that *all* of the part-list items have been included. Because of this uncertainty, the experimental subjects may raise their *criterion* for responding and thus withhold responses that would have been correct.

A second list-discrimination hypothesis has been proposed by J. R. Anderson and Bower (1972) and Schwartz and Humphreys (1973). The Anderson and Bower hypothesis is that the negative transfer obtained in the part/whole-transfer paradigm is due to the experimental subjects' difficulties in associating List 2 markers (list tags) with items previously associated with several List 1 markers. The result is that the learning of new list tags for "old" words in List 2 is retarded. In a comparison of all of these hypotheses, R. J. Sternberg and Bower (1974) have concluded that the pattern of results best favors their version of list discrimination and fails to support either version of organization theory.

Coding Processes

We have emphasized that information is not processed directly but is encoded in some fashion. We also noted that humans selectively attend to their environment, that they process information in serial or parallel fashion or both, and that they store information in the form of memory codes. In this section we will examine some selected issues in coding.

Rehearsal Strategies

Perhaps the simplest type of coding strategy involves the rehearsal of verbal information. It has generally been assumed that humans do rehearse information to be remembered by simply repeating the material either covertly or overtly. Rehearsal may also involve attempts to relate the information to be learned to an existing store of knowledge. Thus, rehearsal can be an *elaborative* process.

The experimental study of rehearsal has expanded with the development of an overt-rehearsal procedure by Rundus and Atkinson (1970) and Rundus (1971). This procedure was briefly described in Chapter 9, but we will discuss it in greater detail here. Their procedure allows a rather direct study of rehearsal by minimizing the complications of mediational processes that may normally occur. They asked their subjects to rehearse aloud the words from a list while it was presented and then recorded the overt rehearsals on tape. The usual serial-position curve was obtained, showing primacy and recency effects. The early items on the list were rehearsed more frequently than the other items, and except for the last few items on the list, correct recall of the items was closely related to the number of rehearsals.

Once it was clear that rehearsal is an important factor in storing information in LTM, an obvious issue was the role of different rehearsal strategies in recall. Atkinson and Shiffrin (1971) have provided clear evidence that the particular strategy a subject uses during rehearsal affects recall. In their experiment two groups of subjects were used: one group rehearsed each word three times prior to the presentation of the next word (one-word strategy), whereas the other group rehearsed the three most recent items (three-word strategy). The important point is that using the second strategy results in more rehearsals for the early items than does the first strategy. This will be obvious if you think about how you would actually rehearse in the two conditions. For example, in a list consisting of *apple, car, chair,* and *pencil,* the one-word strategy would result in the following rehearsal sequence: "apple, apple, apple; car, car, car; chair, chair, chair; pencil, pencil, pencil." In contrast, the three-word strategy would result in the following rehearsal sequence: "apple, apple, apple; car, car, apple; chair, car, apple; pencil, chair, car." Keep in mind that rehearsal occurs after the presentation of each word, which explains the sequence of the second strategy. Thus, in the second strategy *apple* is rehearsed five times, *car* is rehearsed four, and so on. With the second procedure the usual primacy effect in recall is obtained, whereas no primacy effect occurs with the first strategy.

Release from Proactive Inhibition

Another approach to the study of coding processes stems from a procedure developed by Wickens, Born, and Allen (1963) called release from proactive inhibition (PI). It has been proposed by several psychologists (G. H. Bower, 1967; Norman & Rumelhart, 1970; Underwood, 1969; Wickens, 1970) that memories of verbal information are coded in terms of attributes. The basic idea is that our memory of a word may be represented as a bundle of attributes, including physical, semantic, and other characteristics. Thus, when we store a particular word in memory, we may actually encode many features of the word, such as number of syllables, number of phonemes, taxonomic category, and sense impression, to mention only a few.

The basic procedure used by Wickens (1970, 1972) involves the study of short-term memory (Peterson & Peterson, 1959). The procedure for the control groups begins with a brief presentation of a group of three words (a triad) belonging to a common class, such as *apple, banana,* and *orange.* This is followed by a rehearsal-prevention task of counting backward by 3s for 20 seconds. Then the subjects are asked to recall the words. Finally, a new triad of items is presented, and the process is repeated. The control group continues in this fashion for four trials, with the triads always belonging to the same class. For example, a list would appear as follows: *apple, banana, orange; pear, grape, lemon; peach, lime, grapefruit; tangerine, plum, pineapple.* In contrast, the experimental group receives different triads for the first three trials but is shifted on the fourth trial to a new class of words

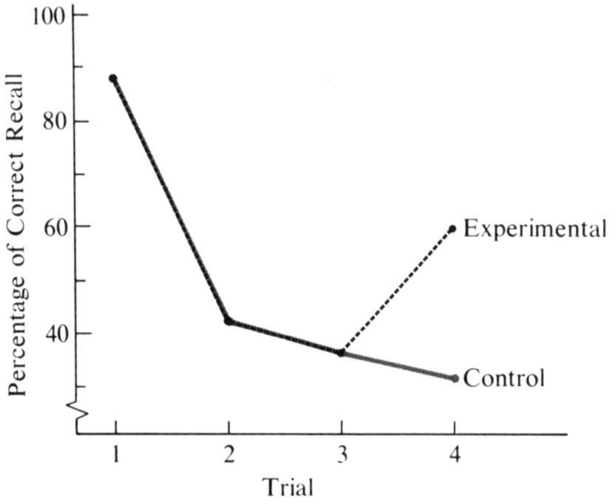

Figure 12–4. Illustration of release from proactive inhibition, showing the percentage of correct recall for experimental and control groups. (From "Characteristics of Word Encoding," by D. D. Wickens. In A. W. Melton and E. Martin (Eds.), *Coding Processes in Human Memory.* Copyright 1972 by H. V. Winston. Reprinted by permission of the publisher, Hemisphere Publishing Corporation.)

that is the same as that given the experimental subjects. Figure 12–4 shows typical results from a large number of studies. The control group shows a steady reduction in recall over all trials, which Wickens attributes to the build-up of PI in the recall of related words. The same pattern is shown in the experimental group for the first three trials, but on the fourth trial the experimental group shows a dramatic improvement in recall. Since on this trial the subjects have been shifted to a new class of items, Wickens attributes the improvement to a release from PI.

The importance of this procedure is that it allows investigation of the attributes that have been encoded by switching from various classes of materials. Wickens (1970) concludes that when a PI release is obtained, the subjects were encoding predominantly on the same attributes over successive triads during the PI build-up. Accordingly, the identification of an attribute depends upon having both a PI build-up and a PI release (Underwood, 1972). The results of a large number of studies indicate that humans are sensitive to (and thus encode) a large number of word attributes but are insensitive to certain other aspects. Humans are quite sensitive to semantic attributes of words, moderately sensitive to physical characteristics, and rather insensitive to syntactical features (Wickens, 1972).

Context Effects and Memory

The study of context effects in memory is of interest because such effects can throw light on the way humans encode as well as retrieve information. Our memory of some event or target item can be very dependent on the prevailing context at the time the information was encoded. The prevailing context can be any or all other events at the time of encoding. For instance, if you meet someone while drinking beer in a particular bar, you may not be able to recall that person in any other context. In short, your memory can be contextually dependent, although it may not be as extreme as in this example. You may recall the person the next time you drink another beer even in another location; moreover, recall may be even less cue-dependent, so that you recall the person when you are in another social situation. The more general significance of context effects in encoding is that the prediction as well as the explanation of human behavior is dependent upon the way information is represented in memory. For instance, the representation of the word *punch* in memory will depend upon the way in which it is encoded. Depending upon whether the verbal context is *spiked* or *hefty,* different features will be stored.

The general approach in context studies has been to present a to-be-remembered item embedded in some verbal context during training. The context can consist of words, phrases, sentences, or any other material. At testing, the to-be-remembered word can be presented with the same context as during training, with a new context, or with context completely omitted. In general, changing the context produces poorer recognition of the to-be-remembered word than keeping the context the same (see, for example, R. R. Hunt & Ellis, 1974; Light & Carter-Sobell, 1970; Tulving & Thomson, 1971; Winograd & Conn, 1971). For example, if the training context is *strawberry* and the target item is *jam,* changing the context during testing to *traffic* will produce a decrease in recognition. This decrease is particularly marked when, as in this example, the new context implies a different meaning. Deletion of all context in testing usually results in recognition performance intermediate between that produced by keeping the same context and that produced by context changes that alter the meaning of the target item (Hunt & Ellis, 1974; Thomson, 1972). Winograd and Conn (1971) have reported that the effect of adding new context at testing depended upon the semantic relation between the context and the target item (a noun). For instance, a new context that implies a familiar meaning of the noun (for example, *round/ball)* produces greater recognition than a new context that implies a less familiar meaning (for example, *dance/ball*).

Context and Encoding Specificity

The study of contextual factors and memory is interesting not only because it reveals something about the nature of encoding but also because it may reveal something about retrieval processes. If contextual information is presented with a target noun at input (for example, *vigorous/health*), and if the contextual information actually influences the way the target noun is encoded, then the context should serve as an effective retrieval cue when an attempt is made to recall the target noun. In short, the cue word *vigorous* should permit easy access to *health*.

In a study of context cues in recall, Tulving and Osler (1968) found that cue words (context cues) facilitated recall of target words when the cue words were present at both study and testing, whereas retrieval cues did not enhance recall of the target words when presented only at testing. In other words, if a retrieval cue was to be effective, it had to be present at input. From these results Tulving and Osler concluded that specific retrieval cues aid recall *if and only if* the information about them and their relation to the target words are stored at input. This generalization has come to be known as the *encoding-specificity principle,* and in its strongest form it contends that context cues will be effective in retrieving information only to the extent that the cues were encoded with the to-be-remembered information (Tulving & Thomson, 1973). For example, the cue *table* will aid recall of the target word *chair* if and only if the encoding of the target word includes the semantic relation between the cue and target words.

The results of several experiments dealing with *extralist* retrieval cues (for example, Bahrick, 1969; Bilodeau, 1967; Fox, Blick, & Bilodeau,1964) appear to disprove this principle. In these studies retrieval cues were provided to subjects *only* at the time of recall, but the cues nevertheless facilitated recall. Tulving and Thomson (1973) give several possible interpretations of these results. One possibility is simply that during encoding the subjects stored the target word in relation to a cue that was not present during training but was present during testing. For example, Tulving and Osler (1968) note that if the to-be-remembered word is *bulb,* at least some subjects are likely to think of it as having something to do with light even though *light* is not actually presented as the context. They argue that if *light* is presented as a retrieval cue, it will be as effective for those subjects who thought of it at input as for subjects who might have been given *light* as context. In response to this argument, R. R. Hunt and Ellis (1974) have noted that it may, in some sense, compromise the principle of encoding specificity if we are allowed to specify the encoding of the target item in this fashion. If an extralist cue is effective, we must *assume* that it was encoded at input. Thus, the Tulving and Osler argument may run the risk of being circular.

Santa and Lamwers (1974) have suggested that when extralist cues have failed to be effective (Thomson & Tulving, 1970), the subjects may simply have been confused about what to do when presented with extralist retrieval cues that were strong associates of the target words. Santa and Lamwers found that extralist cues that are strong associates of the target words can serve as retrieval cues when the subjects are informed about the relation between the target and cue words. In response to this finding, Wiseman and Tulving (1976) agree that strong target associates can serve effectively as retrieval cues but argue that the encoding-specificity principle still holds. We can expect to see continued evaluation of this principle by further experimental work.

Stimulus Variability, Perceptual Grouping, and Memory

A traditional assumption in human learning and memory is that no two nominally identical stimulus events are functionally identical on successive presentations. Although the exact identity of stimulus events is in part a matter of psychologists' inability to control the precise conditions of stimulation on successive presentations, it is also true that humans do not always attend to the same aspects of stimulation and may encode on different features of nominally identical events.

Although our theories of human learning and memory have focused largely on *encoding* variability (G. H. Bower, 1972b; Martin, 1972), which concerns the variability of the hypothetical representation in memory, another approach to the study of coding processes has been to examine the effects of nominal stimulus variations on recognition and recall. This line of research can be easily appreciated by considering the following question: Is it better to reread the same article on a given topic several times in order to retain the information, or is it better to read different versions of the same topic? In a similar vein consider this question: Is it better to study the same photograph of a person's face in order to remember the face, or is it better to study several photographs of the same face that vary in, say, background? As you can see, the issue is one of repetition versus varied input, where *varied input* refers to situations in which contextual and/or structural variations of stimuli are introduced in the course of study and subjects are then tested for recall of the events.

The study of varied input versus repetition in memory has been approached in two ways. In the first case only *contextual* stimuli present during training are varied, and subjects are tested for memory of a consistently associated response. This approach is typical of the work of Bevan and his colleagues. For example, in one study (Dukes & Bevan, 1967), stimuli of the class *Ax, Bx, Cx, Dx,* and so on were presented, where *x* was the common feature and *A, B, C,* and *D* were the modifying elements. Thus, *x* could represent the photograph of a particular person, and *A, B, C,* or *D* could represent his or her appearance in different poses or dress. In this instance, pictures of models from a Sears catalog were used as stimuli. For each picture of the same class (the same model), subjects learned a particular name and were then tested for recall of the name when shown either one of the old training pictures (for example, *Bx*) or a new picture of the same model (for example, *Mx*). Different models, of course, received different names. The effect of varied training depended upon whether the test stimulus (picture) was truly an old one seen in training or a new picture from the same category. Varying the stimuli during training produced superior cued recall (using either old or new pictures) compared to that produced by repetition training but with new pictures presented at recall. In contrast, repetition training always produced superior recall compared to all other conditions when the test pictures were old.

The second approach to the study of variability has been to vary directly the structural properties of the *entire stimulus* to be placed in memory, as distinct from varying only the contextual elements. This approach is exemplified by the work of G. H. Bower and his colleagues (for example, Bower & Springston, 1970; Bower & Winzenz, 1969; Winzenz, 1972; Winzenz & Bower, 1970) and of Ellis and his colleagues (for example, Ellis, Parente, Grah, & Spiering, 1975; Ellis, Parente, & Walker, 1974; R. R. Hunt, Parente, & Ellis, 1974).

Bower's approach has typically examined the effects of constant input (repetition training) versus variable input in the learning of digit and letter series. For example, a digit sequence such as 856742931564 may have been presented auditorily as 856—7—4293—1564, where the dashes represent pauses in presentation. The sequences were presented successively either as consistently grouped or as differently grouped prior to a test of immediate recall of the digit strings. A basic finding throughout Bower's studies was that when pauses were imposed on a digit (or letter) string, recall depended upon whether the pauses were in the same position over successive presentations. When the pauses remained the same on each presentation of the string, recall of the sequences improved over successive trials, whereas there was no improvement in recall when the same items were presented in a variable manner. Typical results are given in Figure 12–5, which shows a decrease in errors only when the same groupings were presented.

Another issue has been raised in studies of perceptual grouping and memory: How does the structure of the to-be-remembered material affect recognition and recall? Using

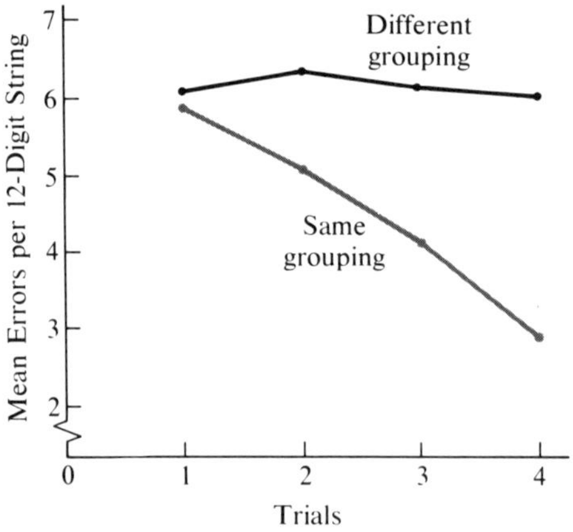

Figure 12–5. Effects of different versus same grouping on recall of number strings. (From "Group Structure, Coding, and Memory for Digit Series," by G. H. Bower and D. Winzenz, *Journal of Experimental Psychology Monographs,* 1969, *80*(2)2, 1–17. Copyright 1969 by the American Psychological Association. Reprinted by permission.)

the approach of varying the spatial groupings of letter sequences, Ellis and his colleagues (1974) examined the effect of varied versus constant input on both recognition and recall. The letter sequences consisted of strings such as *rumwig,* which were grouped into three chunks, such as *r umw ig,* and presented either consistently on successive presentations (same group structure) or variably on successive presentations (for example, *r umwi g, ru mw ig, r umw ig, ru mwi g*). Each subject was presented with a list of 12 such letter sequences under conditions of either constant or varied input. In the constant condition a given letter sequence was presented with the same grouping, whereas four different grouping structures were used in the varied condition. The subjects' task was to recall the letter sequence in the appropriate order. The basic results are given in Figure 12–6, which shows the probability of recall for the varied and constant conditions over eight trials. The figure shows a clear superiority in recall due to varied input and reveals that the difference became progressively greater with practice.

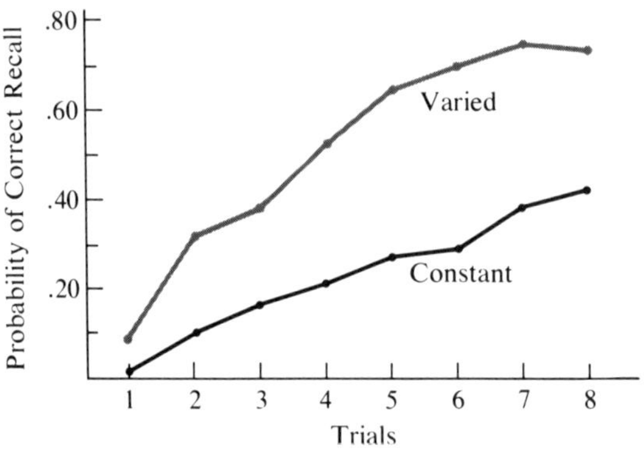

Figure 12–6. Effect of variable versus constant input on the probability of recall of letter strings. (From "Coding and Varied Input versus Repetition in Human Memory," by H. C. Ellis, F. J. Parente, and C. W. Walker, *Journal of Experimental Psychology,* 1974, *102,* 284–290. Copyright 1974 by the American Psychological Association. Reprinted by permission.)

The experimenters proposed the following interpretation of superior recall under conditions of varied input:

> An explanation of the general superiority of varied input on recall is reasonably straightforward and can be accounted for by what we call a *perceptual regrouping hypothesis*. This process is viewed as operating in the following manner. When a subject is shown varied groupings on successive presentations, he eventually learns to ignore the experimenter-imposed groupings, since they change on successive presentations and are not a relevant feature. In addition, it is assumed that varied input leads the subject to adopt the strategy of seeking a new and overall grouping which, if successful, will facilitate recall because the particular letter sequences can be grouped as a unit. Since the letter sequences contained an inherent grouping structure in the form of pronounceable or easy-to-integrate units, detection and encoding of this overall structure must facilitate recall. Moreover, the recall data suggest the general principle that variability in nominal-stimulus input leads to greater stability in the subject's functional encoding under conditions in which the subject can achieve an overall or unitary encoding of the input sequence. In contrast, if no existing or inherent structure were present, varied input would not be expected to facilitate recall. Search for such a structure and the corresponding development of subject encodings would be fruitless, and performance in such instances would be degraded [p. 288].[1]

Although the superiority of recall under varied input may appear to contradict the results reported by Bower and his associates, this is not the case. Bower's studies have established the fact that recall improves only under conditions of repetition when the subject is apparently unable to recode the sequence. In contrast, Ellis and his associates have established that variable input is facilitative under conditions in which the subject can apparently recode the sequence; the point is that subjects must discover and encode a sequence containing an inherent structure if variable input is to enhance recall.

Constructive Processes in Memory

One general approach to the study of memory has emphasized quantitative changes, a tradition stemming from Ebbinghaus (1885), whereas a second approach has emphasized qualitative changes in the representation of events in memory over time. This latter approach emphasizes that the memory of an event may not only weaken but that it may also be distorted or modified in such a way as to reflect a qualitative change. An example was seen in Bartlett's (1932) studies of memory for prose passages such as folk tales. As noted in the previous chapter, Bartlett stressed the notion that humans acquire or use a cognitive structure as the basis for abstracting the meaning of a passage. Thus, this second tradition has emphasized memory for meaning, for general ideas or gist, and the ways in which a person's memory for meaning can change as a result of constructive processes in memory. This second approach has received less attention than the other until relatively recently. New developments in memory research (Cofer, 1973; Kintsch, 1974) have led to an increase of interest in the approach.

But what does it mean to assert that *constructive* processes operate in memory? In general, this means that humans somehow integrate information (such as prose passages, stories, and so forth) into a more or less coherent and organized structure; this structure is usually referred to as a schema (Bartlett, 1932). Once the schema is established, it can determine whether a person will judge a sentence or other information as having been previously encountered. In other words, recognition (or recall) of previously presented in-

[1] From "Coding and Varied Input versus Repetition in Human Memory," by H. C. Ellis, F. J. Parente, and C. W. Walker, *Journal of Experimental Psychology*, 1974, *102*, 284–290. Copyright 1974 by the American Psychological Association. Reprinted by permission.

formation is influenced by the schema that a person uses to organize information. We can say that the schema is a kind of contextual framework into which information is integrated.

The results of recent experimental work (for example, Bransford & Franks, 1971; Franks & Bransford, 1971; Jarvella, 1971; Sachs, 1967) have lent support to the notion of constructive processes in memory. Let us consider two examples. Bransford and Franks conducted experiments on the abstraction of linguistic ideas that served to show how schematic information in memory can be constructed so as to represent information that is only implicit in the material as actually presented. In other words, these researchers demonstrated that under certain conditions humans will recognize information that was not actually presented but was only implicit. What this finding suggests is that you can remember something that you never actually experienced, as long as part of the information presented could be recombined into new portions. Such a finding supports the constructive view of memory.

In the Bransford and Franks study, subjects were presented with a group of simple sentences that, if combined, would represent a single sentence with four components expressing a "whole idea." For example, a sentence expressing the whole idea would be "The rock that rolled down the mountain crushed the tiny hut at the edge of the woods." This complex sentence can be broken down into four simple sentences: (a) "The rock rolled down the mountain"; (2) "The rock crushed the hut"; (3) "The hut was tiny"; and (4) "The hut was at the edge of the woods."

During the study phase of the experiment, the subjects heard a list of sentences containing only one, two, or three of the components. They *never* heard the sentence containing all four components. For example, they would hear sentences such as "The rock rolled down the mountain" (one component, or idea); "The tiny hut was at the edge of the woods" (two ideas); or "The rock crushed the tiny hut at the edge of the woods" (three ideas). During the recognition test the subjects were presented with several kinds of sentences. Some of the sentences had been presented during study (old sentences), some of the sentences had not been heard during study but were consistent with the ideas presented (new sentences), and some sentences were inconsistent with the ideas presented during study (noncases). The sentences that the subjects had heard before consisted of one, two or three components; the sentences they had *not* heard before consisted of one, two, three, or *four* components. (Keep in mind that no four-component sentences had ever been heard during study). The subjects' task was to attempt to recognize those sentences that they had actually heard during study and to rate their degree of confidence in having heard the sentence before on a five-point rating scale.

The major finding was that the more parts of a whole idea a test sentence contained, the more confident the subjects were of having heard the sentence during study. Thus, the subjects were most confident of having heard the four-component whole idea—which, of course, they had never actually heard. The basic results are presented in Figure 12–7, which shows the confidence ratings plotted as a function of the number of components in the test sentences. These results strongly suggest that people integrate information from several sentences and retain a general idea rather than specific sentences as such (compare Cofer, 1973).

Studies on the memory of semantic content have shown similar results. For example, an experiment by Sachs (1967) indicates that meaning is well remembered over time whereas specific wording is not. In her experiment, subjects listened to and tried to understand prose passages. Unknown to the subjects, each passage contained a key sentence, memory for which was tested after they heard the passage. One passage consisted, for example, of a story about the telescope in which a Dutch optician who discovered the principle of the telescope is communicating this information to Galileo. The key sentence in the story was "He sent a letter about it to Galileo, the great Italian scientist." The

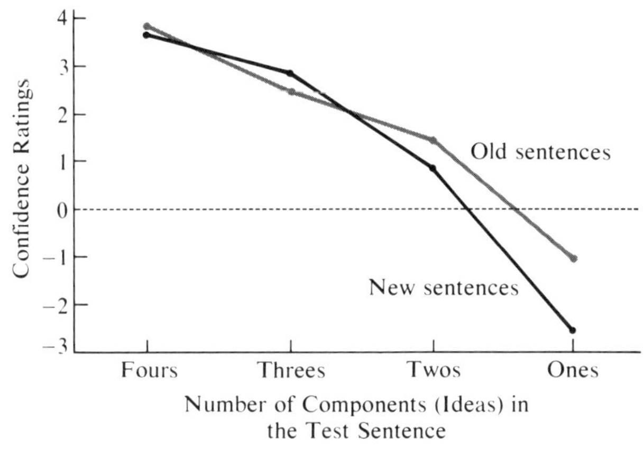

Figure 12–7. Confidence ratings that a test sentence had been seen before as a function of the number of components in the sentence. (From "The Abstraction of Linguistic Ideas," by J. D. Bransford and J. J. Franks, *Cognitive Psychology,* 1971, *2,* 331–350. Reprinted by permission of Academic Press, Inc.)

sentence was inserted as either the last sentence of the passage or 80 or 160 syllables from the end of the passage. Thus, the objectives of the experiment were to examine memory for the key sentence as a function of amount of interpolated activity and to examine the type of information forgotten.

Following presentation of the story, the subjects were given a test sentence and asked whether it was identical to one in the story or whether it had been changed. Four types of test sentences were used. One type was a semantic change: "Galileo, the great Italian scientist, sent him a letter about it." A second type of change was from the active to the passive voice (or the converse): "A letter about it was sent to Galileo, the great Italian scientist." A third type of change was a word-order, or formal, change: "He sent Galileo, the great Italian scientist, a letter about it." The fourth test condition involved no change in the original sentence.

Figure 12–8 shows the percentages of correct judgments on the four kinds of test sentences as a function of the amount of interpolated material. The figure indicates that the subjects could detect a semantic change fairly well even when other material was interpolated. In other words, memory for meaning was reasonably good. In contrast, a change in voice or a change in word order produced a substantial reduction in the accuracy of identification. Even the identical sentence did not fare well. These data strongly support the argument that the meaning, or deep structure, of a sentence is what is remembered.

Mediational Strategies and Mnemonics

Mediational strategies also play an important role in learning and memory. The significance of mediation has been thoroughly documented, and excellent summaries of the research on it can be found in a number of sources (for example, J. J. Jenkins, 1963; H. H. Kendler & Kendler, 1968; Montague, 1972; Schultz, 1972). As we noted earlier, the term *mediation* sometimes refers to situations in which the subject interjects a third term between the stimulus-and-response pair. At a more general level, however, the term *mediation* refers to efforts by the subject to link two items. The process of mediation is frequently thought of as a verbal process, but it may involve mental imagery and perceptual processes

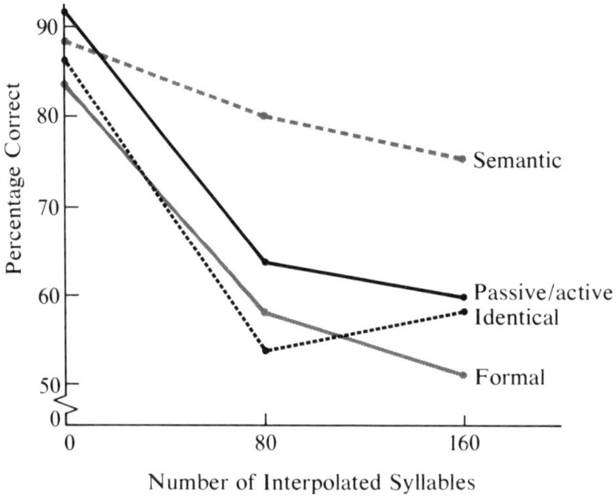

Figure 12–8. The percentages of correct judgments for the four kinds of test sentences as a function of the amount of interpolated material. (From "Recognition Memory for Syntactic and Semantic Aspects of Connected Discourse," by J. S. Sachs, *Perception and Psychophysics,* 1967, *2,* 437–442. Reprinted by permission of the Psychonomic Society.)

as well. One important feature of mediation is that, just as we saw with stimulus selection, humans actively control the way in which they learn. Moreover, mediation represents another instance of organizational processes in learning and memory.

Mediation in Paired-Associate Learning

A great variety of approaches to the study of mediation have been employed. In one approach, experimenters have studied verbal mediation in paired-associate learning either by inferring mediators on the basis of association norms or by supplying subjects implicitly or explicitly with mediators so as to prime performance. An example of an experiment using free-association norms to study mediation is one conducted by Wood and Bolt (1968). In this study, subjects learned a paired-associate list consisting of single-letter stimuli paired with responses that were high-frequency words. The experimental subjects were told that they would be given a mediator to help them associate each letter/word pair. The mediator was written out next to each letter. Moreover, each mediator began with the same letter as the stimulus. For example, the pairs *t/chair, k/queen,* and *m/lamb* had mediating responses of *table, king,* and *mutton,* so that the pairs appeared during study as *t/(table)/chair, k/(king)/queen,* and *m/(mutton)/lamb.* A control group did not receive the mediators. The study/recall method was used; during testing, the experimental group did not see the mediators and were required to recall from the letters alone. As might be expected, the experimental group correctly recalled substantially more words than did the control group.

In a second experiment Wood and Bolt (1968) altered their procedure in two ways so that the mediator was inappropriate for the task. In one case the subjects received the same mediating responses as in the first experiment, but the task responses were changed. For example, the mediators *table, king,* and *mutton* were used as before but with the pairs *t/doctor, k/sour,* and *m/afraid.* In the second case the mediators were changed, but the same pairs were used as in the first experiment. When compared with a no-mediator control, both groups showed poorer recall, indicating that mediators can interfere with as well as facilitate learning.

Natural-Language Mediation

Another approach to the study of mediation examines the way humans use language in generating their own mediators. An example of this research is an experiment by Montague, Adams, and Kiess (1966). They gave subjects a single presentation of 25 CVC pairs and asked them to report the natural-language mediators (if any) they used. The subjects returned to the laboratory 24 hours later and were asked to recall both the response terms in each pair and the natural-language mediators used on the prior day. The recall of the mediator was important because the mediator is a response that can be forgotten just like any other response.

One purpose of the study was to see how recall of the response item was related to recall of the mediator. Independent judges scored the natural-language mediator as correct if it was judged as being sufficiently similar to the mediator produced during the first test. When the experimental conditions were combined, Montague and his colleagues found that when the mediator was recalled correctly, 72.6% of the response terms were recalled correctly. However, only *1.8%* of the response terms were recalled when the mediator was incorrectly recalled. If no mediator was produced during original learning (rote?), recall was only 5.8%. Thus, the effects of natural-language mediation in recall are quite substantial. The use of such mediators represents one instance of the general use of mnemonics.

Mediation via Rules

Humans can also successfully mediate on the basis of rules or principles that are built into the material to be learned. The importance of rules has been shown in a number of learning tasks, including paired-associate learning. As G. H. Bower (1970a) has noted, humans look for relations among several or all of the pairs they are learning. In short, given the stimulus term, humans look for a rule for calculating the response term. These rules can be built into the paired-associate lists in several ways, such as having the response word rhyme with the stimulus. In general, such built-in rules increase the ease with which learning occurs. Bower further notes that if subjects discover and use rules when the rules are experimentally built-in, we can have some confidence that subjects search for and probably find some rules even when they are not explicitly built into a list.

But why do rules aid learning? An experiment by Bower and Bolton (1969) on the learning of rhymes suggests an answer. Rhymes, of course, are well-known as effective mnemonic devices, and words that rhyme are generally easier to learn than nonrhyming words. Bower and Bolton have proposed that in the context of paired-associate learning, rhymes aid learning because the rhyming relation restricts the search for a response to a few alternatives. One way they tested this *response-restriction hypothesis* was to show that a nonrhyming rule that equally restricts response alternatives will facilitate paired-associate learning as much as a rhyming rule. Experimental subjects learned a 36-pair list in which half the pairs conformed to a general rule and half did not. In one case the rule half of the list consisted of rhyming pairs, such as *hat* and *fat*. In the second case an assonance rule was used in which the response was related to the stimulus by a change in its last phoneme; examples are *hat* and *hag* and *pit* and *pin*. The 18 rule pairs were emphasized by being printed in red type, while the nonrule pairs were printed in black type. In both cases the control subjects learned a list of unrelated pairs.

Figure 12–9 compares the experimental subjects' recall on both lists. The left-hand panel shows the effects of the rhyming rule, and the right-hand panel shows the effects of the assonance rule. In both cases, learning was facilitated with the rule lists, and the superiority was roughly equal. Thus, an assonance rule that restricts the number of response alternatives about as much as a rhyming rule produces about the same advantage in learning. In short, there is nothing particularly unique about the ease of learning rhymes; if a list simply restricts the number of response alternatives, learning should be facilitated.

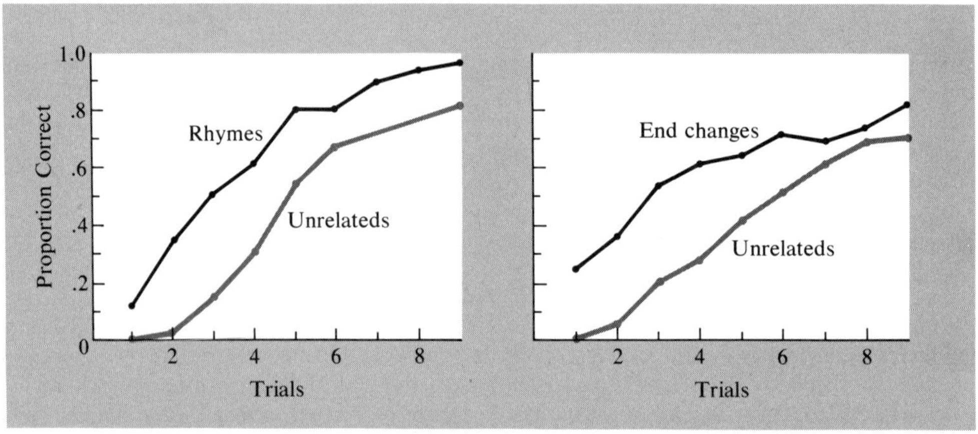

Figure 12–9. Mean correct recall of word pairs with a rhyming rule and an assonance rule. (From "Why Are Rhymes Easy to Learn?" by G. H. Bower and L. Bolton, *Journal of Experimental Psychology,* 1969, *82,* 453–461. Copyright 1969 by the American Psychological Association. Reprinted by permission.)

Imagery and Mediation

Finally, let us consider a source of mediation that stems from mental imagery. We saw in the previous chapter that imagery is an important factor in learning. Our concern here is with why imagery is so effective.

Two kinds of explanations for the effect of stimulus imagery in paired-associate learning have been proposed. One is a mediational interpretation, and the other is a stimulus-differentiation interpretation. Several versions of each theory have been suggested, but we will consider only one version of each type of theory. Mediational theory is an attempt to explain the effects of stimulus imagery in terms of mediating images employed by subjects during paired-associate learning. One version is Paivio's (1969) *conceptual-peg hypothesis,* which he describes as follows:

> The argument is that the stimulus member of a pair serves as a "conceptual peg" (a term first introduced by Lambert and Paivio, 1956) to which its associate is hooked during learning trials when the stimulus and response members are presented together, and from which the response member can be retrieved on recall trials when the stimulus member is presented alone. On the assumption that imagery can serve a mediating function, as the imagery memory technique suggests, it follows that the ease of learning the stimulus–response association will depend partly on the image-arousing capacity of the individual nouns and of the stimulus member in particular. The imagery value of both stimulus and response would contribute to the formation of a compound image, consisting of images evoked by the individual items when the two are presented together, thereby affecting the formation of the mediated association. On recall trials, however, when the stimulus is presented alone, its image-arousing value would be particularly important, for the stimulus member must serve as the cue that reinstitutes the

compound image from which the response component can be retrieved and recoded as a word. The hypothesis leads to the prediction that a positive effect of noun imagery will be greater on the stimulus side than on the response side of pairs. Assuming, further, that concrete nouns such as "house" elicit images more readily than abstract nouns such as "truth," it would be expected that [paired-associate] learning of nouns will be particularly facilitated when the stimulus noun is concrete [p. 244].[2]

The alternative account, stimulus-differentiation theory, emphasizes that the stimulus terms themselves become more distinctive and less confusing. The basic idea is that when a set of stimuli tends to evoke strong mental images, these stimuli become better differentiated than a set of stimuli that does not tend to evoke strong mental images. Although the results of several studies (for example, Dominowski & Galdin, 1968; Wicker, 1970) support differentiation theory, Paivio (1971, pp. 291–293) has argued that these results do not necessarily rule out mediation.

Substantial support for a mediational interpretation comes from a number of other studies (for example, G. H. Bower, 1970b; Tatum, 1976). Tatum has shown that the facilitating effects of stimulus imagery are maintained even when response recall is conditional on stimulus recognition. Tatum in effect equated stimulus-recognition performance for high and low imagery conditions.

Imagery and Mnemonics

As a last example of organizational processes in learning and memory, we will examine two types of imagery techniques. These techniques are special cases of mnemonic devices in memory—that is, devices that enable us to encode information effectively and that hence are aids to memory. One type of mnemonic device is the *method of loci,* and the other is the *peg-word method.*

The method of loci was known to the ancients and is nicely illustrated in a story reported by Cicero. In the story a Greek poet named Simonides was commissioned to read a poem at a banquet in honor of a wealthy Roman nobleman. After his presentation of the poem, Simonides was called outside the banquet hall by a messenger. In his absence the roof caved in, killing all those at the banquet table. All the bodies were so completely crushed as to be unrecognizable. Nevertheless, Simonides was able to identify each person for purposes of separate burial because he was able to recall the *place* of each guest reclining at the table. His interpretation of this remarkable feat of memory was that he had formed a mental image of the place where each person reclined and of the person such that person and location were fixed in memory. Thus, this procedure has come to be known as the method of loci, since it involves the development of distinctive visual images of things to be remembered within a spatial framework. Recall of the information is basically a matter of mentally moving through the locations in the spatial image.

G. H. Bower (1970a) describes how the method of loci can be used in remembering a series of items such as a grocery list. Imagine that your task is to remember a list consisting of hot dogs, cat food, tomatoes, bananas, and whiskey. The method of loci would involve constructing a vivid image in which each item is located in a particular place. This can be accomplished by imagining that you are taking a walk through surroundings that are very familiar, such as a walk from home to campus. Assume that in your walk you pass a picket fence, a huge tree, the entrance to an elegant house, a park with a slide, and the main entrance to the campus, marked by pillars on either side. You could thus imagine the fol-

[2]From "Mental Imagery in Associative Learning and Memory," by A. Paivio, *Psychological Review,* 1969, *76,* 241–263. Copyright 1969 by the American Psychological Association. Reprinted by permission.

lowing scenes: long chains of hot dogs topping the fence, a cat eating cat food in the tree, tomatoes having replaced the doorknob and the door knocker on the elegant house, a bunch of bananas sliding down the slide, and bottles of whiskey topping the pillars at the campus entrance. The examples may suggest that the images must be bizarre for effective memory, but that is not the case. Wollen, Weber, and Lowry (1972) have demonstrated that the effectiveness of imagery resides in the images' allowing an interaction between items and not in bizarreness itself.

Although the method of loci may seem complicated or unnecessary for good memory, experimental studies of the method have shown it to be quite effective. For example, Groninger (1971) assigned subjects to an imagery condition in which they had to construct a spatial image with 25 different locations; thus, the subjects constructed their own spatial image. Then they were given a pack of 25 cards with different words and instructed to learn them in order using the method of loci. Control subjects were simply instructed to learn the cards in any order they wished. All the subjects knew all the words at the end of the study. Both groups of subjects were given tests of retention 1 week and 5 weeks later. The imagery group recalled 92% and 80% of the words correctly after 1 and 5 weeks, respectively, whereas the control group recalled only 64% and 36%.

The peg-word method for remembering information requires knowledge of the following little series: "One is a bun, two is a shoe, three is a tree, four is a door, five is a hive, six is sticks, seven is heaven, eight is a gate, nine is a line, and ten is a hen." Once this has been learned, you can learn any series of items using imagery. If the items consist of words such as *cigar, woman, book, bicycle,* and so on, you might construct images consisting of a cigar lying on a bun, a woman trying on a shoe, a book lying beside a tree, a bicycle being carried through a door, and so forth. Experimental evidence (for example, Bugelski, 1968) indicates that the peg-word method is also effective for remembering.

Summary

This chapter examined the role of organizational processes and coding in memory. Organizational processes operate in free recall—particularly in clustering and subjective organization. Clustering is the tendency either to recall sequences of words that are categorically related or to recall words that are associatively related, even though they were not presented together at input. Subjective organization refers to the tendency to group words more consistently in output, according to subjective or idiosyncratic criteria. Finally, the part/whole transfer effect in free recall was initially interpreted in terms of organizational processes but is currently viewed in terms of a list-discrimination hypothesis based on confusion between list tags.

Coding processes were discussed in some detail. Rehearsal—especially elaborative rehearsal—is particularly important. Rehearsal and recall are clearly related. Humans may code on several dimensions, and proactive interference will build up in short-term memory in which subjects must learn items of the same class. Context is especially important in determining how information is represented in memory. The issue of encoding specificity appears to be still unresolved. Stimulus variability plays an important role in memory. Variable input facilitates retention of information for which a "high-order" structure can be discovered. Only where no obvious structure exists is repetition superior to variable input.

Memory is constructive. Under certain conditions humans may be more confident that they have heard sentences that they never actually heard than sentences actually heard. We tend to remember gist and meanings rather than detailed information.

Finally, humans use mnemonic devices in remembering information. Mediational strategies involving natural language, rules, and mental imagery are also important.

Chapter 13

Transfer of Training

In this chapter we will look at the way new learning is influenced by prior learning. When we acquire new skills or knowledge, we usually do not start from scratch but benefit or sometimes suffer from prior learning experiences. Indeed, it would be difficult to think of any adult learning that is not, at least in some minimal way, influenced by previous learning. Thus, the study of transfer represents a continuation of the study of learning but focuses on the role of prior learning as the major independent variable.

Many of the early studies of transfer were directed toward answering questions about educational psychology and classroom practice. One of the earliest issues centered around the breadth of transfer effects. The question was to what extent training in one subject will carry over to other subjects. At one extreme on this issue was the doctrine of *formal discipline,* in which the results of certain kinds of training are expected to have widespread transfer effects. In this view the mind is composed of several "faculties," such as memory, reasoning, and judgment, and these faculties can be strengthened through the study of certain types of subject matter. For example, Latin and other languages are regarded as effective subjects for strengthening the powers of memory, and geometry is thought to be effective for strengthening the powers of logical reasoning. Strengthening these general faculties, or powers, should carry over into other areas. Since geometry and law, for example, both involve the individual's reasoning powers, the study of one should aid in mastery of the other. This notion that the study of certain content areas imparts mental discipline exerted considerable influence on thinking about school curricula.

This doctrine came under attack early in this century by Thorndike and Woodworth (1901), who failed to find any substantial evidence in support of it. They proposed an alternative theory, *identical elements,* in which training in one area is thought to transfer to another as long as certain elements of the two are identical. Thorndike and Woodworth did not place a narrow connotation on the notion of elements; they included aims, methods, and approaches of the two areas. The results of early experimental studies appeared to favor this more restricted view of transfer, although Osgood (1953) has questioned the soundness of these early studies. Contemporary research on transfer has shifted away from these early conceptions, but the distinction between the two extreme positions is reflected in our current distinction between general and specific transfer effects.

Current research on transfer has focused on transfer processes and on the component analysis of transfer effects in laboratory tasks. This emphasis can be seen in the shift from classroom to laboratory studies of transfer, efforts at analyzing the dimensions of transfer tasks, and the use of more analytic research designs. For a summary of these trends, see the reviews by Ellis (1969) and Postman (1971).

Concept of Transfer

Because transfer concerns the effect of prior learning on new learning, studies of the process involve two stages of practice. Subjects are given some kind of controlled practice on a first task followed by practice on a second, or transfer, task. The fundamental issue is how practice on the first task affects performance on the second task. Transfer effects can be positive, negative, or zero.

Positive transfer occurs when first-task learning aids performance on the second task. If, for example, mastery of one foreign language aids you in learning a new language, positive transfer is said to occur. Negative transfer occurs when first-task learning interferes with second-task performance. Although having learned to drive one type of car can aid in learning to drive another type, some interference may initially be encountered if certain features differ, such as type of transmission or location of controls. Zero transfer can occur in either of two ways: first-task learning may have no effect on second-task learning, or both positive and negative transfer may occur and cancel each other out.

Transfer studies have one of two general objectives. The traditional objective has been to determine which of the effects just discussed has occurred. In contrast, in other studies the *transfer test* has been used as a way of determining what has been learned in the training phase. The transfer test serves as an analytic probe designed to illuminate the nature of sets, habits, strategies, and so on that may have been established in training.

We saw examples of this second approach in Chapter 11. For instance, recall that in investigating the role of contiguity in verbal-discrimination learning, Spear, Ekstrand, and Underwood (1964) used a paired-associate transfer test to determine whether subjects were strengthening associations just on the basis of contiguity of items. Similarly, we noted that in studies of stimulus selection (for example, C. T. James & Greeno, 1967; Richardson, 1971) a transfer test was employed to determine what functional cues or stimuli subjects were using. In Chapter 12 we examined studies of part/whole transfer (for example, Tulving, 1966) in which a transfer test was used to explore the nature of organizational strategies established in part-list learning. In all these instances a transfer test was used to infer the development of particular processes in first-task learning. Thus, you have already been exposed to the study of transfer from this second perspective.

Research Procedures in Transfer

The concept of transfer can be most clearly understood by examining the ways in which transfer has been studied in the laboratory. Transfer has been studied in several basic ways (see Ellis, 1969; Postman, 1971). In this section we will look at the design of transfer experiments, the measurement of transfer, and the basic transfer paradigms.

The Design of Transfer Experiments

The simplest experimental design used in transfer studies compares the performance of an experimental and a control group as follows. The experimental group learns some initial task, designated as Task A, followed by a transfer task, designated as Task B. The control group learns only Task B. Thus, the test task is the same for both groups, and the only difference between them is the presence (or absence) of prior training on Task A; the two groups are assumed to be comparable in ability. The performance of the two groups on Task B is compared in order to assess transfer effects. If the performance of the experimental group is superior to that of the control group, we infer positive transfer from A to B. In contrast, if the performance of the experimental group is inferior, we conclude that the transfer from A to B is negative. If the two groups are equivalent in Task B performance, we have a case of zero transfer. This experimental design is shown in Table 13–1.

Table 13–1. Basic transfer design.

Group	*Initial Task*	*Transfer Task*
Experimental	A	B
Control	—	B

This simple design illustrates the study of *gross* transfer effects. It allows us only to conclude whether there is transfer from A to B; it does not necessarily specify any of the processes that may be involved in the transfer. If training on A does transfer to performance on B, at least two sources of transfer may be operating. On the one hand, the transfer from A to B may be the result of *specific* skills, habits, and knowledge. On the other hand, the transfer may result from *general* factors, such as adaptation to the experimental situation and requirements of the task. These factors must be separated if we wish to identify the specific skills, habits, and so forth that produce a given transfer effect.

Consider a simple example of transfer from Latin to French. You might in this instance expect that facility in Latin would transfer to the learning of a Romance language such as French. Part of the transfer, however, could be due to the specific similarities between the two languages, such as common word roots. In contrast, part of the transfer could be due to general habits, such as having learned how to learn a foreign language. Therefore, many transfer experiments employ a second type of control group in which subjects learn an initial task that is not specifically related to the transfer task but nevertheless provides for general practice—that is, practice in learning how to learn tasks of the same class. This type of design is shown in Table 13–2.

Table 13–2. Basic transfer design controlling for general transfer effects.

Group	*Initial Task*	*Transfer Task*
Experimental	A	B
Control	X	B

In this case the control group learns X and then B; the experimental group learns A and then B as before. For example, in an experiment designed to study the transfer effects of training on Latin to learning French, the control subjects might learn another language (such as Russian, Arabic, or Chinese) that is not specifically related to French yet provides practice in learning how to learn a language. In this type of transfer design, a comparison of the experimental and control groups' performance on Task B provides a measure of specific transfer effects that are no longer mixed with general effects. This second type of design is used more frequently, since it is usually desirable to separate specific from general effects.

Other basic designs have been employed, such as those that match the experimental and control groups on some prior test. However, matching designs have their limitations, as noted by Postman (1971), and have not been widely used in recent years.

The Measurement of Transfer

The direction as well as the amount of transfer is measured by the difference between the performances of the experimental and control groups on Task B, the test task. Since transfer can be measured at any or all stages during test-task learning and since transfer effects may appear during different stages of the test task, it is generally advantageous to carry practice on the test task to a substantial level and to obtain measures at several stages. Transfer effects may, for example, appear only during the first few trials on the transfer task and dissipate during the latter trials. Or the effect of a given variable may be on the *rate* of learning the transfer task but not on the initial level of transfer performance.

Postman (1971) has noted that there are a priori reasons for expecting measures obtained during the early portion of the test task to be especially sensitive to transfer effects. The difference in prior learning of the experimental and control groups is greatest at the beginning of the transfer test. Since the two groups are treated alike during the transfer stage, the relative effects of earlier training can, in general, be expected to diminish with additional practice on the transfer task. Nevertheless, if the previously acquired habits and skills come into play late in the transfer task, we can expect measures of transfer to show these effects at a later stage. Since we may not be entirely sure when these effects will appear, the use of a stringent criterion during transfer is clearly desirable.

Transfer researchers sometimes measure the amount and direction of transfer using formulas, although transfer effects are usually quite evident in acquisition curves for the control and experimental conditions. For any given measure obtained, such as the number of correct responses for a fixed number of trials, the performance difference between the control and the experimental group defines the amount of transfer in terms of the scoring unit. On the other hand, transfer formulas permit comparison of findings from studies that used different levels of criterion achievement or different kinds of transfer tasks.

A simple and widely used transfer formula appears below. In this formula E represents the mean performance of the experimental group on the transfer task, and C represents the mean performance of the control group. By comparing the difference between the two groups with C itself, the percentage of transfer can be expressed as follows:

$$\text{Percentage of transfer} = \frac{E - C}{C} \times 100.$$

If the scores vary inversely with the level of performance, as is the case, for example, with the number of errors, the numerator becomes $C - E$.

Several alternative formulas have been suggested by Murdock (1957), but space limitations prevent a discussion of them. In any case, the use of relative measures derived from transfer measures has declined in recent years (Postman, 1971), so a detailed examination would be unnecessary.

Basic Transfer Paradigms

Transfer can be studied in any of the laboratory tasks discussed so far—serial learning, paired-associate learning, free-recall learning, recognition learning, or discrimination learning. In principle, transfer between any two learning tasks can be experimentally studied. Moreover, transfer between different kinds of tasks can be studied, such as the transfer from verbal-discrimination to paired-associate learning (see, for example, Spear et al., 1964) or the transfer from paired-associate learning to stimulus recognition (see, for example, Ellis & Muller, 1964).

The most widely used paradigm is paired-associate learning because it permits independent variation of stimulus and response factors. Subjects can be given two paired-associate tasks in succession in which (1) the stimuli and responses of the two lists differ completely; (2) the stimuli remain the same, but the responses differ; (3) the stimuli differ, but the responses remain the same; or (4) the stimuli and/or responses are varied in some degree of similarity. Variations in the relationships between two successive paired-associate lists define what are known as *transfer paradigms;* a paradigm is simply a shorthand way of describing these relationships. Let us examine the basic transfer paradigms.

The A/B, C/D *Paradigm.* The *A/B, C/D* paradigm is the basic control paradigm for the evaluation of specific transfer effects. In this paradigm, as in all others, subjects learn two successive paired-associate lists. The first list is designated *A/B,* where *A* stands for the stimulus terms of the list and *B* designates the response terms. The second list is designated *C/D,* where *C* represents the stimuli and *D* the response terms. This representation simply means that there is no obvious similarity between the stimuli (*A* and *C*) or the responses (*B* and *D*) of the two lists. The paradigm is illustrated as follows, using two pairs in each list:

Initial List	*Transfer List*
A/B	*C/D*
XUL/DOG	*JOQ/ICE*
BOJ/SKY	*WYX/RUG*

There are few letters common to the two sets of stimuli. Moreover, they are not meaningfully related. The same holds for the response terms. Therefore, any transfer from learning the *A/B* list to learning the *C/D* list is due to general transfer effects, such as learning how to learn lists. For this reason, this paradigm serves as the basic control for evaluating specific transfer effects when compared to other paradigms.

Postman (1971) has noted some problems in the uncritical use of this paradigm as a baseline control. For example, although complete dissimilarity of both the stimulus and the response terms is the defining feature of the paradigm, this dissimilarity may not always be easy to accomplish, especially with syllables, for there are only a limited number of letters available. Despite these problems, however, the *A/B, C/D* paradigm remains the typical control in transfer studies.

The A/B, A/D *Paradigm.* This is the classic paradigm for negative transfer, in which subjects learn to attach new responses to old stimuli. Nevertheless, it is important to note that either negative or positive transfer can occur with this paradigm depending on experimental conditions. Negative transfer has been reported in many experiments (for example, Postman, 1962b; Twedt & Underwood, 1959), but both negative and positive transfer have been reported by Ellis and Shaffer (1974) with variations in intralist stimulus similarity.

The *A/B, A/D* paradigm is illustrated as follows, again using two pairs in each list:

Initial List	*Transfer List*
A/B	*A/D*
XUL/BAN	*XUL/RUG*
BOJ/NET	*BOJ/LIP*

The A/B, C/B *Paradigm.* In this paradigm the subjects' task is to associate the old response terms with new stimuli. The classic studies of transfer (for example, Bruce, 1933;

R. J. Hamilton, 1943) found that with this paradigm positive transfer typically occurs. Later experiments (for example, Postman, 1962; Twedt & Underwood, 1959) yielded negative transfer. These differences were nicely reconciled in a study by J. Jung (1963), who found that either positive or negative transfer occurred depending on the meaningfulness of the response terms. His subjects learned two six-pair lists consisting of adjectives as stimuli and trigrams as responses with two levels of response meaningfulness. The experimental subjects learned an *A/B, C/B* sequence, whereas the control subjects learned an *A/B, C/D* sequence.

The mean numbers of correct responses on the transfer task on Trials 1–10 for the two levels of response meaningfulness are shown in Figure 13–1. The figure indicates a clear interaction between response meaningfulness and type of paradigm, with positive transfer in the *C/B* paradigm under low response meaningfulness and negative transfer under high response meaningfulness. We will discuss the interpretation of these results later, but for now we emphasize that either positive or negative transfer effects can occur in this paradigm depending upon the experimental conditions.

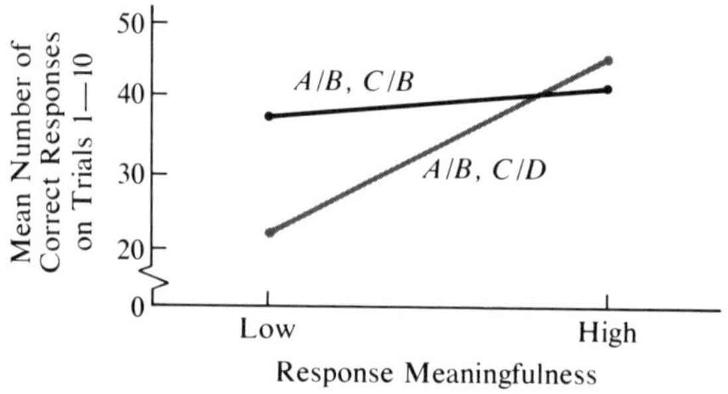

Figure 13–1. Mean number of correct responses on a transfer task as a function of response meaningfulness and transfer paradigm. (From "Effects of Response Meaningfulness (*m*) on Transfer of Training under Two Different Paradigms," by J. Jung, *Journal of Experimental Psychology,* 1963, *65,* 377–384. Copyright 1963 by the American Psychological Association. Reprinted by permission.)

The *A/B, C/B* paradigm is illustrated as follows:

Initial List	*Transfer List*
A/B	*C/B*
XUL/DOG	*JOQ/DOG*
BOJ/SKY	*WYX/SKY*

The A/B, A/B_r *Paradigm.* *In the A/B, A/B_r* paradigm the lists are arranged so that the same responses are present in the transfer list but are *re-paired* with the stimuli, requiring the subject to learn new associations. With this paradigm negative transfer is obtained especially if the response terms are meaningful (see, for example, Kausler & Kanoti, 1963; Porter & Duncan, 1953; Postman, 1962b). Positive transfer can be obtained with this paradigm using low-meaningfulness CCCs for response terms (G. Mandler & Heinemann, 1956). In a direct comparison of the effects of response meaningfulness in this paradigm, Merikle and Battig (1963) and Merikle (1968) found that the characteristic negative transfer occurred when the response terms were high in meaningfulness but that positive transfer occurred with low-meaningfulness responses. This paradigm is illustrated as follows:

Initial List	*Transfer List*
A/B	A/B_r
XUL/DOG	*XUL/SKY*
BOJ/SKY	*BOJ/DOG*

Comparison of the Paradigms. In an early study Twedt and Underwood (1959) compared all four paradigms and established their rank order. Subjects learned an *A/B* list followed by lists conforming to either *C/D*, *C/B*, *A/D*, or A/B_r. The lists were constructed so that all subjects learned the *same* transfer list, which was accomplished by having the subjects learn different *A/B* lists. The lists consisted of 12 pairs of adjectives, with learning on the first list taken to a criterion of one perfect trial and ten trials on the transfer list. Mean correct responses as a function of trials for the four paradigms are shown in Figure 13–2. With the *C/D* paradigm serving as the basic control, the groups in all three paradigms showed negative transfer in that performance was inferior to that of the control. The ordering of the paradigms in terms of increasing negative transfer was *C/B*, *A/C*, and A/B_r. In addition, both mixed and unmixed lists were varied in this experiment, and comparable results were found in the rank ordering of the paradigms. However, not all studies have shown comparable differences between mixed and unmixed lists (see, for example, Postman, 1966; Wickens & Cermak, 1967), so it cannot be taken for granted that the two types of lists are always comparable.

Although the rank ordering of the paradigms reported by Twedt and Underwood (1959) is typically found with meaningful responses, we have already cautioned that the absolute level of transfer can vary with the conditions of the experiment. Moreover, the abso-

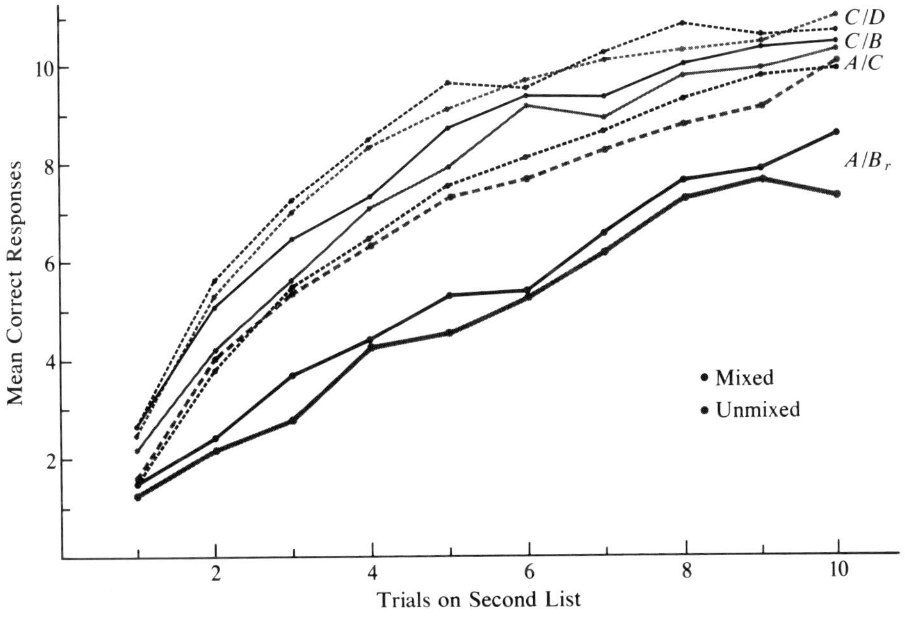

Figure 13–2. Comparison of the four transfer paradigms. (From "Mixed vs. Unmixed Lists in Transfer Studies," by H. M. Twedt and B. J. Underwood, *Journal of Experimental Psychology,* 1959, *58,* 111–116. Copyright 1959 by the American Psychological Association. Reprinted by permission.)

lute level of performance can vary with the nature of the test itself. These qualifications are noted simply to reemphasize that the transfer effects are not identical across all experimental and test conditions.

Transfer Paradigms and Conditioning

An interesting line of research is tests of the generality of the results of verbal-transfer paradigms in animal conditioning. Instead of asking whether results of animal-learning studies generalize to humans, the reverse question is asked: Do principles from human-learning research generalize to animal conditioning? In a clever series of experiments, Wickens (1973) attempted to mimic the standard verbal-transfer paradigms in classically conditioning cats to a shock stimulus.

The basic procedure is quite straightforward. Cats are placed in a comfortable sling with an electrode attached to either of the two forepaws. The shock serves as the US, and the CR is a paw flexion. The procedure allows the study of *two* URs, the response of the right paw and the response of the left paw; either or both responses can be used. The CS is either a light or a tone.

The analogy with the verbal-transfer paradigms can now be seen. The flexions of the right and left paws can be designated as the *B* and *D* responses, respectively, and the light and the tone can be designated as the *A* and *C* stimuli, respectively. Thus, conditioning of a right-paw response to a light followed by conditioning of a left-paw response to a tone would mimic the *A/B, C/D* paradigm; in this case a new response is associated with a new stimulus. Similarly, we can regard the conditioning of a right-paw response to a light followed by conditioning of the same response to a tone as analogous to the *A/B, C/B* paradigm. In turn, the *A/B, A/D* paradigm would involve conditioning a different paw to the same stimulus. The basic results are similar to the verbal-transfer results. With the *C/D* paradigm as a baseline control, negative transfer is found in both the *C/B* and *A/D* paradigm, with greater negative transfer in the latter.

Specific and Nonspecific Transfer

We noted earlier that transfer effects may be due to either specific or general factors. Now that we have examined the ways in which transfer is studied, let us examine the distinction between these factors in greater detail and look at several instances of each type of transfer.

Nonspecific Transfer

By the term *nonspecific transfer* we mean those sources of transfer attributable to practice effects that are independent of the specific features or similarities of the training and transfer tasks. For instance, if subjects learn a series of successive paired-associate lists, each list consisting of entirely new items, the subjects will show progressive improvement in performance (see, for example, Long, 1971; J. L. Rogers, 1968). Since the improvement in performance is independent of the specific features of the lists (new lists are used in each successive session), such improvement is called nonspecific transfer. There are two kinds of nonspecific transfer: warm-up and learning to learn.

Warm-Up. Warm-up and learning to learn are related processes, but a basic difference between the two is that warm-up is a transitory effect. In warm-up a "set" is activated that includes such things as postural adjustments, rhythmic behavior, and "attentive" habits that carry over from one task to another and thus facilitate learning. Warm-up effects appear in motor learning as well as verbal learning. You are probably aware of these effects in various skills such as bowling, tennis, or skiing, where warm-up is identified with the establishment of the appropriate postural set required for efficient performance of the particular skill. Warm-up is different from learning to learn in that the latter involves the acquisition of more permanent instrumental skills and habits that carry over from one task to another (see Postman & Schwartz, 1964).

The concept of warm-up can be easily understood by examining two experiments by Thune (1950). In the first experiment each subject was given ten trials on each of two paired-associate lists; List A consisted of adjective pairs, and List B consisted of noun pairs. Six groups of subjects were employed in the experiment, as shown in Table 13–3. On Day 1 subjects were given either 10, 8, 6, 4, 2, or 0 trials on List A; on Day 2 they received 0, 2, 4, 6, 8, or 10 trials on List A, respectively, for a *total* of ten trials in any condition, but with the amount of practice varied on successive days. Following practice on List A on Day 2, the subjects practiced on the second list, List B. The sequence thus conformed to an *A/B, C/D* paradigm.

Table 13–3. Outline of Thune's experiment on warm-up, showing practice conditions on Day 1 and Day 2.

	Day 1			*Day 2*		
Condition	*Practice List*	*Rest*	*List A*	*List A*	*Cartoon Sorting*	*List B*
0	6 trials	1′	10 trials	0 trials	10′	10 trials
2	6 trials	1′	8 trials	2 trials	10′	10 trials
4	6 trials	1′	6 trials	4 trials	10′	10 trials
6	6 trials	1′	4 trials	6 trials	10′	10 trials
8	6 trials	1′	2 trials	8 trials	10′	10 trials
10	6 trials	—	—	10 trials	10′	10 trials

(From "The Effects of Different Types of Preliminary Activities on Subsequent Learning of Paired-Associate Material," by L. E. Thune, *Journal of Experimental Psychology,* 1950, *40,* 423–438. Copyright 1950 by the American Psychological Association. Reprinted by permission.)

Thune's reasoning was as follows. He first assumed that learning to learn itself is a relatively permanent process—that is, that whatever is involved in learning to learn will not be forgotten. This assumption means that a group that had eight trials on Day 1 and two trials on Day 2 had as much learning to learn as a group that had two trials on Day 1 and eight trials on Day 2. More generally, all of the groups were assumed to be equal in learning to learn because they all had an equal amount of practice over the 2 days. In contrast, Thune assumed that warm-up dissipates over time, evidence for which has been shown by C. E. Hamilton (1950). Whatever warm-up would be generated from practice on Day 1 Thune assumed would be lost by Day 2. Therefore, he reasoned that by varying the amount of practice on List A on Day 2, any effect on the learning of List B would reflect the action of warm-up itself. Figure 13–3 shows the results of this experiment and indicates the effect of the number of trials on List A (Day 2) on the total number of correct responses on List B. As can be seen, there was a direct relationship between the number of warm-up trials and performance on List B.

Thune's first experiment demonstrated the effectiveness of an associative-learning task in providing warm-up effects. In the second experiment he demonstrated comparable warm-up effects from a color-guessing task. Subjects attempted to guess which one of five

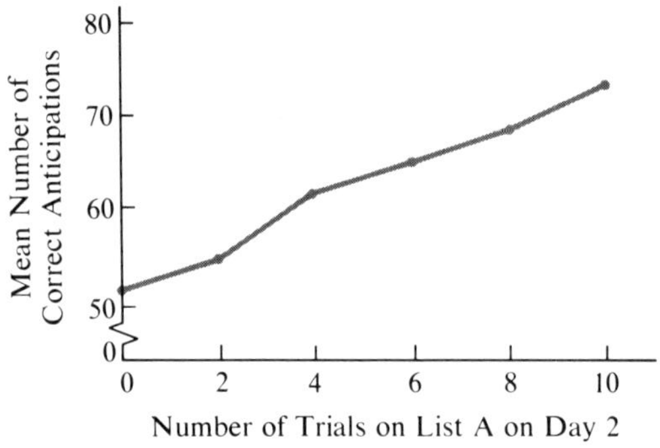

Figure 13–3. Thune's warm-up effects as a function of number of trials on List A (Day 2). (From "The Effects of Different Types of Preliminary Activities on Subsequent Learning of Paired-Associate Material," by L. E. Thune, *Journal of Experimental Psychology,* 1950, *40,* 423–438. Copyright 1950 by the American Psychological Association. Reprinted by permission.)

colors would appear as a warm-up task and then were given a test list. He found that test-list performance was much greater if the color-guessing task was given just prior to the test task than if it was given a day earlier.

That a nonassociative task provided as much warm-up as an associative task seemed surprising, and this finding was further examined by Schwenn and Postman (1967). They found that for naïve subjects familiarization with a learning (associative) task provided greater gains in test performance than a nonassociative task (letter guessing). Schwenn and Postman suggested that the difference between their results and Thune's was due to his subjects' having prior experience with the associative task whereas their subjects were naïve; for experienced subjects they suggested that either an associative or a nonassociative task would provide comparable warm-up effects.

In the Schwenn and Postman study, subjects learned a common test task of a paired-associate list of adjectives. The prior activity consisted of either learning a list of unrelated adjectives or number guessing for four or ten trials. A control group received no prior activity. The results are shown in Figure 13–4, which is a plot of the mean number of correct responses to the test task. The figure clearly shows that a learning task produced greater facilitation than a nonlearning task and that greater warm-up effects occurred with ten rather than four trials. Four trials of number-guessing practice had no effect, whereas four trials of learning produced substantial effects.

In an experiment similar to Thune's, C. E. Hamilton (1950) examined the speed with which warm-up effects dissipate. The experiment consisted of nine groups of subjects; each received ten trials of practice in learning a list of paired adjectives, followed by rest intervals of 8 seconds or 5, 10, 20, 40, 60, 120, 180, or 240 minutes. The transfer test consisted of ten trials of practice in learning a list of paired nouns. Figure 13–5 shows the performance on the test list as a function of the delay between training and test lists. As the interval was lengthened, performance dropped fairly rapidly at first and then began to level off at about 60 minutes. Thus, the notion that warm-up effects are transitory is clearly supported by Hamilton's study.

Learning to Learn. We have noted that learning to learn involves the acquisition of instrumental skills, habits, and strategies that carry over into the learning of successive tasks. The progressive improvement in performance commonly noted when subjects learn successive tasks of the same class is evidence for learning to learn. An early study by Ward

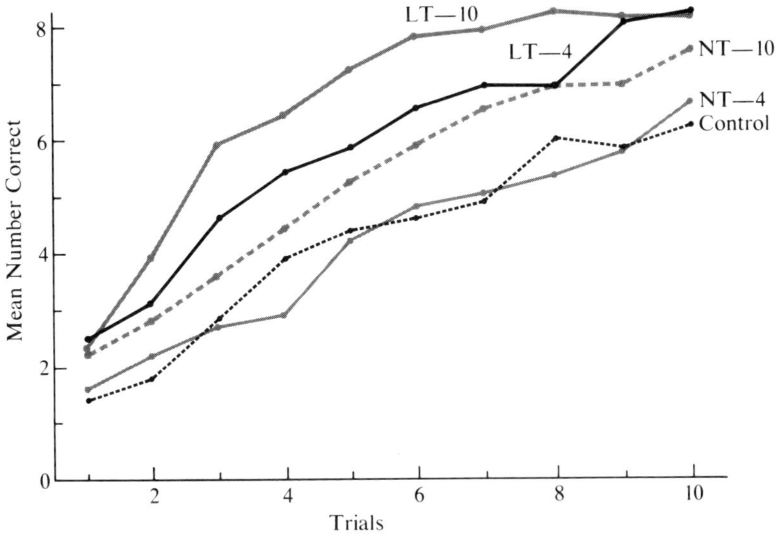

Figure 13–4. Transfer-list learning as a function of type and amount of practice. *LT* indicates learning task, and *NT* indicates nonlearning task. (From "Studies of Learning to Learn: V. Gains in Performance as a Function of Warm-Up and Associative Practice," by E. A. Schwenn and L. Postman, *Journal of Verbal Learning and Verbal Behavior,* 1967, *6,* 565–573. Reprinted by permission of Academic Press, Inc.)

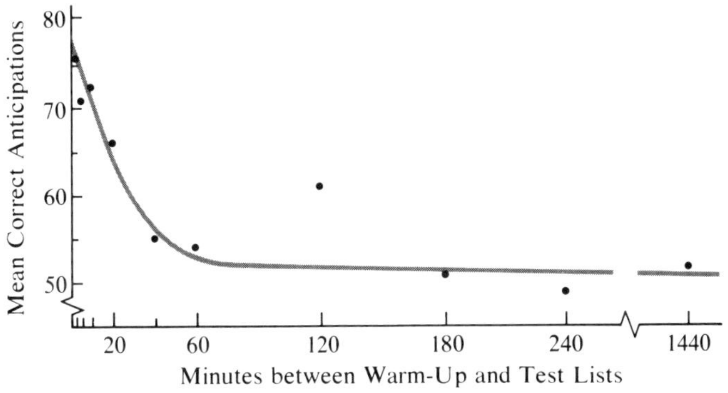

Figure 13–5. Mean correct anticipations on the test list following different intervals of rest between warm-up and test lists. The point above 240 minutes is taken from Thune's (1950) study. (From "The Relationship between Length of Interval Separating Two Learning Tasks and Performance on the Second Task," by C. E. Hamilton, *Journal of Experimental Psychology,* 1950, *40,* 613–621. Copyright 1950 by the American Psychological Association. Reprinted by permission.)

(1937) illustrates this process. He required subjects to learn 16 successive serial lists at the rate of one list each day. Each serial list consisted of 12 CVCs, and the subjects learned by the anticipation method. The results of this experiment are shown in Figure 13–6, which indicates the progressive improvement in learning serial lists. The last list required less than half the number of trials to learn than did the first list. The figure also shows that the bulk of the improvement occurred in the early lists.

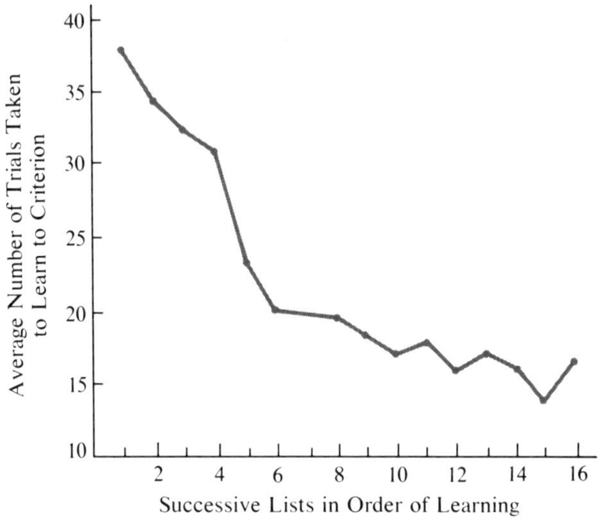

Figure 13–6. Learning-to-learn effects as reflected in progressively fewer trials taken to reach criterion as a function of practice on successive lists. (From "Reminiscence and Rote Learning," by L. B. Ward, *Psychological Monographs,* 1937, *49,* No. 220.)

Similar results have been reported by Keppel, Postman, and Zavortink (1968) in studies of paired-associate learning. Using the study/recall procedure, their subjects learned up to 36 lists consisting of word pairs. One list was learned every 48 hours. The actual improvement in learning was roughly a halving of the rate of learning from the beginning to the end. Although these results are similar to Ward's, exact comparisons are not possible because of differences in the tasks, lists, and criterion of learning employed.

Evidence for the relative permanence of learning-to-learn effects comes from several experiments. In an early study by Bunch and McCraven (1938), transfer effects remained approximately constant as a function of the interval between the training task and the test of transfer. Ellis and Hunter (1961) have demonstrated that this transfer constancy over time occurs in the case of nonspecific transfer using the *A/B, C/D* paradigm. Subjects learned two successive paired-associate lists with either no delay between the first and the second list or a delay of 2, 14, or 28 days. A second group of subjects merely relearned the first list after the same intervals. In this fashion a comparison of transfer and retention over time could be made. The basic results are presented in Figure 13–7, which shows the mean number of trials needed to reach criterion for both the transfer and the relearning group as a function of the interval between training and the test. Except for the immediate-test condition, transfer was approximately constant regardless of the time interval, whereas progressively more trials were required to relearn the task with the passage of time. The slight superiority in transfer in the zero-delay condition was perhaps due to the effects of both warm-up and learning to learn, since the transfer test immediately followed the training test; otherwise, the transfer effects were strikingly comparable. These results suggest that learning-to-learn effects are relatively permanent whereas specific information is forgotten over the course of time.

A detailed examination of learning to learn has been carried out by Postman and his colleagues (for example, Keppel & Postman, 1966; Postman, 1964, 1969; Postman, Burns, & Hasher, 1970; Postman & Schwartz, 1964; Postman & Stark, 1967). This line of research represents the most comprehensive effort to understand nonspecific transfer. In the

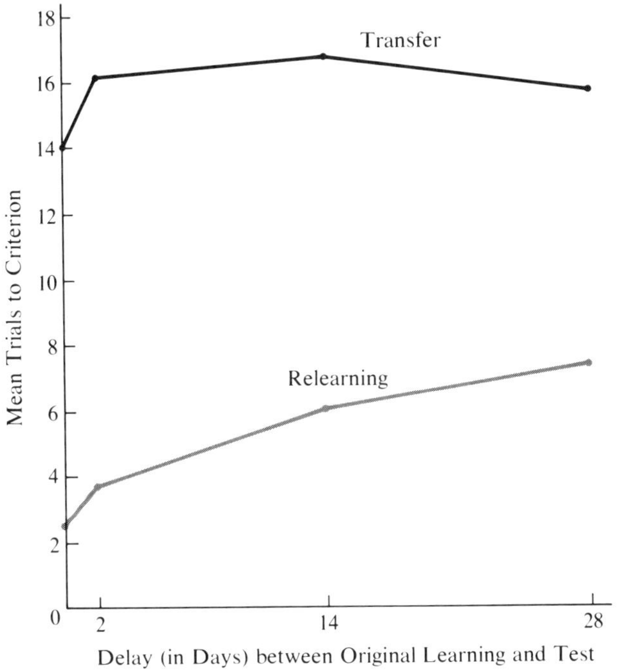

Figure 13–7. Comparison of nonspecific transfer and relearning (retention) over time. (From "A Comparison of the Temporal Course of Retention and Nonspecific Transfer," by H. C. Ellis and J. E. Hunter, *Technical Report,* 1961, No. 4. Reprinted by permission of the Sandia Corporation.)

first study in this series, Postman and Schwartz investigated learning to learn as a function of method of practice and class of verbal materials. Their subjects learned either one paired-associate list or one serial list consisting of either adjectives or trigrams. Half the subjects in each of these four conditions were then shifted to a second list of paired associates, while the remaining half learned a new serial list. A control group received no prior training. There was evidence for learning to learn in all conditions in that all the experimental subjects showed gains in speed of learning the transfer task. Nevertheless, the improvement was significantly greater when the method of practice remained the same than when it changed. The findings were similar for the type of materials but were less pronounced. In general, Postman and Schwartz concluded that transfer effects from one list to another are based in part upon specific instrumental habits that are carried over from one task to another.

Subsequent studies in this series dealt with a variety of problems. Postman (1964), for example, examined the effects of different transfer paradigms on learning to learn. The results showed learning-to-learn effects in all paradigms, although the degree of improvement varied as a function of paradigm. This study did not, however, make it possible to determine whether differences in improvement reflected the learning of skills specific to each paradigm (so that the paradigms differed in effectiveness) or the learning of general transfer skills that were used with varying degrees of success as a function of the paradigm.

In a follow-up study Keppel and Postman separated these two possible interpretations by training subjects on four different paradigms and testing them under the same conditions of transfer. The paradigms were C/D, A/D, A/B_r, and A/B'. In the last paradigm the responses on the second list are similar to those on the first list. Two test paradigms were used, *A/D* and *A/B'*. Thus, in both test situations the paradigm remained the same for one group and changed for the other three groups. The basic finding was that the type of transfer paradigm did not affect performance differentially on the test paradigm. This finding led to the conclusion that transfer skills acquired during the training phase were general in their effects. In short, whatever subjects are learning in the different paradigms appears to carry over equally well regardless of whether the test paradigm is the same or is changed. The more general importance of Postman's series of studies is their demonstration that rule-governed behavior and learning strategies can be brought under control and systematically studied.

Learning to learn is also seen in animal learning. This was described in Chapter 6 in the section on learning sets, so we will review it here. A series of experiments by Harlow (1949) served to call attention to the importance of this principle and to its relevance to much of human learning. In the typical Harlow experiment, monkeys were trained on relatively simple discrimination problems. For example, a monkey was presented with two objects, a cube and a solid triangle, with a raisin always hidden under one object and never under the other. The position of the objects was randomized, so the monkey had to learn which of the two stimuli hid the raisin. After the monkey mastered this discrimination problem, another was presented using new stimuli. With successive discrimination problems, the monkeys became progressively more efficient in learning them. The learning curves for the early discrimination problems showed the typical improvement in performance seen in many situations—that is, a gradual and steady improvement—whereas the learning curves for the later problems showed a rapid improvement, with more than 95% correct discriminations on the second test trial. The monkey learned how to learn this class of materials and then appeared to learn in a rapid, insightful manner—not by trial and error.

Learning to learn has also been extensively studied in young children. The pattern of results is similar. Early learning shows the gradual, cumulative picture, whereas later learning is more rapid and seems insightful. What appears to be most important in learning to learn is identification of and attention to the important cues in the situation. For example, the monkey must learn that it is the shape and not the position of the object that determines reward in one situation, whereas it is the color of the object in another situation. This ability to identify the relevant features is a matter of learning a general principle, and it is general principles than can be so readily transferred.

Specific Transfer

As noted earlier, when transfer effects depend upon similarities between the components of the training and transfer tasks, the transfer effects are generally designated as specific. In this section we will examine several sources of specific transfer in paired-associate learning.

Response Learning. An important source of specific transfer stems from response learning. As we have noted, part of what subjects learn in an *A/B* paired-associate test is making the response terms available as recallable units. This process is especially important if the response terms are unfamiliar or low in meaningfulness. Therefore, we should expect a source of positive transfer due to response learning in paradigms in which the response terms remain the same in the transfer task. In the case of the *A/B, C/B* paradigm, we can therefore expect that positive-transfer effects due to response learning can occur if the responses are low in meaningfulness, because whatever response learning occurs in the first list will carry over to the second list. We have already noted this deduction in discussing J. Jung's (1963) experiment (see Figure 13–1). On the other hand, if the response terms are highly meaningful or familiar, we can expect little, if any, positive transfer due to response learning. The reason is that such responses require little effect to make them available as recallable units during *A/B* learning; therefore, little response-learning effect is available for transfer to the *C/B* list.

Stimulus Differentiation. Another source of positive-transfer effects is stimulus differentiation. In Chapter 11 we noted that one process in paired-associate learning is differentiation among the stimulus terms (E. J. Gibson, 1940). If the stimuli are highly similar or confusing, part of what subjects must learn is to distinguish among the stimuli, so that each can reliably function as a cue for the appropriate response. If the stimuli in the training and transfer tasks are kept identical, as in the *A/B, A/D* paradigm, a potential source of transfer due to differentiation among the stimuli is present.

A longstanding view (E. J. Gibson, 1940) has been that positive transfer should be greater as the intralist similarity of the stimuli increases. In short, if subjects expend considerable effort in distinguishing among difficult-to-discriminate stimuli, then stimulus differentiation should provide for greater transfer compared with a situation in which the stimuli are easy to distinguish. This view predicts that in the *A/B, A/D* paradigm there will be greater positive transfer when the stimuli are high than when they are low in intralist stimulus similarity. To test this view, the performance of the *A/B, A/D* group is compared with that of a group in the *A/B, C/D* paradigm, the control for nonspecific transfer effects. No transfer of differentiation specific to the stimuli can occur in the control condition, since the stimuli are new and quite different from those in the first task.

Early attempts to prove this hypothesis on the transfer of stimulus differentiation were largely unsuccessful (see reviews by Arnoult, 1957; Ellis, 1969). The results of experiments by Del Castillo and Ellis (1968) and Underwood and Ekstrand (1968) are representative of the negative findings. Using lights of varying brightness, Del Castillo and Ellis found no reliably greater transfer when the stimuli were high than when they were low in intralist similarity. Underwood and Ekstrand found no greater transfer with high-similarity than with low-similarity stimuli consisting of trigrams. These findings were puzzling because it was not immediately obvious why learned discriminations among stimuli would not transfer to a second task when the stimuli were nominally identical.

In an effort to understand these negative results, Ellis and Shaffer (1974) further explored the transfer-of-differentiation hypothesis by examining the effects of type and complexity of stimuli. They found that the transfer of differentiation depends critically upon the complexity of the stimuli. Three experiments were conducted, all focusing on properties of the stimuli as the critical factor. In all instances, subjects learned lists conforming to the *A/B, A/D* paradigm with appropriate *A/B, C/D* controls and lists in which the stimuli were either high or low in intralist similarity. In all the experiments the responses were three-letter common words in the first list and digits in the second list. In the first experiment the stimuli were trigrams, as in the study by Underwood and Ekstrand; here no evidence for transfer of stimulus differentiation was found. In contrast, in the remaining two experiments, which used complex visual shapes and 3×3 letter matrixes, clear evidence was found for transfer of differentiation. Here positive transfer in the *A/B, A/D* paradigm resulted when the stimuli were high in intralist similarity, whereas the usual negative transfer occurred with low-similarity stimuli. These results are summarized in Figure 13–8, which shows the mean total correct responses over ten trials for all three kinds of stimuli as a function of high versus low similarity.

Ellis and Shaffer suggested that the basis for the transfer differentiation with *complex* but not with simple stimuli may be the result of multiple redundant cues in the complex

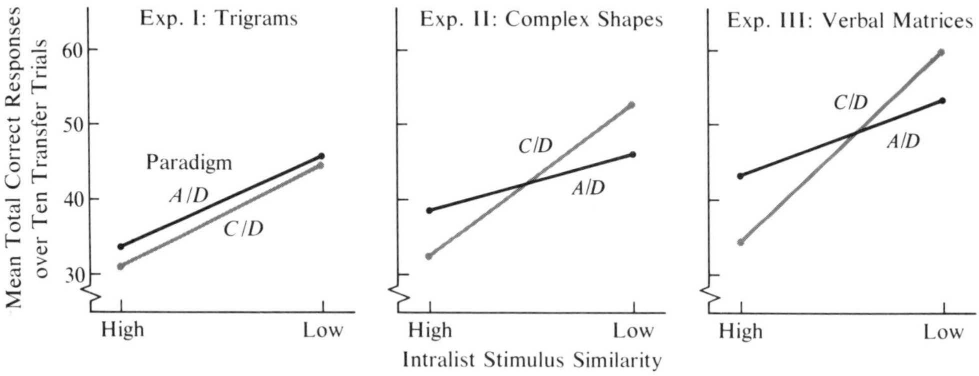

Figure 13–8. Transfer of stimulus differentiation as a function of intralist stimulus similarity and complexity of stimuli. (From "Stimulus Encoding and the Transfer of Stimulus Differentiation," by H. C. Ellis and R. W. Shaffer, *Journal of Verbal Learning and Verbal Behavior,* 1974, *13,* 393–400. Reprinted by permission of Academic Press, Inc.)

stimuli. If subjects have to search among alternative features of a complex stimulus for one on which to base a discrimination, they are more likely to retain these discriminations in a second task containing the same nominal stimuli.

Response Differentiation. A parallel process on the response side of the paired-associate task can also occur. If the responses are difficult to discriminate, there will be a source of positive transfer when the responses are identical, as in the *A/B, C/B* paradigm.

Forward Associations. When you learn an *A/B* association, it can transfer to the second task and produce interference, or negative transfer. This can occur with the *A/B, A/D* and *A/B*, A/B_r paradigms, where new or re-paired responses must be learned to the same stimuli. Suppose, for example, that all the people you knew were suddenly given new names; for instance, the person you knew as Karen Smith was renamed Susan Bennett. You can see the confusion that would result because the old association between the person and the name would have to be suppressed while the new association was learned. Similar examples occur in motor-skills learning. For instance, suppose that in one car the automatic transmission is so arranged that the lever must be pulled down all the way for the car to be put in reverse. Suppose that another car has just the opposite arrangement, requiring that the lever be pushed up for reverse. Changing from one car to the other could present difficulties through interference, since the reversal responses are opposite responses made to the same stimuli.

In verbal paired-associate learning the *B* response rarely intrudes during *A/D* learning. Nevertheless, since the *A/B* forward association is inappropriate to learning the *A/D* association, it provides a source of interference. In a similar vein, interference from forward associations occurs in the *A/B*, A/B_r paradigm. Although the response terms come from the same pool of responses, new pairings are required.

Backward Associations. Another source of negative transfer stems from backward associations, which can be established during *A/B* learning. As we noted in the previous chapter, backward associations are usually weaker than forward associations, but they may nevertheless produce negative-transfer effects. Consider the *A/B, C/B* paradigm. If *B/A* backward associations are established during *A/B* learning, they can interfere with the *B/C* backward associations during C/B learning. In short, the backward associations of the first list may interfere with the backward associations of the second list to produce negative transfer. Note that in this case the backward associations of the two lists form the paradigm B/A, B/C, which is the same as an A/B, A/D paradigm that produces interference.

Consider the A/B, A/B_r paradigm, which already suffers from interference due to forward associations. In a similar vein, it also suffers from interference due to backward associations. The B/A backward association can interfere with the B_r/A association. Since this paradigm suffers from the negative effects of both forward and backward associations, we can now better understand why it typically yields the greatest amount of negative transfer.

Overview

Let us now review what we have been saying about the components of transfer for the various transfer paradigms. These results are summarized in Table 13–4, which describes the specific components associated with the four paradigms, C/D, A/D, C/B, and A/B_r. The components include response learning, response differentiation, stimulus differentiation, forward associations, backward associations, and list discrimination. We have not discussed the last component but will describe it shortly. The table identifies the component processes that are thought to operate in each of the basic paradigms. A + sign indicates a positive-transfer effect, a − sign indicates a negative-transfer effect, and 0 indicates zero transfer. A ++ sign indicates a very strong positive-transfer effect, and a −− sign indicates a very strong negative-transfer effect.

Table 13–4. A summary of transfer effects for the major transfer paradigms.

	Paradigm			
Component	C/D	A/D	C/B	A/B_r
Response learning	0	0	+	+
Response differentiation	0	0	+	+
Stimulus differentiation	0	+	0	+
Forward associations	0	−	0	−
Backward associations	0	0	−	−
List differentiation	++	−+	+−	−−

(Adapted from "Transfer, Interference, and Forgetting," by L. Postman. In J. W. Kling and L. A. Riggs (Eds.), *Woodworth and Schlosberg's Experimental Psychology,* Third Edition. Copyright © 1971 by Holt, Rinehart and Winston. Used by permission.)

The table makes clear why the C/D paradigm serves as the appropriate baseline control for assessing transfer effects. The specific components of transfer are assumed to be nonoperative, since both the stimuli and the responses are new; hence, all these factors are weighted zero in the C/D paradigm. The nonspecific factors of warm-up and learning to learn are regarded as the same for all the paradigms, which is a quite reasonable assumption (Keppel & Postman, 1966). The ability of subjects to distinguish items from the two separate lists, which is list differentiation, is assumed to be maximal because the two lists are entirely dissimilar (compare Postman, 1971).

In turn, consider, for example, the A/B_r paradigm. A positive weight is associated with response learning and response differentiation, since the responses are identical in the two lists. Similarly, a positive factor is present with stimulus differentiation, since the stimuli are identical. Both forward and backward associations produce a negative effect, and list differentiation is heavily negative because it is difficult to distinguish between the two lists.

Transfer and Similarity

An important effort in transfer research has been to relate transfer effects to the variable of similarity. We have already noted instances of transfer based upon the similarity of two tasks, such as learning two foreign languages or learning to drive two kinds of automobiles. In this research either formal or meaningful similarity of items in paired-associate lists is typically varied. For instance, a pair of items in a training list might be *happy/cat,* and in transfer the pair might be *contented/cat*. In this instance the similarity of the stimulus terms is high, while the response terms remain identical. More generally, in studies of paired-associate transfer, the similarity between the stimulus terms of the two lists can be varied, the similarity of the response terms of the two lists can be varied, or both stimulus and response similarity can be jointly varied. A considerable amount of research has been conducted on the effects of stimulus and response similarity on transfer. However, we can note only a few examples. Let us first consider the role of stimulus similarity in transfer.

Stimulus Similarity and Transfer

The typical approach in experiments on the effects of stimulus similarity is to vary the level of interlist stimulus similarity through several degrees and observe the effects on transfer. In general, when stimuli are varied and the responses are kept identical, positive transfer increases with increasing stimulus similarity. This generalization has been supported by the results of a number of investigations (for example, Bruce, 1933; Ellis & Burnstein, 1960; McKinney, 1933).

In the classic study by Yum (1931), subjects learned an initial list of 14 paired associates consisting of syllable pairs as stimuli and familiar words as responses. For example, the subjects were taught to say the word *jury* to the stimulus item *toq/bex*. A test was given 24 hours later in which the stimulus items were either identical, varied by changing one letter, or varied by changing two letters. For example, in a change of one letter, *toq/bex* became *tiq/bex*. A measure was taken of the extent to which the subjects responded to the modified stimuli as though they were the original stimuli. Transfer, as measured by the recall of the original response to the various stimulus conditions, was always positive, but it varied with the degree of similarity of the stimuli. Specifically, when the stimuli were identical, 50% of the words were recalled correctly; with a one-letter variation, only 33% were recalled; and with a two-letter variation, only 11% were recalled. Thus, the less the amount of change in the stimuli—that is, the greater their similarity—the greater the amount of transfer. Yum repeated this experiment with visual-pattern stimuli and found quite comparable results.

So far, we have seen that similarity of both verbal and visual-pattern stimuli facilitates positive transfer. In these experiments the responses were always identical in the training and transfer tasks. Thus, a question immediately arises: What is the effect of stimulus similarity when the response terms change? A comparison of two experiments (E. J. Gibson, 1941; R. J. Hamilton, 1943) provides an answer to this question. Hamilton's study required subjects to associate nonsense-syllable responses with visual patterns as stimuli during training. The transfer list required the subjects to associate the same responses with variations of the training-list stimuli, which were varied through three degrees of similarity.

In Gibson's study the stimulus items were the same as Hamilton's, but the transfer list had new responses. In both experiments the subjects learned the original and transfer lists to a criterion of eight out of 12 correct responses. The basic results of the two experiments appear in Table 13–5. The table shows that all groups were performing at about the same level in original learning, which is to be expected. This is simply to say that all groups were comparable prior to the test of transfer.

Table 13–5. Comparison of the transfer results of studies by Gibson and Hamilton.

	Mean Trials to Learn 8 of 12 Responses			
	Hamilton		*Gibson*	
Group	*Original List*	*Transfer List*	*Original List*	*Transfer List*
I	6.73	1.27	6.86	7.43
II	7.40	2.08	7.00	5.43
III	7.40	2.35	7.07	5.71
IV	7.44	3.48	7.14	3.93

(From "Retroactive Inhibition as a Function of Degree of Generalization between Tasks," by E. J. Gibson, *Journal of Experimental Psychology,* 1941, *28,* 93–115, and "Retroactive Facilitation as a Function of Degree of Generalization between Tasks," by R. J. Hamilton, *Journal of Experimental Psychology,* 1943, *32,* 363–376. Copyright 1941 and 1943 by the American Psychological Association.)

Let us examine Hamilton's results first because these show the effect of variations in stimulus similarity when the responses in the two lists are identical. As can be seen in Table 13–5, the subjects in Group I learned the transfer list in slightly more than one trial, which is not surprising, since this group continued to learn the original list. With increasing stimulus dissimilarity, the subjects required progressively more trials to learn the list. In short, with increasing stimulus similarity there is increasing positive transfer, but this is true only when the responses on the two lists are kept identical. Gibson's results show what happens when responses are new or changed.

In Gibson's study the subjects in Group I learned to make new responses to the same stimuli (an *A*/*B*, *A*/*D* paradigm). As indicated in Table 13–5, in this case learning was the slowest, requiring an average of 7.43 trials to reach criterion. The subjects in Groups II and III, where stimulus similarity was intermediate, required about 5.5 trials. The subjects in Group IV, where stimulus similarity was lowest, required the fewest trials to learn the transfer list. The more general significance of the Gibson study is that it demonstrated a restriction on the general principle that stimulus similarity aids transfer. If the responses in the transfer task are *different* from those in the training task, then the greater the similarity of the stimuli, the less the transfer.

Theoretical interpretations of the transfer effects due to stimulus similarity have traditionally employed the concept of stimulus generalization (see E. J. Gibson, 1940). Such accounts have assumed that during the learning of a stimulus–response pair, there is some tendency for stimuli similar to a training stimulus also to acquire some tendency toward evoking the response. This is simply to say that there is some spread of habit strength to stimuli that share one or more dimensions of the training stimulus. Thus, when subjects begin learning a second list consisting of similar stimuli, the process of stimulus generalization can account for the transfer effects. We will return to a fuller discussion of this account later, but note it now as one of the first kinds of interpretations of transfer effects.

Response Similarity and Transfer

Similar studies have been conducted on the effects of interlist response similarity on paired-associate transfer. There is some evidence from a study by Underwood (1951) that when the stimuli are kept identical on the two lists and the responses are varied along a continuum of similarity, performance improves with increasing response similarity. In this study Underwood required subjects to learn an initial paired-associate list of adjectives and then learn a second list in which the stimuli were kept identical but the responses were varied through three degrees of meaningful similarity: high, moderate, and low. The basic finding was that performance on the transfer task, in terms of the number of trials to reach criterion, progressively improved with increasing response similarity. In addition, Underwood found that performance on the very first transfer test increased with increasing response similarity.

A similar study by Osgood (1946) points out some of the complications associated with response similarity. In this study, subjects learned paired-associate lists in which two letters served as stimuli and adjectives were used as responses. In the transfer list the stimuli were kept identical, but the responses were varied in three ways: they were either similar in meaning to the responses on the first list, unrelated in meaning, or opposite in meaning. The similarity dimension was the "feeling tone" associated with the words. For example, *elated* and *high* were similar words, whereas *elated* and *low* were regarded as opposite in feeling tone. A mixed-list design was used, with five pairs for each similarity condition. The similar pairs were learned better than either the unrelated or the opposed pairs, but no difference was found between the last two pairs. Moreover, the negative transfer occurred in all conditions, and the differences among all three conditions were not large. Thus, you are alerted to some of the complexities associated with response similarity.

Osgood's Transfer Surface

In an effort to integrate the results of stimulus and response similarity on transfer, Osgood (1949) presented an empirical summary of the literature in the form of a surface. His analysis of the literature led him to make three empirical generalizations about the effects of similarity on transfer and on interference effects in retention. These generalizations are as follows. (1) In transfer paradigms in which the stimuli are varied and the responses are kept identical, we find that positive transfer is obtained and increases with increasing stimulus similarity. Support for this generalization came from several studies (for example, R. J. Hamilton, 1943; McKinney, 1933). (2) In transfer paradigms in which the responses are varied and the stimuli remain the same, negative transfer is obtained, which decreases as the similarity between the responses increases. According to Osgood, this generalization is also supported by several studies (for example, Bruce, 1933; E. J. Gibson, 1941). (3) Finally, when both the stimuli and the responses are varied, negative transfer is obtained, which increases as the similarity of the stimuli increases (see, for example, E. J. Gibson, 1941; Melton & Von Lackum, 1941).

These three generalizations are represented in the well-known transfer and retroaction surface (Osgood, 1949), which is shown in Figure 13–9. The figure is a three-dimensional diagram that represents the effect of stimulus and response similarity on amount and direction of transfer. The vertical dimension represents the direction and amount of transfer, going from maximum positive transfer through zero transfer to maximum negative transfer. The width dimension represents stimulus similarity, ranging from functional identity of stimuli, similarity, to neutrality (unrelatedness) of stimuli. The length dimension represents response similarity, ranging from functional identity of responses through neutral, or unrelated, responses to responses that are opposite and finally antagonistic. The rectangular (median horizontal) plane, which is anchored on the left at the point of zero transfer, represents zero transfer throughout the surface. To "read" the surface, you project the degree of stimulus and response similarity for a given combination until the projections intersect and then judge whether the point of intersection is above, below, or on the reference plane. If it is above the reference plane, transfer is positive; if it is below the plane, transfer is negative; if it coincides with the plane, transfer is zero.

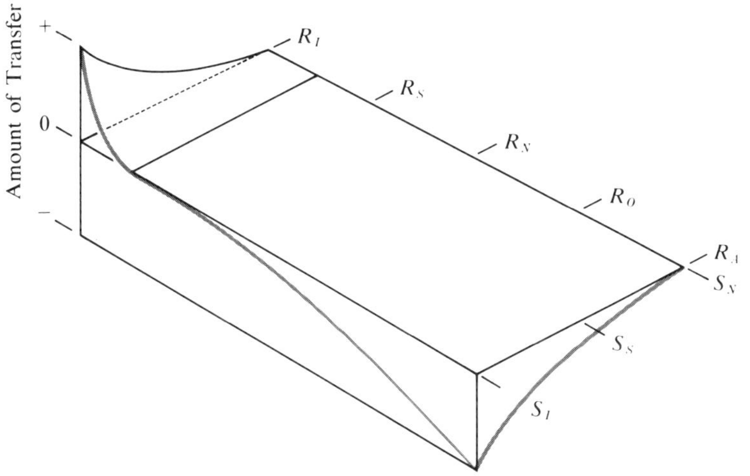

Figure 13–9. Osgood's transfer and retroaction surface. The medial plane represents the effects of zero magnitude, response relations are distributed along the length, and stimulus relations are distributed along the width. (From "The Similarity Paradox in Human Learning: A Resolution," by C. E. Osgood, *Psychological Review,* 1949, *56,* 132–143. Copyright 1949 by the American Psychological Association. Reprinted by permission.)

In order better to understand the Osgood surface, consider a few cases. For example, the figure indicates that the conditions for maximum positive transfer consist of a transfer task in which both the stimuli and the responses are identical to those of the training task (S_I, R_I). This is quite reasonable, since under these conditions the transfer task is simply a continuation of the training task. The figure also shows that as long as the responses are identical (R_I), any degree of stimulus similarity will yield some positive transfer and that transfer increases with increasing stimulus similarity. Finally, the figure indicates that the condition of maximum negative transfer is having to make antagonistic responses to identical stimuli (S_I, R_A).

Although in 1949 the existing data on transfer and similarity appeared to approximate Osgood's surface, the results of subsequent studies raised doubts about its adequacy. In an elaborate study designed to verify Osgood's formulations, Bugelski and Cadwallader (1956) found evidence in support of the effects of stimulus similarity but failed to find support for Osgood's predictions about response similarity. Here they used identical, similar, neutral, and opposite responses. Indeed, Osgood (1946) had not found evidence entirely consistent with predictions about response similarity. In contrast, Dallett (1962) found results consistent with Osgood's formulation when he restricted himself to investigating only identical, similar, and unrelated responses. What this suggests, of course, is a basic problem in measuring response similarity. Moreover, it is difficult to distinguish between "opposite" and "antagonistic" responses, which makes this portion of the surface of dubious value.

Several attempts (for example, Dallet, 1965; Houston, 1964; C. P. Thompson, 1966; Wimer, 1964) have been made either to revise Osgood's surface or to develop new surfaces. These variations appear limited in one way or another and have been critically evaluated by Postman (1971). For a number of reasons, psychologists have turned away from efforts at building transfer surfaces based simply on stimulus and response similarity. What has been found to be far more useful is a description of the *components* of transfer, many of which we have already discussed. The most promising effort so far is Martin's (1965) attempt to describe the component processes of transfer and to conceptualize them in a surface.

Martin's Component Surface

Martin has proposed that transfer effects can be more efficiently analyzed and interpreted by examining the component processes that make up transfer than by examining only the similarity dimension in transfer, as Osgood did. In effect, Martin analyzed Osgood's transfer surfaces in terms of three component processes: response learning, forward associations, and backward associations. Since there are three components (processes) to be considered, Martin has suggested that there should be three separate surfaces, each describing how a particular component is transferred for each of four paradigms.

Martin examined the following transfer paradigms: *A/B, A/B* (which is simply the continuation of the same list); *A/B, C/B; A/B, A/D;* and *A/B, C/D*. These paradigms represent the limiting case of variations in stimulus and response similarity. Martin's component surfaces are shown in Figure 13–10, each surface indicating how a particular component operates.

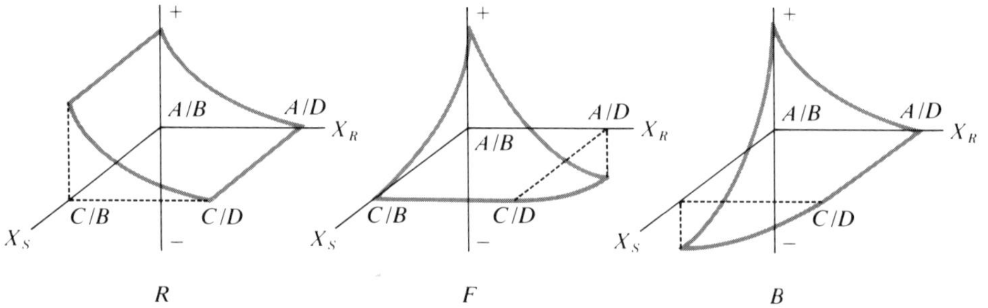

Figure 13–10. Martin's component-transfer surfaces. The surfaces *R, F,* and *B* represent the transfer of response availability, forward associations, and backward associations, respectively. (From "Transfer of Verbal Paired Associates," by E. Martin, *Psychological Review,* 1965, *72,* 327–343. Copyright 1965 by the American Psychological Association. Reprinted by permission.)

To make these component surfaces clearer, let us examine the left-hand surface, which shows the effects of response learning (*R*) for the four different paradigms. The direction and degree of transfer are indicated by the vertical axis going from + to −. The degree of stimulus similarity is along the X_S axis, and the degree of response similarity is along the X_R axis. For example, the X_S axis describes stimulus similarity going from the *A/B* paradigm to the *C/B* paradigm, where *A* represents identical stimuli and *C* represents dissimilar (unrelated) stimuli; the same holds for the dimension from *A/D* to *C/D*. The response-similarity dimension (X_R) goes from *A/B* to *A/D*, where *B* represents identical responses and *D* represents new or unrelated responses; the same holds for the dimension from *C/B* to *C/D*. Still considering only the effects of response learning, Figure 13–10 shows that the positive-transfer effect due to response learning occurs in the *A/B* and *C/B* paradigms and that the positive-transfer effect systematically declines from a maximum to zero as the responses change from identity to dissimilarity.

The influence of forward and backward associations is depicted in the middle and right-hand figures, respectively. Considering only the diagram showing the effects of forward associations, there is a positive-transfer effect only in the *A/B* paradigm, a negative-transfer effect in the *A/D* paradigm, and a zero-transfer effect in the *C/B* and *C/D* paradigms.

The advantage of Martin's surface over Osgood's is that Martin's shows the effects of three separate components, which can have different weights depending upon the particular paradigm. In contrast, Osgood's surface deals implicitly with only the forward-association component. Martin's surface deals, of course, with only three components, and we have already seen that there are additional components of transfer. Nevertheless, it is this type of component surface that more adequately portrays our knowledge of transfer effects.

Transfer and Mediation

We saw the importance of mediation in Chapters 11 and 12 and noted the role that it can play in associative learning, memory, and transfer. In this section we will examine the role of mediation in transfer in greater detail and see how it has been studied in the laboratory. The ease with which one learns a transfer task may depend upon the type of associations that exist between the training and transfer tasks. The study of such associations and of the way humans use such associations in learning a transfer task comprises the research area of mediation.

The study of mediation can be readily illustrated by examining a study by Bugelski and Scharlock (1952), which shows how language serves to mediate the learning of a paired-associate list of words. These researchers demonstrated that the ease of learning a third paired-associate list was dependent upon having learned two previous lists containing words that would facilitate, or mediate, the learning of a third list. The task of the subjects was to learn three successive lists that conformed to the sequence *A/B*, *B/C*, and *A/C*, as shown in Table 13–6. The table contains a representative pair of words for each list.

Table 13–6. Representative pairs of words in a three-stage mediation study.

List I	*List II*	*List III*
S_1 R_1 fish/hat	S_2 R_2 hat/book	S_1 R_2 fish/book

(From "An Experimental Demonstration of Unconscious Mediated Association," by B. R. Bugelski and D. P. Scharlock, *Journal of Experimental Psychology,* 1952, *44,* 334–338. Copyright 1952 by the American Psychological Association. Reprinted by permission.)

The learning of the first list (for example, *fish/hat*) served only to establish the desired associations. The response terms were then used as the stimulus terms of the second list. For example, the response term *hat* became a stimulus term. This was assumed to strengthen the associative connection between *fish* and *book,* even though these words were never directly paired. The learning of the third list served as a test of this reasoning, since if the association between *fish* and *book* was strengthened by the chain *fish/hat/book,* the *fish/book* association should be easier to learn via mediation than an appropriate control pair. Performance was indeed better on the mediated test pairs. Moreover, the subjects indicated no awareness that mediators were being developed when given a posttest interview. This study illustrates one type of mediational paradigm, the three-stage *chaining paradigm,* in which all the associations are experimentally acquired.

Mediation has also been shown when the mediating associations are assumed or inferred rather than experimentally acquired. An early demonstration was conducted by W. A. Russell and Storms (1955). They inferred the operation of a mediational chain by selection of words known to be associatively related. By selecting words that are associatively related, such as flower and stem or smell and flower, the mediational process could be studied. They reasoned that if subjects were first taught a paired-associate list consisting of pairs such as *cek/stem*, there would be positive transfer to the learning of a second list consisting of pairs such as *cek/smell* because of the known chain of associations, *stem/flower/smell*.

These relations are outlined in Table 13–7. Subjects learned an initial *A/B* list. The associative chain *B/C/D* is known to exist. Thus, it was expected that the subjects would perform better on the transfer list, *A/D,* than subjects who learned a control list in which the mediational chain would not facilitate the learning of an *A/X* list; the expectation proved correct. This sequence represents a four-stage chaining paradigm, in which two stages (*B/C, C/D*) are assumed to operate.

Table 13–7. Schematic outline of the conditions in a four-stage mediation study.

	Original List	*Inferred Chain*	*Transfer List*
Experimental			
Group	Learn *A/B*	(*B/C/D*)	Learn *A/D*
Example	cek/stem	(stem/flower/smell)	cek/smell
Control			
Group	Learn *A/B*	(*B/C/D*)	Learn *A/X*
Example	cek/stem	(stem/flower/smell)	cek/joy

(From "Implicit Verbal Chaining in Paired-Associate Learning," by W. A. Russell and L. H. Storms, *Journal of Experimental Psychology,* 1955, *49,* 287–293. Copyright 1955 by the American Psychological Association. Reprinted by permission.)

So far, we have illustrated what are known as chaining paradigms in mediation. Two other mediation paradigms are frequently used: *stimulus equivalence* and *response equivalence.* Stimulus-equivalence paradigms involve the formation of associations for a common response term with different stimuli. Subjects learn a first list, *A/B,* and then a second list, *C/B,* in which the same response terms are used but paired with new stimuli. The assumption is that the *A* and *C* stimuli of the two lists acquire equivalence due to their association with the common response, *B*. If the subjects are then given a test list, *A/C,* it is assumed that *B* will be evoked by both *A* and *C* and will thus serve to mediate the association between *A* and *C*.

The response-equivalence paradigm also involves the formation of associations for common stimuli with different responses. For example, subjects first learn a *B/A* list followed by a *B/C* list; the assumption is that the *A* and *C* responses will acquire equivalence by being associated with the common stimuli, *B*. Thus, learning of the test list, *A/C,* will be facilitated.

Schulz and Lovelace (1964) have suggested an important distinction between two aspects of mediation: discovery of the mediational rule and use of the mediational rule. This distinction assumes that discovery of the mediational rule does not ensure its automatic use.

To evaluate this distinction, Schulz and Weaver (1968) varied the length of the *A/C* test interval in a three-stage chaining paradigm. The basic assumption was that the length of the test interval is an important factor in using the mediating response because its use would presumably require more time than is the case when the mediating association is not operating. They found that as the test interval was increased, the superiority in performance due to mediation increased. They also varied the length of the *A/C* study interval, which presumably would allow for the discovery of the mediating response; here they found that performance was a direct function of the study interval for both experimental and control conditions.

Our survey of mediation has necessarily been brief. This literature has been reviewed extensively and frequently during the past decade (B. Earhard & Mandler, 1965; Horton, 1967; J. J. Jenkins, 1963; Kjeldergaard, 1968; Postman, 1971). A review of programmatic research in mediation has been conducted by Schulz (1972). The interested reader is encouraged to read these reviews.

Transfer Theory

Psychologists have long been interested in developing theoretical accounts of transfer phenomena. Several varieties, ranging from classical stimulus–response conceptions to cognitive interpretations, have been developed. Each of these types of theories has dealt with a limited range of empirical findings, and thus no single comprehensive theory has emerged. In this section we will briefly survey several types of transfer theory: classical stimulus–response theory, mediation theory, stimulus-encoding-variability theory, and cognitive theory.

Classical Stimulus–Response Theory

Classical stimulus–response theory accounts for transfer in terms of the process of generalization. The theory encompasses both stimulus and response generalization as explanatory concepts and represents an extension of generalization concepts to verbal learning and transfer (see E. J. Gibson, 1940). We have already briefly noted how stimulus generalization has been used to account for transfer. Let us now examine this account in greater detail.

A stimulus-generalization interpretation of transfer assumes that during the learning of a stimulus–response pair a *single stage*—that is, association formation—is involved. This single-stage conception of associative learning is principally what distinguishes it from two-stage mediation theory; we will return to this point later. During association formation in the learning of a particular *A/B* pair, it is assumed that stimuli similar to *A*, such as *A′*, *A″*, and so on, acquire some associative connection with the *B* response, such that *A′/B* and *A″/B* associations also become strengthened, although not to the level of the directly practiced association (*A/B*) itself. Therefore, in an *A/B*, *A′/B* paradigm (or in an *A/B*, *A″/B* paradigm), the subject begins the second list with some of this learning accomplished by virtue of stimulus-generalization tendencies. More generally, the basic notion is that a generalization gradient spreads around the training stimuli, such that other stimuli that lie along some dimension shared with the training stimuli acquire some associative strength. The gradient of generalization is thought to operate like that in conditioning, except that the stimuli are usually multidimensional.

Classical transfer theory would thus predict maximum positive transfer in the *A/B*, *A/B* paradigm, in which the stimuli and responses are identical because generalization should be virtually complete. High positive transfer should occur in the *A/B*, *A′B* paradigm, less positive transfer should occur in the *A/B, A''/B* paradigm, and zero transfer should occur in the *A/B, C/B* paradigm because there is no generalization from the *A* to the *C* stimuli. Yet we have already seen that negative transfer occurs in the *A/B, C/B* paradigm, which indicates that classical theory using the generalization concept is at best incomplete as an account of transfer (compare Kausler, 1974).

A parallel principle of response generalization has been used to account for the effects of response similarity in transfer. In this case it is assumed that during the learning of an *A/B* pair, responses similar to *B*, such as *B'* and *B''*, also acquire some strength by virtue of response generalization. Therefore, we should expect positive transfer in an *A/B, A/B'* paradigm.

Mediation Theory

Mediation theory is an extension of single-stage stimulus–response theory in that it assumes the operation of an intermediate, or mediating, process as the basis for observed transfer phenomena. Although the use of generalization to explain transfer effects due to stimulus or response similarity is reasonable when the stimuli vary along clearly defined physical dimensions, when the stimuli vary along the more complex dimension of meaningful similarity, a mediation interpretation is more reasonable.

Let us consider the *A/B, A/B'* paradigm, which we have seen leads to positive transfer. Underwood (1951) had interpreted this result in terms of response generalization on the assumption that *B'* and *B''* responses would acquire some strength during *A/B* associative learning. But it also is possible to interpret such positive transfer in terms of mediation, especially when the responses are words (Barnes & Underwood, 1959). Suppose, for example, that a set of pairs in an *A/B, A/B'* list consists of the sequence *xuf/warm, xuf/hot*. Since *warm* and *hot* are conceptually related, the transfer list will be easy to learn because of the mediating chain *A/B/B'* (*xuf/warm/hot*). Thus, we see that a mediational interpretation can account for certain transfer effects quite simply without resorting to generalization mechanisms.

Mediational theories are still part of a stimulus–response theory, but they represent an elaboration of classical one-stage theory by postulating an additional stage. In this sense mediational theory is more flexible than classical one-stage theory and thus can account for a wider range of transfer phenomena. It is important because of its recognition of *implicit* or covert processes that intervene between stimulus events and overt responses of the organism.

Encoding-Variability Theory

Encoding-variability theory moves one additional step toward a more complex, cognitive type of theory. Theories employing the concept of coding (or encoding) emphasize that nominal-stimulus events are not necessarily the stimuli that organisms use in learning situations. Coding processes are similar to mediation, and on occasion they have been treated as largely synonymous concepts. They nevertheless differ in an important way in that mediating responses are treated theoretically as being tied in some fairly direct manner to nominal stimulation, in the sense of being stimulus-determined. In contrast, coding responses are determined by both the stimulus conditions and learner states, such as sets and instructions. In short, the main difference between coding and mediation lies in the contribution of the organism's activity to coding, a contribution that allows for even greater flexibility in accounting for complex behavior (compare Ellis, 1973; Lawrence, 1963).

The coding concept emphasizes that stimulus events affect behavior, not as nominal events themselves, but in terms of the way events are encoded by the organism. This notion harks back to classical Gestalt psychology (see, for example, Koffka, 1935), which emphasized that the important stimulus is the stimulus-as-perceived, not the physical stimulus. In current terms, this argument emphasizes the stimulus-as-coded as the important determinant of behavior.

Martin (1968) has extended Lawrence's (1963) ideas about coding to the analysis of certain transfer phenomena. In his formulation, the encoding-variability hypothesis, a nominal stimulus is encoded as a perceptual-encoding representation, which serves as the stimulus-as-coded. Thus, the encoded version of a nominal stimulus may vary from situation to situation.

A central feature of Martin's theory is the assumption that encodings vary as a function of the meaningfulness of the stimuli, where meaningfulness is thought to be related to the fragmented/integrated character of the stimulus. More specifically, Martin proposes that variability in encoding a given nominal stimulus is inversely related to its meaningfulness. Stimuli high in meaningfulness can be readily encoded as a unit; stimuli low in meaningfulness are likely to be variably encoded on successive trials because of the fragmented character of the stimuli. For instance, *dog* is likely to be encoded as "dog" immediately, whereas the trigram *xwm* is more likely to be variably encoded on successive trials.

Given the assumption that a nominal stimulus, A, may be variably encoded on successive trials, such that the encoding may be a_1 on one trial, a_2 on another, a_3 on another, and so forth, we can now examine the implications of variable encoding for transfer outcomes. In the A/B, A/D and A/B, A/B_r paradigms, where the nominal stimuli remain identical, we can assume that the *encoded version* of A is not necessarily identical in the two lists. If, say, in the A/B, A/D paradigm, the encoded version of A in the second list is different from the encoded version of A in the first list, the A/D list becomes functionally like a C/D list because the first-list stimuli are *recoded* in the second list.

This assumption that subjects will recode nominally identical stimuli allows the prediction that the usual interference, or negative transfer, in the A/D or A/B_r paradigm can be overcome or minimized, since the usual interference from forward associations is no longer operative. This is simply to say that if the transfer list is in fact like a new list, then the interference should be minimal. There are additional features of the encoding-variability hypothesis; however, we are here concerned primarily with the *recoding* process.

How do tests of this hypothesis fare in the laboratory? In general, there is little evidence for the hypothesis on the basis of current experimental research. According to the hypothesis, subjects who recode the A stimuli during transfer should perform better than subjects who retain the same encodings in negative-transfer paradigms. Yet precisely the opposite results were obtained by Goggin and Martin (1970) in a study of "forced" stimulus recoding. Similarly, R. F. Williams and Underwood (1970) found no evidence for the recoding hypothesis using stimuli that were "highlighted" by special cuing techniques. Postman and Stark (1971), Ellis (1973), and Mueller, Gautt, and Evans (1974) also found no support for the hypothesis.

It should be pointed out that there is evidence that subjects will spontaneously recode stimuli (Houston, 1967; Merryman & Merryman, 1971). The issue, however, is whether recoding will lead to reduced negative transfer, and, as noted, the evidence is not supportive of this view. Before we dismiss the recoding corollary of the encoding-variability hypothesis, we should note that Martin (1971) has questioned the appropriateness of some of the experimental tests of recoding on the grounds that they lack sensitivity. Nevertheless, the usefulness of the recoding hypothesis depends on the extent to which effective experimental tests can be derived from it (Postman & Underwood, 1973). In general, encoding-variability theory applied to transfer has not been promising.

Cognitive Theory

The area of transfer has long been represented by theoretical interpretations stemming largely from stimulus–response associationistic conceptions and their extensions, as seen in mediation and encoding theories. Use of the paired-associate procedure, with its separation of stimulus and response, has, of course, readily lent itself to an S–R analysis. In contrast, cognitive theories of transfer have been more recently developed, and only a few scattered attempts have been made. Therefore, we will touch on only a few developments in cognitive theory, but we can expect to see more developments in this area.

An early cognitive theory designed to account for the effects of overlearning (learning beyond some criterion) on transfer was proposed by G. Mandler (1962). In this theory cognitive structures emerge from associative processes. During overlearning, analogic structures develop of the overt responses made during learning; these structures develop during the course of response integration, in which discrete parts of a response unit come to develop as a functional unit. In other words, once a response sequence has been integrated and acts as a unit, it develops, according to Mandler, some form of structural representation that he identifies as a "central" analog, or analogic structure. This analog of the response unit can function independently of the overt response sequence and permits symbolic activity to occur without emission of the response units. In effect, structures are developed on the basis of associationistic stimulus–response connections, and once they are established they enable the organism to behave cognitively. This issue has been further debated by J. Jung (1965) and Mandler (1965), and a study by J. T. Spence and Schulz (1965) has not supported Mandler's ideas in the context of verbal learning. Although Mandler has not attempted to develop his ideas further, the problem of going from discrete associations to complex structure is still unresolved.

A more recent effort is a cognitive theory of negative transfer proposed by Greeno, James, and DaPolito (1971), which begins by redefining the successive stages of associative learning. The first stage involves the storing of a stimulus–response pair as a unit. The assumption is that the response can influence the encoding of the stimulus and that the stimulus can influence the encoding of the response. In the second stage, subjects learn to retrieve the pair from memory. Once the pairs are stored, the subjects must develop some retrieval plan that enables them to assess these stored units. Characteristics of the stimuli play the primary role in determining the effectiveness of retrieval.

Negative transfer in the *A/B, A/D* paradigm is regarded as the result of interference from two sources. In the first case, interference is expected to develop to the extent that the stimuli, the responses, or both are encoded in the same way on successive lists. It is assumed that such encodings will transfer, and it is this stability of encodings that produces negative transfer. This feature of the argument is, interestingly enough, just the reverse of Martin's. The second source of interference stems from a disruption of the first-list retrieval plan when the stimuli are now paired with new responses. This requires that the subjects develop a new retrieval plan, which acts to suppress or disrupt the old retrieval plan and thus leads to forgetting of the *A/B* associations.

It is not clear how fundamental a change this theory is from classical association theory. The language system is obviously different, and several assumptions are changed. Yet it remains to be seen whether this account more effectively characterizes negative transfer than do stage-analysis concepts. For a detailed evaluation of this theory, the interested reader should see Postman and Underwood (1973).

Other types of cognitive theories have stressed the learning of *rules* or principles that transfer either positively or negatively in new situations. For example, we noted in Chapter 12 that subjects can acquire and use coding strategies. Recall that Ellis, Parente, and Walker (1974) found that subjects recall letter strings that are variably grouped substantially better than the same letter strings consistently grouped over successive presentations.

The superiority of varied input is referred to as the variability effect in free recall and has been interpreted in terms of the perceptual-regrouping hypothesis mentioned in Chapter 12. This hypothesis assumes that variation in the experimenter-imposed grouping rule or structure for letter sequences (for example, *ba nc ow; b anco w*) will increase the likelihood that subjects will discover the underlying structure (*bancow*). Since the spatial grouping of the letter strings changes on successive presentations for the subjects in the varied-input condition, it is assumed that they are more likely to recognize the irrelevancy of the experimenter-imposed grouping and will therefore attempt to encode the letter sequence as an intact unit (*bancow*), which will obviously enhance recall.

The basic argument here is that subjects acquire a rule or strategy for encoding the letter sequences as an intact, pronounceable unit. Once these rules or strategies have been acquired, it is proposed that they will readily transfer to new lists of sequences. Clear evidence for these transfer effects was found in two recent experiments (Ellis, Parente, Grah, & Spiering, 1975; Hunt, Parente, & Ellis, 1974). In these experiments, subjects trained under varied input successfully transferred whatever encoding strategies or rules they achieved during first-list learning, regardless of whether they were shifted to a second list consisting of variably grouped or consistently grouped letter strings. In contrast, subjects trained under constant input appeared unable to alter their strategies when shifted to varied input and performed equally poorly when shifted to either constant or varied input. Thus, in one case we see that varied experience provides for strong positive transfer, while in the other case constant experience leads to transfer suppression.

Summary

In this chapter we described some of the principal procedures, empirical findings, and theoretical interpretations of transfer. Early studies of transfer focused on practical educational problems, whereas later studies have focused on analytic research and the development of theoretical conceptions of transfer. The influence of previous learning on performance in new learning situations defines the study of transfer.

The study of transfer involves the comparison of experimental-group and control-group performance on some common transfer task. Transfer measurement is usually direct, and transfer formulas are infrequently used in current research. Transfer in paired-associate learning typically involves the use of four basic paradigms: *A/B, C/D; A/B, A/D; A/B, C/B;* and *A/B*, A/B_r. Other paradigms include *A/B, A′/B* and *A/B, A/B′*.

Transfer effects can be divided into nonspecific (general) and specific categories. Nonspecific transfer includes warm-up and learning to learn. Nonspecific transfer was seen to be stable over the course of time in which information is typically forgotten. Specific transfer is transfer based upon the similarities of the training and transfer tasks. Instances of specific factors in transfer are response learning, stimulus differentiation, response differentiation, foward associations, and backward associations.

Similarity was seen as an important factor in transfer. Both stimulus and response similarity affect transfer. An early attempt to integrate the effects of similarity is Osgood's transfer and retroaction surface. A more successful empirical summary is Martin's component surface which deals with response learning, forward associations, and backward associations.

Mediational processes were also seen to be important in transfer. Three basic types of mediation paradigms were described: chaining, stimulus equivalence, and response equivalence. Transfer theories were briefly discussed, including classical stimulus–response theory, mediation theory, encoding-variability theory, and cognitive theory.

Chapter 14

Perceptual Learning and Memory

It is relatively easy to locate a friend in the midst of hurrying people at a busy air terminal. In this situation we are rapidly scanning a large number of unfamiliar faces and obtaining enough information to make sure that they are not the friend until that person is located. Such search tasks are an everyday experience. More important, however, is that our skill in making searches for such things as telephone numbers, location of streets, and so on appears to improve with practice. This improvement with practice is one kind of evidence for the process known as perceptual learning.

In this chapter we will consider some of the relations between perception, learning, and memory, with an emphasis on how various conditions of practice come to influence our perception of objects and events. There is substantial evidence (for example, Epstein, 1967; E. J. Gibson, 1969; Vanderplas, 1970) that our perception of environmental stimuli can be modified by past experiences. For instance, a sophisticated winetaster can make fine discriminations among wines that cannot be made by a novice. Similarly, a trained physician can recognize features in an x-ray that are not readily detected by a beginning medical student. Finally, a skilled driver can make rapid judgments about many features of driving, such as the speed of approaching cars or the amount of space available to negotiate a turn, that a beginning driver may not be able to make. In all of these examples, judgments about environmental events are made that are subject to improvement with practice.

We examined some aspects of the process by which discriminations improve with practice in Chapter 6. We have also noted the significance of perceptual processes as they relate to learning and development in other chapters. The focus of this chapter, however, is on the way learning influences perception.

The Concept of Perceptual Learning

At a general level the term *perceptual learning* refers to any modification of perception that can be attributed to learning (Ellis, 1978). We use the word *modification* rather than *improvement* because under certain conditions humans may actually show decrements in perceptual performance. Normally, however, we think of perception as becoming better in the sense of becoming more accurate as the result of practice. This definition is both descriptive and functional in that it describes perceptual learning as a relationship involving perception and learning, but it does not describe how perceptual learning evolves.

E. J. Gibson (1969, p. 3) has noted three characteristics of perceptual learning. First, perceptual learning implies an interaction between the organism and the environment. Second, because we are concerned with learning, perceptual learning emphasizes modification of behavior. Third, because we are also focusing on perception, the modification that occurs is in the organism's ability to *extract information* from the environment rather than to do something to the environment. Presumably, in the process of extracting information from the stimulus environment, perception should come into increasing correspondence with the events and objects of the physical world.

Any discussion of perceptual learning requires that a distinction be made between learning and perception. It is generally agreed that learning is a relatively permanent effect that is inferred from performance changes due to practice. The condition of practice serves to distinguish learning from performance changes attributable to other conditions, such as maturation, fatigue, or drug states. Similarly, perception is inferred from performance changes due to stimulation. Both perception and learning are inferred processes tied to performance changes, but they differ in their antecedents.

Perceptual learning can be readily understood by examining how learning and perception relate. Consider again the example of searching for a familiar face in a crowded air terminal. You search until you correctly identify the familiar face, which illustrates the process of perception. If, however, you were required to go to the air terminal every day and locate a new but familiar person, your skill in locating familiar faces would quickly improve. Such an improvement in search skills with practice would be an instance of perceptual learning.

Another instance of perceptual learning can be seen in the effects of practice on the judgment of distance. In a classic study E. J. Gibson and Bergman (1954) demonstrated that verbal estimates of distance improved simply as a result of practice in making judgments. Moreover, the effects of practice transferred to making judgments involving a new range of stimuli. Again, perceptual learning is seen as some change in perception due to practice. Gibson (1969) provides another illustration, one from everyday experience:

> Thinking about something substantive in one's own experience often helps pin down a problem. Let me describe what I heard as I woke up this morning, for it points to an everyday aspect of perceptual learning that is not so apparent in James' examples of sensory "virtuosity." In my window came a medley of sounds. They divided for me into two kinds. One was the sound of the neighbor's lawn mower. I knew that one. The rest was a conglomeration (for me) of many bird songs. Suddenly a new one was added to the conglomeration and I could pick it out from the rest—it was the mourning dove. I knew it, as I did the lawn mower. What does it mean to say that I knew it? An easy answer would be to say that I had identified it by learning the name for it. But that would be no answer, for it would not explain how I differentiated that particular pattern of sound from the rest of the medley. An ornithologist could no doubt have separated out all the patterns and named them for me. I know the names, too; there are wrens, robins, cardinals, finches, and so on. But I cannot differentiate the songs. In the case of the mourning dove, the fact that I know the name is incidental. I could call it a paloma just as well and still recognize the pattern of its song. I can go with the ornithologist to his field laboratory and listen to the sounds from the marsh. The patterns of physical energy coming to his ears and mine are the same. But from this burst of sound impinging on the eardrum, he can detect patterns and invariants where I cannot. He can describe to me some of the qualities—"listen to that low rhythmical rumbling sound"; but I cannot hear them separated from the rest of the buzzes and whirs even when he tells me their characteristics. How has he learned to detect the critical features which make the pattern distinct from all the others? This question is a central problem for perceptual learning [p. 5][1]

[1] From *Principles of Perceptual Learning and Development*, by E. J. Gibson. Copyright © 1969. Reprinted by permission of Prentice-Hall, Inc., Englewood Cliffs, New Jersey.

Categories of Perceptual Tasks

To understand perceptual learning, psychologists study a number of perceptual tasks. A taxonomy of five basic perceptual tasks has been described by Hake (1957) and elaborated on by Vanderplas (1963). This taxonomy categorizes the types of perceptual tasks on the basis of the decision each requires the individual to make. The classification is also hierarchical. In order of increasing complexity, the five basic tasks are detection, discrimination, recognition, identification, and judgment.

Detection

A detection task is one in which an observer reports the presence or absence of a stimulus. For example, when you respond to the ring of the telephone, you do so because you detect the sound. Detection may also occur with a flash of light, pressure on the skin, movement of some object, or, more generally, some signal presented in the context of background stimulation.

A classic example of detection research is a study of the two-point threshold by Volkmann (1858), reported in Woodworth (1938). Volkmann applied two points of pressure about the size of a pencil point to the tip of subjects' middle finger of the left hand. The

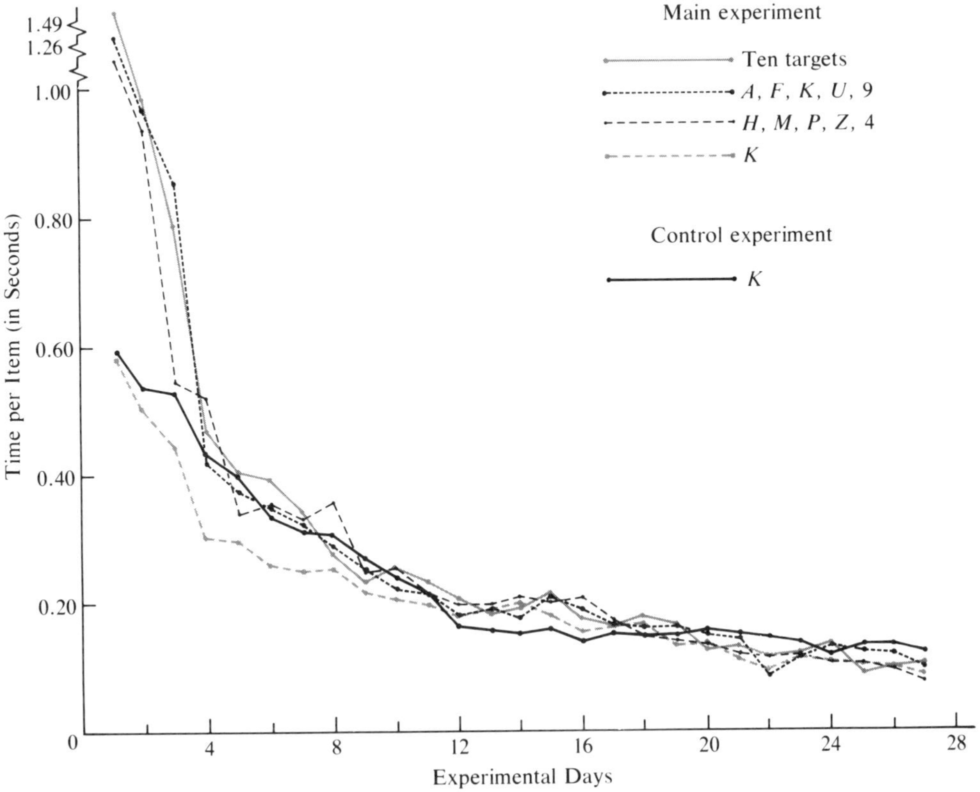

Figure 14–1. Learning curves showing the effect of sustained practice on detection of various classes of targets. (Reprinted with permission of author and publisher from: Neisser, U., Novick, R., and Lazar, R. Searching for ten targets simultaneously, *Perceptual and Motor Skills,* 1963, *17,* 955–961.)

subjects were required to make judgments of twoness—that is, to report when they actually felt two points of stimulation as the distance between the points was varied over successive presentations. Volkmann's main finding was a steady decrease in the two-point threshold with practice.

Another example of detection can be seen in search tasks. These tasks, as noted earlier, require subjects to search among some set of stimuli for a designated target item. Neisser (1964) has shown the dramatic improvement in the speed with which humans locate targets in a list as a result of sustained practice. In one study Neisser, Novick, and Lazar (1963) investigated the effects of practice over a 27-day period in which subjects scanned for different types of items. The tasks were to search for a *K*; to search for one of the five items *A, F, K, U,* or 9; to search for *H, M, P, Z,* or 4; or to search for any one of the ten letters and numbers used in the other conditions. The basic results are presented in Figure 14–1, which shows the time needed per item in each of the four experimental conditions. The performance of the subjects in all the conditions improved with practice, but the greatest improvement occurred in the multiple-target conditions.

What accounts for such enormous improvement in the ability to detect targets? One explanation has been suggested by E. J. Gibson (1969, p. 171), who contends that subjects must be learning to focus their search on a minimal set of features that distinguishes the target items from the general context. This is essentially a selective-attention interpretation. However, the details of this process are not completely clear.

Discrimination

When a winetaster reports that two wines differ in some feature, such as body or acidity, the winetaster has been engaging in the process of discrimination. It is not necessary that the two wines be named or identified; all that must be reported is that they are perceived as different. Similarly, a person may report that two flashes of light differ in that one is brighter or that two tones differ in that one is louder. Thus, discrimination is the discernment of a difference between two stimuli. In the typical discrimination experiment, subjects are presented with two stimuli, either simultaneously or successively, and asked to report whether they are the same or different. If the stimuli lie along the same continuum, the subjects may give responses of "more" or "less."

Improvement in discrimination performance is taken as evidence for perceptual learning. Classic studies in the improvement of discrimination with practice have shown a reduction in the differential threshold for various classes of stimuli (see E. J. Gibson, 1969). In an illustrative study in this tradition, Björkman and Ottander (1959) examined the differential threshold for lifted weights. Subjects practiced making discriminations in lifted weights over 5 days without knowledge of results. Over this period of practice, the differential threshold was considerably reduced. In an important study by Pick (1965), children were given practice in discrimination of visual and tactual forms. The basic task was to distinguish between standard forms and various transformations of the forms. Not only did the children learn to discriminate among the forms, but they were able to transfer to new forms that were similar.

Recognition

In recognition tasks, subjects must report whether a particular target item is old (familiar) or new (unfamiliar) following a training session in which the subjects were exposed to a number of stimuli. The important difference between recognition and discrimination is that a recognition decision is based upon a judgment of familiarity. There are two basic types of recognition tasks: a single-item procedure and a multiple-item forced-choice procedure. In either type, subjects are shown a series of items in a training session and given instructions to remember the items. This session is followed by a recognition test.

A number of recognition experiments have been conducted in which subjects are given various kinds of training conditions and then tested for stimulus recognition. Many of these experiments have examined the role of verbal labeling of the stimuli (see Ellis, 1973). Early experiments of this type demonstrated that the effect of practice on improvement in shape recognition depended upon the type of training administered. For example, Vanderplas and Garvin (1959) gave subjects paired-associate training in labeling random shapes with nonsense syllables of 0% association value. With increasing amounts of practice, no improvement in shape recognition occurred. In contrast, Ellis and Muller (1964) found that shape recognition systematically improved with practice when words were used as responses during paired-associate training.

The effects of varying amounts and types of practice are illustrated in an experiment by Ellis (1968). Subjects were given paired-associate training in labeling random shapes and then given either a shape-recognition test or a paired-associate transfer test; here we are concerned only with the shape-recognition test. In the shape-recognition test four factors were varied: shape complexity (six-point or 24-point random shapes—random shapes are straight-sided shapes that vary in the number of sides, and hence points, they may possess); association value of the shapes (low or high); type of response associated with the stimulus (meaningful and relevant word, meaningful but irrelevant word, or CVC trigram); and amount of practice (two, eight, or 16 paired-associate trials). The response variable was of interest because it allowed separation of the effects of response relevance (meaningful and relevant words versus meaningful and irrelevant words) and the effects of response meaningfulness (meaningful and irrelevant words versus CVC trigrams).

The results of the recognition test following the various conditions of pretraining are shown in Figure 14–2. The upper two panels show the results for the six-point (low-complexity) shapes, and the lower two panels show the results for the 24-point (high-complexity) shapes. First, recognition improved with practice (pretraining) for all conditions, although the rate of improvement appeared faster for the high-complexity shapes. Second, response relevance (representativeness) was generally a more potent influence on recognition than was response meaningfulness. The role of the response variable was interpreted in terms of the relevant response's directing the subjects' attention to distinctive features of the stimulus and suggesting a particular encoding of the shape by virtue of the shape/label relationship. For example, if a particular shape was labeled "mountain" and the label was judged to be representative of the shape, then the label could facilitate encoding of the stimulus. It should be added that labeling practice does not always facilitate recognition as compared with the performance of control subjects who merely *observe* the shapes during pretraining. For example, Ellis and Muller (1964) found that labeling (versus observation) facilitated recognition with complex but not with simple shapes.

In an interesting line of research, Malpass and his associates (for example, Malpass & Kravitz, 1969; Malpass, Lavigueur, & Weldon, 1973) examined the effects of training on recognition of faces. In the latter study, subjects were asked to describe verbally both Black and White faces. In the first experiment, although verbal training affected verbal usage and verbal-recognition performance, such changes did not parallel changes in face-recognition performance. Black subjects obtained higher recognition scores for Black faces than for White faces; similarly, White subjects obtained higher recognition scores for White faces. In a second experiment White subjects practiced for 100 training trials in the recognition of both Black and White faces. After this extensive training the differences in recognition of Black versus White faces disappeared. In this case we have an instance of perceptual learning of complex visual stimuli.

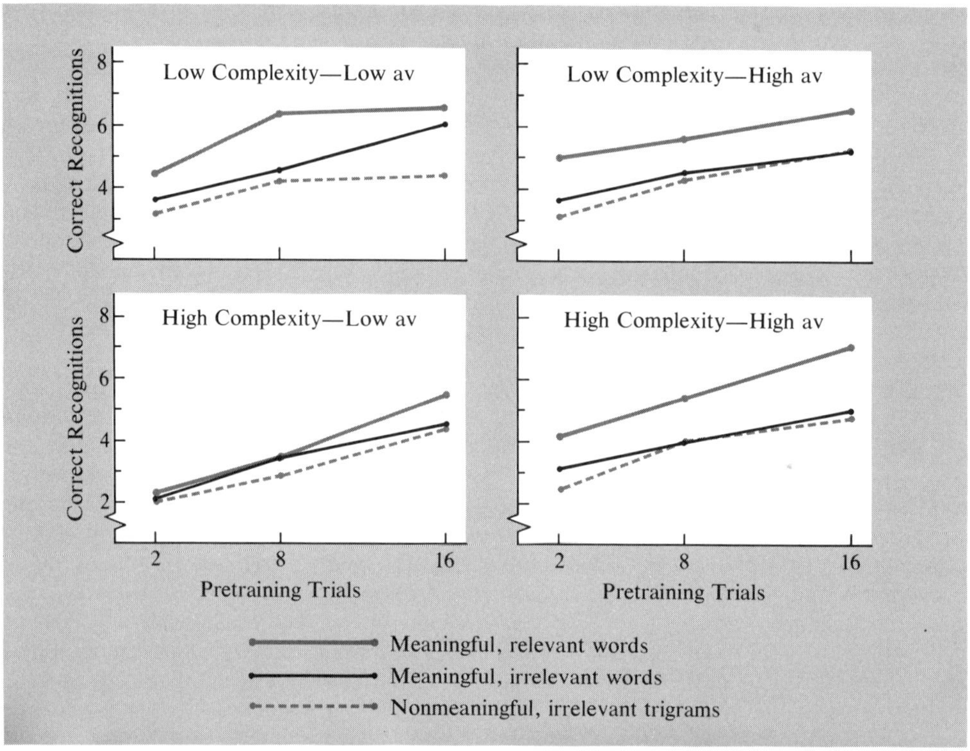

Figure 14–2. Effects of three kinds of verbal-labeling practice on shape recognition. (From "Transfer of Stimulus Predifferentiation to Shape Recognition and Identification Learning: Role of Properties of Verbal Labels," by H. C. Ellis, *Journal of Experimental Psychology,* 1968, *78,* 401–409. Copyright 1968 by the American Psychological Association. Reprinted by permission.)

Identification

An identification task requires that a specific identifying response be made to a stimulus. Since this task requires a unique response to be made to each stimulus, it goes one step beyond the task of recognition. The responses are usually names, letters of the alphabet, or numbers, but they may involve simple motor responses, such as pulling different switches on a panel. An example is learning Morse code, which requires identifying auditory patterns as letters of the alphabet.

As Vanderplas (1970) notes, most studies of perceptual identification have used verbal materials. Typical studies include those on thresholds of identification for words (for example, Colegate & Eriksen, 1972; Goldiamond & Hawkins, 1958; Postman, Bruner, & McGinnies, 1948). For instance, Postman and his colleagues studied the influence of personal values on the recognition of words and demonstrated that the subjects' personal value system, as assessed by the Allport and Vernon value scale, predicted the ease with which words would be identified. For example, if a subject scored high in, say, economic values, then words belonging to this class were more readily recognized.

Other studies have used nonword stimuli, such as auditory sequences. For example, Neisser and Hirst (1974) presented subjects with four signals, consisting of a high tone, a low tone, a hiss sound, and a scratch sound. The task of the subjects was to identify the order of signal presentation on a typewriter keyboard. Over 21 days of training, the subjects' ability to identify the sequences improved enormously.

Judgment

In tasks involving judgment, subjects are typically presented with a series of stimuli and asked to rate them on some scale of judgment, such as size, beauty, complexity, and so on. One line of research has been to examine changes in preferences for shape complexity associated with developmental and age changes. For example, Munsinger and Weir (1967) have shown that preference for complex random shapes increases in young children between the ages of 9 and 41 months.

Theories of Perceptual Learning

In this section we will focus on accounting for the way in which perception improves with practice. A variety of theories of perceptual learning have been proposed (see E. J. Gibson, 1969). However, only two have been strongly influential in generating research. These are mediation and differentiation theory.

Mediation Theory

In general, mediation theory assumes that perception is modified as the result of mediating responses that become associated with stimuli. Other terms for mediation theory include *acquired-compound theory* (see Saltz, 1971) and *enrichment theory* (see J. J. Gibson & E. J. Gibson, 1955).

Fundamental to mediation theory is the belief that verbal responses can affect discriminatory/perceptual processes. William James (1890) was perhaps the first psychologist to write systematically about the role of language in perception. According to James, discrimination improves with practice because differential associations are developed and become attached to the different stimuli experienced. The essence of James's position can be seen in his discussion of how one might learn to distinguish burgundy from claret:

> Probably they have been drunk on different occasions. When we first drank claret we heard it called by that name, we were eating such and such a dinner, etc. Next time we drink it, a dim reminder of all these things chimes through us as we get a taste of the wine. When we try burgundy our first impression is that it is a kind of claret; but something falls short of full identification and presently we hear it called burgundy. During the next few experiences, the discrimination may still be uncertain—"which," we ask ourselves, "of the two wines is this present specimen?" But at last the claret-flavor recalls pretty distinctly its own name, "claret," "that wine I drank at so-and-so's table," etc.; and the burgundy-flavor recalls the name "burgundy" and someone else's table. And only when this different setting has come to each is our discrimination between the two flavors solid and stable. After a while the tables and other parts of the setting, besides the name, grow so multifarious as not to come up distinctly into consciousness; but *pari passu* with this, the adhesion of each wine with its own name becomes more and more inveterate, and at last each flavor suggests instantly and certainly its own name and nothing else. The names differ far more than the flavors, and help to stretch these latter further apart. Some such process as this must go on in all our experience [p. 511].

James argued that the verbal labels *claret* and *burgundy* become associated with the appropriate wine. Since the verbal labels are more distinctive than the wines themselves, the verbal label *plus* wine is a more distinctive stimulus compound than the wine alone.

In their development of mediation theory, Dollard and Miller (1950) and Goss (1955) assume that an organism receives sensory feedback from any response that it makes, whether overt or covert, motor or verbal. For example, when you walk, you feel the sensory input from walking; when you talk, you hear yourself talking. Thus, any response generates its own characteristic stimulation. If a response is made to some external (nominal) stimulus, the external stimulus and the response-produced (feedback) stimulus combine to form a new compound stimulus that is mediated by the response. In the example cited by James, the cue properties of the response of saying "burgundy" to the wine itself combine to form a compound, and this compound is presumably more distinctive than the wine itself. Dollard and Miller have proposed two hypotheses incorporating the concept of a response-produced cue: *acquired distinctiveness of cues* and *acquired equivalence of cues.*

Acquired Distinctiveness of Cues. Incorporating the above general assumptions, the hypothesis of acquired distinctiveness of cues contends that attaching distinctive response-produced cues to two stimuli that are initially similar provides for learned distinctiveness, as reflected in a decrease in the extent to which instrumental responses will generalize from one stimulus to another. For example, suppose we have two external stimuli, S_1 and S_2, that are to be discriminated. S_1 is associated with the overt response R_A, and S_2 is associated with the overt response R_K. Since each overt response produces its own implicit response-produced cues, s_A and s_K, the effective stimulus compounds are now $S_1 + s_A$ and $S_2 + s_K$, respectively. On the assumption that s_A differs from s_K more than S_1 does from S_2, the addition of response-produced cues to the external stimuli should increase the distinctiveness of the compound.

Acquired Equivalence of Cues. The complement of acquired distinctiveness is the acquired equivalence of cues. In this case, associating identical or similar response-produced cues with two initially distinctive stimulus events gives them some learned equivalence, increasing the extent to which instrumental repsonses will generalize from one stimulus to another. For example, suppose we have two external stimuli, S_1 and S_2, that are associated with two responses, R_A and R_A (the responses are identical). In this case the response-produced cue of s_A is added to both S_1 and S_2, thus making the compounds less distinctive, or more equivalent. Let us now examine a few tests of the mediation theory of perceptual learning; these tests will help to clarify and amplify the theory.

Experimental Tests of Acquired Distinctiveness. The great majority of tests have used the *stimulus-predifferentiation paradigm.* In general, studies of stimulus predifferentiation are designed to determine what is learned about the pretraining stimuli in an *A/B, A/D* transfer paradigm. Experiments of this kind typically involve two stages, training and testing. In the training phase, subjects are generally given practice in attaching specific responses, usually verbal labels, such as names or words, to a set of stimuli. In the test phase the subjects are given a task that requires them to make new and even qualitatively different responses to the stimuli. Frequently, the test task requires making motor responses to the stimuli, such as pushing different buttons. The assumption is that if attaching different verbal responses to stimuli during training makes them more distinctive, then such training should transfer in the test phase, where the same stimuli are used.

For this interpretation to be valid, at least two features must be present in the experiment. First, the responses in the training and test phases must be as dissimilar as possible, so that there will be no transfer based simply on the similarity of the responses or on mediation via the response terms. Second, an appropriate control group must be used in which the subjects are given comparable training in the first phase with a set of stimuli unrelated to those used in the transfer task.

There are a number of variations on this basic design. For example, subjects may be required to inspect the stimuli during pretraining rather than to label them. In addition, three kinds of tests have been most frequently used (see Ellis, 1969). These are as follows: (1) having subjects attach new responses to the training stimuli following training in labeling the stimuli (Gagné & Baker, 1950; Goss & Greenfeld, 1958), which is the basic transfer task just described; (2) taking more direct measures of perceptual performance, such as detection, discrimination, or recognition of the stimuli (Arnoult, 1956; Ellis, 1968); and (3) measuring the change in the probability of generalization tendencies following labeling practice (Birge, 1941; Malloy & Ellis, 1970). For a more comprehensive review of this research, the reader should see Arnoult (1957) or Ellis (1969).

Studies of stimulus predifferentiation using transfer tasks requiring subjects to learn new responses to the stimuli have generally yielded results at least consistent with the acquired-distinctiveness-of-cues interpretation. Unfortunately, some of the studies that provide the most support lacked appropriate controls, and other studies have yielded results that can be interpreted in different ways. But despite these complexities, let us examine a typical experiment.

In an early study by Gagné and Baker (1950), one group of subjects was given training in learning to associate different letters of the alphabet with lights varying in color and position on a display panel, whereas a control group received no training. Both groups were then transferred to a task requiring them to pull a particular switch in the presence of the lights. The subjects given practice in associating different letters with the lights were superior in learning the transfer task compared to the control subjects. This superiority was interpreted to mean that label training served to reduce the generalization among the stimuli, thus making them more distinctive and facilitating performance on the transfer task. Unfortunately, the lack of an appropriate control group makes this interpretation open to question; any facilitation due to verbal-label training could have been due to the general-transfer effects of warm-up and learning to learn.

In a similar study Goss and Greenfeld (1958) compared the effects of a variety of label-training conditions with the performance of subjects who only saw the stimuli. All labeling conditions led to superior transfer compared with that of the subjects who only observed the stimuli. Although these results are more convincing, the control condition was not ideal because we do not know whether the subjects were paying comparable attention to the stimuli. In brief, a number of experiments of this type have been conducted on the effects of label training on transfer tasks, and though the majority of them do show positive-transfer effects due to labeling (compare Ellis, 1969; E. J. Gibson, 1969), there is considerable doubt whether the results are *simply* attributable to an acquired-distinctiveness-of-cues mechanism.

Studies of the distinctiveness-of-cues component of mediation theory fare more poorly in light of the results of experiments using more direct perceptual tests. In general, these experiments compare the effects of label training with attending to the stimuli and then require the subjects to discriminate among the stimuli or recognize the stimuli. The results of experiments using same/different discrimination tasks have frequently been negative. We need look at only one study for illustration.

Robinson (1955) assigned subjects to four different conditions—three experimental conditions and one control condition. In one experimental condition, designed to produce acquired distinctiveness of cues, subjects were trained in labeling ten fingerprint stimuli with different names. In another condition, designed to produce acquired equivalence, subjects labeled half the stimuli with one response and the remaining half with another response. The third group made same/different discriminations among the fingerprints. The control group subjects had no experience with the stimuli. All four groups were then given a test requiring them to make discriminations between the various training stimuli and new but similar stimuli. Although all the experimental groups made fewer errors than the control group, no differences in performance were found among the experimental groups. Since the group labeling the stimuli with distinctive names performed no better than the group receiving same/different training, the importance of verbal labels is minimized here.

It should be noted, however, that this experiment suffers from the fact that the same/different group benefited from practice on a task most like the transfer task, which may have inflated its performance relative to that of the distinctive-labeling group. Despite this flaw, this study illustrates the generally negative findings resulting from labeling when a same/different discrimination task is used. Mere looking at or attending to the stimuli yields as good results as does labeling training.

The pattern of results with recognition studies differs from that of discrimination studies. As noted earlier, in several experiments (for example, Ellis & Muller, 1964), verbal labeling of stimuli facilitated their recognition compared to observing the stimuli. These results can, however, be interpreted in terms of the labels directing the subjects' attention to the distinctive aspects of the stimuli rather than increasing the distinctiveness of the stimuli themselves.

In summary, the experimental evidence provides little support for the acquired-distinctiveness-of-cues notion. The experiments appear either to lack the appropriate controls or to permit equally plausible alternative interpretations of the data. Given this situation, let us now look at the acquired-equivalence-of-cues hypothesis.

Experimental Tests of Acquired Equivalence. Experimental tests of acquired equivalence have focused on the issue of whether common (or similar) labels increase the equivalence of the stimuli. Again, the pattern of results appears to depend in part on the nature of the test task. For example, in the Robinson (1955) study just described, labeling the fingerprints with common labels did not reduce the discriminability of the stimuli compared with the performance of the subjects who had made same/different discriminations during training. In short, no evidence for an acquired-equivalence effect was obtained. This finding is of some interest because experimenters using recognition measures have reported data consistent with the acquired-equivalence-of-cues hypothesis.

Ellis and his colleagues have reported two experiments that yielded results consistent with, although *not demanded by,* the hypothesis. In the first experiment (Ellis, Bessemer, Devine, & Trafton, 1962), subjects were given training with eight random shapes constructed of vinyl tile. The subjects were allowed to feel the shapes but could not see them. One group, in a *distinctiveness*-training condition, learned to associate distinctive and representative verbal labels with each of the eight shapes. A second group, in an *equivalence*-training condition, learned the response "wide" to the four wide stimuli and "narrow" to the four narrow stimuli. A third group merely *inspected* the shapes tactually for an equal amount of time without instructions to label them. Following training, the subjects were given a tactual shape-recognition task. Although the group who had learned distinctive verbal labels performed no better than did the observation group, the common-labeling group did not perform as well as the observation group, which is limited evidence for an equivalence effect. A follow-up experiment (Ellis, Feuge, Long, & Pegram, 1964), in which the type of observing responses made during tactual manipulation of the shapes was controlled, yielded the same results.

As Ellis (1973) has noted, the principal problem with this type of finding is interpretation. On the one hand, the data can be regarded as consistent with a mediational interpretation in which the stimuli become more equivalent through the addition of common response-produced cues. Ellis has, however, questioned this interpretation and has indicated that at least two alternative interpretations of the poorer recognition following equivalence training are plausible. One interpretation is that the labels, since they were representative of one physical feature (width) of the shapes, might simply have encouraged the subjects to observe primarily the width of the shapes and to ignore other features. Since accurate shape recognition is dependent upon more features than width cues, the subjects in the equivalence-training condition might have been expected to show poorer performance simply because they had picked up less information about the shapes. This account emphasizes the possible role of *observing responses*. The second account emphasizes the importance of *selective attention,* in which the label affects attentional processes. In either case, the point is that the poorer recognition performance resulting from practice in labeling shapes does not *demand* an interpretation in accordance with the acquired-equivalence-of-cues hypothesis. More generally, these findings illustrate the difficulties in distinguishing between mediational and attentional interpretations.

Saltz (1971) has argued that it is important to distinguish between a "strong" and a "weak" version of the acquired-equivalence hypothesis. A strong form of the hypothesis predicts that labeling different stimuli with common labels (equivalence training) will lead to transfer performance inferior to that of subjects who have never seen the stimuli. Evidence of this kind would be regarded as support for the general S–R theory from which the hypothesis is derived. A weak form of the hypothesis predicts only a relative decrease in performance due to confusion over similarity among the responses. Studies have not produced any evidence for the strong form of the hypothesis; in no case has equivalence training led to an absolute reduction in performance as compared with that of appropriate controls. In short, experience with the stimuli, even when they are assigned common labels, produces some positive transfer.

In contrast, several studies (for example, Ellis et al., 1962; Ellis et al., 1964; P. A. Katz, 1963) have provided evidence for a weak equivalence effect. Nevertheless, the results can all be interpreted in terms of attentional or observing-response formulation. In all cases it is possible that the label suggested that the subjects should attend to certain features of the stimulus. Thus, the evidence in favor of the weak version of the hypothesis is not unequivocal.

To evaluate verbal mediational versus attentional interpretations of the kind just described, Malloy and Ellis (1970) attempted to determine whether verbal responses attached to stimuli during training produce a transfer effect *over and above* whatever effect is produced by simply attending to the stimuli. If not, then the usefulness of a cue-producing-response concept would be seriously weakened, principally because it would become unnecessary in accounting for the data. On the other hand, if it could be demonstrated that verbal-pretraining procedures do produce an additional effect, then there would be more cogent evidence for a cue-producing-response (mediational) interpretation of the effects of verbal-labeling practice with stimuli.

Malloy and Ellis used a mediated-generalization procedure because it is directly pertinent to the Dollard and Miller theory. The procedure consisted of three stages. The first stage was designed to establish acquired-equivalence (E) and acquired-distinctiveness (D) effects by having subjects attach a common CVC response to two different stimuli and different CVC responses to different stimuli, respectively. The experiment was entirely within-subject, requiring subjects to learn both an E and a D condition, together with controls for attentional effects. Like the subjects in the E condition, the subjects in one attention control saw two similar stimuli and had only to observe these stimuli. Thus, this condition was designated an observation/observation (OO) control. A similar control for attention in the D condition was employed, requiring subjects to respond to one of the pairs of stimuli and not to respond to the other (OD condition). Finally, a no-pretraining control (C) was employed to provide a baseline measure. During the second stage each subject learned a new identifying response (noun) to one stimulus from each set of each of the four conditions; this phase simply established a to-be-generalized response, which was measured in the third, or test, phase of the experiment. In the test phase the subjects were shown all eight stimuli and asked to give the identifying response learned in Phase 2. The principal objective was to examine the extent to which the subjects would respond to the stimuli not shown in Phase 2 (but shown in Phase 1) as though they had been seen during Phase 2. For example, if the subjects in the E (equivalence) condition responded to both stimuli with a roughly comparable frequency, then we would have evidence for an equivalence effect.

The basic results appear in Figure 14–3. The left-hand panel shows the equivalence comparisons, and the right-hand panel shows the distinctiveness comparisons. The most interesting and important finding appears in the left-hand panel, which shows substantially greater generalization following E pretraining than in the OO control for attention. This simply means that attaching identical verbal labels to similar stimuli increases the likelihood that the stimuli will be treated alike as compared with the OO control. In short, practice with common verbal labels produces greater generalization than does attention to the stimuli alone. The right-hand panel shows, in contrast, no effect due to distinctiveness training, a finding consistent with those of previous experiments.

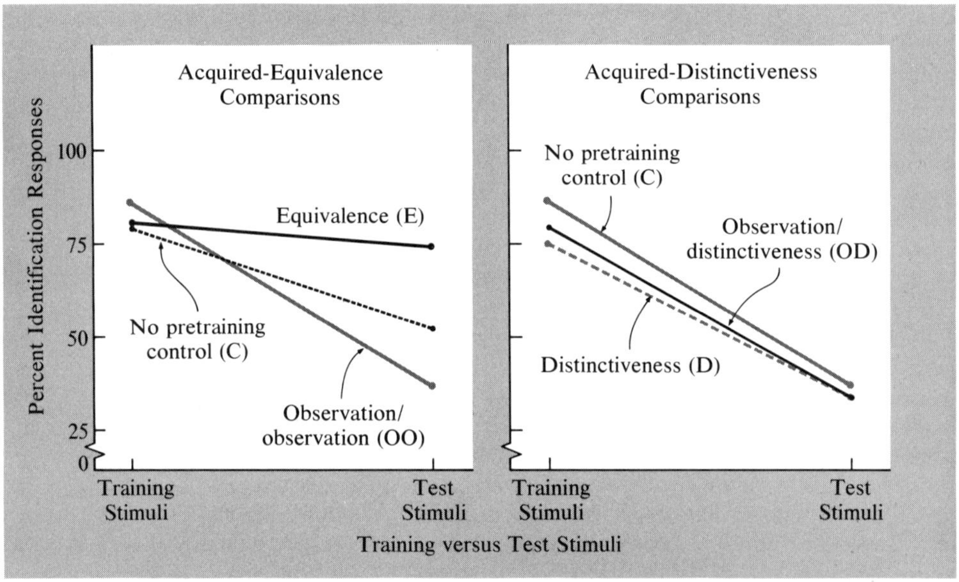

Figure 14–3. The generalization of verbal identifying responses to visual stimuli following acquired-equivalence and acquired-distinctiveness pretraining. (From "Attention and Cue-Producing Responses in Response-Mediated Stimulus Generalization," by T. E. Malloy and H. C. Ellis, *Journal of Experimental Psychology,* 1970, *83,* 191–200. Copyright 1970 by the American Psychological Association. Reprinted by permission.)

Overview. The acquired-equivalence hypothesis in mediation theory fares somewhat better than its acquired-distinctiveness corollary. Support for the hypothesis is clearly dependent upon the type of test task used. Recognition-memory experiments provide data consistent with but not demanded by the hypothesis. The strongest evidence for the hypothesis stems from the mediated-generalization results obtained by Malloy and Ellis. More generally, the overall pattern of experimental results does not provide strong support for mediation theory. Let us now turn to the second major theory of perceptual learning.

Differentiation Theory

Differentiation theory was first formulated by E. J. Gibson in 1940. In the original version of the theory, Gibson applied the concepts of differentiation and generalization as used in conditioning to the analysis of verbal-learning phenomena. According to Gibson, the fundamental process underlying discrimination learning is a steepening of the generalization gradients surrounding each stimulus as the result of reinforcement of responses to one stimulus and nonreinforcement of responses to other stimuli. This process, stimulus differentiation, leads to reduced confusion among the stimuli after a training session. Gibson extended the idea of differentiation to verbal learning using the paired-associate task, in which part of what is learned (when two or more pairs are present) is distinguishing among the stimulus terms. Theoretically, subjects learn to establish consistent, differentiating, representational responses to each stimulus in the list.

If the stimulus terms are readily distinguishable, this process should take only a small portion of the total learning time, whereas if the stimuli are difficult to distinguish, this process becomes increasingly important. Furthermore, Gibson assumed that once stimulus differentiation had occurred, it would transfer to a second paired-associate list containing the same stimuli. Hence, Gibson referred to this process as the "transfer of differentiation" among stimuli.

The significance of differentiation theory in the 1940s was the implication of a presumably *nonassociative* process in learning. According to traditional theories of learning, learning is the strengthening of S–R associations; Gibson's theory posited an additional factor, stimulus differentiation.

The theory was reformulated in 1955 and more fully developed in 1969. The original S–R theory in the Hullian tradition was abandoned, and the importance of differential reinforcement to differentiation was minimized. In the revised theory (J. J. Gibson & Gibson, 1955), the process of perceptual learning is thought of as differentiation, by which an organism becomes increasingly sensitive to dimensions of stimulation not previously detected. In this view, organisms learn to differentiate various aspects of stimulation that are already present in the stimulus environment. Thus, perceptual learning consists of responding·to various stimuli not previously responded to rather than *adding* associations or response-produced cues to stimuli. Accordingly, perceptual learning is viewed as a *discriminative* process rather than an *associative* or additive process.

E. J. Gibson (1969) has marshalled an array of evidence in support of her theory, and it is beyond the scope of this chapter to consider all of it. Rather, we will briefly focus on representative examples of research results that appear to be consistent with the theory and note some conceptual/methodological issues.

The original theory was criticized on systematic grounds by Postman (1955, 1963), who pointed out that it is insufficient to contend that an organism comes to respond to new aspects of stimulation as a result of practice because this process is what a theory of perceptual learning must explain. In her expansion of the theory, Gibson (1969) has, however, attempted to outline some of the fundamental ways by which perceptual learning occurs. The proposed processes are abstraction, filtering, and attention.

The process of abstraction involves the discovery of an invariant relation among a number of objects and events. In essence, the organism discovers some regularity or principle. Filtering involves the selection or rejection of stimuli for input. Once stimulus information gets into the nervous system, the information may or may not be ignored as the result of the third process, attention. At present, these mechanisms are somewhat descriptive and are therefore only possibilities in Gibson's theory. Nevertheless, they represent an effort to align differentiation theory with information-processing conceptions of behavior.

The studies that support Gibson's theory are of several kinds. One class of experiments (for example, Robinson, 1955) demonstrates that practice in observing the stimuli yields just as great an improvement in perceptual performance as does labeling the stimuli. Similarly, Pick's (1965) results suggest that subjects learn to distinguish dimensions of difference among stimuli and that they use these as the basis of transfer rather than learning some prototype or schema.

Another kind of experiment that has recently yielded some support for Gibson's theory is the transfer-of-differentiation experiment in which the intralist similarity of the stimuli is varied. Suppose that two groups of subjects each learn a paired-associate list. In one list the stimuli are highly similar and difficult to discriminate. In the other list they are dissimilar and thus easy to discriminate. If each group of subjects then learns a second list containing the same type of stimuli as in their respective first lists, transfer should be greater in the high-similarity list (see Ellis, 1973). The reason is that greater effort must be given to discriminating among the stimuli high in intralist similarity. As noted in Chapter 13, earlier studies (Del Castillo & Ellis, 1968; Underwood & Ekstrand, 1968) demonstrated negative evidence for this proposition when simple stimuli, such as light-intensity differences and trigrams, were used. However, in a more recent study Ellis and Shaffer (1974), using the complex stimuli of 24-point random shapes or 3×3 letter matrixes, obtained clear positive transfer of differentiation. Although these data are consistent with one aspect of the theory, the original theory placed no restrictions on classes of stimuli.

We will not discuss the animal studies of perceptual learning here; they were described in Chapter 7. It is sufficient to say that the results of these experiments have not ruled out nondifferential reinforcement and thus question this aspect of Gibson's theory. Nevertheless, on balance, the data appear to be reasonably consistent with some form of differentiation theory. Both mediation and differentiation theory have suffered from a lack of explicitness regarding some features, but we can expect the theories to be sharpened and refined on the basis of new experimental findings.

Task and Stimulus Considerations

One final point should be underlined before we leave our discussion of theories of perceptual learning. Support for either theory is partly dependent upon the nature of the test task and upon properties of the stimuli. The role of task variables has been fully demonstrated by Ellis and Muller (1964) and Vanderplas, Sanderson, and Vanderplas (1964). For example, Ellis and Muller have shown that although labeling training facilitates transfer to a task in which subjects learn new responses to the stimuli, such training does not facilitate recognition of the same stimuli. As they point out, if pretraining with stimuli with distinctive verbal labels makes the stimuli more distinctive in a transfer task, then why does not the same training make the stimuli more discriminable in same/different or recognition tasks? The point of the question is that theories of perceptual learning must consider the nature of the test task itself.

In a similar vein, characteristics of the stimuli themselves affect the outcome of such experiments. For example, labeling does facilitate the subsequent recognition of complex but not simple shapes (Ellis & Muller, 1964). Further, the transfer-of-differentiation effect is obtained with complex stimuli containing multiple redundant cues but not with simple stimuli (Ellis & Shaffer, 1974). These results suggest that psychologists must evaluate the properties of stimuli used in learning and memory experiments with greater concern than in the past. There is evidence (for example, Bevan, 1968; Garner, 1974) that such concern is growing.

Relations among Learning, Perception, and Memory

In this section we will look at several representative categories of relations among learning, perception, and memory. These categories are the role of practice, cross-modal transfer, adaptation to transformed stimulation, schema learning, and memory for form.

The Role of Practice

A large number of perceptual-learning studies have been conducted on the role of practice in perception. This research has been reviewed rather extensively by E. J. Gibson (1953) and summarized more recently by Epstein (1967). Such studies generally involve repeated presentations of stimulus objects during a training session, followed by some kind of test such as discrimination or recognition. The training and test sessions may be separated into two distinct phases (see, for example, T. L. Bennett & Ellis, 1968; E. J. Gibson & Walk, 1956; Vanderplas et al., 1964), or the training and test sessions may alternate, as in, say, paired-associate training. Normally, it is assumed in such studies that the subjects actually do attend to the stimuli, although the assumption of comparable attention for different training conditions is not always warranted (L. S. James, 1973; Malloy & Ellis, 1970). Gibson (1953) has pointed out that the training session does not require any reinforcement or use of correction procedures; all that is specifically required in studies of perceptual learning is that the subjects do attend to the stimuli during the training phase.

We have already noted examples of experiments in which practice served to reduce search time (Neisser, 1964; Neisser & Hirst, 1974), to improve recognition performance (Ellis, 1968), and to improve distance estimates (E. J. Gibson & Bergman, 1954). Although a number of studies have demonstrated improved perception with practice, not all studies have consistently done so (see Epstein, 1967). The important question is not whether perception improves with practice but what the mechanisms are that account for changes or improvements. As we have just seen, this is the fundamental issue plaguing theories of perceptual learning.

Cross-Modal Transfer

Cross-modal transfer provides additional evidence for perceptual learning. In cross-modal transfer, learning in one sensory system, such as the visual modality, transfers to another sensory system, such as the tactual modality. One way of thinking about cross-modal transfer is to ask yourself how you might perform in visual tasks if you were blind for a long time and then your sight was suddenly restored. If you were blind virtually from birth, so that you had learned the alphabet through Braille (tactual input), would there be any transfer to the visual system when your sight was restored?

Gregory and Wallace (1963) have described a case history of such an instance. The patient lost his sight at 10 months of age, and he was blind until he was over 50, when surgery restored his sight. Even though he had depended primarily on touch for making discriminations, he quickly learned to respond to the visual world. Of special relevance to cross-modal transfer was that he could visually recognize any upper-case letter *without* training. Transfer was immediate and accurate. Moreover, he could readily identify numbers, leading Gregory and Wallace to conclude that transfer from the earlier tactual experience must have occurred. Such learning is perceptual and suggests to J. J. Gibson (1966) a kind of "unity of the senses"; this implies that there are certain properties of stimuli, such as form, that have the same features regardless of the sensory system in which they are learned.

The ability of organisms to transfer information about stimuli across sensory modalities has been well documented. This literature has been extensively reviewed by E. J. Gibson (1969) and Wright (1970). In addition, Birch and Lefford (1963) have shown that such transfer appears to increase with development. However, despite the massive amount of evidence for intersensory transfer, the processes that underlie it are still unclear.

Two different though not completely exclusive accounts of cross-modal transfer have been advanced. One position emphasizes the role of mediational processes and assumes that cross-modal stimulus equivalence results from making common mediating responses to the stimuli. In contrast, the invariant-features hypothesis (J. J. Gibson, 1966) assumes that the organism responds to some kind of "higher-order" stimuli that are invariant with sensory modality.

The mediational hypothesis has been invoked post hoc as one possible explanation of the transfer effects (see, for example, Gaydos, 1956; Holmgren, Arnoult, & Manning, 1966). A more recent experiment by Shaffer and Howard (1974) was an attempt to compare the two accounts. These researchers' strategy was to give subjects practice with unfamiliar-form stimuli in one sensory modality and then administer a transfer task in which the same stimuli were presented in another modality. The assumption was that the use of unfamiliar forms would minimize the likelihood of the subjects' using common mediating responses. The forms were dot patterns (Posner & Keele, 1968), and the subjects were trained either visually or tactually and then transferred to the other stimulus form. In contrast to the results of previous experiments, Shaffer and Howard failed to find any evidence for cross-modal transfer. They attributed this failure to the difficulty of verbally encoding the dot-pattern stimuli and interpreted the data as not supporting the invariant-features hypothesis, since if the subjects had been learning invariant features, positive transfer should have occurred. Given the low verbal codability of the stimuli, Shaffer and Howard argued by inference that had verbal mediating responses been present, some positive transfer should have resulted. They suggest that in studies showing positive-transfer effects (for example, Gaydos, 1956; Lobb, 1970; Shaffer and Ellis, 1974), the stimuli were higher in verbal codability and thus allowed a greater possibility of verbal mediational processes. Although this argument is indirect and is based upon null findings, the studies by Shaffer and his colleagues appear to mark the beginning of more analytic studies of intersensory transfer.

Adaptation to Transformed Stimulation

Another class of perceptual-learning phenomena occurs when humans adapt to stimulation that is transformed in some fashion. Early work in the study of adaptation to transformed stimulation was conducted by Stratton (1896, 1897). He wore a lens system that inverted his visual field for 8 days and made anecdotal reports of his experiences in readjusting to daily activities. Among his many experiences was that he began to visualize the world as inverted and to develop new sensorimotor coordination. For example, Stratton reported that it became standard practice to start with the right hand rather than the left hand in attempting to grasp an object that was seen on the left, even though objectively, it lay to the right. According to Stratton, things eventually came to look normal and upright.

Although important research occurred subsequent to Stratton's work, modern interest in the study of adaptation appears to have been stimulated by the work of I. Kohler (1964). Kohler's work has focused on adaptation to prismatic lenses and colored spectacles. A prism is a wedge of glass that bends light passing through it. The retinal image of an object viewed through a prism will be distorted in several ways, including laterally. Kohler found that upon first inspecting objects through a prismatic lens, perception is confusing but that it eventually becomes stabilized and perceptual/motor coordination is restored.

In another area of research in adaptation, Held and his associates (for example, Held & Hein, 1958; Held & Schlank, 1959) have examined the way humans adapt to transformed stimulation by having subjects manually locate a target while looking through a prism. The prism has the effect of displacing the image of the subject's hand, and the subject is allowed to observe his or her hand movements or the target, but not both. The subject's task is to locate the target on repeated trials. The results indicate not only that localization gradually improves but that the improvement is dependent upon active movement of the subject's hand rather than passive movement of the hand by the experimenter or no movement.

Schema Learning

Schema learning also appears to involve perceptual learning. According to Bartlett (1932) and Oldfield (1954), a schema is a kind of concept that is abstracted from a class of stimuli having some common features. For example, you can be said to acquire a schema for sailboats, faces, houses, or cars on the basis of your experience with a range of instances in each class. Your schema is thus some abstracted representation of the events experienced. Schema theory was first described informally by Bartlett, who used the concept to account for his findings on memory for prose. The concept was further developed by Hebb (1949), Oldfield (1954), and Woodworth (1938). Woodworth emphasized that a new pattern was learned in terms of a "schema plus correction," indicating that a given pattern may be judged to conform to the schema but with some adjustment. As an example, Attneave (1957) notes that a "square with a nick on the side" is easier to learn than most seven-sided polygons because the schema "square" is simple, familiar, and unambiguous and the correction ("with a nick on the side") is easily identified.

Attneave's (1957) study provides a good demonstration of schema learning. An experimental group received training with a prototype stimulus (a visual pattern). The subjects were then given a paired-associate task in which the stimuli were variations (similar stimuli) of the prototype; the prototype itself was not used during the paired-associate learning. In contrast, a control group did not see the prototype during preliminary training but simply reproduced an unrelated pattern. They were then given the same paired-associate transfer task as the experimental group. Attneave found that the experimental subjects, who had learned the class schema, performed better than the control subjects on the paired-associate task. He argued that their superior performance was due to their knowledge of the schema.

A more recent line of attack on schema learning stems from the work of Evans and his associates (for example, Evans, 1967; Evans & Arnoult, 1967). In Evans's (1967) development of schema theory, a schema is defined as a characteristic or central tendency of some population of objects. A schema is also thought to be a rule or set of rules for generating a population prototype. However, schemata are probabilistic in that no member of a schema family necessarily need follow the schema rule in all respects. The essential difference between Evans's view and Bartlett's or Oldfield's is that Evans defines a schema in advance of an experiment, based on the characteristics of the stimulus population, as distinct from inferring the schema on the basis of performance. Posner (1969) has defined a schema in a similar fashion.

Schemata have been found to occur in the absence of knowledge of results. For example, Evans and Arnoult (1967) examined schema learning using statistical concepts in a free-sorting task. The subjects were told only that there were two concepts and that they should sort the 60 stimuli into two piles corresponding to what they thought were the two concepts. Even though no information about the concepts was given to the subjects prior to the task and no knowledge of results was given, learning occurred. This type of finding received considerable emphasis in early studies, in part because it seemed to contradict assumptions of traditional learning theory.

Other experiments (for example, Posner & Keele, 1970) have examined the retention of schemata over time. These studies are of interest because they allow comparison of the ability of subjects to classify stimuli in accord with a schema with the memory of specific patterns. Although retention of the latter has been found to decline with time, subjects show no loss in the ability to classify stimuli according to a learned schema.

Memory for Form

Studies of memory for form have generally been concerned with the relation between memory and perception. Learning has been implicated in studies using verbal labels on the assumption that language may influence both the perception and the memory of form. Research on the memory for form has been thoroughly reviewed by H. W. Hake (1957) and Riley (1962); selected aspects of the literature have been more recently summarized by Zusne (1970) and Ellis (1973). We will therefore note only a few highlights of this research.

One issue in these studies has been the attempt to specify the role of verbal labels in memory for form. To clarify the mechanisms underlying the effect of verbal labels, let us again examine the classic study by Carmichael, Hogan, and Walter (1932). As we noted in Chapter 9, this experiment required subjects to label various semiambiguous drawings with words that might influence the way the drawings were encoded. The results of the experiment indicated that the reproductions of the drawings were influenced by the verbal labels that had been assigned to the stimuli. Roughly three-fourths of the experimental subjects' reproductions were distorted in the direction of the labels, whereas the control group's reproductions showed no systematic distortion. The control group received no labels. The general conclusion was that the encoding of the visual forms, and hence their reproduction, was influenced not only by the forms themselves but by the verbal context present at input. The findings are quite reliable and have been replicated in other experiments.

It was subsequently noted, however, that the findings could be interpreted in at least two ways. First, the labels could be influencing the encoding of the stimuli at the time of presentation. Alternatively, the labels could be exerting their influence at recall and thus affecting *retrieval* of the stimuli. Of course, both explanations could be valid, but it was argued that the experiment did not allow a distinction between these alternatives.

Hanawalt and Demarest (1939) challenged the encoding interpretation and argued for the retrieval interpretation. They modified the procedure used in the earlier experiment by presenting the labels only at the time of recall. The principal result was that the reproductions were influenced by the labels presented at recall. According to Hanawalt and Demarest, the labels functioned as retrieval cues. However, the subjects could have drawn their reproductions based on the labels themselves rather than reproducing stimulus figures based upon some memory trace. Moreover, in postexperiment interviews the vast majority of the subjects reported associating the figures with objects during training, and most of the reproductions were judged to be similar to the associations. This result parallels the findings of Carmichael and his colleagues and is consistent with an encoding interpretation.

Because of difficulties associated with interpreting the reproduction measure (see H. W. Hake, 1957; Prentice, 1954), later investigations used recognition-memory tasks. A large number of experiments have shown that verbal labels can affect recognition memory when the labels are representative of the stimuli (see, for example, Ellis, 1968; Price & Slive, 1970), when the stimuli are complex but not simple (Ellis & Muller, 1964), and even when the labels are implicit (Ellis & Homan, 1968). High-association-value stimuli are better recognized than low-association-value stimuli (see, for example, Clark, 1965; Ellis, Muller, & Tosti, 1966; Feuge & Ellis, 1969; Price & Slive, 1970). Moreover, the effects of labels persist over long periods (Daniel & Ellis, 1972; Ellis & Daniel, 1971). We have discussed a number of these studies elsewhere and will simply summarize by noting that the results of many experiments indicate that verbal-labeling practice enables subjects to encode stimuli efficiently (see Ellis, 1973).

The results of recognition-memory experiments have led Ellis (Ellis, 1973; Ellis & Muller, 1964) to propose the conceptual-coding hypothesis mentioned in Chapter 11. According to this hypothesis, when a verbal label is associated with a shape, the label, if representative of the shape, will enable encoding of the stimulus and hence facilitate subsequent stimulus recognition. This occurs when the label allows the subject to relate the stimulus to some available concept that is representative of the visual form. The label may actually serve as a concept, or the label may suggest a concept. An important assumption of this hypothesis is that the effect of associating verbal labels with stimuli is dependent upon the inherent codability of the stimuli. The effects of verbal-labeling practice are greater with less codable, more complex, less meaningful, or more ambiguous stimuli.

Five features of this hypothesis should be noted. (1) Subjects achieve a representation of the stimulus that is not simply the verbal label. (2) The effect of labeling is localized in the encoding process rather than retrieval, because stimulus-recognition memory over time is not conditional upon memory of the labels (Ellis & Daniel, 1971; Ellis & Shumate, 1973). (3) The hypothesis applies only to stimulus recognition and not to recall or reproductive memory (Ellis & Daniel, 1971). (4) The properties of a label are important only insofar as they are representative of the shapes or allow a belongingness relationship to be established (Ellis & Shumate, 1973; Ellis & Tatum, 1973). (5) The important mechanism that underlies conceptual coding is selective attention (Ellis, 1968; 1973).

Evidence for this hypothesis comes from several sources. For example, Ellis and Muller (1964) have reported that recognition of only complex visual forms is facilitated by verbal-labeling practice. Similarly, Santa and Ranken (1972) found that labeling practice increasingly facilitated recognition as number of forms increased. In addition, Ellis, Parente, and Shumate (1974) found greater facilitation of letter-sequence recognition with less meaningful stimuli. Finally, Dempster and Rohwer (1974) have reported facilitation of noun recognition by appropriate encoding instructions. However, the hypothesis proposes only that the effects of labeling will be greater with less meaningful stimuli.

There is some evidence (Del Castillo & Gumenik, 1972; L.S. James, 1973; Paivio & Csapo, 1971; Santa & Ranken, 1972) that verbal labels also have a rehearsal function. These experimenters have reported that the presence of labels during the learning of unfamiliar forms leads to improved serial-recognition performance. The basic assumption is that labels permit the subject to rehearse serial-position information.

Finally, it has been proposed that verbal-labeling practice enables retrieval of visual information. The evidence on this issue is complex and appears to depend on the nature of the memory task. Ellis and Daniel (1971) and Daniel and Ellis (1972) have argued that the primary function of verbalization is to facilitate encoding of the stimuli and that the verbal label appears not to be an effective retrieval cue for recognition. For example, Ellis and Daniel found that following paired-associate training, recognition of shapes was essentially constant over intervals of up to 28 days, whereas memory for the associated verbal labels declined during this period. These data undermine the view that recognition of visual forms is mediated by verbal labels at the time of recognition testing and hence the view that verbal labels act as retrieval cues in *recognition*-memory tasks.

In contrast to the recognition findings, Santa and his colleagues (Nicosia & Santa, 1975; Santa, 1975; Santa & Ranken, 1968) have reported some impressive results supporting the view that labeling training does bring retrieval processes into play when *recall* tasks are used. Santa has shown in studies of reintegrative memory, which require the subject to remember a whole shape when only a part is presented in the test, that labels do facilitate memory when the subjects are required to use them during the retention task. Similarly, Nicosia and Santa have shown that the effect of verbal coding in recall tasks involves not only encoding but retrieval processes as well.

Summary

In this chapter we have outlined some of the major empirical findings and theories on perceptual learning. That perception is modifiable by practice is evidence for the process of perceptual learning. We also discussed relations between perception and memory.

The five major categories of perceptual tasks are detection, discrimination, recognition, identification, and judgment. Throughout the chapter we saw that a particular variable can affect one of the measures while not necessarily affecting others. For example, we saw that a variable might effect performance in a generalization task but not in a same-difference discrimination task.

Theories of perceptual learning were classified into mediational and differentiation theories. Mediation theory emphasizes that stimuli become more distinctive or equivalent as the result of the addition of distinctive or common response-produced cues, respectively. Experimental tests have provided little evidence for acquired distinctiveness of cues, whereas there is some evidence for acquired equivalence. Differentiation theory has fared better, but many of its details are yet to be developed. At present, it is in an informal and largely descriptive stage. It places emphasis on the detection of distinctive features and attending to stimuli.

Studies of relations among perception, learning, and memory have examined a wide range of variables, including the effects of practice, cross-modal transfer, adaptation to transformed stimulation, schema learning, and memory for form. Memory for form was seen to involve both encoding and retrieval processes.

Chapter 15

Concept Formation, Problem Solving, and Decision Making

Human beings think. We often engage in covert, cognitive activities variously referred to as contemplation, reflection, deliberation, or reasoning—in a word, thinking. Although organisms lower on the evolutionary ladder almost certainly "think," thought is most characteristic of humans. Sometimes thinking is rather aimless, especially on long summer days, but more often our thoughts are directed. We may be planning future activities, reviewing past successes and failures, or attempting to make a decision or to solve some problem that we are confronting in the present. Thought is generally a complex activity only partly revealed by overt behavior.

Although we sometimes experience flashes of "insight" or have ideas "pop" into consciousness, thought is usually progressive, involving several stages. There are no clear dividing lines between the various stages or components of thinking, but it is useful to distinguish at least three broad categories of cognitive activity: *concept formation, problem solving,* and *decision making*.

The formation and use of concepts is an important component of thought, especially in its early stages. Information must be collected, classified, categorized, and organized before it can be used. When some goal is desired or some problem confronted, the available (organized) information may be called upon. The processes by which information is used in discovering or formulating the several courses of action implied by the desired goal or by the problem situation are referred to as problem solving. Finally, after information has been organized and several possible courses of action determined, some decision may be required; one of the several alternative actions must be chosen.

These stages or component processes can be identified in many cognitive activities that you must perform on a daily basis:

What shall I eat for breakfast?
Where am I most likely to find a parking space at this time of day?
Why won't my car start?
Is there an easier way to meet the foreign-language requirement?

In each case you must be able to draw upon appropriate sets of information, formulate alternative courses of action, and then choose and implement one of those possible actions.

Certainly, all of these situations require that you think. Often, however, you are not very conscious of the processes that are involved in these relatively simple and routine situations. But when a particularly difficult and important problem is presented, the complex cognitive processes involved may become more apparent.

Suppose, for example, that you are going to purchase a new automobile. (We will ignore, for now, the rational or irrational processes that led you to this decision.) Before you can decide which car to buy, you must determine what relevant information you have, or can obtain, and how it should be organized. Automobiles come in a dazzling assortment of types and styles. There are sports cars, luxury cars, and family cars; subcompacts, compacts, intermediate-sized, and full-sized cars; sedans, hardtops, and wagons; foreign and domestic cars; red cars, blue cars, two-tones, and custom trims; economical, "reliable," and high-performance cars; and so on. Each car claims membership in one or more of the categories, but, advertising notwithstanding, no car simultaneously fits all of them. You will have to determine what features of cars are important for your needs and what combinations of features are actually represented by the various cars that are available.

To simplify the problem, suppose that you are going to consider only economy. Now, you must determine what an economical car is. Is it a car that gets good gasoline mileage? Is 15 miles per gallon good, or do you require 25 miles per gallon? What about maintenance costs? If a particular car gets 25 miles per gallon but requires relatively expensive service every 3000 miles, would it be more economical to buy one that gets 15 miles per gallon and requires less expensive service every 12,000 miles? On the other hand, what if the initial cost of the latter is $500 more than that of the former and neither has as high a resale value as an intermediate-priced third alternative that gets 20 miles per gallon and requires moderately expensive service every 6000 miles? Even after greatly simplifying the situation, then, a great many factors have to be considered before a rational decision can be made. It is no wonder that we often resolve such complex problems in less than an optimal fashion, as follows:

> I won't buy a Chevrolet because my dad always said they rattle and fall apart. A Plymouth is definitely out because my Aunt Natty had one and it never ran very well. Volkswagens are out because they are unpatriotic. I think I'll buy a Ford. My friend George has always had good luck with them, and this year's model is very nice looking, especially that metallic-gold job with the alligator-vinyl top. If I buy it this week, the dealer will throw in the lightning-bolt chrome trim and raised-letter tires for free. Besides, my cousin played football at North State with Awe G. Whiz, the owner of the local Ford dealership, and he says Awe is a great guy.

Psychologists studying the processes involved in thinking have generally tended to avoid extremely complex situations, such as that posed by the purchasing of an automobile. Their reasons should be clear from the above example; there are just too many factors involved, and many of them are highly idiosyncratic to the particular "thinker" who is dealing with the situation. Research has instead focused on a rather small set of somewhat limited thinking situations in which the variables involved can be better identified and more easily controlled. In this way the component cognitive processes can be isolated and studied more systematically.

Although concept formation, problem solving, and decision making are all simultaneously involved in any human thinking situation, psychologists have attempted to focus upon these processes separately. In experiments concerned primarily with concept formation, a set of stimuli varying in several identifiable, and usually independent, characteristics is presented, and the subjects are required to group the individual stimuli into categories. Usually only two stimulus categories are involved, and the response required of the subjects is completely specified and rather elementary (for example, "This stimulus is an A, and that is a B"). In problem-solving studies the response alternatives are generally much more complicated, and the subjects must discover for themselves what they are. Further, many aspects of the task are not entirely specified. Anagrams exemplify these characteristics of problem solving (for instance, rearrange the letters in *hogutt* to make a word.) Interest is focused upon how the subjects determine for themselves what the relevant aspects of the situation are and how they formulate a plan of attack on the problem. Decision-making studies have usually emphasized choice among a relatively small number of clearly specified alternatives. The alternatives usually vary in their value, utility, or likelihood of being successful or "correct" (for example, would you rather have $1 right now or a 1-in-4 chance of getting $5 tomorrow?).

Concept formation, problem solving, and decision making will each be discussed separately in the following sections of this chapter. It should be kept in mind, however, that there is a great deal of overlap in the processes involved and that most thinking simultaneously involves elements of all three processes.

Concept Formation

The term *concept* can have a number of different meanings. In our everyday usage the term may refer to any notion or idea, such as the concept of truth, the concept of flight, the concept of humanity. More often, and especially in psychology, *concept* refers to a category, or set—the set of all living things, the set of all things that are edible, the set of all things that are both red and square. By some definitions, whenever two or more things are reacted to in the same way or are called by the same name, a concept is indicated. None of these uses of the term is exactly like the others, but neither are they completely distinguishable.

By narrowing the definition of the term and by adding some conditions for its use, this ambiguity can be reduced and the task of describing concept formation greatly simplified. First, *concept* can be restricted and used only to refer to sets of identifiable things. Abstract ideas such as truth would have to be excluded unless some agreement was reached on how individual truths are to be identified. Living things would be much easier to identify, and things that are both red and square could be identified quite unambiguously. As a further requirement, sets that are formed by a random or completely arbitrary assignment process would not qualify as concepts. In other words, there must be some specifiable (in principle, at least) features that are shared by members of the set but not by nonmembers. Living things, for example, share the properties of reproducing and metabolizing, while nonliving things do not exhibit these features. Alternatively, the requirement might be imposed that there be some statable rule (perhaps stated in language, mathematics, or some other symbol system) by which membership in the concept set can be determined. For the concept *all things that are red and square,* the rule might be:

> Members include all closed figures having four equal sides and reflecting light radiation in the spectral range from 650 to 700 nanometers.

By these rather stringent requirements, a concept is a set of identifiable objects (or "things") that share some specifiable properties and/or are related by some statable rule.

This definition, though admittedly somewhat restricted, does provide a rule for determining what is a concept and what is not. It does apply to a great variety of sets that are generally referred to as concepts, and it is sufficient to cover the majority of concepts that have typically been studied by psychologists.

Components of a Concept

Before discussing the formation of concepts, it will be helpful to introduce more formally the general constituents of a concept. The definition just presented refers to sets of "things." These "things" are usually called *instances*. A *positive instance* is any member of the concept set, and a *negative instance* is any nonmember. A pine tree, for example, is a positive instance of the concept *living things*. At the same time it is generally regarded as a negative instance of the concept *things that are edible* (followers of the late Ewell Gibbons notwithstanding).

Instances are the most elementary components of a concept. Each instance can be thought of as a constellation of individual characteristics, or *attributes*. Pine trees have a number of attributes; they metabolize, reproduce, grow, are green, are upright, and are somewhat conical in shape, to name just a few.

Although attributes generally are viewed as individual properties of instances, they may themselves be concepts. Thus, *green* is an attribute of pine trees, but it is also a concept. *Green* is the set of all wavelengths of light between about 510 and 560 nanometers.

Attributes may be *relevant* to deciding an instance's membership in a set (for example, *all living things*), or they may be *irrelevant*. The pine tree's attributes of reproducing and metabolizing, for example, are relevant to the concept *living things*, while being large and conical in shape are irrelevant. Thus, knowing that an instance has the attributes (properties) of metabolizing and reproducing is sufficient to classify that instance as a member of the concept set (positive instance). Instances that do not have those attributes are nonmembers (negative instances). On the other hand, knowing that an instance is large (or small) or conical (or any shape) will not help to determine whether it is a member of the concept set *living things*.

Attributes can be organized into *dimensions*, each attribute being one of several possible values along some dimension such as size, shape, or color. Thus, *green* is one value (or set of values) along the color dimension (red, yellow, green, blue, purple), and *conical* is a value on the shape dimension (cube, cylinder, cone, sphere). Just as attributes may be relevant or irrelevant, dimensions may be relevant or irrelevant. Shape, for example, is an irrelevant dimension in defining the concept *living things*. Knowing the shape of an instance would provide little, if any, indication of whether it is living.

Naturally occurring ("real-world") concepts are often very complex. Usually a large number of interrelated dimensions are involved, and the specific defining attributes may only partially (probabilistically) determine positive instances. Determining how such complex concepts are formed and modified is extremely difficult. For this reason, experimental studies of concept formation have generally employed "artificial" concepts. By constructing their own concepts, experimenters can be reasonably certain of their subjects' previous experience with and knowledge of the concepts. More important, the relevant dimensions and defining attributes can be precisely determined and independently manipulated to produce specific positive and negative instances of the concepts.

Sets of simple geometric figures have frequently been used in studies of concept formation. Geometric figures can be systematically varied along a number of dimensions—for example, size, shape, color, orientation, and location. Further, each of these dimensions can be varied independently from the others. Every shape (for example, square, circle, or triangle) can be green, red, black, or white; small, medium, or large; located at the top, bottom, left, or right of an array; and so on. A large number of concepts can be defined in terms of attributes from any one of these dimensions or combinations of the dimensions.

Rules

The attribute or combination of attributes that defines positive instances of a concept can be described by a *rule*. The rules for most concepts (*living things, animals, economy cars,* and so forth) would be very complex and would involve a large number of attributes. However, psychologists have generally studied relatively simple concepts for which the rules can be precisely stated. For example, geometric figures are typically used to study relatively simple concepts, such as that defined by the rule

All square figures, regardless of size, color, orientation, and so on are positive instances.

More complex rules, involving a number of attributes, have also been used:

All figures that are small and red and square are positive instances.

Five possible rules for determining positive and negative instances of concepts are illustrated in Figure 15–1. In this example three independent dimensions—shape, size, and color—are each represented by two attributes—*square* and *triangle, large* and *small,* and *black* and *white.* These attributes are combined to produce eight distinguishable instances. The concepts specified by the rules divide these instances into two categories, positive instances (+) and negative instances (−).

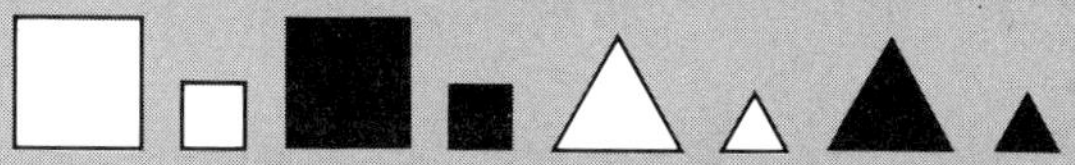

Rule	Instances							
1. Large: unidimensional	+	−	+	−	+	−	+	−
2. Both large and white: conjunctive	+	−	−	−	+	−	−	−
3. Either large or white or both: disjunctive	+	+	+	−	+	+	+	−
4. Either large or white but not both: exclusive disjunctive	−	+	+	−	−	+	+	−
5. If large, then white; if small, then square: conditional	+	+	−	+	+	−	−	−

Figure 15–1. Schematic illustration of five basic concept rules for simple geometric figures.

The first rule might be stated as

All figures that are large are positive instances.

Only one relevant dimension is employed, size; all others are irrelevant. Figures having the attribute *large* on the size dimension are classified as positive instances, and those having the attribute *small* are negative instances. This type of rule is called *unidimensional* because only one dimension needs to be considered in order to classify an instance.

Although unidimensional rules can be relatively simple, as in this illustration, they may be much more complex. Often the single dimension specified in a rule is itself composed of several other dimensions. In the automobile-purchase example presented earlier, economy might be viewed as one dimension on which cars can be classified. However, the economy dimension itself involves a complex combination of a number of other dimensions, such as gasoline consumption, maintenance costs, initial investment, and resale value.

The second rule requires that two dimensions be considered. It is a *conjunctive rule,* specifying that a figure must have both attributes, *large and white,* to qualify as a positive instance. Only the large white square and the large white triangle, then, are positive instances of the concept specified by the conjunctive rule. Notice that the dimension of shape (square or triangle) is irrelevant to the assignment of instances according to this rule. Thus, the two values (attributes) from that dimension may appear in either positive or negative instances. In the situation illustrated in Figure 15–1, one square and one triangle are positive instances, and three squares and three triangles are negative instances.

More than two dimensions may be included in a conjunctive rule. The principal feature is that positive instances must simultaneously have all the designated attributes from all the specified dimensions. In our automobile-selection example the desired car might be specified by the conjunctive rule *four-door, domestic, economy car*. Now for any vehicle to be acceptable, it must be economical, have four doors, *and* be made in the United States. In comparison to a unidimensional rule (for example, *economy car*), a conjunctive rule generally reduces the number of positive instances possible in a given set. Indeed, if a conjunctive rule were to combine mutually exclusive attributes (for example, *economical, four-door, Cadillac El Dorado*), the number of positive instances may be reduced to none.

Rule 3 is an either/or rule, usually referred to as a *disjunctive rule.* As in the conjunctive rule, at least two dimensions are required, but for this rule items need not have the designated attributes from all dimensions at once. Any item having the required attributes from one of the dimensions, several of the dimensions, or all of the dimensions would be classified as a positive instance of the concept. In the geometric-figures example any figure that is large *or* white *or* both large and white would be a positive instance. Only the small black triangle and the small black square are excluded from this set.

Closely related to Rule 3 is Rule 4, the *exclusive disjunctive rule.* This, too, is an either/or rule, but items containing more than one of the designated attributes are excluded from the positive set. As illustrated in the figure, the large white square and the large white triangle do not qualify as positive instances of the concept defined by this rule. Shapes must be either large *or* white but not both.

The last rule illustrated is a *conditional rule.* The main characteristic of conditional rules is that the attribute or attributes determining item classification depend upon (are made conditional upon) the represented value of some other dimension. These are if/then rules. *If* an item is large, *then* it must be white to be classified as a positive instance of the concept.

A number of conditional rules can be formed by varying the way in which instances that fail to meet the first "if" condition are classified. The rule illustrated in the figure specifies that small items (that is, those that are not large) must be square if they are to be included as positive instances. Other conditional rules might specify that nonlarge items are allowed to be positive instances (if small, then positive) or all negative (if small, then negative) or some combination in between (if small, then black).

Conditional rules can be applied to categorize "acceptable" automobiles in our car-buying example:

If it is an economy car, *then* it must have custom trim (otherwise, the standard trim will do).
If it is a full-sized car, *then* it must have power steering and power brakes (otherwise, only power brakes are required).
If it is a foreign car, *then* it must be a sports car (otherwise, it must be a van).

The five rules just discussed do not exhaust the possible categorization rules, even for simple geometric figures. Certainly, the number and complexity of rules that would be needed to describe the various categories of events, objects, and relationships that we deal with daily must be very great. Systematic studies of these five rather simple types of rules for combining attributes from several well-defined dimensions to classify a restricted set of instances have, however, provided a considerable amount of information about the complex cognitive processes involved in concept formation.

The Acquisition of a Concept

In a typical laboratory experiment in which subjects are required to learn a concept, they are presented with a number of instances and asked to categorize them. This procedure is called the *reception paradigm*. Usually only two categories are required. After each instance is categorized (as a positive or a negative instance), the subjects are informed whether their response was correct. The concept is considered to be learned when the subjects have correctly assigned all instances to the appropriate category. Sometimes more stringent criteria are imposed. For example, the subjects may be required to state the rule that determines instance classification or to categorize correctly some instances that have not been encountered before. Interest is focused upon how much time (or how many trials or instances) is required or how many errors are made before the concept is learned.

Although this procedure is much more structured than that by which we usually learn concepts in our natural environment, it does share many features with more common, nonlaboratory, concept-learning situations. Consider how you might have learned the concept *compact car*. Certainly, you did not go down the street labeling cars "compact" or "not compact" and have someone tell you "right" or "wrong." However, you probably did acquire the concept progressively by having experiences with a variety of cars, both instances and noninstances. Ads presented instances with labels (feedback), such as "Introducing the new compact car from Ford, the Pinto!" Friends might have brought their new compacts over for you to see. You might have seen an unfamiliar car on the street and guessed that it was a new compact car of some kind and then found out later that you were wrong (it was a new U.S. "sports" car). In time, you learned the concept; you were eventually able to classify compact cars correctly whenever you saw them.

A number of characteristics of the concept, and of the concept-formation task, have been found to affect the difficulty of concept acquisition. Of particular importance are the type and number of dimensions along which instances may vary, the number and similarity of attributes (values) represented for each dimension, and the proportion of those dimensions and/or attributes that are relevant or irrelevant. The complexity of the rule that defines the concept is also a very important factor in any concept-learning task.

In general, the more dimensions on which instances may vary, the more difficult the concept will be to learn. In Figure 15–1, for example, there are three binary dimensions (two attributes each) represented. Thus, the number of different instances (geometric figures) is limited to eight. The number of possible rule-determined categorizations of these instances (into positive and negative sets) is also limited. Three unidimensional rules are possible (one each based upon size, shape, or color). Possible conjunctive rules include three two-dimensional rules (shape + size, shape + color, size + color) and one three-dimensional rule (shape + size + color). Because each dimension is represented by two attribute values, there are eight possible combinations of one attribute for each dimension (small black triangle, small black square, . . . large white square). The number of disjunctive-rule and conditional rule divisions of the eight-instance set in Figure 15–1 would also be limited to combinations of the three dimensions, with two attributes available for each dimension.

If the number of dimensions were increased from three to four, for example, the total number of possible instances would be increased to 16. (In general, the number of distinguishable instances that can be generated from N independent dimensions, each having two attribute values, is 2^N; $2^3 = 8$, and $2^4 = 16$.) There would be four possible unidimensional classification rules, six two-dimensional conjunctive rules, three three-dimensional conjunctive rules, and one four-dimensional conjunctive rule. Each of these rules could vary with regard to which attributes were chosen to represent the relevant dimensions. The number and complexity of disjunctive-rule and conditional-rule categories that could be formed would also increase greatly as the number of dimensions was increased.

The effect of increasing the number of stimulus dimensions on concept learning has been empirically demonstrated a number of times. Depending upon characteristics of the concept-learning task and of the concept (rule) being learned, increasing the number of relevant and/or irrelevant dimensions affects the ease of learning the task. The difficulty of concept learning, gauged in terms of the number of errors before concept attainment, for a number of combinations of relevant and irrelevant dimensions is illustrated in Figure 15–2. Notice that as the proportion of irrelevant to relevant dimensions increases, the number of errors tends to increase. There is clear indication that increasing irrelevant dimensions has a detrimental effect.

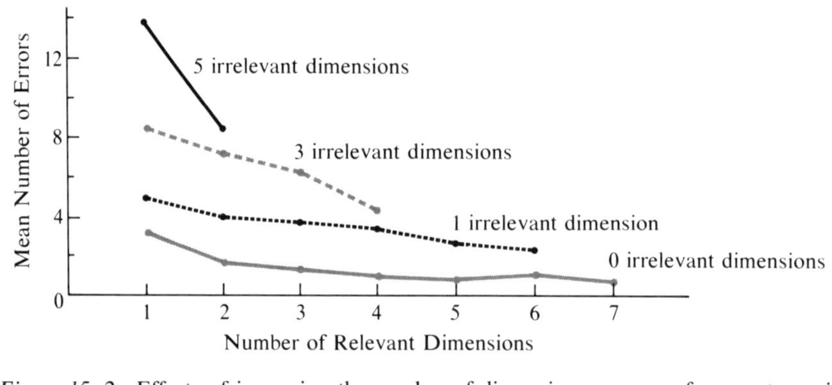

Figure 15–2. Effects of increasing the number of dimensions on ease of concept acquisition. (From *Human Conceptual Behavior,* by L. E. Bourne, Jr. Copyright 1966 by Allyn & Bacon, Inc. Reprinted by permission.)

Increasing the number of attributes on each dimension has a similar effect on concept learning. If each of the three dimensions in Figure 15–1 were represented by three attributes (rather than two), as is illustrated in Figure 15–3, the number of distinguishable instances would be greatly increased ($3^3 = 27$ instances). A unidimensional concept could specify as relevant any one of the three attributes from any of the three dimensions (for example, *small* is positive; *large* and *medium* are negative). Alternatively, three response categories might be required (for example, *small* is A, *medium* is B, and *large* is C). The number of specific conjunctive classifications of instances that could be formed by three dimensions would also increase. The number of different two-dimensional conjunctive categories that could be formed by combining size and color, for example, is four with two

Figure 15–3. Set of instances generated from three stimulus dimensions each represented by three attribute values. Compare this illustration to Figure 15–1, in which three dimensions are represented by only two attribute values each.

attributes per dimension (small + white, small + black, large + white, large + black) and nine with three attributes per dimension (small + white, medium + white, large + white, . . . medium + grey, . . . large + black). The number and complexity of disjunctive and conditional rules are similarly increased by the addition of more attributes to represent each dimension in a concept-learning situation.

Increasing the number of dimensions and/or attributes, then, greatly increases the complexity of a concept-formation task. The number of distinguishable instances is increased, and a greater number of concepts or specific classification rules becomes possible. As a consequence, learning the correct classification of any instance provides less information about the rule defining the concept. Also, memory requirements are increased as the number of instances in the set increases; positive and negative assignments for a larger number of items must be remembered. All of these factors are affected by increases in the number of dimensions and/or attributes involved, and the acquisition of concepts generally becomes much more difficult.

Escalation of dimensions and/or attributes, and thus instances (or vice versa), frequently is the cause of difficulty in the acquisition or retention of natural concepts. For example, the concept *compact car* has become much more complex because of the addition of a large number of new variations in automobiles. At one time, size was the principal dimension for determining whether a car was a compact. There were only a few values on this dimension, and virtually all small cars were classified as positive instances of *compact.* Other relevant attributes included *small, economical engines, modest interior and exterior trims,* and *relatively low initial cost.* In recent times this concept has become much more complex, to the point that *compact car* is probably no longer a specific category at all. There are mini-compacts, subcompacts, compact station wagons, and, more recently, personal-sized luxury cars. The size dimension, then, has been greatly expanded, resulting in the addition of many new attribute values. Other dimensions, such as initial cost and economy of operation, have similarly been expanded and combined in new ways. The result is considerable confusion about what a compact car is. For example, is a personal-sized luxury car an expensive compact that gets poor gas mileage?

Redundancy and Salience

Adding dimensions and/or attributes does not always increase the difficulty of concept learning. If the additional dimensions are completely *redundant* in relation to the other dimensions, whether relevant or irrelevant, they may add very little to the difficulty of learning. Indeed, in some situations the addition of relevant redundant dimensions may actually make concept learning easier.

A simple example of dimension redundancy is presented in the first row of Figure 15–4. Note that a correct classification of instances could be accomplished on the basis of either shape (all squares are positive) or color (all white figures are positive). The shape and color dimensions are both relevant, and they are redundant—all squares are also white, and all non-squares (triangles) are black. Concept learning is generally easier when there is this kind of redundancy.

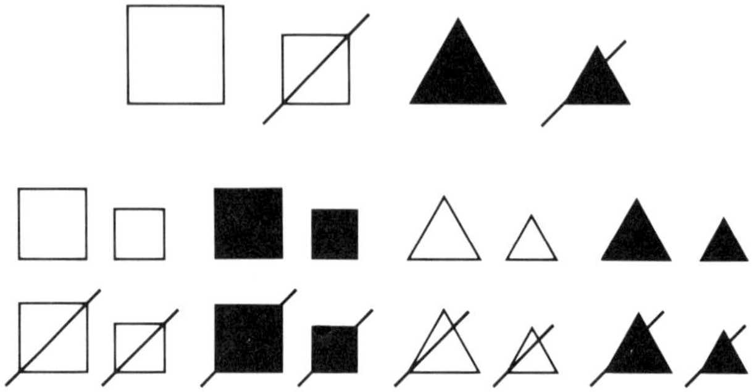

Figure 15–4. Instance sets generated by four dimensions (shape, size, color, and line) when these dimensions are redundant (first row) and when they are independent (second and third rows).

A third redundant dimension is also illustrated in the first row of Figure 15–4, the oblique-line dimension with two attributes, *present* or *absent*. The oblique-line dimension is redundant in relation to the size dimension; all the small figures also have an oblique line through them. Both size and oblique line are irrelevant to the correct categorization, so they are irrelevant/redundant dimensions. In some, more complex situations the addition of irrelevant dimensions, even when redundant, can retard concept learning. Generally, however, the addition of irrelevant redundant dimensions has little effect.

One important reason for the relatively small effects of adding redundant dimensions can be seen by comparing the stimulus set in the first row of Figure 15–4 with that in the other two rows. Both sets represent combinations of four stimulus dimensions. In the first row, however, shape is redundant with color, and size is redundant with line. As a result, there are only four distinguishable instances in the set. All four dimensions are independent (*not* redundant) in the other two rows, resulting in 16 different instances. Obviously, adding redundant dimensions does not increase the complexity of the concept-learning situation nearly so much as adding new independent dimensions.

Interestingly, when several dimensions of a stimulus set are redundant, subjects often fail to notice more than one of the dimensions. For example, everyone knows that you should stop when a traffic light is red and go when it is green. You could, however, have learned to stop and go on the basis of the position of the lights rather than their color. The position and color dimensions are (usually) redundant. When asked the question "When should you stop, when the top light is on or when the bottom light is on?" many people either give the wrong answer or say that they do not know. (You can check your own answer at the nearest traffic light.) Apparently, most of us have learned this concept on the basis of the color dimension without noticing the redundant position dimension.

The traffic-light example suggests another factor that can alter the effect of adding dimensions: the *salience* of the additional dimensions. A highly salient dimension is one that learners will notice and, perhaps because of previous experience, one that they will attempt to use in classifying instances. For example, young children often group objects on the basis of color, which is generally a highly salient dimension for children. In fact, children may persist in categorizing instances on the basis of color even though that dimension is irrelevant. They may settle for being correct half of the time on the basis of color (an irrelevant dimension) rather than shift to another (relevant) dimension that would allow them to be correct all of the time. (This tendency has occasionally been a source of great frustration for psychologists studying concept learning in children.)

Similar salience effects can also affect adult concept formation. Salience can be varied in several ways, the most direct being to make the attributes sampled from a dimension more or less similar to one another. Color will be a more salient dimension if it is represented by red, green, and yellow than by pink, red, and orange. The notion of salience thus relates to the process of stimulus selection discussed in Chapter 11 and to the more general process of encoding.

The learner's previous experience is another important determinant of dimension salience. If color has frequently been an important, relevant dimension in the past, the learner may be predisposed to attend to the color dimension in new situations. Alternatively, if color has generally been irrelevant or unreliable as a basis for responding, color attributes (even when relevant) may tend to be overlooked.

Both redundancy and salience, then, are important determinants of the effect of added dimensions or attributes. Salience and redundancy often interact in concept-learning situations; when two relevant dimensions are redundant, the more salient of the two will usually be chosen as the basis for categorization. Frequently, little will be learned about the less salient dimension.

Our recent (and continuing) energy crisis provides an illustration of how altering the salience of stimulus dimensions can have very profound effects on concepts. For example, the miles-per-gallon dimension, along which automobiles have always varied, has recently taken on new importance (salience). Advertising, production, and consumption all show that a new categorization rule is in effect, one that emphasizes the gasoline-use dimension. A particularly bizarre example of how changing the salience of dimensions can alter classification of instances is an advertisement that was run by a prominent manufacturer of motor homes during the height of the gasoline shortage. The ad pointed out a previously overlooked attribute of their product, its 75-gallon-capacity gas tank. It was suggested that one could store precious gasoline in its tank and siphon it out for use in the family car. Changing the salience of redundant dimensions in this case apparently changed a "personal luxury hotel on wheels" into a $25,000 gasoline-storage tank.

Rule Complexity

One of the most important influences on the difficulty of concept learning is the nature of the rule that defines the concept. If instances are to be categorized on the basis of a simple, unidimensional rule, concept learning is usually relatively easy. If, on the other hand, a more complex rule (that is, disjunctive or conditional) is involved, learning may be much more difficult.

An experiment by Bourne (1967) directly investigated the effects of rule complexity on concept learning. Instances of geometric figures that varied independently along four dimensions (color, shape, size, and number, each having three attribute values) were presented singly to subjects. The task was to learn to classify each instance as a member or nonmember of a concept set. Feedback was given after each instance, and the number of trials (instances) required to learn the concept was recorded.

By changing the assignment of relevant dimensions and/or attributes, five different concepts were created for each rule. For example, one conjunctive concept might have been

Positive instances are both large and square.

By changing the relevant attributes, a different conjunctive-rule concept could be defined using the same dimensions:

Positive instances are both small and triangular.

Additional conjunctive concepts could be created by combining different dimensions—color + number, size + color, and so forth. The subjects successively learned all five concepts defined by either a conjunctive rule, an inclusive disjunctive rule, or a conditional rule.

Some of the results of this experiment are shown in Figure 15–5. Clearly, the concepts defined by a conjunctive rule were learned more readily than the other concepts; the first conjunctive concept required fewer than 20 trials, on the average, for mastery. Disjunctive and conditional rules resulted in concepts that were more difficult to learn. More than 40 trials were required to learn the first concepts employing these rules.

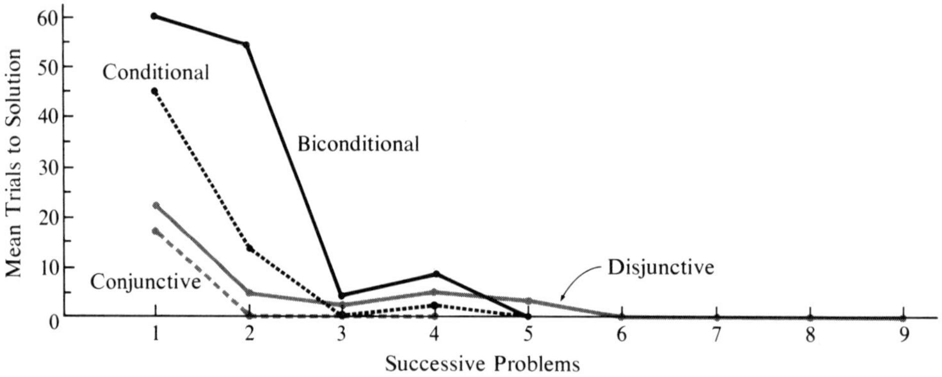

Figure 15–5. Learning to learn concepts defined by four basic concept rules. (From "Learning and Utilization of Conceptual Rules," by L. E. Bourne, Jr. In B. Kleinmuntz [Ed.], *Concepts and the Structure of Memory.* Copyright 1967 by John Wiley & Sons, Inc. Reprinted by permission.)

The results of this experiment show that rule complexity is an important determinant of the difficulty of concept learning. The results also indicate that subjects *learn how to learn* concepts that are defined by different rules. After some practice, disjunctive and conditional rules were learned in fewer than half of the trials required to learn the first concept. This finding was extended in a subsequent experiment investigating learning to learn concepts.

Bourne (1970) required subjects to learn three successive concepts, each defined by the same bidimensional rule, but with different attributes being relevant. This experiment used a *rule-learning procedure.* The subjects were told in advance which attributes were relevant and then had only to learn what the rule was for combining them. After the subjects had learned the first set of three concepts, they were then given three more concepts to learn that were defined by a different bidimensional rule. In all, the subjects learned four sets of concepts, each set using a different rule. Conjunctive, inclusive disjunctive, and two different conditional rules were learned in different orders by different groups of subjects.

The results of this study are shown in Figure 15–6. As in the previous experiment, successive concepts employing the same rule were progressively easier to learn. Also, practice in learning concepts defined by one rule resulted in faster learning of concepts defined by a different rule, regardless of the order in which different concept rules were learned. Apparently, subjects not only learn how to learn concepts defined by one rule but learn to learn concepts more generally, even concepts defined by different rules.

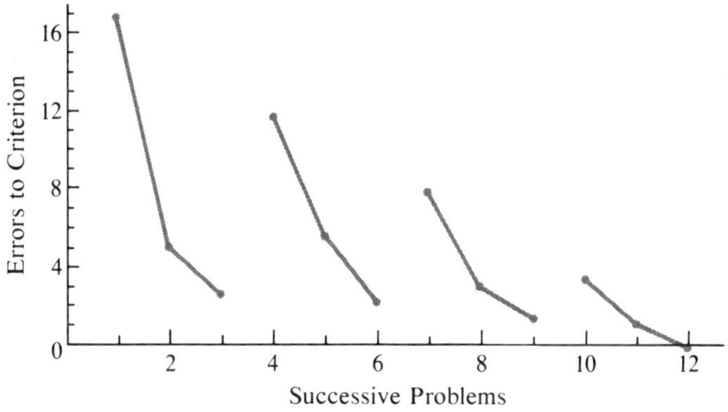

Figure 15–6. Transfer of concept learning from trial to trial within a rule and between different rules. Problems are blocked into sets of three, each block being based on one of the four primary bidimensional rules. (From "Knowing and Using Concepts," by L. E. Bourne, Jr., *Psychological Review,* 1970, *77*(6), 546–556. Copyright 1970 by the American Psychological Association. Reprinted by permission.)

Transfer of Concept Learning

Previous concept-learning experiences have a very important influence on subsequent concept-learning performance. Sometimes the effect is positive, producing improved performance in later learning, and sometimes the effect is negative, retarding the acquisition of subsequent concepts. There are rather obvious practical reasons for studying the factors that affect transfer of concept learning. For example, much of our education system assumes positive transfer of concept learning. Learning concepts in the classroom should aid in the acquisition of new concepts in the "real world." In addition, psychologists have studied transfer because analyses of performance on a second concept-learning task can provide important insights into what was learned during the first concept-formation task.

There are a number of ways to approach the study of transfer of concept learning. The studies of learning how to learn concepts (Bourne, 1967, 1970) reviewed earlier provide one example. Perhaps the most intensively studied type of concept transfer, however, has been that using the *concept-shift* or *solution-shift procedure.* Usually the first concept learned is relatively simple—a unidimensional-rule concept, for example. The second concept might employ the same basic rule, but the relevant dimension and/or attributes are changed. When the second concept employs the same relevant dimension as the first, the transfer task is referred to as an *intradimensional shift.* For example, the first concept might be defined by the rule

Squares are positive instances; circles are negative instances.

For the second concept the rule might be

Triangles are positive; diamonds are negative.

Notice that both concepts are defined (by a unidimensional rule) in terms of the same relevant dimension, shape. The second concept simply uses different attributes than the first. A special instance of an intradimensional shift is the *reversal shift.* Here, both the relevant dimension and the attributes are kept the same, but the assignment of attributes to category designations is reversed. For example, if squares were positive and circles were negative in the first concept task, circles are positive and squares negative in the second (reversal) task. Intradimensional and other types of concept shifts are schematically illustrated in Figure 15–7.

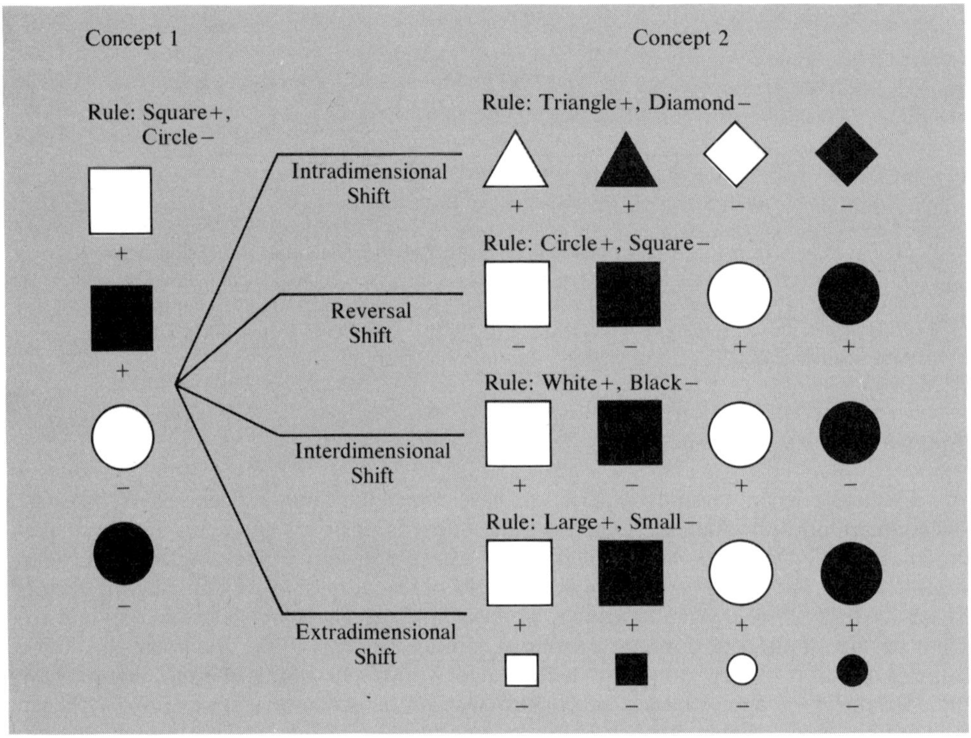

Figure 15–7. Schematic illustration of four basic solution-shift transfer conditions.

When the second concept is based on a dimension that was present but irrelevant in the first concept-learning task, an *interdimensional shift* has occurred. In Figure 15–7, color was irrelevant for Concept 1 but relevant for Concept 2. Another type of shift indicated is an *extradimensional shift.* The new dimension, size, was not present during the learning of Concept 1; it was added and made relevant for the second concept.

Other types of shifts are possible. Examples include extradimensional shifts in which both relevant and irrelevant dimensions are new, intradimensional shifts in which one of the first concept attributes (either the positive or the negative) is retained, and interdimensional shifts in which the attributes for the previously irrelevant (but now relevant) dimension are changed. There are other possibilities as well, but few have been investigated to any extent. Most of the research interest has focused upon comparisons of the effects of reversal shifts with those of one or more of the other types of shifts illustrated in Figure 15–7.

The emphasis upon reversal shifts has been motivated primarily by theoretical concerns; performance in the second (reversed) concept-learning situation is analyzed in order to determine the nature of the learning that took place in the formation of the first concept. One possibility is that the subject learns to categorize each instance separately during the learning of the first concept; that is, the concept may be learned in a rote fashion. If this is true, the reversal shift should prove to be very difficult. The subject would have to stop responding as in the first task and learn to make the opposite response to every instance in the second task. Learning, by this account, proceeds instance by instance.

In some situations lower animals (for example, rats) seem to learn concepts in a rote fashion. As a result, reversal shifts are usually found to be much harder for these animals to learn than are interdimensional shifts. Very young children sometimes exhibit this same type of learning and transfer in concept-formation situations. With extra training on the first concept (overtraining), however, both rats and young children will learn the second concept faster when it is a reversal shift (the *overtraining reversal effect*). Older children and adults almost always learn a reversal shift faster than interdimensional or extradimensional shifts.

A number of theoretical accounts have attempted to explain and incorporate these concept-shift findings, but no one account has yet achieved general support. Among the more popular accounts are the developmental S–R mediation theory (H. H. Kendler & Kendler, 1962, 1968); several attention theories (for example, Trabasso & Bower, 1968; Zeaman & House, 1963); and a perceptual-differentiation theory (E. J. Gibson, 1969; Tighe & Tighe, 1966). A complete discussion and comparison of these theoretical approaches is beyond the scope of this chapter, but it may be useful to consider briefly some of the general characteristics of one of these accounts, for the theories have some important implications for the understanding of concept learning.

The S–R mediation account evolved from simpler S–R theories that were developed in the context of the study of discrimination learning in lower animals. An implicit (covert) response and its implicit stimulus consequences (or response-produced cues) are assumed to intervene between the overt stimulus (instance/object) and the overt categorization response. The exact nature of these implicit mediating events cannot be determined directly but must be inferred from the observed relationships between overt stimulus and response events. Mediating responses often appear to be verbal (for human subjects, at least) and can be characterized as labels or descriptions that emphasize relevant aspects of the overt stimulus objects. For example, an instance such as a large white square might produce the mediating response "shape is square."

A schematic illustration of the general features of the S–R mediation conceptualization is presented in Figure 15–8. Implicit mediating events, covert responses (r), and their stimulus consequences (s) are assumed to intervene between the overt instances (S) and the category-assignment responses ($R+$ and $R-$). These mediating responses (and their associated stimulus components) are related to the dimensions/attributes of the instances. Notice in the figure that as the concept is learned, only the size-related mediators are consistently associated with responses assigning instances to categories; that is, r (size)/s ("large") is always associated with $R+$, and r (size)/s ("small") is always associated with $R-$. All the other mediators are equally often associated with both $R+$ and $R-$.

According to the mediation account, associations between instances and size-related mediating responses, and between size-related mediating stimuli and the overt category responses, will be progressively strengthened during concept acquisition. Other mediating r/s events (those related to shape or color) will be extinguished (or at least become relatively

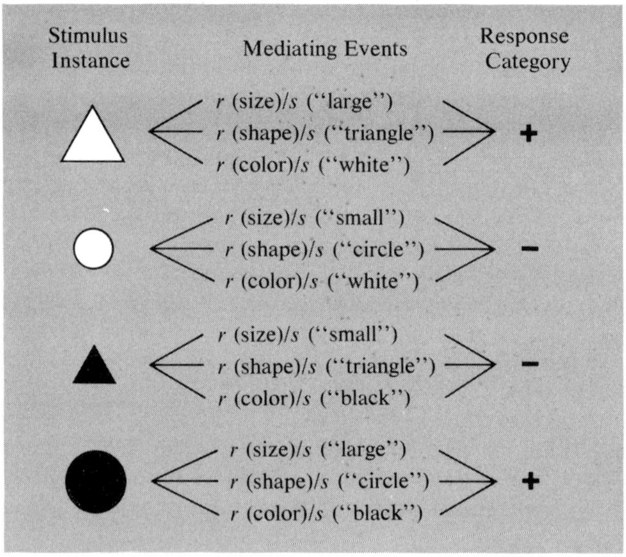

Figure 15–8. Schematic illustration of the S–R mediation account of concept learning.

weaker) because they are only inconsistently associated with the category responses. Subjects will develop a strong (learned) tendency to produce size-related mediating responses to all instances, and the overt category responses will thus be associated primarily with the attendant implicit mediating stimuli; *s* ("large") will elicit $R+$, and *s* ("small") will elicit $R-$. When some new instance is encountered, such as a large white square, it will tend to produce a size-related mediator (large) and thus the correct category assignment ($R+$).

The mediation account of concept learning postulates that the overt response is associated with a covert stimulus event rather than being associated directly with the nominal instance. This conceptualization has important implications for the concept-shift situation. If a second concept-learning task employs the same relevant dimensions (intradimensional shift), the previously learned mediating responses will still be appropriate, and acquisition of the second concept should be facilitated. Even when the second concept represents a reversal shift, as is illustrated in Figure 15–9, the previously learned mediating responses remain correct. Only the new (reversed) category assignments, the overt responses to the implicit mediating stimuli, need to be relearned. Note that in Figure 15–9 the old associative connection between the mediating stimulus and the category response, *s* (square)/$R+$, must be replaced by a new learned connection, *s* (square)/$R-$. If a different relevant dimension is employed (for example, the interdimensional shift shown in Figure 15–9), both the mediating responses and the category assignments must be relearned. In the lower right-hand section of Figure 15–9, both the old mediating response to the instance/stimulus, *S*/*r* (shape), *and* the connection between the old mediating stimulus and the overt category response, *s* ("square")/$R+$, must be replaced by new learned connections, *S*/*r* (color) and *s* ("white")/$R+$, respectively.

By adding the assumption that mediational responses are less available (less likely to occur) or more difficult to learn for rats and young children than for adults, the S–R mediation theory provides an explanation for the differences between these groups in reversal-shift performance. Rats and young children, it is argued, tend to learn to categorize objects more directly (by rote), without the aid of mediating responses. When presented with a reversal shift, they must extinguish (or unlearn) the old instance assign-

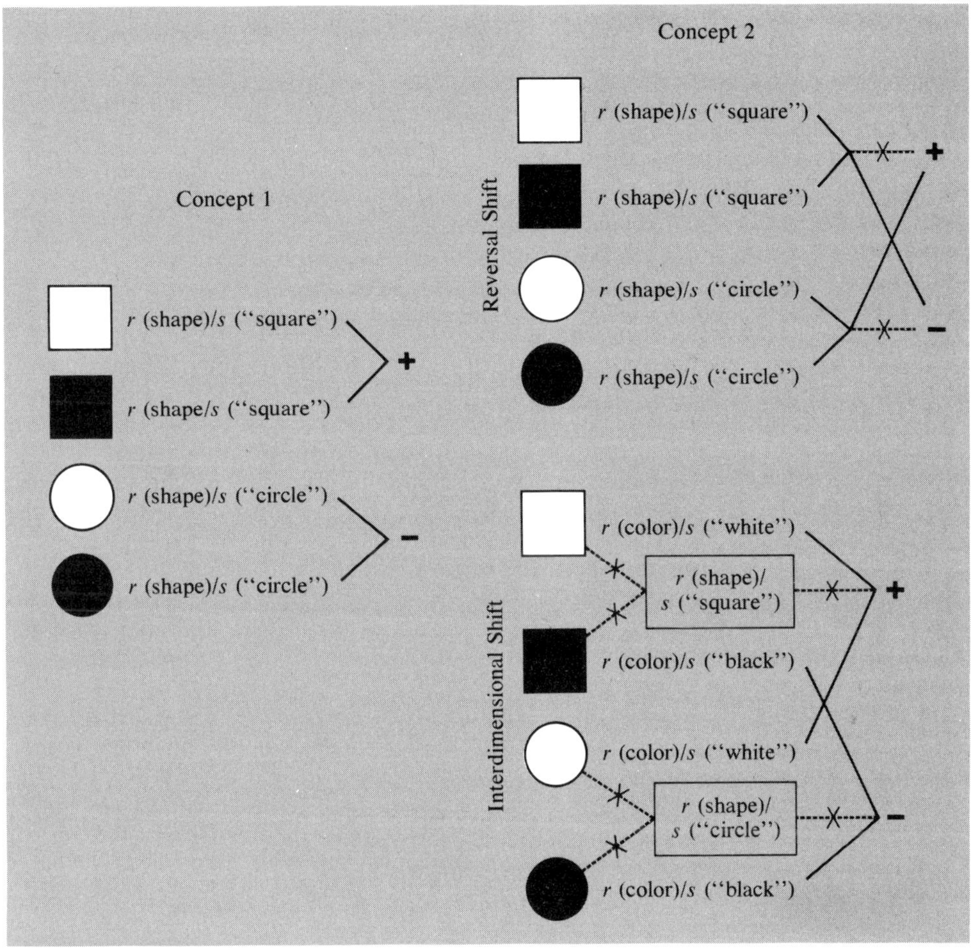

Figure 15–9. Schematic illustration of the S–R mediation account of solution-shift performance.

ments and learn the new ones. Thus, rats and young children would find the reversal shift more difficult than an interdimensional shift because more old, competing responses must be unlearned. Adults (and overtrained rats and children) tend to establish strong mediating responses in the first task and need only change their attribute assignments in the second, reversal-shift, task. When the second task requires the learning of a new mediating response as well as new attribute assignments, adults tend to do worse than in a reversal shift.

S–R mediation theories have been and continue to be important contenders among the various attempts at systematic explanation of concept learning and shift phenomena. There are several versions of mediation theory, but all share the basic postulate that some covert, *r*/*s* events intervene between the overt instances and the observed category responses. The mediation approach has fared relatively well as a theoretical conceptualization of concept learning. It has the advantage of being directly related to other S–R association accounts of the behavior of both humans and lower animals, and it has served as an effective framework for a great deal of research in concept learning and related areas. There are, however, several aspects of the mediation analysis that require further development. Perhaps the most important of these is some specification of the processes by which appropriate common mediating responses come to be elicited by widely differing instances. In other words, how do such very diverse sets of objects as large white circles, large red triangles, and large black globs elicit the single, common mediating response of *r* (size)/ *s* ("large")? In effect, the S–R mediation account of concept learning postulates a covert process that is itself concept learning.

Overview

Concept formation has been viewed here as the categorization of rule-defined *sets* of instances. The discussion was generally restricted to various aspects of the formation of set relationships among simple geometric figures. The choice of this context was based upon the same considerations that have led researchers to choose these stimuli and relations for systematic study of concept learning and use; geometric figures can be categorized and distinguished on the basis of a number of well-defined, independent stimulus dimensions. Thus, concept sets can be defined unambiguously with relatively simple rules, and the processes involved in concept formation can more readily be isolated and analyzed.

Further, there is reason to believe that acquisition and use of simple geometric concepts may reflect the same basic processes that are involved in the learning of more complex natural concepts. Certainly, the more concrete concepts that we deal with every day can be viewed as sets defined by rules relating attribute values from a number of relevant dimensions. Concepts such as *mammal, economy car, table, fruit,* and so on can be understood in these terms. Each word/label refers to a set of instances or "things" that have a particular, though perhaps not completely defined, combination of attributes (*small, medium,* or *large; living* or *dead; animal, vegetable, mineral;* and so forth).

Consider again, for example, the concept *economy car.* What are the relevant dimensions and attributes for determining whether an instance (a car) is a member of the concept set *economy car*? A few of the relevant dimensions and their associated attributes (dichotomized for simplicity) are listed in Table 15–1. Other dimensions might be added, some relevant, some partially relevant, or some having various degrees of redundancy with those listed (for example, horsepower, size, comfort). Many other dimensions are largely irrelevant to the economy-car classification (color, number of doors, country of manufacture, maker/importer). Many of the dimensions that are listed are not totally independent of one another. The major difference between the economy-car concept and the geometric-figure concepts, however, is in the complexity of the rule for combining these attributes so as to specify the set of positive instances.

Table 15–1. Relevant dimensions and attributes for the concept *economy car* (1978 figures).

Relevant Dimensions	*Attributes (Dichotomized)*	
Initial cost	Under $4000	Over $4000
Depreciation (2 yrs.)	Under 50%	Over 50%
Fuel requirements	Regular	Ethyl
Fuel consumption	Over 25 mpg	Under 25 mpg
Maintenance costs	Under $200 per 12,000 mi.	Over $200 per 12,000 mi.

There is no simple conjunctive, disjunctive, or conditional rule for combining the listed attributes to form the concept set *economy car.* A complex compound of conjunctive, disjunctive, and conditional rules would be required. A reasonable rule (or rules) for defining *economy car* might be

> *If* a car costs more than $4000, *then* it must depreciate less than 50% in 2 years *and* use regular gasoline *and* get more than 25 miles per gallon *and* have maintenance costs under $200 per 12,000 miles.
> *If* a car costs less than $4000, *then,* if it depreciates more than 50% in 2 years, it must use regular gasoline *and* get more than 25 miles per gallon *and* have maintenance costs under $200 per 12,000 miles;
> *If* the car depreciates less than 50%, *then* it must use regular gasoline *or* ethyl gasoline *and* get more than 25 miles per gallon *and/or* have maintenance costs under $200 per 12,000 miles.

This does present a noticeably more complex picture than "red and square," but the basic principle is essentially the same; relevant attributes are combined, according to a rule, to designate positive (and thus negative) instances of the concept. Presumably, the relevant attributes and the rule may all be acquired in the context of various experiences (with feedback) with positive and negative instances of *economy car*. As in many laboratory experiments, the concept may be applied to classify instances correctly even though the learner cannot actually state the rule.

How would you determine whether an unfamiliar automobile (instance) is an economy car? If you refer to the stated rule and to the lists of relevant dimensions and attributes in Table 15–1, you may not be able to see immediately how to proceed. The required relationships among the various relevant attributes can be clarified somewhat by representing the rule as a tree diagram. In this case, because all the dimensions are reduced to exactly two attributes each, the binary tree in Figure 15–10 can be used to represent the concept.

To determine whether a particular instance is an economy car, one need only ask a series of yes/no questions. First,

> Does the car cost more than $4000?

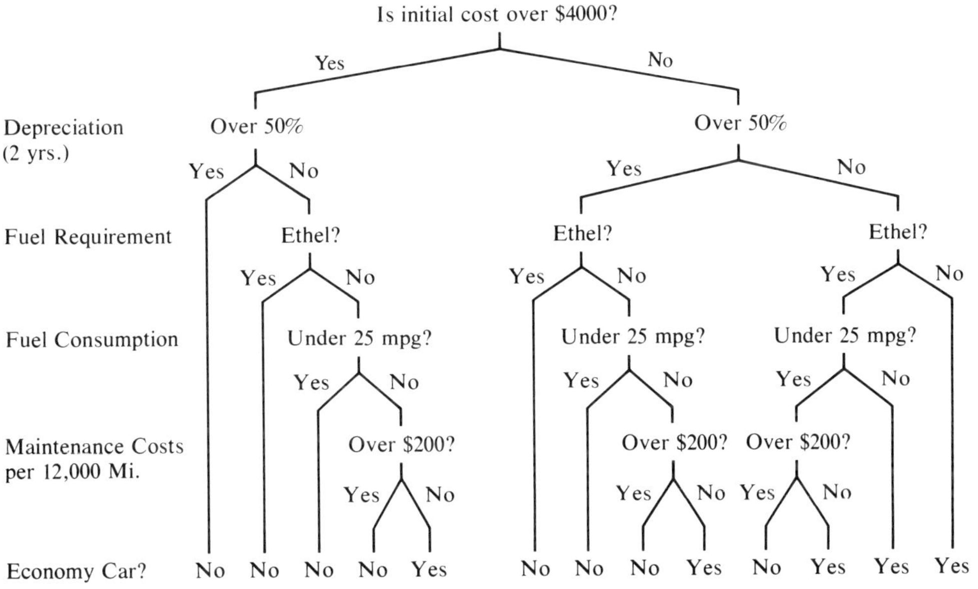

Figure 15–10. Tree diagram for the concept *economy car*.

If the answer to this question is yes, then the next question should be

> Does the car depreciate more than 50% in the first 2 years?

If the answer to this question is also yes, the car is *not* an economy car. If the answer to the second question is no, further questions must be considered before the car can be categorized as a positive or a negative instance. Thus, the complex, multidimensional concept *economy car* can be reduced to a hierarchical combination of much simpler concepts (*cost, maintenance,* and so forth).

Binary coding systems of the type just described are very effective and can be used to represent very complex concepts. The digital computer, for example, uses ordered binary relations to represent complex information (concepts) and procedures. More abstract concepts (such as *love, truth, morality*) are, no doubt, much more complex, but they can also be viewed as sets of instances (statements, actions, feelings, and so on). For such concepts, however, the determination of relevant attributes may be extremely difficult, and the rules for combining these attributes are likely to be very complex.

Concepts do not "exist" in the external environment but must be formed "on demand." The nature of a concept—the attributes that are relevant and the rule by which they are combined—is largely determined by the set of instances that the concept former confronts and by the type and number of categories that are required. In laboratory experiments, such as those reviewed in the preceding pages, the set of instances is usually shown or described to the subjects, and they are thoroughly instructed about the type of rules and response categories that are admissible. In the formation of natural concepts, the relevant attributes and rules must be discovered, often with very little knowledge of what the total instance set may be like. As new instances are encountered and their classification learned, the list of relevant attributes may be altered and the rules for combining them amended. In these complex circumstances concept formation begins to require the kind of cognitive activities that are usually referred to as problem solving.

Problem Solving

Problem solving cannot be distinguished completely from concept formation. Certainly, the cognitive processes that underlie performance in both of these situations overlap greatly, and there are many similarities in the nature of the tasks and in the behaviors required. A distinction can be made, however, on the basis of the relative emphasis placed upon certain features of the tasks and on the types of behaviors that are of primary interest in each.

In concept-formation tasks almost complete information is provided about the characteristics of instances, the nature and number of categories, and the type of category-identification responses that are required. Further, only a very small number of responses (often only two) are allowed; the primary focus is upon how subjects learn to make an arbitrarily assigned response to a number of distinguishable stimuli (instances). In problem-solving situations there is generally much more uncertainty. Often the statement of the task that is provided to subjects is ambiguous, allowing a number of different interpretations. Rather than a specified, small number of response alternatives, an unspecified and potentially large number of responses are usually possible (although only one of those may be "correct").

Concept formation, then, can be characterized as involving a large number of different stimuli to which a very limited and completely specified set of responses must be made. Problem solving, on the other hand, typically involves a single stimulus (albeit a complex stimulus) to which an unspecified, large number of responses can be made. Some, one, or none of these responses may be the "correct" response.

Problems

What is a problem? A number of different definitions have been offered. Davis (1973) gives the psychological definition of a problem as "a stimulus situation for which an organism has no ready response." In less psychological terms, Webster's New Collegiate Dictionary (1974) defines a problem as "a question raised for inquiry, consideration, or solution." For most purposes there is little difference between the "stimulus" definition and the "question" definition. The essential features of both are alike: a problem is an action-inducing situation (stimulus/question) for which the required action (response/answer) is not immediately available. To make a sufficient response or to provide an acceptable answer is to solve the problem. The selection or formulation of appropriate responses/answers is accomplished by a set of processes that is generally referred to as problem solving.

Problem solving is a very frequent, perhaps continuous, activity that we engage in every day. The problems that we encounter and solve, or attempt to solve, vary in complexity and difficulty. Some are satisfactorily solved with little effort and in a rather short time. Others may require a great deal of concentrated effort and perhaps are never satisfactorily resolved.

An example of a relatively simple problem that is confronted daily is

What shall I have for breakfast?

In principle, there are a very large number of possible solutions to this problem. Most of these possibilities have been eliminated, however, and do not have to be seriously considered. Social/cultural conventions dictate that only certain alternatives are appropriate (for example, whale blubber and french-fried ants are generally not considered breakfast fare), and long-established personal habits tend to limit the set of alternatives (for example, eggs and bacon, waffles, or granola). A number of other factors, such as the time available for preparation and consumption and the momentary availability of various alternatives, may also combine to limit further the set of solutions that have to be considered. Thus, what might have been a difficult problem is reduced to a rather routine choice among a very few alternatives.[1]

At the other extreme are some very complex problems that may occupy much time and energy but are rarely, if ever, fully solved:

Be happy!
Make something of yourself.
Benefit humanity.

These serious problems are very difficult to deal with, largely because the solutions are not very well defined. When the nature of the solution is unclear, it is difficult to determine whether any given approach to the problem may be successful. Further, with a problem such as these, it is virtually impossible to know when you have solved it.

Systematic studies of problem solving have generally not been directed at either very simple ("What shall I have for breakfast?") or very complex ("Be happy!") problems.

[1] Although breakfast may not seem to pose a problem, you need only visit your local pancake house some Sunday morning to convince yourself otherwise. Here the usual constraints of time and good sense are lifted, and you will hear intense and lengthy problem-solving efforts: "Shall I have the sour-cream and blueberry waffles, the cherry/pecan pancake roll with whipped cream, or the boysenberry wheat cakes with hot apple/raisin sauce?"

Psychologists have tended to concentrate their efforts on problems of approximately intermediate difficulty in which the solutions are not immediate but the solution requirements are relatively well defined. Within this range of difficulty, a very large number of different problems and different problem-solving situations have been studied. Perhaps as a result of the diversity of the problems studied, no single, unifying conceptualization of problem solving has as yet emerged. There are, however, some general characteristics that most psychologists would agree are essential to any problem-solving situation. To solve any problem, the individual must determine:

1. What the problem is.
2. What the solution will be like.
3. One or more ways to get from the problem to the solution.

The Stages of Problem Solving

Understanding the problem is the first, and often the most important, step toward solving the problem. If you misinterpret the problem, there is little chance that you will be able to solve it. Many problems are posed in such a way that the solver is very likely to misinterpret the problem. Posner (1973) offers the following example of a problem in which the proper interpretation greatly simplifies the finding of a solution:

> Two train stations are fifty miles apart. At 2 P.M. one Saturday afternoon two trains start toward each other, one from each station. Just as the trains pull out of the stations, a bird springs into the air in front of the first train and flies ahead to the front of the second train. When the bird reaches the second train it turns back and flies toward the first train. The bird continues to do this until the trains meet.
>
> If both trains travel at the rate of twenty-five miles per hour and the bird flies at a hundred miles per hour, how many miles will the bird have flown before the trains meet [p. 150–151].

There are several ways to represent this problem. If you choose to think of the problem directly in terms of the distance covered by the bird (as the statement of the problem seems to indicate you should), you will find it very difficult to solve. For example, you might try to calculate how far the bird flies on its first trip, add to that how far it flies on its second trip, and so on. If you choose a less direct representation—how much time does the bird spend in flight?—the problem becomes very simple. You need only note that it will take 1 hour for the two trains to converge (50 miles at a closing speed of $25 + 25 = 50$ miles per hour) and that the bird, flying at 100 miles per hour, will cover 100 miles in that hour.

Your anticipation of what the essential characteristics of a problem's solution are going to be can also greatly affect your success in solving the problem. Your representation of the desired solution not only guides your efforts at solving the problem but also tells you when to stop—that is, when the problem has been satisfactorily solved. A good example of a problem whose successful solution turns on whether an appropriate representation of the correct solution is established is presented in Figure 15–11. This problem was posed in an experiment in Scheerer (1963), and it often proved difficult to solve because subjects incorrectly assumed that the solution required that all lines intersect at one of the dots. In fact, the only way to solve the problem is to extend the lines past the dots (see Figure 15–12).

Once an interpretation of a problem is decided upon and some general representation of a solution established, a strategy must be formulated for achieving a specific solution to the problem. Some types of problems, such as anagrams and many mechanical puzzles, admit only a blind trial-and-error strategy for finding a solution. Other problem situations (for example, a chess game) may require that a rather elaborate, multistage plan be formu-

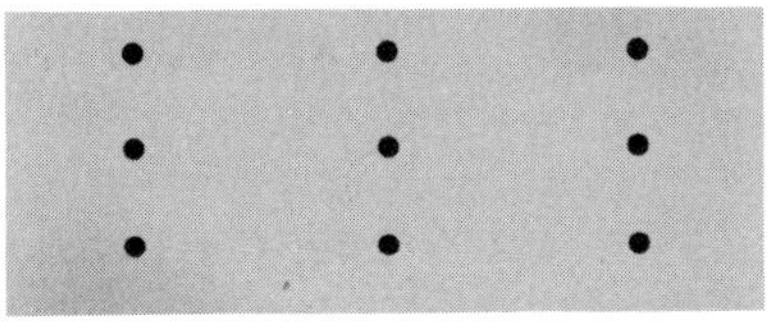

Figure 15–11. Nine-dot problem. Connect the dots using only four straight lines. Do not lift your pencil. (From "Problem Solving," by M. Scheerer, *Scientific American,* 1963, *204*(4), 118–128. Copyright © 1963 by Scientific American, Inc. Reprinted by permission.)

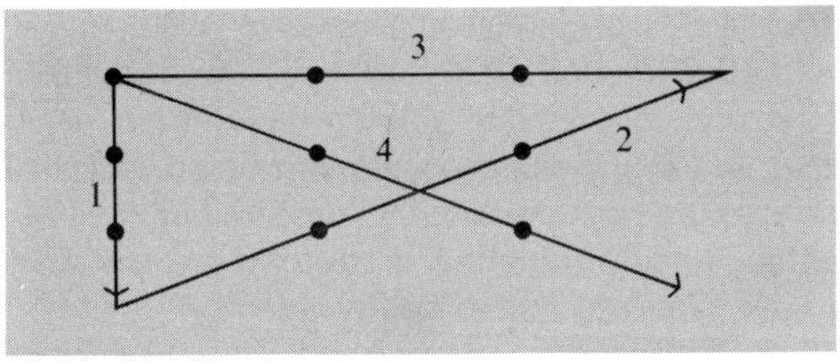

Figure 15–12. The solution to the nine-dot problem.

lated in order to achieve some specific solution (for example, a particular checkmate configuration). In both cases the basic problem and the general nature of the solution may be quite clear; the major problem-solving task is to discover a plan that will lead to a specific successful solution.

Psychologists have studied the formulation of problem-solving strategies in a variety of ways. One of the more effective procedures is to present subjects with a series of problems that are different in details but are all similar in terms of strategy that will produce a correct solution. An example of this approach is provided by the seven water-jar problems in Table 15–2. The basic task is, given three plain jars, each having a different capacity, to measure out exactly some specified amount of water. The first problem,

Obtain exactly 100 quarts of water,

can be solved by filling Jar B (127 quarts) and then pouring off enough to fill one Jar A (21 quarts) and two Jar Cs (3 + 3 = 6 quarts). This will leave exactly 100 quarts in Jar B. See whether you can solve Problems 2 through 7.

Table 15–2. Water-jar problems.

	Three jars are present with the listed capacity (in quarts)			*Obtain exactly this amount of*
Problem Number	*Jar A*	*Jar B*	*Jar C*	*water (in quarts)*
1	21	127	3	100
2	14	163	25	99
3	18	43	10	5
4	9	42	6	21
5	20	59	4	31
6	23	49	3	20
7	10	36	7	3

If you did try to solve all of the problems in Table 15–2, you probably found each successive problem (up to Problem 7) easier to solve. The reason is that all of the problems except the seventh can be solved by using the same strategy:

$$\text{Jar B} - \text{Jar A} - 2\ \text{Jar C} = \text{solution}.$$

Problem 7 probably took you longer to solve than Problem 6, even though in many ways Problem 7 is much easier. Problem 7 can be solved very easily by simply filling Jar A and then pouring off enough to fill Jar C. In this case the strategy learned in the preceding problems does not work and thus interferes with finding the correct solution. Did you notice that the same simple strategy that worked for Problem 7 also works for Problem 6? Most likely you solved Problem 6 by the same strategy that was applied to Problems 1 through 5, even though there is a simpler strategy that would have worked just as well. Sometimes, applying old strategies to a new problem can facilitate finding a solution, and at other times it can substantially hinder problem solving. It is clear, however, that the formulation of a strategy is an important component of problem solving.

The three basic stages of problem solving, understanding the problem, determining the nature of the solution, and formulating a strategy, are characteristic of virtually all problem-solving situations. The ease or difficulty and the success or failure of problem-solving efforts can usually be traced to one or another of these aspects of the task. In the following section we will briefly consider some problems that have often been studied in the laboratory. The problems differ substantially in format and complexity, and each tends to place different amounts of emphasis on one or another of the three basic stages of problem solving. After reviewing some of the more typical laboratory problems, we will turn to some practical, "real-world," problem-solving situations.

Problem Solving in the Laboratory

One class of problems that has been studied extensively, using both animals and humans, can be termed *insight problems*. Wolfgang Köhler's (1925) widely cited studies of problem solving by chimpanzees provide an excellent example of this type of problem. Köhler described many different problems that all had the basic feature of a barrier of some kind standing between a chimpanzee and some desired goal (for example, a banana).

In a typical insight problem one or several chimpanzees were placed in a room. A piece of fruit was suspended from the ceiling so as to be out of reach from the floor. After a number of unsuccessful efforts (for example, attempting to jump up and grab the fruit), the chimps were able to solve this problem in several ways. Sometimes chimps would drag boxes under the suspended fruit, stand on one box, or several boxes piled one upon the other, and reach the fruit. After fairly extensive practice with this basic problem, some chimps exhibited rather ingenious novel solutions to the problem. For example, one chimp might stand on the shoulders of another, or, after enticing Köhler to come under the fruit, a chimp might climb up on his shoulders to reach the prize.

Köhler's book *The Mentality of Apes* (1925) is filled with fascinating accounts of the problem-solving behavior of his chimpanzee subjects. His observations led him to conclude that the solution of many of these problems was accomplished suddenly and as a whole. For example, he provides the following description of a chimp's solution of the suspended-fruit problem:

> Koko stretched toward the prize for a while in vain; he stared away, saw the box, and stared at it for a moment. He went up to it and seized it; for a minute it looked as if he were about to attack it again; but instead, he dragged it hurriedly beneath the objective, mounted it and pulled down the prize [p. 42].

This seemingly sudden appreciation of the solution to a problem (the "Aha!" phenomenon), which frequently occurred in Köhler's studies, he termed insight. In his analysis of problem solving, the emphasis was upon perception-like processes—"seeing" the solution to the problem. Once the basic solution configuration is perceived, any number of specific strategies may be employed to achieve the desired objective. For example, the chimps stood on boxes, each others' shoulders, or Köhler's shoulders; in one instance a chimp dragged a ladder from another room to accomplish the solution. The emphasis in Köhler's experiments, then, was more upon understanding the problem and "perceiving" the general nature of the solution than upon the development and testing of problem-solving strategies.

There are many examples of problem solving by human subjects that exhibit the same perception-like characteristics. Perhaps the most famous example is the *pendulum problem* used by N. R. F. Maier (1931). In the basic problem there are two strings hanging down from the ceiling of a room. The task is to tie the two strings together. The barrier to a solution is that the strings are too far apart to allow grasping one of them and then walking over to the other.

How can you get the two strings together? One answer is suggested by the title "pendulum problem." You could attach something heavy to one of the strings (for example, your shoe) and start it swinging toward the other string like a pendulum. Then you could grab the free string with one hand and when the pendulum string swings within reach, catch it with the other hand.[2] The critical aspect of the problem is the perception (insight) that by swinging one of the strings toward the other you can catch hold of both of them. Once this is realized, any means of swinging the string will do. In Maier's experiments, for example, a number of objects were available in the room. Some subjects solved the problem by tying a pair of pliers to one of the strings.

One key to solving problems of the insight type is to be able to use familiar objects in unfamiliar ways. Using your shoe (which normally covers your foot) as a pendulum weight is a good example. K. Dunker (1945) pointed out that it is often difficult to think of an object as serving something other than its usual function. He referred to this tendency as *functional fixity.*

Experiments have shown that functional fixity is particularly difficult to overcome if an object is serving in its usual capacity. For example, you are much less likely to use your shoe for a pendulum weight when you are wearing it than when it is lying on a table or on the floor. Scheerer (1963) reported several experiments that confirmed this aspect of functional fixity. In one problem the solution required that the subjects tie two short sticks together to form a longer pole. This problem was solved rather easily if the required piece of string was hanging by itself on a wall. The problem was much more difficult, however, when the string was being used to hold up a picture or a calendar. Subjects failed to notice the string in the latter case, even though it was clearly visible and hanging on the same nail as before. Some subjects actually searched around the room for "something to tie the sticks together with" but failed to notice the string. Apparently, the string's serving a familiar hang-something-with function made it more difficult to consider its possible use for tying something together.

In all the above examples insight problems have emphasized the first two stages of problem solving, understanding the problem and achieving a general representation of the solution. Once the subject perceives these aspects of the problem correctly, a specific solution may be reached very quickly. Arranging the problem situation so as to call attention to

[2] Other solutions are possible. For example, you might lengthen one of the strings by tying a belt or something to it. This additional length could allow you to walk over and grab the other string without losing your hold on the first string.

elements that are important to the solution (such as placing the shoe on a table or hanging the string on the wall by itself) will generally facilitate the solving of these problems. Disguising the important elements, as by having the required objects serve their usual functions, will generally interfere with problem solving.

Other problems studied in the laboratory place less emphasis on perceiving the correct form of the problem and solution and focus more on the development of strategies. The water-jar problems discussed earlier and chess problems are good examples of problems that emphasize strategy. Newell and Simon (1972) have studied *crypt-arithmetic problems,* such as

$$\begin{array}{r} \text{D O N A L D} \\ +\ \underline{\text{G E R A L D}} \\ \text{R O B E R T} \end{array} \qquad D = 5$$

Solution of these problems depends upon the ability to develop and carry out systematic problem-solving plans. The problem itself is easily understood (find unique integer values for the letters), and the general form of the solution is also clear (the problem is solved when substitution of integers for letters yields an arithmetically correct sum). The difficult part of this problem is finding a way to determine which specific integers should be substituted for which letters.

One possible approach to solving the above problem is to try all possible integer-to-letter assignments. This approach is doomed, however, because of the enormous number of possible combinations (3,628,800). A blind trial-and-error approach is not likely to succeed, so some other, more systematic strategy would seem to be required. In fact, human problem solvers do approach such problems quite systematically. Psychologists who present these problems to human subjects are primarily interested in studying how human problem solvers formulate, test, and reject or modify strategies.

A direct approach to studying problem-solving strategies is to require subjects to solve problems like DONALD + GERALD out loud—that is, to report verbally each step of their attempts to solve the problem. By studying the resulting *verbal protocols* and other, accompanying problem-solving behaviors, important insights into problem-solving processes can be gained.

As an illustration of this research technique—and of the type of strategy formation and testing involved in this type of problem—consider the following protocol of a solution to the DONALD + GERALD = ROBERT (D = 5) problem.

$$\text{(Start) 1.} \quad \begin{array}{r} \text{D O N A L D} \\ +\ \underline{\text{G E R A L D}} \\ \text{R O B E R T} \end{array} \qquad D = 5$$

First, substitute 5 for D, to give

$$\text{2.} \quad \begin{array}{r} \text{5 O N A L 5} \\ +\ \underline{\text{G E R A L 5}} \\ \text{R O B E R T} \end{array}$$

If D = 5 and T = D + D, then T must be 1$\emptyset$, or actually it is T = $\emptyset$ and carry a 1:

$$\text{3.} \quad \begin{array}{r} 1\ \ \\ \text{5 O N A L 5} \\ +\ \underline{\text{G E R A L 5}} \\ \text{R O B E R}\ \emptyset \end{array}$$

Now then, $R = 2L + 1$. Because two times any number is always an even number, the carried 1 means that R must be an odd number, 1, 3, 5, 7, or 9. But from the first column ($5 + G = R$), R must be at least 5 because G must be at least $\emptyset$. Thus, $L + L + 1 = R = 5$, 7, or 9, and L must be 2, 3, or 4. However, each letter has to have its own number assigned, and D is already 5, so $R = 7$ or 9 and $L = 3$ or 4. Try $R = 7$, $L = 3$. That gives

$$\begin{array}{lcccccc} 4. & & 5 & O & N & A & 3 & 5 \\ & + & G & E & 7 & A & 3 & 5 \\ \hline & & 7 & O & B & E & 7 & \emptyset \end{array}$$

So far, so good. Now, if $A + A = E$, E must be even, so $E = \emptyset$, 2, 4, 6, or 8. Because $T = \emptyset$, I can eliminate that one. If $E = 2$, 4, 6, or 8, $A = 1$, 2, 3, or 4, but $L = 3$, so A cannot be 3 and E cannot be 6. Try $E = 2$, $A = 1$.

$$\begin{array}{lccccccc} & & & & & 1 & & \\ 5. & & 5 & O & N & 1 & 3 & 5 \\ & + & G & 2 & 7 & 1 & 3 & 5 \\ \hline & & 7 & O & B & 2 & 7 & \emptyset \end{array}$$

That looks OK. Now, for N, I am left with $N + 7 = B$. Also, I have $O + 2 = O$. Oops! How can that be, $O + 2 = O$? Perhaps a carry would help. What could be carried? Even if $N = 9$, $9 + 7 = 16$, and the carry would only be 1, leaving $1 + O + 2 = O$. That does not seem to work. Better back up and have another go. Maybe $E = 4$ and $A = 2$? If that were true, I would be left with $O + 4 = O$ or $1 + O + 4 = O$. Either way, it will not work. Is there any number that could satisfy $O + ? = O$ or $1 + O + ? = O$? Aha! Only $\emptyset$ and 9 will work! $T = \emptyset$, so E must be 9. So now I have

$$\begin{array}{lccccccc} 6. & & 5 & O & N & A & 3 & 5 \\ & + & G & 9 & 7 & A & 3 & 5 \\ \hline & & 7 & O & B & 9 & 7 & \emptyset \end{array}$$

Which means that A must be 4½. Nuts! But wait. If $L = 8$, R would still be 7, and there would be a 1 to carry. Now, $A = 4$ and $4 + 4 + 1$ carry $= 9$.

$$\begin{array}{lccccccc} 7. & & 5 & O & N & 4 & 8 & 5 \\ & + & G & 9 & 7 & 4 & 8 & 5 \\ \hline & & 7 & O & B & 9 & 7 & \emptyset \end{array}$$

Things are looking up! Now what numbers do I have left?

$$\begin{array}{cccccccccc} \emptyset & 1 & 2 & 3 & 4 & 5 & 6 & 7 & 8 & 9 \\ T & - & - & - & A & D & - & R & L & E \end{array}$$

N must be one of the numbers that is left. But what one? I need to have a carry to the $O + 9 = O$, if that is going to work, so N must be equal to or greater than 3. Only 3 and 6 are left, so $N = 3$ or 6. Try $N = 3$. OK, $3 + 7 = 1\emptyset$, so that would mean that $B = \emptyset$, but T is already $\emptyset$—N must be 6. Therefore $6 + 7 = 13$, carry a 1, so $B = 3$. That leaves

$$\begin{array}{lccccccc} & & & 1 & & 1 & 1 & \\ 8. & & 5 & O & 6 & 4 & 8 & 5 \\ & + & G & 9 & 7 & 4 & 8 & 5 \\ \hline & & 7 & O & 3 & 9 & 7 & \emptyset \end{array}$$

Only the numbers 1 and 2 are left, and the letters O and G. If O = 1, 1 + 1 + 9 = 11, carry the 1, and 1 + 5 + 2 = 7, which will not work! OK, if O = 2, then 1 + 2 + 9 = 12, carry the 1, 1 + 5 + 1 = 7. Hurrah! The problem is solved:

```
9.   D O N A L D            5 2 6 4 8 5
   + G E R A L D     =      1 9 7 6 8 5
   -------------          -------------
     R O B E R T            7 2 3 9 7 Ø
                            R O B E R T
```

Which checks!

In their analysis of many protocols similar to this one, Newell and Simon found a number of common elements; different subjects seem to use similar strategies and procedures in solving these problems. Newell and Simon characterize the solution process as a *means/ends analysis*. Subjects seem to be attempting to change (by various means) from one state of knowledge about a problem (an end) to another. In particular, their efforts can generally be viewed as an attempt to change from the initial, problem state to the desired goal (solution) state. For complex problems (for example, DONALD + GERALD), the desired end cannot be accomplished all at once. Rather, subjects must establish *subgoals* (for example, find out what R is), the attainment of which will produce a change toward the ultimate goal. As each subgoal is accomplished, or appears to be accomplished, the subjects checks the new state of the problem against their representation of the ultimate solution. If the new state appears to be closer to the solution than the beginning state, the subjects will continue with the plan or set of procedures that they have been following. If, at some point, the new state is incompatible with the desired solution, or seems not to be leading toward the solution, the subjects must *back up* and find where they went wrong. Then a new plan must be formulated, implemented, and tested. When the obtained state finally matches the desired solution, the problem is solved, and the subjects can cease their problem-solving efforts.

G. A. Miller, Galanter, and Pribram (1960) characterized these features of the problem-solving process in terms of the *TOTE* unit, *test/operate/test/exit*. Problem solvers successively *test* their knowledge of a problem against their representation of the solution. If knowledge and representation do not match, the solvers must perform some *operation* in an effort to make their state of knowledge closer to the solution. Test/operate/test sequences must be repeated until a test reveals a satisfactory match with the solution. At that point the problem solvers can *exit* from the problem.

This problem-solving protocol illustrates many of the features referred to by Newell and Simon. Several general characteristics of the protocol should be noted. First, it clearly represents an organized, systematic problem-solving effort. Operations begin at the right and generally proceed column by column toward the left. This procedure is appropriate for solving simple multiple-digit addition problems, and its application to the crypt-arithmetic problem reflects the solver's previous learning. The solution of the problem is accomplished in steps, by the attainment of subgoals. Though there are some instances of essentially blind trial and error (for example, R must be either 7 or 9; try 7), a strategy is usually discernible.

In terms of the TOTE unit analysis, the first test in the protocol can be represented by the statement of the problem (1). A simple operation of substituting the given information (D = 5) produces the second statement (2) to be tested. A subgoal, find the value of T, is then defined, and the necessary operation (D + D = 5 + 5 = T = 1Ø) is performed. The subsequent test (3) reveals progress toward the ultimate objective. A new subgoal, find R, is now approached. At this point the solver makes use of knowledge gained earlier in a context outside the problem—that is, that twice any number is an even number. After determining that R must be an odd number (any even number plus 1 must be an odd number), the solver looks ahead to the first column (D + G = R) and uses that information to reduce the number of possibilities for R. After the possibilities for R are reduced to two values (7 or 9), an arbitrary trial value, 7, is selected. Substitution (operation) produces a new statement of the problem (4), which again shows progress toward the desired solution. Similarly, new operations directed at the subgoal of finding A and E produce another positive test result (5). In establishing the next subgoal, the solver looks ahead again and finds O + 2 = O. Difficulties with this subgoal (5), which is essential to the attainment of the final solution, lead the solver to back up and reevaluate solutions to previous subgoals. A new solution for the subgoal of finding L produces State 7, a test of which seems to indicate a change toward the solver's representation of the final solution. Several additional operations produce the statement of the problem (8), which reveals that only a few more changes are needed to accomplish a match with the solution state. These operations are accomplished, yielding State 9, which matches the desired solution state, and the weary problem solver is finally able to exit.

By elaborating on this basic approach, Newell and Simon and their colleagues have developed computer programs that can successfully perform a wide variety of problem-solving tasks. The programs generally follow the means/ends or TOTE procedures just discussed. Because every step of the procedures must be fully specified if the computer program is to work, efforts to build problem-solving machines have contributed greatly to psychologists' understanding of the processes involved.

> How is a problem "understood" and some representation of its general solution established?
> How are subgoals determined?
> What are the necessary steps for comparing a statement of the problem with a representation of its solution; that is, how is a test performed?
> How are operations selected and implemented?

These and many other questions must be answered in detail in the process of programming a computer to solve problems. If the machine is programmed so as to *simulate* the performance of the human problem solver—that is, to achieve the same interpretation of a problem and its solution, to select the same subgoals, to make the same errors, and so on—the program can be offered as a *model* of human problem solving. In that respect the program and its component procedures and functions can serve as a *theory* of problem solving, and the validity of that theory can be tested.

Can the program (model) be used to *predict* human problem-solving performances? Does the model provide a useful *analysis* of the components of problem solving? These and other tests have been applied, and computer models have generally stood the test rather well. Still, some psychologists have expressed reservations about the use of computer programs and their information-representation formats and information-processing routines as theories of human problem solving. Others have argued that although the approach appears promising, we are still very far from having the ability to program a problem-solving machine that has anything like human capabilities.[3] Most psychologists would agree, however, that computerized information-processing models have contributed greatly to our understanding of human problem solving.

Problem Solving in the "Real" World

What can we learn from the laboratory analysis of problem solving that will help us solve real problems? Successful problem solving is crucial:

[3] Some of the more recent accomplishments in this domain, however, suggest that this gap is narrowing rather rapidly.

> How can I be happy?
> How do we get people to buy new cars?
> What measures can government take to cure inflation without precipitating a depression?
> What are the viable alternatives to fossil-fuel sources of energy?

These are very complex problems, and the welfare of individuals, corporations, nations, and, perhaps, all of humanity may depend upon finding satisfactory solutions. Hopefully, systematic studies of problem solving conducted in the laboratory can provide some guidance on how we might proceed to solve such pressing real-world problems.

Perhaps efforts to apply the scientific knowledge of problem solving should begin by adopting the component analysis that has proved useful in the laboratory. Recall that the three basic stages of problem solving are understanding the problem, characterizing the solution, and developing a strategy. Presumably, these same components will be found in real-world problem-solving situations. Difficulties in problem solving, whatever the context, should be traceable to one or another of these components. Also, any actions or procedures that will increase understanding of a problem, clarify the general characteristics of the solution, or increase the effectiveness of solution strategies should improve the chances of successful solution of the problem.

Understanding the Problem. There can be little doubt that a problem that has been misinterpreted will be difficult or impossible to solve. The initial statement or definition of the problem was found to be an essential determinant of ease and effectiveness of efforts to solve laboratory problems (recall Posner's converging-train/flying-bird problem). There are many ways that the interpretation or statement of a problem can impede a successful solution. The problem, as understood, may be too general or too complex. If you initially state a problem as, for example,

> How can we conserve energy?

you may have considerable difficulty determining what steps to take toward finding a solution. In this situation it may help to break the problem down into subproblems or subgoals:

> How can we reduce electric-power consumption?

Or, reducing even further,

> How can we reduce residential use of electric power?

The subproblems may themselves be very complex and difficult to solve, but because they are more limited in scope and more clearly defined, progress toward successful solutions may be more likely. Of course, subgoals must be selected and formulated so that their solution will represent actual progress toward the solution of the more general problem.

At the opposite extreme the statement of a problem may be too narrow, placing undue restrictions on the types of solutions that will be attempted. Davis (1973) offers the example

> How can we build a better mouse trap?

Stating the problem in this way may lead to only a very narrow approach to finding a solution to the actual problem (presumably, the problem is an abundance of unwanted mice). The above statement of the problem tends to restrict solutions to some form of a trap. If the problem were stated as

How can we get rid of mice?

the door might be opened to more creative and effective solutions.

Problems might be misinterpreted in a variety of ways, some of them more debilitating than others. A problem may be well defined and elegantly stated, producing vigorous and apparently appropriate progress toward a solution, but simply be the *wrong* problem. An example might be the automobile manufacturers' problem in the early 1970s:

How can we get people to buy more new cars?

The basic problem seemed to be that people were not purchasing a sufficient number of new cars to support the manufacturers' needs. Approaches to solving this problem tended to be intensified advertising campaigns, discounts on the purchase price, and cash rebates to purchasers. These solutions were at least somewhat successful. However, other types of solutions might have been tried if a different statement of the problem had been decided upon. For example,

What alternative product would people be more likely to buy?

So long as the problem that you are working on is poorly stated or incorrectly interpreted, solving it may be very difficult or your solutions may be less than satisfactory. Thus, considerable care should be exercised to understand your problem before you begin to attempt to solve it. Whenever you find that you are not making progress on solving a problem or you are experiencing a great deal of difficulty, perhaps you should back up and take another look at the problem. You may have misinterpreted the problem in the first place.

Characterizing the Solution. Another major deterrent to finding effective solutions to problems is the premature formulation of the type of solution that is sought. Obviously, the type of solution that is deemed acceptable will have a very strong influence on the specific solutions that may be tried. For one reason or another, the type of solution first hit upon is usually very similar to the "solutions" that have been used in similar situations in the past. History is sometimes *not* the best teacher.

Many creative problem-solving procedures recognize this danger and emphasize the importance of postponing decisions about the nature of a solution to a problem. The brainstorming approach (Osborn, 1963), for example, specifically requires that large numbers of "solutions" be brought forth, regardless of how bizarre some of them may sound, without requiring elaboration and without allowing any criticism. The purpose is to air as many possible types of solutions before allowing yourself (or your group) to focus on a particular type. Once the general form of an "acceptable" solution has been established, it may be very difficult even to consider other, perhaps better, forms of solution.

The insight problems, especially, point to the importance of the representation (perception) of a problem and its solution. In the suspended-fruit situation studied by Köhler (1925), for example, one might imagine that a chimp could perceive the problem's solution to be of the form

Get the fruit down here with me.

However, only after changing the representation of the solution to something like

Get me up there with the fruit

does the specific solution of standing on a box become likely.

The *incubation phenomenon,* often observed in natural problem-solving settings and confirmed in the laboratory, may be related to the importance of achieving a good representation of a solution. If you have been struggling with a problem for some time and are not making much progress, getting away from the problem for a while may be beneficial. Sometimes while you are away from the problem and not thinking about it, a solution will suddenly pop into your mind. This sudden occurrence of a solution after an inactive, incubation period may in part be a result of a change in your representation of the form of the solution. The time away from the problem may allow you to break out of an unsuccessful solution pattern and increase the likelihood that you will be able to entertain other, potentially more successful, types of solutions.

Perhaps the most important lesson to be learned from laboratory studies of insight-type problems is that functional fixity may prevent optimal use of problem-solving resources. In the pendulum problem (Maier, 1931) and in problems studied by Scheerer (1963), functional fixity was a major barrier to successful solution. One way to help overcome this obstacle is to list everything that is available to you in the problem situation, without any regard for their potentials for solving the problem. Once a list of objects (clothing, furniture, other people, and so forth) is made, all of the possible uses of each object might be listed, especially unusual uses. Some studies (for example, Glucksburg, 1964; Glucksburg & Weisberg, 1966) have shown that considering thc parts of objects separately (for instance, a shoe has a heel, a sole, a tongue, strings or a buckle, and so on) may be helpful. Although most objects (and their parts) and uses listed will be of no value in solving the problem, inventorying your resources may reveal or suggest an otherwise unnoticed element that can be used to effect a solution.

Developing a Strategy. Developing a plan of attack on a problem is probably the most complex part of problem solving. The strategy adopted will, of course, depend greatly upon the statement of the problem and the general representation of the solution. Means/ends analysis, the procedure that characterizes the information-processing/computer-model approach to problem solving, suggests several ways that a problem-solving strategy might be formulated. Often, the best strategies are found by working backward from the general solution or goal. This is especially effective when the goal is relatively well defined, as in mathematical proofs or chess games or when the objective is to reach some known destination. Consider, for example, the problem

> How can I spend spring vacation in Mazatlan?

Working backward from the goal, it will be noted that an essential step is to get to Mazatlan. Thus, some means of transportation will be required. Transportation costs money, so the next step backward is to determine how to accumulate the needed funds. Eventually, this working-backward strategy may lead you to forego a planned ski trip so as to save money, to purchase transportation, to get to Mazatlan, to enjoy your spring break. Working backward can be an effective strategy, but it does require that you have a good idea of where you are eventually trying to go.

Working backward is actually a special case of the more general strategy of dividing a large problem into subgoals. Some of the more serious and complex problems that are confronted by each of us are perhaps only approachable by determining appropriate subgoals.

> How can I be happy?

This is a problem that most people wish to resolve successfully, but the ultimate solution or goal is not at all well defined. By establishing some smaller, more precisely defined subgoals, such as

> Have a good job.
> Make friends.
> Be healthy.

some approach to the ultimate goal may be made. Obtaining a desirable job may require that you get an education, serve an apprenticeship, or change your location. Making friends may involve joining organizations or just introducing yourself to your neighbors. In any event, when the ultimate goal is unclear, it is often difficult to develop strategies for accomplishing the objective. Subgoals can be established, however, that are more specific, and some progress toward a solution can be made. Of course, the subgoals that you select must be such that achieving them will actually represent progress toward the more general, ultimate goal.

A number of very interesting, creative, and even successful problem-solving methods have been developed. Many of these methods are based on principles uncovered by laboratory studies of problem solving. Davis, in the last half of his book *Psychology of Problem Solving: Theory and Practice* (1973), describes several of these real-world problem-solving techniques. Among these are idea-generating check lists; a series of questions designed to elicit new ways of viewing a problem or its solution; systems that emphasize metaphorical or analogical reasoning, such as "synectics" and "bionics"; and some freewheeling brainstorming techniques. These approaches have proved helpful in solving some difficult problems encountered by industry and government. A feature common to all of these techniques is that they attempt to ensure that many possible interpretations of the problem have been considered, that a large number of general solutions have been proposed before any one type is focused on, and that several potentially successful strategies, often borrowed from other problem areas, will be tried.

Decision Making

Both concept formation and problem solving contain elements of decision making. When an instance is encountered in a concept-formation task, subjects must decide whether it is a positive or a negative instance. Problem solving requires many decisions. Solvers must decide upon an interpretation of the problem, select subgoals and strategies, and determine when the problem has been satisfactorily solved. Because there are a great many factors affecting subjects' behavior in these situations (Do they know the concept rule? Do they understand the problem?), psychologists have found it more effective to study decision making separately.

In studies of human decision making, the approach has generally been to specify some set of alternatives rather completely, including an indication of the relative costs and gains associated with each, and then require subjects to choose among those alternatives. The focus is upon the factors that determine the subjects' decision. An example given at the beginning of this chapter,

> Would you rather have $1 right now or a 1-in-4 chance of getting $5 tomorrow?

illustrates these general features. Both alternatives are clearly stated; the interest is in the way the subjects weigh one alternative against the other and decide which they would prefer.

Research has tended to concentrate on two general decision-making situations, choice among different-valued alternatives and gambles. There are, of course, many similarities between these two situations, but gambles generally have a special element of *risk*. In the above example, subjects stand a 3-in-4 chance of not getting anything if they choose the $5 alternative. Choice situations, though they do have certain elements of uncertainty, generally do not involve this type of risk. For example, subjects might be asked:

> Which would you prefer, a new Cadillac or a new Lincoln?

Although subjects may be uncertain about which car they ought to choose, there is not really any risk. They presumably will be given whichever they choose.

The Cadillac/Lincoln choice points to another important aspect of most decision-making research. For the most part these decisions are made in a *game* context; that is, subjects are rarely asked to make real gambles or to make choices among real alternatives. The game context is primarily a result of the experimenters' limited resources (they can hardly afford actually to give away Lincolns and Cadillacs), and there are also ethical constraints (if subjects gamble and lose, experimenters cannot insist that they pay up). Some caution must be exercised, then, when attempting to apply the results of laboratory studies to real decision-making situations. Nonetheless, these systematic studies do provide insight into the more fundamental processes involved in human decision making.

Value and Choice

The first step in making a decision is to determine the alternatives that are available to be chosen. For the most part, however, this component of decision making is a problem-solving task, and the processes involved have already been described. To focus more directly on the elements of decision, we will assume that the alternatives open to the decision maker have been provided by an experimenter or have otherwise already been specified. For present purposes, the decision-making process begins when some set of alternative actions or goals has been established and the task is to choose from among those alternatives.

A rational decision maker chooses among alternatives on the basis of their *value*. The value of an alternative is composed of both *gain* (positive) and *cost* (negative) elements. The net value, or *utility*, of an alternative is found by subtracting the costs associated with that alternative from the gains, or more simply, finding the algebraic sum of the positive and negative values. Determining the utility of alternatives is often quite difficult because many of the costs and gains are uncertain and intangible. For example,

> Should you continue in college or get a job?

Although there are some tangible values associated with both alternatives (for example, costs of tuition and fees, gains of salary), many of the costs and gains are intangible (Will you like what you are doing? What will your parents or friends think? What is the value of intellectual growth? Will you get more intellectual stimulation at school or on a job?). Sometimes the values of alternatives seem more tangible, so decisions may be somewhat easier to make:

> Would you prefer to have $.10 or $1?

It seems clear that the value of the dollar is greater than that of the dime. However, there are circumstances in which the reverse may be true. Consider the same choice as it might be offered to a 3-year-old child by an older sibling:

Would you rather have this wrinkly old paper dollar or this shiny new dime?

The point is that values are determined by the judgment processes of the decision maker. The utility of any alternative, however tangible and "absolute" it may seem, will vary from one decision maker to another and from one situation to another.[4]

The fundamental principle of rational decision making, then, is rather simple: *choose the alternative with the greatest utility.* The difficulty, of course, is that you must first determine the costs and gains that should be assigned to each alternative.[5] Though there are no sure-fire methods for evaluating alternatives in complex decision-making situations, there are ways at least to approach the task systematically. Some of these methods are illustrated in the following example.

Suppose that you are planning to make a trip over the Christmas recess. You have 10 days, and you have saved enough money either to go north for a skiing vacation or to go south to the beach. Each of these alternatives has different costs and gains. Moreover, some are rather concrete, and others are less tangible. How might you proceed to determine the relative utility of these two alternatives, so that you could make a rational decision? Because the two general alternatives are very different, it is difficult to compare them directly. You might, however, analyze each into a number of more specific positive and negative components. Perhaps then some common basis for comparison of the two alternatives could be discovered (this may be analogous to the establishment of subgoals in a problem-solving situation).

One possible listing of the costs and gains associated with the two trip alternatives is presented in Table 15–3. Listing specific costs and gains for each alternative may not immediately suggest a decision, but it does provide some grounds for making comparisons of the values associated with each alternative.

One feature common to the two alternatives is that there are expenses to be considered. This particular dimension is quite concrete, and the value (in this case a negative

Table 15–3. Dimensions for comparison (costs and gains) of ski trip and beach trip.

Ski Trip	*Beach Trip*
Gains	*Gains*
Skiing	Swimming and boating
Snow and forest scenery	Sun, sand, and surf
Ski-lodge atmosphere	Beach house
European cuisine	Seafood
Hot wine	Cold beer
Fireplace get-togethers	Beach parties
Costs	*Costs*
Transportation	Transportation
Room and board	Room and board
Cold and weariness	Heat and sand
Danger of injury	Danger of sunburn
Lift tickets and equipment	Fees and boat rental

[4] An interesting and common example of situational determination of values is provided by the change-maker machine. Whereas a dollar bill is usually worth (valued at) exactly 100 cents, there are situations—such as having to make an important phone call from a public booth and not having any change—in which you would be willing to exchange a paper dollar for 90 cents.

[5] This principle is somewhat akin to the basic principle for stock-market investing: "Buy low; sell high." The principle is clear enough; the implementation is the hard part.

value, or cost) for each alternative can be determined relatively easily and precisely. Expenses for the ski trip might be

Transportation	$ 40
Room rent (lodge)	120
Lift and equipment	96
Food	100
Miscellaneous	25
Total expenses	$381

These costs can be compared to those for going to the beach:

Transportation	$ 80
Beach cottage	120
Boat rental	50
Food	75
Miscellaneous	35
Total expenses	$360

Thus, if the two alternatives are compared on the expense dimension, the cost of the ski trip is found to be greater than that of the beach trip. But should you decide just on the basis of expenses? Only if all other relevant features are the same. We have determined that the ski trip is more expensive (by $21), but what about the positive values associated with each alternative? The primary purpose of either trip is to "do something." In one case the main activity is skiing (and perhaps sitting around the lodge telling lies about how well you did on that last run). For the beach trip the primary activities are sunning on the sand and swimming in the ocean. You must somehow determine which of these activities you enjoy more.

Even after you have found some means of comparing the alternatives on each dimension, you must somehow combine these dimensions to make a final choice. This brings up some difficult questions. How should you *weight* the various dimensions? If you like skiing more than swimming, does that outweigh the fact that the ski trip costs more money? Which is more important, the activity itself or the environment in which the activity is performed? You may like skiing better than swimming but find the warm sun, sand, and sea more appealing surroundings than the cold snow and the forest. Thus, even if you can determine which alternative is better on each dimension, you cannot necessarily just choose the alternative that is better on the majority of the dimensions. Some dimensions are more important (weighted more heavily) than others.

Perhaps it is no wonder that we rarely actually go through such an elaborate, headache-producing procedure every time we are faced with a difficult decision. More often, we may focus upon one or two dimensions (such as how much money each trip will cost or whether warmth is preferable to cold) and, even then, not compare them very systematically. Of course, being human decision makers, we always have the option of making an irrational choice (recall the decision to buy a Ford from Awe G. Whiz).

Decisions Involving Risk

Placing a bet, investing in a business venture, and buying a used car all involve an element of risk. The risk is that you may lose; you might lose the money that you put down on your bet, you might lose the opportunity to make more moneyon a different investment, or you might lose more in repair bills and grief than you saved by buying a cheaper car. These are all gambling situations. There are costs and gains to be considered, as in choice situations, but there is an additional element of *chance*. There is uncertainty about the particular costs and gains associated with each decision alternative.

In laboratory studies of risk-type decision making, subjects are usually required to make hypothetical bets or to choose which of several bets they would rather make. Which bet would you prefer to try?

> Roll a die. If it is a six, you win $5;
> if not, you lose $2.
> Toss a coin. If it is heads, you win $5;
> if not, you lose $5.

A rational decision would be to make the bet with the greater expected payoff; that is, to choose the bet that, in the long run, will pay greater gains against smaller losses. To make it easier to determine which bet is better, a *payoff matrix* can be constructed.

	Die Bet	Coin Bet
Win	Gain $5	Gain $5
Lose	Cost $2	Cost $5

Each bet, then, has two possible outcomes; you might win or you might lose. In determining the long-run, *expected value (EV)* of each bet, you must consider both the amount to be gained or lost and the *probability (P)* of winning or losing. The expected value of a bet is the probability of winning times the amount to be won, minus the probability of losing times the amount to be lost. Thus:

$$\begin{aligned} EV \text{ (die bet)} &= [p(6) \times \$5] - [p(\bar{6}) \times \$2] \\ &= (^1/_6 \times \$5) \quad - (^5/_6 \times \$2) \\ &= \$.83 \qquad\quad - \$1.67 \\ &= -\$.84 \end{aligned}$$

$$\begin{aligned} EV \text{ (coin bet)} &= [p(\text{H}) \times \$5] - [p(T) \times \$5] \\ &= (½ \times \$5) \quad - (½ \times \$5) \\ &= \$2.50 \qquad - \$2.50 \\ &= \$0 \end{aligned}$$

Given a choice between these two bets, the coin bet is to be preferred—at least you would expect to break even in the long run. The die bet will lead to a net loss in the long run of approximately $.84 per bet—the kind of bet that pays the light bills in Las Vegas.

A good example of a risk-type decision that many people encounter in the real world is to buy or not to buy insurance. You might consider buying a medical-insurance policy, for example, to protect yourself against the possibility of encountering medical expenses that are greater than you wish to pay. The policy does, of course, cost money, and you might stay well. In the latter case you will be out the cost of the insurance. Should you buy such a policy or not? This actually is a rather complex decision involving several kinds of risk, but if simplified, the situation can be represented by a payoff matrix:

	Buy Insurance	Do Not Buy Insurance
Catastrophic Sickness	Costs: Policy premiums Gains: Covered medical expenses, and so on	Costs: Expenses of treatment Gains: Policy premiums
Remain Well	Costs: Policy premiums Gains: Comfort and security of having coverage	Costs: Comfort and security Gains: Policy premiums

In this simplified situation only four possible outcomes are represented: you might buy the insurance and get sick, buy and stay well, do not buy and get sick, or do not buy and stay well. Each of these four outcomes has costs and gains associated with it, and whether you buy or do not buy insurance, there is some probability that you will get sick and encounter large medical expenses. To determine which alternative action, buying or not buying, has the greatest overall utility, we must be able to assign actual values to the costs and gains in the payoff matrix. As is usually true in such complex decision-making situations, neither the individual costs and gains nor the probabilities of occurrence can be determined exactly. The more closely these values can be estimated, however, the better the basis for making a rational decision.

Some of the values for this hypothetical example, could, in principle, be determined rather directly. The price of the insurance policy, for example, would generally be a known quantity. This premium price could be adjusted by subtracting your estimate of medical expenses that you can reasonably expect to incur in future years (perhaps based on prior years' expenses). Just to have some real numbers for our example, suppose the policy costs \$480 per year. Your expected medical expenses are \$600 per year, but \$100 of that would not be covered by the policy (for example, dental bills), and the insurance policy has a \$300 deductible (you have to pay that before the insurance begins to pay for anything). Thus, the actual cost of the policy can be estimated to be \$280 per year (\$480 premium minus \$200 covered medical expenses).

Other costs and gains are not so easily determined. What if you actually encountered a large unexpected medical expense? Some catastrophic illness might occur, and you would somehow have to pay the costs of treatment. Although such costs cannot be predicted with any precision, they can be represented in the payoff matrix as an unknown value. Let C (for catastrophic cost) stand for this cost. Related to the catastrophe problem is the positive value of security associated with knowing that such events are provided for. This unknown subjective factor, S, might also be recognized as a benefit of buying the insurance, whether you become ill or stay well.

There are, no doubt, other factors that should be considered (tax advantage of buying insurance, possibility that some government welfare agency would bail you out if a catastrophe actually occurred, and so forth), but the hypothetical values we have developed should be sufficient to illustrate the application of the payoff matrix in this complex decision-making situation.

Hypothetical values can now be substituted for the costs and gains in the payoff matrix, and the utility of each outcome can be determined.

	Buy	$\overline{\text{Buy}}$
Sick	Cost: \$280 Gain: $C + S$	Cost: $S + C$ Gain: \$280
Well	Cost: \$280 Gain: S	Cost: S Gain: \$280

For the outcome buy/get sick, for example, the gains are the expenses for the catastrophe, C, and the psychological value of the security of being covered against such losses, S. The cost is the actual price of the policy, \$280 per year. The utilities (U) for all four outcomes can be represented as:

$$
\begin{array}{lll}
 & \text{Gain} & \text{Cost} \\
U\ (\text{buy/sick}) = & (C + S) & - \$280 \\
U\ (\text{buy/well}) = & S & - \$280 \\
U\ (\overline{\text{buy}}/\text{sick}) = & \$280 & - (S + C) \\
U\ (\overline{\text{buy}}/\text{well}) = & \$280 & - S
\end{array}
$$

These utility values must be adjusted to take into account the different probabilities of occurrence of each outcome. The probability of a major illness, for example, should be rather small, and this fact should play some part in making the decision. Although the actual probability cannot be determined for any specific individual, you can make your own subjective estimate. Your estimate of the probability of encountering catastrophic medical expenses can be represented in the example by the unknown value, p (the probability of staying well, then, would be $1 - p$). The utility values can now be multiplied by their estimated probabilities to find *expected utilities* (EU) for each outcome:

$$
\begin{aligned}
EU\ (\text{buy/sick}) &= p[(C + S) - \$280] \\
EU\ (\text{buy/well}) &= (1-p)(S - \$280) \\
EU\ (\overline{\text{buy}}/\text{sick}) &= p[\$280 - (S + C)] \\
EU\ (\overline{\text{buy}}/\text{well}) &= (1-p)(\$280 - S)
\end{aligned}
$$

To complete the example, we must now determine the expected utility of the two alternatives, to buy or not to buy. This is sometimes referred to as the *marginal expected utility* (MEU) and is simply the total expected utility for each alternative.

$$
\begin{aligned}
MEU\ (\text{buy}) &= EU\ (\text{buy/sick}) + EU\ (\text{buy/well}) \\
&= p\ [(C + S) - \$280] + (1 - p)(S - \$280) \\
&= pC + pS - p(\$280) + S - \$280 - pS + p(\$280) \\
&= pS = pS + p(\$280) - p(\$280) + S + pC + S - \$280 \\
&= S + pC - \$280
\end{aligned}
$$

$$
\begin{aligned}
MEU\ (\overline{\text{buy}}) &= EU\ (\overline{\text{buy}}/\text{sick}) + EU\ (\overline{\text{buy}}/\text{well}) \\
&= p\ [\$280 - (S + C)] + (1 - p)(\$280 - S) \\
&= p(\$280) - pS - pC + \$280 - S - p(\$280) + pS \\
&= p(\$280) = p(\$280) + pS - pS + \$280 = pC - S \\
&= \$280 - pC - S
\end{aligned}
$$

The rather reasonable conclusion is that you should buy the policy if, in your estimation, the value of security plus the value of catastrophe costs (adjusted by its presumably low probability) is greater than \$280 per year. If security and expected catastrophe costs are worth less than \$280 per year, do not buy the policy.

As in the previous decision example, a human decision maker probably rarely goes to the trouble of such a process. Nonetheless, the computation of marginal expected utilities may represent some of the processes, however covert, that people use in making decisions that involve risk. Certainly, the factors that were found to be important in the example of buying medical insurance are the ones on the basis of which a rational decision would be made. How the necessary subjective values (such as security) and probabilities are estimated by a particular human decision maker remains largely a mystery. This general model of decision making, however, has served as a guide for much of the systematic research on the topic and may eventually lead to a better understanding of the processes employed by the human decision maker.

Summary

Thinking is among the most characteristic activities of human beings. Thought is often revealed in overt behaviors, but for the most part thinking is a covert activity. In this chapter concept formation, problem solving, and decision making were discussed as separable but highly interrelated components of thinking.

Psychologists have generally treated concept formation as the process (or processes) by which distinguishable objects or "things" (instances) are organized into different categories. Instances that vary along some identifiable dimensions (for example, color size, shape) are assigned to different or the same categories on the basis of their specific attributes (for example, *red* versus green, large versus *small, square* versus *circular*. The correct assignment of instances is usually determined by a rule (for example, "All red objects are positive instances"). Concept formation is demonstrated by the correct assignment of instances that have not previously been encountered.

This experimental approach to concept formation does seem to encompass many of the features of concept learning outside the laboratory. The example of the acquisition of the concept *economy car* certainly requires the categorization of instances (autos) on the basis of their dimensions of variation. Some of the dimensions along which auto instances vary are relevant to their categorization; cars that are small, have good fuel economy, and are relatively low in cost are more likely to be economy cars. Other dimensions, such as color and country of origin, are irrelevant in determining whether a car is an economy car. Of course, real-world concepts generally involve much more complex rules than concepts typically studied in the laboratory. But the basic processes for learning the concepts are very similar: individual instances are encountered, some feedback is obtained on the proper categorization of these instances, and finally, new instances can be correctly categorized when they are encountered for the first time.

Problem solving can be distinguished from concept formation in the following way. Concept formation generally requires that some large number of readily identified instances be consistently categorized by the assignment of one of a small number of specified responses. Problem solving is generally initiated by a single complex stimulus to which some unspecified, perhaps large number of responses may be made. A situation presents a problem when the most immediately available responses are not correct.

A great many problem situations have been studied in the laboratory. Some are more complex than others, and most are rather artificial when compared to problems encountered outside the laboratory. The procedures necessary for successfully solving either type of problem, however, do share some characteristics. Solving any problem requires that the problem be properly defined, that some notion of at least the general form of the desired solution be anticipated, and that some viable means for getting from the problem situation to the solution be discovered. Successful problem-solving strategies recognize the importance of each of these stages and employ systematic procedures for ensuring that each is accomplished.

The study of decision making has generally focused upon the processes by which subjects choose among a set of reasonably well specified alternatives. Generally, the alternatives vary in value and/or likelihood of success. For example, subjects may be asked to choose between getting $1 immediately and having a 1-in-4 chance of getting $5 later. It is usually assumed that the choice will be made on the basis of expected subjective utility of the alternatives—the alternative that is perceived as the most valuable and the most certain will be the one chosen.

Although the laboratory analysis of decision making has resulted in some important insights into human decision making, it has some limitations. First, laboratory studies almost invariably deal with clearly specified alternatives having known probabilities of success. The most difficult and often the most important decisions that people face are full of unknowns. Not all of the alternative courses of action are known, their respective values are undetermined, and the likelihood of the various possible outcomes can only be guessed at. Deciding whether to buy health insurance was presented as an example of a realistic decision in which many of the important bases for making a choice are unknown. Another important limitation of laboratory analyses is that the decision maker is usually assumed to be rational; that is, the individual will always choose the alternative that is judged to have the highest expected utility. It takes little observation of human behavior to discover that this assumption is suspect outside the laboratory. If the systematic procedures of rational decision making were more nearly followed, many of our decisions might be made with greater likelihood of success.

References

Adams, H. E., & Calhoun, K. S. Indices of memory recovery following electroconvulsive shock. *Physiology and Behavior,* 1972, *9,* 783–787.

Adams, J. A. *Human memory.* New York: McGraw-Hill, 1967.

Adelman, H. M., & Maatsch, J. L. Resistance to extinction as a function of the type of response elicited by frustration. *Journal of Experimental Psychology,* 1955, *50,* 61–65.

Ader, R., & Belfer, M. R. Prenatal maternal anxiety and offspring emotionality in the rat. *Psychological Reports,* 1962, *10,* 711–718.

Ader, R., & Conklin, P. M. Handling of pregnant rats: Effects on emotionality of their offspring. *Science,* 1963, *142,* 411–412.

Adey, W. R. Neurophysiological correlates of information transaction and storage in brain tissue. In E. Stellar & J. M. Sprague (Eds.), *Progress in physiological psychology* (Vol. 1). New York: Academic Press, 1966.

Adey, W. R., Dunlop, C. W., & Hendrix, C. E. Hippocampal slow waves: Distribution and phase relationships in the course of approach learning. *Archives of Neurology,* 1960, *3,* 74–90.

Adey, W. R., & Walter, D. O. Application of phase detection and averaging techniques in computer analysis of EEG records in the cat. *Experimental Neurology,* 1963, *7,* 186–209.

Adler, N., & Hogan, J. A. Classical conditioning and punishment of an instinctive response in *Betta splendens. Animal Behaviour,* 1963, *11,* 351–354.

Agranoff, B. W., & Klinger, P. D. Puromycin effect on memory fixation in the goldfish. *Science,* 1964, *146,* 952–953.

Ainsworth, M. D. *Infancy in Uganda: Infant care and the growth of attachment.* Baltimore: Johns Hopkins University Press, 1967.

Alberts, E., & Ehrenfreund, D. Transposition in children as a function of age. *Journal of Experimental Psychology,* 1951, *41,* 30–38.

Allen, M. Rehearsal strategies and response cuing as determinants of organization in free recall. *Journal of Verbal Learning and Verbal Behavior,* 1968, *7,* 58–63.

Alpern, H. P., & McGaugh, J. L. Retrograde amnesia as a function of duration of electroshock stimulation. *Journal of Comparative and Physiological Psychology,* 1968, *65,* 265–269.

Altman, J., & Das, G. D. Autoradiographic examination of the effects of enriched environments on the rate of glial multiplication in the adult rat brain. *Nature,* 1964, *204,* 1161–1163.

Ambrose, J. A. The development of the smiling response in early infancy. In B. M. Foss (Ed.), *Determinants of infant behavior* (Vol. 1). London: Methuen, 1961.

Amsel, A. The role of frustrative nonreward in noncontinuous reward situations. *Psychological Bulletin,* 1958, *55,* 102–119.

Amsel, A. Partial reinforcement effects on vigor and persistence. In K. W. Spence & J. T. Spence (Eds.), *The psychology of learning and motivation* (Vol. 1). New York: Academic Press, 1967.

Amsel, A. Positive induction, behavioral contrast, and generalization of inhibition in discrimination learning. In H. H. Kendler & J. T. Spence (Eds.), *Essays in neobehaviorism: A memorial volume to Kenneth W. Spence.* New York: Appleton-Century-Crofts, 1971.

Amsel, A. Behavioral habituation, counterconditioning, and a general theory of persistence. In A. H. Black & W. F. Prokasy (Eds.), *Classical conditioning II: Current research and theory.* New York: Appleton-Century-Crofts, 1972.

Amsel, A., Hug, J. J., & Surridge, C. T. Number of food pellets, goal approaches, and the partial reinforcement effect after minimal acquisition. *Journal of Experimental Psychology,* 1968, *77,* 530–534.

Amsel, A., & Roussel, J. Motivational properties of frustration: I. Effect on a running response of the addition of frustration to the motivational complex. *Journal of Experimental Psychology,* 1952, *43,* 363–368.

Amsel, A., Surridge, C. T., & Hug, J. J. Number of food pellets and the partial reinforcement extinction effect after extended acquisition. *Journal of Experimental Psychology,* 1969, *82,* 578–580.

Anderson, C.O., Denenberg, V. H., & Zarrow, M. X. Effects of handling and social isolation upon the rabbit's behavior. *Behaviour,* 1972, *43,* 165–175.

Anderson, J. R. *Language, memory, and thought.* Hillsdale, N.J.: Erlbaum, 1976.

Anderson, J. R., & Bower, G. H. Recognition and retrieval processes in free recall. *Psychological Review,* 1972, *11,* 594–605.

Anderson, J. R., & Bower, G. H. *Human associative memory.* Washington, D.C.: Hemisphere, 1973.

Anrep, G. V. Pitch discrimination in the dog. *Journal of Physiology,* 1920, *53,* 367–385.

Appel, J. B. Punishment and shock intensity. *Science,* 1963, *141,* 528–529.

Appel, J. B. Fixed-interval punishment. *Journal of Experimental Analysis of Behavior,* 1968, *11,* 803–808.

Appel, J. B., & Peterson, N. J. Effects of shock intensity on response suppression. *Psychological Reports,* 1965, *16,* 721–730.

Archer, E. J. A re-evaluation of the meaningfulness of all possible CVC trigrams. *Psychological Monographs,* 1960, *74*(10, Whole No. 497).

Arnoult, M. D. Recognition of shapes following paired associate pretraining. In G. Finch & F. Cameron (Eds.), *Symposium on Air Force human engineering, personnel, and training research* (Vol. 1) (NAS/NRC Publication No. 455). Washington, D.C.: National Academy of Sciences/National Research Council, 1956.

Arnoult, M. D. Stimulus predifferentiation: Some generalizations and hypotheses. *Psychological Bulletin,* 1957, *54,* 339–350.

Asch, S. E., & Ebenholtz, S. M. The principle of associative symmetry. *Proceedings of the American Philosophical Society,* 1962, *106,* 135–163.

Atkinson, R. C., & Shiffrin, R. M. Human memory: A proposed system and its control processes. In K. W. Spence and J. T. Spence (Eds.), *The psychology of learning and motivation* (Vol. 2). New York: Academic Press, 1968.

Atkinson, R. C., & Shiffrin, R. M. The control of short-term memory. *Scientific American,* 1971, *225,* 82–90.

Attneave, F. Transfer of class experience with a class-scheme to identification learning of patterns and shapes. *Journal of Experimental Psychology,* 1957, *54,* 81–88.

Ayllon, T., & Azrin, N. H. Punishment as a discriminative stimulus and conditioned reinforcer with humans. *Journal of the Experimental Analysis of Behavior,* 1966, *9,* 411–419.

Azrin, N. H. Some effects of immediate and nonimmediate punishment. *Journal of Psychology,* 1956, *42,* 3–21.

Azrin, N. H. Effects of punishment intensity during variable-interval reinforcement. *Journal of the Experimental Analysis of Behavior,* 1960, *3,* 123–142.

Azrin, N. H. Punishment of elicited aggression. *Journal of the Experimental Analysis of Behavior,* 1970, *14,* 7–10.

Azrin, N. H., Hake, D. F., Holtz, W. C., & Hutchinson, W. R. Motivational aspects of escape from punishment. *Journal of the Experimental Analysis of Behavior,* 1965, *8,* 31–44.

Azrin, N. H., & Holz, W. C. Punishment. In W. R. Honig (Ed.), *Operant behavior: Areas of research and application.* New York: Appleton-Century-Crofts, 1966.

Azrin, N. H., Holz, W. C., & Hake, D. Fixed-ratio punishment. *Journal of the Experimental Analysis of Behavior,* 1963, *6,* 141–148.

Bacon, W. E. Partial reinforcement extinction effect following different amounts of training. *Journal of Comparative and Physiological Psychology,* 1962, *55,* 998–1003.

Baddeley, A. D. The influence of acoustic and semantic similarity on long-term memory for word sequences. *Quarterly Journal of Experimental Psychology,* 1966, *18,* 302–309.

Baddeley, A. D., & Dale, H. C. The effect of semantic similarity on retroactive interference in long- and short-term memory. *Journal of Verbal Learning and Verbal Behavior,* 1966, *5,* 417–420.

Baenninger, R., & Grossman, J. C. Some effects of punishment on pain-elicited aggression. *Journal of the Experimental Analysis of Behavior,* 1969, *12,* 1017–1022.

Bahrick, H. P. Measurement of memory by prompted recall. *Journal of Experimental Psychology,* 1969, *79,* 213–219.

Banks, R. K., & Vogel-Sprout, M. Effects of delayed punishment on an immediately rewarded response in humans; *Journal of Ex-*

perimental Psychology, 1965, *70,* 357–359.
Barnes, J. M., & Underwood, B. J. "Fate" of first-list associations in transfer theory. *Journal of Experimental Psychology,* 1959, *58,* 97–105.
Barnett, S. A. *The rat: A study of behavior.* Chicago: Aldine, 1963.
Baron, A. Delayed punishment of a runway response. *Journal of Comparative and Physiological Psychology,* 1965, *60,* 131–134.
Barondes, S. H., & Cohen, H. D. Comparative effects of cyclohexamide and puromycin on cerebral protein synthesis and consolidation of memory in mice. *Brain Research,* 1967, *4,* 44–51.
Barondes, S. H., & Jarvik, M. E. The influence of actinomycin-D on brain RNA synthesis and on memory. *Journal of Neurochemistry,* 1964, *11,* 187–195.
Barry, H., III, Wagner, A. R., & Miller, N. E. Effects of alcohol and amobarbital on performance inhibited by experimental extinction. *Journal of Comparative and Physiological Psychology,* 1962, *55,* 464–468.
Bartlett, F. C. *Remembering.* London: Cambridge University Press, 1932.
Battig, W. F. Paired associate learning. In T. R. Dixon & D. L. Horton (Eds.), *Verbal behavior and general behavior theory.* Englewood Cliffs, N.J.: Prentice-Hall, 1968.
Beach, F. A., Conovitz, M. W., Steinberg, F., & Goldstein, A.C. Experimental inhibition and restoration of mating behavior in male rats. *Journal of Genetic Psychology,* 1956, *89,* 165–181.
Beck, S. B. Eyelid conditioning as a function of CS intensity, UCS intensity, and manifest anxiety scale score. *Journal of Experimental Psychology,* 1963, *66,* 429–438.
Behrend, E. R., & Bitterman, M.E. Sidman avoidance in the fish. *Journal of the Experimental Analysis of Behavior,* 1963, *13,* 229–242.
Bennett, E. L., Rosenzweig, M. R., & Diamond, M. C. Rat brain: Effects of environmental enrichment on wet and dry weights. *Science,* 1968, *163,* 825–826.
Bennett, E. L., Rosenzweig, M. R., & Diamond, M. C. Time courses of effects of differential experience on brain measures and behavior of rats. In W. L. Byrne (Ed.), *Molecular approaches to learning and memory.* New York: Academic Press, 1969.
Bennett, T. L. Evidence against the theory that hippocampal theta is a correlate of voluntary movement. *Communications in Behavioral Biology,* 1969, *4,* 165–169.
Bennett, T. L. Hippocampal EEG correlates of behavior. *Electroencephalography and Clinical Neurophysiology,* 1970, *28,* 17–23.
Bennett, T. L. Hippocampal theta activity and behavior—A review. *Communications in Behavioral Biology,* 1971, *6,* 37–48.
Bennett, T. L. The effects of centrally blocking hippocampal theta activity on learning and retention. *Behavioral Biology,* 1973, *9,* 541–552.
Bennett, T. L. *Brain and Behavior.* Monterey, Calif.: Brooks/Cole, 1977.
Bennett, T. L., Anton, B. S., & Levitt, L. Stimulus relevancy and transfer of perceptual learning. *Psychonomic Science,* 1971, *25,* 159–160.
Bennett, T. L., & Ellis, H. C. Tactual–kinesthetic feedback from manipulation of visual forms and nondifferential reinforcement in transfer of perceptual learning. *Journal of Experimental Psychology,* 1968, *77,* 495–500.
Bennett, T. L., & Gottfried, J. Hippocampal theta and response inhibition. *Electroencephalography and Clinical Neurophysiology,* 1970, *29,* 196–200.
Bennett, T. L., Hébert, P. N., & Moss, D. E. Hippocampal theta activity and the attention component of discrimination learning. *Behavioral Biology,* 1973, *8,* 173–181.
Bennett, T. L., Nunn, P. J., & Inman, D. P. Effects of scopolamine on hippocampal theta and correlated discrimination performance. *Physiology and Behavior,* 1971, *7,* 451–454.
Berger, H. Uber des Elektrenkephalogramm des Menschen. *Archiv für Psychiatrie und Nervenkrankheiten,* 1929, *87,* 527–570.
Berlyne, D. E. The influence of the albedo and complexity of stimuli on visual fixation in the human infant. *British Journal of Psychology,* 1958, *49,* 315–318.
Berlyne, D. E. The reward-value of indifferent stimulation. In J. T. Tapp (Ed.), *Reinforcement and behavior.* New York: Academic Press, 1969.
Berry, F. M., Joubert, C. E., & Baumeister, A. A. Stimulus selection and meaningfulness at different stages of paired associate learning. *Journal of Experimental Psychology,* 1971, *95,* 189–194.
Bersh, P. J. The influence of two variables upon the establishment of a secondary reinforcer for operant responses. *Journal of Experimental Psychology,* 1951, *41,* 62–73.
Bertsch, G. J. Punishment of consummatory and instrumental behavior: Effects on licking and bar pressing in rats. *Journal of Comparative*

and Physiological Psychology, 1972, *78,* 478–484.

Bessemer, D. W., & Stollnitz, F. Retention of discriminations and an analysis of learning set. In A. M. Schrier & F. Stollnitz (Eds.), *Behavior of nonhuman primates* (Vol. 4). New York: Academic Press, 1971.

Bevan, W. The contextual basis of behavior. *American Psychologist,* 1968, *23,* 701–714.

Bilodeau, E. A. Experimental interference with primary associates and their subsequent recovery with rest. *Journal of Experimental Psychology,* 1967, *73,* 328–332.

Birch, H. G., & Lefford, A. Intersensory development in children. *Monographs of the Society for Research in Child Development,* 1963, *28,* (5, Serial No. 89).

Birge, J. S. *The role of verbal responses in transfer.* Unpublished doctoral dissertation, Yale University, 1941.

Birnbaum, I. M. Free-recall learning as a function of prior-list organization. *Journal of Verbal Learning and Verbal Behavior,* 1968, *7,* 1037–1042.

Bitterman, M. E. Phyletic differences in learning. *American Psychologist,* 1965, *20,* 396–410.

Bitterman, M. E., & Schoel, W. M. Instrumental learning in animals: Parameters of reinforcement. *Annual Review of Psychology,* 1970, *21,* 367–436.

Björkman, M., & Ottander, C. Improvement of discriminative ability by training. *Reports from the psychological laboratories* (No. 66). Stockholm: University of Stockholm, 1959.

Black, A. H., & Morse, P. Avoidance learning in dogs without a warning stimulus. *Journal of the Experimental Analysis of Behavior,* 1961, *4,* 17–23.

Black, M., & Suboski, M. D. Incubation and ECS-produced gradients in one-trial and multitrial discriminated-avoidance conditioning in rats. *Journal of Comparative and Physiological Psychology,* 1971, *74,* 325–330.

Black, R. W. Incentive motivation and the parameters of reward in instrumental conditioning. In W. J. Arnold & D. Levine (Eds.), *Nebraska Symposium on Motivation.* Lincoln: University of Nebraska Press, 1969.

Black, R. W., & Ekstand, P. Instrumental and consummatory behavior as a function of length of reward period. *Psychonomic Science,* 1964, *1,* 301–302.

Boe, E. E. The effect of punishment duration and intensity on the extinction of an instrumental response. *Journal of Experimental Psychology,* 1966, *72,* 125–131.

Bolinger, D. The atomization of meaning. *Language,* 1965, *41,* 555–573.

Bond, E. K. Perception of form by the human infant. *Psychological Bulletin,* 1972, *77,* 225–245.

Bonner, J. Molecular biological approaches to the study of memory. In J. Gaito (Ed.), *Macromolecules and behavior.* New York: Appleton-Century-Crofts, 1966.

Boring, E. G. *A history of experimental psychology.* New York: Appleton-Century-Crofts, 1950.

Boroczi, G., Storms, L. H., & Broen, W. E. Response suppression and recovery of responding at different deprivation levels as functions of intensity and duration of punishment. *Journal of Comparative and Physiological Psychology,* 1964, *58,* 456–459.

Bourne, L. E., Jr. *Human conceptual behavior.* Boston: Allyn & Bacon, 1966.

Bourne, L. E., Jr. Learning and the utilization of conceptual rules. In B. Kleinmuntz (Ed.), *Memory and the structure of concepts.* New York: Wiley, 1967.

Bourne, L. E., Jr. Knowing and using concepts. *Psychological Review,* 1970, *77*(6), 546–556.

Bourne, L. E., Jr., Ekstrand, B. R., & Dominowski, R. L. *The psychology of thinking.* Englewood Cliffs, N.J.: Prentice-Hall, 1971.

Bousfield, A. K., & Bousfield, W. A. Measurement of clustering and of sequential constancies in repeated free recall. *Psychological Reports,* 1966, *19,* 935–942.

Bousfield, W. A. The occurrence of clustering in the recall of randomly arranged associates. *Journal of General Psychology,* 1953, *49,* 229–240.

Bousfield, W. A., Whitmarsh, G. A., & Berkowitz, H. Partial response identities in associative clustering. *Journal of General Psychology,* 1960, *63,* 233–238.

Bousfield, W. A., & Wicklund, D. A. Rhyme as a determinant of clustering. *Psychonomic Science,* 1969, *16,* 183–184.

Bower, G. H. Partial and correlated reward in escape learning. *Journal of Experimental Psychology,* 1960, *59,* 126–130.

Bower, G. H. A contrast effect in differential conditioning. *Journal of Experimental Psychology,* 1961, *62,* 196–199.

Bower, G. H. A multicomponent theory of the memory trace. In K. W. Spence & J. T. Spence (Eds.), *The psychology of learning and motivation* (Vol. 1). New York: Academic Press, 1967.

Bower, G. H. Analysis of a mnemonic device. *American Scientist,* 1970, *58,* 496–510. (a)
Bower, G. H. Organizational factors in memory. *Cognitive Psychology,* 1970, *1,* 18–46. (b)
Bower, G. H. Mental imagery and associative learning. In L. Gregg (Ed.), *Cognition in learning and memory.* New York: Wiley, 1972. (a)
Bower, G. H. Stimulus sampling theory of encoding variability. In A. W. Melton & E. Martin (Eds.), *Coding processes in human memory.* Washington, D.C.: Winston, 1972. (b)
Bower, G. H., & Bolton, L. Why are rhymes easy to learn? *Journal of Experimental Psychology,* 1969, *82,* 453–461.
Bower, G. H., Fowler, H., & Trapold, M. A. Escape learning as a function of amount of shock reduction. *Journal of Experimental Psychology,* 1959, *58,* 482–484.
Bower, G. H., & Lesgold, A. M. Organization as a determinant of part-to-whole transfer in free recall. *Journal of Verbal Learning and Verbal Behavior,* 1969, *8,* 501–506.
Bower, G. H., & Springston, F. Pauses as recoding points in letter series. *Journal of Experimental Psychology,* 1970, *83,* 421–430.
Bower, G. H., & Winzenz, D. Group structure, coding, and memory for digit series. *Journal of Experimental Psychology Monographs,* 1969, *80,* (2, Pt. 2), 1–17.
Bower, T. G. R. The object in the world of the infant. *Scientific American,* 1971, *225,* 30–38.
Braine, M. D. S. The autogeny of English phrase structure: The first phase. *Language,* 1963, *39,* 1–13.
Bransford, J. D., & Franks, J. J. The abstraction of linguistic ideas. *Cognitive Psychology,* 1971, *2,* 331–350.
Brattgård, S. O. The importance of adequate stimulation for the chemical composition of retinal ganglion cells during early postnatal development. *Acta Radiologica,* 1952, *96,* 1–80. (Supplement)
Brazier, M. A. B. *A history of the electrical activity of the brain: The first half-century.* London: Pitmar, 1961.
Breland, K., & Breland, M. The misbehavior of organisms. *American Psychologist,* 1961, *16,* 681–684.
Breland, K., & Breland, M. *Animal behavior.* New York: Macmillan, 1966.
Brennan, W. M., Ames, E. W., & Moore, R. W. Age differences in infants' attention to patterns of different complexities. *Science,* 1966, *151,* 354–366.
Broadbent, D. E. A mechanical model for human attention and immediate memory. *Psychological Review,* 1957, *64,* 205–215.
Broadbent, D. E. Flow of information within the organism. *Journal of Verbal Learning and Verbal Behavior,* 1963, *2,* 34–39.
Broadbent, D. E. *Decision and stress.* New York: Academic Press, 1971.
Broadhurst, P. L. Emotionality and the Yerkes–Dodson law. *Journal of Experimental Psychology,* 1957, *54,* 345–352.
Broen, W. E., Jr., Stroms, L. H., & Goldberg, D. H. Decreased discrimination as a function of increased drive. *Journal of Abnormal and Social Psychology,* 1963, *67,* 266–273.
Brown, J. Some tests of the decay theory of immediate memory. *Quarterly Journal of Experimental Psychology,* 1958, *10,* 12–21.
Brown, J. S. Generalization and discrimination. In D. I. Mostofsky (Ed.), *Stimulus generalization.* Stanford, Calif.: Stanford University Press, 1965.
Brown, J. S., & Jacobs, A. The role of fear in the motivation and acquisition of responses. *Journal of Experimental Psychology,* 1949, *39,* 747–759.
Brown, P. L., & Jenkins, H. M. Auto-shaping of the pigeon's key-peck. *Journal of the Experimental Analysis of Behavior,* 1968, *11,* 1–8.
Brown, R. T., & Wagner, A. R. Resistance to punishment and extinction following training with shock or nonreinforcement. *Journal of Experimental Psychology,* 1964, *68,* 503–507.
Brown, R. W., & McNeill, D. The "tip of the tongue" phenomenon. *Journal of Verbal Learning and Verbal Behavior,* 1966, *5,* 325–337.
Bruce, R. W. Conditions of transfer of training. *Journal of Experimental Psychology,* 1933, *16,* 343–361.
Buckholtz, N. S., & Bowman, R. E. Incubation and retrograde amnesia studied with various ECS intensities and durations. *Physiology and Behavior,* 1972, *8,* 113–117.
Bugelski, B. R. Images as mediators in one-trial paired-associate learning: II. Self-timing in successive lists. *Journal of Experimental Psychology,* 1968, *77,* 328–334.
Bugelski, B. R. Words and things and images. *American Psychologist,* 1970, *25,* 1002–1012.
Bugelski, B. R., & Cadwallader, T. C. A reappraisal of the transfer and retroaction surface.

Journal of Experimental Psychology, 1956, *52,* 360–366.

Bugelski, B. R., & Scharlock, D. P. An experimental demonstration of unconscious mediated association. *Journal of Experimental Psychology,* 1952, *44,* 334–338.

Bunch, M. E. Cumulative transfer of training under different temporal conditions. *Journal of Comparative Psychology,* 1944, *37,* 265–272.

Bunch, M. E. Experimental extinction in learning and memory. *Journal of General Psychology,* 1963, *69,* 275–291.

Bunch, M. E., & McCraven, V. Temporal course of transfer in the learning of memory material. *Journal of Comparative Psychology,* 1938, *25,* 481–496.

Bureš, J., & Burešová, O. Cortical spreading depression as a memory disturbing factor. *Journal of Comparative and Physiological Psychology,* 1963, *56,* 268–272.

Burns, B. D. *The mammalian cerebral cortex.* London: Arnold, 1958.

Burt, D. E., & Wike, E. L. Effects of alternating partial reinforcement and alternating delay of reinforcement on a runway response. *Psychological Reports,* 1963, *13,* 439–442.

Camp, D. S., Raymond, G. H., & Church, R. M. Temporal relationships between response and punishment. *Journal of Experimental Psychology,* 1967, *74,* 114–123.

Campbell, D. T., & Krael, T. P. Transposition strength as a function of drive level and amount of drive reduction. *Journal of Experimental Psychology,* 1953, *45,* 97–101.

Campbell, D. T., & Krael, T. P. Transposition away from a rewarded stimulus card to a non-rewarded one as a function of a shift in background. *Journal of Comparative and Physiological Psychology,* 1958, *51,* 592–595.

Campbell, P. E., Crumbaugh, C. M., Rhodus, D. M., & Knouse, S. B. Magnitude of partial reward and amount of training in the rat: A hypothesis of sequential effects. *Journal of Comparative and Physiological Psychology,* 1971, *75,* 120–128.

Capaldi, E. D. Simultaneous shifts in reward magnitude and level of food deprivation. *Psychonomic Science,* 1971, *23,* 357–359.

Capaldi, E. D. Enhancement of rats' single-alternation performance by high food deprivation. *Psychonomic Science,* 1972, *26,* 10–12.

Capaldi, E. J. Partial reinforcement: A hypothesis of sequential effects. *Psychological Review,* 1966, *73,* 459–477.

Capaldi, E. J. A sequential hypothesis of instrumental learning. In K. W. Spence & J. T. Spence (Eds.), *The psychology of learning and motivation* (Vol. 1). New York: Academic Press, 1967.

Capaldi, E. J. An analysis of the role of reward and reward magnitude in instrumental learning. In J. H. Reynierse (Ed.), *Current issues in animal learning.* Lincoln: University of Nebraska Press, 1970.

Capaldi, E. J. Successive negative contrast effect: Intertrial interval, type of shift, and four sources of generalization decrement. *Journal of Experimental Psychology,* 1972, *96,* 433–438.

Capaldi, E. J., & Capaldi, E. D. Magnitude of partial reward, irregular reward schedules, and a 24-hour ITI: A test of several hypotheses. *Journal of Comparative and Physiological Psychology,* 1970, *72,* 203–209.

Capaldi, E. J., & Lynch, D. Repeated shifts in reward magnitude: Evidence in favor of an associational and absolute (noncontextual) interpretation. *Journal of Experimental Psychology,* 1967, *75,* 226–235.

Capaldi, E. J., & Spivey, J. E. Stimulus consequences of reinforcement and nonreinforcement: Stimulus traces or memory. *Psychonomic Science,* 1964, *1,* 403–404.

Capaldi, E. J., & Stanley, L. R. Temporal properties of reinforcement aftereffects. *Journal of Experimental Psychology,* 1963, *65,* 169–175.

Capaldi, E. J., & Waters, R. W. Conditioning and nonconditioning interpretations of small trial phenomena. *Journal of Experimental Psychology,* 1970, *84,* 518–522.

Carlson, J. J., & Black, A. H. Traumatic avoidance learning: The effects of preventing escape responses. *Canadian Journal of Psychology,* 1960, *14,* 21–28.

Carlton, P. L., & Markiewicz, B. Studies on the physiological bases of memory. In E. Stellar & J. M. Sprague (Eds.), *Progress in physiological psychology* (Vol. 5). New York: Academic Press, 1973.

Carmichael, L., Hogan, H. P., & Walter, A. A. An experimental study of the effect of language on the reproduction of visually perceived form. *Journal of Experimental Psychology,* 1932, *15,* 73–86.

Castellucci, V., & Goldring, S. Contribution to steady potential shifts of slow depolarization in cells presumed to be glia. *Electroencephalography and Clinical Neurophysiology,*

1970, *28,* 109–118.

Caton, R. The electrical current of the brain. *British Medical Journal,* 1875, *2,* 278–296.

Caul, W. F., & Barrett, R. J. Electroconvulsive shock effects on conditioned heart rate and suppression of drinking. *Physiology and Behavior,* 1972, *8,* 287–290.

Cerletti, V., & Bini, L. Electric shock treatment. *Bulletin of the Academy of Medicine of Rome,* 1938, *64,* 36.

Cermak, L. S. *Human memory: Research and theory.* New York: Ronald Press, 1972.

Chapouthier, G. Behavioral studies of the molecular basis of memory. In J. A. Deutsch (Ed.), *The physiological basis of memory.* New York: Academic Press, 1973.

Chase, S. *The tyranny of words.* New York: Harcourt Brace Jovanovich, 1938.

Cherkin, A. Kinetics of memory consolidation: Role of amnesic treatment parameters. *Proceedings of the National Academy of Science,* 1969, *63,* 1094–1101.

Cherry, E. C. Some experiments on the recognition of speech with one and two ears. *Journal of the Acoustical Society of America,* 1953, *25,* 975–979.

Cheselden, W. An account of some observations made by a young gentleman who was born blind, or lost his sight so early, that he had no remembrance of ever having seen, and was couched between 13 and 14 years of age. *Philosophical Transactions of the Royal Society,* 1728, *35,* 447–450. (a)

Cheselden, W. An explication of the instruments used, in a new operation on the eyes. *Philosophical Transactions of the Royal Society,* 1728, *35,* 451–452. (b)

Chevalier, J. A. Permanence of amnesia after a single posttrial electroconvulsive seizure. *Journal of Comparative and Physiological Psychology,* 1965, *59,* 125–127.

Chomsky, N. *Syntactic structures.* The Hague: Mouton, 1957.

Chomsky, N. Verbal behavior (a review of Skinner's book). *Language,* 1959, *35,* 26–58.

Chomsky, N. *Aspects of the theory of syntax.* Cambridge, Mass.: MIT Press, 1965.

Chomsky, N. *Language and mind.* New York: Harcourt Brace Jovanovich, 1968.

Chomsky, N. Deep structure, surface structure, and semantic interpretation. In D. Steinberg & L. Jakobovits (Eds.), *Semantics: An interdisciplinary reader in philosophy, linguistics, anthropology, and psychology.* London: Cambridge University Press, 1971.

Chomsky, N. *Language and mind.* New York: Harcourt Brace Jovanovich, 1972.

Chorover, S. L., & Schiller, P. H. Short-term retrograde amnesia in rats. *Journal of Comparative and Physiological Psychology,* 1965, *59,* 73–78.

Chorover, S. L., & Schiller, P. H. Reexamination of prolonged retrograde amnesia in one-trial learning. *Journal of Comparative and Physiological Psychology,* 1966, *61,* 34–41.

Church, R. M. The varied effects of punishment on behavior. *Psychological Review,* 1963, *70,* 369–402.

Church, R. M. Response suppression. In B. A. Campbell & R. M. Church (Eds.), *Punishment and aversive behavior.* New York: Appleton-Century-Crofts, 1969.

Church, R. M., Raymond, G. A., & Beauchamp, R. D. Response suppression as a function of intensity and duration of a punishment. *Journal of Comparative and Physiological Psychology,* 1967, *63,* 39–44.

Church, R. M., Wooten, C. L., & Matthews, T. J. Contingency between a response and an aversive event in the rat. *Journal of Comparative and Physiological Psychology,* 1970, *72,* 476–485.

Cieutat, V. J., Stockwell, F. E., & Noble, C. E. The interaction of ability and amount of practice with stimulus and response meaningfulness (*m, m'*) in paired associate learning. *Journal of Experimental Psychology,* 1958, *56,* 193–202.

Cilluffo, A., & Black, R. W. Runway performance maintained by multiple rewards per trial. *Psychonomic Science,* 1970, *19,* 19–21.

Clark, H. J. Recognition memory for random shapes as a function of complexity, association value, and delay. *Journal of Experimental Psychology,* 1965, *69,* 590–595.

Cofer, C. N. Does conceptual organization influence the amount retained in immediate free recall? In B. Kleinmuntz (Ed.), *Concepts and the structure of memory.* New York: Wiley, 1967.

Cofer, C. N. Properties of verbal materials and verbal learning. In J. W. Kling & L. A. Riggs (Eds.), *Woodworth and Schlosberg's experimental psychology.* New York: Holt, Rinehart and Winston, 1971.

Cofer, C. N. Constructive processes in memory. *American Scientist,* 1973, *61,* 537–543.

Cofer, C. N., & Bruce, D. R. Form-class as the basis for clustering in the recall of nonassociated words. *Journal of Verbal Learning and Verbal Behavior,* 1965, *4,* 386–389.

Cofer, C. N., Bruce, D. R., & Reicher, G. M.

Clustering in free recall as a function of certain methodological variations. *Journal of Experimental Psychology,* 1966, *71,* 858–866.

Cofer, C. N., Chmielewski, D. L., & Brockway, J. F. Constructive processes and the structure of human memory. In C. N. Cofer (Ed.), *The structure of human memory.* San Francisco: Freeman, 1975.

Cohen, H. D., & Barondes, S. H. Further studies of learning and memory after intracerebral actinomycin-D. *Journal of Neurochemistry,* 1966, *13,* 207–211.

Cohen, H. D., Erwin, F., & Barondes, S. H. Puromycin and cyclohexamide: Different effects on hippocampal electrical activity. *Science,* 1966, *154,* 1557–1558.

Colegate, R. L., & Eriksen, C. W. Form of redundancy as a determinant of tachistoscopic word recognition. *Perception and Psychophysics,* 1972, *12,* 477–481.

Collins, A. M., & Loftus, E. F. A spreading-activation theory of semantic processing. *Psychological Review,* 1975, *82,* 407–428.

Collins, A. M., & Quillian, M. R. Retrieval time from semantic memory. *Journal of Verbal Learning and Verbal Behavior,* 1969, *8,* 240–247.

Collins, A. M., & Quillian, M. R. How to make a language user. In E. Tulving & W. Donaldson (Eds.), *Organization of memory.* New York: Academic Press, 1972.

Conrad, C. Cognitive economy in semantic memory. *Journal of Experimental Psychology,* 1972, *92,* 149–154.

Conrad, R. Acoustic confusions in immediate memory. *British Journal of Psychology,* 1974, *55,* 75–84.

Coons, F. E., & Miller, N. E. Conflict vs. consolidation of memory traces to explain "retrograde amnesia" produced by ECS. *Journal of Comparative and Physiological Psychology,* 1960, *53,* 524–531.

Craik, F. I. M., & Lockhart, R. S. Levels of processing: A framework for memory research. *Journal of Verbal Learning and Verbal Behavior,* 1972, *11,* 671–684.

Crespi, L. P. Quantitative variation of incentive and performance in the white rat. *American Journal of Psychology,* 1942, *55,* 467–517.

Crespi, L. P. Amount of reinforcement and level of performance. *Psychological Review,* 1944, *51,* 341–357.

Cross, H., Halcomb, C. G., & Matter, W. W. Imprinting or exposure in rats given early auditory stimulation. *Psychonomic Science,* 1967, *7,* 223–234.

Dale, H. C. A., & McGlaughlin, A. Evidence of acoustic coding in long-term memory. *Quarterly Journal of Experimental Psychology,* 1971, *23,* 1–7.

Dallett, K. M. The transfer surface re-examined. *Journal of Verbal Learning and Verbal Behavior,* 1962, *1,* 91–94.

Dallett, K. M. Number of categories and category information in free recall. *Journal of Experimental Psychology,* 1964, *68,* 1–12.

Dallett, K. M. A transfer surface in which second-list S–R pairings do not correspond to first-list pairings. *Journal of Verbal Learning and Verbal Behavior,* 1965, *4,* 528–534.

Daly, H. B. Learning of a hurdle-jump response to escape cues paired with reduced reward or frustrative nonreward. *Journal of Experimental Psychology,* 1969, *79,* 146–157. (a)

Daly, H. B. Supplementary reports: Is instrumental responding necessary for nonreward following reward to be frustrating? *Journal of Experimental Psychology,* 1969, *80,* 186–187. (b)

Daly, H. B. Learning to escape cues paired with reward reduction following single-or-multiple-pellet rewards. *Psychonomic Science,* 1972, *26,* 49–52.

Daly, H. B., & McCroskery, J. H. Acquisition of a bar-press response to escape frustrative nonreward and reduced reward. *Journal of Experimental Psychology,* 1973, *98,* 109–112.

Daniel, T. C. The nature of the effect of verbal labels on recognition memory for form. *Journal of Experimental Psychology,* 1972, *96,* 152–157.

Daniel, T. C., & Ellis, H. C. Stimulus codability and long-term recognition memory for visual form. *Journal of Experimental Psychology,* 1972, *93,* 83–89.

Darwin, C. A. *The origin of species by means of natural selection.* London: Murray, 1859.

Davenport, R. K., & Menzel, E. W. Stereotyped behavior of the infant chimpanzee. *Archives of General Psychiatry,* 1963, *8,* 99–104.

Davenport, R. K., & Rogers, C. M. Intellectual performance of differentially reared chimpanzees: I. Delayed response. *American Journal of Mental Deficiency,* 1968, *72,* 674–680.

Davenport, R. K., Rogers, C. M., & Menzel, E. W. Intellectual performance of differentially reared chimpanzees: II. Discrimination-learning set. *American Journal of Mental Deficiency,* 1969, *73,* 963–969.

Davis, G. A. *Psychology of problem solving: Theory and practice.* New York: Basic Books, 1973.

Debold, R. C., Firshein, W., Carrier, S. C., III, & Leaf, R. C. Changes in RNA in the occipital cortex of rats as a function of light and dark during rearing. *Psychonomic Science,* 1967, *7,* 379–380.

Del Castillo, D. M., & Ellis, H. C. The role of response-produced cues in paired-associate transfer as a function of stimulus similarity. *Psychonomic Science,* 1968, *10,* 197–198.

Del Castillo, D. M., & Gumenik, W. E. Sequential memory for familiar and unfamiliar forms. *Journal of Experimental Psychology,* 1972, *95,* 90–96.

Delgado, J. M. R., Johnston, V. S., Wallace, J. D., & Bradley, R. J. Operant conditioning of amygdala spindling in the free chimpanzee. *Brain Research,* 1970, *23,* 347–362.

Dember, W. N. *The psychology of perception.* New York: Holt, Rinehart and Winston, 1960.

Dempster, F. N., & Rohwer, W. D., Jr. Component analysis of the elaborative encoding effect in paired-associate learning. *Journal of Experimental Psychology,* 1974, *103,* 400–408.

Denenberg, V. H. An attempt to isolate critical periods of development in the rat. *Journal of Comparative and Physiological Psychology,* 1962, *55,* 813–815.

Denenberg, V. H. Stimulation in infancy, emotional reactivity, and exploratory behavior. In D. C. Glass (Ed.), *Neurophysiology and emotion.* New York: Rockefeller University Press and Russell Sage Foundation, 1967.

Denenberg, V. H., & Karas, G. G. Interactive effects of age and duration of infantile experience on adult learning. *Psychological Reports,* 1960, *7,* 313–322.

Denenberg, V. H., & Morton, J. R. C. Effects of preweaning and post-weaning manipulations upon problem-solving behavior. *Journal of Comparative and Physiological Psychology, 1962, 55,* 1096–1098.

Denenberg, V. H., & Morton, J. R. C. Infantile stimulation, prepuberal sexual–social interaction and emotionality. *Animal Behavior,* 1964, *12,* 11–13.

Denenberg, V. H., & Smith, S. A. Effects of infantile stimulation and age upon behavior. *Journal of Comparative and Physiological Psychology,* 1963, *56,* 307–312.

Denenberg, V. H, Woodcock, J. M., & Rosenberg, K. M. Long-term effects of preweaning and postweaning free-environment experience on the rat's problem solving behavior. *Journal of Comparative Physiological Psychology,* 1968, *66,* 533–535.

Denenberg, V. H., Wyly, M. V., Burns, J. K., & Zarrow, M. X. Behavioral effects of handling rabbits in infancy. *Physiology and Behavior,* 1973, *10,* 1001–1004.

Diamond, M. C. Extensive cortical depth measurements and neuron size increases in the cortex of environmentally enriched rats. *Journal of Comparative Neurology,* 1967, *131,* 357–364.

Diamond, M. C., Law, F., Rhodes, H., Lindner, B., Rosenzweig, M. R., Krech, D., & Bennett, E. L. Increases in cortical depth and glia numbers in rats subjected to enriched environment. *Journal of Comparative Neurology,* 1966, *128,* 117–125.

Diamond, M. C., Rosenzweig, M. R., & Bennett, E. L. Unpublished data cited by Rosenzweig, M. R., in Effects of environment on development of brain and behavior. In E. Tobach, L. R. Aronson, & E. Shaw (Eds.), *The biopsychology of development.* New York: Academic Press, 1971.

DiCara, L. V., Braun, J. J., & Pappas, B. A. Classical conditioning and instrumental learning of cardiac and gastrointestinal responses following removal of neocortex in the rat. *Journal of Comparative and Physiological Psychology,* 1970, *73,* 208–216.

DiCara, L. V., & Miller, N. E. Changes in heart-rate instrumentally learned by curarized rats as avoidance responses. *Journal of Comparative and Physiological Psychology,* 1968, *65,* 8–12. (a)

DiCara, L. V., & Miller, N. E. Instrumental learning of systolic blood pressure responses by curarized rats: Dissociation of cardiac and vascular changes. *Psychosomatic Medicine, 1968, 30,* 489–494. (b)

DiCara, L. V., & Miller, N. E. Instrumental learning of vasomoter responses by rats: Learning to respond differentially in the two ears. *Science,* 1968, *159,* 1485–1486. (c)

Dingman, W., & Sporn, M. B. The incorporation of 8-azaguanine into rat brain RNA and its effect on maze learning by the rat: An inquiry into the biochemical bases of memory. *Journal of Psychiatric Research,* 1961, *1,* 1–11.

Dingman, W., & Sporn, M. B. Molecular theories of memory. *Science,* 1964, *144,* 26–29.

Dodson, J. D. The relation of strength of stimulus to rapidity of habit formation in the kitten. *Journal of Animal Behavior,* 1915, *5,* 330–336.

Dolinsky, R. Clustering and free recall with alternative organizational cues. *Journal of Experimental Psychology,* 1972, *95,* 159–163.

Dollard, J., & Miller, N. E. *Personality and psychotherapy.* New York: McGraw-Hill, 1950.

Dominowski, E. L., & Galdin, H. Imagery and paired-associate learning. *Canadian Journal of Psychology,* 1968, *22,* 336–348.

Douglas, R. J. The hippocampus and behavior. *Psychological Bulletin,* 1967, *67,* 416–442.

Douglas, R. J., & Pribram, K. H. Learning and limbic lesions. *Neuropsychologia,* 1966, *4,* 197–220.

Douglas, W. W. Autocoids. In L. S. Goodman & A. Gillman (Eds.), *Pharmacological basis of therapeutics.* New York: Macmillan, 1970.

Doyle, G., & Yule, E. P. Grooming activities and freezing behavior in relation to emotionality in albino rats. *Animal Behavior,* 1959, *7,* 18–22.

Dukes, W. F., & Bevan, W. Stimulus variation and repetition in the acquisition of naming responses. *Journal of Experimental Psychology,* 1967, *74,* 178–181.

Duncan, C. P. The retroactive effect of electroshock on learning. *Journal of Comparative and Physiological Psychology,* 1949, *42,* 32–44.

Dunker, K. On problem solving. *Psychological Monographs,* 1945, *58* (5, Whole No. 270).

Dyck, D. G., Mellgren, R. L., & Seybert, J. A. Within-subject partial reinforcement effects: Differential extinction following nondifferential percentage of reinforcement in acquisition. *Journal of Experimental Psychology,* 1973, *97,* 391–394.

Earhard, B., & Mandler, G. Mediated associations: Paradigms, controls, and mechanisms. *Canadian Journal of Psychology,* 1965, *19,* 346–378.

Earhard, M. Subjective organization and list organization as determinants of free-recall and serial-recall memorization. *Journal of Verbal Learning and Verbal Behavior,* 1967, *6,* 501–507.

Ebbinghaus, H. *Memory* (H. A. Ruger & C. E. Bussenuis, trans.). New York: Dover Books, 1964. (Originally published, 1885)

Eccles, J. C. *The neurophysical basis of mind.* Oxford: Clarendon Press, 1953.

Ehrenfreund, D. Experimental test of the continuity theory of discrimination learning with pattern vision. *Journal of Comparative and Physiological Psychology,* 1948, *41,* 408–422.

Ekstrand, B. R. Backward associations. *Psychological Bulletin,* 1966, *65,* 50–64.

Ekstrand, B. R. Effects of sleep on memory. *Journal of Experimental Psychology,* 1967, *75,* 64–72.

Ekstrand, B. R. To sleep, perchance to dream (about why we forget). In C. P. Duncan, L. Seechrest, & A. W. Melton (Eds.), *Human memory: Festschrift in honor of Benton J. Underwood.* New York: Appleton-Century-Crofts, 1972.

Ekstrand, B. R., Wallace, W. P., & Underwood, B. J. A frequency theory of verbal discrimination learning. *Psychological Review,* 1966, *73,* 566–578.

Elazar, Z., & Adey, W. R. Spectral analysis of low frequency components in the electrical activity of the hippocampus during learning. *Electroencephalography and Clinical Neurophysiology, 1967, 23,* 225–240.

Ellen, P., & Aitken, W. C., Jr. Analysis of DRL responding by rats with septal damage. *Physiological Psychology,* 1973, *1,* 16–20.

Ellen, P., & Braggio, J. T. Reactions to DRL schedule changes in rats with septal damage. *Physiological Psychology,* 1973, *1,* 267–272.

Ellen, P., & Butter, J. External cue control of DRL performance in rats with septal lesions. *Physiology and Behavior,* 1969, *4,* 1–6.

Ellen, P., Wilson, A. S., & Powell, E. W. Septal inhibition and timing behavior in the rat. *Experimental Neurology,* 1964, *10,* 120–132.

Ellis, H. C. Transfer of stimulus predifferentiation to shape recognition and identification learning: Role of properties of verbal labels. *Journal of Experimental Psychology,* 1968, *78,* 401–409.

Ellis, H. C. Transfer and retention. In M. H. Marx (Ed.), *Learning: Processes.* New York: Macmillan, 1969.

Ellis, H. C. Stimulus encoding processes in human learning and memory. In G. H. Bower (Ed.), *The psychology of learning and motivation* (Vol. 7). New York: Academic Press, 1973.

Ellis, H. C. *Fundamentals of human learning, memory, and cognition.* Dubuque, Iowa: Brown, 1978.

Ellis, H. C., Bessemer, D. W., Devine, J. V., & Trafton, C. L. Recognition of random tactual shapes following predifferentiation training.

Perceptual and Motor Skills, 1962, *10,* 99–102.

Ellis, H. C., & Burnstein, D. D. The effect of stimulus similarity and temporal factors in perceptual transfer of training. *Technical report,* 1960, No. 1, Sandia Corp., Albuquerque, N.M.

Ellis, H. C., & Daniel, T. C. Verbal processes in long-term stimulus recognition memory. *Journal of Experimental Psychology,* 1971, *90,* 18–26.

Ellis, H. C., Feuge, R. L., Long, K. K., & Pegram, V. G. Evidence for acquired equivalence of cues in a perceptual task. *Perceptual and Motor Skills,* 1964, *19,* 159–162.

Ellis, H. C., & Homan, L. Implicit verbal responses and the transfer of stimulus predifferentiation. *Journal of Experimental Psychology,* 1968, *76,* 486–489.

Ellis, H. C., & Hunter, J. E. A comparison of the temporal course of retention and nonspecific transfer. *Technical report,* 1961, No. 4, Sandia Corporation, Albuquerque, N.M.

Ellis, H. C., & Muller, D. G. Transfer in perceptual learning following stimulus predifferentiation. *Journal of Experimental Psychology,* 1964, *68,* 388–395.

Ellis, H. C., Muller, D. G., & Tosti, D. T. Stimulus meaning and complexity as factors in the transfer of stimulus predifferentiation. *Journal of Experimental Psychology,* 1966, *71,* 629–633.

Ellis H. C., Parente, F. J., Grah, C. R., & Spiering, K. Coding strategies, perceptual grouping, and the "variability effect" in free recall. *Memory and Cognition,* 1975, *3,* 226–232.

Ellis, H. C., Parente, F. J., & Shumate, E. C. Meaningfulness, perceptual grouping, and organization in recognition memory. *Journal of Experimental Psychology,* 1974, *102,* 308–313.

Ellis, H. C., Parente, F. J., & Walker, C. W. Coding and varied input versus repetition in human memory. *Journal of Experimental Psychology,* 1974, *102,* 284–290.

Ellis, H. C., & Shaffer, R. W. Stimulus encoding and the transfer of stimulus differentiation. *Journal of Verbal Learning and Verbal Behavior,* 1974, *13,* 393–400.

Ellis, H. C., & Shumate, E. C. Encoding effects of response belongingness and stimulus meaningfulness on recognition memory of trigram stimuli. *Journal of Experimental Psychology,* 1973, *98,* 70–78.

Ellis, H. C., & Tatum, B. C. Stimulus encoding and the relationship between stimulus recognition and association formation. *Journal of Verbal Learning and Verbal Behavior,* 1973, *12,* 174–184.

Epstein, W. *Varieties of perceptual learning.* New York: McGraw-Hill, 1967.

Epstein, W., Rock, I., & Zuckerman, C. B. Meaning and familiarity in verbal learning. *Psychological Monographs,* 1960, *74,* No. 491.

Eriksen, C. W., & Collins, J. F. Some temporal characteristics of visual pattern perception. *Journal of Experimental Psychology,* 1968, *74,* 476–484.

Estes, W. K. An experimental study of punishment. *Psychological Monographs,* 1944, *57* (3, Whole No. 263).

Estes, W. K. The statistical approach to learning theory. In S. Koch (Ed.), *Psychology: A study of a science* (Vol. 2). New York: McGraw-Hill, 1959.

Estes, W. K. Learning theory and the new "mental chemistry." *Psychological Review,* 1960, *67,* 207–223.

Estes, W. K. Phonemic coding and rehearsal in short-term memory for letter strings. *Journal of Verbal Learning and Verbal Behavior,* 1973, *12,* 360–373.

Evans, S. H. A brief statement of schema theory. *Psychonomic Science,* 1967, *8,* 87–88.

Evans, S. H., & Arnoult, M. D. Schematic concept formation: Demonstration in a free sorting task. *Psychonomic Science,* 1967, *9,* 221–222.

Fantino, E., Kasdon, D., & Stringer, N. The Yerkes–Dodson law and alimentary motivation. *Canadian Journal of Psychology,* 1970, *24,* 77–84.

Fantz, R. L. Pattern vision in young infants. *Psychological Record,* 1958, *8,* 43–47.

Fantz, R. L. The origin of form perception. *Scientific American,* 1961, *204,* 66–72.

Fantz, R. L. Pattern vision in newborn infants, *Science,* 1963, *140,* 296–297.

Fantz, R. L. Visual perception from birth as shown by pattern selectivity. *Annals of the New York Academy of Sciences,* 1965, *118,* 793–814.

Fantz, R. L., & Nevis, S. Pattern preferences and perceptual–cognitive development in early infancy. *Merrill-Palmer Quarterly,* 1967, *13,* 77–108.

Feder, R., & Ranck, J. B., Jr. Studies on single neurons in dorsal hippocampal formation and septum in unrestrained rats: II. Hippocampal slow waves and theta cell firing during bar pressing and other behaviors. *Experimental*

Neurology, 1973, *41,* 532–555.

Feirstein, A. R., & Miller, N. E. Learning to resist pain and fear: Effects of electric shock before versus after reaching goal. *Journal of Comparative and Physiological Psychology,* 1963, *56,* 797–800.

Ferraro, D. P., & Branch, K. M. Variability of response location during regular and partial reinforcement. *Psychological Reports,* 1968, *23,* 1023–1031.

Ferster, C. B., & Skinner, B. F. *Schedules of reinforcement.* New York: Appleton-Century-Crofts, 1957.

Festinger, L. The psychological effects of insufficient rewards. *American Psychologist,* 1961, *16,* 1–11.

Fetz, E. E. Operant conditioning of cortical unit activity. *Science,* 1969, *163,* 955–958.

Feuge, R. L., & Ellis, H. C. Generalization gradients in recognition memory of visual form. *Journal of Experimental Psychology,* 1969, *79,* 288–294.

Fillmore, C. J. The case for case. In E. Bach & R. T. Harms (Eds.), *Universals in linguistic theory.* New York: Holt, Rinehart and Winston, 1968.

Fillmore, C. J. Toward a modern theory of case. In D. A. Reibel & S. A. Schane (Eds.), *Modern studies in English.* Englewood Cliffs, N.J.: Prentice-Hall, 1969.

Flescher, G. I. L'amnesia retrograda dopo l'elettroshock: Contributo allo studio della patogenesi delle amnesie in genere. *Schweizer Archiv für Neurologie, Neurothirurgie, und Psychiatrie,* 1941, *48,* 1–28.

Flexner, J. B., & Flexner, L. B. Restoration of memory lost after treatment with puromycin. *Proceedings of the National Academy of Sciences,* 1967, *57,* 1651–1654.

Flexner, J. B., & Flexner, L. B. Further observations on restoration of memory lost after treatment with puromycin. *Yale Journal of Biology and Medicine,* 1970, *42,* 235–240.

Flexner, J. B., Flexner, L. B., & Stellar, E. Memory in mice as affected by intracerebral puromycin. *Science,* 1963, *141,* 57–59.

Flexner, L. B., & Flexner, J. B. Effects of acetoxycyclohexamide and of an acetoxycyclohexamide–puromycin mixture on cerebral protein synthesis and memory in mice. *Proceedings of the National Academy of Sciences,* 1966, *55,* 369–374.

Flexner, L. B., & Flexner, J. B. Intracerebral saline: Effect on memory of trained mice treated with puromycin. *Science,* 1968, *159,* 330–331.

Flexner, L. B., Flexner, J. B., Roberts, R. B., & De la Haba, G. Loss of recent memory in mice as related to regional inhibition of cerebral protein synthesis. *Proceedings of the National Academy of Sciences,* 1964, *52,* 1165–1169.

Flood, J. F., Rosenzweig, M. R., Bennett, E. L., & Orme, A. E. The influence of duration of protein synthesis inhibition on memory. *Physiology and Behavior,* 1973, *10,* 555–562.

Forgays, D. G., & Read, J. M. Crucial periods for free-environmental experience in the rat. *Journal of Comparative and Physiological Psychology,* 1962, *55,* 816–818.

Forrester, W. E., & King, D. J. Effects of semantic and acoustic relatedness on free recall and clustering. *Journal of Experimental Psychology,* 1971, *88,* 16–19.

Fowler, H. Suppression and facilitation by response contingent shock. In F. R. Brush (Ed.), *Aversive conditioning and learning.* New York: Academic Press, 1971.

Fowler, H., & Trapold, M. A. Escape performance as a function of delay of reinforcement. *Journal of Experimental Psychology,* 1962, *63,* 464–467.

Fox, P. W., Blick, K. A., & Bilodeau, E. A. Stimulation and prediction of verbal recall and misrecall. *Journal of Experimental Psychology,* 1964, *68,* 321–322.

Franchina, J. J., & Brown, T. S. Reward magnitude shift effects in rats with hippocampal lesions. *Journal of Comparative and Physiological Psychology,* 1971, *76,* 365–370.

Franks, J. J., & Bransford, J. D. Abstraction of visual patterns. *Journal of Experimental Psychology,* 1971, *90,* 65–74.

Fried, P. A. Effects of septal lesions on conflict resolution in rats. *Journal of Comparative and Physiological Psychology,* 1969, *69,* 375–380.

Fried, P. A. Limbic system lesions in rats: Differential effects in an approach-avoidance task. *Journal of Comparative and Physiological Psychology,* 1971, *74,* 349–353.

Friedman, M. H. Electroconvulsive shock as a traumatic (fear-producing) experience in the albino rat. *Journal of Abnormal and Social Psychology,* 1953, *48,* 555–562.

Fuller, J. L., Rosvold, H. E., & Pribram, K. H. The effect on affective and cognitive behavior in the dog of lesions of the pyriform-amygdala hippocampal complex. *Journal of Comparative and Physiological Psychology,* 1957, *50,* 89–96.

Fuster, J. M., & Uyeda, A. A. Reactivity of limbic neurons of the monkey to appetitive and aversive signals. *Electroencephalography and Clinical Neurology,* 1971, *30,* 281–293.

Gagné, R. M., & Baker, K. E. Stimulus predifferentiation as a factor in transfer of training. *Journal of Experimental Psychology,* 1950, *40,* 439–451.

Gamboni, W. R. Anticipatory errors in rats as a function of delayed reward. *Journal of Experimental Psychology,* 1973, *97,* 98–104.

Garcia, J., Hankins, W. G., & Rasiniak, K. W. Behavioral regulation of the *milieu interne* in man and rat. *Science,* 1974, *185,* 824–831.

Garcia, J., Kimeldorf, D. J., & Hunt, E. L. The use of ionizing radiation as a motivating stimulus. *Psychological Review,* 1961, *68,* 383–395.

Garcia, J., Kimeldorf, D. J., Hunt, E. L., & Davies, B. P. Food and water consumption of rats during exposure to gamma radiation. *Radiation Research,* 1956, *4,* 33–41.

Garcia, J., & Koelling, R. A. The relation of cue to consequence in avoidance learning. *Psychonomic Science,* 1966, *4,* 123–124.

Garner, W. R. *The processing of information and structure.* Hillsdale, N.J.: Erlbaum, 1974.

Gault, F. P., & Leaton, R. N. Electrical activity of the olfactory system. *Electroencephalography and Clinical Neurophysiology,* 1963, *15,* 299–304.

Gaydos, H. F. Intersensory transfer in the discrimination of forms. *American Journal of Psychology,* 1956, *69,* 107–110.

Gazzaniga, M. S. *The bisected brain.* New York: Appleton-Century-Crofts, 1970.

Gentner, D. Evidence for the psychological reality of semantic components: The verbs of possession. In D. Normal & D. Rumelhart (Eds.), *Explorations in cognition.* San Francisco: Freeman, 1975.

Gerbrandt, L. K., & Thomson, C. W. Competing response and amnestic effects of electroconvulsive shock under extinction and incentive shifts. *Journal of Comparative and Physiological Psychology,* 1964, *58,* 208–211.

Ghent, L. *Age changes in the mode of perceiving geometric forms.* Paper presented at the meeting of the Eastern Psychological Association, Philadelphia, April 1964.

Gibbs, F. A., Davis, H., & Lennox, W. G. The electroencephalogram in epilepsy and in conditions of impaired consciousness. *Archives of Neurology and Psychiatry,* 1935, *34,* 1133–1148.

Gibson, E. J. A systematic application of the concepts of generalization and differentiation to verbal learning. *Psychological Review,* 1940, *47,* 196–229.

Gibson, E. J. Retroactive inhibition as a function of the degree of generalization betweeen two tasks. *Journal of Experimental Psychology,* 1941, *28,* 93–115.

Gibson, E. J. Improvement in perceptual judgments as a function of controlled practice or training. *Psychological Bulletin,* 1953, *50,* 401–431.

Gibson, E. J. *Principles of perceptual learning and development.* New York: Appleton-Century-Crofts, 1969.

Gibson, E. J., & Bergman, R. The effect of training on absolute estimation of distance over the ground. *Journal of Experimental Psychology,* 1954, *48,* 473–482.

Gibson, E. J., & Walk, R. D. The effect of prolonged exposure to visually presented patterns on learning to discriminate them. *Journal of Comparative and Physiological Psychology,* 1956, *49,* 239–242.

Gibson, E. J., Walk, R. D., Pick, H. L., & Tighe, T. J. The effect of prolonged exposure to visual patterns on learning to discriminate similar and different patterns. *Journal of Comparative and Physiological Psychology,* 1958, *51,* 584–587.

Gibson, J. J. *The senses considered as perceptual systems.* Boston: Houghton Mifflin, 1966.

Gibson, J. J., & Gibson, E. J. Perceptual learning: Differentiation or enrichment? *Psychological Review,* 1955, *62,* 32–41.

Glanzer, M. Storage mechanisms in recall. In G. H. Bower (Ed.), *The psychology of learning and motivation* (Vol. 5). New York: Academic Press, 1972.

Glanzer, M., & Cunitz, A. R. Two storage mechanisms in free recall. *Journal of Verbal Learning and Verbal Behavior,* 1966, *5,* 351–360.

Glass, D. C., & Singer, J. E. Behavioral aftereffects of unpredictable and uncontrollable aversive events. *American Scientist,* 1972, *60*(4), 457–465. (a)

Glass, D. C., & Singer, J. E. *Urban stress: Experiments in noise and social stressors.* New York: Academic Press, 1972. (b)

Glassman, E., Henderson, A., Cordle, M., Moon, H. M., & Wilson, J. E. Effect of cyclohexamide and actinomycin-D on the behavior of the headless cockroach. *Nature,* 1970, *225,* 967–968.

Glaze, J. A. The association value of nonsense syllables. *Journal of Genetic Psychology,* 1928, *35,* 255–267.

Glickman, S. E. Perseverative neural processes and consolidation of the memory trace. *Psychological Bulletin,* 1961, *58,* 218–233.

Glucksburg, S. Effects of verbal behavior on problem solving: Labeling the functionally fixed object. *American Psychologist,* 1964, *19,* 575. (Abstract)

Glucksburg, S., & Weisberg, R. W. Verbal behavior and problem solving: Some effects of labeling in a functional fixedness problem. *Journal of Experimental Psychology,* 1966, *71,* 659–664.

Goggin, J., & Martin, E. Forced stimulus encoding and retroactive interference. *Journal of Experimental Psychology,* 1970, *84,* 131–136.

Goldiamond, I., & Hawkins, W. F. Vexierversuch: The log relationship between word-frequency and recognition obtained in the absence of stimulus words. *Journal of Experimental Psychology,* 1958, *56,* 457–463.

Gonzalez, R. C., Bainbridge, P., & Bitterman, M. E. Discrete trials lever pressing in the rat as a function of pattern of reinforcement, effortfulness of response and amount of reward. *Journal of Comparative and Physiological Psychology,* 1966, *61,* 110–122.

Gonzalez, R. C., & Champlin, G. Positive behavioral contrast, negative simultaneous contrast and their relation to frustration in pigeons. *Journal of Comparative and Physiological Psychology,* 1974, *87,* 173–187.

Goodrich, K. P. Performance in different segments of an instrumental response chain as a function of reinforcement schedule. *Journal of Experimental Psychology,* 1959, *57,* 57–63.

Gorman, A. M. Recognition memory for nouns as a function of abstractness and frequency. *Journal of Experimental Psychology,* 1961, *61,* 23–29.

Gormezano, I., & Moore, J. W. Classical conditioning. In M. H. Marx (Ed.), *Learning: Processes.* New York: Macmillan, 1969.

Goss, A. E. A stimulus–response analysis of the interaction of cue-producing and mediating responses. *Psychological Review,* 1955, *62,* 20–31.

Goss, A. E., & Greenfeld, N. Transfer to a motor task as influenced by conditions and degree of prior discrimination training. *Journal of Experimental Psychology,* 1958, *55,* 258–269.

Grandine, L., & Harlow, H. F. Generalization of the characteristics of a single learned stimulus by monkeys. *Journal of Comparative and Physiological Psychology,* 1948, *41,* 327–338.

Grant, D. A. Cognitive factors in eyelid conditioning. *Psychophysiology,* 1973, *10,* 75–81.

Grant, D. A., & Schneider, D. E. The intensity of the conditioned stimulus and strength of conditioning: II. The conditioned galvanic skin response to the auditory stimulus. *Journal of Experimental Psychology,* 1949, *39,* 35–40.

Grastyán, E., Karmos, G., Vereczkey, L., & Kellényi, L. The hippocampal electrical correlates of the homeostatic regulation of motivation. *Electroencephalography and Clinical Neurophysiology,* 1966, *21,* 34–53.

Grastyán, E., Lissák, K., Madarász, L., & Donhoffer, H. Hippocampal electrical activity during the development of conditioned reflexes. *Electroencephalography and Clinical Neurophysiology,* 1959, *11,* 409–430.

Greeno, J. G. The structure of memory and the process of solving problems. In R. L. Solso (Ed.), *Contemporary issues in cognitive psychology.* Washington, D.C.: Winston, 1973, 103–134.

Greeno, J. G., James, C. T., & DaPolito, F. J. A cognitive interpretation of negative transfer and forgetting of paired associates. *Journal of Verbal Learning and Verbal Behavior,* 1971, *10,* 331–345.

Greenough, W. T., & Schwitzgebel, R. L. Effect of a single ECS on extinction of a bar-press. *Psychological Reports,* 1966, *19,* 1227–1230.

Gregory, R. L., & Wallace, J. G. Recovery from early blindness: A case study. *Experimental Psychology Monographs,* 1963, No. 2.

Grice, G. R. The acquisition of a visual discrimination habit following response to a single stimulus. *Journal of Experimental Psychology,* 1948, *38,* 633–642. (a)

Grice, G. R. The relation of secondary reinforcement to delayed reward in visual discrimination learning. *Journal of Experimental Psychology,* 1948, *38,* 1–16. (b)

Grice, G. R. Stimulus intensity and response evocation. *Psychological Review,* 1968, *75,* 359–373.

Grice, G. R. Conditioning and a decision theory of response evocation. In G. H. Bower (Ed.),

The psychology of learning and motivation (Vol. 5). New York: Academic Press, 1972.

Grice, G. R. Information-processing dynamics of human eyelid conditioning. *Journal of Experimental Psychology: General,* 1977, *106,* 71–93.

Grice, G. R., & Hunter, J. J. Stimulus intensity effects depend upon the type of experimental design. *Psychological Review,* 1964, *71,* 247–256.

Grice, G. R., & Saltz, E. The generalization of an instrumental response to stimuli varying in the size dimension. *Journal of Experimental Psychology,* 1950, *40,* 702–708.

Groninger, L. D. Mnemonic imagery and forgetting. *Psychonomic Science,* 1971, *23,* 161–163.

Gumnit, R. J. The distribution of direct responses evoked by sounds in the auditory cortex of the cat. *Electroencephalography and Clinical Neurophysiology,* 1961, *13,* 889–895.

Guthrie, E. R. *The psychology of learning.* New York: Harper & Row, 1935.

Guttman, N. Operant conditioning, extinction, and periodic reinforcement in relation to concentration of sucrose used as reinforcing agent. *Journal of Experimental Psychology,* 1953, *46,* 213–224.

Guttman, N., & Kalish, H. I. Discriminability and stimulus generalization. *Journal of Experimental Psychology,* 1956, *51,* 79–88.

Haber, A., & Kalish, H. I. Prediction of discrimination from generalization after variations in schedule of reinforcement. *Science,* 1963, *142,* 412–413.

Haber, R. N. Eidetic images. *Scientific American,* 1969, *220,* 36–44.

Haggard, D. F. Acquisition of a simple running response as a function of partial and continuous schedules of reinforcement. *Psychological Records,* 1959, *9,* 11–18.

Hake, D. F., Azrin, N. H., & Oxford, R. The effects of punishment on squirrel monkeys. *Journal of the Experimental Analysis of Behavior,* 1967, *10,* 95–107.

Hake, H. W. *Contributions of psychology to the study of pattern vision* (Report No. 57–621). Wright Air Development Center, 1957.

Hall, J. F. *Classical conditioning and instrumental learning.* Philadelphia: Lippincott, 1976.

Hamilton, C. E. The relationship between length of interval separating two learning tasks and performance on the second task. *Journal of Experimental Psychology,* 1950, *40,* 613–621.

Hamilton, L. W. Intrabox and extrabox cues in avoidance responding: Effect of septal lesions. *Journal of Comparative and Physiological Psychology,* 1972, *78,* 268–273.

Hamilton, R. J. Retroactive facilitation as a function of degree of generalization between tasks. *Journal of Experimental Psychology,* 1943, *32,* 363–376.

Hamilton, W. F., & Coleman, T. B. Trichromatic vision in the pigeon as illustrated by the spectral hue discrimination curve. *Journal of Comparative Psychology,* 1933, *15,* 183–191.

Hammes, J. A. Visual discrimination learning as a function of shock-fear and task difficulty. *Journal of Comparative and Physiological Psychology,* 1956, *49,* 481–484.

Hanawalt, N. B., & Demarest, I. H. The effect of verbal suggestion in the recall period upon the reproduction of visually perceived forms. *Journal of Experimental Psychology,* 1939, *25,* 159–174.

Hanson, H. M. Effects of discrimination training on stimulus generalization. *Journal of Experimental Psychology,* 1959, *58,* 321–333.

Harlow, H. F. The formation of learning sets. *Psychological Review,* 1949, *56,* 51–65.

Harlow, H. F. The nature of love. *American Psychologist,* 1958, *13,* 673–685.

Harlow, H. F. The development of learning in the rhesus monkey. *American Scientist,* 1959, *47,* 459–479.

Harlow, H. F. The heterosexual affectional system in monkeys. *American Psychologist,* 1962, *17,* 1–9.

Harlow, H. F., Harlow, M. K., & Meyer, D. R. Learning motivated by a manipulation drive. *Journal of Experimental Psychology,* 1950, *40,* 228–234.

Harlow, H. F., Harlow, M. K., Schlitz, K. A., & Mohr, D. J. The effect of early adverse and enriched environments on the learning ability of rhesus monkeys. In L. E. Jarrard (Ed.), *Cognitive processes of nonhuman primates.* New York: Academic Press, 1971.

Harlow, H. F., Harlow, M. K., & Suomi, S. J. From thought to therapy: Lessons from a primate laboratory. *American Scientist,* 1971, *59,* 538–549.

Hartman, T. F., & Grant, D. A. Effects of intermittent reinforcement on acquisition, extinction, and spontaneous recovery of the conditioned eyelid response. *Journal of Experimental Psychology,* 1960, *60,* 89–96.

Haycock, J. W., Gold, P. E., Macri, J., & McGaugh, J. L. Noncontingent footshock attenuation of retrograde amnesia: A generalization effect. *Physiology and Behavior,* 1973, *11,* 99–102.

Haycock, J. W., & McGaugh, J. L. Retrograde amnesia gradients as a function of ECS intensity. *Behavioral Biology,* 1973, *9,* 123–127.

Hayes, K. J. The backward curve: A method for the study of learning. *Psychological Review,* 1953, *60,* 269–275.

Hearst, E., Besley, S., & Farthing, G. W. Inhibition and the stimulus control of behavior. *Journal of the Experimental Analysis of Behavior,* 1970, *14,* 373–409.

Hearst, E., & Jenkins, H. M. Sign-tracking: The stimulus–reinforcer relation and directed action. *Psychonomic Society Monographs,* 1974, 1–49.

Hearst, E., & Koresko, M. B. Stimulus generalization and the amount of prior training on variable-interval reinforcement. *Journal of Comparative and Physiological Psychology,* 1968, *66,* 133–138.

Hearst, E., Koresko, M. B., & Poppen, R. Stimulus generalization and the response-reinforcement contingency. *Journal of the Experimental Analysis of Behavior,* 1964, *7,* 369–380.

Hebb, D. O. *The organization of behavior.* New York: Wiley, 1949.

Hebb, D. O., & Williams, K. A method of rating animal intelligence. *Journal of General Psychology,* 1946, *34,* 59–65.

Heber, R., Garber, H., Harrington, S., & Hoffman, C. Rehabilitation of families at risk for mental retardation. Unpublished progress report, University of Wisconsin at Madison Research and Training Center, 1972.

Hein, A., & Diamond, R. M. Contrasting development of visually triggered and guided movements in kittens with respect to interocular and interlimb equivalence. *Journal of Comparative and Physiological Psychology,* 1971, *76,* 219–224.

Hein, A., Gower, E., & Diamond, R. Exposure requirements for developing the triggered component of the visual-placing response. *Journal of Comparative and Physiological Psychology,* 1970, *73,* 188–192.

Heinze, W. J. *Quantitative genetic analysis of learning and induced retrograde amnesia in the rodent* Rattus norvedicus. Unpublished doctoral dissertation, University of California, Berkeley, 1970.

Held, R., & Hein, A. Adaptation of disarranged hand–eye coordination upon re-afferent stimulation. *Perceptual and Motor Skills,* 1958, *8,* 87–90.

Held, R., & Hein, A. Movement-produced stimulation in the development of visually guided behavior. *Journal of Comparative and Physiological Psychology,* 1963, *56,* 872–876.

Held, R., & Schlank, M. Adaptation to disarranged eye–hand coordination in the distance dimension. *American Journal of Psychology,* 1959, *72,* 603–605.

Henker, B. A., Asano, S., & Kagan, J. An observational system for studying visual attention in the infant. *Journal of Experimental Child Psychology,* 1968, *6,* 391–394.

Herrnstein, R. J. Superstition: A corollary of the principles of operant conditioning. In W. K. Honig (Ed.), *Operant behavior: Areas of research and application.* New York: Appleton-Century-Crofts, 1966.

Hershenson, M. Visual discrimination in the human newborn. Unpublished doctoral dissertation, Yale University, 1964.

Hershenson, M. Development of the perception of form. *Psychological Bulletin,* 1967, *67,* 326–336.

Hershenson, M., Munsinger, H., & Kessen, W. Preferences for shapes of intermediate variability in the newborn human. *Science,* 1965, *147,* 630–631.

Hine, B., & Paolino, R. M. Retrograde amnesia: Production of skeletal but not cardiac response gradients by electroconvulsive shock. *Science,* 1970, *169,* 1224–1226.

Hockman, C. H. Prenatal maternal stress in the rat: Its effects on emotional behavior in the offspring. *Journal of Comparative and Physiological Psychology,* 1961, *54,* 679–684.

Holmes, J. E., & Adey, W. R. Electrical activity of the entorhinal cortex during conditioned behavior. *American Journal of Physiology,* 1960, *199,* 741–744.

Holmgren, G. L., Arnoult, M. D., & Manning, W. H. Intermodal transfer in a paired-associates learning task. *Journal of Experimental Psychology,* 1966, *71,* 254–259.

Holz, W. C., & Azrin, N. H. Discriminative properties of punishment. *Journal of the Experimental Analysis of Behavior,* 1961, *4,* 225–232.

Holz, W. C., & Azrin, N. H. Interactions between the discriminative and aversive properties of punishment. *Journal of the Experimental Analysis of Behavior,* 1962, *5,* 229–234.

Holz, W. C., Azrin, N. H., & Ulrich, R. E. Punishment of temporally spaced responding. *Journal of the Experimental Analysis of Behavior,* 1963, *6,* 115–122.

Homme, L. E., deBaca, P. C., Devine, J. V., Steinhorst, R., & Rickert, E. J. Use of the Premack principle in controlling the behavior of nursery school children. *Journal of the Experimental Analysis of Behavior,* 1963, *6,* 544.

Honig, W. K., Boneau, C. A., Burstein, K. R., & Pennypacker, H. S. Positive and negative generalization gradients obtained under equivalent training conditions. *Journal of Comparative and Physiological Psychology,* 1963, *56,* 111–116.

Horton, D. L. Mediation or pseudomediation: A reply to Earhard and Mandler. *Canadian Journal of Psychology,* 1967, *21,* 471–489.

Hothersall, D., & Brener, J. Operant conditioning of changes in heart rate in curarized rats. *Journal of Comparative and Physiological Psychology,* 1969, *68,* 338–342.

House, E. L., & Pansky, B. *A functional approach to neuroanatomy.* New York: McGraw-Hill, 1967.

Houston, J. P. Verbal transfer and interlist similarities. *Psychological Review,* 1964, *71,* 563–566.

Houston, J. P. Stimulus selection as influenced by degrees of learning, attention, prior association, and experiences with stimulus components. *Journal of Experimental Psychology,* 1967, *73,* 509–516.

Hovland, C. I. The generalization of conditioned responses: I. The sensory generalization of conditioned responses with varying frequencies of tone. *Journal of General Psychology,* 1937, *17,* 125–148. (a)

Hovland, C. I. The generalization of conditioned responses: II. The sensory generalization of conditioned responses with varying intensities of tone. *Journal of Genetic Psychology,* 1937, *51,* 279–291. (b)

Hovland, C. I. The generalization of conditioned responses: IV. The effects of varying amounts of reinforcement upon the degree of generalization of conditioned responses. *Journal of Experimental Psychology,* 1937, *21,* 261–276. (c)

Howard, J. L., Galosy, R. A., Gaebelien, C. J., & Obrist, P. A. Some problems in the use of neuromuscular blockade. In P. A. Obrist, H. R. Black, J. Brener, & L. V. DiCara (Eds.), *Cardiovascular psychophysiology.* Chicago: Aldine, 1974.

Howes, D. A word count of spoken English. *Journal of Verbal Learning and Verbal Behavior,* 1966, *5,* 572–604.

Hubel, D. H. Effects of distortion of sensory input on the visual system of kittens. *Physiologist,* 1967, *10,* 17–45.

Hughes, R. A. Retrograde amnesia in rats produced by hippocampal injections of potassium chloride: Gradient of effect and recovery. *Journal of Comparative and Physiological Psychology,* 1969, *68,* 637–644.

Hughes, R. A., Barrett, R. J., & Ray, O. S. Retrograde amnesia in rats increases as a function of ECS-test interval and ECS intensity. *Physiology and Behavior,* 1970, *5,* 27–30. (a)

Hughes, R. A., Barrett, R. J., & Ray, O. S. Training to test interval as a determinant of a temporally graded ECS-produced response decrement in rats. *Journal of Comparative and Physiological Psychology,* 1970, *71,* 318–324. (b)

Hull, C. L. *Principles of behavior.* New York: Appleton-Century-Crofts, 1943.

Hull, C. L. *A behavior system.* New Haven, Conn.: Yale University Press, 1952.

Hulse, S. H., Jr. Amount and percentage of reinforcement and duration of goal confinement in conditioning and extinction. *Journal of Experimental Psychology,* 1958, *56,* 48–57.

Humphreys, L. G. The effect of random alternation of reinforcement on the acquisition and extinction of conditioned eyelid reactions. *Journal of Experimental Psychology,* 1939, *25,* 141–158.

Hunt, H. F., & Brady, J. V. Some effects of punishment and intercurrent anxiety on a simple operant. *Journal of Comparative and Physiological Psychology,* 1955, *48,* 305–310.

Hunt, R. R., & Ellis, H. C. Recognition memory and the degree of semantic contextual change. *Journal of Experimental Psychology,* 1974, *103,* 1153–1159.

Hunt, R. R., Parente, F. J., & Ellis, H. C. Transfer of coding strategies in free recall with constant and varied input. *Journal of Experimental Psychology,* 1974, *103,* 619–624.

Hurwitz, H. M. B. Conditioned responses in rats reinforced by light. *British Journal of Animal Behaviour,* 1956, *4,* 31–33.

Hutchings, D. E. Early handling in rats: The effects of body-temperature reduction and stimulation on adult emotionality. *Proceedings of the American Psychological Association,* 1965, 183–184.

Hyde, T. S. Differential effects of effort and type of orienting task on recall and organization of highly associated words. *Journal of*

Experimental Psychology, 1973, *79,* 111–113.

Hyde, T. S., & Jenkins, J. J. Differential effects of incidental tasks on the organization of recall of a list of highly associated words. *Journal of Experimental Psychology,* 1969, *82,* 472–481.

Hyde, T. S., & Jenkins, J. J. Recall for words as a function of semantic, graphic, and syntactic orienting tasks. *Journal of Verbal Learning and Verbal Behavior,* 1973, *12,* 471–480.

Hydén, H. Quantitative assay of compounds in isolated, fresh nerve cells and glial cells from control and stimulated animals. *Nature,* 1959, *184,* 433–435.

Hydén, H., & Egyházi, E. Nuclear RNA changes of nerve cells during a learning experiment in rats. *Proceedings of the National Academy of Sciences,* 1962, *48,* 1366–1373.

Hydén, H. & Egyházi, E. Glial RNA changes during a learning experiment with rats. *Proceedings of the National Academy of Sciences,* 1963, *49,* 618–624.

Hydén, H., & Egyházi, E. Changes in RNA content and base composition in cortical neurons of rats in a learning experiment involving transfer of handedness. *Proceedings of the National Academy of Sciences,* 1964, *52,* 1030–1035.

Hydén, H., & Lange, P. W. A differentiation in RNA response in neurons early and late in learning. *Proceedings of the National Academy of Sciences,* 1965, *53,* 946–952.

Hydén, H., & Lange, P. W. Brain-cell protein synthesis specifically related to learning. *Proceedings of the National Academy of Sciences,* 1971, *65,* 898–904. (a)

Hydén, H., & Lange, P. W. S-100 brain protein: Correlations with behavior. *Proceedings of the National Academy of Sciences,* 1971, *67,* 1959–1966. (b)

Hymovich, B. The effects of experimental variations on problem-solving in the rat. *Journal of Comparative and Physiological Psychology,* 1952, *45,* 313–321.

Isaacson, R. L., Douglas, R. J., & Moore, R. J. The effect of radical hippocampal ablation on acquisition of avoidance response. *Journal of Comparative and Physiological Psychology,* 1961, *54,* 625–628.

Isaacson, R. L., & Kimble, D. P. Lesions of the limbic system: Their effects upon hypotheses and frustration. *Behavioral Biology,* 1972, *7,* 767–793.

Ison, J. R. Experimental extinction as a function of the number of reinforcements. *Journal of Experimental Psychology,* 1962, *64,* 314–317.

Jackson, W. J., & Strong, P. N. Differential effects of hippocampal lesions upon sequential tasks and maze learning by the rat. *Journal of Comparative and Physiological Psychology,* 1969, *68,* 442–450.

Jacobson, A. L. Learning in flatworms and annelids. *Psychological Bulletin,* 1963, *60,* 74–94.

James, C. T., & Greeno, J. G. Stimulus selection at different stages of paired-associate learning. *Journal of Experimental Psychology,* 1967, *74,* 75–83.

James, L. S. Serial learning of nonsense shapes as a function of instructions controlling labeling. *Perception and Psychophysics,* 1973, *13,* 313–318.

James, W. *The principles of psychology.* New York: Holt, Rinehart and Winston, 1890.

Jarvella, R. J. Syntactic processing of connected speech. *Journal of Verbal Learning and Verbal Behavior,* 1971, *10,* 409–416.

Jenkins, H. M. Generalization gradients and the concept of inhibition. In D. Mostofsky (Ed.), *Stimulus generalization.* Stanford, Calif.: Stanford University Press, 1965.

Jenkins, H. M., & Harrison, R. H. Effect of discrimination training on auditory generalization. *Journal of Experimental Psychology,* 1960, *59,* 246–253.

Jenkins, H. M., & Harrison, R. H. Generalization gradients of inhibition following auditory discrimination learning. *Journal of the Experimental Analysis of Behavior,* 1962, *5,* 435–441.

Jenkins, H. M., & Sainsbury, R. S. The development of stimulus control through differential reinforcement. In N. J. Macintosh & W. K. Honig (Eds.), *Fundamental issues in associative learning.* Halifax, Nova Scotia: Dalhousie University Press, 1969.

Jenkins, J. G., & Dallenbach, K. M. Oblivescence during sleep and waking. *American Journal of Psychology,* 1924, *35,* 605–612.

Jenkins, J. J. Mediated associations: Paradigms and situations. In C. N. Cofer & B. S. Musgrave (Eds.), *Verbal behavior and learning.* New York: McGraw-Hill, 1963.

Jenkins, J. J., & Russell, W. A. Associative clustering during recall. *Journal of Abnormal and Social Psychology,* 1952, *47,* 818–821.

Jenkins, W. O. A temporal gradient of derived reinforcement. *American Journal of Psychology,* 1950, *63,* 237–243.

John, E. R. *Mechanisms of memory.* New York:

Academic Press, 1967.

John, E. R. Brain mechanisms of memory. In J. L. McGaugh (Ed.), *Psychobiology: Behavior from a biological perspective*. New York: Academic Press, 1971.

Johnson, D. A. Developmental aspects of recovery of function following septal lesions in the infant rat. *Journal of Comparative and Physiological Psychology,* 1972, *78,* 331–348.

Johnson, N. F. Chunking: Associative chaining versus coding. *Journal of Verbal Learning and Verbal Behavior,* 1969, *8,* 725–731.

Johnson, N. F. Chunking and organization in the process of recall. In G. H. Bower (Ed.), *The psychology of learning and motivation* (Vol. 4). New York: Academic Press, 1970.

Johnston, J. M. Punishment of human behavior. *American Psychologist,* 1972, *27,* 1033–1054.

Jung, J. Effects of response meaningfulness (*m*) on transfer of training under two different paradigms. *Journal of Experimental Psychology,* 1963, *65,* 377–384.

Jung, J. Comments on Mandler's "From association to structure." *Psychological Review,* 1965, *72,* 318–322.

Jung, R., & Kornmüller, A. E. Eine Methodik der Abkitung lokalisierter Potentialschwankungen aus subcorticalen Hirngebieten. Archiv für Psychiatrie und Nervenkrankheiten, 1938, *109,* 1–30.

Kaada, B. R. Somato-motor, autonomic and electrocorticographic responses to electrical stimulation of "rhinencephalic" and other structures in primates, cat and dog. *Acta Scandinavian Physiology,* 1951, *24,* Supplement 83, 1–258.

Kaada, B. R., Rasmussen, E. W., & Kviem, O. Effects of hippocampal lesions on maze learning and retention in rats. *Experimental Neurology,* 1961, *3,* 333–355.

Kagan, J. Attention and psychological change in the young child. *Science,* 1970, *170,* 826–832.

Kalish, H. I., & Haber, A. The prediction of discrimination from generalization following variations in deprivation level. *Journal of Comparative and Physiological Psychology,* 1965, *60,* 125–128.

Kamin, L. J. The delay-of-punishment gradient. *Journal of Comparative and Physiological Psychology,* 1959, *52,* 434–437.

Kanak, N. J., & Neuner, S. D. Associative symmetry and item availability as a function of five methods of paired-associate acquisition. *Journal of Experimental Psychology,* 1970, *86,* 288–295.

Kanfer, F. H., & Phillips, J. S. *Learning foundations of behavior therapy.* New York: Wiley, 1970.

Kapp, B. S., & Schneider, A. M. Selective recovery from retrograde amnesia produced by hippocampal spreading depression. *Science,* 1971, *173,* 1149–1151.

Karas, G. G., & Denenberg, V. H. The effects of duration and distribution of infantile experience on adult behavior. *Journal of Comparative and Physiological Psychology,* 1961, *54,* 170–174.

Karpicke, J., & Hearst, E. Inhibitory control and errorless discrimination learning. *Journal of the Experimental Analysis of Behavior,* 1975, *23,* 159–166.

Karsh, E. B. Effects of number of rewarded trials and intensity of punishment on running speed. *Journal of Comparative and Physiological Psychology,* 1962, *55,* 44–51.

Karsh, E. B. Changes in intensity of punishment: Effect on running behavior of rats. *Science,* 1963, *140,* 1084–1085.

Katona, G. *Organizing and memorizing.* New York: Columbia University Press, 1940.

Katz, J. J., & Fodor, J. A. The structure of a semantic theory. *Language,* 1963, *39,* 170–210.

Katz, J. J., & Postal, P. N. *An integrated theory of linguistic descriptions.* Cambridge, Mass.: MIT Press, 1964.

Katz, P. A. Effects of labels on children's perception and discrimination learning. *Journal of Experimental Psychology,* 1963, *66,* 423–428.

Kausler, D. H. *Psychology of verbal learning and memory.* New York: Academic Press, 1974.

Kausler, D. H., & Kanoti, G. A. R–S learning and negative transfer effects with a mixed list. *Journal of Experimental Psychology,* 1963, *65,* 201–205.

Kemble, E. D., & Tapp, J. T. Passive and active avoidance performance following small amygdaloid lesions in rats. *Physiology and Behavior,* 1968, *3,* 713–718.

Kendler, H. H., & Kendler, T. S. Vertical and horizontal processes in problem solving. *Psychological Review,* 1962, *69,* 1–16.

Kendler, H. H., & Kendler, T. S. Mediation and conceptual behavior. In K. W. Spence & J. T. Spence (Eds.), *The psychology of learning and motivation* (Vol. 2). New York: Academic Press, 1968.

Kendler, T. S. An experimental investigation of transposition as a function of the difference between training and test stimuli. *Journal of Experimental Psychology,* 1950, *40,* 552–562.

Keppel, G., & Postman, L. Studies of learning to learn: III. Conditions of improvement in the performance of successive transfer tasks. *Journal of Verbal Learning and Verbal Behavior,* 1966, *5,* 260–267.

Keppel, G., Postman, L., & Zavortink, B. Studies of learning to learn: VIII. The influence of massive amounts of training upon the learning and retention of paired-associate lists. *Journal of Verbal Learning and Verbal Behavior,* 1968, *7,* 790–796.

Keppel, G. & Underwood, B. J. Proactive inhibition in short-term retention of single items. *Journal of Verbal Learning and Verbal Behavior,* 1962, *1,* 153–161.

Kerpelman, L. C. Preexposure to visually presented forms and nondifferential reinforcement in perceptual learning. *Journal of Experimental Psychology,* 1965, *69,* 259–262.

Kerpelman, L. C., & Pollack, R. H. Developmental changes in the location of form discrimination cues. *Perceptual and Motor Skills,* 1964, *19,* 375–382.

Kesner, R. P., Gibson, W. E., & LeClair, M. J. ECS as a punishing stimulus: Dependency on route of administration. *Physiology and Behavior,* 1970, *5,* 683–686.

Kessler, J. W. *Psychopathology of childhood.* Englewood Cliffs, N.J.: Prentice-Hall, 1966.

Keyes, J. B. ECS perseveration effect following varying amounts of training. *Physiological Psychology,* 1973, *1,* 2–4.

Kimble, D. P. The effects of hippocampal lesions in rats. *Journal of Comparative and Physiological Psychology,* 1963, *56,* 273–283.

Kimble, D. P. The hippocampus and internal inhibition. *Psychological Bulletin,* 1968, *70,* 285–295.

Kimble, D. P., & Kimble, R. J. Hippocampectomy and response perseveration in the rat. *Journal of Comparative and Physiological Psychology,* 1965, *60,* 474–476.

Kimble, D. P., & Kimble, R. J. The effect of hippocampal lesions on extinction and "hypothesis" behavior in rats. *Physiology and Behavior,* 1970, *5,* 735–738.

Kimble, D. P., & Pribram, K. H. Hippocampectomy and behavior sequences. *Science,* 1963, *139,* 824–825.

Kimble, G. A. *Hilgard and Marquis' conditioning and learning.* New York: Appleton-Century-Crofts, 1961.

Kimble, G. A. Cognitive inhibition in classical conditioning. In H. H. Kendler & J. T. Spence (Eds.), *Essays in neobehaviorism: A memorial volume to Kenneth W. Spence.* New York: Appleton-Century-Crofts, 1971.

King, R. H., & Glasser, R. L. Duration of electroconvulsive shock-induced retrograde amnesia in rats. *Physiology and Behavior,* 1970, *5,* 335–339.

Kintsch, W. *Learning, memory, and conceptual processes.* New York: Wiley, 1970.

Kintsch, W. *The representation of meaning in memory.* Hillsdale, N.J.: Erlbaum, 1974.

Kjeldergaard, P. M. Transfer and mediation in verbal learning. In T. R. Dixon & D. L. Horton (Eds.), *Verbal behavior and general behavior theory.* Englewood Cliffs, N.J.: Prentice-Hall, 1968.

Klee, J. B. The relation of frustration and motivation to the production of abnormal fixations in the rat. *Psychological Monographs,* 1944, *56,* 257.

Kleinmuntz, B. *Concepts and the structure of memory.* New York: Wiley, 1967.

Klüver, H., & Bucy, P. C. "Psychic blindness" and other symptoms following bilateral temporal lobectomy in rhesus monkeys. *American Journal of Physiology,* 1937, *119,* 352–353.

Klüver, H., & Bucy, P. C. Preliminary analysis of the functions of the temporal lobes in monkeys. *Archives of Neurology and Psychiatry,* 1939, *42,* 979–1000.

Koffka, K. *The growth of the mind.* London: Routledge and Kegan Paul, 1924.

Koffka, K. *Principles of Gestalt psychology.* New York: Harcourt Brace Jovanovich, 1935.

Kohlenberg, R. & Trabasso, T. Recovery of a conditioned emotional response after one or two electroconvulsive shocks. *Journal of Comparative and Physiological Psychology,* 1968, *65,* 270–273.

Kohler, I. The formation and transformation of the perceptual world. *Psychological Issues,* 1964, *3*(4).

Köhler, W. *The mentality of apes.* New York: Harcourt Brace Jovanovich, 1925.

Köhler, W. Simple structural functions in the chimpanzee and in the chicken. In W. D. Ellis (Ed.), *A source book of Gestalt psychology.* New York: Harcourt Brace Jovanovich, 1939.

Köhler, W., & Wegener, J. Currents of the human auditory cortex. *Journal of Cellular and Comparative Physiology,* 1955, Supplement 1, 25–54.

Kopp, R., Bohdanecky, Z., & Jarvik, M. E. Proactive effect of a single electro-convulsive shock (ECS) on one-trial learning in mice. *Journal of Comparative and Physiological Psychology,* 1968, *65,* 514–517.

Koppenall, R. J., Jagoda, E., & Cruce, J. A. F. Recovery from ECS-produced amnesia following a reminder. *Psychonomic Science,* 1967, *9,* 293–294.

Kraeling, D. Analysis of amount of reward as a variable in learning. *Journal of Comparative and Physiological Psychology,* 1961, *54,* 560–565.

Krasner, L., & Ullman, L. P. *Research in behavior modification.* New York: Holt, Rinehart and Winston, 1965.

Krech, D., Rosenzweig, M. R., & Bennett, E. L. Effects of complex environment and blindness on rat brain. *Archives of Neurology,* 1963, *8,* 403–412.

Krechevsky, I. A note concerning the nature of discrimination learning in animals. *Psychological Review,* 1937, *44,* 97–104.

Krechevsky, I. A study of the continuity of the problem-solving process. *Psychological Review,* 1938, *45,* 107–133.

Kučera, H., & Francis, W. N. *Computational analysis of present-day American English.* Providence, R.I.: Brown University Press, 1967.

Kuenne, M. P. Experimental investigation of the relation of language to transposition behavior in young children. *Journal of Experimental Psychology,* 1946, *36,* 471–490.

Kviem, O., Setekleiv, J., & Kaada, B. R. Differential effects of hippocampal lesions on maze and passive-avoidance learning in rats. *Experimental Neurology,* 1964, *9,* 59–72.

Lacey, J. I., Smith, R. L., & Green, A. The use of conditioned autonomic responses in the study of anxiety. *Psychosomatic Medicine,* 1955, *17,* 208–217.

Lakoff, G. Linguistics and natural logic. *Synthése,* 1970, *22,* 151–271.

Lakoff, G. On generative semantics. In D. Steinberg & L. Jakobovits (Eds.), *Semantics: An interdisciplinary reader in philosophy, linguistics, anthropology, and psychology.* London: Cambridge University Press, 1971.

Lambert, W. E., & Paivio, A. The influence of noun–objective order on learning. *Canadian Journal of Psychology,* 1956, *10,* 9–12.

Lashley, K. S. The problem of serial order in behavior. In L. A. Jeffress (Ed.), *Cerebral Mechanisms in Behavior.* New York: Wiley, 1951.

Lashley, K. S. Cerebral organization and behavior. *Research Publication Association Nervous Mental Disease,* 1958, *36,* 1–18.

Lashley, K. S., & Wade, M. The Pavlovian theory of generalization. *Psychological Review,* 1946, *53,* 72–87.

Lawrence, D. H. Acquired distinctiveness of cues: I. Transfer between discriminations on the basis of familiarity with the stimulus. *Journal of Experimental Psychology,* 1949, *39,* 770–784.

Lawrence, D. H. Acquired distinctiveness of cues: II. Selective association in a constant stimulus situation. *Journal of Experimental Psychology,* 1950, *40,* 175–188.

Lawrence, D. H. The transfer of a discrimination along a continuum. *Journal of Comparative and Physiological Psychology,* 1952, *45,* 511–516.

Lawrence, D. H. The applicability of generalization gradients to the transfer of discrimination. *Journal of General Psychology,* 1955, *52,* 37–48.

Lawrence, D. H. The nature of a stimulus: Some relationships between learning and perception. In S. Koch (Ed.), *Psychology: A study of a science* (Vol. 5). New York: McGraw-Hill, 1963.

Lawrence, D. H., & DeRivera, J. Evidence for relational transposition. *Journal of Comparative and Physiological Psychology,* 1954, *47,* 465–471.

Lawrence, D. H., & Festinger, L. *Deterrents and reinforcements.* Stanford, Calif.: Stanford University Press, 1962.

Lee-Teng, E., & Sherman, S. M. Memory consolidation of one-trial learning in chicks. *Proceedings of the National Academy of Sciences,* 1966, *56,* 926–931.

Lefcourt, H. M. The functions of the illusions of control and freedom. *American Psychologist,* 1973, *28,* 417–425.

Leicht, K. L., & Kausler, D. H. Functional stimulus learning as related to degree of practice and meaningfulness. *Journal of Experimental Psychology,* 1965, *69,* 100–101.

Leiman, A. L., & Christian, C. N. Electrophysiological analyses of learning and memory. In J. A. Deutsch (Ed.), *The physiolog-*

ical basis of memory. New York: Academic Press, 1973.

Leonard, D. J., & Zavala, A. Electroconvulsive shock, retroactive amnesia, and the single-shock method. *Science,* 1964, *146,* 1073–1074.

Lesse, H. Rhinencephalic electrophysiological activity during "emotional behavior" in cats. *Psychiatric Response Reports,* 1960, *12,* 332–333.

Levine, S. A further study of infantile handling and adult avoidance behavior. *Journal of Personality,* 1956, *25,* 70–80.

Levine, S. Infantile experience and consummatory behavior in adulthood. *Journal of Comparative and Physiological Psychology,* 1957, *50,* 609–612.

Levine, S. Noxious stimulation in infant and adult rats and consummatory behavior. *Journal of Comparative and Physiological Psychology,* 1958, *51,* 230–233.

Levine, S. The effects of differential infantile stimulation on emotionality at weaning. *Canadian Journal of Psychology,* 1959, *13,* 243–247.

Levine, S., Alpert, M., & Lewis, G. W. Differential maturation of an adrenal response to cold stress in rats manipulated in infancy. *Journal of Comparative and Physiological Psychology,* 1958, *51,* 774–777.

Levine, S., Chevalier, J. A., & Korchin, S. J. The effects of early shock and handling on later avoidance learning. *Journal of Personality,* 1956, *24,* 475–493.

Levine, S., Haltmeyer, G. C., Karas, G. G., & Denenberg, V. H. Physiological and behavioral effects of infantile stimulation. *Physiology and Behavior,* 1967, *2,* 55–59.

Levine, S., & Wetzel, A. Infantile experiences, strain differences, and avoidance learning. *Journal of Comparative and Physiological Psychology,* 1963, *56,* 879–881.

Lewis, D. J. Partial reinforcement: A selective review of the literature since 1950. *Psychological Bulletin,* 1960, *57,* 1–28.

Lewis, D. J., & Maher, B. A. Neural consolidation and electroconvulsive shock. *Psychological Review,* 1965, *72,* 225–239.

Lichtenstein, P. E. Studies of anxiety: I. The production of a feeding inhibition in dogs. *Journal of Comparative and Physiological Psychology,* 1950, *43,* 16–29.

Lickey, M. E., & Fox, S. S. Localization and habituation of sensory evoked DC responses in cat cortex. *Experimental Neurology,* 1966, *15,* 437–454.

Liddell, H. S. Conditioning and emotions. *Scientific American,* 1954, *190,* 48–57.

Light, L. L., & Carter-Sobell, L. Effects of changed semantic context on recognition memory. *Journal of Verbal Learning and Verbal Behavior,* 1970, *9,* 1–11.

Lindholm, B. W. Critical periods and the effects of early shock on later emotional behavior in the white rat. *Journal of Comparative and Physiological Psychology,* 1962, *55,* 597–599.

Lindsay, P. H., & Norman, D. A. *Human information processing: An introduction to psychology.* New York: Academic Press, 1972.

Lindsley, D. B., Bowden, J., & Magoun, H. W. Effect upon EEG of acute injury to the brain stem activating system. *Electroencephalography and Clinical Neurophysiology,* 1949, *1,* 475–486.

Lobb, H. Asymmetrical transfer of form discrimination across sensory modalities in human adults. *Journal of Experimental Psychology,* 1970, *86,* 350–354.

Loftus, E. F. Reconstructing memory: The incredible eyewitness. *Psychology Today,* 1974, *8,* 116–119.

Loftus, E. F., & Palmer, J. C. Reconstruction of automobile destruction: An example of the interaction between language and memory. *Journal of Verbal Learning and Verbal Behavior,* 1974, *13,* 585–589.

Loftus, E. F., & Zanni, G. Eyewitness testimony: The influence of the wording of a question. *Bulletin of the Psychonomic Society,* 1975, *5,* 86–88.

Logan, F. A. *Incentive.* New Haven, Conn.: Yale University Press, 1960.

Logan, F. A. Transfer of discrimination. *Journal of Experimental Psychology,* 1966, *71,* 616–618.

Logan, F. A. Incentive theory and changes in reward. In K. W. Spence & J. T. Spence (Eds.), *The psychology of learning and motivation* (Vol. 2). New York: Academic Press, 1968.

Logan, F. A. Essentials of a theory of discrimination learning. In H. H. Kendler & J. T. Spence (Eds.), *Essays in neobehaviorism: A memorial volume to Kenneth W. Spence.* New York: Appleton-Century-Crofts, 1971.

Logan, F. A. *Fundamentals of learning and motivation* (2nd ed.). Dubuque, Iowa: Brown, 1976.

Logan, F. A., & Wagner, A. R. *Reward and punishment.* Boston: Allyn & Bacon, 1965.

Long, K. K. Transfer from teaching to learning.

Journal of Educational Psychology, 1971, *62,* 167–178.

Lorenz, K. Der Kumpan in der Unwelt des Vogels. *Journal für Ornithologie,* 1935, *83,* 137–213; 289–314.

Lovaas, O. I., & Simmons, J. Q. Manipulation of self-destruction in three retarded children. *Journal of Applied Behavior Analysis,* 1969, *2,* 143–157.

Lovelace, E. A., & Blass, E. M. Utilization of stimulus elements in paired associate learning. *Journal of Experimental Psychology,* 1968, *76,* 596–600.

Lubar, J. F. Effect of medial cortical lesions on the avoidance behavior of the cat. *Journal of Comparative and Physiological Psychology,* 1964, *58,* 38–46.

Luttges, M. W., & McGaugh, J. L. Permanence of retrograde amnesia produced by electroconvulsive shock. *Science,* 1967, *156,* 408–410.

MacDougall, J. M., Van Hoesen, G. W., & Mitchell, J. C. Anatomical organization of septal projections in maintenance of DRL behavior in rats. *Journal of Comparative and Physiological Psychology,* 1969, *68,* 568–575.

Mackintosh, N. J. Selective attention in animal discrimination learning. *Psychological Bulletin,* 1965, *64,* 292–300.

Mackintosh, N. J. *The psychology of animal learning.* New York: Academic Press, 1974.

Macrides, F., & Chorover, S. L. *Neuroelectrical disturbances produced by intracerebral injection of puromycin dihydrochloride in rats.* Paper presented at the meeting of the Eastern Psychological Association, Washington, D.C., April 1968.

Madsen, M. C., & Kimble, D. P. The maze behavior of hippocampectomized rats under massed and distributed trials. *Psychonomic Science,* 1965, *3,* 193–194.

Madsen, M. C., & Luttges, M. W. Effect of electroconvulsive shock (ECS) on extinction of an approach response. *Psychological Reports,* 1963, *13,* 225–226.

Maier, N. R. F. Reasoning in humans: II. The solution of a problem and its appearance in consciousness. *Journal of Comparative Psychology,* 1931, *12,* 181–194.

Maier, S. F. Failure to escape electric shock: Incompatible skeletal–motor responses or learned helplessness? *Learning and Motivation,* 1970, *1,* 157–169.

Maier, S. F., Albin, R. W., & Testa, T. J. Failure to escape in rats previously exposed to inescapable shock depends on nature of escape response. *Journal of Comparative and Physiological Psychology,* 1973, *80,* 581–592.

Maier, S. F., Seligman, M. E. P., & Solomon, R. L. Pavlovian fear conditioning and learned helplessness. In B. A. Campbell & R. M. Church (Eds.), *Punishment and aversive behavior.* New York: Appleton-Century-Crofts, 1969.

Malloy, T. E., & Ellis, H. C. Attention and cue-producing responses in response-mediated stimulus generalization. *Journal of Experimental Psychology,* 1970, *83,* 191–200.

Malpass, R. S., & Kravitz, J. Recognition for faces of own and other "race." *Journal of Personality and Social Psychology,* 1969, *13,* 330–335.

Malpass, R. S., Lavigueur, H., & Weldon, D. E. Verbal and visual training in face recognition. *Perception and Psychophysics,* 1973, *14,* 285–292.

Mandler, G. From association to structure. *Psychological Review,* 1962, *69,* 415–427.

Mandler, G. Subjects do think: A reply to Jung's comments. *Psychological Review,* 1965, *72,* 323–326.

Mandler, G. Organization and memory. In K. W. Spence & J. T. Spence (Eds.), *The psychology of learning and motivation* (Vol. 1). New York: Academic Press, 1967.

Mandler, G. Association and organization: Facts, fancies, and theories. In T. R. Dixon & D. L. Horton (Eds.), *Verbal behavior and general behavior theory.* Englewood Cliffs, N.J.: Prentice-Hall, 1968.

Mandler, G. Organization and recognition. In E. Tulving & W. Donaldson (Eds.), *Organization of memory.* New York: Academic Press, 1972.

Mandler, G., & Heinemann, S. H. Effect of over-learning of a verbal response on transfer of training. *Journal of Experimental Psychology,* 1956, *51,* 39–46.

Mandler, J. M., & Mandler, G. *Thinking: From association to Gestalt.* New York: Wiley, 1964.

Margolius, G. Stimulus generalization of an instrumental response as a function of the number of reinforced trials. *Journal of Experimental Psychology,* 1955, *49,* 105–111.

Marks, L. E., & Miller, G. A. The role of semantic and syntactic constraints in the memorization of English sentences. *Journal of Verbal Learning and Verbal Behavior,* 1964, *3,* 1–5.

Marr, J. N., & Gardner, L. E., Jr. Early olfactory experience and later social behavior in the rat: Preference, sexual responsiveness, and care of young. *Journal of Genetic Psychology,* 1965, *107,* 167–174.

Marr, J. N., & Lilliston, L. G. Social attachment in rats by odor and age. *Behaviour,* 1969, *33,* 277–282.

Marsh, G. D. Inverse relationship between discriminability and stimulus generalization as a function of number of test stimuli. *Journal of Comparative and Physiological Psychology,* 1967, *64,* 284–289.

Martin, E. Transfer of verbal paired associates. *Psychological Review,* 1965, *72,* 327–343.

Martin, E. Relation between stimulus recognition and paired-associate learning. *Journal of Experimental Psychology,* 1967, *74,* 500–505. (a)

Martin, E. Stimulus recognition in aural paired-associate learning. *Journal of Verbal Learning and Verbal Behavior,* 1967, *6,* 272–276. (b)

Martin, E. Stimulus meaningfulness and paired-associate transfer: An encoding variability hypothesis. *Psychological Review,* 1968, *75,* 421–441.

Martin, E. Verbal learning theory and independent retrieval phenomena. *Psychological Review,* 1971, *78,* 314–332.

Martin, E. Stimulus encoding in learning and transfer. In A. W. Melton & E. Martin (Eds.), *Coding processes in human memory.* Washington, D.C.: Winston, 1972.

Martin, E., & Melton, A. W. Meaningfulness and trigram recognition. *Journal of Verbal Learning and Verbal Behavior,* 1970, *9,* 126–135.

Masserman, J. H. *Behavior and neurosis.* Chicago: University of Chicago Press, 1943.

Masserman, J. H., & Pechtel, C. Neuroses in monkeys: A preliminary report of experimental observations. *Annals of the New York Academy of Sciences,* 1953, *56,* 253–265.

McAllister, W. R., & McAllister, D. E. Variables influencing the conditioning and measurement of acquired fear. In W. F. Prokasy (Ed.), *Classical conditioning: A symposium.* New York: Appleton-Century-Crofts, 1965.

McCain, G. Partial reinforcement effects following a small number of acquisition trials. *Psychonomic Monograph Supplement,* 1966, *1,* 251–270.

McCain, G. Different levels of performance with equivalent weights of reward. *Psychonomic Science,* 1969, *14,* 2–3.

McCain, G. Reward magnitude and instrumental responses: Consistent and partial reward. *Psychonomic Science,* 1970, *19,* 139–141.

McCain, G., Dyleski, K., & McElvain, G. Reward magnitude and instrumental responses: Consistent reward. *Psychonomic Monograph Supplements,* 1971, *3*(16, Whole No. 48).

McCain, G., & Garrett, B. L. Generalization to stimuli of different brightness in three straight alley studies. *Psychological Reports,* 1964, *15,* 368–370.

McCleary, R. A. Response-modulation functions of the limbic system: Initiation and suppression. In E. Stellar & J. M. Sprague (Eds.), *Progress in physiological psychology* (Vol. 1). New York: Academic Press, 1966.

McCollough, C. Color adaptation of edge detectors in the human visual system. *Science,* 1965, *149,* 1115–1116.

McCulloch, T. C., & Pratt, J. C. A study of the pre-solution period in weight discrimination by white rats. *Journal of Comparative Psychology,* 1934, *18,* 271–290.

McGaugh, J. L. Time-dependent processes in memory storage. *Science,* 1966, *153,* 1351–1358.

McGaugh, J. L., & Alpern, H. P. Effects of electroshock on memory: Amnesia without convulsions. *Science,* 1966, *152,* 665–666.

McGaugh, J. L., & Herz, M. J. *Memory consolidation.* San Francisco: Albion, 1972.

McGaugh, J. L., Landfield, P. W., & Dawson, R. G. Delayed development of amnesia following electroconvulsive shock: A further examination. Unpublished manuscript cited in J. L. McGaugh & M. J. Herz, *Memory consolidation.* San Francisco: Albion, 1972.

McGeoch, J. A. Forgetting and the law of disuse. *Psychological Review,* 1932, *39,* 352–370.

McGeoch, J. A. *The psychology of human learning.* New York: Longmans, Green, 1942.

McGuire, W. J. A multiprocess model for paired-associate learning. *Journal of Experimental Psychology,* 1961, *62,* 335–347.

McIver, A. H., & Camp, B. Early cold stress: I. Effects on emotional reactivity in rats. *Proceedings of the American Psychological Association,* 1966, *1,* 155–156.

McIver, A. H., Jeffrey, W. E., Stevenson, M., & Nielson, H. C. Infantile handling and body temperature in the rat: III. Early temperature change and its implications for later responses. *Transactions of the New York Academy of Sciences,* 1968, *30,* 992–1000.

McKinney, F. Quantitative and qualitative essential elements of transfer. *Journal of Experimental Psychology,* 1933, *16,* 854–864.

McLaurin, W. A. Postirradiation saccharin avoidance in rats as a function of the interval between ingestion and exposure. *Journal of Comparative and Physiological Psychology,* 1964, *57,* 316–317.

McLaurin, W. A., Farley, J. A., Scarborough, B. B., & Rawlings, T. D. Postirradiation saccharin avoidance with non-coincident stimuli. *Psychological Reports,* 1964, *14,* 507–512.

Means, L. W., Huntley, D. H., Anderson, H. P., & Harrell, T. H. Deficient acquisition and retention of a visual–tactile discrimination task in rats with medial thalamic lesions. *Behavioral Biology,* 1973, *9,* 435–450.

Means, L. W., Leander, J. D., & Isaacson, R. L. The effects of hippocampectomy on alternation behavior and response to novelty. *Physiology and Behavior,* 1971, *6,* 17–22.

Meehl, P. E. On the circularity of the law of effect. *Psychological Bulletin,* 1950, *47,* 52–75.

Mellgren, R. L., & Dyck, D. G. Partial reinforcement effect, reverse partial reinforcement effect, and generalized partial reinforcement effect within subjects. *Journal of Experimental Psychology,* 1972, *92,* 339–346.

Melton, A. W. Implications of short-term memory for a general theory of memory. *Journal of Verbal Learning and Verbal Behavior,* 1963, *2,* 1–21.

Melton, A. W., & Irwin, J. McQ. The influence of degree of interpolated learning on retroactive inhibition and the overt transfer of specific responses. *American Journal of Psychology,* 1940, *53,* 173–203.

Melton, A. W., & Von Lackum, W. J. Retroactive and proactive inhibition in retention: Evidence for a two-factor theory of retroactive inhibition. *American Journal of Psychology,* 1941, *54,* 157–173.

Melvin, K. B., & Ervey, D. H. Facilitative and suppressive effects of punishment on species-typical aggressive display in *Betta splendens. Journal of Comparative and Physiological Psychology,* 1973, *83,* 451–457.

Mendoza, J. E., & Adams, H. E. Does electroconvulsive shock produce retrograde amnesia? *Physiology and Behavior,* 1969, *4,* 307–309.

Menzel, E. W., Davenport, R. K., & Rogers, C. M. Tool using in wild and restriction-reared chimpanzees. *Folia Primatologica,* 1970, *12,* 273–283.

Merikle, P. M. Paired-associate transfer as a function of stimulus and response meaningfulness. *Psychological Reports,* 1968, *22,* 131–138.

Merikle, P. M., & Battig, W. F. Transfer of training as a function of experimental paradigm and meaningfulness. *Journal of Verbal Learning and Verbal Behavior,* 1963, *4,* 485–488.

Merryman, C. T., & Merryman, S. S. Stimulus encoding in the *A–B′*, *Ax–B* and the *A–B′*$_r$, *Ax–B* paradigms. *Journal of Verbal Learning and Verbal Behavior,* 1971, *10,* 681–685.

Migler, B. Experimental self-punishment and superstitious escape behavior. *Journal of the Experimental Analysis of Behavior,* 1963, *6,* 371–385.

Migler, B. Effects of averaging data during stimulus generalization. *Journal of the Experimental Analysis of Behavior,* 1964, *7,* 303–307.

Miller, G. A. The magical number seven, plus or minus two: Some limits on our capacity for processing information. *Psychological Review,* 1956, *63,* 81–97.

Miller, G. A., Galanter, E., & Pribram, K. H. *Plans and the structure of behavior.* New York: Holt, Rinehart and Winston, 1960.

Miller, N. E. Studies of fear as an acquirable drive: I. Fear motivation and fear reduction as reinforcement in the learning of new responses. *Journal of Experimental Psychology,* 1948, *38,* 89–101.

Miller, N. E. Liberalization of basic S–R concepts: Extensions to conflict behavior, motivation and social learning. In S. Koch (Ed.), *Psychology: A study of a science* (Vol. 2). New York: McGraw-Hill, 1959.

Miller, N. E. Learning resistance to pain and fear: Effects of overlearning, exposure, and rewarded exposure in context. *Journal of Experimental Psychology,* 1960, *60,* 137–145.

Miller, N. E. Some recent studies of conflict behavior and drugs. *American Psychologist,* 1961, *16,* 12–24.

Miller, N. E. Learning of visceral and glandular responses. *Science,* 1969, *163,* 434–446.

Miller, N. E. Applications of learning and biofeedback to psychiatry and medicine. In A. M. Freedman, H. I. Kaplan, & B. J. Sadock (Eds.), *Comprehensive textbook in psychiatry* (Vol. 2). Baltimore: Williams and Wilkins, 1975.

Miller, N. E., & Banuazizi, A. Instrumental learning by curarized rats of a specific visceral response, intestinal or cardiac. *Journal of Comparative and Physiological Psychology,* 1968, *65,* 1–7.

Miller, N. E., & Carmona, A. Modification of a visceral response, salivation in thirsty dogs, by instrumental training with water reward. *Journal of Comparative and Physiological Psychology,* 1967, *63,* 1–6.

Miller, N. E., & DiCara, L. V. Instrumental learning of heart-rate changes in curarized rats: Shaping, and specificity to discriminative stimulus. *Journal of Comparative and Physiological Psychology,* 1967, *63,* 12–19.

Miller, N. E., & DiCara, L. V. Instrumental learning of urine formation in rats: Changes in renal blood flow. *American Journal of Physiology,* 1968, *215,* 677–683.

Miller, N. E., & Dollard, J. *Social learning and limitation.* New Haven, Conn.: Yale University Press, 1941.

Miller, N. E., & Dworkin, B. R. Visceral learning: Recent difficulties with curarized rats and significant problems for future research. In P. A. Obrist, A. H. Black, J. Brener, & L. V. DiCara (Eds.) *Cardiovascular psychophysiology.* Chicago: Aldine, 1974.

Miller, N. E., & Kessen, M. L. Reward effects of food via stomach fistula compared with those of food via mouth. *Journal of Comparative and Physiological Psychology,* 1952, *45,* 555–564.

Milner, B. The memory defect in bilateral hippocampal lesions. *Psychiatric Research Report,* 1959, *11,* 43–52.

Milner, B. Amnesia following operation on the temporal lobes. In C. M. W. Whitty & O. L. Zangwill (Eds.), *Amnesia.* London: Butterworth, 1966.

Monné, L. Functioning of the cytoplasm. In F. F. Nord (Ed.), *Advances in enzymology* (Vol. 8). New York: Interscience, 1948.

Montague, W. E. Elaborative strategies in verbal learning and memory. In G. H. Bower (Ed.), *The psychology of learning and memory* (Vol. 6). New York: Academic Press, 1972.

Montague, W. E., Adams, J. A., & Kiess, H. O. Forgetting and natural language mediation. *Journal of Experimental Psychology,* 1966, *72,* 829–833.

Montgomery, K. C. The role of exploratory drive in learning. *Journal of Comparative and Physiological Psychology,* 1954, *47,* 60–64.

Moore, J. W., & Gormezano, I. Effects of omitted versus delayed UCS on classical eyelid conditioning under partial reinforcement. *Journal of Experimental Psychology,* 1963, *65,* 248–257.

Morra, M. Level of maternal stress during two pregnancy periods on rat offspring behavior. *Psychonomic Science,* 1965, *3,* 7–8.

Moruzzi, G., & Magoun, H. W. Brain stem reticular formation and activation of the EEG. *Electroencephalography and Clinical Neurophysiology,* 1949, *1,* 455–473.

Moss, D. E. *Puromycin and memory.* Unpublished doctoral dissertation, Colorado State University, 1973.

Mueller, J. H., Gautt, P., & Evans, J. H. Stimulus encoding in A–B_r transfer. *Journal of Experimental Psychology,* 1974, *103,* 54–61.

Muenzinger, K. F. Motivation in learning: I. Electric shock for correct responses in the visual discrimination habit. *Journal of Comparative Psychology,* 1934, *17,* 267–278.

Müller, G. E., & Pilzecker, A. Experimentelle Beitrage zur Lehre vom Zedachtnis. *Zeitschrift für Psychologie,* Ergbd., 1900, *1,* 1–300.

Mullin, A. D., & Mogerson, G. J. Effects of fear conditioning on avoidance learning. *Psychological Reports,* 1963, *13,* 707–710.

Munsinger, H., & Weir, M. W. Infants' and young children's preference for complexity. *Journal of Experimental Child Psychology,* 1967, *5,* 69–73.

Murdock, B. B., Jr. Transfer designs and formulas. *Psychological Bulletin,* 1957, *54,* 313–326.

Murdock, B. B., Jr. The retention of individual items. *Journal of Experimental Psychology,* 1961, *62,* 618–625.

Murdock, B. B., Jr. The serial position effect of free recall. *Journal of Experimental Psychology,* 1962, *64,* 482–488.

Murdock, B. B., Jr. *Human memory: Theory and data.* Hillsdale, N.J.: Erlbaum, 1974.

Myer, J. S. Punishment of instinctive behavior: Suppression of mouse-killing by rats. *Psychonomic Science,* 1966, *4,* 385–386.

Myer, J. S. Prior killing experience and the suppressive effects of punishment on the killing of mice by rats. *Animal Behaviour,* 1967, *15,* 59–61.

Myer, J. S. Associative and temporal determinants of facilitation and inhibition of attack by pain. *Journal of Comparative and Physiological Psychology,* 1968, *66,* 17–21.

Myer, J. S. Effects of noncontingent aversive stimulation. In F. R. Brush (Ed.), *Aversive conditioning and learning.* New York: Academic Press, 1971.

Myer, J. S., & Baenninger, R. Some effects of punishment and stress on mouse killing by rats. *Journal of Comparative and Physiological Psychology,* 1966, *62,* 292–297.

Myer, J. S., & Ricci, D. Delay of punishment

gradients for the goldfish. *Journal of Comparative and Physiological Psychology,* 1968, *66,* 417–421.

Neisser, U. Decision time without reaction time: Experiments in visual scanning. *American Journal of Psychology,* 1963, *76,* 376–385.

Neisser, U. Visual search. *Scientific American,* 1964, *210*(6), 94–102.

Neisser, U. *Cognitive psychology.* New York: Appleton-Century-Crofts, 1967.

Neisser, U., & Beller, H. K. Searching through word lists. *British Journal of Psychology,* 1965, *56,* 349–358.

Neisser, U., & Hirst, W. Effect of practice on the identification of auditory sequences. *Perception and Psychophysics,* 1974, *15,* 391–398.

Neisser, U., Novick, R., & Lazar, R. Searching for ten targets simultaneously. *Perceptual and Motor Skills,* 1963, *17,* 955–961.

Nelson, T. O., & Rothbart, R. Acoustic savings for items forgotten from long-term memory. *Journal of Experimental Psychology,* 1972, *93,* 357–360.

Newell, A., & Simon, H. A. *Human problem solving.* Englewood Cliffs, N.J.: Prentice-Hall, 1972.

Newman, J. R., & Grice, G. R. Stimulus generalization as a function of drive level, and the relation between two measures of response strength. *Journal of Experimental Psychology,* 1965, *69,* 357–365.

Nicholls, M. F., & Kimble, G. A. Effect of instructions upon eyelid conditioning. *Journal of Experimental Psychology,* 1964, *67,* 400–402.

Nicosia, G. J., & Santa, J. L. Words and the reproduction of nonsense things. *Journal of Experimental Psychology: Human Learning and Memory,* 1975, *4,* 369–375.

Niki, H. The effects of hippocampal ablation on the behavior in the rat. *Japanese Psychological Research,* 1962, *4,* 139–153.

Nissen, H. W., Chow, K. L., & Semmes, J. Effects of restricted opportunity for tactual, kinesthetic, and manipulative experience on the behavior of a chimpanzee. *American Journal of Psychology,* 1951, *64,* 485–507.

Noble, C. E. An analysis of meaning. *Psychological Review,* 1952, *59,* 421–430.

Noble, C. E. Measurements of association value (*a*), rated associations (*a'*), and scaled meaningfulness (*m'*) for the 2100 CVC combinations of the English alphabet. *Psychological Reports,* 1961, *8,* 487–521.

Noble, M., & Adams, C. K. The effect of length of CS–US interval as a function of body temperature in a cold-blooded animal. *Journal of General Psychology,* 1963, *69,* 197–201.

Norman, D. A. Memory, knowledge, and the answering of questions. In R. L. Solso (Ed.), *Contemporary issues in cognitive psychology: The Loyola Symposium.* Washington, D.C.: Winston, 1973.

Norman, D. A. *Memory and attention.* New York: Wiley, 1976.

Norman, D. A., & Rumelhart, D. E. A system for perception and memory. In D. A. Norman (Ed.), *Models of human memory.* New York: Academic Press, 1970.

Norman, D. A., Rumelhart, D. E., & LNR Research Group. *Explorations in cognition.* San Francisco: Freeman, 1975.

Norris, E. B., & Grant, D. A. Eyelid conditioning as affected by verbally induced inhibitory set and counter reinforcement. *American Journal of Psychology,* 1948, *61,* 37–49.

Notterman, J. M., & Mintz, D. E. *Dynamics of response.* New York: Wiley, 1965.

Novinski, L. S. A reexamination of the part/whole effect in free recall. *Journal of Verbal Learning and Verbal Behavior,* 1972, *11,* 228–233.

Nurnberger, J. I. Direct enumeration of cells of the brain. In W. F. Windle (Ed.), *Biology of neuroglia.* Springfield, Ill.: Thomas, 1958.

Oldfield, R. C. Memory mechanisms and the theory of schemata. *British Journal of Psychology,* 1954, *45,* 14–23.

Olds, J. Operant conditioning of single unit responses. *Proceedings of the XXIII International Congress of Physiological Science,* 1965, *4,* 372–380.

Olds, J., & Hirano, T. Conditioned responses of hippocampal and other neurons. *Electroencephalography and Clinical Neurophysiology,* 1969, *26,* 159–166.

Olds, J., & Milner, P. Positive reinforcement produced by electrical stimulation of septal area and other regions of the rat brain. *Journal of Comparative and Physiological Psychology,* 1954, *47,* 419–427.

Olds, J., Mink, W. D., & Best, P. J. Single unit patterns during anticipatory behavior. *Electroencephalography and Clinical Neurophysiology,* 1969, *26,* 144–158.

Olds, J., & Olds, M. E. Interference and learning in paleocortical systems. In J. F. Delafresnaye (Ed.), *Brain mechanisms in learning.* Oxford: Blackwell, 1961.

Olton, D. S., & Isaacson, R. L. Hippocampal lesions and active avoidance. *Physiology and*

Behavior, 1968, *3,* 719–724.

Orwell, G. *1984.* New York: New American Library, 1949.

Osborn, A. F. *Applied imagination* (3rd ed.). New York: Scribner's, 1963.

Osgood, C. E. Meaningful similarity and interference in learning. *Journal of Experimental Psychology,* 1946, *36,* 244–301.

Osgood, C. E. The similarity paradox in human learning: A resolution. *Psychological Review,* 1949, *56,* 132–143.

Osgood, C. E. *Method and theory in experimental psychology.* New York: Oxford University Press, 1953.

Oshima, K., Gorbman, A., & Shimada, H. Memory-blocking agents: Effects on olfactory discrimination in homing salmon. *Science,* 1969, *165,* 86–88.

Overmier, J. B. Interference with avoidance behavior: Failure to avoid traumatic shock. *Journal of Experimental Psychology,* 1968, *78,* 340–343.

Overmier, J. B., & Leaf, R. C. Effects of discriminative Pavlovian fear conditioning upon previously or subsequently acquired avoidance responding. *Journal of Comparative and Physiological Psychology,* 1965, *60,* 213–217.

Overmier, J. B., & Seligman, M. E. P. Effects of inescapable shock upon subsequent escape and avoidance responding. *Journal of Comparative and Physiological Psychology,* 1967, *63,* 28–33.

Padilla, A. M. Analysis of incentive and behavioral contrast in the rat. *Journal of Comparative and Physiological Psychology,* 1971, *75,* 464–470.

Padilla, S. G. Further studies on the delayed pecking of chicks. *Journal of Comparative Psychology,* 1935, *20,* 413–443.

Pagano, R. R., Bush, D. F., Martin, G., & Hunt, E. B. Duration of retrograde amnesia as a function of electroconvulsive shock intensity. *Physiology and Behavior,* 1969, *4,* 19–21.

Paivio, A. Learning of adjective–noun paired associates as a function of adjective–noun word order and noun abstractness. *Canadian Journal of Psychology,* 1963, *17,* 370–373.

Paivio, A. Mental imagery in associative learning and memory. *Psychological Review,* 1969, *76,* 241–263.

Paivio, A. *Imagery and verbal processes.* New York: Holt, Rinehart and Winston, 1971.

Paivio, A., & Csapo, K. Short-term sequential memory for pictures and words. *Psychonomic Science,* 1971, *24,* 50–51.

Paivio, A., Smythe, P. C., & Yuille, J. C. Imagery versus meaningfulness of nouns in paired-associate learning. *Canadian Journal of Psychology,* 1968, *22,* 427–441.

Paivio, A., Yuille, J. C., & Madigan, S. A. Concreteness, imagery, and meaningfulness values for 925 nouns. *Journal of Experimental Psychology Monograph,* 1968, *76* (1, Pt. 2).

Paolino, R. M., & Hine, B. EEG seizure anomalies following supramaximal intensities of cortical stimulation. *Journal of Comparative and Physiological Psychology,* 1973, *82,* 285–293.

Paolino, R. M., & Levy, H. M. Amnesia produced by spreading depression and ECS: Evidence for time-dependent memory trace localization. *Science,* 1971, *172,* 746–749.

Paolino, R. M., Quartermain, D., & Levy, H. M. Effect of electroconvulsive shock duration on the gradient of retrograde amnesia. *Physiology and Behavior,* 1969, *4,* 147–149.

Parkinson, S. R., Kroll, N. E., & Parks, T. E. Short-term retention of superimposed and of spatially distinct multi-letter visual arrays. *Memory and Cognition,* 1973, *1,* 301–303.

Pavlov, I. P. *Conditioned reflexes* (G. V. Anrep, trans.). London: Oxford University Press, 1927.

Pavlov, I. P. *Lectures on conditioned reflexes.* New York: International Publishers, 1928.

Pearl, J. The effects of preshock and additional punishment on general activity. *Psychological Reports,* 1963, *12,* 155–161.

Pearl, J., Walters, G. C., & Anderson, D. C. Suppressive effects of aversive stimulation on subsequently punished behavior. *Canadian Journal of Psychology,* 1964, *18,* 343–355.

Peeke, H. V. S., McCoy, F., & Herz, M. J. Drive consummatory response effects on memory consolidation for appetitive learning in mice. *Communications in Behavioral Biology,* 1969, *4,* 49–53.

Pellegrino, L. J. Amygdaloid lesions and behavioral inhibition in the rat. *Journal of Comparative and Physiological Psychology,* 1968, *65,* 483–491.

Pellegrino, L. J., & Clapp, D. R. Limbic lesions and externally cued DRL performance. *Physiology and Behavior,* 1971, *7,* 863–868.

Penfield, W. The interpretative cortex. *Science,* 1959, *129,* 1719–1725.

Penfield, W. Speech, perception and the uncommitted cortex. *Pontifasiae Academiae Scientarum, Scripta Varia,* 1965, *30,* 319–347.

Penfield, W., & Milner, B. Memory deficits produced by bilateral lesions in the hippocampal zone. *Archives of Neurology and Psychiatry,* 1958, *79,* 475–497.

Penfield, W., & Perot, P. The brain's record of auditory and visual experience: A final summary and discussion. *Brain,* 1963, *86,* 595–696.

Penny, R. K. Children's escape performance as a function of schedules of delay of reinforcement. *Journal of Experimental Psychology,* 1967, *73,* 109–112.

Perfetti, C. A. Lexical density and phrase structure depth as variables in sentence retention. *Journal of Verbal Learning and Verbal Behavior,* 1969, *8,* 719–724.

Perin, C. T. The effect of delayed reinforcement upon the differentiation of bar responses in white rats. *Journal of Experimental Psychology,* 1943, *32,* 95–109.

Peterson, L. R., & Peterson, M. Short-term retention of individual items. *Journal of Experimental Psychology,* 1959, *58,* 193–198.

Pfaffman, C. The pleasures of sensation. *Psychological Review,* 1960, *67,* 253–268.

Phillips, M. I., & Olds, J. Unit activity: Motivation-dependent responses from midbrain neurons. *Science,* 1969, *165,* 1269–1271.

Pick, A. D. Improvement of visual and tactual form discrimination. *Journal of Experimental Psychology,* 1965, *69,* 331–339.

Pinckney, G. Avoidance learning in fish as a function of prior fear conditioning. *Psychological Reports,* 1967, *20,* 71–74.

Porter, L. W., & Duncan, C. P. Negative transfer in verbal learning. *Journal of Experimental Psychology,* 1953, *46,* 61–64.

Posner, M. I. Abstraction and the process of recognition. In J. T. Spence & G. H. Bower (Eds.), *The psychology of learning and motivation* (Vol. 3). New York: Academic Press, 1969.

Posner, M. I. *Cognition: An introduction.* Glenview, Ill.: Scott, Foresman, 1973.

Posner, M. I., & Keele, S. W. On the genesis of abstract ideas. *Journal of Experimental Psychology,* 1968, *77,* 353–363.

Posner, M. I., & Keele, S. W. Retention of abstract ideas. *Journal of Experimental Psychology,* 1970, *83,* 304–308.

Posner, M. I., & Konick, A. F. On the role of interference in short-term retention. *Journal of Experimental Psychology,* 1966, *72,* 221–231.

Posner, M. I., & Mitchell, R. F. Chronometric analysis of classification. *Psychological Review,* 1967, *74,* 392–409.

Postman, L. The history and present status of the law of effect. *Psychological Bulletin,* 1947, *44,* 489–563.

Postman, L. Association theory and perceptual learning. *Psychological Review,* 1955, *62,* 438–446.

Postman, L. The effects of language habits on the acquisition and retention of verbal associations. *Journal of Experimental Psychology,* 1962, *64,* 7–19. (a)

Postman, L. Transfer of training as a function of experimental paradigm and degree of first-list learning. *Journal of Verbal Learning and Verbal Behavior,* 1962, *1,* 109–118. (b)

Postman, L. Perception and learning. In S. Koch (Ed.), *Psychology: A study of a science* (Vol. 5). New York: McGraw-Hill, 1963.

Postman, L. Studies of learning to learn: II. Changes in transfer as a function of practice. *Journal of Verbal Learning and Verbal Behavior,* 1964, *3,* 437–447.

Postman, L. Differences between unmixed and mixed transfer designs as a function of paradigm. *Journal of Verbal Learning and Verbal Behavior,* 1966, *5,* 240–248.

Postman, L. Experimental analysis of learning to learn. In G. H. Bower & J. T. Spence (Eds.), *The psychology of learning and motivation* (Vol. 3). New York: Academic Press, 1969.

Postman, L. Transfer, interference and forgetting. In J. W. Kling & L. A. Riggs (Eds.), *Woodworth and Schlosberg's experimental psychology.* New York: Holt, Rinehart and Winston, 1971.

Postman, L. A pragmatic view of organization theory. In E. Tulving & W. Donaldson (Eds.), *Organization of memory.* New York: Academic Press, 1972.

Postman, L., Bruner, J. S., & McGinnies, E. Personal values as organizing factors in perception. *Journal of Abnormal and Social Psychology,* 1948, *43,* 142–154.

Postman, L., Burns, S., & Hasher, L. Studies of learning to learn: X. Nonspecific transfer effects in free recall learning. *Journal of Verbal Learning and Verbal Behavior,* 1970, *9,* 707–715.

Postman, L., & Greenbloom, R. Conditions of cue selection in the acquisition of paired-associate lists. *Journal of Experimental Psychology,* 1967, *73,* 91–100.

Postman, L., & Phillips, L. W. Short-term temporal changes in free recall. *Quarterly Journal of Experimental Psychology,* 1965, *17,* 132–138.

Postman, L., & Schwartz, M. Studies of learning to learn: I. Transfer as a function of method of practice and class of verbal materials. *Journal of Verbal Learning and Verbal Behavior,* 1964, *3,* 37–49.

Postman, L., & Stark, K. Studies of learning to learn: IV. Transfer from serial to paired-associate learning. *Journal of Verbal Learning and Verbal Behavior,* 1967, *6,* 339–353.

Postman, L., & Stark, K. Role of response availability in transfer and interference. *Journal of Experimental Psychology,* 1969, *79,* 168–177.

Postman, L., & Stark, K. Encoding variability and transfer. *American Journal of Psychology,* 1971, *84,* 461–472.

Postman, L., & Underwood, B. J. Critical issues in interference theory. *Memory and Cognition,* 1973, *1,* 19–40.

Premack, D. Toward empirical behavior laws: I. Positive reinforcement. *Psychological Review,* 1959, *66,* 219–233.

Premack, D., & Premack, A. J. Increased eating in rats deprived of running. *Journal of the Experimental Analysis of Behavior,* 1963, *6,* 209–212.

Prentice, W. C. H. Visual recognition of verbally labeled figures. *American Journal of Psychology,* 1954, *67,* 315–320.

Price, R. H., & Slive, A. B. Verbal processes in shape recognition. *Journal of Experimental Psychology,* 1970, *83,* 373–379.

Pritchard, R. M. Stabilized images on the retina. *Scientific American,* 1961, *204,* 72–78.

Prokasy, W. F., & Hall, J. F. Primary stimulus generalizations. *Psychological Review,* 1963, *70,* 310–322.

Pschirrer, M. E. Goal events as discriminative stimuli over extended intertrial intervals. *Journal of Experimental Psychology,* 1972, *96,* 425–432.

Puff, C. R. Clustering as a function of the sequential organization of stimulus word lists. *Journal of Verbal Learning and Verbal Behavior,* 1966, *5,* 503–506.

Puff, C. R. Role of clustering in free recall. *Journal of Experimental Psychology,* 1970, *87,* 384–386.

Purtle, R. B. Peak shift: A review. *Psychological Bulletin,* 1973, *80,* 408–421.

Quartermain, D., Paolino, R. M., & Miller, N. E. A brief temporal gradient of retrograde amnesia independent of situational change. *Science,* 1965, *149,* 1116–1118.

Quillian, M. R. Semantic memory. In M. Minsky (Ed.), *Semantic information processing.* Cambridge, Mass.: MIT Press, 1968.

Quillian, M. R. The teachable language comprehender. *Communications of the Association for Computing Machinery,* 1969, *12,* 459–476.

Rabe, A., & Haddad, R. K. Acquisition of two-way shuttlebox avoidance after selective hippocampal lesions. *Physiology and Behavior,* 1969, *4,* 319–323.

Rabinowitz, F. M., & Witte, K. L. Stimulus selection as a function of letter color. *Journal of Verbal Learning and Verbal Behavior,* 1967, *6,* 167–168.

Ranck, J. B., Jr. A movable microelectrode for recording from single neurons in unrestrained rats. In M. I. Phillips (Ed.), *Brain unit activity during behavior.* Iowa City: University of Iowa Press, 1973. (a)

Ranck, J. B., Jr. Studies on single neurons in dorsal hippocampal formation and septum in unrestrained rats: I. Behavioral correlates and firing repertoires. *Experimental Neurology,* 1973, *41,* 461–555. (b)

Rappoport, D. A., & Daginawala, H. F. Changes in nuclear RNA of brain induced by olfaction in catfish. *Journal of Neurochemistry,* 1968, *15,* 991–1006.

Ray, O. L., & Barrett, R. J. Disruptive effects of electroconvulsive shock as a function of current level and mode of delivery. *Journal of Comparative and Physiological Psychology,* 1969, *67,* 110–116.

Ray, O. S., & Bivens, L. W. Reinforcement magnitude as a determinant of performance decrement after electroconvulsive shock. *Science,* 1968, *160,* 330–332.

Raymond, G. A. *Accentuation and attenuation of punishment by prior exposure to aversive stimulation.* Unpublished doctoral dissertation, Brown University, 1968.

Razran, G. Stimulus generalization of conditioned responses. *Psychological Bulletin,* 1949, *46,* 337–365.

Razran, G. The observable unconscious and the inferable conscious in current Soviet psychophysiology: Interoceptive conditioning, semantic conditioning, and the orienting reflex. *Psychological Review,* 1961, *68,* 81–147.

Razran, G. *Mind in evolution.* Boston: Houghton Mifflin, 1971.

Rescorla, R. A. Pavlovian conditioning and its proper control procedures. *Psychological Review,* 1967, *74,* 71–80.

Rescorla, R. A. Second-order conditioning: Implications for theories of learning. In F. J. McGuigan & D. B. Lumsden (Eds.), *Contemporary approaches to conditioning and learning*. Washington, D.C.: Winston, 1973.

Rescorla, R. A., & Wagner, A. R. A theory of Pavlovian conditioning: Variations in the effectiveness of reinforcement and nonreinforcement. In A. H. Black & W. F. Prokasy (Eds.), *Classical conditioning II: Current research and theory*. New York: Appleton-Century-Crofts, 1972.

Reynolds, G. S. Behavioral contrast. *Journal of the Experimental Analysis of Behavior*, 1961, *4*, 57–71.

Richardson, J. Cue effectiveness and abstraction in paired-associate learning. *Psychological Bulletin*, 1971, *75*, 73–91.

Richardson, J. Encoding and stimulus selection in paired-associate verbal learning. In A. W. Melton & E. Martin (Eds.), *Coding processes in human memory*. Washington, D.C.: Winston, 1972.

Rickert, E. J. Role of feedback stimuli in response discrimination and differentiation. *Journal of Experimental Psychology*, 1969, *82*, 148–155.

Rickert, E. J., & Bennett, T. L. Performance of hippocampectomized rats on discontinuous negatively correlated reward. *Behavioral Biology*, 1972, *7*, 375–382.

Rickert, E. J., Bennett, T. L., Anderson, G. J., Corbett, J., & Smith, L. Differential performance of hippocampally ablated rats on nondiscriminated and discriminated DRL schedules. *Behavioral Biology*, 1973, *8*, 597–609.

Riesen, A. H. Arrested vision. *Scientific American*, 1950, *183*, 16–19.

Riley, D. A. The nature of the effective stimulus in animal discrimination learning. *Psychological Review*, 1958, *65*, 1–7.

Riley, D. A. Memory for form. In L. Postman (Ed.), *Psychology in the making*. New York: Knopf, 1962.

Riley, D. A. *Discrimination learning*. Boston: Allyn & Bacon, 1968.

Riopelle, A. J. Transfer suppression and learning sets. *Journal of Comparative and Physiological Psychology*, 1953, *46*, 61–64.

Rizley, R. C., & Rescorla, R. A. Associations in second-order conditioning and sensory preconditioning. *Journal of Comparative and Physiological Psychology*, 1972, *81*, 1–11.

Robbins, D. Partial reinforcement: A selective review of the alleyway literature since 1960. *Psychological Bulletin*, 1971, *76*, 415–431.

Robinson, J. S. The effect of learning labels for stimuli on their later discrimination. *Journal of Experimental Psychology*, 1955, *49*, 112–115.

Rock, I. The role of repetition in associative learning. *American Journal of Psychology*, 1957, *70*, 186–193.

Roenker, D. L., Thompson, C. P., & Brown, S. C. Comparison of measures for the estimation of clustering in free recall. *Psychological Bulletin*, 1971, *76*, 45–48.

Rogers, C. M., & Davenport, R. K. Effects of restricted rearing on sexual behavior of chimpanzees. *Developmental Psychology*, 1969, *1*, 200–204.

Rogers, J. L. Input and output components of learning to learn. *Journal of Experimental Psychology*, 1968, *78*, 233–241.

Rosenzweig, M. R. Effects of environment on development of brain and behavior. In E. Tobach, L. R. Aronson, & E. Shaw (Eds.), *The biopsychology of development*. New York: Academic Press, 1971.

Ross, L. E. The decremental effects of partial reinforcement during acquisition of the conditioned eyelid response. *Journal of Experimental Psychology*, 1959, *57*, 74–82.

Rowland, V. Cortical steady potential (direct current potential) in reinforcement and learning. In E. Stellar & J. M. Sprague (Eds.), *Progress in physiological psychology* (Vol. 2). New York: Academic Press, 1968.

Rowland, V., & Anderson, R. Brain steady potential shifts. In E. Stellar & J. M. Sprague (Eds.), *Progress in physiological psychology* (Vol. 4). New York: Academic Press, 1971.

Rowland, V., Bradley, H., School, P., & Deutschman, D. Cortical steady potential shifts in conditioning. *Conditional Reflex*, 1967, *2*, 3–22.

Rumelhart, D. E., Lindsay, P. H., & Norman, D. A. A process model for long-term memory. In E. Tulving & W. Donaldson (Eds.), *Organization of memory*. New York: Academic Press, 1972.

Rundus, D. Analysis of rehearsal processes in free recall. *Journal of Experimental Psychology*, 1971, *89*, 63–77.

Rundus, D., & Atkinson, R. C. Rehearsal processes in free recall: A procedure for direct observation. *Journal of Verbal Learning and Verbal Behavior*, 1970, *9*, 99–105.

Runquist, W. N. Performance in eyelid conditioning following change in reinforcement schedule. *Journal of Experimental Psychology*, 1963, *65*, 617–618.

Runquist, W. N. Verbal learning. In J. B. Sidowski (Ed.), *Experimental methods and instrumentation in psychology.* New York: McGraw-Hill, 1966.

Runquist, W. N. Functions relating intralist similarity in paired-associate learning. *Journal of Experimental Psychology,* 1968, *7,* 549–553.

Runquist, W. N., & Joinson, P. A. Rated similarity of low association value CVC trigrams. *Journal of Verbal Learning and Verbal Behavior,* 1968, *7,* 317–320.

Russell, P. A. Infantile stimulation in rodents: A consideration of possible mechanisms. *Psychological Bulletin,* 1971, *75,* 192–202.

Russell, W. A., & Storms, L. H. Implicit verbal chaining in paired-associate learning. *Journal of Experimental Psychology,* 1955, *49,* 287–293.

Sachs, J. S. Recognition memory for syntactic and semantic aspects of connected discourse. *Perception and Psychophysics,* 1967, *2,* 437–442.

Salama, A. A., & Hunt, J. Fixation in the rat as a function of infantile shocking, handling, and gentling. *Journal of Genetic Psychology,* 1964, *105,* 131–162.

Salapatek, P. Visual scanning of geometric figures by the human newborn. *Journal of Comparative and Physiological Psychology,* 1968, *66,* 247–258.

Salapatek, P., & Kessen, W. Visual scanning of triangles by the human newborn. *Journal of Experimental Child Psychology,* 1966, *3,* 155–167.

Saltz, E. *The cognitive bases of human learning.* Homewood, Ill.: Dorsey Press, 1971.

Sandler, J., & Davidson, R. S. Punished avoidance behavior in the presence of a nonpunished alternative. *Psychonomic Science,* 1967, *8,* 297–298.

Sandler, J., Davidson, R. S., Greene, W. E., & Holzschuh, R. D. Effects of increasing punishment frequency on Sidman avoidance behavior. *Psychonomic Science,* 1966, *5,* 103–104. (a)

Sandler, J., Davidson, R. S., Greene, W. E., & Holzschuh, R. D. Effects of punishment intensity on instrumental avoidance behavior. *Journal of Comparative and Physiological Psychology,* 1966, *61,* 212–216. (b)

Sandler, J., Davidson, R. S., & Malagodi, E. F. Durable maintenance of behavior during concurrent avoidance and punished–extinction conditions. *Psychonomic Science,* 1966, *6,* 105–106.

Santa, J. L. Verbal coding and redintegrative memory for shapes. *Journal of Experimental Psychology,* 1975, *104,* 286–294.

Santa, J. L., & Lamwers, L. L. Encoding specificity: Fact or artifact? *Journal of Verbal Learning and Verbal Behavior,* 1974, *13,* 412–423.

Santa, J. L., & Ranken, H. B. Language and memory: Redintegrative memory for shapes facilitated by naming. *Psychonomic Science,* 1968, *13,* 109–110.

Santa, J. L., & Ranken, H. B. Effects of verbal coding on recognition memory. *Journal of Experimental Psychology,* 1972, *93,* 268–278.

Schaefer, T. *The effects of early experience: Infant handling and later behavior in the white rat.* Unpublished doctoral dissertation, University of Chicago, 1957.

Schaefer, T., Weingarten, F. S., & Towne, J. C. Temperature change: The basic variable in the early handling phenomenon? *Science,* 1962, *135,* 41–42.

Schaeffer, A. A. Habit formation in frogs. *Journal of Animal Behavior,* 1911, *1,* 309–335.

Scheerer, M. Problem solving. *Scientific American,* 1963, *204*(4), 118–128.

Schiller, P. H., & Chorover, S. L. Short-term amnestic effects of electroconvulsive shock in one-trial maze learning paradigm. *Neuropsychologia,* 1967, *5,* 155–163.

Schmaltz, L. W., & Isaacson, R. L. The effects of preliminary training conditions upon DRL performance in the hippocampectomized rat. *Physiology and Behavior,* 1966, *1,* 175–182.

Schneider, A. M., Kapp, B., Aron, C., & Jarvik, M. E. Retroactive effects of transcorneal and transpinnate ECS on step-through latencies of mice and rats. *Journal of Comparative and Physiological Psychology,* 1969, *69,* 506–509.

Schreiner, L. H., & Kling, A. Behavioral changes following rhinencephalic injury in the cat. *Journal of Neurophysiology,* 1953, *16,* 643–659.

Schulz, R. W. Mediation. In C. P. Duncan, L. Sechrest, & A. W. Melton (Eds.), *Human memory: Festschrift for Benton J. Underwood.* New York: Appleton-Century-Crofts, 1972.

Schulz, R. W., & Lovelace, E. A. Mediation in verbal paired-associate learning: The role of temporal factors. *Psychonomic Science,* 1964, *1,* 95–96.

Schulz, R. W., & Weaver, G. E. The *A–B, B–C, A–C* mediation paradigm: The effects of variation in *A–C* study- and test-interval lengths and strength of *A–B* or *B–C*. *Journal of Experimental Psychology,* 1968, *76,* 303–311.

Schwartz, R. M., & Humphreys, M. S. List differentiation in part/whole free recall. *American Journal of Psychology,* 1973, *86,* 79–88.

Schwartzbaum, J. S., Kellicutt, M. H., Spieth, T. M., & Thompson, J. B. Effect of septal lesions in rats on response inhibition associated with food-reinforced behavior. *Journal of Comparative and Physiological Psychology,* 1964, *58,* 217–224.

Schwenn, E. A., & Postman, L. Studies of learning to learn: V. Gains in performance as a function of warm-up and associative practice. *Journal of Verbal Learning and Verbal Behavior,* 1967, *6,* 565–573.

Scoville, W. B., & Milner, B. Loss of recent memory after bilateral hippocampal lesions. *Journal of Neurology, Neurosurgery and Psychiatry,* 1957, *20,* 11–21.

Scragg, G. W. Answering questions about processes. In D. Norman & D. Rumelhart (Eds.), *Explorations in cognition.* San Francisco: Freeman, 1975.

Sechenov, I. M. *Reflexes of the brain.* Cambridge, Mass.: MIT Press, 1965.

Selfridge, O., & Neisser, V. Pattern recognition by machine. *Scientific American,* 1960, *203,* 60–80.

Seligman, M. E. P., & Beagley, G. Learned helplessness in the rat. *Journal of Comparative and Physiological Psychology,* 1975, *88,* 534–541.

Seligman, M. E. P., & Campbell, B. A. Effect of intensity and duration of punishment on extinction of an avoidance response. *Journal of Comparative and Physiological Psychology,* 1965, *59,* 295–297.

Seligman, M. E. P., & Groves, D. P. Nontransient learned helplessness. *Psychonomic Science,* 1970, *19,* 191–192.

Seligman, M. E. P., & Maier, S. F. Failure to escape traumatic shock. *Journal of Experimental Psychology,* 1967, *74,* 1–9.

Seligman, M. E. P., Maier, S. F., & Geer, J. The alleviation of learned helplessness in the dog. *Journal of Abnormal Psychology,* 1968, *73,* 256–262.

Seligman, M. E. P., Maier, S. F., & Solomon, R. L. Unpredictable and uncontrollable aversive events. In F. R. Brush (Ed.), *Aversive conditioning and learning.* New York: Academic Press, 1971.

Seligman, M. E. P., Rosellini, R. A., & Kozak, M. Learned helplessness in the rat: Reversibility, time course, and immunization. *Journal of Comparative and Physiological Psychology,* 1975, *88,* 542–547.

Senden, M. von. *Space and sight: The perception of space and shape in the congenitally blind before and after operation* (P. Heath, trans.). London: Methuen, 1960.

Seybert, J. A., Mellgren, R. L., Jobe, J. B., & Eckert, E. Sequential effects in discrete-trials instrumental escape conditioning. *Journal of Experimental Psychology,* 1974, *102,* 473–483.

Shaffer, R. W., & Ellis, H. C. An analysis of intersensory transfer of form. *Journal of Experimental Psychology,* 1974, *102,* 948–953.

Shaffer, R. W., & Howard, J. The transfer of information across sensory modalities. *Perception and Psychophysics,* 1974, *15,* 334–348.

Sheer, D. E. Electrophysiological correlates of memory consolidation. In G. Ungar (Ed.), *Molecular mechanisms in learning and memory.* New York: Plenum Press, 1970.

Sheffield, F. D. Relation between classical conditioning and instrumental learning. In W. F. Prokasy (Ed.), *Classical conditioning: A symposium.* New York: Appleton-Century-Crofts, 1965.

Sheffield, F. D. A drive induction theory of reinforcement. In R. N. Haber (Ed.), *Current research in motivation.* New York: Holt, Rinehart and Winston, 1966.

Sheffield, F. D., & Roby, T. B. Reward value of a non-nutritive sweet taste. *Journal of Comparative and Physiological Psychology,* 1950, *43,* 471–481.

Sheffield, F. D., Roby, T. B., & Campbell, B. A. Drive reduction versus consummatory behavior as determinants of reinforcement. *Journal of Comparative and Physiological Psychology,* 1954, *47,* 349–355.

Sheffield, F. D., Wulff, J. J., & Backer, R. Reward value of copulation with sex drive reduction. *Journal of Comparative Physiological Psychology,* 1951, *44,* 3–8.

Sheffield, V. F. Extinction as a function of partial reinforcement and distribution of practice. *Journal of Experimental Psychology,* 1949, *39,* 511–527.

Shepard, R. N. Comments on Professor Underwood's paper. In C. N. Cofer & B. B. Musgrave (Eds.), *Verbal behavior and learning.* New York: McGraw-Hill, 1963.

Shepard, R. N. Recognition memory for words, sentences, and pictures. *Journal of Verbal Learning and Verbal Behavior,* 1967, *6,* 156–163.

Shettleworth, S. J. Reinforcement and the organization of behavior in golden hamsters:

Hunger, environment, and food reinforcement. *Journal of Experimental Psychology: Animal Behavior Processes,* 1975, *104,* 56–87.

Shiffrin, R. M., & Geisler, W. S. Visual recognition in a theory of information processing. In R. L. Solso (Ed.), *Contemporary issues in cognitive psychology: The Loyola Symposium.* Washington, D.C.: Winston, 1973.

Shulman, H. G. Semantic confusion errors in short-term memory. *Journal of Verbal Learning and Verbal Behavior,* 1972, *11,* 221–227.

Sidman, M. A note on functional relations obtained from group data. *Psychological Bulletin,* 1952, *49,* 263–269.

Siegel, A. I. Deprivation of visual form definition in the ring dove: I. Discriminatory learning. *Journal of Comparative and Physiological Psychology,* 1953, *46,* 115–119.

Silbiger, F. F. *Facedness and complexity as determiners of attention in the human infant.* Unpublished doctoral dissertation, Wayne State University, 1968.

Simpson, G. G. The biological nature of man. *Science,* 1966, *152,* 472–478.

Skinner, B. F. *The behavior of organisms.* New York: Appleton-Century-Crofts, 1938.

Skinner, B. F. "Superstition" in the pigeon. *Journal of Experimental Psychology,* 1948, *38,* 168–172.

Skinner, B. F. *Verbal behavior.* New York: Appleton-Century-Crofts, 1957.

Skinner, B. F. Teaching machines. *Science,* 1958, *128,* 969–977.

Skinner, B. F. Teaching machines. *Scientific American,* 1961, *205,* 90–120.

Skinner, B. F. *About behaviorism.* New York: Knopf, 1974.

Slamecka, N. J. Recall and recognition in list-discrimination tasks as a function of the number of alternatives. *Journal of Experimental Psychology,* 1967, *74,* 187–192.

Slamecka, N. J., Moore, T., & Carey, S. Part-to-whole transfer and its relation to organization. *Journal of Verbal Learning and Verbal Behavior,* 1972, *11,* 73–82.

Slaughter, J., Hahn, W., & Rinaldi, P. Instrumental conditioning of heart rate in the curarized rat with varied amount of pretraining. *Journal of Comparative and Physiological Psychology,* 1970, *72,* 356–359.

Sluckin, W. *Imprinting and early experience.* Chicago: Aldine, 1965.

Smith, S. M., Brown, H. O., Toman, J. E. P., & Goodman, L. S. The lack of cerebral effects of d-tubocurarine. *Anesthesiology,* 1947, *8,* 1–14.

Smythe, P. C., & Paivio, A. A comparison of the effectiveness of word imagery and meaningfulness in paired-associate learning of nouns. *Psychonomic Science,* 1968, *10,* 49–50.

Sokolov, E. N. *Perception and the conditioned reflex.* New York: Pergamon Press, 1963.

Solomon, R. L. Punishment. *American Psychologist,* 1964, *19,* 239–253.

Solso, R. L. Functional stimulus selection as related to color versus verbal stimuli. *Journal of Experimental Psychology,* 1968, *78,* 382–387.

Solso, R. L. (Ed.) *Theories in cognitive psychology.* Hillsdale, N. J.: Erlbaum, 1974.

Spalding, D. A. Instinct with original observations on young animals. *British Journal of Animal Behaviour,* 1954, *2,* 1–11. (Originally published, 1873).

Spear, N. E., Ekstrand, B. R., & Underwood, B. J. Association by contiguity. *Journal of Experimental Psychology,* 1964, *67,* 151–161.

Spears, W. C. Assessment of visual preference and discrimination in the four-month-old infant. *Journal of Comparative and Physiological Psychology,* 1964, *57,* 381–386.

Spence, J. T., & Schulz, R. W. Negative transfer in paired-associate learning as a function of first-list trials. *Journal of Verbal Learning and Verbal Behavior,* 1965, *4,* 397–400.

Spence, K. W. The nature of discrimination learning in animals. *Psychological Review,* 1936, *43,* 427–449.

Spence, K. W. The differential response in animals to stimuli varying within a single dimension. *Psychological Review,* 1937, *44,* 430–444.

Spence, K. W. Continuous versus non-continuous interpretations of discrimination learning. *Psychological Review,* 1940, *47,* 271–288.

Spence, K. W. The basis of solution by chimpanzees of the intermediate size problem. *Journal of Experimental Psychology,* 1942, *31,* 257–271.

Spence, K. W. An experimental test of the continuity and non-continuity theories of discrimination learning. *Journal of Experimental Psychology,* 1945, *35,* 253–266.

Spence, K. W. The role of secondary reinforcement in delayed reward learning. *Psychological Review,* 1947, *54,* 1–8.

Spence, K. W. *Behavior theory and conditioning.* New Haven, Conn.: Yale University Press, 1956.

Spencer, H. *Principles of psychology.* New York: Appleton-Century-Crofts, 1855.

Sperling, G. A. The information available in

brief visual presentations. *Psychological Monographs,* 1960, *74*(11, Whole No. 498).

Sperling, G. A. A model for visual memory tasks. *Human Factors,* 1963, *5,* 19–31.

Sperling, G. A. Successive approximations to a model for short-term memory. *Acta Psychologica,* 1967, *27,* 285–292.

Spevack, A. A., & Suboski, M. D. Retrograde effects of electroconvulsive shock on learned responses. *Psychological Bulletin,* 1969, *72,* 66–76.

Spiegel, T. A., Hostetter, G., & Thomas, G. J. Effects of bilateral lesions in the hippocampus on acquisition of two-maze problems. *Psychonomic Science,* 1966, *6,* 205–206.

Spielberger, C. D., & DeNike, L. D. Descriptive behaviorism versus cognitive theory in verbal operant conditioning. *Psychological Review,* 1966, *73,* 306–326.

Spitz, R. A., & Wolf, K. M. Anaclitic depression. In *Psychoanalytic study of the child* (Vol. 2). New York: International Universities Press, 1946.

Spivey, J. E. *Influence of small numbers of partial reinforcement training trials on resistance to extinction.* Unpublished doctoral dissertation, University of Texas, 1964.

Spooner, A., & Kellogg, W. N. The backward conditioning curve. *American Journal of Psychology,* 1947, *60,* 321–334.

Staats, A. W. *Learning, language, and cognition.* New York: Holt, Rinehart and Winston, 1968.

Staats, A. W. Linguistic–mentalistic theory versus an explanatory S–R learning theory of language development. In D. Slobin (Ed.), *The ontogenesis of grammar.* New York: Academic Press, 1971.

Staddon, J. E. R., & Simmelhag, V. L. The "superstition" experiment: A reexamination of its implications for the principles of adaptive behavior. *Psychological Review,* 1971, *78,* 3–43.

Stebbins, W. C. Response latency as a function of amount of reinforcement. *Journal of the Experimental Analysis of Behavior,* 1962, *5,* 305–307.

Stein, D. G., & Kimble, D. P. Effects of hippocampal lesions and posttrial strychnine administration on maze behavior in the rat. *Journal of Comparative and Physiological Psychology,* 1966, *62,* 243–249.

Sternberg, R. J., & Bower, G. H. Transfer in part–whole and whole–part free recall: A comparative evaluation of theories. *Journal of Verbal Learning and Verbal Behavior,* 1974, *13,* 1–26.

Sternberg, S. High-speed scanning in human memory. *Science,* 1966, *153,* 652–654.

Sternberg, S. Memory-scanning: Mental processes revealed by reaction-time experiments. *Acta Psychologica,* 1969, *30,* 276–315.

Storms, L. H., Boroczi, G., & Broen, W. E. Effects of punishment as a function of strain of rat and duration of shock. *Journal of Comparative and Physiological Psychology,* 1963, *56,* 1022–1026.

Storms, L. H., Boroczi, G., & Broen, W. E. Recovery from punishment of bar pressing maintained on fixed and variable interval reward schedules. *Psychonomic Science,* 1965, *3,* 289–290.

Stratton, G. M. Some preliminary experiments on vision without inversion of the retinal image. *Psychological Review,* 1896, *3,* 611–617.

Stratton, G. M. Upright vision and the retinal image. *Psychological Review,* 1897, *4,* 182–187.

Stromeyer, C. F. Further studies of the McCollough effect. *Perception and Psychophysics,* 1969, *6,* 105–110.

Stromeyer, C. F., & Mansfield, R. J. Colored aftereffects produced with moving images. *Perception and Psychophysics,* 1970, *7,* 108–114.

Strong, P. N., Jr. Memory for object discriminations in the rhesus monkey. *Journal of Comparative and Physiological Psychology,* 1959, *52,* 333–335.

Surridge, C. T., & Amsel, A. Performance under a single alternation schedule of reinforcement at 24-hour intertrial interval. *Psychonomic Science,* 1965, *3,* 131–132.

Surridge, C. T., & Amsel, A. Acquisition and extinction under single alternation and random partial-reinforcement conditions with a 24-hour intertrial interval. *Journal of Experimental Psychology,* 1966, *72,* 361–368.

Surridge, C. T., & Amsel, A. Confinement duration on rewarded and nonrewarded trials and patterning at 24-hour ITI. *Psychonomic Science,* 1968, *10,* 107–108.

Sutherland, N. S., Mackintosh, N. J., & Mackintosh, J. Simultaneous discrimination training on Octopus and transfer of discrimination along a continuum. *Journal of Comparative and Physiological Psychology,* 1963, *56,* 150–156.

Tatum, B. C. Stimulus imagery effect in associative learning: Differentiation or mediation? *Journal of Experimental Psychology: Human*

Learning and Memory, 1976, *2,* 252–261.

Teitelbaum, H. A comparison of effects of orbitofrontal and hippocampal lesions upon discrimination learning and reversal in the cat. *Experimental Neurology,* 1964, *9,* 452–462.

Terrace, H. S. Wavelength generalization after discrimination learning with and without errors. *Science,* 1964, *144,* 78–80.

Terrace, H. S. Behavioral contrast and the peak shift: Effects of extended discrimination training. *Journal of the Experimental Analysis of Behavior,* 1966, *9,* 613–617. (a)

Terrace, H. S. Discrimination learning and inhibition. *Science,* 1966, *154,* 1677–1680. (b)

Terrace, H. S. Stimulus control. In W. K. Honig (Ed.), *Operant behavior: Areas of research and application.* New York: Appleton-Century-Crofts, 1966. (c)

Terris, W., & Barnes, M. Learned resistance to punishment and subsequent responsiveness to the same and novel punishments. *Psychonomic Science,* 1969, *15,* 49–50.

Terris, W., & Rahhal, D. K. Learning to resist mild and intense punishment and subsequent resistance to air-blast punishment. *Psychonomic Science,* 1969, *15,* 45–46.

Terris, W., & Wechkin, S. Learning to resist the effects of punishment. *Psychonomic Science,* 1967, *7,* 161–162.

Theios, J. The partial reinforcement effect sustained through blocks of continuous reinforcement. *Journal of Experimental Psychology,* 1962, *64,* 1–6.

Thomas, D. R., & Switalski, R. W. Comparison of stimulus generalization following variable-ratio and variable-interval training. *Journal of Experimental Psychology,* 1966, *71,* 236–240.

Thomas, G. J. Maze retention by rats with hippocampal lesions and with fornicotomies. *Journal of Comparative and Physiological Psychology,* 1971, *75,* 41–49.

Thomas, G. J., Hostetter, G., & Barker, D. J. Behavioral functions of the limbic system. In E. Stellar & J. M. Sprague (Eds.), *Progress in physiological psychology* (Vol. 2). New York: Academic Press, 1968.

Thomas, G. J., & Slotnik, B. Impairment of avoidance responding by lesions in cingulate cortex in rats depends on food drive. *Journal of Comparative and Physiological Psychology,* 1963, *56,* 959–964.

Thomas, H. Visual-fixation responses of infants to stimuli of varying complexity. *Child Development,* 1965, *36,* 629–638.

Thompson, C. P. On the incompatibility of the Houston and Osgood transfer surfaces. *Psychological Review,* 1966, *73,* 586–588.

Thompson, C. P., Hamlin, V. J., & Roenker, D. L. A comment on the role of clustering in free recall. *Journal of Experimental Psychology,* 1972, *94,* 108–109.

Thompson, J. B., & Schwartzbaum, J. S. Discrimination behavior and conditioned suppression (CER) following localized lesions in the amygdala and putamen. *Psychological Reports,* 1964, *15,* 587–606. (Monograph Supplement 4–v15)

Thompson, R. The effects of degree of learning and problem difficulty on perseveration. *Journal of Experimental Psychology,* 1958, *55,* 496–500.

Thompson, R. Localization of the "visual memory system" in the white rat. *Journal of Comparative and Physiological Psychology,* 1969, *69,* 1–29.

Thompson, R., & Massopust, L. C. The effect of subcortical lesions on retention of a brightness discrimination in rats. *Journal of Comparative and Physiological Psychology,* 1960, *53,* 488–496.

Thompson, R., & McConnell, J. Classical conditioning in the planarian. *Journal of Comparative and Physiological Psychology,* 1955, *48,* 65–68.

Thompson, R. F. *Foundations of physiological psychology.* New York: Harper & Row, 1967.

Thompson, W. R. Influence of prenatal maternal anxiety on emotionality in young rats. *Science,* 1957, *125,* 698–699.

Thomson, D. M. Context effects in recognition memory. *Journal of Verbal Learning and Verbal Behavior,* 1972, *11,* 497–511.

Thomson, D. M., & Tulving, E. Associative encoding and retrieval: Weak and strong cues. *Journal of Experimental Psychology,* 1970, *86,* 255–262.

Thorndike, E. L. Animal intelligence: An experimental study of the associative processes in animals. *Psychological Review Monograph Supplements,* 1898, *2* (Whole No. 8).

Thorndike, E. L. *Animal intelligence.* New York: Macmillan, 1911.

Thorndike, E. L. *Educational psychology* (Vol. 2). New York: Teachers College Press, Columbia University, 1913.

Thorndike, E. L. *The fundamentals of learning.* New York: Teachers College Press, Columbia University, 1932.

Thorndike, E. L., & Lorge, I. *The teacher's word book of 30,000 words.* New York:

Teachers College Press, Columbia University, 1944.

Thorndike, E. L., & Woodworth, R. S. The influence of improvement in one mental function upon the efficiency of other functions (I). II. The estimation of magnitudes. III. Functions involving attention, observation and discrimination. *Psychological Review,* 1901, *8,* 247–261, 384–395, 553–563.

Thune, L. E. The effects of different types of preliminary activities on subsequent learning of paired-associate material. *Journal of Experimental Psychology,* 1950, *40,* 423–438.

Tighe, L. S., & Tighe, T. J. Discrimination learning: Two views in historical perspective. *Psychological Bulletin,* 1966, *66,* 353–370.

Trabasso, T., & Bower, G. H. *Attention in learning: Theory and research.* New York: Wiley, 1968.

Trafton, C. L. Effects of lesions in the septal area and cingulate cortical areas on conditioned suppression of activity and avoidance behavior in rats. *Journal of Comparative and Physiological Psychology,* 1967, *68,* 191–197.

Trapold, M. A., & Spence, K. W. Performance change in eyelid conditioning as related to the motivational and reinforcing properties of the UCS. *Journal of Experimental Psychology,* 1960, *59,* 209–213.

Traupmann, K. L. Acquisition and extinction of an instrumental running response with a single- or multiple-pellet reward. *Psychonomic Science,* 1971, *22,* 61–63.

Travis, R. P., Jr., Hooten, T. F., & Sparks, D. L. Single unit activity related to behavior motivated by food reward. *Physiology and Behavior,* 1968, *3,* 309–318.

Travis, R. P., Jr., & Sparks, D. L. Changes in unit activity during stimuli associated with food and shock reinforcement. *Physiology and Behavior,* 1967, *2,* 171–177.

Travis, R. P., Jr., Sparks, D. L., & Hooten, T. F. Single unit response related to sequences of food motivated behavior. *Brain Research,* 1968, *7,* 455–458.

Treisman, A. M. Verbal cues, language, and meaning in selective attention. *American Journal of Psychology,* 1964, *77,* 206–219.

Truax, T., & Thompson, R. Role of the hippocampus in performance of easy and difficult discrimination tasks. *Journal of Comparative and Physiological Psychology,* 1969, *67,* 228–234.

Tulving, E. Subjective organization in free recall of "unrelated" words. *Psychological Review,* 1962, *69,* 344–354.

Tulving, E. Subjective organization and effects of repetition in multi-trial free-recall learning. *Journal of Verbal Learning and Verbal Behavior,* 1966, *5,* 193–197.

Tulving, E. Theoretical issues in free recall. In T. R. Dixon & D. L. Horton (Eds.), *Verbal behavior and general behavior theory.* Englewood Cliffs, N.J.: Prentice-Hall, 1968.

Tulving, E., & Donaldson, W. (Eds.). *Organization of memory.* New York: Academic Press, 1972.

Tulving, E., & Madigan, S. A. Memory and verbal learning. *Annual Review of Psychology,* 1970, *21,* 437–484.

Tulving, E., & Osler, S. Effectiveness of retrieval cues in memory for words. *Journal of Experimental Psychology,* 1968, *77,* 593–601.

Tulving, E., & Pearlstone, Z. Availability versus accessibility of information in memory for words. *Journal of Verbal Learning and Verbal Behavior,* 1966, *5,* 381–391.

Tulving, E., & Thomson, D. M. Retrieval processes in recognition memory: Effects of associative context. *Journal of Experimental Psychology,* 1971, *87,* 116–124.

Tulving, E., & Thomson, D. M. Encoding specificity and retrieval processes in episodic memory. *Psychological Review,* 1973, *80,* 352–373.

Turner, C. H., Davenport, R. K., & Rogers, C. M. The effect of early deprivation on the social behavior of adolescent chimpanzees. *American Journal of Psychiatry,* 1969, *125,* 1531–1536.

Twedt, H. M., & Underwood, B. J. Mixed vs. unmixed lists in transfer studies. *Journal of Experimental Psychology,* 1959, *95,* 375–381.

Ulrich, R. E., Hutchinson, R. R., & Azrin, N. H. Pain-elicited aggression. *Psychological Record,* 1965, *15,* 111–126.

Ulrich, R. E., Wolff, P. C., & Azrin, N. H. Shock as an elicitor of intra- and inter-species fighting behaviour. *Animal Behaviour,* 1964, *12,* 14–15.

Underwood, B. J. Associative transfer in verbal learning as a function of response similarity and degree of first-list learning. *Journal of Experimental Psychology,* 1951, *42,* 44–54.

Underwood, B. J. Interference and forgetting. *Psychological Review,* 1957, *64,* 49–50.

Underwood, B. J. Individual and group predictions of item difficulty for free learning.

Journal of Experimental Psychology, 1966, *71,* 673–679.

Underwood, B. J. Attributes of memory. *Psychological Review,* 1969, *76,* 559–573.

Underwood, B. J. Are we overloading memory? In A. W. Melton & E. Martin (Eds.), *Coding processes in human memory.* Washington, D.C.: Winston, 1972.

Underwood, B. J., & Ekstrand, B. R. Differentiation among stimuli as a factor in transfer performance. *Journal of Verbal Learning and Verbal Behavior,* 1968, *7,* 172–175.

Underwood, B. J., Ekstrand, B. R., & Keppel, G. An analysis of intralist similarity in verbal learning with experiments on conceptual similarity. *Journal of Verbal Learning and Verbal Behavior,* 1965, *4,* 447–462.

Underwood, B. J., Ham, M., & Ekstrand, B. R. Cue selection in paired-associate learning. *Journal of Experimental Psychology,* 1962, *64,* 405–409.

Underwood, B. J., & Keppel, G. One-trial learning? *Journal of Verbal Learning and Verbal Behavior,* 1962, *1,* 1–13.

Underwood, B. J., Runquist, W. N., & Schulz, R. W. Response learning in paired-associate lists as a function of intralist similarity. *Journal of Experimental Psychology,* 1959, *58,* 70–78.

Underwood, B. J., & Schulz, R. W. *Meaningfulness and verbal learning.* Philadelphia: Lippincott, 1960.

Ungar, G. Molecular mechanisms in information processing. *International Review of Neurobiology,* 1970, *13,* 223–253.

Unna, K. R., & Pelikan, E. W. Evaluation of curarizing drugs in man: VI. Critique of experiments on unanesthetized subjects. In A. R. McIntyre (Ed.), Curare and anti-curare agents. *Annals of the New York Academy of Sciences,* 1951, *54,* 297–530.

Ursin, H. Effect of amygdaloid lesions on avoidance behavior and visual discrimination in cats. *Experimental Neurology,* 1965, *11,* 298–317.

Vanderplas, J. M. Associative processes and task relations in perceptual learning. *Perceptual and Motor Skills,* 1963, *16,* 501–509.

Vanderplas, J. M. Perception and learning. In M. H. Marx (Ed.), *Learning: Interactions.* New York: Macmillan, 1970.

Vanderplas, J. M., & Garvin, E. A. Complexity, association value, and practice as factors in shape recognition following paired-associates training. *Journal of Experimental Psychology,* 1959, *57,* 155–163.

Vanderplas, J. M., Sanderson, W. A., & Vanderplas, J. N. Some task-related determinants of transfer in perceptual learning. *Perceptual and Motor Skills,* 1964, *18,* 71–80.

Vanderwolf, C. H. Limbic–diencephalic mechanisms of voluntary movement. *Psychological Review,* 1971, *78,* 83–113.

Wagner, A. R. Effects of amount and percentage of reinforcement and number of acquisition trials on conditioning and extinction. *Journal of Experimental Psychology,* 1961, *62,* 234–242.

Walk, R. D., & Gibson, E. J. A comparative and analytical study of visual depth perception. *Psychological Monographs,* 1961, *75*(15).

Walk, R. D., Gibson, E. J., Pick, H. L., & Tighe, T. J. The effectiveness of prolonged exposure to cutouts vs. painted patterns for facilitation of discrimination. *Journal of Comparative and Physiological Psychology,* 1959, *52,* 519–521.

Walsh, D. A., & Jenkins, J. J. Effects of orienting tasks on free recall in incidental learning: "Difficulty," "effort," and "process" explanations. *Journal of Verbal Learning and Verbal Behavior,* 1973, *12,* 481–488.

Walter, W. G. The location of cerebral tumours by electroencephalography. *Lancet,* 1936, *2,* 305–308.

Walter, W. G. Slow potential waves in the human brain associated with expectancy, attention and decision. *Archiv für die Psychiatrie und Zeitschrift für die gesamte Neurologie,* 1964, *206,* 309–322.

Ward, L. B. Reminiscence and rote learning. *Psychological Monographs,* 1937, *49*(220).

Warren, J. M., & Brookshire, K. H. Stimulus generalization and discrimination learning by primates. *Journal of Experimental Psychology,* 1959, *58,* 348–351.

Warrington, E. K., & Weiskrantz, L. An analysis of short-term and long-term memory defects in man. In J. A. Deutsch (Ed.), *The physiological basis of memory.* New York: Academic Press, 1973.

Watson, J. B. *Behavior: An Introduction to Comparative Psychology.* New York: Holt, Rinehart & Winston, 1914.

Watson, J. B. *Behaviorism.* New York: Norton, 1924.

Waugh, N. C., & Norman, D. A. Primary memory. *Psychological Review,* 1965, *72,* 89–104.

Webster, D. B., & Voneida, R. J. Learning deficits following hippocampal lesions in split-brain cats. *Experimental Neurology,* 1964, *10,* 170–182.

Weiss, J. M., Kriekhaus, E. E., & Conte, R. Effects of fear conditioning on subsequent avoidance behavior. *Journal of Comparative and Physiological Psychology,* 1968, *65,* 413–421.

Whiting, J. W. M., & Mowrer, O. H. Habit progression and regression—A study of some factors relevant to human socialization. *Journal of Comparative Psychology,* 1943, *36,* 229–253.

Whorf, B. L. *Language, thought, and reality* (J. B. Carroll, Ed.). New York: Wiley, 1956.

Wickens, D. D. Encoding categories of words: An empirical approach to meaning. *Psychological Review,* 1970, *77,* 1–15.

Wickens, D. D. Characteristics of word encoding. In A. W. Melton & E. Martin (Eds.), *Coding processes in human memory.* Washington, D.C.: Winston, 1972.

Wickens, D. D. Classical conditioning, as it contributes to the analyses of some basic psychological processes. In F. J. McGuigan & D. B. Lumsden (Eds.), *Contemporary approaches to conditioning and learning.* Washington, D.C.: Winston, 1973.

Wickens, D. D., Born, D. G., & Allen, C. K. Proactive inhibition and item similarity in short-term memory. *Journal of Verbal Learning and Verbal Behavior,* 1963, *2,* 440–445.

Wickens, D. D., & Cermak, L. S. Transfer effects of synonyms and antonyms in mixed and unmixed lists. *Journal of Verbal Learning and Verbal Behavior,* 1967, *6,* 832–839.

Wickens, D. D., Schroder, H. M., & Snide, J. D. Primary stimulus generalization of the GSR under two conditions. *Journal of Experimental Psychology,* 1954, *47,* 52–56.

Wicker, F. W. On the locus of picture–word differences in paired-associate learning. *Journal of Verbal Learning and Verbal Behavior,* 1970, *9,* 52–57.

Wike, E. L. Secondary reinforcement: Some research and theoretical issues. In W. J. Arnold & D. Levine (Eds.), *Nebraska Symposium on Motivation.* Lincoln: University of Nebraska Press, 1969.

Wild, J. M., & Blampied, N. M. Hippocampal lesions and stimulus generalization in rats. *Physiology and Behavior,* 1972, *9,* 505–511.

Williams, D. R., & Williams, H. Automaintenance in the pigeon: Sustained pecking despite contingent nonreinforcement. *Journal of the Experimental Analysis of Behavior,* 1969, *12,* 511–520.

Williams, R. F., & Underwood, B. J. Encoding variability: Tests of the Martin hypothesis. *Journal of Experimental Psychology,* 1970, *86,* 317–324.

Williams, S. B. Resistance to extinction as a function of number of reinforcements. *Journal of Experimental Psychology,* 1938, *23,* 506–522.

Wilson, M., Warren, J. M., & Abbott, L. Infantile stimulation, activity, and learning by cats. *Child Development,* 1965, *36,* 843–853.

Wilson, P. D., & Riesen, A. H. Visual development in rhesus monkeys neonatally deprived of patterned light. *Journal of Comparative and Physiological Psychology,* 1966, *61,* 87–95.

Wilson, W., Weiss, E. J., & Amsel, A. Two tests of the Sheffield hypothesis concerning resistance to extinction, partial reinforcement, and distribution of practice. *Journal of Experimental Psychology,* 1955, *50,* 51–60.

Wimer, R. Osgood's transfer surface: Extension and test. *Journal of Verbal Learning and Verbal Behavior,* 1964, *3,* 274–279.

Winograd, E., & Conn, C. P. Evidence from recognition memory for specific encoding of unmodified homographs. *Journal of Verbal Learning and Verbal Behavior,* 1971, *10,* 199–206.

Winson, J. Inter-species differences in the occurrence of theta. *Behavioral Biology,* 1972, *7,* 479–487.

Winzenz, D. Group structure and coding in serial learning. *Journal of Experimental Psychology,* 1972, *92,* 8–19.

Winzenz, D., & Bower, G. H. Subject-imposed coding and memory for digit series. *Journal of Experimental Psychology,* 1970, *83,* 52–56.

Wischner, G. J., & Fowler, H. Discrimination performance as affected by duration of shock for either the correct or incorrect response. *Psychonomic Science,* 1964, *1,* 239–240.

Wiseman, S., & Tulving, E. Encoding specificity: Relation between recall superiority and recognition failure. *Journal of Experimental Psychology: Human Learning and Memory,* 1976, *2,* 349–361.

Wisenfeld, Z. *Steady potential correlates of T-maze learning in the rat.* Unpublished master's thesis, Case Western Reserve University, 1969.

Wollen, K. A. Effects of instructional set and materials upon forward and backward learning. *Journal of Experimental Psychology,* 1970, *85,* 275–277.

Wollen, K. A., Weber, A., & Lowry, D. H. Bizarreness versus interaction of mental image as determinants of learning. *Cognitive Psychology,* 1972, *3,* 518–523.

Wood, G. Organizational processes and free recall. In E. Tulving & W. Donaldson (Eds.), *Organization of memory.* New York: Academic Press, 1972.

Wood, G., & Bolt, M. Mediation and mediation time in paired-associate learning. *Journal of Experimental Psychology,* 1968, *78,* 15–20.

Woods, P. J., Davidson, E. H., & Peters, R. J. Instrumental escape conditioning in a water tank: Effects of variations in drive, stimulus intensity and reinforcement magnitude. *Journal of Comparative and Physiological Psychology,* 1964, *57,* 466–470.

Woods, P. J., Markman, B. S., Lynch, W. C., & Stokely, S. N. Partial reinforcement effects in instrumental escape conditioning. *Learning and Motivation,* 1972, *3,* 279–292.

Woodworth, R. S. *Experimental psychology.* New York: Holt, Rinehart and Winston, 1938.

Woody, C. D., Vassilevsky, N. N., & Engle, J. Conditioned eye-blink unit: Activity at coronal–precruciate cortex of the cat. *Journal of Neurophysiology,* 1970, *33,* 838.

Wright, J. M. Cross-modal transfer and sensory equivalence—A review. *Scandinavian Journal of Psychology,* 1970, *11,* 22–30.

Wulf, F. Uber die Veranderung von Vorstellungen. *Psychologische Forsch,* 1922, *1,* 333–373.

Yarrow, L. J. The development of focused relationships during infancy. In J. Hellmuth (Ed.), *The exceptional infant* (Vol. 1). Seattle: Special Child Publications, 1967.

Yates, F. A. *The art of memory.* Chicago: University of Chicago Press, 1966.

Yum, K. W. An experimental test of the law of assimilation. *Journal of Experimental Psychology,* 1931, *14,* 68–82.

Zeaman, D. Response latency as a function of the amount of reinforcement. *Journal of Experimental Psychology,* 1949, *39,* 466–483.

Zeaman, D., & House, B. J. The role of attention in retardate discrimination learning. In N. R. Ellis (Ed.), *Handbook of mental deficiency: Psychological theory and research.* New York: McGraw-Hill, 1963.

Zeiberger, J., Sampen, S., & Sloane, H. N. Modification of a child's problem behaviors in the home with mother as therapist. *Journal of Applied Behavior Analysis,* 1968, *1,* 47–53.

Zener, K. The significance of behavior accompanying conditioned salivary secretion for theories of the conditioned response. *American Journal of Psychology,* 1937, *50,* 384–403.

Ziff, D. F., & Capaldi, E. J. Amytal and the small trial partial reinforcement effect: Stimulus properties of early trial nonrewards. *Journal of Experimental Psychology,* 1971, *87,* 263–269.

Zinkin, S., & Miller, A. J. Recovery of memory after amnesia induced by electroconvulsive shock. *Science,* 1967, *155,* 102–104.

Zornetzer, S. F., & McGaugh, J. L. Retrograde amnesia and brain seizures in mice. *Physiology and Behavior,* 1971, *7,* 401–408. (a)

Zornetzer, S. F., & McGaugh, J. L. Retrograde amnesia and brain seizures in mice: A further analysis. *Physiology and Behavior,* 1971, *7,* 841–845. (b)

Zucker, I. Effect of lesions of the septal–limbic area on the behavior of cats. *Journal of Comparative and Physiological Psychology,* 1965, *60,* 344–352.

Zusne, L. *Visual perception of form.* New York: Academic Press, 1970.

Name Index

Subject Index